LENIN

COLLECTED WORKS

42

ИНСТИТУТ МАРКСИЗМА-ЛЕНИНИЗМА при ЦК КПСС

В. И. ЛЕНИН

СОЧИНЕНИЯ

Издание четвертое

ИЗДАТЕЛЬСТВО
ПОЛИТИЧЕСКОЙ ЛИТЕРАТУРЫ
МОСКВА

V. I. LENIN

COLLECTED WORKS

VOLUME
42
October 1917–March 1923

PROGRESS PUBLISHERS
MOSCOW

TRANSLATED FROM THE RUSSIAN
BY BERNARD ISAACS

First printing 1969
Second printing 1971
Third printing 1977

11-17-78

Л $\dfrac{10102-211}{014\,(01)-77}$ без объявл.

CONTENTS

October 1917-July 1918

CONTENTS

APPENDIX

PREFACE

Volume Forty-Two contains items written after the October Revolution, which were first published in the Complete Russian Edition of Lenin's *Collected Works* or which were published in *Lenin Miscellanies*, magazines and newspapers. These documents form an important supplement to the works included in the various volumes of this edition.

The first group of documents dates to the period from November 1917 to July 1918—the period of continued development of the socialist revolution and consolidation of Soviet power. Mention should be made first of all of "Theses on the Tasks of the Party + the Present Situation", the article "Plekhanov on Terror", the "Draft Resolution for the C.C., R.S.D.L.P.(B.) Concerning the Expulsion from the Party of S. A. Lozovsky", the "Outline of a Programme of Economic Measures" and a number of chapters of the original version of the article "The Immediate Tasks of the Soviet Government". These deal with the tasks that faced the working class after the conquest of power, stress the necessity for strengthening the dictatorship of the proletariat and suppressing the resistance of the overthrown exploiting classes, and sharply criticise the Right-opportunist elements within the Party.

Several documents relate to Lenin's fight to get Russia out of the war, to conclude the Brest peace treaty ("Speech at a Joint Meeting of the Bolshevik and Left S.R. Groups in the All-Russia Central Executive Committee, February 19, 1918", "Speech to the Lettish Riflemen, February 20, 1918" and others). The numerous decisions for the Council of People's Commissars drafted by Lenin reflect the first steps of the Communist Party and the Soviet Government in the field of political, economic and cultural activities.

A large part of the materials relate to the period of foreign military intervention and the civil war, among them: notes on "The Tasks and Organisation of the Work of the Council of Defence", "Notes at a Meeting of the Commission on Cartridges", "Draft Resolution for the C.C., R.C.P.(B.) on Sending Groups of Workers Out on Food Transportation Jobs", "Draft Decision for the Council of Defence on the Mobilisation of Soviet Employees", "Draft Decisions for the C.C. Politbureau on Measures to Fight Mamontov", "Proposals on Military Questions", "Decisions of the Politbureau of the C.C., R.C.P.(B.) on the Order of the Revolutionary Military Council of the Western Front" and Lenin's speeches: "Speech to Ivanovo-Voznesensk Communist Workers Leaving for the Front, October 24, 1919", "Speech at the Eleventh Issue of Red Commanders of the First Moscow Machine-Gunners Training Courses, May 12, 1920", "Report on the Internal and External Position of the Republic at a Meeting of Activists of the Moscow Organisation of the R.C.P.(B.), October 9, 1920". These and many other documents strikingly illustrate the gigantic activities of the Central Committee and the Soviet Government, headed by Lenin, in organising the defeat of the interventionists and whiteguards.

A considerable part of the volume is made up of items and documents written after the war, when the problems of economic rehabilitation and socialist construction bulked large. Industry, agriculture, science and technology, public education, improvement of the machinery of state, the national question, foreign policy—all these problems were dealt with daily by Lenin, who directed the activities of the Party and the Government.

The items included in this volume contain important supplementary material showing how Lenin worked on the plan of socialist construction.

Of great significance are the chapters of the original version of "The Immediate Tasks of the Soviet Government" (the end of Chapter IV, chapters V-IX and the beginning of Chapter X) which were first published in 1962. In these chapters Lenin sets forth in greater detail than in the final text a number of questions relating to the task of starting construction of a new society and reveals the importance

of solving economic problems and the need for proper
management of the national economy during the period
of transition from capitalism to socialism. In interviews
given to Lincoln Eyre, correspondent of the American
newspaper *The World*, and to the correspondent of the
Japanese newspaper *Osaka Asahi* and in his "Notes on
Electrification" Lenin characterises the role of electrification
in building the economic foundation of socialism and developing the productive forces. Questions of the New Economic
Policy are dealt with in the "Reply to the Debate on the
Report on Concessions" at the meeting of the Communist
group of the All-Russia Central Council of Trade Unions
on April 11, 1921, in speeches made at the Tenth All-Russia
Conference of the R.C.P.(B.) during the debate on the
resolution on questions of the New Economic Policy, and in
a letter "To the Russian Colony in North America".

Consistent application of democratic centralism in running
the economy, scientific planning, rational and efficient
management, proper organisation of labour, the introduction
of cost accounting, the running of enterprises on a paying
basis, and the use of moral and material incentives
for developing production were considered by Lenin to be
the most vital principles and methods of socialist management. Mention can here be made of such documents as the
"Speech at a Meeting of the Presidium of the S.E.C., April 1,
1918", "Comments on the Draft 'Regulations for the
Management of the Nationalised Enterprises'", "Salaries for
Specialists", "Addendum to the Draft Regulations on Subbotniks", "Draft of the Main Point of the C.L.D. Decision on
the General Planning Commission", "Plan of an Article
'Commercial Organisation'", "Motion to the Politbureau of
the C.C., R.C.P.(B.) on Bonuses for Enterprises" and others.

Defining the tasks of economic construction in his "Plan
of a Speech at the Trade Union Congress", Lenin wrote:
"Work discipline, higher labour productivity, work organisation, increased output, relentless fight against slipshod
work and red tape. By this sign shall ye conquer" (p. 308).

Materials such as: "Addendum to the Draft Decision for
the C.P.C. 'On the Distribution of Agricultural Machines'",
"Draft Decision for the C.L.D. on Fowler Ploughs", the
draft decision on "Measures for Improving the Organisation

of State Farms" and others show Lenin's concern for the revival of agriculture, for the supply of the peasants with machines, for the development of the state farms, for support of the co-operatives on the part of the state and for the creation of conditions for the socialist transformation of the village.

A number of materials deal with questions of cultural development: the draft decision for the C.P.C. on "Library Organisation", "Instructions for Compiling a Reading Book for Workers and Peasants", "Draft Decision for the Polit-bureau of the C.C., R.C.P.(B.) on the Chief Committee for Political Education", "Rough Draft of a Resolution on Proletarian Culture", "Addendum to the Draft Decision for the C.P.C. on an Obligatory Science Minimum in the Higher Schools", "Draft Decision for the Plenum of the C.C., R.C.P.(B.) on the Reorganisation of the People's Commissariat for Education", "Directives on the Film Business". These and other documents contain important propositions regarding the substance and ways of effecting a cultural revolution, the communist education of the working people, the political enlightenment of the masses.

Of exceptionally great significance is the letter "On the Establishment of the U.S.S.R." in which Lenin put forward the idea of creating a Union of Soviet Socialist Republics as a single multinational socialist state based on a voluntary association of equal and sovereign Soviet Republics. Questions concerning the national policy of the Communist Party and the Soviet Government are dealt with also in the "Notes at a Meeting of Delegates to the Second All-Russia Congress of Communist Organisations of the Peoples of the East", "Draft Decision for the Politbureau of the C.C., R.C.P.(B.) on the Tasks of the R.C.P.(B.) in Turkestan", "Draft Decision for the Politbureau of the C.C., R.C.P.(B.) on the Tasks of the R.C.P.(B.) in Localities Inhabited by Eastern Peoples" and other items, in which Lenin urges the need for unity and fraternal co-operation among all the nationalities of the Soviet land and for waging a vigorous fight against chauvinism and nationalism.

The speech winding up the debate on the report on concessions at the meeting of the R.C.P.(B.) group at the Eighth Congress of Soviets contains Lenin's important thesis on

Soviet patriotism: "The patriotism of a person who is prepared to go hungry for three years rather than surrender Russia to foreigners is genuine patriotism, without which we could not hold out for three years. Without this patriotism we would not have succeeded in defending the Soviet Republic, in doing away with private property.... This is the finest revolutionary patriotism" (p. 245).

In his note "The Democratism and Socialist Nature of Soviet Power" and his "Speech at a Meeting in Presnya District, July 26, 1918", Lenin characterises the Soviets and reveals the genuine democratism of the Soviet Constitution.

Many documents reflect Lenin's efforts to improve the working of the machinery of state, and strengthen state, Party and public control: "Proposals for the Distribution of Functions Between the Deputy Chairmen of the C.P.C. and the C.L.D.", "Proposals Concerning the Work Routine of the Deputy Chairmen and the Chairman of the C.P.C.", "Letter to L. B. Kamenev, A. I. Rykov and A. D. Tsyurupa on the Distribution of Work Between the Deputy Chairmen of the C.P.C. and the C.L.D.", "Politbureau of the C.C., R.C.P.(B.) Directives on a Workers' Inspection", "Materials to the Article 'How We Should Reorganise the Workers' and Peasants' Inspection'", etc. A number of documents are devoted to the strengthening of socialist legality: "Rough Theses of a Decision on the Strict Observance of the Laws", "Proposals Concerning the Work of the Vecheka", "Speech at the Fourth Conference of Gubernia Extraordinary Commissions, February 6, 1920" and others.

Lenin regarded the Communist Party as the guiding and directing force of Soviet society. He never relaxed his efforts to strengthen the ideological and organisational unity of the Party, he urged the need for doing everything to develop inner-Party democracy, to rigidly adhere to the principle of collective leadership and to strengthen the Party's ties with the masses. These questions are dealt with in many documents included in this volume: "Speech on the Immediate Tasks of Party Development" at the Ninth All-Russia Conference of the R.C.P.(B.), draft resolution and proposals for the resolution on this question, speech to the R.C.P.(B.) group at the Eighth Congress of

Soviets during the debate on the report of the All-Russia C.E.C. and C.P.C. concerning home and foreign policies, "Speech at a Meeting of Moscow Party Activists, February 24, 1921", "Draft of a Letter of the C.C., R.C.P.(B.) on the Attitude to Non-Party Workers", "Outline of a Speech at a Meeting of Supporters of the 'Platform of Ten'"—delegates to the Tenth Congress of the R.C.P.(B.), "Remarks Concerning the Work Plan of the C.C., R.C.P.(B.)".

Lenin's draft resolution for the Politbureau of the C.C. concerning Maxim Gorky's articles in the magazine *Communist International* is a striking illustration of his high-principled attitude, his intolerance towards the cult of personality.

Of great importance is the series of documents dealing with the Soviet state's foreign policy: the interviews with foreign correspondents, the "Draft Directives to the Deputy Chairman and All Members of the Genoa Delegation", "Draft Directives of the C.C., R.C.P.(B.) for the Soviet Delegation to the Genoa Conference", "Draft Decision for the C.C.,R.C.P.(B.) on the Tasks of the Soviet Delegation at Genoa", "Amendments and Remarks to the Draft Declaration of the Soviet Delegation at the Genoa Conference" and others, which formulate the fundamental principles of the Soviet Republic's foreign policy and the aims and methods of Soviet diplomacy.

These documents show how consistently the Soviet Government, headed by Lenin, pursued its policy of peace and establishment of business relations with the capitalist countries. In his interview given to an American correspondent, Lenin said: "I know of no reason why a socialistic commonwealth like ours cannot do business indefinitely with capitalistic countries" (p. 177). At the same time the Soviet Government strongly rebuffed all attempts of the imperialist powers to interfere in the internal affairs of the Soviet Republic or to impose upon it fettering terms of an economic agreement. Lenin said: "We have reiterated and reiterated our desire for peace.... But we do not propose to be strangled to death for the sake of peace" (ibid.).

Notable items in this volume are the documents which reveal the friendly fraternal relations between the Soviet state and the countries where the people had come to power. This volume contains the draft decisions for the C.P.C.

concerning a treaty with the Socialist Workers' Republic of Finland. This was the first treaty in history to be signed between two socialist republics, and represented a new type of international relations between equal sovereign states. The text of Lenin's "Talk With a Delegation of the Mongolian People's Republic" contains important guidelines on the paths of development towards socialism for countries with a pre-capitalist social system, and on the specific features of the tactics which the revolutionary parties in these countries should adopt.

The writings included in this volume are a valuable supplement to the well-known works of Lenin dealing with the international labour and communist movements. Mention should first of all be made of Lenin's letter to Chicherin (at the end of December 1918) outlining the basic ideological platform and organisational principles of the Communist International. Of considerable interest are the materials relating to the Second Congress of the Comintern—the "Plan of a Resolution Concerning the Meaning of the Concept 'Dictatorship of the Proletariat' and the Fight Against the 'Fashionable' Distortion of This Slogan", "Remarks on the Report of A. Sultan-Zade Concerning the Prospects of a Social Revolution in the East" and others. A number of documents deal with the Third Congress of the Comintern and show what a tremendous job Lenin performed in preparing the basic decisions of the Congress and guiding its proceedings. These include: "Letter to O. W. Kuusinen and Remarks on the Draft 'Theses on the Organisational Activities of the Communist Parties, on the Methods and Content of Their Work'", "Remarks on the Draft Theses on Tactics for the Third Congress of the Communist International", "Speeches at a Meeting of Members of the German, Polish, Czechoslovak, Hungarian and Italian Delegations".

These documents reflect the irreconcilable struggle which Lenin carried on against Right-wing opportunism, reformism and revisionism, and at the same time against Leftism, adventurism, dogmatism and sectarianism in the international communist movement. They contain very important guidelines on questions of the strategy and tactics of the international communist movement. The Communist Parties, Lenin emphasised, should focus their attention on the task

of winning over the majority of the working class, the bulk
of the working masses, and prepare them for the socialist
revolution. In a number of documents—"Draft Decision
of the Politbureau of the C.C., R.C.P.(B.) on the Tactics
of the United Front", "Letter to Members of the Politbureau
of the C.C.,R.C.P.(B.) with Remarks to the Draft Resolution
for the First Extended Plenary Meeting of the Comintern
Executive on Participation in a Conference of the Three
Internationals", "Proposal to the Draft Resolution for the
Eleventh Party Congress on the Report of the R.C.P.(B.)
Delegation in the Comintern"—Lenin argues the case for
the tactics of a united front, the adoption of a united action
by the working class.

The Appendix to the volume contains questionnaires
filled in by Lenin in the capacity of delegate to Communist
Party congresses and conferences, in the course of reregistration of members of the Moscow organisation of the R.C.P.
and under the All-Russia census of the R.C.P. members.

Of considerable interest are the records of Lenin's official
orders and instructions, reception of visitors and other
facts entered in the Journal of Lenin's Duty Secretaries.
This document reveals how manfully Lenin fought his
illness, giving all his strength to the cause of the Party,
the cause of the working class.

*Institute of Marxism-Leninism
of the C.C. of the C.P.S.U.*

October 1917-July 1918

SPEECH AT A MEETING
OF THE COUNCIL OF PEOPLE'S COMMISSARS
NOVEMBER 3 (16), 1917

Comrade Lenin objects to any agreement whatsoever with Vikzhel,[1] which tomorrow will be overthrown in a revolutionary manner, from below. Moscow must be given creative, organising, revolutionary reinforcements from Petrograd—the sailor element, to be exact. The food problem: we are getting supplies from the north. After winning Moscow and overthrowing Vikzhel from below we shall be getting food supplies from the Volga.

First published November 6-7, 1927
in *Pravda* No. 255, in an article
by N. Gorbunov
"How the Working Staff
of the Council of People's Commissars
Was Created During the October Days"

Printed from the handwritten copy
of the minutes

ADDENDA TO THE DRAFT DECREE
ON THE REQUISITION OF ARTICLES
OF WARM CLOTHING
FOR THE SOLDIERS AT THE FRONT

The following to be added:
Heading: +... *and on the requisition of flats of the rich to relieve the needs of the poor....*

§ 1. ... plus one article of warm clothing in addition to a blanket (overcoat, winter coat, jacket, felt boots, etc.).

§ 2. ... The term rich flat applies to any flat in which the number of rooms equals or exceeds the number of permanent occupants.

The owners of rich flats are obliged immediately, under threat of confiscation of all their property, to draw up in duplicate a statement listing the articles of warm clothing they have and of those supplied by them to the front, one copy of which is to be handed to the House Committee, the other to the district Soviet of Workers' and Soldiers' Deputies.

The owners of rich flats, under similar threat, are obliged immediately to submit in duplicate to the same institutions a statement to the effect that they are vacating one of two rich flats for the needs of the poor population of the capital (that is, two rich families having two rich flats are obliged to move into one of their flats during the winter, giving the other up to the use of the poor population in view of the extreme need created by the war).

The house committees shall immediately draw up lists of rich flats subject to requisition, and the district Soviets of Workers' Deputies shall endorse these lists and define the conditions and order in which families of the poor population are to move into these flats.[2]

Written in November,
prior to 8th (21st), 1917

First published in 1933
in *Lenin Miscellany XXI*

Printed from the manuscript

INTERVIEW GIVEN TO GREGORI YARROS, CORRESPONDENT
OF THE *ASSOCIATED PRESS AGENCY*

NOVEMBER 15 (28), 1917

In connection with the results of the elections in Petrograd in which the Bolsheviks won six seats,[3] the *Associated Press* correspondent interviewed Lenin, the President of the Council of National Commissioners, who was elated over the great victory of his party.

"What do you think of the results of the elections to the Constituent Assembly?" the correspondent asked.

"I think that these elections have proved a great victory for the Bolshevik Party. The number of votes cast for it in the elections in May, August and in September is constantly growing.[4] To get six seats out of twelve in a city in which the bourgeoisie (Cadets[5]) are strongest, means to win in Russia."

"Do you suppose that the Constituent Assembly of such composition as the results of the elections in Petrograd indicate will sanction all the measures of the Government of National Commissioners?"

"Yes, it will sanction, because there will be no majority, according to your supposition, against us, and together with the left social revolutionists[6] we shall constitute a majority in Petrograd (seven out of twelve)."

"What parties will enter into the new Council of National Commissioners?"

"I do not know positively, but I think that only the left social revolutionists, besides the Bolsheviks."

First published in part
in 1962
in the journal *Istoria SSSR*
(*History of the USSR*) No. 2

First published in full in 1965
in the Fifth Russian Edition
of the *Collected Works*, Vol. 54

Printed from the typewritten copy
of the English original

THE SALARIES OF HIGH-RANKING
OFFICE EMPLOYEES
AND OFFICIALS

DRAFT DECREE FOR THE C.P.C.[7]

Recognising the need for energetic measures to reduce the salaries of high-ranking office employees and officials in all state, public and private institutions and enterprises, the Council of People's Commissars decrees:

1) that the salary limit for people's commissars be fixed at 500 rubles a month where there are no children, and 100 rubles extra for each child; housing to be at the

rate of not more than 1 room for each member of the
family; 2) that all local Soviets of Workers', Soldiers'
and Peasants' Deputies be asked to prepare and carry out
revolutionary measures to impose special taxes on high-
ranking employees; 3) that the Ministry for Finance be
instructed to draft a general law concerning this reduction;
4) that the Ministry for Finance and all the respective
commissars be instructed to immediately study the estimates of the ministries and cut all excessively high salaries
and pensions.

Written November 18
(December 1), 1917

First published in 1933   Printed from the manuscript
in *Lenin Miscellany XXI*

DRAFT DECISION FOR THE C.P.C.
ON THE QUESTION OF THE WAR MINISTRY[8]

In view of the fact that General Manikovsky has issued
a counter-revolutionary order to the Moscow Military
District not to have appointed commanders replaced by
elected ones,

in view of the fact that General Marushevsky has been
conducting negotiations with Dukhonin aimed against
the Council and has made a criminal attempt at sabotage
during the organisation of a delegation for conducting
armistice negotiations,*

1) Manikovsky and Marushevsky are to be arrested
immediately and not released without the permission of
the Council of People's Commissars[9];

2) a thorough screening of the War Ministry personnel
to be started immediately and all unreliable elements
among the high command to be discharged;

3) reliable elements from among the commanders of the
Lettish rifle regiments to be ordered out at once to Petrograd;

---

* The first two paragraphs are in Trotsky's handwriting.—*Ed.*

4) one Lettish rifle regiment to be ordered out to Petrograd at once[10];

5) fulfilment of the above measures to be reported daily to the C.P.C.

This decision is not to be published.

Written November 19
(December 2), 1917

First published in 1965
in the Fifth Russian Edition
of the *Collected Works*, Vol. 54

Printed from the manuscript

THESES FOR A LAW ON THE CONFISCATION OF APARTMENT AND TENEMENT HOUSES[11]

1) *All* land (urban) shall become the property of the nation.

2) Houses which are *systematically* let to tenants shall be confiscated and become the property of the nation.

3) Owners of houses that are *not* let to tenants shall, pending the decision of the Constituent Assembly, remain in possession without any change in their rights of ownership.

4) Several-months compensation (2 to 3 months) to owners of confiscated houses who can prove their ... *

5) Rent shall be collected by (whom?) the *Soviets* (paid into the current accounts of the Soviets).

6) Building committees (the trade unions + building offices) shall take charge also of house supplies (fuel, etc.).

7) Rent payment to come in force immediately.

8) The building and house committees shall come into force gradually as and when they are set up by the trade unions and the Soviets.

9) The heating of the houses and their normal upkeep shall be the duty of the house committees and other institutions (trade unions, Soviets, fuel departments of the town council, etc.).

Written November 20
(December 3), 1917

First published in 1933
in *Lenin Miscellany* XXI

Printed from the manuscript

---

* The sentence is unfinished.—*Ed.*

DRAFT DECISION FOR THE C.P.C.
ON THE QUESTION
OF FOLLOWING A SOCIALIST POLICY
IN THE ECONOMIC FIELD[12]

1) Two or three engineers shall be sent to the Special Defence Council for the purposes of control and the drafting of a general plan of industrial demobilisation (Kozmin to be charged with forming this group);[13]

2) A 3-5-man commission of C.P.C. members (and non-members) shall be set up to discuss the major problems of the Government's economic policy (Pyatakov and Bukharin to be charged with forming this commission);

3) A conference of food-supply men shall be organised to discuss practical measures for combating marauding and improving the condition of the most needy sections of the population (Shlyapnikov + Manuilsky to be charged with organising this conference).

Written November 27
(December 10), 1917

First published in 1933   Printed from the manuscript
in *Lenin Miscellany XXI*

OUTLINE OF A PROGRAMME
OF ECONOMIC MEASURES

Nationalisation of banks

Drawing money back into the treasury

New money for large denominations

Revolutionary measures for switching factories to useful production

Centralisation of consumption by compulsory association in consumers' societies

State monopoly of foreign trade
Nationalisation of industry

State loans.

Written not before
November 27
(December 10), 1917

First published in 1933
in *Lenin Miscellany* XXI   Printed from the manuscript

DEMONSTRATION SLOGANS[14]

To the demonstration slogans published on 28.XI.,
I advise adding:

Shame to the Right S.R.s and Chernovites[15] who have
broken away from the peasant congress!

Long live the Second All-Russia Congress of Peasant
Deputies, which has sided with the Soviet power!

The working people demand that the Constituent Assembly recognise Soviet power and the Soviet Government!

Long live the nationalisation of the banks!

Down with the saboteurs and striking officials! Boycott
them, use revolutionary terrorism against them!

Lenin

Written November 28
(December 11), 1917

First published in 1957
in the journal
Voprosi Istorii KPSS No. 3   Printed from the manuscript

LIABILITY FOR UNFOUNDED ACCUSATIONS

DRAFT RESOLUTION FOR THE C.C., R.S.D.L.P.(B.)[16]

The C.C. establishes the principle:

that in all squabbles and personal accusations, the person who makes such accusations without bringing specific
charges before a court shall be considered a slanderer;

that those who consider themselves affected by such
accusations shall be invited to take legal action.

Written November 29
(December 12), 1917

First published in 1945   Printed from the manuscript
in *Lenin Miscellany XXXV*

THE CONVERSION OF MUNITION WORKS
TO ECONOMICALLY USEFUL WORK

DECREE OF THE COUNCIL OF PEOPLE'S COMMISSARS

Comrade Raskolnikov is instructed to immediately
contact the Commissariat for Trade and Industry, as well
as the Commissariat for Food (Machine Supply Department),
for the purpose of immediately arranging for orders to be
placed with the works engaged in naval installations
and repairs. Especially urgent is the production of farm
implements and machines, and the building and repair
of locomotives. Primary attention to be paid to the
St. Petersburg Metalworks, which is well stocked with
fuel and metal.

The Chief Naval Economic Board is instructed to immediately revise the estimates of the Ministry for Marine
for 1917 with a view to stopping all expenditure on the
naval construction programme and all unproductive expenditure in general, and reallocating the corresponding sums
to useful national economic work. Comrade I. E. Gukovsky
is delegated to take part in this work in the capacity of
plenipotentiary commissar in charge of the revision of the
estimates of all departments.

Daily reports to the Council of People's Commissars
on the fulfilment of this order shall be made by Comrade
Raskolnikov and the person authorised by the Chief Naval
Economic Board (or by Comrade Gukovsky), as well as
by the authorised agent of the Commissariat for Trade
and Industry.

                                    V. Ulyanov (Lenin)
                        Chairman, Council of People's Commissars

Written November 29
(December 12), 1917

First published in 1933   Printed from the manuscript
in *Lenin Miscellany XXI*

THESES ON THE TASKS OF THE PARTY
+ THE PRESENT SITUATION

(α) Recognition of the revolution of 25.X. as a socialist revolution.

(β) Rejection of all limitations to this in the spirit of reversion to the bourgeois-democratic revolution (gradual transition; "stage" of the bloc with the petty bourgeoisie, etc.).

(γ) Dictatorship of the proletariat, its special features as compared with "general", formal (bourgeois) democracy, its tactics.

(δ) Soviet power and the power of the Bolsheviks.

(ε) Agreement with the petty bourgeoisie not in the sense of a bloc for a bourgeois-democratic revolution, not in the sense of restricting the tasks of the socialist revolution, but exclusively in the sense of the *forms* of transition to socialism on the part of *different* sections of the petty bourgeoisie.

(ι) Bourgeois liberties versus suppression of the exploiters.

(χ) Saboteurs and capitalists; capitalists and "public opinion" of the bourgeoisie.

(ζ) The Constituent Assembly and its subordination to the Soviet power, to the interests and conditions of the civil war.

(η) Top organisations (Vikzhel, Peasants' Central Executive Committee, etc.) and the struggle against them.

(ϑ) Struggle against reformism in its *modern* presentation:
  (1) the proletariat's hands tied by fellow-travellers from among the petty bourgeoisie
  (2) restricted scope of the revolutionary struggle of the rank and file
  (3) rejection of terrorism.

Written November 1917

First published in 1957
in the journal
Voprosi Istorii KPSS No. 1

Printed from the manuscript

ANSWERS TO QUESTIONS
PUT BY A WORKERS' DELEGATION
OF ALEXANDRO-GRUSHEVSKY DISTRICT[17]

1) Re the sequestration of mines and works in the Alexandro-Grushevsky District.

Mines and works may be confiscated only after the district is liberated from Kaledin's troops and influence.

2) Should the workers now quit the mines and go away to Central Russia?

They should not quit but go on working as long as possible. Resolution on this question by the Council of People's Commissars: the workers of the Alexandro-Grushevsky District to be instructed to contact Kharkov for the arming of the Red Guard. The comrades to be asked to hold out to the last, as long as they can, and not throw up their work.

3) On sending guards to the mines.

Our troops are moving in the direction of Kaledin's troops in sufficient numbers.

4) Re a subsidy of 3,000,000 rubles to carry on the work.

The question of Monotop[18] will be settled on the arrival of Comrade Artyom from Kharkov.

5) Are the bank-notes issued by Kaledin's government to be considered valid?

The bank-notes are to be considered invalid.

V. Ulyanov (Lenin)
Chairman, Council of People's Commissars

Written December 11 (24), 1917

First published in 1959   Printed from the typed copy
in *Lenin Miscellany XXXVI*

DRAFT DECISION FOR THE C.P.C.
ON STAFF SALARIES
IN GOVERNMENT OFFICES[19]

The Council of People's Commissars decrees that the rates of pay recognised by the Government Office Staffs Commission and accepted by the All-Russia Convention of Junior Employees of Government Institutions shall be recognised as a norm to be guided by.

Written December 13 (26), 1917

First published in 1965
in the Fifth Russian Edition
of the *Collected Works*, Vol. 54

Printed from the manuscript

THE ORGANISATION OF A COMMISSION
OF PRACTITIONERS

DRAFT DECISION FOR THE C.P.C.[20]

The Council of People's Commissars directs the Supreme Economic Council to organise immediately a Commission of Practitioners to be charged with collecting orders for useful products from all departments, institutions and organisations, passing these orders on to factories that are at a standstill or are being closed down, and checking to what extent these orders are being passed on and carried out. The Commission, guided by the general economic plan of the Supreme Economic Council, is to submit to the Council of People's Commissars revolutionary measures for the immediate fulfilment of its task and report on its activities twice a week.

Written December 15 (28), 1917

First published in 1933
in *Lenin Miscellany XXI*

Printed from the manuscript

INSTRUCTIONS ON THE PROCEDURE
FOR TABLING QUESTIONS IN THE C.P.C.

Every commissar tabling a question in the Council of People's Commissars shall be required to submit a *written* statement specifying:

a) what the question is (briefly) [this statement cannot be confined to a mere reference to the subject, but must *set forth the gist* of the matter].

b) what exactly the Council of People's Commissars is being asked to do (give money; adopt *such-and-such* a resolution, etc. The person introducing the question must state clearly *what* he wants)

c) whether the question involves departments under other commissars. If so, exactly which; whether they have given their findings in writing.[21]

Lenin

Written December 16 (29), 1917

First published in 1933   Printed from the manuscript
in *Lenin Miscellany XXI*

DRAFT DECISION FOR C.P.C.
ON THE IRREGULAR ACTIONS
OF PEOPLE'S COMMISSAR FOR JUSTICE
I. Z. STEINBERG AND MEMBER OF THE BOARD
OF THE PEOPLE'S COMMISSARIAT FOR JUSTICE
V. A. KARELIN[22]

The Council of People's Commissars considers that no changes in the decisions of the Dzerzhinsky Commission or any other commission appointed by the Soviets[23] are permissible other than by way of appeal to the Council of People's Commissars, and on no account by way of personal order of the Commissar for Justice.

The Council of People's Commissars considers further that the act of comrades Steinberg and Karelin, who released the arrested men on the night of 18.XII was illegal both in form and substance, since it contravened not only the privileges of the Dzerzhinsky Commission but the direct decision of the Council of People's Commissars adopted on the evening of 18.XII which ordered the arrested men to be detained for identification.

*Lenin**

Written December 19, 1917
(January 1, 1918)

First published in 1933   Printed from the manuscript
in *Lenin Miscellany XXI*

PLEKHANOV ON TERROR

There was a time when Plekhanov was a socialist, a prominent exponent of revolutionary socialism.

At that time—now, alas, in the limbo of forgotten things—Plekhanov expressed his opinion on a subject which happens to have vital significance in the present period.

It happened in 1903, when the Russian Social-Democrats were framing their programme at the Second Party Congress.

The minutes of this Congress contain the following very informative entry, that might have been written specially for the present day:

"*Posadovsky.* The statements made here for and against the amendments strike me as being not a dispute over details but a serious difference of opinion; without a doubt we disagree on the following fundamental question: *should our future policy be governed by certain basic democratic principles, admitted to have absolute value,* or *are all democratic principles to be governed exclusively by what is profitable for our party?* I definitely declare for the latter. There is no democratic principle that we could not make subservient to the *interests of our party.* (*Interjection*: "Even inviolability of the person?") Yes! Inviolability of the person as well! As a revolutionary party striving towards its ultimate goal—that of a social revolution—we must regard democratic principles exclusively from the point of view of the speediest possible achievement of that goal, from the point of view of our party's interests. If one or another demand does not turn out to our advantage we shall not use it.

"Therefore I oppose any amendments that are likely in future to narrow our freedom of action."

"*Plekhanov. I fully support what Comrade Posadovsky has said. Every given democratic principle should be examined not on its own*

* This document was also signed by J. V. Stalin.—*Ed.*

merits in the abstract, but in its bearing on what may be called the basic principle of democracy, namely, on the principle that says: salus populi suprema lex*. Translated into the language of the revolutionary, this means that the success of the revolution is the highest law. If it were necessary for the success of the revolution to restrict the effect of one or another democratic principle, it would be criminal to stop at such a restriction. As my own personal opinion I would say that even the principle of universal suffrage should be regarded from the point of view of this basic principle of democracy I have just mentioned. Hypothetically it is conceivable that we, Social-Democrats, may have occasion to come out against universal suffrage. The bourgeoisie of the Italian republics once deprived persons belonging to the nobility of political rights. The revolutionary proletariat could restrict the political rights of the upper classes the way these classes once restricted the political rights of the proletariat. The fitness of such a measure could only be judged by the rule: salus revolutionis suprema lex. The same point of view should be adopted by us on the question of the duration of parliaments. If, on an impulse of revolutionary enthusiasm, the people were to elect a very good parliament, a sort of Chambre Introuvable, we should try and make it a long parliament; and if the elections turned out to be unfavourable w e s h o u l d t r y a n d d i s m i s s i t n o t i n t w o y e a r s' time, but if possible in two w e e k s" (Minutes of the Second Congress of the R.S.D.L.P., pp. 168-69).

The enemies of socialism may be deprived for a time not only of inviolability of the person, and not only of freedom of the press, but of universal suffrage as well. A bad parliament should be "dismissed" in two weeks. The good of the revolution, the good of the working class, is the highest law. That was how Plekhanov spoke when he was a socialist. That was how the great majority of the present-day Mensheviks spoke, those same Mensheviks who are now screaming about "Bolshevik terror".

The "good of the revolution" now demands a grim fight against saboteurs, organisers of military cadet insurrections, and newspapers run by bankers. When the Soviet authorities embark upon such struggle, the so-called socialists from the camp of the Mensheviks and S.R.s shout from all the house-tops against civil war and terror.

When that Kerensky[24] of yours reintroduced capital punishment at the front, that was not terror, gentlemen, was it?

When your coalition cabinet, with the hands of the Kornilovs,[25] machine-gunned whole regiments for showing

---

* The welfare of the people is the highest law.—*Ed.*

insufficient enthusiasm for the war, that was not civil war, gentlemen, was it?

When those Kerenskys and Avksentyevs[26] of yours threw 3,000 soldiers into a single prison in Minsk for "harmful agitation", that was not terror, gentlemen, was it?

When you suppressed the *workers'* newspapers, that was not terror, gentlemen, was it?

The only difference is that the Kerenskys, Avksentyevs and Lieberdans,[27] hand in glove with the Kornilovs and Savinkovs,[28] have practised terror *against the workers, soldiers and peasants* in the interests of a handful of landowners and bankers, while the Soviet government is taking strong measures against the landowners, marauders and their underlings—*in the interests of the workers, soldiers and peasants.*

Pravda, No. 221, January 4, 1918
(December 22, 1917)
and *Izvestia* No. 259,
December 23, 1917

Printed from *Pravda* text collated
with that of *Izvestia*

DRAFT RESOLUTION FOR THE C.C., R.S.D.L.P.(B.) CONCERNING THE EXPULSION FROM THE PARTY OF S. A. LOZOVSKY

Resolution of the C.C., R.S.D.L.P.(Bolsheviks)

Taking into consideration

1) that Comrade Lozovsky, from the very beginning of the October Revolution, has expressed opinions which radically diverge from those of the Party and of the revolutionary proletariat in general, but coincide on all major points with the petty-bourgeois negation of the dictatorship of the proletariat as an essential phase in the transition to socialism;

2) that by his statement of November...* in the newspaper *Novaya Zhizn*,[29] which has gone over to the bourgeoisie, Comrade Lozovsky has aroused general indignation not

---

* Lenin has left a space in the manuscript for the date.—*Ed.*

only among all Party people, but among the class-conscious workers at large,[30] and that the resolution of the C.C. of the R.S.D.L.P. concerning Comrade Lozovsky's expulsion from the Party, passed soon after this statement had been made, was not announced and carried out only because of the hopes expressed by some comrades that the vacillations of Comrade Lozovsky were of a temporary nature caused by his inability to quickly grasp the significance of the historic upheaval that was taking place with such extraordinary speed;

3) that the expectations of the comrades who wished to give Comrade Lozovsky time to fully grasp the significance of the revolution that took place, have not been justified and that Comrade Lozovsky's entire political conduct and especially his articles in Nos. 7 and 8 of *Professionalny Vestnik*[31] point to this comrade's complete divergence from the cardinal principles of socialism in his approach to the role of the proletariat in the socialist revolution;

4) that membership of the Party by a person who holds an important post in the trade union movement and is debauching that movement with shoddy bourgeois ideas, not only compromises the Party and demoralises all organisational work among the proletariat, but causes enormous practical harm to the urgent task of organising socialist production by the trade unions;

5) that joint work in the ranks of a single Party is impossible with a person who does not understand the necessity for the dictatorship of the proletariat, which is recognised by our Party Programme, who does not understand that without such a dictatorship, that is, without a systematic, ruthless suppression of the resistance of the exploiters, which sticks at no bourgeois-democratic formulas, one cannot conceive of any consistently democratic, leave alone socialist, revolution, nor of any serious measures for coping with the crisis and economic chaos caused by the war;

6) that joint work in the ranks of a single Party is impossible with a person who repudiates the socialist tasks of the proletariat, which has won political power; with a person who refuses to accept the idea that it is the duty of the trade unions to take upon themselves state functions and carry through with the greatest vigour and determination

the socialist reorganisation of production and distribution on a nation-wide scale,

the C.C. of the R.S.D.L.P. resolves: that Comrade Lozovsky be expelled from the R.S.D.L.Party (Bolsheviks) and this resolution be published without delay.

Written December 30, 1917
(January 12, 1918)

Published in 1959
in *Lenin Miscellany XXXVI*   Printed from the manuscript

DECISION OF THE C.P.C.
ON THE FIGHT AGAINST KALEDIN[32]

1

DECISION OF THE C.P.C.

The Council of People's Commissars approves Comrade Antonov's[33] vigorous measures against the Kaledinites and their accomplices, and at the same time rules that the Commander-in-Chief has the right to take repressive measures, including sentences of forced labour in the mines, against capitalist saboteurs who threaten to cause unemployment and famine.

2

ADDENDUM TO THE DECISION OF THE C.P.C.

As soon as it becomes possible to set up revolutionary tribunals they will immediately examine each case of forced labour assignment, and will either fix the term of such labour or release the persons from custody.

Written:
the Decision — December 30, 1917
(January 12, 1918); the Addendum—
January 1 (14), 1918

First published: Printed from the manuscript
the Decision—in 1942
in *Lenin Miscellany XXXIV*
the Addendum—in 1959
in *Lenin Miscellany XXXVI*

RATES OF PAY
FOR HIGH-RANKING OFFICIALS

DRAFT DECISION FOR THE C.P.C.[34]

Re Comrade Shlyapnikov's inquiry concerning rates of pay for high ranking officials, the C.P.C.

1) confirms that the decree establishing 500-ruble monthly salaries for members of the Council of People's Commissars is to be interpreted as an *approximate* norm for top salaries and contains no prohibition to pay specialists more;

2) calls attention once more to the fact that the decree of the C.P.C. contains a demand for revolutionary measures to be taken to reduce excessively high salaries;[35]

3) directs all People's Commissars immediately to report what has been done in fulfilment of this decree;

4) directs the Commissar for Finance to submit a report as to whether resolute measures have been taken to collect income tax and eliminate evasions in the payment of this tax;

5) directs the local Soviets of Workers', Soldiers' and Peasants' Deputies to take more energetic measures to collect the special tax on excessively high incomes.

Written January 2 (15), 1918

First published in 1933   Printed from the manuscript
in *Lenin Miscellany XXI*

MEASURES FOR IMPROVING THE FOOD SITUATION

DRAFT DECISION FOR THE C.P.C.[36]

Having decided to postpone publication of the decrees concerning the Food Council pending the food congress, and while persistently urging all food supply workers not to leave their posts and to avoid partial conflicts,

The Council of People's Commissars directs the All-Russia Food Council and the Commissariat for Food to send out more and numerically larger armed detachments as well as commissars to take the most revolutionary measures to expedite shipments, collect and store grain, etc., as well as to wage a ruthless struggle against profiteers, even to the extent of calling on the local Soviets to shoot convicted profiteers and saboteurs on the spot.

The Council of People's Commissars decrees that rations shall not be increased and that the dispatch of through goods-trains shall be stepped up and their progress carefully controlled.

Urgent steps shall be taken to clear the Petrograd railway junction, the All-Russia Food Council to be made responsible for this work.

The All-Russia Food Council shall report daily to the C.P.C. on the progress of food supply work and to submit a plan of food operations.

Written January 14 (27), 1918

First published in 1931
in *Lenin Miscellany* XVIII   Printed from the manuscript

INQUIRY OF THE C.P.C.
TO THE C.C. OF THE LEFT S.R. PARTY[37]

Following the decision of the Council of People's Commissars dated 14.I (night)—extract from the journal is herewith enclosed—we ask the C.C. of the Left Socialist-Revolutionary Party to answer the following questions:

1) When did the Petrograd Committee of the Left S.R.s pass its resolution refusing to have any members on the staff of the Committee of Inquiry so long as Kozlovsky was on it?

2) What is the text of that resolution?

3) Was the C.C. of the Left S.R. Party aware of this resolution and was it commented on in the C.C. of the Left S.R.s?

4) When and by whom (of the Left S.R.s) in the Petrograd Soviet or its Executive Committee was it reported that the Left S.R.s would not join the Committee of Inquiry so long as Kozlovsky was on it?

5) Did the Left S.R.s carry out the decision of the Petrograd Soviet, which asked them to present evidence against Kozlovsky within a definite period?

Written January 15 (28), 1918

First published in 1933
in *Lenin Miscellany XXI*

Printed from the manuscript

DRAFT DECISION FOR THE C.P.C.
ON THE ORDER OF SUBORDINATION
OF THE BALTIC AND BLACK SEA FLEETS[38]

Considering the wording of the note to § 51 to be inexact or based on a misunderstanding, since the text, if taken literally, implies a refusal to recognise the supremacy of the Soviet state authority,[39] the C.P.C. asks the Navy's legislative organ to revise the wording of this note.

The C.P.C. takes into consideration the statement by representatives of the Navy that the note in question in no way signifies any repudiation of the central Soviet authorities, and instructs comrades Proshyan and Lunacharsky to draw up on behalf of the Council of People's Commissars a well-reasoned memorandum to the legislative organ of the Navy clarifying the point of view of the Council of People's Commissars.

Written January 15 (28), 1918

First published in 1959
in *Lenin Miscellany XXXVI*

Printed from the manuscript

ON SALARIES

DRAFT DECISION FOR THE C.P.C.[40]

The Council of People's Commissars endorses the estimates of the Commissariat for Post and Telegraph temporarily, for two months, in order that immediate steps be taken in the meantime to revise and adjust the rates of pay and salaries for all professions and all areas in the country.

This revision to be made by the Commissariat for Labour by arrangement with all the other commissariats and workers' organisations.

Written January 16 (29), 1918

First published in 1933   Printed from the manuscript
in *Lenin Miscellany XXI*

DRAFT DECISIONS FOR THE C.P.C.
ON THE ORGANISATION OF FOOD SUPPLY[41]

The Council of People's Commissars asks the Food Congress immediately, not later than tomorrow morning, to appoint at least three of the most experienced food supply workers to take part at once in the work of the existing top food supply bodies and in the discussion of the most vigorous and revolutionary steps for coping with the famine.

The Council of People's Commissars asks the Food Congress to elect a committee to receive reports from all the groups, institutions and workers in the food business who are now in conflict, and to forward the committee's findings to the C.P.C.

Written January 16 (29), 1918

First published in 1931   Printed from the manuscript
in *Lenin Miscellany XVIII*

DRAFT DECISION FOR THE C.P.C.
ON THE ACTIVITIES OF THE COMMITTEE
OF INQUIRY UNDER THE PETROGRAD SOVIET

Meeting of 21.I.1918

Having heard the report of the commission investigating the Committee of Inquiry, the C.P.C. resolves:

That two extra members be added to the commission, one of them Comrade Algasov, the other a Bolshevik recommended by Sverdlov.

That the commission be given the right to make searches, seizures and arrests without preliminary arrangements with any other institutions.

That the commission be given technical facilities and the right to draw on funds provided by the Commissariat for Justice.

That the commission be asked to work faster and more energetically in order to single out more quickly those whose innocence, in view of the slanderous nature of the accusations against them, is now obvious.[42]

First published in 1933   Printed from the manuscript
in *Lenin Miscellany XXI*

THE CONVERSION OF MUNITION WORKS
TO ECONOMICALLY USEFUL WORK

DRAFT DECISION FOR THE C.P.C.

Expressing its extreme regret that the proper commissariats are extremely slow in taking practical steps towards switching over the metalworks to useful work, the C.P.C. asks the Petrograd Metalworkers Trade Union, in co-operation with the Commissariat for Labour, the Petrograd Soviet and the Supreme Economic Council, to start immediately converting the metalworks to repair work on and production of railway equipment as well as to the production of goods suitable for exchange for grain, etc.

All military orders to be suspended.

Written January 23 (February 5),
          1918
     First published in 1933   Printed from the manuscript
     in *Lenin Miscellany XXI*

ADDENDUM TO THE DRAFT
OF THE "FUNDAMENTAL LAW
ON THE SOCIALISATION OF THE LAND"[43]

When the land is to be used for purposes other than farming (building, cultural and educational purposes, special industries and crafts, etc.), the size of the allotment is determined by the local Soviets in conformity with the requirements of the persons or institutions applying for permission, depending on the social necessity of the purpose for which the land is required.

Written in January, prior to the 27th
(February 9), 1918

First published in 1933   Printed from the manuscript
in *Lenin Miscellany XXI*

ADDENDUM TO THE DRAFT DECREE ON THE INSTITUTION OF AN ALL-RUSSIA INTER-DEPARTMENTAL EXTRAORDINARY COMMISSION FOR GUARDING THE RAILWAYS[44]

A special duty of the guard is ruthlessly to combat profiteering and the illicit transportation of food.

Written January 30
(February 12), 1918

First published in 1931   Printed from the manuscript
in *Lenin Miscellany XVIII*

PROPOSALS ON MEASURES TO IMPROVE THE FOOD SITUATION IN PETROGRAD

The Council of People's Commissars directs the Commissariat for Railways immediately to draw up and submit to it a draft decree banning free travelling on the railways except one trip home for every soldier returning from his place of service after demobilisation.

V. Ulyanov (Lenin)
Chairman, Council of People's Commissars

The C.P.C. instructs the Manager of the State Bank to dispatch to the South immediately and without fail 200 million rubles at the disposal of Yakubov's expedition for supplying grain to the needy areas as directed by the People's Commissariat for Food.

The Food Commissariat is to urgently make arrangements with the Military Commissariat for enlisting the services of the road units operating at the front. These units are to be sent to the grain-producing areas in the greatest possible numbers to take urgent measures for laying down rails and other means of improving and expediting the transportation, collection and storing of grain.

Written January 30
(February 12), 1918

First published in 1931   Printed from the manuscripts
in *Lenin Miscellany XVIII*

DECISION OF THE C.P.C.
CONCERNING THE EMPLOYMENT OF SABOTEURS[45]

The Council of People's Commissars resolves that no negotiations whatever are to be carried on with saboteurs.

The respective People's Commissariats may employ, as individuals, such saboteurs whose services are considered essential for the various departments provided that they fully submit to Soviet power and support it.

Written January 31
(February 13), 1918

Published February 14 (1), 1918   Printed from the manuscript
in *Pravda* No. 25

SPEECH AT A JOINT MEETING OF THE BOLSHEVIK AND LEFT S.R. GROUPS IN THE ALL-RUSSIA CENTRAL EXECUTIVE COMMITTEE
FEBRUARY 19, 1918

BRIEF NEWSPAPER REPORT

In a long speech lasting two hours, Lenin propounded the theses that there was no way out for Russia, that it was necessary immediately to conclude a separate peace, since the Germans were advancing all along the front en masse and we were powerless to offer any resistance to this million-strong pressure. Having concluded peace, we would be able to start putting things in order at home and deepening the socialist revolution, and we would succeed in completing the radical reforms that would bring us nearer to the introduction in Russia of a socialist system.

Sotsial-Demokrat No. 28
February 20 (7), 1918

Printed from the text
of the newspaper *Sotsial-Demokrat*

SPEECH TO THE LETTISH RIFLEMEN
FEBRUARY 20, 1918

BRIEF NEWSPAPER REPORT

Lenin made a long speech in which he called on the Letts to support Soviet power on the question of peace. The worn-out Russian people had to be given peace at all costs. In doing so we would strengthen the revolution and start building a new young Russia. In any case, the surrendered territories would not remain occupied, because the Russian revolution in the near future would spread not only to Germany, but to the other belligerent powers. The impact of the world social revolution would compel German imperialism to give up all its conquests.

Novaya Zhizn No. 30,
February 21 (8), 1918

Printed from the text
of *Novaya Zhizn*

TELEPHONE MESSAGE TO
THE EXECUTIVE COMMISSION
OF THE PETROGRAD COMMITTEE AND TO ALL
DISTRICT COMMITTEES
OF THE BOLSHEVIK PARTY[46]

21(8).II.1918. 12.20 p.m.

In accordance with decisions of the Petrograd Soviet to be passed this evening, we advise you, without losing an hour, to rally all the workers in order to organise tens of thousands of workers and get all the bourgeoisie, everyone of them to a man, under the control of these workers, to dig trenches outside the city. This is the only hope for the revolution. The revolution is in danger. The line of trenches will be marked out by the military. Prepare the implements, most important of all organise and mobilise one and all.

Lenin

First published in 1962
in the Fifth Russian Edition
of the *Collected Works,* Vol. 35

Printed from the manuscript

DECISION OF THE C.P.C.
ON THE ACCEPTANCE
OF THE GERMAN PEACE TERMS[47]

In accordance with the decision adopted by the Central Executive Committee of the Soviets of Workers', Soldiers' and Peasants' Deputies at 4.30 a.m. on February 24, the Council of People's Commissars has resolved that the terms of peace proposed by the German Government be accepted and a delegation sent to Brest-Litovsk

V. Ulyanov (Lenin)
Chairman, Council of People's Commissars

Written February 24, 1918

Published February 25 (12), 1918
in the evening edition
of *Pravda* No. 35,
and in the special evening edition
of *Izvestia* No. 33

Printed from the manuscript

TREATY WITH THE FINNISH
SOCIALIST WORKERS' REPUBLIC[48]

1

DRAFT DECISION OF THE C.P.C.

The Council of People's Commissars resolves:
To acknowledge in principle the justice of the Finnish comrades' desire that part of the territory mentioned in the Finnish addendum to § 6 of the draft treaty be handed over to the Finnish Socialist Workers' Republic.

The Conciliation Board is instructed to work out ways for the practical implementation of this transfer.[49]

Written February 25, 1918

2

DIRECTIVE OF THE C.P.C.
TO THE RUSSO-FINNISH CONCILIATION BOARD

The Council of People's Commissars gives the following directive to the Board:
That it be fair and necessary to ensure full political rights for the citizens of both republics residing in the other republic.

Written February 25, 1918

3

DRAFT DECISION FOR THE C.P.C.

Taking into consideration
first, that next to Finland there is a great city with an extremely high percentage of the bourgeois population;
second, that Finland usually has about thirty thousand Finnish workers living in Petrograd;

third, that the bourgeoisie of Petrograd usually has about two hundred thousand bourgeois living in Finland;

fourth, that therefore formal equality among Finnish and Russian citizens (in the matter of enjoying political rights abroad) would in practice be an obvious privilege for the Russian bourgeoisie,

the C.P.C. recommends the Russo-Finnish Conciliation Board to alter § 13 of the draft to read as follows:

either have § 13 refer, not to citizens, but only to workers and to peasants who do not exploit other people's labour;

or add to the former wording of § 13 a reservation to the effect that Russian citizens coming to Finland who are unable to prove that they belong to the two above-mentioned categories of working people, shall not enjoy political rights in Finland.[50]

Written February 27, 1918

First published in 1933
in *Lenin Miscellany XXI*

Printed from the manuscript

ADDENDUM TO THE DRAFT DECISION FOR THE C.P.C. CONCERNING THE ACTIVITIES OF THE COMMITTEE OF INQUIRY UNDER THE PETROGRAD SOVIET

In view of the statement by Comrade Schroeder that he was firmly convinced, despite the commission's opinion, that Comrade Mitzgendler was guilty of bribery, the C.P.C. considers Comrade Schroeder in duty bound, first, to repeat this statement in writing, and secondly, to bring his accusation against Mitzgendler before a court of law immediately in his own name.[51]

Written February 26, 1918

First published in 1933
in *Lenin Miscellany XXI*

Printed from the manuscript

SPEECHES AT THE MEETING OF THE C.P.C.
MARCH 4, 1918[52]

1

I fully agree with Comrade Trutovsky that the tendencies and attempts of which we have heard here are completely at variance with the aims of the workers' and peasants' government and have nothing in common with socialism.[53] The aim of socialism is to turn all the means of production into the property of the whole people, and that does not at all mean that the ships become the property of the ship workers or the banks the property of the bank clerks. If people take such paltry things seriously, then we must do away with nationalisation,[54] because the whole thing is preposterous. The task, the aim of socialism, as we see it, is to convert the land and the industrial enterprises into the property of the Soviet Republic. The peasant receives land on condition that he works it properly. If the river transport workers receive ships, it is on condition that they take a proprietary interest in them: they must submit their estimates if only in order to have income and expenditure endorsed, and they must take proper care of the ships. If they cannot do this, we shall remove them. Seeing that they have been arguing for three weeks, I would propose removing all of them from the management, because this shows an utter inaptitude for organisation, a complete failure to grasp the vital tasks facing the Soviet Republic. It is chaos, disorganisation, even worse—it borders on sabotage. They have started a sort of organised crusade in the Union and come complaining. Meanwhile, the boats on the Volga stand unrepaired. What is this? What is it—a madhouse? I am perfectly sure that they realise that if we go on existing in this chaos we shall bring still greater calamities down on our heads. The chief condition with us is discipline and the organised transfer of all property to the people, the transfer of all sources of wealth to the Soviet Republic, and their strictly disciplined disposal. So when we are told that the river transport workers will be private managing proprietors, we obviously cannot agree to it. Soviet power is to do the managing. But you organise a sort of debate preventing unity among all organisations....* If they are dissatisfied, they could have asked for the order to be rescinded. But they are proposing again that it should be decided first whom the ships belong to, so that the ship workers should demand a 140 per cent rise.

2

I fully agree with many things, but as to the make-up of the Board, I think the proposal of the river transport comrades is absolutely unacceptable. For one thing, that is not the question we are dealing with. The question at issue is that the men are not receiving their money. That's simply scandalous, of course. What are we allocating money for? For it to remain on paper? We have heard a thousand complaints, that unless the money is sent, our transport will collapse. If the money was assigned on February 21, and on the 22nd it was not received, then they should have come on the 23rd complaining. We are suffering from a money famine, we are short of currency notes, the treasury cannot print all we need. If we assign money and you unassign it, then actually nothing is sent. You should have come here on February 23, and not March 3. We demanded that these tens of millions should be given. I don't know who is more to blame. I believe the representatives of the Economic Council. We cannot satisfy everybody. While we are supplying Petrograd, Moscow is hungering for currency notes...** If people only wrote assignments and did not take any measures, they should have come here, or called me to the phone or somebody else, and complained about it. It is a rare week when I do not receive a complaint about money not being paid out, but from you I never received a single complaint. The people in charge should be made to answer for it, at least reprimanded. Under the ruling of February 21 the congress of river transport workers is obliged to submit the estimates. As regards the composition of the Management

---

* Part of the shorthand report has not been deciphered.—*Ed.*
** Part of the shorthand report has not been deciphered.—*Ed.*

Board, I think we should have corrected our decree rather in the vein Comrade Shlyapnikov suggested. Paragraph 3 provides for a Board of seven members. Why this wasn't inserted is incomprehensible. A number of trade union representatives could be included in it. I propose that resolute measures be taken to have this money forwarded immediately by through goods trains. Then notification should be sent in the usual way saying the money has been dispatched. As regards the second point I believe the only Board possible in this instance and most acceptable for everyone, for the Council of People's Commissars—the only possible Board is the one appointed yesterday by the Council of People's Commissars. There are no grounds for changing this. I believe we should put this through. And if it's really true about the 200 rubles salary, which was adopted as definite and made a condition for the nationalisation of transport—if that's a fact, and if demands are made for levelling up with other organisations, then I personally raise the question of cancelling nationalisation. There may come a time shortly when there will be no money at all. We had a single guarantee on the basis of which we wanted to carry out nationalisation, and this is being taken away from us. If that's the case, this measure should be revoked. Unless this is done we shall be taking on another responsibility incurring enormous losses.

3

I find the appointment of a commissar inconvenient in many respects. We have no indisputable candidate for this post. Therefore we shall not satisfy all requirements, inasmuch as both sides will be dissatisfied. The appointment of a commissar will mean setting aside the Union, and that form is undemocratic. We shall pass a decision for them to submit a proposal by the morning. If the Board is too unwieldy it could elect an executive committee. We can implement that organisationally tomorrow or the day after and have the thing put through organisationally at once within a fixed period. In appointing an executive committee, certain people could perhaps be appointed to it. This would

be correct, as we would not be setting aside the river transport workers. They can have no objection to co-operation
by the trade unions. If this doesn't go through, we can then
go ahead with the appointment of a commissar. The members
of this Council know that the question of a candidate is, of
course, a difficult one, and to decide now on appointing
a commissar is to decide nothing, as we quite often waste
a whole week over it. It is best to use this method. There
remains one proposal—to revoke points 5, 6 and 7. Adopted.
Under Paragraph 3 six Board members will be replaced by
temporary representatives from the trade unions.

First published in 1962   Printed from the shorthand record
in the Fifth Russian Edition
of the *Collected Works*, Vol. 35

DRAFT DECISION FOR THE C.P.C.
ON THE SETTING UP OF A WATER TRANSPORT
MANAGEMENT BOARD[55]

That comrades Milyutin, Shlyapnikov and Aprelev be
charged with organising, not later than tomorrow, a Board
in pursuance of § 3[56], each special function to be handled
by a specially authorised agent answerable to the Board as
a whole and to the C.P.C.

That in pursuance of § 3 any six Board members at the
choice of the Supreme Economic Council and representatives
of the regional councils be replaced by representatives of the
all-Russia trade unions.

That two comrades, one from the Water Transport Union
and one from the S.E.C., shall be appointed immediately
and report not later than tomorrow to Spunde in order to
have the currency notes dispatched without delay.[57]

Written March 4, 1918
First published in 1933   Printed from the manuscript
n *Lenin Miscellany XXI*

INTERVIEW WITH ARTHUR RANSOME,
CORRESPONDENT OF THE *DAILY NEWS* [58]

One of the weakest spots in Balfour's speech is the statement that the Japanese are going to help the Russians. [59] *Which Russians?*

In Russia today there is one power, which by its nature is destined to wage a life and death struggle against the attacks of international imperialism—that is the Power of the Soviets. The first step, however, of those Russians, whom the Japanese intend to "help", as soon as they heard rumours of the advance of the latter, was to demand the abolition of the Soviet Power. Should the Japanese move into Siberia, these same "Russians" whom the Japanese are going to "help", will demand the abolition of the Soviets throughout the whole of Siberia. What can take the place of the Soviet Power?

The only power that can take its place is a bourgeois government. But the bourgeoisie in Russia has proved clearly enough that it can only remain in power with foreign help. If a bourgeois government, supported by outside help, should establish itself in power in Siberia, and Eastern Russia become lost to the Soviet, then in Western Russia the Soviet Power would become weakened to such an extent that it could hardly hold out for long; it would be followed by a bourgeois government, which would also need foreign help. The Power to give this help would, of course, not be England. It is easy to understand what avenues are opened up by this possibility.

I confirm that I really said this in a conversation with Ransome, and I give permission for it to be printed.

Lenin

Moscow 23.III.1918

First published in 1932 in Russian (as an illustration) and in English in the book: R. H. Bruce Lockhart, *Memoirs of a British Agent*, London

Printed from the typewritten text with a postscript in Lenin's own hand

RE DRAFT DECREE CONCERNING
THE ESTABLISHMENT OF STATE CONTROL
OVER ALL FORMS OF INSURANCE [60]

The composition of the Insurance Council to be changed in the direction of increasing the number of representatives of the working classes to approximately two-thirds of the total number of members.

The Chief Commissariat for Insurance Affairs to maintain contact with the C.P.C. by its chief Commissar attending the meetings of the C.P.C. with a consultative voice.

Add*

Written March 23, 1918
First published in 1933   Printed from the manuscript
in *Lenin Miscellany XXI*

ORIGINAL VERSION OF THE ARTICLE
"THE IMMEDIATE TASKS
OF THE SOVIET GOVERNMENT" [61]

CHAPTER IV

...**

Today this task—which is, of course, not yet sufficiently completed and can never be fully accomplished—no longer stands first among the tasks facing the Soviet government. The recent congresses of the Soviets, notably the All-Russia Congress held in Moscow, have shown that the overwhelming majority of the labouring classes have firmly and consciously sided with the Soviet power in general and with the Bolshevik Party in particular. It goes without saying that for any government that is at all democratic the task of convincing the masses can never be wholly overshadowed—on the contrary, it will always be among the important tasks of government. As a key issue, however, it will only have significance for parties of the opposition or for parties that

---

* Here the manuscript breaks off.—*Ed.*
** The beginning of the shorthand record has not been found.—**Ed.**

are fighting for ideals of the future. After the Bolsheviks, first under tsarism and then under Kerensky, had succeeded in winning over to their side the majority of the class-conscious active elements of the working masses, our Party was faced with the task of conquering power and suppressing the resistance of the exploiters. The task that came to the fore was that of winning, instead of convincing, Russia. From the end of October 1917 approximately up to February 1918 the militant or military task held first place, as it naturally should for any political party making a bid for power in conditions of sharp and extremely bitter struggle. Obviously, for the Party of the proletariat, the task of suppressing the resistance of the exploiters becomes a crucial issue, because the working masses who side with the proletariat are opposed here by the united members of the propertied classes armed both with the power of capital, the power of knowledge and the long-standing, if not age-old, habit and practice of government. Owing to the special conditions that were created in Russia under the influence of the unforgotten lessons of the revolution of 1905 and the influence of the far more painful and harsher lessons of the present war—owing to these conditions the Bolsheviks succeeded with comparative ease in solving the problem of winning power both in the capital and in the chief industrial centres of Russia. But in the provinces, in places far removed from the centre, and especially in districts known to have the greatest concentration of a comparatively backward population rooted in the traditions of the monarchy and medievalism—the Cossack regions, for instance—Soviet power had to contend with a resistance that took on military forms and is only now, more than four months after the October Revolution, coming to an end. At the present time the task of overcoming and suppressing the resistance of the exploiters in Russia is, in the main, completed. Russia has been won by the Bolsheviks chiefly because—as that prominent leader of the counter-revolutionary Don Cossacks, Bogayevsky himself, recently admitted—the overwhelming majority of the people even among the Cossacks have consciously, firmly and definitely sided with the Bolsheviks. But the special conditions in which the propertied classes are placed economically enable them naturally to organise not only

passive resistance (sabotage), but to repeat the attempt at
military resistance to Soviet power. For that reason the
task of suppressing the resistance of the exploiters cannot be
regarded as having been finally completed. At any rate,
it has now obviously been dealt with in its main aspects and
is retreating into the background. The Soviet government
will never for a moment allow itself to forget about this task
and will under no circumstances let itself be diverted from
it by any political or so-called socialist names or decla-
mations. We have to speak about this because both the Mensheviks and the Right S.R.s act as the most mobile, sometimes even as the most brazen-faced counter-revolutionaries,
who wage a sharper struggle against the Soviet government
than the one they had allowed themselves to wage against
the reactionary and landowner governments, and rely on
their party's label and designation to protect them. Naturally, the Soviet government will never falter in its task of
suppressing the resistance of the exploiters, no matter what
party banners or what popular and specious names this
resistance may be covered up with. However, at the present
time the task of suppressing resistance has, in the main,
been completed, and the task now confronting us is that of
administering the state.

This transition from what was once the priority task of
convincing the masses, a transition from the task of winning
power and crushing the resistance of the exploiters by
military force to what is now the primary task of administering the state—this transition is the main feature of the
present moment. The difficulty which the Soviet government
is experiencing is that of bringing home the essentials of
this transition to all the class-conscious elements of the
working masses as well as the people's political leaders.
For it is self-understood that the transition to the peaceful
tasks of governing the whole population irrespective of
classes, a transition that is taking place in conditions when
the civil war is still going on in some places, when grave
military dangers are threatening the Soviet Republic from
both the West and the East, and when the war has caused
untold havoc throughout the country—it is self-understood
that such a transition is beset with tremendous difficulties.

CHAPTER V

The task of administering the state, which now confronts the Soviet government, has this special feature, that, probably for the first time in the modern history of civilised nations, it deals pre-eminently with economics rather than with politics. Usually the word "administration" is associated chiefly, if not solely, with political activity. However, the very basis and essence of Soviet power, like that of the transition itself from capitalist to socialist society, lie in the fact that political tasks occupy a subordinate position to economic tasks. And now, especially after the practical experience of over four months of Soviet government in Russia, it should be quite clear to us that the task of administering the state is primarily a purely economic task—that of healing the country's wounds inflicted by the war, restoring its productive forces, organising accountancy in and control over production and distribution, raising the productivity of labour—in short, it boils down to the task of economic reorganisation.

This task can be said to fall under two main headings: 1) accounting and control over production and distribution in the broadest, most widespread and universal forms of such accounting and control, and 2) raising the productivity of labour. These tasks can be handled by any form of collective effort or any form of state passing over to socialism only on condition that the basic economic, social, cultural and political preconditions for this have been created in a sufficient degree by capitalism. Without large-scale machine production, without a more or less developed network of railways, postal and telegraph communications, without a more or less developed network of public educational institutions, neither of these tasks can be carried out in a systematic way on a national scale. Russia is in a position when quite a number of these initial preconditions for such a transition actually exist. On the other hand, quite a number of these preconditions are absent in our country, but can be borrowed by it fairly easily from the experience of the neighbouring, far more advanced countries, whom history and international intercourse have long since placed in close contact with Russia.

CHAPTER VI

The basic aim of every society going over to a socialist
system consists in the victory of the ruling class—or rather
the class that is growing up to be the ruling class—namely,
the proletariat, over the bourgeoisie as described above.
And this task is set before us in a substantially new way,
quite unlike the way it stood in the course of many decades
of the proletariat's world-wide experience of struggle against
the bourgeoisie. Now, after the gains of the October Revolution, after our successes in the civil war, victory over the
bourgeoisie should stand for something much bigger, albeit
more peaceful in form: namely, victory over the bourgeoisie,
now that it has been secured politically and made good
militarily, should now be achieved in the sphere of organisation of the national economy, in the sphere of organisation
of production, in the sphere of country-wide accounting and
control. The problem of accounting and control over production was dealt with by the bourgeoisie all the more effectively
in proportion as production expanded and the network of
national economic institutions embracing tens and hundreds
of millions of the population of a large modern state became
more ramified. We must handle this task now in a new way,
backed by the predominating position of the proletariat,
supported by the bulk of the working and exploited masses,
making use of those elements of organising talent and technical knowledge which have been accumulated by the preceding
society, and nine-tenths, perhaps even ninety-nine hundredths
of which belong to a class hostile and opposed to the
socialist revolution.

CHAPTER VII

German imperialism, which has made the greatest advance
not only in military power and military techniques, but in
big industrial organisations within the framework of
capitalism, has incidentally given proof of its economic
progressiveness by being the first country to introduce labour
conscription. Naturally, in the conditions of capitalist

society in general and particularly when the monarchist states are waging an imperialist war, labour conscription is nothing more than a military convict prison for the workers, a new means of enslaving the working and exploited masses, a new system of measures for suppressing all protest on the part of these masses. Nevertheless, there is no question that it is only because of the economic preconditions created by big capitalism that such a reform could be put forward and effected. And now we, amid conditions of appalling post-war economic disorganisation, are obliged to consider the urgency of a similar reform. Naturally, Soviet power, which is passing from a capitalist to a socialist organisation of society, must tackle this problem of labour conscription from the other end, opposite to that of German imperialism. For the capitalists and imperialists of Germany labour conscription meant enslavement of the workers. For the workers and peasant poor in Russia labour conscription should mean, first and foremost, recruitment of the rich and propertied classes for the discharge of their social duties. We should start labour conscription with the rich.

This is necessitated, generally speaking, not only by the fact that the Soviet Republic is a socialist republic. The necessity arises also from the fact that it was precisely the wealthy and propertied classes who, by their resistance, both military and passive (sabotage), mostly prevented Russia from healing the wounds inflicted upon her by the war, hampered the country's economic rehabilitation and progress. That is why accounting and control, which should be now considered a problem of paramount importance in the whole business of state administration, must be applied first of all to the wealthy and propertied classes. It was the members of these classes who enjoyed the tribute they collected from the working people, especially during the war; it was they who used this tribute to evade a task which is the duty of every citizen, namely, that of lending a hand in healing the country's wounds and putting it on its feet again; it was they who used the plundered tribute to retire and entrench themselves behind impregnable walls and offer every possible resistance to the victory of the socialist principle over the capitalist principle of society's organisation. One of the chief weapons of such struggle against the Soviets and against socialism on the part of the wealthy and propertied classes was their possession of considerable hoards of currency notes. The propertied classes in capitalist society derived most of their wealth from the land and other means of production, such as factories, mills, etc., which they owned. The Soviet government had no difficulty, thanks to the support of the workers and the great majority of the peasants, in abolishing the right of the landowners and the bourgeoisie to these basic items of the country's wealth. It was not difficult to decree the abolition of private property in land. It was not difficult to nationalise most of the factories and mills. There is no doubt that the nationalisation of other big industrial enterprises and transport facilities is a problem that will easily be dealt with in the very near future.

Capitalist society, however, has created another form of wealth, which is by no means so easy for the Soviet government to deal with. This is wealth in the form of money, or rather, currency notes. Currency notes during the war were issued in very great numbers. Russia was cut off by a wall of military operations from commerce with a number of countries who had been her largest importers and exporters. The amassment of currency notes in the hands of the wealthy and propertied classes, practically all of whom, directly or indirectly, had speculated on the high prices for military contracts and supplies, is one of the chief means by which the propertied classes amassed wealth and accumulated power over the working people. Today the economic position of Russia, as probably of every capitalist country that has gone through three years of war, is characterised by the fact that enormous amounts of paper money are concentrated in the hands of and hoarded by a comparatively small minority, the bourgeoisie and propertied classes, and this paper money, though greatly depreciated through massive emission, still represents a claim to levy tribute on the working population.

During the transition from capitalist to socialist society it is absolutely impossible to do without currency notes or to replace them with new ones in a short space of time. The Soviet government is now confronted with a difficult task, which nevertheless has to be dealt with at all costs—the task of combating the resistance of the wealthy, a resistance that takes the form of hoarding and concealing the proofs of their claim to levy tribute on the working people. These proofs are currency notes. Naturally, while these currency notes previously gave the right to acquire and purchase the means of production, such as land, factories, mills, etc., their significance today has diminished and even been reduced to naught. The purchase of land has become impossible in Russia after promulgation of the law on the socialisation of the land, while the purchase of factories and mills and similar large-scale means of production and transport has become practically impossible owing to the rapid process of nationalisation and confiscation of all such large enterprises. And so, it becomes more and more difficult and almost impossible for members of the bourgeoisie and propertied classes (including the peasant bourgeoisie) to acquire money for the purchase of the means of production. But in defending their old privileges and trying to retard and obstruct as much as they can the business of socialist reforms within the country, the bourgeoisie are hoarding and concealing the proofs of their claim to a share in the social wealth, their claim to levy tribute on the working people, hoarding and concealing currency notes in order to have a chance, however slender, of maintaining their position and recovering their old privileges in the event of difficulties or crises of a military or commercial nature that might yet beset Russia.

As regards consumer goods, the possibility of buying them with the sums of paper money they have accumulated through speculations during the war remains almost fully with the bourgeoisie and propertied classes, since the problem of proper rationing and distribution of these goods in a country like Russia, with her huge population of small peasants, petty artisans or handicraftsmen, presents tremendous difficulties, and in the prevailing state of economic chaos caused by the war this problem still remains practically unsolved. Thus, the Soviet government is obliged to start the business of accounting and control over production and distribution by an organised struggle against the wealthy and propertied classes who are hoarding vast sums in currency notes and evading state control.

It is estimated that currency notes to the value of about thirty thousand million rubles have been issued in Russia to date. Of this sum probably no less than twenty thousand million, or maybe considerably more, are excess hoards unneeded for trade turnover, which are kept hidden away by members of the bourgeoisie and propertied classes for motives of self-interest—or class self-interest.

The Soviet government will have to combine the introduction of labour conscription with the registration, in the first place, of people belonging to the bourgeoisie and propertied classes; it will have to demand truthful statements (declarations) concerning the amount of currency notes available; it will have to take a number of measures to make sure that this demand will not remain on paper; it will have to consider transitional measures for concentrating all stocks of currency notes in the State Bank or its branches. Unless these measures are taken, the business of accounting and control over production and distribution cannot be effectively carried through.

CHAPTER VIII

The introduction of labour conscription, however, cannot be confined to accounting and control over the sums of currency notes concentrated in the hands of the propertied classes. The Soviet government will have to apply the principles of labour conscription also to the direct activities of the bourgeoisie and propertied classes in the sphere of factory management and the servicing of enterprises by all kinds of subsidiary labour such as book-keeping, accountancy, clerical work, technical, administrative and other jobs. In this respect, too, the task of the Soviet government is now shifting from the sphere of direct struggle against sabotage to the sphere of business organisation in the new conditions, since after the victories won by the Soviets in the civil war, beginning with October and ending February, a breach has virtually been made in the passive forms of resistance, namely, in the sabotage by the bourgeoisie and the bourgeois intellectuals. It is no accident that at the present time we are witnessing a sweeping, one might say widespread, change of sentiment and political behaviour in the camp of the former saboteurs, i.e., the capitalists and bourgeois intellectuals. In all spheres of economic and political life we now find a great number of bourgeois intellectuals and capitalist businessmen offering their services to the Soviet power. And it is up to the Soviet power now to make use of these services, which are definitely necessary for the transition to socialism, especially in a peasant country like Russia, and should be utilised on condition that the Soviet government has complete ascendancy, direction and control over its new assistants and co-operators (who had often acted in defiance of this same Soviet power in the secret hope of protesting it).

To show how necessary it is for the Soviet government to make use of the services of bourgeois intellectuals for the transition to socialism, we venture to use an expression that may at first glance seem paradoxical: we must to a considerable extent, take a lesson in socialism from the trust managers, we must take a lesson in socialism from capitalism's big organisers. That this is no paradox anyone can easily see who realises that it is the big factories, big machine industry, which developed exploitation of the working people to an unheard-of degree, that it is precisely the big factories that are the centres of concentration of that class which alone has been able to destroy the rule of capital and begin the transition to socialism. It is not surprising, therefore, that in order to solve the practical problems of socialism, when the organisational aspects of it are pushed to the fore, we must enlist to the service of the Soviet power a great number of bourgeois intellectuals, especially from among those who were engaged in the practical work of organising large-scale capitalist production, that is to say, first and foremost, those engaged in organising syndicates, cartels and trusts. Tackling this problem will require of the Soviet government an exertion of energy and initiative by the working masses in all fields of the national economy, since the old position held by the so-called captains of industry—the old position of the masters and exploiters— this old position the Soviet government will never let them have. The former captains of industry, the former masters and exploiters, must be employed as technical experts, managers, consultants, advisers. A new, difficult, but extremely gratifying problem must be solved, that of combining all the experience and knowledge which these

members of the exploiting classes have accumulated, with
the initiative, energy and work of the broad masses of the
working people. For only by this combination is it possible
to build the bridge leading from the old capitalist to the new
socialist society.

If the socialist revolution had won simultaneously
throughout the world or, at least, in a number of advanced
countries, then the task of enlisting the services of the best
technician specialists from among the leaders of old capitalism to the process of the new organisation of production
would have been made considerably easier. Backward
Russia would not have to wrestle with this problem on her
own, as the advanced workers of the West-European
countries would have come to her help and relieved her of
most of the complexities involved in that most difficult
of all tasks arising in the period of transition to socialism
known as the organisational task. In the present situation,
when the socialist revolution in the West is slow and late
in coming, and Russia has to speed up measures for her
reorganisation, if only in order to save the population from
starvation and afterwards the whole country from a possible
foreign military invasion—in the present situation we have
to borrow from the advanced countries, not their help in
socialist organisation and the support of the workers, but
the help of their bourgeoisie and capitalist intellectuals.

Things have so shaped themselves that we are able to get
this help by organising the assistance of the bourgeois
intellectuals in solving the new organisational problems of
the Soviet power. This assistance can be secured by paying
high salaries to the best specialists in every field of knowledge, both to the citizens of this country and to those invited
from abroad. Naturally, in a developed socialist society
it would appear quite unfair and incorrect for members of
the bourgeois intelligentsia to receive considerably higher
pay than that received by the best sections of the working
class. Under the conditions of practical reality, however...*
we must solve this pressing problem by means of this (unfair)
remuneration for bourgeois specialists at much higher rates.

---

* Part of the sentence illegible and has been omitted.—*Ed.*

If, for example, we found that in order to organise production in Russia on new lines, in order to raise the productivity of labour and train our people in the art of working in better conditions—if we had to employ for this purpose, say two thousand big specialists in different fields of knowledge, specialists from among Russian and still more from among foreign, let us say, American sources—if we had to pay them fifty or a hundred million rubles a year, such an expense, from the point of view of the interests of the national economy, and generally from the point of view of abandoning out-worn methods of production for newer and more up-to-date methods, would be fully warranted. Such a sum is worth paying to have our people trained in better methods and techniques of production, and we shall have to pay it because, short of the victory of the socialist revolution in other countries, there is no other possibility of getting this leadership.

Of course, employment of the labour and guidance of the bourgeois intellectuals in combination with proper control by the democratic organisations of the working people and the Soviets, will create a number of new problems, but these problems will be quite solvable. No difficulties can stop us from solving these problems, as we have no other way out towards a higher organisation of production under the present situation.

I shall go further. Big capitalism has created systems of work organisation, which, under the prevailing conditions of exploitation of the masses, represent the harshest form of enslavement by which the minority, the propertied classes, wring out of the working people surplus amounts of labour, strength, blood and nerves. At the same time they are the last word in the scientific organisation of production, and as such, have to be adopted by the Socialist Soviet Republic and readjusted to serve the interests of our accounting and control over production on the one hand, and raising the productivity of labour, on the other. For instance, the famous Taylor system, which is so widespread in America, is famous precisely because it is the last word in reckless capitalist exploitation. One can understand why this system met with such an intense hatred and protest on the part of the workers. At the same time, we must not for a moment

forget that the Taylor system represents the tremendous
progress of science, which systematically analyses the process
of production and points the way towards an immense
increase in the efficiency of human labour. The scientific
researches which the introduction of the Taylor system started
in America, notably that of motion study, as the Americans
call it, yielded important data allowing the working population to be trained in incomparably higher methods of labour
in general and of work organisation in particular.

The negative aspect of Taylorism was that it was applied
in conditions of capitalist slavery and served as a means of
squeezing double and triple the amount of labour out of the
workers at the old rates of pay regardless of whether the
hired workers were capable of giving this double and triple
amount of labour in the same number of working hours
without detriment to the human organism. The Socialist
Soviet Republic is faced with a task which can be briefly
formulated thus: we must introduce the Taylor system and
scientific American efficiency of labour throughout Russia
by combining this system with a reduction in working time,
with the application of new methods of production and work
organisation undetrimental to the labour power of the
working population. On the contrary, the Taylor system,
properly controlled and intelligently applied by the working
people themselves, will serve as a reliable means of further
greatly reducing the obligatory working day for the entire
working population, will serve as an effective means of
dealing, in a fairly short space of time, with a task that
could roughly be expressed as follows: six hours of physical
work daily for every adult citizen and four hours of work
in running the state.

The adoption of such a system would call for very many
new skills and new organisational bodies. Without doubt,
this will create for us many difficulties, and the posing of
such a task will even evoke perplexity if not resistance
among certain sections of the working people themselves.
We may be sure, however, that the progressive elements
among the working class will understand the need for such
a transition, and that the appalling extent of the economic
chaos witnessed in the towns and villages by millions of men
returning from the front who had been torn away from it all

and now saw the full extent of the ravages caused by the war—all this, without doubt, has prepared the ground for shaping public opinion in this direction, and we may be sure that the transition which we have roughly outlined above will be accepted as a practical task by all elements among the working classes who have now consciously sided with the Soviet government.

CHAPTER IX

An economic transition of the above nature calls also for a corresponding change in the functions of Soviet leadership. It is quite natural, in a situation under which the main task was to convince the majority of the nation or to win power and crush the resistance of the exploiters, that among the leaders, too, those who came to the fore should have been agitators in regard to the masses, with whom Soviet power was more closely connected than any other democratic form of government in the past. Naturally, winning over the majority of the population or drawing it into a hard and difficult armed struggle against the exploiters called above all for agitators of ability. Conversely, the tasks outlined above and aimed at establishing accounting and control over production and distribution, advance to the fore practical managers and organisers. Accordingly, a certain reappraisal of leaders, certain shifts among them, should be effected in cases where they are unable to adapt themselves to the new conditions and the new task. Naturally, the leadership of a past period accustomed chiefly to agitators' tasks, would find such a transition very difficult. Naturally, a number of mistakes because of this was unavoidable. Both the leaders and the Soviet electorate at large, that is, the working and exploited masses, must now be made to see the necessity for this change.

Among the working and exploited masses there is far more talent and ability as organisers than as agitators, for the entire work milieu of these classes demanded of them to a much greater extent the ability to organise joint work and a system of accounting and control over production and distribution. Their former conditions of life, on the contrary, provided far less grounds for advancing from their midst leaders possessing the gift of agitators or propagandists. Perhaps that is why we so often see now agitators and propagandists by vocation or calling who are compelled to assume the tasks of organisers, and who have it brought home to them at every step that they are not quite fit for the job and that the workers and peasants are disappointed and dissatisfied with them. These mistakes and failures of the Soviet government often provoke malicious glee among classes that are hostile to the idea of a socialist remodelling of society, among members of the bourgeois parties or those who call themselves socialist parties but who actually serve the bourgeoisie with zeal—people like the Mensheviks and the Right Socialist-Revolutionaries. Clear as the historical inevitability of these mistakes is, it is equally clear that the shortcomings in this respect are merely the growing pains of the new socialist society. There can be no doubt that the representatives of Soviet power all over Russia can and will requalify without great difficulty, that the practical agitators will learn to occupy a befitting leading place. This, however, will take time, and only practical experience by trial and error is capable of bringing a clear realisation of the need for change, capable of bringing to the fore a number of people, or even a whole cross-section, fit to deal with the new tasks. There is probably more organising talent among the workers and peasants than the bourgeoisie imagine. The trouble is that these talents have no chance to develop, make good and win a place for themselves in the conditions of capitalist economy.

On the other hand, if we clearly recognise today the need for enlisting new organising talent on a broad scale to the business of running the state, if we—guided by the principles of Soviet power—start systematically promoting to leading positions people who have practical experience in this business, we shall succeed in a short time in building up a new stratum of practical organisers of production, who, on the basis of the principles evolved by Soviet power, principles cast among the masses and carried into practice by the masses under the control of Soviet bodies representing the mass membership, will win a position for themselves befitting their role of leadership.

CHAPTER X

Soviet government will have to pass over, or rather it will simultaneously have to deal with, the problem of applying corresponding principles to the bulk of the workers and peasants. Here the task of introducing labour conscription presents its other side to us. We must approach this problem differently and highlight different things to those that have to be applied in the case of the wealthy classes. We see no essential need for registering all the working people, for keeping an eye on their stocks of currency notes or their consumption, since all the conditions of life compel the vast majority of these sections of the population to work for their living and give them no chance to hoard anything but the most meagre stocks. Therefore, the task of introducing labour conscription in this field resolves itself into the task of establishing labour discipline and self-discipline.

In the old capitalist society discipline over the working people was enforced by capital through the constant threat of starvation. This threat being combined with excessively heavy toil and the workers' awareness that they were working, not for themselves, but for somebody else's benefit, the conditions of labour became a constant struggle of the great majority of the working people against the organisers of production. This inevitably created a psychology in which public opinion among the working people not only did not frown on poor work or shirkers, but, on the contrary, saw in this an inevitable and legitimate protest against or means of resistance to the excessive demands of the exploiters. If the bourgeois press and its echoers are now shouting so much about anarchy among the workers, about their lack of discipline and excessive demands, the vicious nature of this criticism is so obvious that it is not worth dwelling on. It is only natural that in a country like Russia, where the bulk of the population for the last three years has endured such appalling hunger and privations, there should have been a number of cases of utter despondency and a break-down of organisation. To demand a quick change in this connection or to expect such changes to be achieved by several decrees, would be as absurd as resorting to appeals in an attempt to restore good cheer and energy into a man who had been beaten within an inch of his life. Only the Soviet government, created by the working people themselves, and taking into consideration the growing signs of recovery among them, is in a position to carry out radical changes in this respect.

The need for working out systematic measures to improve self-discipline among the working people has now been fully brought home to the representatives of Soviet power and its supporters—the political-minded trade union leaders, for instance. There is no doubt that in the environment of capitalist society in general, and still more, in the atmosphere of frenzied, unbridled speculation created by the war, there has seeped in among the working class an element of demoralisation that will seriously need coping with. All the more that, owing to the war, the composition of the working-class vanguard itself has not changed for the better either. Therefore, the maintenance of discipline among the working people, the organisation of control over the measure of labour and the intensity of labour, the introduction of special industrial courts for establishing the measure of labour, for prosecuting those guilty of flagrant violations of this measure, and for exercising systematic influence on the majority with the object of raising this measure—all this has now been brought to the fore as one of the most urgent tasks of the Soviet government.

The only thing is to bear in mind that in bourgeois society one of the principal instruments of social education, namely, the press, completely failed to discharge its task in this respect. And to this day our Soviet press, too, is still largely under the influence of the old habits and old traditions of bourgeois society. This is evidenced, among other things, by the fact that our press, like the old bourgeois press, continues to devote too much space and attention to political trivia, to those personal questions of political leadership by which the capitalists of all countries have striven to draw the attention of the masses away from the really important, profound and cardinal questions of their life.

Dictated between March 23
and 28, 1918

First published in 1962   Printed from the shorthand record
in the Fifth Russian Edition
of the *Collected Works*, Vol. 36

THE STATE OF INLAND WATER TRANSPORT
DRAFT DECISION FOR THE C.P.C.[62]

Having heard the report concerning the disastrous state of the inland water transport and acquainted itself with the draft decree drawn up by the Supreme Economic Council in agreement with the Central Committee of the Water Transport Workers' Union and the representatives of the Central Committee of the Volga Fleet,

the C.P.C. endorses this draft as a temporary measure;

—urgently asks the Nizhni-Novgorod Congress of Water Transport Employees to put this draft into effect immediately and without any deviations;

—should the congress consider it necessary in future to make any amendments to the decree, the C.P.C. asks the congress to send its authorised delegation to the C.P.C. to discuss and finally settle the question of such amendments.

The C.P.C. impresses upon the congress that the disastrous state of inland water transport precludes any possibility of delays and makes it absolutely necessary to strictly and conscientiously carry out all the orders of Kavomar.[63] Only on this condition will the C.P.C. be able to justify the allocation of immense sums on the national fleet in the eyes of the country.

V. Ulyanov (Lenin)
Chairman, Council of People's Commissars

Written March 26, 1918

First published in 1933
in *Lenin Miscellany XXI*   Printed from the manuscript

DRAFT DECISION FOR THE C.P.C. ON CONTROL OF S.E.C. EXPENDITURE[64]

The C.P.C. instructs the representatives, one from the State Control and one from the Commissariat for Finance, to form a commission which, not later than tomorrow, shall start an inspection of the books of the accounting office under the Fuel Department of the S.E.C. and also other accounting offices of the S.E.C.

Comrade Bogolepov is charged with summoning the commission.

The same commission is charged with: first, specially examining the question of forms of accountancy; second, demanding precise statements in writing signed by all the persons concerned certifying their participation in the allocation of money and the conduct of business operations of the various departments of the S.E.C.

The commission shall furthermore demand of the people in charge that they present in the near future the appropriate documents from all subordinate institutions and persons through whom expenditure of S.E.C. sums is effected.

The C.P.C. reprimands the S.E.C. and especially its Fuel Department for the extremely irregular manner in which they conduct business.

Written March 26, 1918
First published in 1933   Printed from the manuscript
in *Lenin Miscellany XXI*

SPEECH AT A MEETING OF THE PRESIDIUM
OF THE S.E.C.
APRIL 1, 1918

The question under discussion is a draft resolution concerning labour discipline drawn up by the All-Russia Council of Trade Unions. Comrade Lenin moves a number of amendments and more definite wordings of different points in the draft, which he suggests should be concretised. Piece wages should be fixed for all industries without exception, and in the case of trades where that is not possible, a system of bonuses should be introduced. To keep account of productivity and maintain discipline it is necessary to set up industrial courts, to form groups of controllers of various trades, not at the enterprise, but from outside, and enlisting the co-operation of engineers, book-keepers and peasants. The decree should definitely provide for the introduction of the Taylor system, in other words, every use should be made of the scientific methods of work suggested by this system. Without it, productivity cannot be raised, without it we shall not be able to introduce socialism. In the application of this system American engineers are to be enlisted. Naturally, in introducing it, due consideration should be given to the poor nutrition. The rates of output, therefore, should make allowance for a low diet. Furthermore, it is necessary to organise output...* in the transition to socialism may enable us to reduce the working day. The decree should mention accountancy and the printing of reports concerning the productivity of the various enterprises. As to penal measures for breaches of labour discipline, these are to be stricter. Punishment should go to the length of imprisonment. Dismissal, too, may be applied, but this will be of an entirely different nature. Under the capitalist system dismissal was a breach of a civic agreement. Now, a breach of discipline, especially with the introduction of compulsory labour service, will be a criminal offence subject to a definite punishment.

First published (in part)
in 1940 in the journal
Proletarskaya Revolutsia No. 1

Printed from the typewritten
copy of the minutes

ADDENDA TO THE DRAFT DECREE
ON THE PROCEDURE FOR SENDING COMMISSARS
OUT TO THE PROVINCES[65]

3) The Soviets shall give every assistance to commissars invested with proper authority, within the limits of such authority.

4) The Soviets shall render unconditional assistance to all commissars extraordinary and other commissars who are

---

* An omission in the minutes.—*Ed.*

appointed by the Council of People's Commissars. Execution
of the orders of these commissars is obligatory for all local
and regional Soviets.

Written April 5, 1918

First published in 1933
in *Lenin Miscellany XXI*

Printed from the manuscript

SPEECH AT A JOINT MEETING
OF REPRESENTATIVES
OF THE ALL-RUSSIA CENTRAL COUNCIL
OF TRADE UNIONS,
THE CENTRAL COMMITTEE
OF THE METALWORKERS' UNION
AND THE SUPREME ECONOMIC COUNCIL
APRIL 11, 1918[66]

FROM A NEWSPAPER REPORT

Comrade Lenin urged the complete nationalisation of all
trustified enterprises, with the group of capitalists who
sponsored the project being enlisted in the service of the
state.

Izvestia No. 72
April 12, 1918

Printed from the newspaper text

TO THE PRESIDING COMMITTEE
OF THE FIRST CONGRESS
OF SOVIETS OF THE DON REPUBLIC[67]

Rostov-on-Don

With all my heart I greet the first Congress of Soviets
of the Don Republic.

In particular I heartily subscribe to the words of the
resolution concerning the necessity for carrying through to

victory the mounting struggle against the kulak elements of Cossackdom in the Don region. These words contain an accurate definition of the tasks of the revolution. This is the kind of struggle that now faces us throughout Russia.

Lenin

Written April 13, 1918
First published in 1942   Printed from the manuscript
in *Lenin Miscellany XXXIV*

ADDENDUM TO THE DRAFT DECREE ON THE REGISTRATION OF SHARES, BONDS AND OTHER INTEREST-BEARING SECURITIES[68]

The ban on the alienation of shares as set forth in the law of 29.XII.1917 shall remain in force pending the promulgation of a law introducing a permissive system for the alienation of shares. Only shareholders who have properly and timely registered their shares shall be entitled to receive compensation in the event of the enterprises being nationalised, the amount and conditions of such compensation to be determined by the law on nationalisation.

Similarly, only such shareholders shall be entitled to receive dividends when payment of same, suspended by the law of 29.XII.1917, will be permitted.

Written April 16, 1918
First published in 1933   Printed from the manuscript
in *Lenin Miscellany XXI*

DECISION OF THE C.P.C. ON THE FINANCING OF SUGAR-BEET SOWING CAMPAIGN[69]

Twenty million rubles is allocated to the Supreme Economic Council to be advanced to the peasants for sugar-beet sowing, the S.E.C. to take all the necessary steps

ensuring the proper expenditure of these sums and their
timely repayment.

V. Ulyanov (Lenin)
Chairman, Council of People's Commissars

Written April 17, 1918

First published in 1945
in *Lenin Miscellany XXXV*

Printed from the manuscript

DRAFT DECREE ON THE INSTITUTION
OF AN ALL-RUSSIA EVACUATION COMMISSION[70]

An All-Russia Evacuation Commission shall be instituted
to effect the speediest and planned evacuation of military
and other freights to new points of destination (the general
object of evacuation being the demobilisation of industry
and satisfaction of the needs of the reorganised national
economy, and by no means only military requirements).

The commission shall work according to a plan approved,
amended and supplemented by the Council of People's
Commissars. This plan determines the destination of the
main classes of freight and the comparative urgency of
their evacuation.

The commission shall be headed by an agent extraordinary invested with dictatorial powers. The members of the
commission shall have a consultative voice and the right to
introduce questions in the C.P.C. (if voted for by no less
than one-third of the membership).

The members of the commission are: the deputy agent
extraordinary with the post of chairman, and representatives
of the Military, Naval, Railway, Food and Labour
Commissariats and the Supreme Economic Council.

Written April, not
later than 19, 1918

First published in 1959
in the book
Decrees of the Soviet Government,
Vol. II

Printed from the manuscript

ADDENDUM TO THE DRAFT DECREE FOR THE C.P.C. ON SUPPLYING AGRICULTURE WITH IMPLEMENTS AND METALS[71]

The basic principle to be applied in the distribution of agricultural machines, etc., should be, on the one hand and in the first place, due concern for agricultural production, for cultivation of all the land and for raising the productivity of agriculture, and, on the other, the supply of agricultural machines, etc., first of all to the working and poor sections of the rural population, with the common object of providing a proper and sufficient supply of breadstuff for the whole population.

Written April 23, 1918

First published in 1933
in *Lenin Miscellany XXI*

Printed from the manuscript

ADDENDUM TO THE DRAFT DECREE FOR THE C.P.C. ON A DEPARTMENT FOR ORGANISING THE CULTIVATED AREA[72]

The Commissariats for Agriculture and for Food are directed to take urgent measures to reduce spring crop undersowing to a minimum, to develop market gardening, and to make preparations for winter crop sowing both on peasant lands and by means of organising crop cultivation by the state.

Written May 2, 1918

Published (in part)
May 10, 1918
in *Izvestia* No. 91

First published in full in 1959
in the book
Decrees of the Soviet Government,
Vol. II

Printed from the manuscript

DRAFT DECISION
FOR THE PRELIMINARY CONFERENCE
ON THE LEADERSHIP
OF THE COMMISSARIAT FOR AGRICULTURE[73]

The preliminary conference (on questions raised by Comrades Spiridonova and Karelin) of members of the Agricultural Board, Comrades Sereda and Meshcheryakov, and Lenin, have come to the conclusion that the questions raised must be regarded as serious political issues and should therefore be dealt with by the Central Committee of the Russian Communist Party.

The conference considers it necessary that these questions be put before the C.C. urgently and without delay.

Written May 3, 1918

First published in 1959   Printed from the manuscript
in *Lenin Miscellany XXXVI*

ADDENDUM
TO THE DECREE ON THE FOOD DICTATORSHIP

All owners of breadstuff who have surpluses and do not deliver them to the collecting stations, as well as those who use grain stocks wastefully for the distilling of illicit spirit, are to be proclaimed enemies of the people, put on trial before the Revolutionary Court and sentenced to not less than ten years imprisonment, and are to have all their property confiscated and they themselves to be banished for all time from their community, while the illicit distillers, in addition, are to be sentenced to compulsory social labour.

Written May 9, 1918

First published in 1931   Printed from the manuscript
in *Lenin Miscellany XVIII*

MOBILISATION OF THE WORKERS
TO COMBAT FAMINE
DRAFT DECISION FOR THE C.P.C.[74]

The Commissariat for Labour is authorised to take extraordinary measures in order, by agreement with the trade unions and under the indisputable control of the Commissariat for Food, to mobilise the greatest possible number of public-spirited, organised and class-conscious workers to help the rural poor in their struggle against the rich kulaks and to mercilessly suppress profiteering in grain and attempts to infringe the grain monopoly.

Written May 9, 1918

First published in 1931
in *Lenin Miscellany XVIII*   Printed from the manuscript

DRAFT DECISION FOR THE C.P.C. ON FUEL[75]

The C.P.C. instructs the reporters to draft immediately detailed and concrete practical rules aimed at:
1) increasing fuel output,
2) economy in its consumption,
3) rational distribution of technical personnel in the fuel producing areas,
4) popular agitation and propaganda concerning the importance of saving fuel.

Written May 24, 1918

First published in 1933
in *Lenin Miscellany XXI*   Printed from the manuscript

DRAFT DECISION FOR THE C.P.C.
ON MOTOR TRANSPORT[76]

The drafts of the S.E.C. and Autocentre to be considered again by a commission of the S.E.C., the Military Department, the Railway, State Control, Labour and Food Commissariats and Autocentre.

The commission to be given five days.

All departments, within the same period, to submit accurate information as to the number of motor lorries already handed over to the Commissariat for Food and the number that will be handed over in the immediate future (out of the total number of lorries).

Composition of the Motor Section of the S.E.C. to be ascertained in detail.

Written May 25, 1918

First published in 1931
in. *Lenin Miscellany XVIII*   Printed from the manuscript

DRAFT DECISION FOR THE C.P.C.
ON PRIVATE PURVEYANCE OF FOOD[77]

All the various bodies serving the food organisations of different trades, such as Prodput or Prodvod, etc., are asked to combine their efforts, their staffs, their agents and detachments with the main forces of the Commissariat for Food. Refusal to co-operate signifies or would signify a refusal to support the Soviet authorities, a refusal to assist in the fight against famine by all the workers and all the peasants. The only way to combat famine is to join forces.

Written May 29, 1918

First published in 1931
in *Lenin Miscellany XVIII*   Printed from the manuscript

MEASURES TO COMBAT FAMINE

1. To hoard surpluses of grain and other food products at a time when the people in Petrograd, in Moscow, and in dozens of non-agricultural uyezds are not only suffering from a shortage of bread, but are cruelly starving, is an enormous crime deserving the most ruthless punishment.

2. The task of fighting famine does not only consist in pumping grain out of the grain-producing areas, but in having all grain surpluses, as well as all foodstuffs in general, delivered to and collected by the state. Unless this is done, there can be no question of any socialist reforms or of our being able to wage an effective defensive war.

3. ...*

Written late in May
or early June 1918

First published in 1959
in *Lenin Miscellany XXXVI*

Printed from the manuscript

ROUGH DRAFT
OF AN AGREEMENT WITH THE S.E.C.
AND THE COMMISSARIAT FOR TRADE
AND INDUSTRY ON THE CONDITIONS
OF BARTER BETWEEN TOWN AND COUNTRY

Agreement with the S.E.C. and the Commissariat
for Trade and Industry

Commodities shall be delivered, not to individuals, but to the volost, village or other associations of peasants strictly on condition that the peasant poor preponderate in those associations.

Commodities shall be delivered in exchange for grain on condition that 25 per cent of the sum is paid in goods and that grain is delivered to the full amount of the surplus over local consumption.

Assessment:
1 million households, 1000 rubles per household

Organisation of the peasant poor for the systematic and rigid levying of a high tax on money hoarded by the peasant bourgeoisie.

Military detachments shall be sent to the villages to collect the said taxes and break down the resistance of the rural bourgeoisie.

---

* Here the manuscript breaks off.—*Ed.*

Take from commissary stores: ⎡Available⎤

Publish at least preliminary results of the Ministry for Food up to 25.X.1917.

Apparatus: food   agents   congress?   Moscow   regional apparatus...

(25 people with us; 2000 with them).

Written May or June 1918

First published in 1959   Printed from the manuscript
in *Lenin Miscellany XXXVI*

COMMENTS ON THE DRAFT "REGULATIONS FOR THE MANAGEMENT OF THE NATIONALISED ENTERPRISES"[78]

Communism requires and presupposes the greatest possible centralisation of large-scale production throughout the country. The all-Russia centre, therefore, should definitely be given the right of direct control over all the enterprises of the given branch of industry. The regional centres define their functions depending on local conditions of life, etc., in accordance with the general production directions and decisions of the centre.

To deprive the all-Russia centre of the right of direct control over all the enterprises of the given industry throughout the country, as follows from the commission's draft, would be regional anarcho-syndicalism, and not communism.

Written June 2, 1918

First published in 1959   Printed from the manuscript
in *Lenin Miscellany XXXVI*

LIBRARY ORGANISATION

DRAFT DECISION FOR THE C.P.C.[79]

The Council of People's Commissars reprimands the Commissariat for Public Education for its insufficient attention to library organisation in Russia, and directs the Commissariat to take immediate and energetic measures, first, to centralise the library business in Russia, second, to introduce the Swiss-American system.

The Commissariat for Public Education is instructed to report to the C.P.C. twice a month on its practical steps in this field.

Written June 7, 1918

First published in 1933
in *Lenin Miscellany XXI*

Printed from the manuscript

RE DRAFT DECREE ON THE ORGANISATION AND SUPPLY OF THE VILLAGE POOR[80]

For the purpose of general guidance in the formation, composition and activities of the Committees of Poor Peasants a permanent council is instituted consisting of two representatives from the Commissariat for Food and one representative from the Commissariat for Agriculture.

All local Soviets, food supply agencies and Committees of Poor Peasants, as well as all other Soviet bodies obey the orders of this council on pertinent matters.

... shall be enjoyed by all without restriction, both by local villagers and newcomers, who do not have surpluses of grain or other food products, do not possess trade, industrial or other establishments and do not employ farmhands or day-labourers.[81]

Detailed rules on the relations between the Committees of Poor Peasants and the local Soviets and on the distribution of departmental functions between the two will be issued specially.

Written June 8, 1918

First published in 1931
in *Lenin Miscellany XVIII*

Printed from the manuscript

RE DRAFT DECISION FOR THE C.P.C.
ON THE COMPOSITION OF THE COMMITTEE
OF PUBLIC WORKS[82]

The C.P.C. instructs Comrade Rykov, or the Board of the S.E.C., to publish the fundamental principles of our policy in regard to enlisting the services of engineers both for work in the commissions of specialists and for administrative posts, the conditions of publicity, criticism on the part of the workers' organisations, and so on.

Written June 10, 1918

First published in 1933   Printed from the manuscript
in *Lenin Miscellany XXI*

REHABILITATION OF RAILWAY TRANSPORT

DRAFT DECISION FOR THE C.P.C.[83]

Following an exchange of views on the question of rehabilitating railway transport the Council of People's Commissars resolves: that Comrade Nevsky be instructed, on consultation with colleagues who strictly pursue a Soviet, truly socialist, and not syndicalist, policy, to submit to the C.P.C. in the near future practical proposals of measures for combating syndicalism and indiscipline, measures for disclosing and prosecuting those who contravene Soviet policies, measures defining the exact responsibility of every official in the effective discharge of his duties, and measures for enlisting the services of comrades capable of carrying out administrative work.

The appointment of a Board in the Commissariat for Railways to be postponed in view of non-publication of the decree.[84]

Written June 14, 1918

First published in 1933   Printed from the manuscript
in *Lenin Miscellany XXI*

DRAFT DECISION FOR THE C.P.C.
ON ADVANCING MONEY TO CENTROTEXTIL[85]

1) An advance of 50 million rubles shall be made to the Flax Department of Centrotextil.

2) The Commissariat for Food and the Military Commissariat shall be obliged within 3 days to submit precise information concerning their debt to Centrotextil.

3) The Flax Department shall be obliged, within the same period, to present its accounts to all the commissariats which are indebted to it. From these accounts currency notes shall be issued as and when calls are received from Centrotextil for the purchase of raw material.

4) A commission shall be appointed to urgently examine the estimates, figures and office organisation of the Flax Department of Centrotextil and submit a report to the C.P.C.

One representative each from the Commissariats for Finance, State Control and Food shall be appointed to the commission, the meeting of which is to be called by Comrade Lander. Deadline 3 days, as from Monday 17.VI.

Written June 15, 1918

First published in 1933
in *Lenin Miscellany XXI*

Printed from the manuscript

DRAFT DECISION FOR THE C.P.C.
ON THE FINANCING OF THE CHIEF COMMITTEE
FOR THE TANNING INDUSTRY[86]

Ten million rubles shall be advanced immediately to the Chief Committee for the Tanning Industry pending final endorsement by the C.P.C. of the whole financial plan or the whole estimates for 37 million rubles.

A commission shall be appointed to immediately study this plan and these estimates consisting of

representatives of the Chief Committee for the Tanning
Industry

the Commissariat for Food Supply
,,   ,,   ,,   Finance
,,   ,,   ,,   Control.

The meeting of the commission shall be called by Comrade
Turkestanov, Chairman of the Board of the Chief Committee
for the Tanning Industry, and the commission shall be
required to finish its work within 5 days.

Written June 15, 1918
First published in 1933   Printed from the manuscript
in *Lenin Miscellany XXI*

THE DEMOCRATISM AND SOCIALIST NATURE
OF SOVIET POWER

The democratism of Soviet power and its socialist nature
are expressed in the fact

that the supreme state authority is vested in the Soviets,
which are made up of representatives of the working people
(workers, soldiers and peasants), freely elected and
removable at any time by the masses hitherto oppressed
by capital;

that the local Soviets freely amalgamate on a basis of
democratic centralism into a single federal union as
represented by the Soviet state power of the Russian
Soviet Republic;

that the Soviets concentrate in their hands not only the
legislative power and supervision of law enforcement,
but direct enforcement of the laws through all the members
of the Soviets with a view to a gradual transition to the
performance of legislative functions and state administration
by the whole working population.

Taking, further, into consideration,

that any direct or indirect legalisation of the rights
of ownership of the workers of any given factory or any given
trade on their particular production, or of their right to
weaken or impede the orders of the state authority, is

a flagrant distortion of the basic principles of Soviet power and a complete rejection of socialism....*

Written in the first half of 1918
First published April 22, 1957
    n *Pravda* No. 112

Printed from the manuscript

INTERVIEW GIVEN TO THE CORRESPONDENT OF *FOLKETS DAGBLAD POLITIKEN* JULY 1, 1918[87]

Your correspondent talked today with Lenin concerning the situation in Russia and the general situation in Europe. Lenin emphasised that a revolution is always born in travail. A country making a revolution on its own will always find itself in a serious position. But the situation is difficult everywhere, not only in Russia. There is said to be anarchy in Russia, but that is the fruit of four years of war, and not of the Bolshevik regime. The few remaining weeks until the new harvest will be the most difficult. The harvest promises to be a good one. The counter-revolution is trying its hardest to take advantage of the present situation. The counter-revolution consists of rich peasants and officers, but without foreign support they are powerless. In the towns where the counter-revolutionaries had won, they remained in power only a few days, if not a few hours. The assassination of Volodarsky, organised by the Right Socialist-Revolutionaries, really reveals the weakness of the counter-revolutionaries. The history of the Russian revolution shows that a party always resorts to individual terror when it does not enjoy the support of the masses.

* * *

Opposition within the Bolshevik Party against the peace of Brest has subsided, says Lenin. Bukharin, Radek and the rest are taking part in the work again. Peace is necessary

---

* Here the manuscript breaks off.—*Ed.*

in order to prevent the Germans from seizing the whole
of Russia and strangling the revolution. As regards the
measures taken against the anarchists, these are due to the
fact that the anarchists had been arming and some of them
had been joining up with patently bandit elements. The
anarchists who are dedicated to an ideal have already been
released and their big daily *Anarkhia* is coming out as
usual.[88]

Amid all these difficulties, industry is being organised.
The owners of the enterprises are still sabotaging on a broad
scale, but the workers are taking the management of the
enterprises into their own hands.

Referring to the Czechoslovak revolt, Lenin expressed
confidence that it would be suppressed by the Soviet troops,
although it was dragging out.

* *
*

The Germans in the Ukraine are in a very difficult plight.
They are receiving no grain whatever from the peasants.
The peasants are arming and attacking the German soldiers
in large groups wherever they are met with. This movement
is spreading. Owing to the German occupation Bolshevism
in the Ukraine has become a sort of national movement.
It is rallying around it people who would not hear of
Bolshevism before that. If the Germans occupied Russia,
the result would be the same. The Germans need peace.
It is significant that in the Ukraine the Germans want peace
more than the Ukrainians themselves do. The same applies
to Turkey. The Germans have concluded an advantageous
agreement with the Ukrainian Rada despite the fact that
people in the Ukraine have always criticised the peace of
Brest. Now the Germans are helping to fight the Bolsheviks
in the Caucasus.

* *
*

We in Russia now have to wait for the revolutionary
movement to develop in Europe. The war party in Germany
today is so strong that it speaks with contempt of the
government in Berlin. Resistance to imperialism, however,
is growing even in bourgeois circles. Sooner or later things

everywhere will lead to political and social collapse. The present situation is unstable, but a better order of things cannot be created merely with the aid of war and bloodshed.

Published in Swedish July 4, 1918,
in *Folkets Dagblad Politiken*
No. 152

First published in Russian in 1962
in the journal
Voprosi Istorii KPSS No. 2

Printed from the translated
newspaper text

DRAFT DECISION FOR THE C.P.C.
ON SUPPLYING THE PEASANTS WITH AGRICULTURAL MACHINES[89]

A commission to be set up of representatives of the Commissariat for Agriculture, the Agricultural Machine Department of the S.E.C. and the Commissariat for Food (Comrade Kozmin to be invited with a consultative voice) to consider measures of practical assistance to the peasants in the matter of supplying them with agricultural machines. The commission is to meet tomorrow morning (July 3) and the same day it is to get in touch with the delegates arriving to the Fifth Congress.[90] Comrade Kharlov is charged with calling the commission and reporting to the Council of People's Commissars. Comrade Sereda to check fulfilment.

Written July 2, 1918

First published in 1933
in *Lenin Miscellany XXI*

Printed from the typewritten copy
of the minutes

DRAFT DECISION
FOR THE C.P.C. ON NON-FULFILMENT OF THE "DECREE ON MONUMENTS OF THE REPUBLIC"[91]

The Council of People's Commissars draws the attention of the Commissariats for Public Education and State Properties, as well as of the Presidium of the Moscow

City Soviet to their impermissible inertness in the matter of carrying out the Decree of 14.IV.1918 (No. 416,* Collection of Statutes, No. 31) and orders them not later than tomorrow, 9.VII.1918, to arrange for a responsible person to exercise energetic supervision over the fulfilment and immediate enforcement of the decree and report progress to the Chairman of the C.P.C. twice a week.

Written July 8, 1918

First published in 1933 in *Lenin Miscellany XXI*   Printed from the manuscript

ROUGH DRAFT OF ARTICLE 20, SECTION 2 OF THE CONSTITUTION OF THE R.S.F.S.R.[92]

The R.S.F.S.R. acknowledges that foreigners engaged in productive work on the territory of the Republic shall enjoy full equality of civil and political rights with Russian citizens.

Written in July, prior to 10th, 1918

First published in 1959 in *Lenin Miscellany XXXVI*   Printed from the manuscript

SPEECH AT A MEETING IN PRESNYA DISTRICT JULY 26, 1918[93]

(*Lenin's appearance was greeted with a prolonged standing ovation. The "Internationale" was sung.*) In his speech Lenin, in a clear and popular form, explained the essential features and basic points of the Soviet Constitution. The Soviets were the highest form of democratic government by the people. The Soviets were not something invented out of one's head, they were the product of living reality. They

---

* Meaning Article 416.—*Ed.*

appeared and developed for the first time in history in our backward country, but objectively they should become the form of government by the working people all over the world.

All constitutions that had existed till now safeguarded the interests of the ruling classes. The Soviet Constitution was the only one that served and would constantly serve the working people and was a powerful weapon in the fight for socialism. Comrade Lenin very aptly pointed out the differences between the demands for "freedom of the press and assembly" in bourgeois constitutions and in the Soviet Constitution. There, freedom of the press and assembly was an exclusive monopoly of the bourgeoisie; there the bourgeoisie met in their saloons, issued their big dailies financed by the banks with the aim of sowing lies and slander and poisoning the minds of the masses; there the workers' press was strangled, not allowed to say what it thought about the predatory war; there, those opposed to the war were hounded and their meetings banned. Here in Soviet Russia, however, the workers' press existed and served the working people. In Russia we were taking the sumptuous houses and palaces away from the bourgeoisie and turning them over to the workers to be used by them as clubs, and that was freedom of assembly in practice. Religion was a private concern. Everyone could believe in what he wants or believe in nothing. The Soviet Republic united the working people of all nations and defended the interests of the working people without national discrimination. The Soviet Republic knew no religious distinctions. It stood above all religion and strove to separate religion from the Soviet state. Lenin went on to describe the Soviet Republic's difficult position, surrounded as it was on all sides by imperialist predators. Comrade Lenin expressed his confidence that the Red Army men would defend our Soviet Republic with all their might against all encroachments by international imperialism and would keep it safe until our ally—the international proletariat—came to our aid. (*Comrade Lenin's speech was greeted with prolonged and tumultuous applause. The "Internationale" was sung.*)

First published in 1957 in the journal *Kommunist* No. 5

Printed from the typewritten copy of the minutes

August 1918—October 1920

DRAFT DECISION FOR THE C.P.C.
ON POTATO PRICES[94]

1) Introduction of fixed prices for potatoes to be postponed until 1.X.

2) The Central Statistical Board to be directed:
to immediately mobilise the entire statistical personnel for (α) taking stock of the potato harvest;
(β) taking stock of and registering the medium and big growers of potatoes
first in the chief potato-growing gubernias around Moscow;
then in the remaining potato-growing gubernias.
The Head of the Central Statistical Board to be required not later than tomorrow, Friday, and subsequently twice a week, to report what measures have been taken.

3) The Commissariat for Food (in co-operation with the Commissariat for Internal Affairs and the Moscow Soviet) to urgently consider introducing a demand for signed vouchers (from the owner of the potatoes who has sold them) as a condition for the free transportation of the potatoes by cartage, railway and waterway.

4) The Commissariat for Food to be directed immediately to mobilise all forces for organising by 25.VIII the urgent and mass purchase of not less than 40 million poods of potatoes at market prices and their delivery to government warehouses in the capital and to military bases.

5) Workers to be enlisted for this purpose *en masse* through the trade unions and the Soviets of the industrial gubernias.

6) A report on the progress of this operation and on the measures for its preparation (as well as recorded information

on it) to be made tomorrow, Friday, and subsequently twice a week, by the Commissariat for Food.

7) Five hundred million rubles to be assigned to the Commissariat for Food for the potato purchasing operation.

8) Point 1 of this decision to be published not later than tomorrow.[95]

Written August 22, 1918

First published in 1933
in *Lenin Miscellany XXI*

Printed from the manuscript

CONFISCATION OF SEEDS FROM THE KULAKS BY THE POOR PEASANTS' COMMITTEES

Ought we not add?
let the Committees of Poor Peasants *confiscate* seed grain from the kulaks, and in any case, if confiscation is now impossible, the rich farmers should subsequently be made to supply the seeds that will temporarily be taken for the poor out of the grain stocks of the former landed estates.[96]

Written in August 1918

First published in 1931
in *Lenin Miscellany XVIII*

Printed from the manuscript

RE THE DECREE ON THE IMPOSITION OF A TAX IN KIND ON FARMERS[97]

1

MAIN PROVISIONS OF THE DECREE

The draft to be revised in 4 days as follows:
1) A popular preamble
   (α) surpluses and equalisation

(articles 17, 12 and others of the law on the socialisation of the land[98])

(β) complete expropriation of the bourgeoisie

NB||| (γ) the rich peasant **not** to be expropriated, but *taxed* equitably, heavily

(δ) middle peasants to be taxed lightly

(ε) poor peasants—not at all.

2) The division into poor (no taxes whatever), middle (very light taxes) and rich peasants to be incorporated in the law itself.

3) % of poor to be fixed roughly at < 40%, middle peasants at < 20%.

4) Taxes on middle peasants to be reduced *considerably*.

5) Regional Soviet organisations shall be entitled to raise the question of changing the rates of taxation for the rich.

6) The poor to have the right to receive part of the collected grain (for food and seed).

2

REMARKS ON THE DRAFT DECREE

NB

(1) Not all the 2 million are kulaks.

(2) A rich peasant may be very prosperous, but not an exploiter, etc.

(3) We expropriate and confiscate in the case of the capitalists, but *not* in the case of the rich peasant.

(4) Confiscation to be applied to kulaks who revolt and offer resistance.

Written September 21, 1918

First published: Printed from the manuscript
Main provisions in 1931
in *Lenin Miscellany XVIII*;
Remarks in 1945
in *Lenin Miscellany XXXV*

RE DECISION OF THE C.P.C.
ALLOCATING FUNDS FOR THE UPKEEP
OF THE POOR PEASANTS' COMMITTEES

$$2 \times 6^{1}/_{2} = 13$$

Within a week.

Temporarily and tentatively pending amalgamation with the Soviets or delimitation of jurisdiction.

Instructions on whom to be given to and on what conditions.

Fix the liability of the recipient and under no circumstances issue further sums unless the first is accounted for.

Payment through the Commissariat for Food.[99]

Written October 15, 1918

First published in 1931   Printed from the manuscript
in *Lenin Miscellany XVIII*

RE DECISION OF THE C.P.C. ON LOGGING

Check delivery figures and results for 1917 and 1918.
What part of the logging organisations are united?

Exact information on the structure of the Logging Department in relation to other institutions.

Practical measures for combating profiteering.

Requisition of all stocks of firewood en route and in Moscow.

Effective measures to have grain* carted to the railway stations.[100]

Written October 15, 1918

First published in 1933   Printed from the manuscript
in *Lenin Miscellany XXI*

* Obviously a slip of the pen. The decision adopted by the C.P.C. dealt only with firewood transportation.—*Ed.*

ROUGH THESES OF A DECISION
ON THE STRICT OBSERVANCE OF THE LAWS

I. Legality must be raised (or rigorously observed), since the basis of laws in the R.S.F.S.R. has been established.

II. Emergency measures of *warfare* against counter-revolution should not be restricted by the laws, provided:
(α) that an exact and formal statement be made by the appropriate Soviet body or official to the effect that the special conditions of civil war and the fight against counter-revolution require that the limits of the law be exceeded;
(β) that such a statement in writing be forwarded immediately to the C.P.C. and copies sent to the local authorities concerned.

III. In all conflicts, friction, misunderstandings or disputes as to the limits of jurisdiction, etc., between officials or Soviet government bodies—all such persons and bodies are obliged immediately to draw up the briefest of reports giving the date, place, and names of the officials or bodies and the bare gist of the matter (without details). A copy of the report must be handed to the other party.

IV. Similar brief reports shall be drawn up by every official or Soviet body in the event of any citizen of the Republic complaining against any measure (or red tape, etc.) on the part of the said official or body. A copy must be sent to the citizen lodging the complaint, and another to the body higher up.

V. Anyone making patently groundless statements in the report tantamount to gross abuse shall be liable to prosecution.

VI. Refusal to hand over a report with the clearly written name of the official is a criminal breach of trust.

I propose that the C.C. approve *in principle* and instruct the People's Commissariat for Justice to word this as a decree.[101]

2/XI.1918

Lenin

First published in 1942
in *Lenin Miscellany XXXIV*

Printed from the manuscript

DRAFT DECISION FOR THE C.P.C.
ON CHILDREN'S HOMES[102]

1) The draft decree of the Commissariat for Social Security shall be rejected.

2) The Commissariats for Social Security and Education shall be directed, in accordance with § 3 of the Decree of 5.VI.1918 (Article 507 of the Collection of Statutes, No. 39), to make arrangements as to the order and date of the turnover.[103]

3) The two Commissariats shall be directed to collect and present to the C.P.C. within two months information concerning actual conditions at the orphanages and similar institutions, their number, and so on.

Written November 19, 1918
First published in 1933
in *Lenin Miscellany XXI*

Printed from the manuscript

ADDENDUM TO THE DRAFT DECREE
ON THE ORGANISATION OF SUPPLY
FOR THE POPULATION

e) Co-operative warehouses and shops are not subject to municipalisation.*

---

* The text of the adopted decree reads "nationalisation".—*Ed.*

In places where co-operatives were nationalised or municipalised and stocks of goods in co-operative stores requisitioned or confiscated by the local Soviet authorities before publication of this decree, all such co-operatives shall be re-established, their stocks returned to them, the missing goods accounted for and no further obstructions raised to their legitimate activities.

Note:

In restoring the co-operatives measures must be taken to prevent counter-revolutionary or kulak distortion of their activities and to have strict and absolute control over them exercised by the Poor Peasants' Committees and the local Soviets.[104]

Written November 21, 1918

First published in 1931 in *Lenin Miscellany XVIII*

Printed from the manuscript

THE TASKS AND ORGANISATION OF THE WORK OF THE COUNCIL OF DEFENCE[105]

First Meeting of the Council of Workers' and Peasants' Defence

1

1.XII.1918

1. *General review of tasks.*
2. *Add from trade unions.*
3. Standing order

Subjects *of general review:*

I
1. Food problem
2. Railway problem
3. Military supply

4. Mobilisation of intelligentsia
5.   „   „ technical personnel
6. Fuel
7. **State Control** & Supreme Military Inspection.

2

I. Task for the Food Commissariat —within 4 days present plan for speeding up and increasing purveyance, forward to *Council of Defence* } Militarisation

Set up in the Food Commissariat a Department for improving *distribution* of foodstuffs, for improving the *distributing apparatus.*

Merge Chief Economic Administration with the Food Commissariat ⟨ + Prodput ⟩ . Instruct Food Commissariat to work up the question (a) of delivering foodstuffs to the 3rd shift of the Tula Cartridge Factory

‖ + Simbirsk Cartridge Factory ‖

(b) of introducing Red Army rations for peat and coal workers near Moscow —*also those on firewood jobs.*

II. Bonuses Commission. On question II **3** *commissions*
Collective Liability Com-   set up
mission.

State Control. Flying inspection.

III.

IV. & V. Krasin
          Krasin + Nevsky + Gorbunov[106]

VI.   Fuel Commission: Lenin,
                       Rykov,
                       Volkovsky,
                       Nevsky,
                       Radchenko [107]
      Question of agents vs contractors.

VII. *Supreme Military Inspection.*

3

1) order the Food Commissariat in shortest possible time to submit a plan for greatly intensifying grain purveyance as well as fodder;

2) when increasing the number of trios, local food supply workers to be appointed to them;

3) direct Comrade Krasin to carry out an urgent investigation into the question of utilising the stocks of boots in Petrograd;

   (Khodinsky warehouse ober Food Commissariat*)

4) brief demands or irregularities to be immediately reported to the chairman.

Written December 1, 1918

First published in 1931   Printed from the manuscript
in *Lenin Miscellany XVIII*

DRAFT DECISION
FOR THE DEFENCE COUNCIL'S FUEL COMMISSION[108]

1) Radchenko, as chairman of the 5-man Fuel Commission, devotes no more than 2 hours a day to the Peat Commission.

2) With regard to the red tape in issuing money[109] the Timber Board is to be ordered to lodge a formal complaint this very day.

1) The Timber Board to be directed within 2 days to make arrangements with the Military Department

   a) for a law granting deferment of military service to woodcutters and wood transporters

   b) for a law mobilising the population for logging work.

2) The Commissariat for Agriculture to be ordered immediately to carry out the instructions of the S.E.C. and, under the control of the Timber Board, to issue not later than tomorrow, 3.XII, regulations governing the assignment of cutting areas and the issue of felling licences.

3) The Central Forest Department of the Commissariat for Agriculture to be warned that in the event of further red tape or a single further complaint on the part of the Timber Board, the personnel of the Department will be arrested and prosecuted.

---

* This refers to the warehouse belonging directly to the People's Commissariat for Food of the R.S.F.S.R.—*Ed.*

4) The Timber Board to be given the right to inspect the stores of all departments for saws and axes (i.e., to be allowed to examine books and warehouses).

2/XII. *V. Ulyanov (Lenin)*

Written December 2, 1918

First published in 1933
in *Lenin Miscellany XXI*

Printed from the manuscript

PROPOSALS CONCERNING THE WORK OF THE VECHEKA[110]

To be headed by Party members who have been in the Party for not less than two years.[111]

Regulations on the Railways Cheka[112] to be revised.

Confirm the right of *trade union* and Party organisations *to act as guarantors.*

Stricter measures and capital punishment to be applied to informers giving false information.

The right to act as guarantors to be given to People's Commissars against the signatures of two Board members.

The right to take part in investigations to be granted[113] etc.

In introducing the registration of technical personnel and of the intelligentsia in general, a warning should be issued that those who do not register lose the right to receive a certificate of guarantee.

The Vecheka department dealing with complaints and requests to expedite cases should be expanded immediately.

Written December 3, 1918

First published in 1933
in *Lenin Miscellany XXI*

Printed from the manuscript

ROUGH DRAFT PROPOSALS FOR INTENSIFYING AND INCREASING FOOD PURVEYANCE[114]

1) food-armymen to be replaced
2) special commissars to be assigned to backward areas and other *organisers with special tasks and bonuses....*

3) Food Commissariat staff, reform and "shake up" of staff.

4) *workers' inspection....*

Drafting of concrete detailed tasks for various local economic councils, challenging to emulation....

Oblige local military authorities to give the food organisations *such-and-such* (define which) military units for "food-army" work.

Written December 4, 1918

First published in 1931   Printed from the manuscript
in *Lenin Miscellany XVIII*

RE DRAFT "REGULATIONS ON THE ORGANISATION OF A WORKERS' FOOD INSPECTION"[115]

1

DRAFT DECISION OF THE C.P.C.

Systematically
1) check concrete cases of urgent execution of definite, clearly defined tasks of the Food Commissariat and food organisations;
2) establish contact with workers and working masses and systematically enlist their co-operation in the work of delivering and distributing foodstuffs, first as witnesses, then as members of the inspection;
3) oblige *all* bodies of the workers' inspection to give weekly reports of their activities to the local and central trade union bodies;
4) a consultative voice....*

2

REMARKS ON THE DRAFT "REGULATIONS"

This draft to be revised in the direction of (1) making it the fixed definite task of the Workers' Food Inspection not only to examine the business correspondence of the food

---

* Here the manuscript breaks off.—*Ed.*

supply organisations, but chiefly to verify concrete instances of their activities in connection with the purveyance, delivery and distribution of food products;

—further (2) obliging the Workers' Food Inspection to establish contact between the food policy and the workers and working masses and enlist their services, one and all (through the participation of witnesses as a first step), to the business of food administration.

(3) —making it the duty of the Workers' Food Inspection to report weekly to the broad mass of the working class and the working population primarily through the trade unions.

Written December 5, 1918

First published in 1931 in *Lenin Miscellany XVIII*

Printed from the manuscript

NOTES AT A MEETING
OF THE COMMISSION ON CARTRIDGES[116]

*First meeting of the Commission on Cartridges
December 5, 1918*

Tula Cartridge Factory.

Measures for increasing output:
New management.
Bonuses.
Third shift (+2000 people).
Emancipation from the (Tula) labour exchange.
Extra equipment (from remaining stocks in Petrograd).
Production records and statistics: weekly.
Foreign samples.
How to muster in Russia highly skilled workers?
Inviting specialists from abroad.
Task to the Science and Technical Department
Keeping proper weekly records of production.

Cartridges per worker a day:
1916 : 240
1918 : 225

Factory's output

maximum 1916 : 35 million

```
        1918: months XII —16 —18 —20
                    (perhaps  25-27)  million
1919:                      I —16 —20
                          II —18 —25
                         III —20 —27
                          IV —22 —29
                           V —25 —31
                          VI —28 —33
                         VII —35
```

Within a month or two months introduce three shifts.

Written December 5, 1918
First published in 1942   Printed from the manuscript
in *Lenin Miscellany XXXIV*

RE DRAFT RESOLUTION FOR THE C.C., R.C.P.(B.) ON AN ALL-RUSSIA CONGRESS OF BANK EMPLOYEES

Immediate (within ten days) congress of bank employees (of both unions) with committees on a parity basis for convening the congress.[117]

Similar parity committees to verify, discover and expose sabotage.

Groups of leading members of Banktrud to be charged immediately with precise defined practical tasks in the field of bank nationalisation, with a short period set for their fulfilment.

Written in December,
not later than 6th, 1918
First published in 1959   Printed from the manuscript
in *Lenin Miscellany XXXVI*

PROPOSALS ON THE QUESTION OF FINANCING CENTROTEXTIL[118]

| Weekly account of the number of *cash-* | 1) People's Bank controls deposits and payments—integrated cash-office. |

offices (departments or enterprises) inte-grated.

Weekly account of amount of produce shipped from each Board and from each big factory, and distributed among the population.

2) "Barter" control of produce shipped and delivered to consumer.
3) Personal responsibility of former capitalists or former owners of the enterprises in all boards and centres (under threat of imprisonment, execution of former capitalists, arrest of their families).[119]
4) Instruct the Food Commissariat, in the field of distribution, which is the weakest field, to give definite *practical* assignments to the *union* of Commercial and Industrial Employees under the collective responsibility of the whole union.

Written December 14, 1918

First published in 1933 in *Lenin Miscellany XXI*

Printed from the manuscript

TO G. V. CHICHERIN[120]

Comrade Chicherin,

We must *urgently* (to be endorsed in the C.C. before departure of the Spartacist[121]) prepare an international socialist conference for founding the Third International. (in Berlin (openly) or in Holland (secretly), *say*, *for 1.II.1 9 1 9*)

⌈generally *very* soon⌉

For this we must
(a) formulate platform *principles* (I think we could
  (α) take the theory and practice of *Bolshevism* —have *Bukharin* set this forth in theses, as briefly as possible.

Talk it over with Bukharin —perhaps *take part
of them* from my draft programme*
(β) then take "*Was will der Spartacusbund?*"). α + β
give sufficiently clear *platform principles*;
(b) define the *basis* (organisational) of the *Third International* (nothing in common with the social-patriots);
(c) give a list of parties, roughly under three headings
αα) parties and groups we have good reason to consider as
already sharing the platform of the Third International and as being sufficiently unanimous on the
question of *formally* founding the Third International;
ββ) parties *close* to this, from whom we *expect*
alignment and affiliation;
γγ) *groups* and currents *within* the social-patriotic
parties more or less close to *Bolshevism*.

I am offering a tentative list (p. 4)**; additions should be
made **with care**.

Who are we *inviting* to our conference? Only αα + ββ
+ γγ and only those (1) who resolutely stand for a break
with the social-patriots (i.e., the people who, directly or
indirectly, supported the bourgeois governments during the
imperialist war of 1914-18); 2) who are *for* a socialist
revolution *now* and f o r the dictatorship of the proletariat;
3) who are *in principle* for "Soviet power" and against
limitation of our work by bourgeois parliamentarism, against
subordination to it, and who recognise the fact that the
Soviet *type* of government is *higher* and *closer* to *socialism*.

Perhaps we should add that we do not suggest that the
whole of the Third International immediately start calling
itself "communist", but we **do place** *on the order of the day
(for discussion)* the *question* of resolutely rejecting the names
of "Social-Democratic" and "socialist" parties, and adopting
that of "communist" parties.

Arguments	*theoretical*	Engels and Marx
	historical	breakdown of the Second International
		disgrace of social-patriotism

---

* Lenin is referring to the material for the draft of the Party's new
programme (see Vol. 24, pp. 455-79 and Vol. 27, pp. 152-58 of this edition).—*Ed.*

** The list is given at the end of this letter.—*Ed.*

the U.S.A., of which it formed the core. The Socialist Party today is a small sectarian organisation.   p. 201

228 *The Social-Democratic Party of Switzerland* (known as the *Swiss Socialist Party*) was formed in the seventies of the last century and was affiliated to the First International. The party was re-formed in 1888. The opportunists were very influential in the party, and during the First World War took a social-chauvinist stand. In the autumn of 1916 the party's Right wing broke away to form their own organisation. The majority, headed by Robert Grimm, took a Centrist, social-pacifist stand, while the Left wing took an internationalist stand. The October Revolution in Russia influenced and strengthened the Left wing, which in December 1920 broke away and in 1921 joined the Communist Party of Switzerland.   p. 201

229 Lenin dealt at length with Tanner's speech in his own speech on the role of the Communist Party (see present edition, Vol. 31, pp. 235-39).   p. 202

230 *Shop Stewards* (or *Shop Stewards Committees*)—elected workers' organisations which existed in Britain in a number of industries and became widespread during the First World War. After the October Revolution in Russia the. Shop Stewards Committees came out actively in support of the Soviet Republic against foreign military intervention.   p. 202

231 Lenin wrote his remarks on the typewritten copy of a report (in German) prepared by A. Sultan-Zade, apparently for the Committee on the National and Colonial Questions. Sultan-Zade's report on the prospects of a social revolution in the East was delivered at the plenary meeting of the Second Congress of the Communist International on July 28, 1920.   p. 202

232 The conflict between the Petrograd United Consumers' Commune and the Petrograd Soviet was this. In the summer of 1920 a number of functionaries of the Executive Committee of the Petrograd Soviet headed by G. Zinoviev and the Petrograd Trade Union Council raised the question of issuing bread rations to workers not only for actual work days but also for holidays and non-working days. The Board of the Petrograd Commune (A. Y. Badayev and others) were opposed to this on the grounds that such an extra issue would violate the very principle on which the work ration was based and that, besides, the necessary supplies for this were lacking; in general, it might upset the regular issue of the work ration and shake the workers' trust in the food supply system. The Petrograd Soviet, however, ignored the opinion of the Petrograd Commune Board and announced the issue of rations for holidays. Badayev refused to carry out this order and declared that the Board of the Petrograd Commune could not work under such conditions. On July 5, 1920, the Petrograd Gubernia Committee of the R.C.P.(B.), having discussed "Com-

rade Badayev's refusal to accept the decision of the Large Presidium of June 23 providing for an increase in the bread ration,
the issue of 5 lb. advance and the issue of rations to workers
during holidays" resolved: "1. That all district bureaux and all
functionaries of the Petrograd Commune shall be ordered to
remain at work and discharge their duties without the slightest
hitch until further notice from the Petrograd Party Committee
and the Executive Committee. 2. That it be deemed necessary
to radically change the personnel of the Petrograd Commune
Board and instruct the Bureau of the Gubernia Committee together
with the Presidium of the Executive Committee to appoint new
comrades through the medium of the Control Council of the
Petrograd Commune and to get in touch with Moscow on this
question pending the convocation of a city conference of factory
committees and unions" (Party Archives of the Party History
Institute of the Leningrad Regional Committee of the C.P.S.U.).
p. 203

[233] The conflict between the Petrograd Commune and the Petrograd
Soviet was discussed at a plenary meeting of the C.C., R.C.P.(B.)
on July 16, 1920, at which Lenin wrote his draft decision. Lenin's
motion was adopted. Taking into consideration that the existing
relations between the functionaries of the Petrograd Commune
and the Petrograd Soviet were likely to lead to further conflicts,
the C.C. resolved to have A. Badayev and a number of other
Petrograd Commune workers transferred to Moscow. Badayev
was appointed Chairman of the Moscow Consumers' Society.
p. 203

[234] Lenin wrote these answers on a telegram dated July 17, 1920,
from A. M. Krasnoshchokov, Foreign Minister of the Far-Eastern
Republic and member of the Far-Eastern Bureau of the C.C.,
R.C.P.(B.) in which he reported the signing of an armistice
agreement with Japan on July 15. A special protocol signed by
the representatives of the F.-E.R. and Japan stated that the best
way of establishing peace in the Far East was the creation of
a buffer state based on democratic principles, under a single
government to be formed at a conference attended by representatives from all the regions of the territory. It was in connection
with this conference that Krasnoshchokov asked Lenin for urgent
replies to the questions raised in his telegram.   p. 204

[235] *The four-pointer*—abbreviated name for the democratic four-
point electoral system, namely: universal, equal and direct
suffrage and secret ballot.   p. 204

[236] This probably means securing a majority for Communists in
democratic state institutions.   p. 204

[237] This speech was delivered at a meeting of thousands of people
on Uritsky Square (formerly Palace Square) on the evening of
July 19, after the termination of the first sitting of the Second
Congress of the Communist International.   p. 204

[236] This refers to Maxim Gorky's article «Vladimir Ilyich Lenin» published as an editorial in the journal *The Communist International* No. 12, 1920, and Gorky's letter to H. G. Wells published in the same issue.

Both the article and the letter, though inspired by genuine affection for Lenin and admiration for his activities, were written from erroneous positions of the personality cult and contained a number of politically harmful theses. Gorky gave extremely subjective and virtually idealist appraisals of the role of Lenin and the Russian people, and the nature of the revolution in Russia. He overlooked the leading role of the Communist Party, the decisive role of the working class and the peasantry in the revolution.

Lenin's motion was adopted by the Politbureau of the C.C., R.C.P.(B.) on July 31, 1920.

The Communist International, organ of the Executive Committee of the Communist International, was published in Russian, German, French, English, Spanish and Chinese. The first issue appeared on May 1, 1919.

The journal published theoretical articles and documents of the Comintern and a number of articles by Lenin ("The Third International and Its Place in History", "The Tasks of the Third International", "Ramsay MacDonald on the Third International", "Greetings to Italian, French and German Communists", "The Constituent Assembly Elections and the Dictatorship of the Proletariat", "Notes of a Publicist" and others). All member Parties of the Comintern were represented on the journal's editorial board. The journal dealt with the fundamental questions of Marxist-Leninist theory bearing on the problems of the international labour and communist movements and the experience of socialist construction in the Soviet Union. It also waged a struggle against various anti-Leninist tendencies. Publication ceased in June 1943 following the decision by the Presidium of the Comintern's Executive on May 15, 1943, dissolving the Communist International.   p. 205

[239] The situation on the Polish and Wrangel fronts was discussed at a meeting of the Politbureau on August 19, 1920. The Wrangel front was found to be the main front, and the Politbureau outlined a number of measures aimed at strengthening it, specifically, it passed a decision to transfer the 6th Division of the First Mounted Army to the Wrangel front.

On August 20, 1920, the Commander-in-Chief forwarded a memorandum to the Revolutionary Military Council of the Republic objecting to this transfer on the grounds that the 6th Division formed the core of the First Mounted Army and in quality was equal to the three remaining divisions. The memorandum bears J. V. Stalin's superscription: "This information is *incorrect*: the remaining three divisions have *no less than* 10,000 sabres, and the 4th Cavalry Division remaining in the Mounted Army is older and more indigenous than the 6th".

On reading this memorandum Lenin wrote his proposals. Lenin made the following notes, apparently during the discussion of these proposals: under points 1 and 2 "Krestinsky against", under point 4 "Krestinsky abstained", and under point 5 "Krestinsky is *for*". The numeration of the points has been retained as given in the manuscript.   p. 205

240 This refers to Order No. 1847 dated August 20, 1920, of the Revolutionary Military Council of the Western Front, which stated that the Polish peace delegation consisted entirely of spies and secret service agents and that peace could only be concluded "on the ruins of White Poland".   p. 206

241 On August 23, 1920, the Revolutionary Military Council of the Republic rescinded the order of the R.M.C. of the Western Front and reprimanded the latter for their irregular action. Simultaneously K. Danishevsky, head of the Soviet delegation conducting negotiations with Poland, was directed, in the event of the Polish delegation not feeling satisfied with the explanation already given to the delegation at its meeting, to bring to the notice of this delegation the order of the Revolutionary Military Council of the Republic countermanding that of the R.M.C. of the Western Front.   p. 206

242 *The Ninth All-Russia Conference of the R.C.P.(B.)* held in Moscow from September 22 to 25, 1920, was attended by 241 delegates (116 of them voting delegates and 125 with a consultative voice) representing 700,000 Party members. There were delegates from the gubernia organisations of the R.S.F.S.R. and the Ukraine, from the C.C. of the Communist Parties of Azerbaijan and Armenia. The Red Army was represented by 34 delegates. The agenda consisted of the following items: 1) Report by the delegate from the Polish Communists; 2) Political report of the C.C.; 3) Organisational report of the C.C.; 4) The immediate tasks of Party development; 5) Report of the Party History Studies Committee; 6) Report on the Second Congress of the Communist International.

Lenin opened the conference with the Central Committee's political report (see present edition, Vol. 31, pp. 275-79), which dealt mainly with two questions—that of concluding peace with Poland and organising Wrangel's defeat.

Lenin's report was followed by heated debates, especially on the causes of the Soviet troops' setback near Warsaw. Winding up the debate, Lenin pointed out that the speeches of the delegates provided rich material for drawing necessary lessons and deductions. The conference unanimously passed a resolution on the terms of peace with Poland, and approved the statement by the All-Russia Central Executive Committee concerning the specific peace terms drawn up under Lenin's direction and edited by him (see *Lenin Miscellany XXXVI*, p. 123-26).

A highlight of the Ninth Conference was the discussion of the question of the immediate tasks of Party development. The

anti-Party group of "Democratic Centralism" put forward
T. V. Sapronov as co-reporter to air their views on this question.
They came out against Party discipline and the Party's guiding
role in the Soviets and the trade unions. The conference, like the
Ninth Congress of the R.C.P.(B.), strongly rebuffed the "Democrat-
ic Centralism" group.

The conference adopted a resolution on "The Immediate Tasks
of Party Development" drafted and moved by Lenin (see pp. 212-13
of this volume), who also wrote the "Proposals for the Resolution
on the Immediate Tasks of Party Development (see p. 214 of this
volume). The conference called attention to the need for drawing
the rank-and-file Communists into wider active participation in the
work of gubernia conferences and Gubernia Party Committee plenums. Measures were outlined for eliminating red tape in the work
of Government and economic bodies. To combat various abuses
and examine complaints received from Communists, the conference
deemed it necessary to set up a Control Commission, and under
the gubernia committees—special Party commissions.

On the C.C.'s organisational report the conference adopted
a resolution to step up the work of the C.C.'s Secretariat with
a view to achieving greater familiarity with local activities
and a pooling of experience, and to pay more attention to the work
of the Agitation and Propaganda Department; it also urged the
necessity of improving the C.C.'s direct guidance of the organisational work of the Red Army and Navy Party organisations
and not allowing the work of these organisations to become
detached from public life. p. 207

243 Lenin is referring to the demagogic statement by A. M. Kollontai
alleging persecution for criticism. She said that criticisers were
sometimes offered to go "to nice torrid climes to eat peaches".
p. 209

244 Lenin's proposals concerning the composition of the Control
Commission were, with certain amendments, incorporated in the
resolution of the Ninth All-Russia Conference of the R.C.P.(B.)
"On the Immediate Tasks of Party Development" (see *KPSS
v resolyutsiyakh i resheniyakh syezdov, konferentsii i plenumov
Ts.K.* [The C.P.S.U. in the Resolutions and Decisions of Its Con-
gresses, Conferences and Plenary Meetings of the Central
Committee, Part I, 1954, pp. 506-12).

The last paragraph from the words "As regards transference"
was crossed out by Lenin and omitted from the resolution.
p. 214

245 *P.P.S.—Polska Partia Socjalistyczna* (The Polish Socialist
Party)—a reformist nationalist party founded in 1892. Throughout the party's history Left-wing groups kept springing up
within it as a result of pressure from the rank-and-file workers.
Some of these groups eventually joined the revolutionary wing
of the Polish working-class movement.

In 1906 the party split up into the P.P.S. Left wing and the
Right, chauvinist wing (the so-called "revolutionary faction").

Under the influence of the Bolshevik Party and the Social-Democratic Party of Poland and Lithuania, the Left wing gradually adopted a consistent revolutionary stand.

During the First World War a large part of the P.P.S. Left wing adopted an internationalist stand. In December 1918 it united with the Social-Democratic Party of Poland and Lithuania to form the Communist Workers' Party of Poland (as the Communist Party of Poland was known up to 1925).

During the First World War the P.P.S. Right wing continued the policy of national chauvinism, organising Polish legions on the territory of Galicia to fight on the side of Austro-German imperialism. With the formation of the Polish bourgeois state the Right P.P.S. in 1919 united with the P.P.S. organisations on Polish territories formerly seized by Germany and Austria, and resumed the name of the P.P.S. On becoming the ruling party, it helped transfer power to the Polish bourgeoisie, systematically carried on anti-communist propaganda, and supported a policy of aggression against the Soviet Union, a policy of conquest and oppression against Western Ukraine and Western Byelorussia. Various groups in the P.P.S. who disagreed with this policy joined the Communist Party of Poland.

After Pilsudski's fascist coup (May 1926) the P.P.S. was nominally a parliamentary opposition, but actually it carried on no active fight against the fascist regime, and continued its anti-communist and anti-Soviet propaganda. During that period the Left-wing elements of the P.P.S. collaborated with the Polish Communists and supported united front tactics in a number of campaigns.

During the Second World War the P.P.S. again split up. Its reactionary and chauvinist faction, which assumed the name *Wolność, Równość, Niepodległość* (Liberty, Equality, Independence), joined the reactionary Polish émigré "government" in London. The Left faction, which called itself the Workers' Party of Polish Socialists, under the influence of the Polish Workers' Party, which was founded in 1942, joined the popular front against the Nazi invaders, fought for Poland's liberation, and pursued a policy of friendly relations with the U.S.S.R.

In 1944, after the liberation of Poland's eastern territories and the formation of a Polish Committee of National Liberation, the Workers' Party of Polish Socialists resumed the name of P.P.S. and together with the P.W.P. participated in the building up of a people's democratic Poland. In December 1948 the P.W.P. and the P.P.S. amalgamated and formed the Polish United Workers' Party. p. 215

[246] Lenin wrote this at a meeting of the Politbureau on October 9, 1920, when the question of drafting a resolution for the Proletcult congress was discussed. Lenin's rough draft contains the main theses of his draft resolution on proletarian culture written on the eve, October 8 (see present edition, Vol. 31, pp. 316-17).

Proletcult (Proletarian Culture)—a cultural and educational organisation which arose in September 1917 as an independent workers' organisation. Proletcult continued to uphold its "independence" after the October Revolution, thus setting itself in opposition to the proletarian state. It shunned the leadership of the Communist Party and insisted on keeping its bodies independent from the Soviet authorities, notably the People's Commissariat for Education. Its members virtually denied the cultural legacy of the past, shirked the tasks of cultural and educational work among the masses, and, by isolating themselves from life, aimed at creating a special" proletarian culture" by "laboratory methods". Bogdanov, Proletcult's chief ideologist, paid lip-service to Marxism, but actually expounded subjective idealism, Machism. Proletcult had a mixed membership. In addition to bourgeois intellectuals, who held leading positions in many of its organisations, the membership included young workers who sincerely wished to promote cultural progress in the Soviet state.

The Communist Party came out strongly against the separatist tendencies of Proletcult. In October 1920 Lenin raised the question of Proletcult before the Politbureau of the Central Committee. Following the latter's decision based on Lenin's draft, the Chief Committee for Political Education drafted instructions governing the relations between Proletcult and the Commissariat for Education. These instructions were endorsed by the plenary meeting of the Central Committee on November 10, 1920.

In 1932 Proletcult ceased to exist. p. 217

247 Lenin's draft, with amendments, was adopted by the Politbureau at its meeting on October 14, 1920. p. 218

248 *The Baku Congress of the Peoples of the East* (the First Congress of the Peoples of the East) was held in Baku between September 1 and 7, 1920. It was attended by 1,891 delegates representing 37 nationalities (of the Caucasus, Central Asia, Afghanistan, China, Egypt, India, Iran, Japan, Korea, Syria, Turkey and other countries). Two-thirds of the delegates (1,273) were Communists.

The congress discussed the following questions: 1) The international situation and the tasks of the working peoples of the East; 2) the national and colonial question; 3) the agrarian question; 4) the Soviets in the East; 5) the organisational question and others. Four sections were formed to prepare the material for the congress: the agrarian, the national and colonial, the Soviet activities, and the organisational sections.

The congress supported the decisions of the Second Congress of the Communist International and drew up a number of resolutions based on these decisions. To implement these decisions the congress organised a Council of Propaganda and Action of the Peoples of the East as a permanent body under the Executive Committee of the Comintern.

Speaking of the Second Congress of the Communist International and the First Congress of the Peoples of the East, Lenin pointed out: "These were international congresses which united the Communists and showed that in all civilised countries and in all the backward countries of the East, the banner of Bolshevism, the programme of Bolshevism, the line of Bolshevik action are an emblem of salvation, an emblem of struggle to the workers of all civilised countries and the peasants of all the backward colonial countries. They showed that, during the past three years, Soviet Russia not only beat off those who fell upon her in order to throttle her, but won the sympathy of the working people of the whole world ..." (see present edition, Vol. 31, pp. 329-30). p. 218

249 Lenin's draft decision on the question of restoring the Baltic Fleet was adopted at a meeting of the Council of Labour and Defence on October 23, 1920. p. 220

250 The question of work and food rations for Soviet office employees was discussed at a meeting of the Council of People's Commissars on October 23, 1920. Lenin's proposals were incorporated *in toto* in the decision adopted on this matter. The C.P.C. directed the commission set up for this purpose to make its report on October 26, 1920. p. 220

251 The draft decision with amendments was adopted at a meeting of the Politbureau of the C.C. on October 26, 1920, devoted to the question of "Inner-Party Moods". p. 221

252 The statement concerning the Control Commission set up in accordance with the decision of the Ninth All-Russia Conference of the R.C.P.(B.) was published on October 28, 1920, on the front page of *Pravda*. p. 221

253 This document is part of a decision of the C.P.C. adopted on October 26, 1920, following a discussion of the question of establishing contacts between the economic commissariats.
This question was raised in April 1920 at the Ninth Congress of the R.C.P.(B.), whose corresponding resolution read: "The Congress directs the C.C. to devise in the immediate future a system of organisational connections between the Supreme Economic Council and other commissariats directly engaged in economic affairs (the commissariats for food, railways, and agriculture) in their everyday work with the aim of securing complete unity in the fulfilment of the economic plan approved by the Congress of the Party" (*The C.P.S.U. in Resolutions and Decisions of Congresses, Conferences and Plenary Meetings of the Central Committee*, Part I, 1954, p. 490). In pursuance of the congress decision, Lenin, at the meeting of the Council of People's Commissars on October 26, 1920, made a report "On

Unifying the Work of the Economic Commissariats in Framing an Integrated Economic Plan" and tabled his draft resolution.

p. 222

254 This trio was appointed by the Council of People's Commissars on October 26, 1920, to collect information regarding the inter-departmental commissions.   p. 222

255 Lenin's draft was incorporated *in toto* in the decision on the Chief Committee for Political Education which was adopted at the meeting of the Politbureau on October 28, 1920.

The *Chief Committee for Political Education* was established under the People's Commissariat for Education by a decree of the Council of People's Commissars signed by Lenin on November 12, 1920. Administratively and organisationally part of the Commissariat for Education, it was subordinated directly to the C.C. of the R.C.P.(B.) on matters dealing with the ideological content of its work. The C.C.P.E. was in charge of all activities in the field of political education, agitation and propaganda, directed the mass communist education of adults (the anti-illiteracy movement, schools, clubs, libraries and village reading-rooms) and also Party education (the communist universities and Party schools). Until reorganised (in June 1930) into the Mass Work Sector of the People's Commissariat for Education, the C.C.P.E. was headed by N. K. Krupskaya. p. 223

256 This refers to the resolution of the All-Russia Central Executive Committee "On Measures for Stepping Up the Activities of the People's Commissariat for Education". It was published in *Izvestia* No. 226 for October 10, 1920.   p. 223

257 At the plenary meeting of the C.C. on November 9, 1920, G. M. Krzhizhanovsky was instructed to prepare for the Eighth All-Russia Congress of Soviets a report "On the Electrification of Russia". At the Congress of Soviets held in Moscow from December 22 to 29, 1920, this report, on the proposal of the presiding committee, was included in the agenda of the congress. p. 224

258 Lenin's draft was adopted by the C.C. plenum on November 10, 1920, practically without amendments.   p. 226

259 See Note 255.   p. 226

260 This draft was adopted by the plenum of the C.C. at its evening session, November 10, 1920, on the report of Comrade Artyom (F. A. Sergeyev) "On Enlisting the Co-operation of Legien Unions to Control Execution of Our Orders".   p. 227

261 In the interests of the country's speedy economic rehabilitation and in order to establish peaceful business relations with the capitalist countries the Soviet Government considered it possible to grant concessions to foreign companies. On October 30, 1920,

the Council of People's Commissars set up a special commission to draft a decree on concessions. In a note to Kalinin dated November 12 Lenin wrote his remarks concerning the submitted draft (see *Collected Works*, Fifth [Russian] Edition, Vol. 52, Document 11). On November 16 the draft decree on concessions submitted by the commission was examined at a meeting of the C.P.C. In this connection Lenin wrote this draft decision, which was adopted by the Council. p. 227

262 The Decree on Concessions was endorsed by the C.P.C. on November 23, 1920. Shortly afterwards a booklet appeared entitled *O kontsessiyakh. Dekret S.N.K. ot 23 noyabrya 1920 g. Tekst dekreta. Obyekty kontsessii. Karty.* (*On Concessions. Decree of the Council of People's Commissars of November 23, 1920. Text of the Decree. Concession Objects. Maps.*) The decree, maps of the concessions and articles by leading Soviet specialists were published in the journal *Russische Korrespondenz* No. 1-2.

For concessions see also present edition, Vol. 31, pp. 438-59 and 463-86. p. 227

263 This draft, with slight amendments, was adopted at the meeting of the Politbureau on November 27, 1920. p. 228

264 This refers to the Council of Labour and Defence.

The Council of Workers' and Peasants' Defence was reorganised at the beginning of April 1920 and renamed the Council of Labour and Defence. Under a decision of the Eighth All-Russia Congress of Soviets in December 1920 the Council began to operate as a C.P.C. commission responsible for co-ordinating the work of all economic departments. It was abolished in 1937.
p. 228

265 The *Committees of Poor Peasants* came into being in the Azerbaijan countryside after the proclamation of the Azerbaijan Soviet Socialist Republic. The decision calling for their organisation was adopted by the Politbureau of the C.C. of the Azerbaijan Communist Party (Bolsheviks) in August 1920.

p. 228

266 S.C.T.—Supreme Council for Transport. p. 228

267 On November 27, 1920, the Politbureau examined Zinoviev's theses of a report "On Improving the Activities of the Soviet Local and Central Authorities and on Combating Bureaucratism" for the forthcoming Eighth All-Russia Congress of Soviets. The Politbureau endorsed Lenin's draft and set up a commission which was authorised to revise the theses. These, in their final wording, were published on December 14, 1920, in *Pravda* and *Izvestia*. p. 229

268 L. B. Krasin headed the Soviet delegation sent to negotiate a trade agreement with the British Government. p. 229

269 *Councils of Action* were set up in August 1920 by the British workers to prevent Britain making war on Soviet Russia. The Communist Party of Great Britain was largely instrumental in getting these councils organised. The councils campaigned for Britain's recognition of Soviet Russia and the establishment of normal relations between the two countries.

The Politbureau of the C.C., R.C.P.(B.) adopted Lenin's motion.

See also pp. 232-33 of this volume. p. 229

270 Lenin's draft was adopted by the Council of People's Commissars on November 30, 1920. p. 230

271 *The Economic Commission* for co-ordinating the work of all the economic commissariats under the chairmanship of Lenin was set up on November 26, 1920. The commission drafted a plan for the reorganisation of the Council of Labour and Defence with a view to focussing its work on problems of economic development.

The document published here formed the basis of the Draft Decision on the Council of Labour and Defence submitted by the All-Russia Central Executive Committee and the Council of People's Commissars to the Eighth Congress of Soviets and endorsed by the congress on December 29, 1920. p. 230

272 This draft was adopted at a meeting of the Politbureau on December 4, 1920. See also *Collected Works*, Vol. 52, Fifth [Russian] Edition, Document 22. p. 232

273 This refers to the Memorandum dated June 29, 1920, which the Soviet Government sent to the British Government (see *Dokumenty Vneshnei Politiki SSSR* [U.S.S.R. Foreign Policy Documents], Vol. II, Moscow, 1958, pp. 593-98). p. 232

274 The last sentence in the manuscript is crossed out.

With reference to negotiations with Britain for the conclusion of a trade agreement see present edition, Vol. 31, pp. 492-93. p. 232

275 Lenin has in view the booklet *On Concessions. Decree of the Council of People's Commissars of November 23, 1920. Text of the Decree. Concession Objects. Maps.* Moscow, 1920. p. 233

276 The question of reorganising the work of the People's Commissariat for Education was raised by Lenin in November 1920 (see *Collected Works*, Fifth [Russian] Edition, Vol. 42, p. 376). This reorganisation was necessitated by the fact that the activities and structure of the Commissariat did not meet the new tasks in the field of public education arising from the transition to peaceful socialist construction. In his letter to Lunacharsky dated November 29, 1920, Lenin set forth his preliminary views on this question (see *Collected Works*, Fifth [Russian] Edition,

Vol. 52, Document 37). Lenin's motion calling for the reorganisation of the Commissariat for Education was adopted by the C.C. plenum on December 8, 1920, with the addition of Point 2, which reads: "The work of the People's Commissariat for Education in the sphere of organisation and administrative management on a wide national scale as well as within the apparatus of the Commissariat itself is to be directed by the People's Commissar only through his assistant."

p. 237

277 On January 26, 1921, the C.C. plenum set up a commission headed by Lenin to work out a scheme for the general reorganisation of the Commissariat for Education. On January 28, in a letter to the members of the Board of the Commissariat for Education Lenin asked for urgent information concerning all types of schools together with the text of existing laws governing them (see *Collected Works*, Fifth [Russian] Edition, Vol. 52, Document 99). On Lenin's proposal the Politbureau of the C.C. on February 2 authorised the commission to issue directives to the Board of the Commissariat for Education in the name of the C.C. of the Party. On February 5 *Pravda* (No. 25) published "Instructions of the Central Committee to Communists Working in the People's Commissariat for Education" signed by Lenin (see present edition, Vol. 32, pp. 120-22).

On February 11 the Council of People's Commissars endorsed the Regulations on the People's Commissariat for Education drawn up by members of the commission and signed by Lenin. They were published in *Izvestia* No. 33 for February 15, and in the course of 1921 served as a basis for the reorganisation of the Commissariat for Education.

p. 238

278 This document formed Point 1 of the Decision On Production Propaganda adopted by the plenum of the C.C., R.C.P.(B.) on December 8, 1920.

See also Lenin's "Theses on Production Propaganda" (Vol. 31 of this edition, pp. 404-06).

p. 238

279 These addenda were included in the text of the decision on the question of setting up a special production organ of the press adopted by the plenum of the C.C., R.C.P.(B.) on December 20, 1920.

p. 238

280 *The Eighth All-Russia Congress of Soviets of Workers', Peasants', Red Army and Cossack Deputies* was held in Moscow from December 22 to 29, 1920. There was a record attendance of 2,537 delegates, of whom 1,728 had a vote and 809 a consultative voice. Of the total number of delegates 91.7 per cent were Communists, 2.7 per cent sympathisers, 3.9 per cent non-Party people, 0.3 per cent Mensheviks, 0.3 per cent Bundists, 0.15 per cent Left S.R.s, 0.15 per cent anarchists, and 0.8 per cent from other parties. The questions on the agenda were: Report on the Work of the All-Russia Central Executive Committee and the Council of People's

Commissars; Electrification of Russia; Rehabilitation of Industry and Transport; Development of Agricultural Production and Assistance to Peasant Farming; Improving the Work of Soviet Agencies and Combating Bureaucratism. The principal questions on the agenda were discussed beforehand at meetings of the R.C.P. group. The congress set up three sections, on industry, agriculture and state organisation, to thrash out these problems.

At the plenary sessions of the congress Lenin delivered a report on December 22 on the work of the All-Russia Central Executive Committee and the Council of People's Commissars, and a speech on December 23 winding up the debate on this question. He also took the floor six times at meetings of the Communist group of the congress (December 21, 22, 24 and 27) on the question of concessions and during the debate of the bill on measures to strengthen and develop peasant farming. See also present edition, Vol. 31, pp. 463-534. p. 239

281 By a decision of the plenum of the C.C., R.C.P.(B.) dated December 8, 1920, the Tenth Congress of the Party was to be convened in February 1921. In January, at the request of local organisations, the C.C. decided to postpone the convocation of the Congress till March. p. 241

282 *Sukharevka*—a market-place in Moscow. During the years of foreign military intervention and civil war it was a centre and symbol of black marketeering. It was closed down in 1932.
p. 247

283 Lenin is referring to the Decree of the Council of People's Commissars on Concessions dated November 23, 1920. It was published in *Izvestia* No. 265 (1112) on November 25, 1920. p. 249

284 *Curzon's Note* was a result of the successes of the Red Army, which had ousted the White Polish invaders from the Ukraine and Byelorussia in the summer of 1920. To hold up the advance of the Red Army and prevent a possible collapse of bourgeois Poland and defeat of Wrangel, the British Government sent a Note to Soviet Russia on July 11, 1920, signed by the British Foreign Secretary Lord Curzon. The Note in the form of an ultimatum demanded that the advance of the Red Army be stopped, that an armistice be concluded with Poland, and that the war with Wrangel should be terminated. The British Government offered to act as mediator and on behalf of the Allies' Supreme Council threatened, in the event of the ultimatum being rejected, to assist Poland "with all the means at its disposal".

In its reply, based on Lenin's proposals, the Soviet Government firmly rejected Curzon's mediation and insisted on direct negotiations with Poland. The Soviet Government protested against Britain's attempt to annex the Crimea and agreed to guarantee the personal safety of Wrangel and his troops only on condition that they surrender immediately and completely.
p. 250

[285] This refers to the booklet *Yediny khozyaistvenny plan i yediny khozyaistvenny apparat* (An Integrated Economic Plan and an Integrated Economic Apparatus) by S. I. Gusev, published in 1920 with a view to the forthcoming Eighth All-Russia Congress of Soviets.

p. 250

[286] This figure gives the number of employees in all administrative, economic and cultural institutions, which were then run by the Moscow Soviet.

p. 251

[287] Lenin is referring to Gusev's booklet *Ocheredniye voprosy khozyaistvennogo stroitelstva* (Immediate Problems of Economic Development. *(On C.C., R.C.P. Theses.) Materials for the Ninth Party Congress* published in 1920.

p. 252

[288] This refers to the Far-Eastern Republic. See Note 217.

In the autumn of 1920 Washington Vanderlip, representing the U. S. Vanderlip Syndicate, conducted negotiations in Moscow for a concession on fishing and the prospecting and extraction of oil and coal in Kamchatka and other parts of Siberia east of the 160th meridian. At the end of October an agreement was drafted under which the Syndicate was to receive a concession for a term of sixty years. On the expiry of 35 years the Soviet Government was entitled to buy out all concession enterprises, and on the expiry of the agreed term the enterprises with their equipment in full running order were to be made over without compensation to the R.S.F.S.R. The Syndicate, however, did not receive the support of the U.S. Administration and financial tycoons and the agreement was never signed.

p. 255

[289] Lenin apparently has in mind the following section of the Programme of the Russian Communist Party (Bolsheviks): "In all its work in the countryside the R.C.P. continues to rely on the proletarian and semi-proletarian elements, organises them first of all into an independent force by creating Party cells in the countryside, organisations of the poor peasants, a special type of trade unions with a membership of rural proletarians and semi-proletarians, and so on, bringing them as close together as possible to the urban proletariat and tearing them away from under the influence of the rural bourgeoisie and petty proprietary interests" *(The C.P.S.U. in Resolutions and Decisions of Congresses, Conferences and Plenary Meetings of the Central Committee*, Part I, 1954, p. 425).

p. 256

[290] The full name is Vserabotzemles, standing for Farm and Forest Workers' Trade Union.

p. 256

[291] Lenin is referring to the section of the Bolshevik Party Programme which says: "The participation of the trade unions in running the economy and drawing the broad masses into this activity is at the same time a chief means of struggle against the

bureaucratisation of the economic apparatus of Soviet power and makes for a truly popular control over the results of production" (*The C.P.S.U. in Resolutions and Decisions of Congresses, Conferences and Plenary Meetings of the Central Committee*, Part I, 1954, p. 422). p. 257

²⁹² During the discussion of the draft resolution of the Eighth All-Russia Congress of Soviets "On Measures to Consolidate and Develop Peasant Farming" the Communist group at the congress declared for the elimination of the points concerning personal premiums for individual farmers. On December 27, 1920, the C.C. at a plenary meeting, examined this question, pointed out that the congress group had adopted an erroneous decision and suggested that it be revised. The plenum adopted Lenin's motion defining the conditions and principles for rewarding individual farmers (see pp. 266-67 of this volume). The plenum authorised Lenin to deliver a report on this question before the congress group. After Lenin's speech the group withdrew its former decision. p. 257

²⁹³ The *Order of the Red Banner* was instituted by a decision of the Eighth All-Russia Congress of Soviets as an award to groups of working people and individual citizens who displayed conspicuous devotion, initiative, industry and self-discipline in tackling economic problems. p. 261

²⁹⁴ The person referred to was Yeryomin, a delegate to the Eighth All-Russia Congress of Soviets. p. 262

²⁹⁵ Lenin's speech at the congress group meeting (see p. 257-61 of this volume) was followed by debates, in which Red Armyman Yeryomin, a middle peasant, tried to prove that the kulaks would be able all the same to take the poor peasants' farming implements and horses away from them. He cited an example of Kozlov Uyezd, Tambov Gubernia, where the starving peasant poor were compelled to sell their horses to the kulaks for five poods of grain. p. 263

²⁹⁶ See *The C.P.S.U. in Resolutions and Decisions of Congresses, Conferences and Plenary Meetings of the Central Committee*, Part I, 1954, p. 468. p. 266

²⁹⁷ The points concerning premiums for individual farmers were adopted by the C.C. plenum on November 27, 1920, and were incorporated in the resolution of the Eighth All-Russia Congress of Soviets "On Measures to Consolidate and Develop Peasant Farming". p. 267

²⁹⁸ This refers to what is known as the Federal Commission headed by L. B. Kamenev. The commission was engaged in preparing questions involving state relations among the Soviet Republics. p. 267

[299]   These proposals were written on Chicherin's letter to the Polit-
        bureau dated December 30, 1920. Chicherin reported that
        A. G. Chervyakov, Chairman of the Council of People's Commis-
        sars of Byelorussia, pointed out the extremely abnormal situation
        that existed as a result of the unsettled state relations between
        Byelorussia and the R.S.F.S.R., which made co-operation between
        the Republics difficult. Chicherin expressed the opinion that
        an agreement should be concluded with Byelorussia similar to
        that concluded with the Ukrainé.
            The question of an agreement on alliance between Soviet
        Byelorussia and the R.S.F.S.R. was raised by the Byelorussian
        Party and administrative bodies in the autumn of 1920. Following
        the negotiations at the end of December 1920 and the beginning
        of January 1921, an agreement on workers' and peasants' alliance
        between the R.S.F.S.R. and the Soviet Socialist Republic of
        Byelorussia was signed on January 16, and endorsed by the Cen-
        tral Executive Committee of Byelorussia on January 21, 1921.
                                                                    p. 267

[300]   Lenin's motion was adopted by the Politbureau on January 4,
        1921.   p. 268

[301]   At the Second Session of the All-Russia Central Executive Commit-
        tee of the Eighth Convocation (March 19-20, 1921) the question
        of the People's Commissariat for Agriculture was not discussed.
        The session dealt with the question of regulations governing
        the people's commissariats. In the decision on this question the
        ultimate date was fixed for submitting to the Presidium of the
        All-Russia C.E.C. for approval regulations governing the people's
        commissariats and their agencies.   p. 268

[302]   On January 26, 1921, the C.C. plenum examined the question
        of Georgia (this question stood third on the agenda, hence Lenin's
        heading "To Point 3"). The discussion of this question followed
        hostile acts against the Soviet Republic by the Menshevik Govern-
        ment of Georgia. In violation of her agreement with the R.S.F.S.R.
        of May 7, 1920, Georgia put a ban on the transit of goods from
        the R.S.F.S.R. through her territory, among them food supplies
        for the famine-stricken population of Armenia. She refused to
        return the R.S.F.S.R. the more valuable of the Russian ships
        formerly held by Wrangel, which put in at Georgian ports after
        his defeat. She took repressive measures against members of the
        Russian embassy staff, insulted the national flag of the R.S.F.S.R.
        and provoked and encouraged counter-revolutionary acts against
        the Soviet authorities in the Northern Caucasus. In connection
        with these violations of the agreement representatives of the
        R.S.F.S.R. lodged repeated official protests, but the Georgian
        Government ignored them.   p. 268

[303]   Lenin's draft was incorporated without amendment in the reso-
        lution of the plenum, where it figures as Point "a". Point "b"
        read: "The Caucasian Front to be directed to examine the question

of any real guarantees (a control commission, etc.) that we could demand from the Georgian Government through diplomatic channels as a safeguard against assistance being given by Georgia to insurgents in Daghestan and Chechen" (Central Party Archives of the Institute of Marxism-Leninism of the C.C. of the C.P.S.U.).
p. 269

304 *Tsektran*—Central Committee of the Joint Trade Union of Rail and Water Transport Workers.
On January 26, 1921, thirteen members of Tsektran wrote to the C.C. of the R.C.P.(B.) asking to be relieved of their duties as members of the Union's Central Committee. One of the reasons given was that criticism of Tsektran's methods of work during the trade union controversy allegedly created an impression among railwaymen and water transport workers that the Central Committee of the Party censured the whole past and present activities of Tsektran. The signatories described criticism of the work of Tsektran as persecution on the part of a group of water transport workers as well as of some members of the Party's C.C. and of the Presidium of the A.C.C.T.U.
Lenin's motion in connection with the letter was adopted by the Politbureau on January 31.   p. 269

305 This refers to the negotiations with Royal Dutch for granting it the right to export oil products from Baku and Grozny districts.
On the question of oil concessions the C.P.C. adopted a decision on February 1, 1921, the first two points of which were formulated on the basis of Lenin's proposals: "a) Approve in principle the granting of oil concessions in Grozny and Baku and other operative oilfields and start and speed up negotiations. b) The Supreme Economic Council to be directed to send a highly competent commission of first-class oil-industry experts to Baku and Grozny to investigate the question of ensuring oil extraction and ascertaining the causes of a possible disaster under present methods of exploitation. The S.E.C. is to present a list of commission members to the C.P.C. for endorsement" (Central Party Archives, Institute of Marxism-Leninism of the C.C. of the C.P.S.U.).
For further information on concessions see present edition, Vol. 32, pp. 134-36; pp. 227-80 of the volume; and *Collected Works*, Vol. 52, Fifth Russian Edition, Documents 83 and 90.
p. 269

306 This draft was adopted by the Council of People's Commissars at its meeting on February 1, 1921.   p. 270

307 On February 9, 1921, the Council of Labour and Defence heard the report of V. A. Avanesov on the fuel situation and set up a commission (F. E. Dzerzhinsky, A. A. Andreyev, D. I. Kursky, A. I. Rykov and V. V. Fomin) with instructions to submit a draft decision at the next meeting of the C.L.D. On February 11 Dzerzhinsky submitted a draft decision to the C.L.D., which was

endorsed with amendments and addenda proposed by Lenin. The members of the interim commission mentioned in Lenin's text were Avanesov, Bergauz, Krylenko, Lomov and Messing.

p. 270

308 Lenin's draft was incorporated completely in the decision of the C.P.C. passed on February 15, 1921, in connection with the report of the Import Plan Revision Commission (points "2" and "3").

p. 271

309 The Trotskyists and other oppositionists came out against the GOELRO (the State Commission for the Electrification of Russia) being transformed into a General Planning Commission. At the meeting of the Council of Labour and Defence on February 18 no decision on setting up such a commission was passed. A shorthand record of the meeting was not kept. Only Lenin's brief notes of the debate and his notes for a winding-up speech have come down to us (see *Lenin Miscellany XX*, pp. 20-22). Judging by these notes and the article "Integrated Economic Plan" (see Vol. 32 of this edition, pp. 137-45) the speakers against a planning commission were Y. Larin, V. P. Milyutin, N. Osinsky and A. I. Rykov. This question was referred to the Council of People's Commissars.

The present draft written by Lenin was incorporated completely in the "Regulations on the State Planning Commission", which were endorsed by the C.P.C. on February 22, 1921, together with a list of commission members drawn up by Lenin (see *Lenin Miscellany XX*, p. 24). The State Planning Commission was set up on the basis of the GOELRO and headed by G. M. Krzhizhanovsky.

p. 271

310 The meeting of Party activists was called by the Moscow Committee of the R.C.P.(B.) at an extremely difficult period, when economic dislocation in the country was at its worst.

The purpose of the meeting was to inform the Party activists of the measures taken to improve the supply of Moscow's working people. The meeting decided to have a report on Soviet Russia's international and domestic situation included in the agenda of the plenary session of the Moscow Soviet.

p. 272

311 This refers to the counter-revolutionary revolt of the Dashnaks in Armenia, which started on February 13, 1921. The Dashnaks received aid in arms and money from the imperialist Governments of Britain, the U.S.A., France, Menshevik Georgia and Turkey. They established a regime of terror and tyranny in the areas which they had seized, burning and razing to the ground villages and towns. The working people of Armenia under the leadership of the Bolshevik Party and with the support of units of the 11th Army of Soviet troops quelled the revolt, liberated the capital of Armenia, Yerevan, on April 4, 1921 and drove out the Dashnaks.

p. 273

312 I. N. Smirnov was the Chairman of the Siberian Revolutionary
     Committee.   p. 274

313 This refers to Point 9 of the resolution of the Ninth All-Russia
     Conference of the R.C.P.(B.) "On the Immediate Tasks of Party
     Organisation" (see *The C.P.S.U. in Resolutions, and Decisions
     of Congresses, Conferences and Plenary Meetings of the Central
     Committee*, Part I, 1954, p. 509).   p. 274

314 See present edition, Vol. 31, pp. 408-26.   p. 274

315 The mobilisation of raw material resources was one of the main
     targets of the Soviet Republic's economic policy in connection
     with the plan for rehabilitating industry. This question was
     discussed on February 18, 1921, at a meeting of the C.P.C.'s
     Economic Commission chaired by Lenin. The commission set
     up a special body which was to have dealt in detail with the
     question of collecting raw materials. The notes published here
     were apparently made by Lenin during a meeting of the Raw
     Materials Commission on February 26, 1921.
        The question of raw material was further discussed at the
     C.P.C. on March 1, 1921, and at a meeting of a special parity
     commission of the Supreme Economic Council and the Commis-
     sariat for Food. The draft decision concerning the collection of
     raw materials was endorsed by the C.P.C. on April 7, 1921.
                                                             p. 275

316 The decision of the C.L.D. for improving the supply of the work-
     ers was published in *Pravda* No. 45 on March 1, 1921.
                                                             p. 277

317 The main part of this document (from the words "will not want
     to work ..." to the end) is in the form of notes made during a dis-
     cussion of oil concessions, probably at a plenary meeting of the
     C.C., R.C.P.(B.) on February 24, 1921. Lenin later rearranged
     the notes, numbered them (points 3-14) and used the free upper
     margin for a preliminary plan of his letter (points 1-14). Lenin's
     letter written according to this plan is not in the Central Party
     Archives of the Institute of Marxism-Leninism of the C.C. of
     the C.P.S.U. The chief questions outlined in the plan were dealt
     with in Lenin's letter to A. P. Serebrovsky, Chairman of Aznef-
     tekom, Baku, dated April 2, 1921 (see *Collected Works*, Vol. 52,
     Fifth Russian Edition, Document 219).
        Lower down the page mention is made of the decision of the
     C.P.C. on oil concessions passed on February 1, 1921. The Coun-
     cil adopted Lenin's draft and approved in principle the granting
     of concessions on certain oil districts of Baku and Grozny and
     other oilfields. For oil concessions see also *Collected Works*,
     Vol. 42, Fifth Russian Edition, pp. 334-36, and Vol. 52,
     Documents 143 and 205).   p. 277

318 Lenin here quotes from Krylov's fable "Musicians". In this fable
     a landowner boasts of his serf choir to his neighbour. The singers

had neither ear nor voice, but the landowner did not think this
mattered, as the thing he most appreciated in people was sobriety
and good behaviour.   p. 278

319 This addendum was included in the decision of the C.P.C. on
March 4, 1921, "On the Establishment of an Obligatory General
Science Minimum at All Higher Schools in the R.S.F.S.R."
                                                                 p. 281

320 *The Tenth Congress of the R.C.P.(B.)* was held in Moscow on
March 8-16, 1921. It was attended, according to the report of
the Mandate Commission, by 694 voting delegates and 296 delegates with a voice but no vote, representing 732,521 Party members. The items on the agenda were: 1) Report of the Central
Committee; 2) Report of the Control Commission; 3) The trade
unions and their role in the country's economic life; 4) The Socialist Republic in a capitalist encirclement, foreign trade, concessions, etc.; 5) Food supply, the surplus-appropriation system, the
tax in kind and the fuel crisis; 6) Questions of Party organisation; 7) The Party's current tasks in the national question;
8) Reorganisation of the army and the militia question; 9) The
Chief Committee for Political Education and the Party's propaganda and agitation work; 10) Report of the R.C.P.'s representative in the Comintern and its current tasks; 11) Report of
the R.C.P.'s representative in the International Trade Union
Council; 12) Elections to the Central Committee, the Control
Commission and the Auditing Commission.

The congress passed decisions on cardinal issues pertaining
to the country's political and economic life. The work of the
congress was guided by Lenin, who delivered the opening and
closing speeches and made reports on the political activities
of the C.C., the substitution of a tax in kind for the surplus-
grain appropriation system, Party unity and the anarcho-
syndicalist deviation, the trade unions, and the fuel question.
Lenin drafted the major resolutions for the congress. See also
present edition, Vol. 32, pp. 165-271.   p. 281

321 The meeting of the supporters of the "Platform of Ten" referred
to here apparently took place on the eve of the congress or early
in its proceedings—on March 8 or 9, 1921.   p. 281

322 This point was elaborated by Lenin in Point 7 of his preliminary
draft resolution on Party unity adopted by the Tenth Congress
of the R.C.P.(B.) (see present edition, Vol. 32, pp. 241-44).
                                                                 p. 282

323 The amendment of Rafail (R. B. Farbman) to Point 4 of the resolution on Party unity proposed adding that moot points "be
discussed at general meetings and in the press". The amendment
was rejected.   p. 282

324 A. S. Kiselyov came out against Point 7 of the resolution on
Party unity, in which the Central Committee was authorised to

resort to the extreme measure of expulsion from the Party in the case of C.C. members guilty of factional activities. In his speech Kiselyov stated that Lenin, in describing the significance of this point, had used the expression "mounting machine-guns".
p. 283

325 The amendment of K. I. Marchenko applied to Point 6 of the resolution "On the Syndicalist and Anarchist Deviation in Our Party" (see present edition, Vol. 32, p. 248). Marchenko proposed to include in the resolution that discussion publications be issued only by the C.C. of the R.C.P.(B.) or by the Regional Bureaux of the C.C. The amendment was rejected.   p. 283

326 Lenin's motion was adopted at the meeting of the Politbureau on March 16, 1921.   p. 284

327 This draft decision was endorsed by the Politbureau on March 19, 1921.   p. 284

328 The meeting of the Communist group of the A.C.C.T.U. discussed the question of concessions and the condition of the workers at the concession enterprises. The meeting was called because some trade union functionaries vacillated on this subject, while A. G. Shlyapnikov and D. B. Ryazanov carried on demagogic propaganda against the idea of concessions.
Lenin made a report on this issue (see present edition, Vol. 32, pp. 300-15), argued against Shlyapnikov's and Ryazanov's statements in the debate, and made notes of the debate, which he used in his reply to the debate.   p. 285

329 This refers to the decision on "The Basic Principles of Concessions Agreements" passed by the C.P.C. on March 29, 1921, on the basis of Lenin's draft. This decision was read out by Lenin in his report on concessions made at a meeting of the Communist group of the A.C.C.T.U. (see present edition, Vol. 32, pp. 302-13). In saying that the C.P.C. passed its decision "in spite of the motion by two very prominent trade unionists", Lenin apparently had in view M. P. Tomsky and A. Z. Holtzmann.   p. 286

330 Lenin is referring to the draft of a concession agreement with the AB Svenska Kullager Fabriken in Göteborg (AB SKF). The agreement was signed in April 1923.   p. 287

331 This refers to the agreement signed at Kutaisi between the Georgian Revolutionary Committee and representatives of the Georgian Menshevik Government following negotiations held on March 17 and 18, 1921.   p. 288

332 Lenin is referring to the trade agreement between Soviet Russia and Britain signed on March 16, 1921.   p. 289

333 This refers to the leaders of the Amsterdam International of Trade Unions—the centre of the international association of

reformist trade unions (founded at the congress in Amsterdam called in July 1919; existed up to December 1945).   p. 290

[334] *Vperyod* (Forward)—a Menshevik daily, launched in March 1917 in Moscow as the organ of the Moscow organisation of the Mensheviks, and subsequently as the organ of the R.S.D.L.P. (Menshevik) committees of the Moscow organisation and the Central Region. On April 2, 1918, it became the organ also of the Mensheviks' Central Committee. On May 10, 1918, by an order of the Vecheka the newspaper was closed down owing to its counter-revolutionary activities, and the men in charge were prosecuted. The newspaper resumed publication on May 14 under the name *Vsegda Vperyod!* (Ever·Forward!) The paper was closed down for good in February 1919 by decision of the All-Russia Central Executive Committee.   p. 290

[335] Lenin is referring to the International Council of Trade Unions organised in July 1920 on the initiative of the Executive Committee of the Communist International and the All-Russia Central Council of Trade Unions to serve as the centre of the world revolutionary trade union movement. At the first international congress of trade unions held in July 1921 it was renamed the Red International of Trade Unions (the Profintern).   p. 293

[336] This draft, with certain corrections in the wording, was adopted by the C.P.C. on April 12, 1921. This question was referred to the State Planning Commission for detailed examination, in which connection Lenin wrote two letters to G. M. Krzhizhanovsky (see present edition, Vol. 35, pp. 486-88).   p. 297

[337] *Algemba*—Russian abbreviated name of the Alexandrov-Gai—Emba branch line and oil pipeline construction project, which was to connect the Emba oilfields with the Urals and Saratov. This draft decision was endorsed by the C.L.D. on April 15, 1921. On April 29 the C.L.D. passed a decision suspending construction of the pipeline in view of the fact that its remoteness entailed heavy expenditure on the delivery of materials, machinery and food, and on May 6 decided to switch the Alexandrov-Gai—Emba railway construction from accelerated to ordinary tempo.
                                                                 p. 297

[338] The draft decision was considered at a meeting of the C.P.C. on April 26, and after the insertion of a number of addenda, was referred to the Narrow C.P.C. for revision. The document published here, formulated by Lenin as Point 5 of the draft decision, was accepted as a basis at the same meeting of the Council. The final decision concerning the distribution of agricultural machines was endorsed by the C.P.C. on May 17, 1921.
                                                                 p. 298

[339] This document formed the basis of the draft letter of the C.C., R.C.P.(B.) dated May 1 "On the Attitude to Non-Party Workers"

to which Lenin made a number of amendments and wrote an
addendum (see *Collected Works*, Vol. 43, Fifth Russian
Edition, pp. 390-92).

On May 4 the C.C. endorsed the draft letter with Lenin's
amendments and addendum, and on May 7 it was published in
Pravda No. 97 as a circular to all Gubernia and Uyezd Party
Committees, communist groups and trade unions.   p. 298

340 Lenin added in pencil at the end of the manuscript: "(pamphlet
on the Socialist-Revolutionaries and Mensheviks. On the rights...)."
The last word is illegible. Apparently Lenin meant the rights
of general meetings.   p. 299

341 This draft was adopted by the Politbureau of the C.C., R.C.P.(B.)
at its meeting on May 10, 1921, devoted to the question of "Directives to the Georgian Comrades".   p. 300

342 This decision was passed by the Politbureau of the C.C. with
slight amendments on May 11, 1921.   p. 301

343 The meeting of the Communist group of the Fourth All-Russia
Congress of Trade Unions to discuss the activities of the
A.C.C.T.U. was held on May 18, 1921. The congress Steering
Commission set up by the C.C. of the R.C.P.(B.) drafted a resolution on the activities of the A.C.C.T.U. which was to be used
as a basis for the resolution of the T.U. Congress, and directed
commission member M. P. Tomsky, Chairman of the A.C.C.T.U.,
to put this draft down for discussion by the Communist group.
Tomsky, however, did not do this. The group's meeting adopted
a resolution tabled by D. B. Ryazanov, which ran counter to the
Party decisions concerning the relations between the Party and
the trade unions. The plenum of the C.C., R.C.P.(B.) on May 18
condemned Ryazanov's resolution, decided to remove Tomsky
from the commission and relieve him of his post in the A.C.C.T.U.,
and to remove Ryazanov from trade union work.

On behalf of the Central Committee Lenin took the floor at
a group meeting and revealed the anarcho-syndicalist nature
of Ryazanov's motion. The group, by an overwhelming majority,
rejected Ryazanov's resolution and adopted that of the Central
Committee. There is no record of Lenin's speech in the Central
Party Archives of the Institute of Marxism-Leninism of the C.C.
of the C.P.S.U.   p. 302

344 During the years of industrial breakdown and disorganisation
following the First World War and the civil war some of the industrial workers became declassed. It was said of such people that
they did not do their jobs at the factories, but made "cigarette
lighters" there, that is, they took advantage of the slackening
of labour discipline to make articles of domestic use for the
black market.   p. 302

345 This document was written by Lenin in connection with the
discussion on May 18, 1921, by the C.C. plenum of the question

of implementing Clause 13 of the Party Programme dealing
with measures in the sphere of religious relations.
Lenin's motion was adopted by the plenum.   p. 302

346 Point 7 of the plenum's original draft resolution required that
the question of the Party's attitude to religion "be put before
all Party cells and committees. The Agitation and Propaganda
Department shall draft and send out preliminary theses of a
report. The minutes of meetings and generally all material dealing
with this question are to be collected locally, forwarded to the
Central Committee, and worked up for a report to the Eleventh
Congress of the R.C.P." (Central Party Archives, Institute of
Marxism-Leninism of the C.C. of the C.P.S.U.).   p. 302

347 Point 10 of the original draft resolution spoke of the necessity
of the Party conducting a most decisive struggle against attempts
on the part of "some of the clergy to set up a new church organisation" accommodated to the state organisation.   p. 303

348 *Ekonomicheskaya Zhizn* (Economic Life)—a daily newspaper,
started coming out in November 1918 as the organ of the Supreme
Economic Council and the economic commissariats. It continued publication till November 1937, latterly as the organ of the
Commissariat for Finance of the U.S.S.R., the State Bank and
other financial organisations of the U.S.S.R. and the Central
Committee of the Bank Employees' Trade Union.   p. 304

349 The draft resolution for the C.C.,R.C.P.(B.) on the question
of the decisions of the R.C.P. group at the Fourth Congress of
Trade Unions was written by Lenin in connection with the group's
adoption of A. Z. Holtzmann's theses on the question of wage
rates, which ran counter to the C.C.'s directives. This draft
was adopted by the Politbureau on May 22, 1921. The congress
group, on the motion of delegations from a number of industrial
trade unions (the metalworkers, textile workers and miners) as
well as delegations from the leading proletarian centres (Moscow,
Petrograd and Ivanovo-Voznesensk), revised its decision and by
a majority vote adopted as a basis the theses of V. Y. Chubar,
which were approved by the C.C. The theses adopted by the
group were approved by the Fourth Trade Union Congress on
May 24.   p. 305

350 The draft decision for the C.C. was written by Lenin (see *Lenin
Miscellany XXIII*, p. 142).   p. 305

351 Lenin's remarks were made to Points 6 and 7 of the Central
Committee's work plan, drafted for the Tenth All-Russia Party
Conference. On May 28, 1921, the conference approved the C.C.'s
plan of work (see *The C.P.S.U. in the Resolutions and Decisions
of Its Congresses, Conferences and Plenary Meetings of the Central
Committee*, Part I, 1954, pp. 576-77).   p. 306

352 Lenin is referring to the All-Russia Conference of Managers of
     Organising and Instructor Departments Under the Gubernia
     Party Committees which was to be convened in May 1921 to
     discuss the immediate tasks of the Party's organisational work.
     The conference did not take place.   p. 306

353 Lenin prepared this plan of a speech for the Fourth All-Russia
     Trade Union Congress held from May 17 to 25, 1921. The Insti-
     tute of Marxism-Leninism, of the C.C. of the C.P.S.U. however,
     has no information of Lenin having delivered this speech at the
     congress.   p. 307

354 *Narodnaya Volya*—a secret political organisation of Narodnik
     terrorists, came into being in August 1879. While subscribing to
     views of the Narodnik utopian socialism, its members engaged
     in political struggle, and considered the most important goal
     to be the overthrow of the autocracy and the winning of political
     freedom. They figured on achieving a reorganisation of society
     without the participation of the people, by means of individual
     terrorism. "The Narodnaya Volya members," wrote Lenin, "made
     a step forward when they took up the political struggle but they
     failed to connect it with socialism." (see present edition, Vol. 8,
     p. 72). The organisation was smashed up by the tsarist govern-
     ment after the assassination of Alexander II on March 1, 1881.
                                                                 p. 307

355 *The Peace Treaty of Versailles* was drawn up at the Paris Con-
     ference in 1919 at the end of the imperialist world war of 1914-
     18 between Germany and her adversaries—the U.S.A., the
     British Empire, France, Italy, Japan and other Allied powers.
       Describing this treaty in a speech on October 15, 1920, Lenin
     said, "It is an unparalleled and predatory peace, which has made
     slaves of tens of millions of people, including the most civilised"
     (see present edition, Vol. 31, p. 326). The Versailles Peace Treaty
     was designed to perpetuate the repartition of the capitalist world
     in favour of the victor countries, and to establish a system of rela-
     tionships between countries aimed at strangling Soviet Russia
     and suppressing the revolutionary movement throughout the
     world.   p. 308

356 This letter was written during the visit of I. I. Mezhlauk, then
     Director of the Petrovskoye Metallurgical Works, and was read
     at a meeting of the workers. It created a fresh upsurge of labour
     activity among the miners of the Donbas.   p. 308

357 The *Tenth All-Russia Conference of the R.C.P.(B.)* was held in
     Moscow from May 26 to 28, 1921. It was attended by 239 delegates
     from Party and Soviet organisations. It was a special con-
     ference. The following questions were on the agenda: 1) economic
     policy: a) the tax in kind; b) co-operatives; c) financial reform;
     d) small industry; 2) the role of the Socialist-Revolutionaries
     and Mensheviks in the present situation; 3) the Third Congress

of the Comintern; 4) information on the Fourth Trade Union Congress; 5) organisational question.

The highlight of the conference was the question of implementing the New Economic Policy, on which people in the local areas were not yet quite clear.

Lenin guided the work of the conference. He delivered the opening speech, spoke on the agenda, made a report on the tax in kind and wound up the debate on this question, and took the floor many times during the discussion of the resolution "On Economic Policy". The conference heard supplementary information by Lenin to the main report on the work of the Fourth Trade Union Congress. Lenin also made a closing speech. See present edition, Vol. 32, pp. 399-437. p. 309

358 Lenin is referring to the amendment to Point 1 of the draft resolution (see present edition, Vol. 32, p. 433). The mover of this amendment proposed to add the words: "inasmuch as the conditions for a world revolution have not changed". This amendment was rejected by a majority vote. p. 309

359 Lenin took the floor in connection with a proposed amendment to Point 3 of the draft resolution. The end of this point read: "Anarchic commodity exchange (that is, exchange which eludes all control and state supervision) to be combated by concentration of exchange chiefly in the hands of the co-operatives, without, however, any restrictions on regular free market operations." The mover of the amendment proposed that the end of the sentence from the words "without, however" be replaced by the words: "administration by mere injunction in the case of such exchange to be eliminated". The amendment was rejected. p. 310

360 Lenin took the floor in connection with a proposed amendment to Point 5 of the draft resolution calling for an extension of the independence and initiative of each large establishment in the matter of disposing of financial and material resources. The mover of the amendment proposed that this point should apply to the state farms as well. The amendment was rejected. p. 311

361 This refers to the amendment to Point 9 of the resolution proposing the following addendum: "special attention being paid to factual and material initiative and independence of the local areas". The amendment was rejected. p. 311

362 This refers to the commission set up for drafting the Instructions of the Council of Labour and Defence to local Soviet bodies. It was set up by the Council on May 20, 1921. p. 312

363 This refers to the amendment to Point 10 of the draft resolution calling for the establishment of "special responsibility on the part of the central agencies for any hampering of local initiative and insufficient support of it" (see present edition, Vol. 32,

p. 435). The mover of the amendment proposed the following addendum: "stronger punitive measures to be taken against mismanagement and misappropriation of state property and wasteful use of labour." The amendment was adopted to Point 6 of the resolution.   p. 312

364 Point 6 of the draft resolution concerned the regulation of workers' wages.   p. 312

365 Lenin here took the floor in connection with Kiselyov's proposal that a point be included in the resolution calling for the introduction of a system of collective testimonials (by up to 3 people) for persons handling state property, and listing the penalties incurred by the giver of such a testimonial. The motion was rejected by a majority of votes.   p. 312

366 Lenin took the floor here in connection with the proposed amendment to Point 2 of the resolution (see present edition, Vol. 32, p. 433). The mover of the amendment proposed that the resolution should state that the tax in kind is brought to the fore in economic activities. The amendment was rejected.   p. 312

367 Lenin's proposals were adopted at a meeting of the Politbureau on June 21, 1921, as directives for the Party Purge Commission. They were included, with certain amendments, in the decision of the Politbureau of June 25 concerning the check-up, revision and purge of the Party. In connection with the drafting of this decision Lenin jotted down notes concerning the conditions of admission to the Party (see *Collected Works*, Fifth [Russian] Edition, Vol. 43, p. 362). Lenin's remarks were also taken into consideration in the decision adopted by the Central Committee.
                                                                p. 315

368 *The Third Congress of the Communist International* was held in Moscow from June 22 to July 12, 1921. It was attended by 605 delegates (291 voting delegates and 314 with a consultative voice) representing 103 organisations from 52 countries, namely: 48 Communist Parties, 8 Socialist Parties, 28 Youth Leagues, 4 syndicalist organisations, 2 opposition Communist Parties (the Communist Workers' Party of Germany and the Workers' Communist Party of Spain) and 13 other organisations. The 72 delegates from the Russian Communist Party (Bolsheviks) were headed by Lenin.
        The congress discussed the world economic crisis and the new tasks of the Communist International; the report on the activity of the Executive Committee of the Communist International; the Communist Workers' Party of Germany; the Italian question; the tactics of the Communist International; the attitude of the Red International Council of Trade Unions to the Communist International; the struggle against the Amsterdam International; the tactics of the R.C.P.(B.); the Communist International and the Communist youth movement; the women's

movement; the United Communist Party of Germany, and other questions.

All the work of preparing for the congress and conducting its activities was directed by Lenin. He wrote the "Theses for a Report on the Tactics of the R.C.P.(B.)" which were adopted by the congress; he spoke on the Italian question; in defence of the tactics of the Communist International; delivered a report on the tactics of the R.C.P.(B.); took a leading part in drafting all the key resolutions; spoke in the committees and at the enlarged sittings of the Executive Committee of the Comintern and at the delegates' meetings. See present edition, Vol. 32, pp. 451-96.

The "Theses on the Organisational Activities of the Communist Parties, on the Methods and Content of Their Work" for the Third Congress of the Communist International were drafted by O. W. Kuusinen. On June 6, 1921, he sent Lenin part of the article he had written on the organisational question and the theses on which the article was based. In accordance with Lenin's remarks Kuusinen redrafted the theses and sent them again to Lenin on June 17 (without points 25-29 dealing with the Party press); on June 21 the rest of the theses were sent (points 25-29). Apparently Lenin read this variant of the theses again. On June 27 Kuusinen sent Lenin a third variant of the theses on the organisational question revised on the basis of Lenin's instructions. The theses were revised also with the co-operation of the German Communist Wilhelm Koenen. On July 9 Lenin approved the theses and gave his final remarks and addenda to them. (see pp. 318—19 of this volume). After discussion in the Committee the theses, with slight amendments, were adopted on July 12 by the Third Congress of the Communist International (see *The Communist International in Documents. Decisions, Theses and Appeals of the Congresses of the Comintern and Plenary Meetings of the Executive Committee of the Communist International. 1919-1932*. Moscow, 1933, pp. 201-25).   p. 316

369   The report on the organisational question at the Third Congress of the Communist International on July 10, 1921 was read by the German Communist W. Koenen.   p. 317

370   See also the previous document in this connection.   p. 318

371   Lenin's remarks were taken into consideration by O. W. Kuusinen and W. Koenen (see *The Communist International in Documents. Decisions, Theses and Appeals of the Congresses of the Comintern and Plenary Meetings of the Executive Committee of the Communist International. 1919-1932*. Moscow, 1933, pp. 221 and 223-24.)   p. 319

372   This document was written in connection with the drafting of the theses on tactics for the Third Congress of the Communist International. The work of drafting the theses was entrusted to the Russian delegation to the congress.

On June 1, 1921, K. B. Radek sent Lenin a draft of the theses containing amendments proposed by A. Thalheimer and Béla Kun and their own draft. On the envelope containing these materials Lenin jotted down his initial remarks on the draft theses on tactics (see *Collected Works*, Vol. 44 Fifth Russian Edition, p. 435) and then wrote out his remarks in full as printed lower down.

In accordance with Lenin's directions the draft theses on tactics were revised, discussed at preliminary meetings with a number of delegations and tabled at the Third Congress in the name of the Russian delegation. On July 1, Lenin delivered a speech at the congress in defence of the tactics of the Comintern (see present edition, Vol. 32, pp. 468-77). On July 12, the theses were unanimously adopted by the congress (see *The Communist International in Documents*, etc. Moscow, 1933, pp. 180-201).

p. 319

373 The Open Letter (*Offener Brief*) of the Central Committee of the United Communist Party of Germany to the Socialist Party of Germany, the Independent Social-Democratic Party of Germany, the Communist Workers' Party of Germany and all trade unions was published in *Die Rote Fahne* on January 8, 1921. The U.C.P.G. called on all workers, trade unions and socialist organisations to unite their forces in combating the growing reaction and the capitalists' attack upon the working people's vital rights. Their programme of joint action included demands for higher pensions for disabled war veterans; elimination of unemployment; improvement of the country's finances at the expense of the monopolies; introduction of factory committee control over all stocks of food, raw materials and fuel; restarting of all closed enterprises; control over sowing, harvesting and marketing of all farm produce by the Peasants' Councils together with the agricultural labourers' organisations; immediate disarming and disbanding of all bourgeois militarised organisations; establishment of workers' self-defence; amnesty for all political prisoners; immediate resumption of trade and diplomatic relations with Soviet Russia. Lenin commented very favourably on the Open Letter (see *Lenin Miscellany XXXVI*, p. 221).

The Right-wing leaders of the organisations to which the Open Letter was addressed rejected the proposal for joint action with the Communists, despite the fact that the workers came out for a united front of the proletariat.   p. 321

374 *KAPD (Kommunistische Arbeiter Partei Deutschlands)*—Communist Workers' Party of Germany, was formed in April 1920 by "Left" Communists, who had been expelled from the Communist Party of Germany at the Heidelberg Congress in 1919. In November 1920, in order to facilitate the unification of all German communist forces and meet the wishes of the/ best proletarian elements within it, the C.W.P.G. was temporarily admitted into the Comintern with the rights of a sympathising member. The Executive Committee of the Comintern, however, still regarded

the United Communist Party of Germany as the only fully-authorised section of the Comintern. C.W.P.G.'s representatives were admitted into the Comintern on the condition that they merged with the United Communist Party of Germany and support-ed all its activities. The Third Congress of the Comintern, in. order to win over the workers who still followed the lead of the C.W.P.G., decided to give the latter two to three months to call a congress and settle the question of amalgamation. The Execu-tive Committee, on behalf of the Third Congress, adopted an appeal "To the Members of the Communist Workers' Party of Germany" setting forth the decision of the congress and urging the C.W.P.G. to abandon its sectarian policy and unite with the U.C.P.G. The C.W.P.G. leadership failed to comply with the decision of the Third Congress and continued their splitting activities.: The Executive of the Comintern was compelled to break off relations with the party. The C.W.P.G. thus found itself outside the Communist International. Eventually the C.W.P.G. degenerated into a small sectarian group having no support among, and hostile to, the working class of Germany.   p. 321

375 *The Italian question* was referred to the Third Congress of the Comintern following the protest of the Italian Socialist Party against the decision of the Comintern's Executive to exclude it from the Communist International and recognise the Communist Party of Italy as the only section of the Comintern in Italy.

The Third Congress of the Communist International adopted the following decision on the I.S.P. on June 29, 1921: "The Italian Socialist Party cannot belong to the Communist Interna-tional so long as the participants of the reformists' conference at Reggio-Emilia and their supporters have not been expelled from the party.

"In the event of this preliminary condition being fulfilled the Third World Congress will authorise its Executive to take the necessary steps to bring about a union between the Italian Social-ist Party, after it has cleared its ranks of all reformist and Cen-trist elements, and the Communist Party of Italy, and transform both organisations into a unified section of the Communist Inter-national" (*The Communist International in Documents. Decisions, Theses and Appeals of the Congresses of the Comintern and Plenary Meetings of the Executive Committee of the Communist Interna-tional. 1919-1932.* Moscow, 1933, p. 164). The Italian Socialist Party, however, failed to carry out this decision of the Third Congress.

A Left faction of "Third-Internationalists" (G. M. Serrati, F. Maffi and others) was formed within the Italian Socialist Party in the spring of 1923, which was for amalgamation with the Communist Party of Italy. In August 1924 the Third Interna-tionalists merged with the Communist Party of Italy. p. 322

376 Lenin is apparently referring to the following text of the initial draft theses on the question of the tactics of the Communist

International submitted by K. B. Radek: "Seeing that the Communist International wishes to create only truly revolutionary mass parties, they [what Radek calls Centrist groups in the Communist Parties of a number of countries.—*Ed.*] are making a big noise about the Comintern falling into sectarianism. This is what the Levi group in Germany, the Smeral group in Czechoslovakia, etc., are doing. The nature of these groups is quite clear. They are Centrist groups, who cloak the policy of passive waiting for the revolution with communist phrases and theories. The Šmeral group put off the organisation of a Communist Party in Czechoslovakia at a time when the majority of the Czechoslovak workers had taken a communist stand" (Central Party Archives of the Institute of Marxism-Leninism of the C.C. of the C.P.S.U.). p. 323

377 B. Šmeral's report at the Inaugural Congress of the Communist Party of Czechoslovakia was published in abridged form in the newspaper *Vorwärts*, around which were grouped the Czechoslovak Lefts headed by K. Kreibich.

Lenin's motion was adopted by the Tactics Committee. The section of the theses on tactics dealing with the Communist Party of Czechoslovakia was worded in accordance with his proposal. p. 324

378 At the beginning of July 1921 the employees of Berlin's municipal services decided to call a strike for higher pay. The strike was decided on by a majority of the workers (about 80,000). The reformists, however, succeeded in preventing the strike. Following negotiations between the representatives of the employees and the Berlin Municipal Council, on which sat Social-Democrats, the employees' pay was slightly raised. p. 326

379 Early in July 1921 the cotton-mill workers of Lille (France) went on strike against wage cuts by the mill-owners. The strike spread to a number of departments. Early in September the workers of the Northern district of France declared a general strike. Although the workers staunchly carried on the fight for two months, the strike failed as a result of the reformist tactics of the trade union leadership and unfavourable economic conditions. p. 326

380 The mass meeting of the workers in Rome, which was held on July 8, 1921, was fully reported in *Pravda* No. 149 on July 10, 1921. p. 326

381 *The draft decision on collective pay for employees of state institutions* was discussed in the C.P.C. on June 14, 21 24 and 28 and July 8, 1921. The system of collective supply was designed to replace that of individual supply by ration coupons and lists as well as bonuses paid in kind. The workers and office employees received remuneration exclusively in the form of wages and salaries, the amount of which was fixed for each enterprise as

a whole, i.e., collectively for all the workers and office staffs. On June 24 the C.P.C. passed a decision adopting the system of collective pay for employees of state institutions in Moscow and Petrograd as from July 1 and in the remaining districts of the Republic not earlier than September 1, and set up a commission to complete "the draft in order to determine, on the basis of at least limited approximate data, what the number of Soviet employees will be after the reduction and what their pay is in money and in kind". On June 28, 1921, the C.P.C., following reports by A.B. Khalatov and L. I. Ginsburg, passed its decision on collective pay for employees in state institutions with amendments to Point "A" proposed by Lenin and with his wording of Point "D". The final text of the Council's decision was adopted on July 8, 1921.   p. 329

382 Lenin's motion was made in connection with the decision of the Politbureau, adopted on the report of A.S. Kiselyov on July 7, 1921, "On Speeding Up the Transition of Enterprises and Institutions to a Self-Supporting System of Operation". The decision stated: "Soviet institutions shall be directed to take more energetic steps towards switching over both separate enterprises and Soviet institutions to a self-supporting system of operation."
                                                                              p. 329

383 In view of the famine that attacked the Volga region and south Ukraine in 1921, the Politbureau on July 9, 1921, passed a decision for the transfer of a maximum number of Communists to food supply work.
     Lenin's "Notes" were written apparently in preparation for the discussion of this question at the meeting of the Politbureau.
                                                                              p. 330

384 The question of Centrosoyuz was discussed at a meeting of the C.P.C. on July 15, 1921 which heard reports by L. M. Khinchuk "On the Organisation of Commodity Exchange and the Need for Speeding Up and Expanding Work in This Direction" and N. P. Bryukhanov "On Supervision Over Centrosoyuz in Pursuance of the Decision of the Council of People's Commissars of June 14, 1921, With a View to Obtaining the Maximum Amount of Grain Through Commodity Exchange". A single resolution was adopted on both reports incorporating Lenin's proposals.
                                                                              p. 332

385 This motion was drafted in connection with the theses of the Siberian Bureau of the Central Committee of the R.C.P.(B.) and the Siberian Revolutionary Committee "On the Forms of Organisation of Siberian Soviet Institutions and Siberian Party Bodies". The theses put the case for the necessity of having in Siberia a regional Soviet centre with corresponding economic and military departments, an agency of the Vecheka and a regional Party centre. Both these centres, in the view of the Siberian Bureau and Siberian Revolutionary Committee, were to be built on the principle of appointment.

The covering memorandum stated that the question would
be discussed at the forthcoming Fourth Siberian Regional Party
Conference at which spokesmen of two trends were expected
to state their views: one, which denied the need for Siberian
regional centres, and the other, which recognised the need for
their creation on the elective principle. The theses of the Siberian
Bureau were endorsed as a whole by the Orgbureau of the C.C.
on July 29, 1921.

Points 4 and 5 in the manuscript were crossed out by Lenin.
                                                                      p. 332

386 The Central Committee plenum considered the question of the
state of transport on August 8, 1921, and endorsed the conclusions of F. E. Dzerzhinsky with the amendments proposed by
Lenin.

Point 1 of the conclusions referred to the need for all Party
and administrative bodies to devise measures for improving and
assisting transport.

Points 2-4 called for reinforcement of the apparatus of the Commissariat for Railways with top-level executives, the issue of
a circular to all Gubernia Committees of the R.C.P.(B.) concerning the state of transport, and the organisation of a transport
subdepartment in the C.C.'s Organisation and Instruction
Department to take charge of Party work on the railways.

Point 5 of the conclusions called for all transport servicing
enterprises being turned over to the People's Commissariat for
Railways.   p. 333

387 The question of setting up an information bureau abroad to
collect material on the international labour movement was
discussed at the Presidium of the Executive Committee of the
Comintern on August 17, 1921. Lenin's proposal was adopted.

Shortly afterwards E. Varga sent Lenin his project for the
"Organisation of Information in the Comintern Executive".
This called for the establishment of an Information Institute
which would supply the Comintern Executive with the necessary
material. The project suggested methods of work for the Institute and outlined instructions for compiling socio-economic
reports and political information.

On August 31, 1921, Lenin sent Varga his remarks on the
project—"Tentative Amendments or Theses" (see pp. 337—39
of this volume).

Lenin's letter of September 1, 1921 (see p. 339 of this volume)
was a reply to Varga's letter dated August 31, 1921, on the subject
of Lenin's theses on the organisation of an Information Institute,
in which Varga reported that there were "deep-going basic
differences in regard to the *aims* of such an Institute". Trotsky,
Zinoviev and Radek, wrote Varga, considered that this Institute
was designed primarily to supply information for the internal
use of the Comintern Executive. "In your theses, on the other
hand, *the weight of emphasis seems to be on press information on
the labour movement* in Central Europe, whereas information for

the Comintern Executive is relegated to the background. This change of aim affects all other changes (legality, complete independence of the Comintern)". "Consequently, it would be necessary to decide in principle: is the aim of the Institute to be: a) information for the Comintern Executive? b) influencing the labour press by its publications? c) linking both aims? All questions of organisation depend, it seems to me, on the solution of this question" (Central Party Archives of the Institute of Marxism-Leninism of the C.C., C.P.S.U.). The plan for setting up an Information Institute did not materialise.   p. 336

388   This draft was written on the letter of I. S. Unschlicht, Deputy Chairman of the Vecheka, to the Central Committee of the R.C.P.(B.), which stated: "At the recent session of the All-Russia Central Executive Committee it was decided at the September sitting to hear the report of the commission set up to inspect the Commissariat for Foreign Trade. Please give me your instructions on the following: 1) should such a report be made at all; 2) if it should, then in what direction" (Central Party Archives of the Institute of Marxism-Leninism of the C.C. C.P.S.U.).

Lenin's motion was adopted by the Politbureau at its meeting on August 25, 1921.   p. 336

389   This motion was written in connection with a telegram from the Chairman of the Siberian Revolutionary Committee I. N. Smirnov dated August 26, 1921, reporting the arrest of Baron Ungern. The Politbureau adopted Lenin's motion.

The trial of Baron Ungern took place on September 15. During the hearing a long list of atrocities committed by Ungern and his underlings was revealed. On capturing Urgu (now Ulan-Bator) he ordered all the employees of Centrosoyuz and the Town Council to be shot. On his orders the peaceful inhabitants were robbed and killed and the town was burnt down. The trial brought to light Baron Ungern's ties with the Chinese militarists (Chang Tso-lin) and Japanese interventionists. Baron Ungern was sentenced to death.   p. 336

390   E. Varga's project for the "Organisation of Information in the Comintern   Executive"   contained   two   appendixes: "Appendix A—Instructions on Compiling Socio-Economic Reports" and "Appendix B—Instructions on Compiling Reports on the Political Situation Within the Country". The instructions under Appendix A covered:

1. The purpose of the reports, which was to give a dynamic picture of the development of the revolutionary movement in the country and its analysis.

2. Four factors conditioning revolutionary development:

a) the Communist Party—the motive force of the revolutionary movement;

b) the proletariat—the revolutionary masses;

c) the ruling classes—the enemy;

d) the petty-bourgeois middle strata.

The report must show the alignment of forces.

3. The starting-point should be an account of the economic situation, the social position of the proletariat and the middle strata.

4. The report should consist of a brief review (5-10 pages) with a detailed appendix to it.

The instructions under Appendix B contained the following sections: 1) Communist Parties; II) non-communist proletarian parties; III) bourgeois parties; IV) organisation of the armed forces.

Lenin refers to §§ 3 and 4 of Section I ("Communist Parties") of Varga's instructions (Appendix B) which deal with legal and illegal Party cells, the promulgation of Party literature, appeals, pamphlets and books and the issue of illegal Party literature.   p. 338

[391] Lenin's motion was adopted by the Politbureau on September 2, 1921. The next day, September 3, Lenin wrote to the Secretary of the Comintern Executive asking him to arrange for the collection of information about workers' donations in Europe for the relief of the famine-stricken areas in Russia (see *Collected Works*, Fifth [Russian] Edition, Vol. 53, Document 270). For Soviet press reports on moneys collected among the international proletariat see Document 345 of the same volume.   p. 340

[392] Under the pretence of rendering relief to the famine-stricken areas in Russia the imperialists organised an "International Commission" headed by Noulens, the former French Ambassador to Russia and one of the chief organisers of counter-revolutionary plots and military intervention against Soviet Russia. The commission was made up of former French, English, and Belgian diplomats and big foreign owners of enterprises that had been nationalised in Russia. On September 4, 1921, the Noulens Commission sent a telegram to the People's Commissariat for Foreign Affairs demanding that thirty experts be admitted into Soviet Russia for on-the-spot investigations under a special programme providing for the collection of information of an intelligence nature.

On September 6 the Politbureau approved, with slight amendments, the text of a Note to Noulens drafted in accordance with Lenin's proposals. The answering Note of the Commissariat for Foreign Affairs, published in *Izvestia* on September 8, stated that "Mr. Noulens' Commission, in lieu of relief for the famine-stricken areas, planned to collect information on the internal position of Soviet Russia ... and this was to be done under the guidance of people who had already engaged in such a study with the undisguised aim of engineering revolts and facilitating the advance of foreign armies on the territory of the U.S.S.R." (*U.S.S.R. Foreign Policy Documents*, Vol. IV, Moscow, 1960). The Soviet Government emphatically refused to permit entry of the Noulens Commission into the Soviet Republic.   p. 341

393 Owing to food difficulties, the crop failure and the need for rendering relief to the famine-stricken areas, the Politbureau, on September 6, 1921, adopted a decision on directives to the Food Commissariat with Lenin's amendments. The directives provided for a reduction in the number of recipients of state food supplies as from October 1921, and the establishment of a grain fund.

p. 341

394 The motion concerning spendings from the gold fund was adopted by the Politbureau on September 14, 1921. p. 342

395 Lenin's motion was adopted by the Politbureau on September 13, 1921. Point 4 was crossed out by Lenin and not included in the decision of the Politbureau.

The question of book sales was re-examined by the Politbureau at its meeting on October 15, at which it confirmed its decision of September 13 and outlined concrete practical measures for its implementation; special attention was given to measures for preventing all kinds of anti-Soviet literature from getting into the book trade. p. 342

396 This motion was adopted by the Politbureau on September 14, 1921. p. 343

397 The Party purge was carried out in compliance with the resolution of the Tenth Congress of the R.C.P.(B.) "On Problems of Party Development". It was preceded by long and careful preparation. On June 21, 1921, the Central Committee and the Central Control Commission adopted a Decision on Checking, Revising and Purging the Party (see *Pravda* No. 146 for June 30, 1921), which fixed the date for the purge to be carried out (from August 1 to October 1, 1921), stipulated that working people, both Communists and non-Party, were to be questioned concerning members of the Party who were being checked, and defined the procedure for setting up local verification commissions. During the period of the purge admission into the Party was suspended, an exception being made in the case of workers and peasants who did not exploit outside labour. On July 7 the Politbureau endorsed a Central Verification Commission for checking the Party membership and local verification commissions. The Central Committee of the Party addressed a letter "To All Party Organisations. On the Purging of the Party" (see *Pravda* No. 163 for July 27, 1921) setting forth the aims and methods of the purge. The C.C. recommended the following guidelines: a more indulgent attitude towards workers in the matter of presenting documents, testimonials, etc. As regards peasants, a clear line should be drawn between kulak and proprietary elements and honest working peasants. A stricter approach to "commissarified" elements, to those holding posts which involve any privileges. An especially strict check to be applied to former government officials and bourgeois intellectuals. And strictest of all to former members of other parties, particularly the Mensheviks and Socialist-Revolutionaries. The start of the purge was put off until August 15.

As a result of the purge, which continued up till the Eleventh Congress of the R.C.P.(B.) about 25 per cent of the membership were expelled from the Party. This improved the Party's social composition, strengthened discipline, gave the Party greater prestige among the non-Party worker and peasant masses and freed the Party from elements who discredited it. The Party's ideological and organisational unity was enhanced. p. 343.

398 This directive of Lenin's was incorporated in the C.C.'s decisions. The "Report of the Central Committee of the R.C.P." for September 1921 states that the C.C. passed two decisions concerning the procedure for recommending members of the R.C.P. during the purge. One stated: "Only those comrades have the right to recommend who have known the recommended person not less than one year and have worked with him or observed his work in one or another Party organisation". The other decision spoke about the responsibility of the recommenders for the recommended (see *Izvestia of the C.C., R.C.P.* No. 35, December 1, 1921). p. 344

399 In 1921 various groups of American workers united around the Society for Technical Aid to Soviet Russia expressed a desire to go to Soviet Russia to lend a hand in economic construction. Most of these workers were Russian emigrants who had gone to America before the October Revolution.

On June 22, 1921, the Council of Labour and Defence discussed the question of enlisting the services of members of the industrial emigrant community, and recognised the desirability of "developing individual industrial enterprises or groups of enterprises by handing them over to groups of American workers and industrially developed farmers on a contract basis ensuring them a definite degree of economic autonomy" (*Lenin Miscellany* XX, p. 202). The Council also considered it necessary to regulate industrial immigration of workers from foreign countries. On August 11, 1921, a telegram signed by Lenin was sent to the Society for Technical Aid to Soviet Russia, stating, among other things: "You must bear in mind the hardships existing in Russia, the difficulties in connection with the food supply problem, and other obstacles which would have to be faced. Persons going to Russia should be prepared to meet these conditions.... It would be best to send delegates first for an on-the-spot inspection of settlement land lots, wood lots, mines, factories, etc. to be leased" (*U.S.S.R. Foreign Policy Documents*, Vol. IV, Moscow, 1960, p. 261).

In the latter part of 1921 a group of American workers headed by S. Rutgers, a Dutch engineer and Communist, W. D. Heywood, a prominent leader of the American labour movement and G. S. Calvert, an American worker, carried on negotiations with the Soviet Government for exploitation by this group of a part of the Kuznetsk coal-field in Siberia and the organisation there of an industrial colony. Lenin received delegates of the American workers' colony on September 19 and had a talk with them. A record of this talk, made by Lenin, is given in *Lenin Miscellany XXIII*, p. 39. Lenin's draft engagement was written in connection with this talk. For details concerning the agreement with the sponsor group of the American workers (Rutgers group) see pp. 348-50 of this volume.   p. 344

400 In a letter to the Politbureau dated October 7, 1921, G. V. Chicherin, People's Commissar for Foreign Affairs, wrote that the Government of the Far-Eastern Republic wished to be briefed by the Politbureau on the following points: 1) Is recognition of the F.-E.R. by Japan and America desirable in the absence of simultaneous recognition by them of the R.S.F.S.R.; 2) Should the offer by foreigners to grant state loans to the F.-E.R. be accepted; 3) Is the F.-E.R. independent of the R.S.F.S.R. in fact as well as in form. In the opinion of the Commissariat for Foreign Affairs these questions were to be answered in the following manner: 1) Recognition of the F.-E.R. is desirable, but without the structure of the F.-E.R. being specified in the agreement; 2) Foreign loans are useful provided the sovereign rights of the F.-E.R. are preserved; 3) The F.-E.R. is to be considered independent of the R.S.F.S.R. only in form.

   Lenin's motion was adopted by the Politbureau on October 8, 1921.

   The draft directives to the F.-E.R. proposed by Chicherin were endorsed by the Politbureau on October 10, 1921.   p. 345

401 Lenin's proposal was included in the decision of the C.C. plenum on October 8, 1921, passed in connection with Molotov's report concerning the registration of executives and the order in which they were to be distributed.   p. 346

402 Lenin's draft directives were adopted by the Politbureau on October 10, 1921, following the report of C. G. Rakovsky, V. Y. Chubar and G. I. Petrovsky. "On this question a general orientation was given," stated the C.C. Report for October-November 1921, "in the sense of a more careful and attentive attitude being shown towards the needs of the peasants and securing their co-operation with the state" (*Izvestia of the Central Committee, R.C.P.(B.)* No. 36 for December 15, 1921).   p. 346

403 This motion was adopted by the Politbureau on October 10, 1921. On November 15 the C.P.C. endorsed the Decree on Social Insurance of Employed Persons (see the newspaper *Izvestia* No. 263, November 23, 1921).   p. 347

404 *Yugostal*—a mining metallurgical trust founded in September 1921. It playe dan important part in rehabilitating the country's iron and steel industry.

These notes were written by Lenin in the margin of the newspaper *Yuzhni Metallurg* (the town of Yenakievo) No. 1 for October 11, 1921. A note by Lenin in the top left-hand corner of the paper reads: "Part to Yuzovka and part to Debaltsevo." p. 347

[405] This draft was written in preparation for the meeting of the Politbureau on the question of an agreement with the group of American workers and engineers headed by S. Rutgers, who had arrived in Russia (see Note 399).

On September 23, 1921, the C.L.D. discussed the proposal of the Rutgers group for the Nadezhdinsk Works and a number of enterprises of the Kuznetsk coal-field to be turned over to them for exploitation, and found it desirable to conclude an agreement, the final terms of which were to be drafted by a commission consisting of representatives of the S.E.C., the Commissariat for Labour and the Commissariat for Agriculture. Lenin took part in the negotiations with the Rutgers group and made a number of proposals in connection with the terms of the agreement (see pp. 348-50, 352-53 of this volume, and *Collected Works*, Vol. 53, Fifth Russian Edition, pp. 260-61, 302-03).

The agreement with the sponsor group (the Rutgers group) of the American workers, which was signed on October 20, was endorsed by the C.L.D. on October 21 and by the C.P.C. on October 25. In November the Soviet Government signed a contract with this group, under which the American workers were to bring with them a definite quantity of tools, materials and foodstuffs, while the Soviet Government assigned a sum of $300,000 for the purchase abroad of machines and equipment. Under the terms of this contract an Autonomous Industrial Colony directly subordinated to the C.L.D. was set up in part of the territory of the Kuznetsk coal-field. p. 348

[406] Lenin's proposals formed the basis of the Politbureau's decision of October 15, 1921, concerning the proposals of S. Rutgers, and the Council of Labour and Defence decision of October 17, 1921, "On the Terms of an Agreement with the Rutgers Group". p. 350

[407] Lenin's draft was adopted at the meeting of the Politbureau on October 14, 1921. After hearing the opinion of the Central Control Commission and the Central Verification Commission on the question of assigning Shlyapnikov to food supply work, the Politbureau ruled on October 27: "The period of Comrade Shlyapnikov's work on food supply should be fixed at two months, counting from the date of his departure" (Central Party Archives, Institute of Marxism-Leninism of the C.C. of the C.P.S.U.).

The *Central Verification Commission*, consisting of five members, was set up for the period of the Party purge to direct the work of the local verification commissions (see *Pravda* No. 146, June 30, 1921). p. 350

[408] There having been certain differences of opinion among leading members of the Baku Party organisation and the central organi-

sations of Azerbaijan in applying the national policy, the Central Committee of the R.C.P.(B.) issued instructions for the greatest discretion to be shown by Party workers in Azerbaijan towards the mode of life and way of thinking among the Moslem population. All functionaries of the Azerbaijan Communist Party were directed to take this into consideration in all their activities and strive towards teamwork and co-operation and not allow any factions to be formed within the Party organisation. Lenin's proposals were included in the decision of the C.C.'s Politbureau adopted October 15, 1921.

The directives on the implementation of the Communist Party's national policy in Azerbaijan drafted by J. V. Stalin were endorsed by the Politbureau on October 17.

Point 6 refers to the decision of the Politbureau of October 3, 1921, aimed at preventing any violation by Baku Party workers of the Soviet Government's policy towards Persia (Iran).   p. 351

409 Lenin's draft was adopted by the Politbureau on October 17, 1921.   p. 352

410 Lenin's draft was adopted by the Politbureau on October 20, 1921. His proposals were incorporated in the agreement concluded with the Rutgers group.   p. 352

411 The *A.R.A.* (*American Relief Administration*)—was formed in 1919 to render relief to the population who had suffered from the First World War. The President of the A.R.A. was Herbert Hoover, a big capitalist, who had had close links with Russian capital before 1917. Some of the A.R.A. staff engaged in charitable work with all sincerity and conscientiousness, but the A.R.A. as a whole served as an instrument for spreading the influence of American imperialism and dumping old stocks.

On October 18, 1921, the draft of an agreement with the A.R.A. on the organisation of food parcels to Russia was circulated for voting among members of the Politbureau. The covering letter has the signatures of Politbureau members and a proposal by Stalin that a charge be made for transportation of the parcels from the frontier to the distributing warehouses, and for their storage, since, in his opinion, this was a commercial operation, not charity. Lenin's bracketed remark was made in connection with this proposal. The draft agreement with the A.R.A. was endorsed by the Politbureau on October 19, 1921.

The Soviet Government accepted A.R.A. assistance in connection with famine on the Volga and in south Ukraine in 1921, but repelled its attempts to interfere in the internal affairs of the Soviet Republic and established control over its activities. As subsequent events proved, the A.R.A. personnel, consisting chiefly of American army officers, engaged in espionage and supported counter-revolutionary elements. The A.R.A. ceased its activities in the U.S.S.R. in June 1923.   p. 353

412 This draft was written by Lenin for the meeting of the Politbureau of October 20, 1921, which had before it the request of the People's Commissariat for Finance that representatives of the Commissariat be included in the C.L.D. and the regional and gubernia economic conferences with a right to vote. The Politbureau rejected this request and adopted Lenin's motion. The last sentence in the manuscript is crossed out and was not included in the decision.

A *Finance Commission of the Central Committee, R.C.P.(B.) and the Council of People's Commissars* was set up on Lenin's proposal soon after the Tenth Congress of the Party for dealing with questions of financial policy in the light of the New Economic Policy. p. 355

413 The question of manufacturing Fowler-type motor ploughs was considered repeatedly by the Council of Labour and Defence. The Metal Department of the Supreme Economic Council, which had been charged with the manufacture of these ploughs in May 1920, drew up a production plan without taking into account available metal and fuel resources. The Special Three-Man Commission set up to combine all production of ploughs did not inform the C.L.D. or the C.P.C. as to the actual state of affairs.

This draft decision was adopted at the meeting of the C.L.D. on October 21, 1921. The case of red tape was brought before the Moscow Military Tribunal, which found a number of members of the staffs of the S.E.C. and the Commissariat for Agriculture guilty of negligence. Considering these men's services in the matter of economic reconstruction, however, the Tribunal decided not to punish them. At the suggestion of the Moscow Military Tribunal the C.L.D. reprimanded the Presidium of the S.E.C. and the Board of the Commissariat for Agriculture for giving insufficient attention to the production of Fowler ploughs. See Lenin's letter to P. A. Bogdanov dated December 23, 1921 (present edition, Vol. 36, pp. 556-58). p. 356

414 Following the endorsement by the Presidium of the All-Russia Central Executive Committee on June 30, 1921, of the "Instructions of the Council of Labour and Defence to Local Soviet Bodies" (see present edition, Vol. 32, pp. 375-98) Lenin wrote a letter to the editors of *Izvestia, Pravda, Ekonomicheskaya Zhizn* and other newspapers on July 21 pointing out the importance of "explaining in detail the significance which the local economic conferences and the publication of reports for general information has for both the application of the New Economic Policy in general and for proper economic construction" (*Collected Works*, Vol. 53, Fifth Russian Edition, p. 52).

When reports started coming in from the local areas, Lenin raised the question of studying and utilising these reports. On October 21, 1921, Lenin made a report at the C.L.D. on the subject of reports and diagrams for the C.L.D. and tabled the draft decision as given here. p. 356

415 V. A. Smolyaninov, in his reminiscences, says that the work of the commission dragged out. "Vladimir Ilyich showed a great interest in the results of our commission's work. On his advice and suggestion a draft decision was drawn up, which was endorsed by the Council of Labour and Defence on November 21, 1921. This decision took into account all Lenin's remarks. He attached special importance to having people appointed in the various commissariats and other institutions who were really interested in and understood the importance of studying the local reports" (*Vospominaniya o Vladimire Ilyiche Lenine* [Reminiscences of Lenin], Part 3, Moscow, 1961, p. 367). Lenin's private library contains several dozen reports of gubernia economic conferences. p. 357

416 The Politbureau (on the report of P. A. Bogdanov, N. I. Lebedev, G. N. Melnichansky and I. I. Kutuzov) considered the draft regulations on the management of the cotton industry at its meeting on October 27, 1921, and adopted Lenin's motion. The amended instructions were afterwards endorsed by the Politbureau at its meeting on November 3. p. 357

417 The article under this title was not written. p. 357

418 The draft of a financial plan and of a plan of emission for 1922 was down for discussion at the meeting of the Council of People's Commissars on November 5, 1921. Lenin's motion formed the basis of the decision passed by the Council on this question. Points 2, 4, 5 and 6 are crossed out in the manuscript and were not included in the decision. p. 359

419 Lenin's draft was incorporated in the text of the Council's decision on this question adopted on November 18, 1921. The Council endorsed "tentatively the budgetary appropriations and their distribution among the commissariats as submitted by the Finance Commission" and directed the commissariats "to speed up the work of making up estimates, which should be completed by December 1". The Finance Commission and the State Planning Commission were charged with "completing the calculation of revenues, both monetary and material, within one week" (Central Party Archives of the Institute of Marxism-Leninism of the C.C. of the C.P.S.U.). p. 360

420 The delegation of the Mongolian People's Republic arrived in Moscow on November 2, 1921. Its members were: Danzan, head of the delegation, Minister for Finance and Chairman of the Central Committee of the Mongolian People's Revolutionary Party; Sukhe-Bator, Commander-in-Chief of the People's Revolutionary Army and War Minister; B. Tserendorzh, Deputy Minister for Foreign Affairs; Djon-Van-Shirnin-Dandin, representative of religious circles, unofficial member of the delegation; Batukhan, adviser and head interpreter. The object of the nego-

tiations was to conclude an agreement between the Government of the R.S.F.S.R. and the People's Government of Mongolia. The draft agreement was considered and approved by the Narrow Council of People's Commissars on November 3, 1921 (see *Collected Works*, Vol. 53, Fifth Russian Edition, p. 324). On November 5, 1921, an agreement was signed by representatives of the R.S.F.S.R. and the M.P.R. under which both parties engaged not to allow groups hostile to the other party to stay or be formed on their territories, and made arrangements for the appointment of diplomatic and consular representatives, the fixing of state boundaries, and customs arrangements. The Soviet Government handed over to the Government of the M.P.R. telegraph installations in Mongolia belonging to the R.S.F.S.R.

Lenin's talk with the delegation took place in the Kremlin. A report of the talk was first published in the minutes of the Ninth Congress of the M.P.R.P., which was held from September 28 to October 5, 1934. The publication was reproduced from the reminiscences of B. Shumyatsky and B. Tserendorzh. The latter wrote in his recollections: "Lenin spoke for a long time with the members of the delegation. He lent an attentive ear to our stories, showed a lively interest in the most varied aspects of life in people's Mongolia, and gave some useful advice. In particular, he drew our attention to the need for raising the level of education and culture among the Mongolian people, while at the same time stressing the need for developing the country's economy to the utmost with a view to meeting all the requirements of the peopl." p. 360

421 *The First All-Russia Conference on Trade Union Cultural and Educational Work* was held in Moscow from September 26 to October 1, 1921. It was attended by 173 delegates (122 voting delegates and 51 with a consultative voice), of whom 119 were Communists, 51 non-Party people, 1 Menshevik, 1 Socialist-Revolutionary and 1 inter-party socialist. There were 13 items on the agenda of the conference, which included reports of the A.C.C.T.U.'s Culture Department, the Peoples' Commissariat for Education and its chief administrations, and Proletcult; reports from the local areas (Donbas, Petrograd, Baku); the New Economic Policy and education; the trade union's work of political education; cultural work among the youth, and other items. The conference mapped out ways for improving the trade unions' work of political education, and new forms and methods under the New Economic Policy (cultural work at private and leased enterprises, and so on).

The conference adopted a wrong stand on the question of relations with the Chief Committee for Political Education. Its resolution ("Role and Aims of the Trade Unions' Cultural Work") contained a demand that the trade unions' cultural work should be freed from the influence of the Chief Committee for Political Education. This ran counter to the resolution of the Tenth Congress of the R.C.P. "On the Chief Committee for Political Education and the Agitation and Propaganda Tasks of the Party" (see *The C.P.S.U. in the Resolutions and Decisions of Its Congresses, Conferences and Plenary Meetings of the Central Committee,* Part I, 1954, p. 550).   p. 361

422   Lenin is referring to the resolution of the Second All-Russia Congress of Political Education Departments (held from October 17 to 22, 1921) "On the Reports of the Chief Committee for Political Education", which defined the relations between the political education departments and the trade unions' culture departments centrally and locally. "The trade unions," ran this resolution, "constantly lapse into the entirely erroneous view that educational work in all forms should be the business of the trade unions, that the trade unions would be better able to conduct the business of education than the educational authorities.

"Their point of view is erroneous and stems from misinterpretation of the tasks of the trade unions. Adherence to such a point of view would induce the conclusion that all state functions, the work of all the commissariats, should be turned over to the trade unions" (*Second All-Russia Congress of Political Education Departments. Congress Bulletin* No. 7, October 24, 1921).

The resolution of the congress mapped out concrete measures for the joint ideological, political, cultural and educational work of the Chief Committee for Political Education and the Culture Department of the A.C.C.T.U.   p. 362

423   The Politbureau of the C.C., R.C.P.(B.) decided on November 8, 1921, to adopt as a basis Lenin's resolution. In accordance with this decision regulations were drafted for the joint political education work of the A.C.C.T.U.'s Culture Department and the Chief Committee for Political Education.   p. 362

424   This note was written on Chicherin's letter to the Politbureau in which he reported that the question of denationalising Soviet Russia's foreign trade was raised at the Baltic Economic Conference (held at Riga, from October 28 to 31, 1921). V. P. Milyutin, the head of the R.S.F.S.R. delegation at the conference, submitted a paper on this question which was sent to the Politbureau. Milyutin's plan boiled down to abolishing the monopoly of foreign trade. On November 10 the Politbureau, on Lenin's motion, rejected Milyutin's proposal (see also *Collected Works,* Vol. 44, Fifth Russian Edition, pp. 427-30; present edition, Vol. 33, pp. 375-78 and pp. 455-59).   p. 362

425   Lenin's motion on food work in the Ukraine was adopted by the Politbureau on November 10, 1921.   p. 362

426   This document was written in connection with the drafting of a decree of the Council of People's Commissars "On Penalties for False Denunciations". The decree was signed by Lenin on

November 24, and published in *Izvestia* on December 1, 1921.
Lenin's addenda were included in the text of this decree (see
*Collection of Statutes and Decrees of the Workers' and Peasants'
Government"*, 1921, No. 77, p. 787).   p. 363

427 The decree introducing payment for newspapers was endorsed
by the C.P.C. on November 28, 1921. Under this decree all individuals, public institutions and organisations, and state institutions and enterprises without exception were to be charged
for newspapers. Lenin's motion formed the basis of Point 8 of
the Decree, which directed the People's Commissariat for Education to draw up within a fortnight and publish instructions
covering control over the proper distribution of newspapers to
the network of educational institutions and the supply of newspapers to the population (see *Izvestia* No. 275, December 7,
1921).   p. 364

428 Lenin is referring to his motion on the question of the disagreements between the leading Party functionaries in the Donbas,
which was discussed at a meeting of the Politbureau.   p. 364

429 Lenin's motion on the first and second questions was adopted
by the Politbureau on November 27, 1921.   p. 364

430 This part of Lenin's letter was a draft for the Politbureau. The
latter's decision, adopted on December 1, 1921, on Lenin's
report, stated that "Comrade Tsyurupa shall be relieved of the
post of People's Commissar for Food and appointed Second Deputy
Chairman of the C.L.D. with a casting vote in the C.L.D. and
the C.P.C., the appointment to be endorsed by the Presidium
of the A.C.E.C." (Central Party Archives of the Institute of
Marxism-Leninism of the C.C. of the C.P.S.U.). A similar wording
was used in the decision of the A.C.E.C. confirming the appointment of A. D. Tsyurupa to the post of Second Deputy Chairman
of the C.L.D. (see *Izvestia* No. 272, December 3, 1921).   p. 365

431 In view of the country's transition to peaceful economic construction, Lenin proposed the reorganisation of the Vecheka. On
December 1, 1921, the Politbureau set up a commission consisting of L. B. Kamenev, D. I. Kursky and F. E. Dzerzhinsky
to go into this question within five days with a view to: "a) narrowing the jurisdiction of the Vecheka; b) narrowing its right
of arrest; c) fixing a term of one month for the whole process of
the law; d) giving more weight to the courts of law; e) considering
the question of a change of name; f) preparing and passing through
the All-Russia C.E.C. general regulations covering changes in
the direction of radical relaxations" (Central Party Archives
of the Institute of Marxism-Leninism of the C.C. of the C.P.S.U.).
     Lenin's ideas were embodied also in the Resolution on the
Vecheka passed by the Ninth All-Russia Congress of Soviets
on December 27, 1921. The congress directed the Presidium

of the All-Russia C.E.C. "to revise the Regulations on the Vecheka and its agencies in the direction of its reorganisation, the narrowing of its jurisdiction and the strengthening of the principles of revolutionary legality" (*The Ninth All-Russia Congress of Soviets. Verbatim Report*, 1922, p. 300). On January 23, 1922, the Politbureau examined the question of reorganising the Vecheka into the State Political Administration (Gosudarstvennoye Politicheskoye Upravleniye—G.P.U.) under the People's Commissariat for Internal Affairs and defined the basic tasks and functions of the G.P.U. On February 6 the Presidium of the All-Russia C.E.C. passed a decision for the reorganisation of the Vecheka (see *Izvestia* No. 30, February 8, 1922).

Point 3 of Lenin's draft refers to the period in which the reorganisation was to be carried out.   p. 367

[432] This draft was written in connection with the discussion by the Politbureau on December 1, 1921, of the question of the tactics of a united workers' front. Lenin's proposals were adopted. They formed the basis of the Comintern Executive's theses "On the United Workers' Front and the Attitude to the Workers Belonging to the II, II$^1/_2$ and Amsterdam Internationals, as Well as the Workers Who Support the Anarcho-Syndicalist Organisations". Lenin's remarks on the theses (see p. 368 of this volume) were also taken into consideration. The theses were published in the journal *The Communist International* No. 20 for 1921. The Eleventh All-Russia Conference of the R.C.P.(B.) (December 19-21, 1921) subscribed to these theses. They were discussed and endorsed by the first enlarged plenary meeting of the Comintern Executive (February 21-March 4, 1922) and by the Fourth Congress of the Comintern.

Lenin's "Notes on the History of the R.C.P." (see present edition, Vol. 36, pp. 552-54) were made in connection with the proposal that Bukharin should write an article summing up the experience of the R.C.P.(B.)   p. 367

[433] This refers to the State Planning Commission's draft decision for the C.L.D. concerning the liquidation of the Commission for the Utilisation of Material Resources under the C.L.D.

§§ 2 and 3 of the State Planning Commission's draft stated that the planning of distribution of the goods produced by the state industrial enterprises and the distribution of food resources was to be carried out respectively by the planning commissions of the Supreme Economic Council and the Food Commissariat, while the State Planning Commission was to integrate these plans into a general plan of distribution of material resources and submit it to the C.L.D. § 5 laid down the terminal date and order of liquidation of the Commission for the Utilisation of Material Resources.

Lenin's motion was adopted at the meeting of the C.L.D. on December 2, 1921. The State Planning Commission's revised draft decision on the C.U.M.R. was endorsed by the C.L.D. on December 16.   p. 367

434 Lenin's draft was written in connection with the discussion by
the Politbureau at its meeting on December 5, 1921, of the
S.E.C.'s complaint against the decision of the C.L.D. withdraw-
ing the flour-mills from the jurisdiction of the S.E.C. and placing
them in charge of the Commissariat for Food. The Politbureau
confirmed the decision of the C.L.D. and directed the Narrow
Council of People's Commissars to pass a supplementary decision
as proposed by Lenin.   p. 368

435 Cf. Note 432.   p. 368

436 *The Propaganda and Action Council of the Peoples of the East*
was elected at the First Congress of the Peoples of the East held
in Baku in September 1920. The Council set.itself the task of
supporting and uniting the liberation movement of the peoples
of the East.   p. 369

437 Lenin's remarks on the draft resolution for the Eleventh
Conference of the R.C.P.(B.) on the Party purge were taken
into consideration by the drafting committee.
    The conference discussed the results of the Party purge and
adopted a resolution "On the Question of Strengthening the Party
as a Result of the Verification of Its Membership", which was
drafted in its final version at a meeting of regional committees,
regional bureaux and Gubernia Committees of the R.C.P. and
endorsed by the Central Committee and the Eleventh Congress
of the Party (see *The C.P.S.U. in the Resolutions and Decisions
of Congresses, Conferences and Plenary Meetings of the Central
Committee*, Part I, 1954, pp. 597-98).   p. 370

438 *The Ninth All-Russia Congress of Soviets* sat in Moscow on December 23-28, 1921. It was attended by 1,993 delegates, of whom
1,631 were voting delegates and 362 had a consultative voice.
1,850 delegates were Communists, 139 non-Party people, and
one delegate each with a consultative voice from the Socialist-
Revolutionaries, the Anarcho-Universalists, the Jewish Social-
Democratic Labour Party Poale Zion and the Molokan communities.
    The congress discussed the reports and passed the following
decisions: 1) Resolution on the report of the All-Russia C.E.C.
and the C.P.C. on the Republic's home and foreign policies;
2) Declaration on the international position of the R.S.F.S.R.;
3) Resolution on the building up of the Red Army and Navy;
4) Resolution on relief to the famine-stricken areas; 5) Appeal
for collection of the tax in kind; 6) Instructions on questions
of economic activities; 7) Resolution on the preliminary results
of the New Economic Policy and on the Republic's industry;
8) Resolution on measures for strengthening and developing
agriculture; 9) Resolution on agricultural co-operation; 10) Resolution on finances and the budget; 11) Resolution of the C.P.C.
on electrification endorsed by the Ninth Congress of Soviets;

12) Resolution on Soviet administrative activities; 13) Resolution on the Vecheka.

Lenin put in a great deal of work in preparing for the congress and directing its proceedings (see present edition, Vol. 33, pp. 141-81).

The Meeting of Non-Party Delegates held on the evening of December 26, 1921, discussed two questions: that of the compulsory carting tax (reporter Lemberg, representative of the Commissariat for Labour), and the agrarian question. The meeting was chaired by M. I. Kalinin.

The first two speeches were delivered by Lenin during the discussion of the carting tax question, the second speech following a request by one of the congress delegates asking Lenin to say a few words "about the servicing of Soviet institutions".

Lenin's third speech was delivered during the discussion of the agrarian question following a speech by Kalinin. Lenin made brief notes of the speeches at the meeting (see *Lenin Miscellany XXIII*, pp. 292-94, 297-98).   p. 370

439   *Zheleskoms*—Russian abbreviated name for Railway Logging Committees supervising felling operations and the carting of wood to the railway stations for the needs of industry and transport.   p. 372

440   Pointing out that twenty instead of five non-Party peasants would now be elected to the All-Russia Central Executive Committee, Kalinin said: "Some comrades say that we elect men by their beards. Excuse me, Comrades, but a beard means a lot to a peasant. It stands for his way of life, his thinking, and the best example is the peasant Petrushkin sitting here next to me. If Comrade Lenin says, 'I'll go and burn all the prayer-books', I'd like to know the opinion of a non-Party man, and I'll ask Petrushkin what the peasants will think of my wanting to burn the prayer-books. He'll say, 'Who cares, let them burn'. He's a young man, but if I ask a bearded man he'll say we ought to wait a bit. This means a lot to us" (*Istorichesky Arkhiv* [Historical Archives], No. 2, 1962, p. 76).   p. 373

441   Lenin started writing the *Draft Theses on the Role and Functions of the Trade Unions Under the New Economic Policy* soon after the plenum of the C.C., R.C.P.(B.) on December 28, 1921. The draft theses were discussed by members of the commission (A. A. Andreyev and Y. E. Rudzutak) and members of the Politbureau; in the course of the discussion amendments and addenda were introduced. On January 12, 1922, the draft was discussed at a meeting of the Politbureau, which resolved that "the text of the theses proposed by Lenin be adopted as a basis.... The theses with all the amendments to be referred to an editorial committee consisting of Comrades Lenin, Zinoviev, Andreyev and Bukharin for final endorsement and publication in the name of the Central Committee with mention that the theses are

supported by the Bureau of the Party group at the A.C.C.T.U.
(Central Party Archives, Institute of Marxism-Leninism).

The final text of the theses was published on January 17,
1922, in *Pravda* as a decision of the Central Committee, R.C.P.,
representing the C.C.'s draft theses on the question of the trade
unions for the Eleventh Congress of the Party. The congress
adopted the C.C.'s theses as a basis; during their discussion in
the committee several amendments were introduced (see *The
C.P.S.U. in the Resolutions and Decisions of Congresses, Conferences and Plenary Meetings of the Central Committee*, Part I,
1954, pp. 603-12).

Volume 33 of this edition gives the final text of the Central
Committee's decision on "The Role and Functions of the Trade
Unions Under the New Economic Policy". The present volume
gives Lenin's draft of the theses.   p. 374

442 *Pravda* for January 3, 1922, published a news-item reporting
the "Suicide of Engineer Oldenborger" which stated: "The Moscow Soviet, in agreement with the Moscow Committee of the
R.C.P., appointed a special commission to investigate the causes
of the suicide of V. V. Oldenborger, Chief Engineer of the Moscow Municipal Waterworks. The Commission found that the
deceased was not only a highly skilled employee, but a man
utterly devoted to his work. The cause of suicide were the difficult conditions, which interfered with the daily routine of Oldenborger's work. Some of the members of the Waterworks Special
Trio, instead of trying to improve things at Moscow's Waterworks, made them more difficult and complicated than ever;
Engineer Semyonov, Chief Inspector of the People's Commissariat for Workers' and Peasants' Inspection, who is a member of
this Trio, was rude, cavilling and bureaucratic in his relations
with Oldenborger; Makarov-Zemlyansky, Chief Inspector of the
same commissariat and a former clerk at the Waterworks, carried
on a ceaseless persecution of Oldenborger; and Yelagin and
Merkulov, workers of the Alexeyevsk Pump-House, accused
Oldenborger groundlessly of technical disorganisation of the
Waterworks and of an attitude of disrespect towards the communist group on the part of the employees. All this was bound to
have its effect on the emotional state of the deceased. The commission considers the continued employment of Makarov-Zemlyansky
impermissible not only in the Workers' and Peasants' Inspection, but in Soviet service generally, as being a person who is
alien to the spirit of Soviet service, an intrigant who has earned
among the employees of the Waterworks the reputation of being
a dishonest man. The commission also found that engineer Semyonov of the W.P.I. should not be allowed to continue work at the
Workers' and Peasants' Inspection or to have anything to do
with the Moscow Municipal Waterworks, and likewise considers
it necessary that Yelagin and Merkulov should be dismissed from
the Waterworks and transferred to some other enterprise."

See also pp. 386-87 of this volume.   p. 384

443 Lenin's proposal that a commission be set up to check and replace some of the leading personnel in the trade unions was based on the fact that the trade unions were honeycombed with former Mensheviks and Socialist-Revolutionaries and that it was necessary to fix a longer record of Communist Party membership for leading trade union officials in keeping with the resolution of the Eleventh All-Russia Conference of the R.C.P. "On the Question of Strengthening the Party as a Result of the Verification of Its Membership" (see "*The C.P.S.U. in the Resolutions and Decisions of Congresses, Conferences and Plenary Meetings of the Central Committee*", Part I, 1954, p. 596).

Lenin's motion was adopted by the Politbureau. On January 20, 1922, a commission was set up consisting of M. P. Tomsky, A. A. Andreyev and S. I. Syrtsov. The commission reported its findings to the Eleventh Congress of the R.C.P.(B.) (see *The Eleventh Congress of the R.C.P.(B.) Verbatim Report.*, 1961, pp. 246-52). p. 386

444 Lenin's draft decisions were adopted by the Politbureau at its meeting on January 5, 1922.

The Oldenborger suicide case was examined by the Supreme Tribunal of the All-Russia C.E.C. on March 8-14, 1922, and the guilty parties were sentenced to various punishments. p. 387

445 The question of increased financing for radio developments was examined by the Politbureau at its meeting on January 20, 1922. The Politbureau agreed with Lenin's motion and approved the decision of the Commissariat for Finance on this question. p. 388

446 The Managing Department of the C.P.C. forwarded this document to the Commissariat for Education on January 27, 1922, with the following covering letter: "I am sending you for guidance Vladimir Ilyich's directives on the film business." The Commissariat for Education was instructed: "1) On the basis of these directives to draw up a programme of action and forward it immediately to the Managing Department of the C.P.C. for report to Vladimir Ilyich. 2) To submit to the Managing Department of the C.P.C. within one month a report on what has actually been done in pursuance of these directives and what results have been achieved. 3) To immediately report what functions have been retained by the Commissariat for Education after the promulgation of the last decision of the Council of Labour and Defence on the film business and who is directly in charge of the performance of these functions" (Central Party Archives, Institute of Marxism-Leninism of the C.C. of the C.P.S.U.).

In a conversation with A. V. Lunacharsky in February 1922 Lenin "once more stressed the necessity of establishing a definite proportion between entertainment films and scientific films". Vladimir Ilyich, Lunacharsky writes in his reminiscences, said that the production of new films imbued with communist ideas and reflecting Soviet realities should be started with newsreel, since, in his opinion, the time had not yet come for the production of such films. "If you have a good newsreel, serious and enlightening pictures, it doesn't really matter if you show some worthless film with them of a more or less usual type to attract the public. A censorship, of course, will be needed. Counter-revolutionary and immoral films should be barred." To this Lenin added: "As you find your feet, what with proper handling of the business, and receive certain loans to carry on, depending on the general improvement in the country's position, you will have to expand production, and particularly make headway with useful films among the masses in the cities, and still more in the countryside.... You must remember always that of all the arts the most important for us is the cinema" (*Sovietskoye Kino* No. 1-2, 1933, p. 10). p. 389

447 Lenin's proposal on Kalinin's trip to the Ukraine was adopted by the Politbureau on January 28. Kalinin made the trip on February 7-18 and March 5-18, 1922, with the agittrain "October Revolution" along the route: Poltava—Mirgorod—Kiev—Belaya Tserkov—Kremenchug—Odessa—Zhmerinka—Kamenets Podolsk—Vinnitsa—Berdichev—Zhitomir. p. 389

448 This refers to an article entitled "The Ninth Congress of Soviets and the Peasantry" published in *Pravda* on January 27, 1922, over the signature Bespartiiny (Non-Party-Man). The writer propounded a plan for popularising among the peasantry the decisions of the Ninth All-Russia Congress of Soviets on peasant questions. Lenin's motion was adopted by the Politbureau on January 28, 1922. p. 390

449 The idea of an international conference to deal with all questions concerning the establishment of peace and economic co-operation in Europe, and also the question of Russian debts, was put forward by the Soviet Government, who addressed Notes to this effect to Britain, France, Japan, Italy, and the U.S.A. (see *Collected Works*, Fifth Russian Edition, Vol. 44, pp. 185-88). The decision to convene an international economic and financial conference was taken by the Supreme Allied Council at a conference in Cannes on January 6, 1922. The Allies invited Soviet Russia to the conference in the hope of forcing from her a number of political and economic concessions while at the same time establishing economic relations with her.

The Soviet delegation to the Genoa Conference was elected at an emergency session of the All-Russia Central Executive Committee on January 27. Lenin was appointed head of the delegation with Chicherin as his deputy "vested with all the rights as chairman in the event of circumstances preventing Comrade Lenin from attending the conference". Among the other members of the delegation were L. B. Krasin, M. M. Litvinov, N. N. Narimanov, V. V. Vorovsky and Y. E. Rudzutak. The question of Lenin going to Genoa was widely discussed by the people of the Soviet Republics. Numerous letters were received expressing apprehension for his life and safety and declaring against his going to the conference. The Central Committee of the R.C.P.(B.) passed a special decision on this question, under which Lenin resigned his commission to Chicherin as head of the delegation.

Lenin directed the work of the delegation, drew up the C.C.'s directives for it, and other important documents bearing on Soviet Russia's participation in the Genoa Conference (see pp. 394-95, 396-98, 401-404, 410 of this volume, and volumes 44 and 45 of the Fifth Russian Edition).

The Genoa Conference sat from April 10 to May 19, 1922. It was attended by representatives from 29 countries. The declaration by the Soviet delegation, which was approved by Lenin and endorsed by the Council of People's Commissars, stated: "While remaining true to the principles of communism, the Russian delegation recognises that in the present epoch, which makes the parallel existence of the old and the emergent new social system possible, economic co-operation between states representing the two systems of property is imperatively necessary for universal economic reconstruction" (*Materialy Genuezskoi konferentsii.* [Materials of the Genoa Conference.] Verbatim Report. Moscow, 1922, p. 78).

The Genoa Conference failed to settle the problems confronting it. The Soviet delegation vigorously repelled the attempts of the imperialist powers to impose a colonial status upon Soviet Russia (the establishment of control over Soviet finances, etc.). By proposing talks on a general reduction of armaments and the banning of the most barbarous methods of warfare (poison gases, military aircraft), the Soviet delegation demonstrated to the world the peace-loving nature of Soviet Russia's Leninist foreign policy.   p. 390

450 Lenin here alludes to the policy of partial concessions which the British Government of Lloyd George carried out in the early twenties in order to suppress the revolutionary movement for national liberation in Ireland and Egypt.

The Anglo-Irish Treaty was signed on December 6, 1920, following a long and hard struggle for national independence by the Irish people. The Treaty provided for the establishment of a dominion "Irish Free State" within the British Empire. Six north-eastern counties (Ulster), the most industrially developed part of Ireland, were alienated to Great Britain.

After crushing the rebellion of the Egyptian people against British rule in December 1921, the British Government was compelled in February 1922 to terminate its protectorate and proclaim Egypt an "independent kingdom". Egypt, however, became only nominally "independent", since all her territory remained occupied by Britain, who controlled the Suez Canal zone, ruled Anglo-Egyptian Sudan, etc.   p. 393

451 The reference is to the forthcoming conference of the three Internationals (the II, II$\frac{1}{2}$ and III Communist International). The

Communist International's active fight for the creation of a united
workers' front against the onset of the bourgeoisie and the leaning
towards unity of action on the part of the working masses compelled the leadership of the II$^1/_2$ International on January 19,
1922, to send a proposal to the Comintern Executive for convening an international conference in the spring of 1922 to consider
the problems of Europe's economic position and action by the
working class against the onset of reaction.   p. 393

452 *Smena Vekh* (Change of Landmarks) a weekly journal published
in Paris from October 1921 to March 1922 by a group of White
émigré intellectuals. The same group published a collection of
articles under this title in Prague in July 1921. A socio-
political trend formed around this journal and the collection,
which became known as *Smenovekhism* (its ideologists were N. V.
Ustryalov, Y. V. Klyuchnikov, S. S. Lukyanov, A. V. Bobrishchev-
Pushkin, S. S. Chakhotin, Y. N. Potekhin and others).
  A slight revival of capitalist elements in Soviet Russia following the introduction of the New Economic Policy served as the
social foundation for this trend. The Smena Vekhists regarded
the N.E.P. as an evolution of Soviet rule towards the restoration
of capitalism. They stood for co-operation with the Soviet government in the hope of the Soviet state evolving back into a bourgeois
state. Some of them were prepared loyally to co-operate with
the Soviet government and contribute to the country's economic revival. The Twelfth All-Russia Conference of the R.C.P.(B.)
(August 4-7, 1922), in its Resolution on Anti-Soviet Parties and
Trends, pointed out: "The so-called Smena Vekh trend has so far
played and may still play an objectively progressive role. It is
rallying those groups of émigrés and Russian intellectuals who
have "reconciled" themselves to the Soviet government and are
prepared to work with it for reviving the country. *To this extent* the
Smena Vekh trend merits a favourable attitude towards it. At the
same time it should never for a moment be forgotten that there
are strong tendencies towards bourgeois restoration among its adher-
ents, who share with the Mensheviks and the Socialist-Revolutionaries the hope that economic concessions will be followed by
political concessions towards a bourgeois democracy, etc."
(*The C.P.S.U. in the Resolutions and Decisions of Its Congresses,
Conferences and Plenary Meetings of the Central Committee*,
Part I, 1954, p. 671). Eventually, most of the Smena Vekh
people sided openly with the counter-revolution. A comment
on this trend is given by Lenin in his report to the Eleventh
Congress of the R.C.P. (see present edition, Vol. 33, p. 285-
86).   p. 394

453 Lenin's note to the Politbureau followed the publication on
February 2, 1922, in *Izvestia* of a telegram from Warsaw reporting
the gist of Parvus's pamphlet *Der wirtschaftliche Rettungsweg*
in which its author justified the annexationist plans of German
imperialism in the East, plans for colonial enslavement of the

peoples of Soviet Russia. There, in Eastern Europe, Parvus wrote, "the way is open for German expansion, for German might, for German thrift".

Lenin's motion was adopted by the Politbureau on February 8. After investigations into this matter the Politbureau passed a decision on March 11, 1922 (see the next document).   p. 395

454   The addenda to the directives of the C.C. contained in this document were adopted by the Politbureau on February 8, 1922.
p. 396

455   *Kooperativnoye Dyelo* (Co-operative Business)—a socio-economic, co-operative and trade daily, organ of Centrosoyuz. The Editor-in-Chief was N. L. Meshcheryakov. Publication started on February 1, 1922.

Lenin's motion (see the next document) was put before the Politbureau at its meeting on February 15, 1922. A decision was passed "To require the editorial board of *Kooperativnoye Dyelo* to submit to the Politbureau within three days an explanation in writing concerning the newspaper's publication, its character, the composition of its editorial board, staff and contributors" (Central Party Archives, Institute of Marxism-Leninism of the C.C., C.P.S.U.). The question was dealt with a second time on February 22, when it was decided to postpone the closing down of the newspaper for a fortnight. A final decision was reached in May, the newspaper *Kooperativnoye Dyelo* being converted into a weekly.   p. 398

456   The first extended plenary meeting of the Comintern Executive was held in Moscow from February 21 to March 4, 1922. It was attended by 105 delegates from 36 countries. The highlight of the meeting was the question of the tactics of the united front. In addition, the meeting heard a report on the situation within the various sections of the Comintern, and other questions. The meeting adopted the theses on the struggle against war and the war menace, the theses on the New Economic Policy, a decision on the tactics of the united front, a resolution on the participation of the Comintern in the proposed conference of the three Internationals, and a number of other documents.

Lenin did not sit in at the meeting owing to ill-health, but he took an active part in preparing the meeting and elaborated the tactics for the Comintern delegation to the conference of the three Internationals (see pp. 393—94, 406, etc. of this volume).

Lenin's proposed amendments to the draft resolution on participation in the conference of the three Internationals were adopted by the Politbureau of the C.C. on February 23, 1922.

A resolution on this point was adopted by the first plenary meeting of the Comintern Executive on March 4, 1922.   p. 400

457   Lenin's motion was adopted by the Politbureau on February 28, 1922, with the following amendments moved by Stalin: "1. The question regarding *recognition of the Soviet government* should

be raised not at the beginning but at the close of the conference
(after attempts had been made to reach an economic agreement),
and no ultimatum should be made of it; 2. *Centrosoyuz, the agricultural co-operatives*, etc., should not be put forward at the conference in the capacity of subjects (contracting parties) (as Krasin
suggests), and only a single subject—the Russian state should
be taken into consideration" (Central Party Archives, Institute
of Marxism-Leninism of the C.C., C.P.S.U.).   p. 404

458   The same day the Politbureau adopted Lenin's proposal, and
      Chicherin sent a radio-telegram to the Italian Foreign Minister
      on the question of the date for convening the Genoa Conference
      (see *Izvestia* No. 47, February 28, 1922).   p. 404

459   The new regulations governing the Narrow Council of People's
      Commissars were endorsed by the C.P.C. on October 31, 1922.
                                                                 p. 405

460   Negotiations for a loan were being conducted with the Swedish
      Government and Swedish business circles by representatives of
      Soviet Russia since the autumn of 1921. Lenin wrote his proposal
      after reading the terms of the loan and the views of the People's
      Commissariat for Foreign Trade and of the People's Commissar
      for Finance N. N. Krestinsky on the matter.   p. 405

461   This letter was written in connection with the drafting by the
      Comintern Executive of directives for the Comintern's delega-
      tion to the conference of the three Internationals. It is a comment
      on the directives which G. Y. Zinoviev drafted and sent to Lenin
      on March 14, 1922, with a request to express his opinion on them
      before the draft was submitted to the Comintern Executive.
         These directives, amended in accordance with Lenin's remarks
      and proposals, were approved by the Politbureau, and unani-
      mously endorsed by the Comintern Executive on March 17.
                                                                 p. 406

462   The Politbureau adopted Lenin's proposal on March 18, 1922.
                                                                 408

463   Lenin's letter was written in connection with the following
      incident. Following numerous complaints of abuses practised in
      the Central Housing Department of the Moscow Soviet, an inspec-
      tion of this department was undertaken. Similar complaints
      having been received addressed to Lenin, the inspection was
      carried out with the close co-operation of the C.P.C.'s Business
      Manager (A. A. Divilkovsky). The inspection revealed abuses
      practised by a number of top members of the staff of the Central
      Housing Department with the connivance of the Department
      Chief of the Moscow Communal Services Sovetnikov, a member
      of the Party. The Bureau of the Moscow Committee of the
      R.C.P.(B.), at a joint meeting with the Presidium of the Moscow
      Soviet on March 14, declared the findings of the inspection com-
      mission to be unfounded and decided to refer the matter to a new,

Party commission for revision. In his letter to N. P. Gorbunov dated March 15, copies of which were forwarded to all members of the Politbureau for their information, Divilkovsky stressed that this decision ran counter to Lenin's instructions that "bureaucratic banditism, especially when practised by suspicious elements who have wormed their way into the Party" should be relentlessly prosecuted, and he asked that this decision be reversed and the guilty parties put on trial (Central Party Archives, Institute of Marxism-Leninism of the C.C., C.P.S.U.).

When sending his letter to Molotov for members of the Politbureau, Lenin wrote on it: "Gorbunov, forward immediately, *show to Tsyurupa and Rykov.*"   p. 408

464 This document was written in connection with L. M. Khinchuk's letter dated March 17, 1922, asking Lenin for instructions whether or not the question of voluntary principle of membership of the co-operatives should be raised at the forthcoming Fifth Session of the Delegates' Council of Centrosoyuz. Lenin's proposals were incorporated in the decision of the Politbureau of May 12, 1922, "On Compulsory Membership, Voluntary Contributions and Unity of Consumers' Co-operatives".   p. 409

465 All Lenin's amendments and remarks to the draft declaration for the Soviet delegation to the Genoa Conference submitted by Chicherin were taken into consideration. This declaration was read out by Chicherin at the first plenary session of the Genoa Conference on April 10, 1922.   p. 410

466 Lenin is referring to the following draft speech submitted by Chicherin: "We attach the greatest importance to Point One of the Cannes resolution concerning mutual recognition of the political and economic systems in both camps of the present-day world" (Central Party Archives of the Institute of Marxism-Leninism of the C.C. of the C.P.S.U.). This text in Chicherin's draft is marked off by Lenin in the margin. The words in Chicherin's draft referred to in points 2, 3 and 4 of Lenin's remarks are underlined by Lenin.   p. 410

467 *The Eleventh Congress of the R.C.P. (B.)* was held in Moscow from March 27 to April 2, 1922. It was attended by 522 voting delegates and 164 delegates with a consultative voice.

The items on the agenda were: 1) The political report of the Central Committee; 2) The organisational report of the Central Committee; 3) The report of the Auditing Commission; 4) The report of the Central Control Commission; 5) The report of the R.C.P. delegation in the Comintern; 6) The trade unions; 7) The Red Army; 8) Financial policy; 9) Results of the Party purge and the strengthening of the Party's ranks; co-reports on work with young people and on the press and propaganda; 10) Elections to the Central Committee and the Central Control Commission. In addition, the congress set up a commission to prepare the question of Party work in the countryside for discussion in the

Agrarian Section of the Party Congress and for drafting a resolution.

´ Considerable preparatory work for the congress was carried out
by the C.C. under Lenin's direction. The most important documents of the congress were drafted by Lenin or with Lenin's
help. Lenin opened the congress, delivered the political report
of the C.C., wound up the debate on the report, spoke about
the printing of advertisements in *Pravda*, and made the closing
speech at the congress.

See also present edition, Vol. 33, pp. 259-326.   p. 411

[468] Lenin's wording was incorporated wholly in the resolution of
the Eleventh Congress of the R.C.P.(B.) "On the Report of the
R.C.P. Delegation in the Comintern" adopted on April 2, 1922
(see *The C.P.S.U. in the Resolutions and Decisions of Congresses,
Conferences and Plenary Meetings of the Central Committee*,
Part I, 1954, pp. 601-03).   p. 411

[469] During the discussion of the resolution "On the Press and Propaganda" at the Eleventh Congress of the R.C.P.(B.), D. B. Ryazanov moved an addendum, proposing that advertisements
should not be printed in the Party press. The congress adopted
the motion with the amendment that advertisements were to be
forbidden not in the Party press as a whole, but only in *Pravda*.
Lenin was not in attendance at the moment. Upon hearing of the
congress decision he wrote the following note to L. B. Kamenev
who had chaired that session: "Comrade Kamenev, I hear that
the congress has placed a ban on advertisements in *Pravda*?
Cannot this be mended, it's an obvious mistake?" (*Lenin Miscellany XIII*, 1930, p. 29). Kamenev did not think the decision
could be altered, and suggested that other ways be found for
supporting *Pravda*. However, after the list of members of the
C.C. and the Central Control Commission elected by the congress
had been announced, Lenin took the floor and proposed that this
decision be reversed on the grounds that under the New Economic
Policy it would be incorrect to depend upon appropriations for
the press being made from the gold fund or revenue receipts.
His motion was adopted.

Since Lenin's speech was taken down in shorthand only
partially and inadequately at that, the version printed in this
volume is incomplete.   p. 411

[470] The C.C. plenum on April 3, 1922, adopted this draft with the
following addendum: "... in order that Comrade Stalin may be
completely released from work in the Workers' and Peasants'
Inspection." Following the plenum's decision to appoint Stalin
General Secretary of the C.C. of the R.C.P., he was relieved of his
duties as People's Commissar of the Workers' and Peasants'
Inspection under a decision of the Council of People's Commissars
dated April 25, 1922.   p. 413

[471] The Politbureau adopted Lenin's motion on April 12, 1922.
                                                                p. 414

[472] *The Conference of the Three Internationals* was held in Berlin
from April 2 to 5, 1922.

A sharp struggle developed at the conference between the
representatives of the II and II$^1/_2$ Internationals on the one
hand, and the Communist International on the other. The Comintern delegation put forward a proposal that a world congress
should be convened, in which the trade unions and other organisations of the workers would participate, to discuss questions
concerning the fight against the onset of capital, against reaction,
and against preparations for new imperialist wars, concerning
aid for the rehabilitation of Soviet Russia, the Treaty of Versailles, and the rehabilitation of the devastated areas. The representatives of the II International, supported by the delegation
of the II$^1/_2$ International, tried to impose unacceptable terms on
the Comintern delegation, namely: the separation of Georgia
from the Soviet state, renunciation of communist cells in the mass
workers' organisations and the release of political criminals.
The Comintern delegation (Bukharin, Radek and C. Zetkin),
while rejecting these terms, nevertheless agreed to the condition
that the Soviet authorities would not apply the death penalty
in the case of the Right Socialist-Revolutionaries and would
allow representatives of the II and II$^1/_2$ Internationals to attend
the trial. In his article "We Have Paid Too Much", Lenin severely
criticised these concessions on the part of the Comintern delegation at the Berlin Conference, which he considered erroneous
(see present edition, Vol. 33, pp. 330-34).

A general declaration was adopted at the conference recognising
the possibility of holding joint meetings and issuing joint statements on concrete issues. The declaration called upon all the
working people to hold mass demonstrations during the Genoa
Conference with slogans to fight for an eight-hour day, against
unemployment, against the onset of capital upon the working
class, in defence of the Russian revolution, in aid of Russia's
famine-stricken areas, for the resumption by all states of political and economic relations with Soviet Russia, for the establishment of a united proletarian front in all countries on a national
and international scale. The conference went on record for the
speedy convocation of a world congress and set up a steering
committee of nine members (three from each International) to
prepare further conferences and a congress.

However, the reformist leadership of the II and II$^1/_2$ Internationals who accepted this agreement under pressure from the
broad masses of the working people, torpedoed and sabotaged
the united struggle of the working class. On May 21, 1922, a number of parties of the II and II$^1/_2$ Internationals passed a decision
to call a world congress at the Hague without the Communists.
By this means the reformist leaders blocked the efforts to create
a united front of the workers. In view of this the Comintern
delegation at the meeting of the steering committee on May 23,

1922, in Berlin, announced its withdrawal from the Committee of Nine.

Lenin's remarks and proposals were made to the following draft decision for the Presidium of the Comintern Executive in connection with the Berlin Conference of the Three Internationals: "1) To step up the campaign against the Mensheviks and Socialist-Revolutionaries throughout the international communist press. 2) To start making systematic use of the material of the Berlin Conference for attacking every weak spot of the opponent. 3) The general appeals of the Nine not to be issued for the time being. 4) In agitation during the demonstration on April 20, to be free-spoken in criticising our opponents. 5) The various sections act according to the concrete conditions. 6) Any new steps by the delegation to be postponed until the question of ratifying the Berlin results is dealt with" (Central Party Archives, Institute of Marxism-Leninism of the C.C., C.P.S.U.).

Zinoviev sent this draft to Lenin with a request that he give his opinion on it the same day before the Presidium of the Comintern Executive met.   p. 415

[473] *The New York Herald*—an American daily, organ of the Republican Party. Published in New York from 1835 to 1924.   p. 417

[474] The question of publishing the works of G. V. Plekhanov was tabled in the Politbureau on Lenin's proposal. The Central Party Archives of the Institute of Marxism-Leninism of the C.C. of the C.P.S.U. contain a copy of the agenda of the Politbureau meeting on April 27, 1922, listing 19 items, to which was added in Lenin's hand: "*Plekhanov's Works*".   p. 417

[475] Lenin's motion was adopted by the Politbureau on May 11, 1922.

Following the decision of the Politbureau a joint meeting of representatives of the Central Statistical Board, the State Planning Commission, the Food Commissariat and the Commissariat for Agriculture was held on May 16 at which the form for supplying information on the amount of the tax in kind collected in 1921-22 and expected in 1922-23 was endorsed.   p. 418

[476] This document was written in connection with the discussion of the question of the foreign trade monopoly which was taking place in leading Party circles at the end of 1921 and during 1922.

The monopoly of foreign trade, established by Decree of the Council of People's Commissars of April 22, 1918, was repeatedly reconfirmed in decisions of the Soviet Government. The adoption of the New Economic Policy and expansion of trade relations with foreign countries necessitated legislative amendments in the sphere of foreign trade. The Theses on Foreign Trade, which A. M. Lezhava, Deputy People's Commissar for Foreign Trade, drafted at Lenin's request, stressed the need for strengthening the monopoly of foreign trade and determined the conditions for the export and import of goods under the new conditions. Lenin approved the Theses, which were accepted on January 4, 1922, by the Supreme Economic Commission of the C.P.C. G. Y. Sokolnikov, N. I. Bukharin and G. L. Pyatakov were against retaining the monopoly of foreign trade. Sokolnikov proposed that it be abolished and replaced by a system of trade concessions. J. V. Stalin, G. Y. Zinoviev and L. B. Kamenev stood for a relaxation of the monopoly of foreign trade. The Politbureau of the C.C., R.C.P. approved the Theses on March 4, 1922, with certain amendments. The final version of the Theses was endorsed on March 10. On the basis of these Theses the Presidium of the All-Russia Central Executive Committee on March 13, 1922, passed its decision "On Foreign Trade" (published in *Izvestia* No. 60, March 15, 1922).

Despite the decision of the Politbureau, Sokolnikov continued to press his point of view and proposed a plan under which the state corporations, co-operatives, etc. were to be allowed to buy food abroad; M. I. Frumkin, Deputy People's Commissar for Foreign Trade, also stood for a relaxation of the foreign trade monopoly and proposed leaving only 4 or 5 items of wholesale trade in the hands of the state on the basis of a firm monopoly.

Following the receipt of documents from N. N. Krestinsky the R.S.F.S.R. Ambassador in Germany, testifying to the adverse influence which the Party controversy on the foreign trade monopoly was having on the business negotiations with foreign capitalists, Lenin on May 15 wrote the draft decision printed here, together with a letter to Stalin and Frumkin in which he pointed out that "*a formal ban should be put* on all talk and negotiations and commissions, etc. concerning the relaxation of the foreign trade monopoly" (*Collected Works*, Vol. 54, Fifth Russian Edition, p. 260). Stalin wrote on Lenin's letter: "I have no objections to a 'formal ban' on measures to *mitigate* the foreign trade monopoly at the *present* stage. All the same, I think that *mitigation* is becoming indispensable" (Lenin. *A Biography*, Moscow, 1966, p. 517).

Lenin's draft decision was endorsed by the Politbureau on May 22. See also present edition, Vol. 33, pp. 455-59; Vol. 45, Fifth Russian Edition, pp. 338-39.   p. 418

477 These documents were written by Lenin in connection with the drafting of the Criminal Code of the R.S.F.S.R. by the People's Commissariat for Justice and its discussion at the Third Session of the Ninth Convocation of the All-Russia Central Executive Committee, which took place from May 12 to 26, 1922. The addenda and the first letter were written by Lenin to the draft "Preamble to the Criminal Code of the R.S.F.S.R." sent him by D. I. Kursky, People's Commissar for Justice. After a talk with Kursky on this question, Lenin wrote his second letter with the rough draft of an additional Article to the Criminal Code.

Lenin's proposals were taken into consideration during the later drafting of the section of the Criminal Code dealing with "Counter-Revolutionary Crimes".

The Criminal Code of the R.S.F.S.R. was endorsed by the Third Session of the All-Russia C.E.C. and put in force on June 1, 1922 (see *Collection of Statutes and Decrees of the Workers' and Peasants' Government* (Russ. ed.), Moscow, 1922, No. 15, June 1, Article 153, pp. 202-39).   p. 419

[478] Lenin's letter was a reply to the inquiry of the Secretariat of the C.C., R.C.P., asking whether or not the question of reducing the size of the Red Army should be raised at the Third Session of the All-Russia C.E.C. of the Ninth Convocation. A plan for reducing the size of the Red Army was being drafted by the Revolutionary Military Council of the Republic in connection with the question of a possible general reduction in armaments which had been raised by the Soviet delegation at the Genoa Conference. This question was included in the agenda of the Third Session in a tentative form, depending on the results of the Genoa Conference. On May 24, 1922, the All-Russia C.E.C. passed a resolution which stated: "Thanks to the line pursued by our delegation, the Genoa Conference gives ground for hoping that a serious reduction of the army is possible." The resolution went on to say: "The Genoa Conference, however, has provided no solution to the most pressing problems concerning the relations between the Soviet Republic and the bourgeois states, leaving fundamental issues to be dealt with at the Hague...." In view of this the question of reducing the army was removed from the agenda of the Third Session. The session asked the Government and the People's Commissariat for Military Affairs to table a pertinent motion when the results of the Hague Conference had been ascertained (see *Third Session of the All-Russia Central Executive Committee of the Ninth Convocation. Bulletin No. 10* (Russ. ed.), May 26, 1922, pp. 18-19).   p. 420

[479] The Politbureau discussed Lenin's motion at its meeting on May 26, 1922, and decided to pass it on as material to the commission set up by the C.C. to steer the work of the Third Session of the All-Russia Central Executive Committee of the Ninth Convocation.   p. 420

[480] *The First Congress of Working Women of Transcaucasia* opened in Baku on May 26, 1922. The following reports were made at the congress: development of the women's movement in Soviet Russia and throughout the world and the tasks of the International Women's Secretariat; the working women of Transcaucasia and the Third International; the present situation, and others. The congress closed on May 30.

Lenin's greetings to the congress were written in reply to a message from the working women of Georgia, Armenia and

Azerbaijan notifying him that he had been elected delegate to
the congress of working women of Transcaucasia.

The greetings were read out at the opening meeting of the congress.   p. 421

481 On August 10, 1922, the Politbureau directed the Orgbureau to
set up a commission to go into the question of relations between
the R.S.F.S.R. and the independent national Soviet Republics
in preparation for the next plenary meeting of the Party's Central
Committee. This commission, set up on August 11, consisted
of J. V. Stalin, V. V. Kuibyshev, G. K. Orjonikidze, K. G. Rakovsky, G. Y. Sokolnikov and representatives of the national
republics—S. A. Agamali-ogly (Azerbaijan), A. F. Myasnikov
(Armenia), P. G. Mdivani (Georgia), G. I. Petrovsky (Ukraine),
A. G. Chervyakov (Byelorussia) and others.

Stalin drafted the commission's resolution "On the Relations
Between the R.S.F.S.R. and the Independent Republics", which
provided for the Ukraine, Byelorussia, Azerbaijan, Georgia and
Armenia entering the Russian Federation as autonomous republics. Stalin's draft was forwarded for discussion to the Central
Committees of the Communist Parties of the Soviet national
republics. It was supported by the Central Committees of the
Communist Parties of Azerbaijan and Armenia. The C.C. of
the Georgian Communist Party was against the draft resolution.
At its meeting on September 15, 1922, it passed the following
decision by a majority vote: "The union in the form of auto no-
misation of the independent republics proposed on the basis of
Stalin's theses is premature. A union of economic efforts and
a common policy are necessary, but all attributes of independence
should be preserved." The C.C. of the Byelorussian Communist
Party went on record for the preservation of treaty relations
between the independent republics. The C.C. of the Ukrainian
C.P. did not discuss the draft.

The commission met on September 23 and 24, 1922, with
V. M. Molotov in the chair. It approved Stalin's draft (with
one abstention—the representative from Georgia). In a special
point the commission rejected the resolution of the C.C. of the
Georgian Communist Party. Stalin's draft was gone over point
by point and approved by a majority with certain minor amendments and addenda. Point 2 stating that the decisions of the
All-Russia Central Executive Committee, the Council of
People's Commissars and the Council of Labour and Defence of
the R.S.F.S.R. were binding upon the corresponding bodies
of the national republics was carried by an 8 to 1 majority
(Mdivani voting against and Petrovsky abstaining).

The final wording of the commission's resolution, which Lenin
deals with in his letter to the members of the Politbureau, was
as follows:

"1. It is considered advisable that treaties be concluded between
the Soviet Republics of the Ukraine, Byelorussia, Azerbaijan,
Georgia, Armenia and the R.S.F.S.R. for their formal entry

into the R.S.F.S.R., the question of Bokhara, Kharezm and the Far-Eastern Republic being left open and confined to agreements with them on customs arrangements, foreign trade, foreign and military affairs, and so on.

"Note: Corresponding changes in the constitutions of the Republics mentioned in Point 1 and of the R.S.F.S.R. to be made after enactment by Soviet procedure.

"2. In accordance with this the decisions of the All-Russia Central Executive Committee of the R.S.F.S.R. shall be considered binding upon the central bodies of the republics mentioned in Point 1, while the decisions of the Council of People's Commissars and the Council of Labour and Defence of the R.S.F.S.R. shall be binding upon the unified commissariats of these republics.

"Note: These republics are to be represented on the Presidium of the All-Russia C.E.C. of the R.S.F.S.R.

"3. External affairs (foreign affairs and foreign trade), military affairs, ways of communication (with the exception of local transport) and Potel (the People's Commissariat for Post and Telegraph—*Ed.*) of the republics mentioned in Point 1 shall be merged with those of the R.S.F.S.R., the corresponding commissariats of the R.S.F.S.R. having their agents and a small staff in the republics.

"The agents are appointed by the People's Commissars of the R.S.F.S.R. by arrangement with the Central Executive Committees of the republics.

"It is considered advisable that the republics concerned be represented on the corresponding foreign agencies of the People's Commissariat for Foreign Affairs and the People's Commissariat for Foreign Trade.

"4. The Commissariats for Finance, Food, Labour and National Economy of the republics shall be formally subject to the directives of the corresponding R.S.F.S.R. commissariats.

"5. The remaining commissariats of the republics mentioned in Point 1, namely, the Commissariats for Justice, Education, Internal Affairs, Agriculture, Workers' and Peasants' Inspection, Public Health and Social Security, shall be considered independent.

"Note 1: The agencies fighting counter-revolution in the aforementioned republics shall be subject to the directives of the G.P.U. of the R.S.F.S.R.

"Note 2: The Central Executive Committees of the republics shall be granted the right of amnesty only in civil cases.

"6. This decision, if approved by the C.C. of the R.C.P., shall not be published, but shall be passed on to the national Central Committees as a circular directive to be enacted through the Central Executive Committee or the Congress of Soviets of the aforementioned republics pending the convocation of an All-Russia Congress of Soviets, at which it is to be declared as the desire of these republics" (Central Party Archives of the Institute of Marxism-Leninism of the C.C., C.P.S.U.).

On September 25 the commission's materials (Stalin's draft,
the resolution and minutes of the commission's meetings, and
the resolutions of the Central Committees of the Communist
Parties of Georgia, Azerbaijan and Armenia) were sent to Lenin
at Gorki. Simultaneously, without waiting for Lenin's instructions
and without the question being considered in the Politbureau,
the Secretariat of the C.C. sent the commission's resolution to
all the members and alternate members of the C.C. in preparation
for the latter's plenary meeting fixed for October 5.

After studying the Commission's material Lenin wrote his
letter to the members of the Politbureau which is published in
this volume. The letter is dated September 27; apparently this
is a slip of the pen, since the Registration Book of Lenin's Letters,
Notes and Instructions bears an entry stating that this letter was
forwarded to the members of the Politbureau on Sepember 26;
moreover, Lenin's conversation with Stalin, to which reference
is made in the letter, took place on September 26; it can be
inferred from this that Lenin's letter was written on September 26.

In his letter to the members of the Politbureau Lenin came
out against Stalin's idea of "autonomisation" of the independent
national Soviet Republics and suggested a fundamentally different way of uniting them by creating a Union of Soviet Socialist
Republics (see also Lenin's letter "The Question of Nationalities
or 'Autonomisation'", present edition, Vol. 36, pp. 605-11).

In accordance with Lenin's proposals the resolution drafted
by the C.C.'s Commission was revised.

The new resolution was worded as follows:

"1. It is considered necessary that a treaty be concluded between
the Ukraine, Byelorussia, the Federation of Transcaucasian
Republics and the R.S.F.S.R. for their amalgamation in a Union
of Socialist Soviet Republics, each reserving the right to freely
secede from membership of the Union.

"2. The supreme body of the Union shall be the Union Central
Executive Committee consisting of representatives of the central
executive committees of the R.S.F.S.R., the Transcaucasian
Federation, the Ukraine and Byelorussia pro rata to the population they represent.

"3. The executive organ of the Union C.E.C. shall be the
Union Council of People's Commissars appointed by the Union
C.E.C.

"4. The People's Commissariats for Foreign Affairs, Foreign
Trade, Military Affairs, Railways and Post and Telegraph of
the republics and federations comprising the Union shall be merged
with those of the Union of Soviet Socialist Republics, the corresponding commissariats of the Union of Republics having in
the republics and federations their agents and a small staff appointed by the People's Commissars of the Union by arrangement
with the Central Executive Committees of the federations and
republics.

"Note: It is considered necessary for the republics concerned
to be represented on the corresponding foreign agencies of the

People's Commissariat for Foreign Affairs and the People's Commissariat for Foreign Trade.

"5. The People's Commissariats for Finance, Food, National Economy, Labour and Inspection of the republics and federations comprising the Union of Republics, also the central agencies for fighting counter-revolution shall be subject to the directives of the corresponding People's Commissariats and to the decisions of the Council of People's Commissars and the Council of Labour and Defence of the Union of Republics.

"6. The remaining people's commissariats comprising the Union of Republics, namely, the Commissariats for Justice, Education, Internal Affairs, Agriculture, Public Health and Social Security shall be considered independent" (Central Party Archives of the Institute of Marxism-Leninism of the C.C. of the C.P.S.U.).

On October 6, 1922, the day on which the question of the relations between the R.S.F.S.R. and the independent republics was discussed at the plenary meeting of the C.C., Lenin, who was unable to attend the meeting, wrote a note to Kamenev urging the need for combating dominant-nation chauvinism and proposing an addendum to the resolution saying that representatives of all the uniting republics should take their turn in presiding at the Union Central Executive Committee (see *Collected Works*, Fifth [Russian] Edition, Vol. 45, p. 214).

The C.C. plenum fully supported Lenin, adopted a resolution in the form of C.C. directives based on his proposals, and instructed a new commission to draft a bill on the formation of the U.S.S.R. for submission to the Congress of Soviets. The members of the C.C. in their speeches strongly denounced all manifestations of dominant-nation chauvinism. At the same time the plenum rebuffed Mdivani, who at first objected to the formation of the U.S.S.R. and then insisted on Georgia joining the U.S.S.R. directly, and not through the Transcaucasian Federation.

Guided by Lenin's instructions, the Central Committee of the Party directed all the subsequent work of uniting the republics.

On December 30, 1922, the First All-Union Congress of Soviets met to form the Union of Soviet Socialist Republics. p. 421

[482] *The Fifth All-Russia Congress of the Textile Workers Trade Union* was held in Moscow from October 6 to 11, 1922. It was attended by 350 voting delegates and 117 delegates with voice but no vote. The congress discussed the report of the Trade Unions Central Committee, and reports on the state of the textile industry, on the All-Russia Congress of Trade Unions, on the organisational question, on the conditions of labour, on cultural work and the international labour movement among the textile workers.

At the opening meeting the delegates elected Lenin honorary chairman of the congress and sent him greetings. On October 9, 1922, they invited Lenin to the congress, and he accepted the invitation. He was unable to attend it, however, as his health had taken a turn for the worse.

Lenin's message of greeting was read out at the morning session on October 10. The platform committee, on behalf of the delegates, sent him a letter in reply to his greetings.   p. 423

483 This document is written on Stalin's note to the members of the Politbureau proposing addenda to the terms of the concession agreement with L. Urquhart.   p. 424

484 The question of the Co-operative Bank was discussed at a meeting of the Politbureau attended by Lenin on November 2, 1922. The Politbureau passed the following decision: "The following theses of Comrade Lenin should be referred as a basis to a committee, which is directed to submit to the Politbureau a written report on fulfilment."

The document published in this volume contains Lenin's note: "**Keep** for my talk with *Khinchuk*" (*L. M. Khinchuk* was Chairman of the Board of Centrosoyuz.— *Ed.*).   p. 424

485 Lenin wrote this letter in reply to the greetings and present received from the Petrograd textile workers, who wrote him:

"*Dear and deeply respected Vladimir Ilyich.*

"On the occasion of its anniversary the Petrograd Textile Trust sends you its ardent greetings and begs you to accept a woollen blanket made at one of its mills.

"We, Petrograd textile workers, should like the warmth of our modest present to bring you the warmth of our hearts and also to show you that in spite of the extremely worn-out condition of our equipment, in spite of the devastation, the shortages and crises, we are working no worse than before the war, which proves that we can achieve whatever we set out to do.

"We wish you, dear Comrade Lenin, good health."   p. 425

486 On November 16, 1922, the Politbureau passed a decision to reduce the army in the course of January 1923 from 800,000 to 600,000 men. The plenum of the C.C., R.C.P.(B.) held on December 18, 1922, confirmed this decision and urged the need for compensating this reduction by improving military equipment, for which purpose the C.P.C. was instructed to find means of quickly normalising the work of the munition factories. The plenum recommended that an appeal be issued in the name of the Tenth All-Russia Congress of Soviets to all nations, emphasising once more the striving of the R.S.F.S.R. towards general disarmament and calling upon the peoples to overcome the resistance which this proposal of the Soviet Republic was meeting on the part of other states.

The Tenth All-Russia Congress of Soviets, on behalf of the millions of the working people, once more solemnly confirmed their desire for peace and peaceful labour.

"Working people of the world!" ran the appeal of the congress. "All who desire peaceful labour, join your efforts to the efforts of Soviet Russia in order to secure peace, and safeguard mankind from monstrous and destructive wars!...

"The Tenth Congress of Soviets solemnly confirms its line of peaceful policy and calls upon everyone to support this line. Let all the peoples demand peace of their governments. The cause of peace is in the hands of the peoples themselves. To avert the danger of future wars the working people of all the world must unite their efforts. Worn-out, suffering, ruined and starving mankind must have peace secured to them at all cost."

p. 425

[487] *The Russian Colony in the U.S.A.* was estimated at about three million people in the twenties, most of whom were immigrants who had left Russia before the revolution for political, economic or religious motives. The members of the bourgeoisie, nobility and intelligentsia, who had escaped from Russia after the October Socialist Revolution, were an insignificant minority. The different social and economic status of these groups and their different attitudes towards Soviet Russia led to the division of the Russian colony into two hostile camps. One camp was made up of the Society of Friends of Soviet Russia (Russian section), the Society for Technical Aid for Soviet Russia, the Russian sections of the U. S. trade unions, the joint conference of various Russian mutual benefit societies and other progressive workers' organisations, around which were united the majority of colonists. The other camp was an alliance of various Russian petty-bourgeois and monarchist organisations united around the anti-Soviet newspaper *Novoye Russkoye Slovo* (The New Russian Word).

Lenin's letter was addressed to that part of the Russian colony in the U.S.A. which was grouped around the organisations that stood for friendly relations with Soviet Russia.   p. 425

[488] The agenda of the Fourth Congress of the Communist International, which was held from November 5 to December 5, 1922, contained the question of the programme of the Communist International. The congress had before it the programme drafted by Bukharin and tabled in his own name, and also the draft programmes of the Communist Parties of Bulgaria and Germany and the "Programme of Action of the Italian Communist Party". On November 13, in his report "Five Years of the Russian Revolution and the Prospects of the World Revolution" Lenin suggested holding simply a general discussion on all the programmes, "to make the first reading, so to speak" and to get them printed in order to study and prepare the programme more profoundly and thoroughly (see present edition, Vol. 33, pp. 418-32). During the discussion of these drafts, lively debates revolved around the question of transition and limited demands, as a means of preparing the masses for the socialist revolution, for the struggle for the dictatorship of the proletariat. Bukharin was opposed to the more general transition and limited demands being theoretically substantiated in the programme of the Comintern, and

even accused of opportunism those who urged the inclusion of these propositions. Bukharin's point of view was criticised by the congress delegates. The delegation of the R.C.P. asked the platform committee of the congress to be allowed to discuss the question of the programme within the delegation before the congress passed any decision on it; this request was granted by the congress (see *Bulletin of the Fourth Congress of the Communist International* No. 14-15, p. 31).

A meeting of the R.C.P.(B.) delegation Bureau was held on November 20, 1922, at which the proposals printed in this book were drawn up as a draft resolution for the congress. According to available information, the very important points 4 and 5 were dictated by Lenin almost word for word. p. 427

489 The Bureau of the R.C.P. delegation, at its meeting on November 20, 1922, also drew up the following "Statement of the Russian Delegation": "In view of the fact that the dispute on how the transition demands should be worded and in what part of the programme they should be treated created the wrong impression that the divergence of opinion was on a matter of principle, the Russian delegation lays down unanimously that the inclusion of the transition demands into the programmes of the national sections, their general wording and theoretical substantiation in the general part of the programme cannot be considered as opportunism." This statement was read at the congress meeting on November 21, after which the presiding committee of the congress submitted to the delegates for consideration the proposals drafted by the Bureau of the R.C.P. delegation, to which slight editorial changes had been made. The congress adopted the proposals as a resolution of the congress (see *Bulletin of the Fourth Congress of the Communist International* No. 18, pp. 7-8). p. 428

490 See also present edition, Vol. 33, pp. 247-48, and 335-43; and pp. 431—33 of this volume.

The list referred to lower down is the one given in the Draft Decree on the Functions of the Deputy Chairmen of the C.P.C. and the C.L.D. (see present edition, Vol. 33, pp. 342-43). p. 428

491 Lenin's proposal was included in the decision of the Politbureau on December 7, 1922, on the report of the State Supplies Commission. The C.P.C. was directed to allocate to the People's Commissariat for Education two million gold rubles out of the money economised on the ship-repair programme (see *Collected Works*, Fifth [Russian] Edition, Vol. 45, pp. 311-12). p. 429

492 On the morning of December 13 Lenin had two attacks of illness. The doctors ordered him a complete rest. "The doctors," his sister Maria (M. I. Ulyanova) wrote later, "had great difficulty in persuading Vladimir Ilyich to drop work altogether and go out into the country. Meanwhile he was to lie down for as long as

possible and not go for walks. In the end Vladimir Ilyich agreed to leave town and said 'I'll start winding up my affairs this very day'."

From then on Lenin spent several days at home, dictating letters and giving various instructions, anxious to wind up his affairs, to which he attached great importance.   p. 432

493 This refers to Rykov's suggestion that the reception of visitors by Lenin should, as a general rule, take place after preliminary selection by the Deputy Chairmen of the C.P.C. and the C.L.D. or by the Secretary of the Central Committee, R.C.P.   p. 432

494 This letter deals with the distribution of functions between Deputy Chairmen of the C.P.C. and the C.L.D. Tsyurupa, Kameney and Rykov as planned on December 12. See pp.   428-29 and 430-32 of this volume for Lenin's proposals on this subject.   p. 432

495 This apparently refers to the conference on management normalisation held in September 1922 in Moscow.   p. 439

496 Here allowance should be made for the scale of prices that existed in 1920. Owing to the continuous growth of emission during the early years of Soviet government, paper money was rapidly depreciating. According to the data of the Currency Board of the People's Commissariat for Finance of the U.S.S.R., the value of the gold ruble (taking as equivalent the gold coins of pre-revolutionary times) averaged 1,633 paper rubles in the first half-year of 1920, rising to 4,083 rubles in the second half-year (see *Nashe Denezhnoye Obrashcheniye. Sbornik materialov po istorii denezhnogo obrashcheniya v 1914-1925 gg.* (Our Currency Circulation. A Collection of Materials on the History of Currency Circulation During 1914-1925.) Moscow, 1926, p. 16).   p. 446

497 Lenin was elected to the Tenth Congress of the R.C.P. as a voting delegate by the Fourteenth Petrograd Gubernia Party Conference from the supporters of the "Platform of the Ten". The delegation was unable to attend the congress in its elected form owing to the critical situation in the city and the counter-revolutionary mutiny at Kronstadt which had just started. Apparently it was in the absence of minutes recording the election of the Petrograd delegation that Lenin wrote in the questionnaire that he had a debating voice. Nevertheless he took part in the voting of all the resolutions and figured in the list of delegates to the Tenth Party Congress as a voting delegate (see *Tenth Congress of the R.C.P.(B.), March 8-16, 1921. Verbatim Report.* Moscow, 1963, p. 729).   p. 450

498 *The Journal of Lenin's Duty Secretaries* contains records of Lenin's orders and instructions, reception of visitors and other facts from November 21, 1922 to March 6, 1923.

The entries in the Journal were made by Secretary of the C.P.C. and the C.L.D. L.A. Fotieva, Assistant Secretary of the C.P.C. and the C.L.D. M.A.Volodicheva, secretaries N. S. Alliluyeva, M. I. Glyasser, and S. A. Flakserman, and Lenin's librarian S. M. Manucharyants.

The office book for registering outgoing mail was used for the Journal. Four columns were ruled off in it: date, who was on duty, orders and instructions, and notes on execution. The title page had the inscription: "Please write in this book all orders and instructions and all happenings during duty hours with a note regarding execution of orders. 21/XI—22." p. 463

499 *Gorbunov, N. P.*—Business Manager of the Council of People's Commissars.   p. 465

500 This refers to the meeting of the C.P.C. at which Lenin presided.
p. 465

501 On November 21 the members of the Politbureau voted on the proposal made by the People's Commissar for Foreign Affairs G. V. Chicherin that the Envoy Plenipotentiary of the R.S.F.S.R. in Italy V. V. Vorovsky be included in the delegation to the Lausanne Conference.   p. 465

502 *Haskell*—colonel, Chief of the A.R.A.   p. 465

503 *Zax, B. G.*—Assistant Business Manager of the C.P.C.
p. 465

504 *Nazaretyan, A. M.*—Assistant Secretary of the C.C., R.C.P.
p. 466

505 *Burakova, M. N.*—technical secretary of the Politbureau.
p. 466

506 See present edition, Vol. 33, p. 444.   p. 466

507 Twenty-one questions were dealt with at this meeting of the Politbureau, among them: the Moscow conference of the R.S.F.S.R., Poland, Estonia, Finland, Latvia and Lithuania; reduction of armaments; the trusts; a joint society for the sale of platinum; agricultural loans; and questions relating to the People's Commissariat for Education.   p. 466

508 *Sklyansky, E. M.*—Deputy Chairman of the Revolutionary Military Council of the Republic.   p. 466

509 *Sokolnikov, G. Y.*—Deputy People's Commissar for Finance·
p. 466

510 Lenin was sent a draft resolution for the Fourth Congress of the Comintern "A Rough Draft of an Agrarian Programme of Action" drawn up by E. Varga and a note from the Comintern

Executive asking for his opinion on the draft. Lenin sent his remarks on the morning of November 25. p. 466

511 For Lenin's correspondence with Stalin on the ship-repair programme see *Collected Works*, Vol. 45, Fifth Russian Edition, pp. 311-13. p. 467

512 *Earsman, and Garden, John S.*—delegates to the Fourth Congress of the Comintern from the Communist Party of Australia.
p. 467

513 The members of the Politbureau voted on Chicherin's proposal that the Soviet Government send a note to the sponsors of the Lausanne Conference concerning the participation of the Soviet delegation in the conference proceedings and of Soviet representatives in the deliberations of the Commission on the Straits.
p. 467

514 At the meeting of the Council of Labour and Defence chaired by Lenin thirteen questions were examined, among them: draft regulations on the Committee for Internal Trade; report of the C.L.D. Commission on the preparation of materials for the Tenth All-Russia Congress of Soviets; importation of grain to Turkestan to support the cotton industry. p. 467

515 The voting was on the decision of the Secretariat of the C.C., R.C.P. dated November 24 appointing a commission composed of F. E. Dzerzhinsky (chairman), D. Z. Manuilsky and V. S. Mitskevich-Kapsukas to urgently examine the statement by members of the C.C. of the Communist Party of Georgia, who had handed in their resignations on October 22, and to propose measures for establishing a durable peace in the C.C. of the Georgian Communist Party. Lenin abstained from voting.
p. 467

516 That day the doctors ordered Lenin a week of complete rest.
p. 467

517 Lenin dictated a letter to Stalin on the ship-repair programme (see *Collected Works*, Vol. 45, Fifth Russian Edition, pp. 311-12); a letter to Trotsky (copies to Zinoviev, Bukharin, Radek, Stalin and Kamenev) about a letter to the Italian delegates to the Fourth Congress of the Comintern and about Trotsky's theses on N.E.P. (see *Collected Works*, Vol. 54, Fifth Russian Edition, p. 314); a letter to Trotsky, Zinoviev, Bukharin and Radek criticising the "Rough Draft of an Agrarian Programme of Action" (ibid., p. 313). The same day Lenin also ordered his signature to be put to a letter of greetings to the Fourth All-Russia Congress of the Educational Workers' Union (see present edition, Vol. 33, p. 445). p. 467

518 This apparently refers to the Comintern Executive's letter to Lenin asking him to receive a number of delegations to the

Fourth Congress of the Comintern and Stalin's letter concerning measures for combating the illicit trade in platinum. The same day Lenin instructed Gorbunov to circulate among all members of the Politbureau a draft decision on measures for combating the illicit trade in platinum. See also the interview with Lenin by Michael Farbman, correspondent of the *Observer* and *Manchester Guardian* (present edition, Vol. 33, pp. 388-89). p. 467

519   Lenin asked his C.P.C. and C.L.D. deputy Tsyurupa to take part in the work of the Politbureau commission appointed to draw up draft regulations on the trusts. On November 27 the Politbureau included Tsyurupa in the commission.   p. 468

520   Apparently this refers to the articles published in *Pravda* on February 2, 1923, in connection with the Soviet Government's refusal to conclude a concession agreement with Urquhart, the English industrialist.   p. 468

521   The report of V. P. Milyutin, Deputy Chairman of the Supreme Economic Council, on questions of trade, finance and industry was sent to Lenin as material for his report to the Tenth All-Russia Congress of Soviets.   p. 468

522   *Münzenberg, W.*—Secretary General, Foreign Committee for the Organisation of International Workers' Aid to the famine-stricken people of Soviet Russia.   p. 469

523   *Kramer V. V.*—professor, neuropathologist attending Lenin.
                                                          p. 469

524   The supplementary card said: "Supplementary to the materials on the question of foreign trade monopoly, asked for the minutes of the meeting presided over by Lezhava and others—list of automatic telephone numbers. All taken to his flat. Gave Lydia Alexandrovna instructions for Frumkin, Lezhava and Tsyurupa in connection with the materials on foreign trade monopoly. Talked on the phone with Frumkin, Gorbunov and others. Looked through the C.L.D. agenda." The same day Lenin was sent the minutes of the meeting of the C.L.D. Commission on Internal Trade held on October 13.   p. 469

525   M. Sorokin, *"Nash promyshlenny Komsostav"* ("Our Industrial Captains") (*Ekonomicheskaya Zhizn*, November 26, 1922). The entry wrongly gives the date as November 27.   p. 469

526   Apparently Lenin was interested in the proposals and conclusions of the C.P.C. Commission on the inspection of R.S.F.S.R. trade agencies abroad. V. A. Avanesov, vice chairman of this commission, sent Lenin these materials on December 3 (see entry for December 3, evening).   p. 469

527   *Bogdanov, P. A.*—Chairman, Supreme Economic Council.
                                                          p. 469

[528] *Fomin, V. V.*—Deputy People's Commissar for Railways.
p. 469

[529] See *Collected Works*, Vol. 54, Fifth Russian Edition, pp. 314-15.
p. 469

[530] At its meeting on November 30 the Politbureau heard the report of the Commission of the C.C. plenum on the "Union of Republics" and adopted the basic principles of the U.S.S.R. Constitution.
p. 470

[531] See *Collected Works*. Vol. 45, Fifth Russian Edition, pp. 312-13.
p. 470

[532] On November 30 the Politbureau endorsed the decision of the C.C.'s Orgbureau of November 20 to convene the plenum of the C.C. on December 15.
p. 470

[533] This refers to the article "A Talk with Peshekhonov". p. 471

[534] *Adoratsky, V. V.*—a scholar, prominent propagandist of Marxism. At Lenin's request, prepared a volume of selected letters of K. Marx and F. Engels.
p. 471

[535] F. Engels, *Political Testament* (Unpublished Letters). Moscow, 1923. The Central Party Archives of the Institute of Marxism-Leninism has a copy of this book that belonged to Lenin with his note to the librarian: "Keep on the shelf. 30/XI. 1922. *Lenin*" (see *Biblioteka Lenina v Kremle* [Lenin's Library in the Kremlin], Moscow, 1961, p. 56).
p. 471

[536] *Syrtsov, S. I.*—member of the staff of the C.C., R.C.P.(B.)
p. 471

[537] *Knipovich, N. M.*—professor, head of the Azov Expedition, whose main object was to make a general survey of the Azov-Black Sea Basin for fish industry revival.
p. 471

[538] Apparently Lenin is referring to the article by F. Kin (Frumkin) "Specialists (An Essay at Statistical Survey)" published September 3, 1922 in *Pravda* No. 197.
p. 472

[539] See present edition, Vol. 35, pp. 559-60.
p. 472

[540] The letter to A. I. Svidersky, Member of the Board of the People's Commissariat of the Workers' and Peasants' Inspection, was signed by Lenin on December 5.
p. 472

[541] *Belenky, A. Y.*—member of the staff of the State Political Administration (G.P.U.).
p. 472

[542] On Lenin's instructions M. I. Frumkin, Deputy People's Commissar for Trade and Industry, drew up a report "Brief

Materials on the State of Foreign Trade", which he sent in on December 4.   p. 473

543 This refers to A. G. Mikhailovsky's memorandum on the country's financial and economic position and the theses by A. M. Krasnoshchokov, Deputy People's Commissar for Finance, on the financing of industry.   p. 473

544 V. A. Avanesov had sent the findings of the C.P.C. Commission on the State Monopoly of Foreign Trade. Lenin read them carefully, made corrections, marginal notes and marks   p. 473

545 On December 4 Gorbunov wrote in the book of orders: "Be posted on Kyshtym Works affair, prepare basic figures concerning the financing of the metallurgical industry, ditto the Donbas and Azneft, study the system of working up census data" (apparently the census of Soviet employees in Moscow and Petrograd, carried out in October-November 1922.—*Ed.*) (see *Istoricheski Archiv*, 1961, No. 5, p. 61).

On returning to his office Lenin dictated a letter to I. I. Khodorovsky asking for information concerning patronage by urban cells of the R.C.P. over village cells and vice versa (see *Collected Works*, Vol. 54, Fifth Russian Edition, pp. 315-16). Lenin intended to mention this in his report to the Tenth All-Russia Congress of Soviets (see present edition, Vol. 36, p. 589). He dealt with this in his article "Pages From a Diary" (see present edition, Vol. 33, pp. 465-66).   p. 474

546 A. L. Kolegayev visited Lenin in connection with fulfilment of the decision of the C.P.C. of November 16, 1922, on the question of subsidies to state theatres.   p. 474

547 *Zhukov, I. P.*—a power engineer.   p. 474

548 See Vol. 33 of this edition, p. 446, and Vol. 54 of the Fifth Russian Edition, p. 316.   p. 474

549 *Holtzmann, A. Z.*—Chief of Central Electricity Board of the Supreme Economic Council. *Lavrentyev, P. F.*—his deputy.
                                                               p. 474

550 G. Reyes. *Nuevas y viéjas rutas.* Buenos Aires, 1922 (New and Old Ways). The book was sent to Lenin from the Secretariat of the Comintern Executive, and returned on December 7 for translation (see *Biblioteka Lenina v Kremle* [Lenin's Library in the Kremlin] Moscow, 1961, p. 665).   p. 474

551 See present edition, Vol. 33, pp. 447-51.   p. 475

552 The list contains the following members of the delegation: J. Hans, Chairman of the Trade Unions Association of Czechoslovakia, Hamosta, Chairman of the Municipal Workers Trade

Union, Fráněk, member of the Building Workers Trade Union, Richter, member of the Transport Workers Trade Union, Chapěra, representative of the Gas and Electrical Industry Workers Trade Union. The delegation conveyed to Lenin greetings from the Czechoslovak workers.   p. 475

⁵⁵³ *Popov, P. I.*—Superintendent of the Central Statistical Board.
p. 475

⁵⁵⁴ *Antselovich, N. M.*— an official of the All-Russian Central Council of Trade unions.   p. 475

⁵⁵⁵ L. A. Fotieva sent letters to member of the Board of the People's Commissariat for Education V. N. Yakovleva and to L. B. Kamenev on the question of providing the pupils and teachers of all the schools with bread, and the following letter to Lenin's deputies: "To Kamenev and Tsyurupa. Vladimir Ilyich requests you by Monday (December 9.—*Ed.*) to look through all the materials on the 'Vishnevsky-Popov' question in order to arrange a conference on Monday with Vladimir Ilyich and Rykov to decide our policy in regard to the Central Statistical Board."   p. 475

⁵⁵⁶ *Eiduk, A. V.*—chairman of the Commission on Agricultural and Industrial Immigration. *Dovgalevsky, V. S.*— People's Commissar for Post and Telegraph.   p. 475

⁵⁵⁷ Lenin wanted to see Board Member N. L. Meshcheryakov of the People's Commissariat for Education about a flat for Professor N. I. Averbach, the eye specialist.   p. 475

⁵⁵⁸ See present edition, Vol. 33, pp. 452-53.   p. 476

⁵⁵⁹ Eighteen questions were examined at the meeting of the Politbureau: the Note on the Straits, the proceedings of the Moscow conference on disarmament, the report of the State Supplies Commission, grain exports, agricultural loans, the wage fund for December 1922, the reports at the Tenth All-Russia Congress of Soviets, the question of N. A. Rozhkov, member of the C.C. of the Menshevik party, and other questions.   p. 476

⁵⁶⁰ Fotieva sent the following note to A. M. Nazaretyan: "Vladimir Ilyich suggests that Unschlicht's four proposals on the question of issuing credentials to deportees should be adopted." I. S. Unschlicht, Deputy Chairman of the G.P.U., proposed that the People's Commissariats should be prohibited from issuing credentials to persons subject to administrative deportation.   p. 476

⁵⁶¹ Lenin asked Yakovleva to keep him informed about the work of the commission appointed on his motion by the Politbureau in the morning of December 7 to prepare the calculations for fully providing the pupils and teachers of all the schools with bread (see p. 429 of this volume).   p. 476

[562] Before leaving for Gorki, Lenin also left written orders to Gorbunov and Fotieva on the manner in which he was to be informed of any documents coming in from the C.C. of the R.C.P.(B.) (see *Collected Works*, Vol. 54, Fifth Russian Edition, p. 318). Lenin instructed his secretaries to send Tsyurupa and Rykov his proposals of December 4 concerning distribution of functions among the deputy chairmen of the C.P.C. and the C.L.D. (see pp. 428-29 of this volume).   p. 476

[563] The minutes of the Politbureau meeting on December 7 were sent to Lenin after his talk with Fotieva, who informed him of the decisions the Politbureau had adopted after his departure.
                                                                p. 476

[564] Lenin dictated to Volodicheva a letter to Stalin protesting against the decision of the Politbureau concerning Rozhkov and proposing that this question be referred to the plenum of the C.C., R.C.P.(B.). The letter also dealt with the work of S. A. Lozovsky in the Profintern (see *Collected Works*, Vol. 54, Fifth Russian Edition, pp. 320-21).   p. 476

[565] The telegram referred to asked permission for the Soviet delegation at the Lausanne Conference to declare that the Soviet Government agreed to a conference of Black Sea states on the question of ensuring safety of navigation in the Black Sea.   p. 476

[566] See present edition, Vol. 33, p. 454.   p. 476

[567] See pp. 429-30 of this volume.   p. 476

[568] The C.C., R.C.P.(B.) plenum, scheduled for December 15, was put off to December 17.   p. 476

[569] This evidently refers to Lenin's proposals concerning the distribution of functions among the deputy chairmen of the C.P.C. and the C.L.D. (see pp. 430-32 of this volume) and his letter concerning the routine work of the deputies and chairman of the C.P.C. (ibid., pp. 430-32).   p. 477

[570] This refers to Lenin's letter to Lazzari (see *Collected Works*, Vol. 54, Fifth Russian Edition, pp. 322-23). Boris Souvarine—delegate to the Fourth Congress of the Comintern; Lenin, in this instance, used his services as a translator.   p. 477

[571] See Vol. 33 of this edition, pp. 335-43.   p. 477

[572] The voting was on the Politbureau's decision (on the telegram of December 7) concerning the sentence in the trial of the Socialist-Revolutionaries in Baku. Lenin voted "for". The Politbureau decided on December 14 not to object.   p. 477

573 Frumkin's comments on the theses of the C.P.C. Commission concerning the inspection of R.S.F.S.R. trade agencies abroad were received on December 11 and reported to Lenin on December 13.   p. 477

574 The mail registration book had down Lenin's letter to Frumkin under No. 8605. Under No. 8606 were instructions to Gorbunov to prepare for Lenin by Tuesday (December 12) the proofs of the book *Na Novikh Putyakh. Itogi novoi ekonomicheskoi politiki 1921-1922. Trudi pod redaktsiei komissii STO* (On a New Path. Results of the New Economic Policy for 1921-1922. Papers edited by the C.L.D. Commission). Moscow, C.L.D. Publishing House, 1923 (Instalment II, Finances, Instalment III, Industry).
                                                          p. 477

575 Dzerzhinsky informed Lenin of the results of the Politbureau Commission's trip to Georgia to investigate the conflict between the Transcaucasian Committee and the Mdivani group. Lenin recalled this talk on January 24, 1923 (see p. 484 of this volume).
                                                          p. 478

576 *Stomonyakov, B. S.*—Trade Representative of the R.S.F.S.R. in Germany.   p. 478

577 See Note 492 in this volume.   p. 478

578 In this letter Lenin once more protested against the Politbureau's decision of December 7 by which the Menshevik Rozhkov was allowed to live in Moscow. See also Note 584 in this volume.   p. 478

579 Lenin stated in his letters that he was unable to attend the forthcoming plenum of the C.C. He expressed his views on how his stand on the question of the foreign trade monopoly should be defended at the plenum and emphasised that vacillation on this question was inadmissible.   p. 478

580 See pp. 432-33 of this volume.   p. 478

581 See present edition, Vol. 33, pp. 455-59.   p. 479

582 *Yaroslavsky, Y. M.*—Chairman of the C.P.C. Commission on the inspection of all R.S.F.S.R. trade agencies abroad.   p. 479

583 Lenin asked Avanesov to read his letter to the plenum of the C.C., R.C.P.(B.) on the question of the foreign trade monopoly and send his suggestions (see *Collected Works*, Vol. 54, Fifth Russian Edition, p. 325).   p. 479

584 On December 14, the Politbureau revoked its decision of December 7 and resolved to banish Rozhkov to Pskov, warning him that at his first anti-Soviet act he would be sent out of the country.
                                                          p. 479

⁵⁸⁵ This refers to Lenin's letter to the plenum of the C.C., R.C.P.(B.), concerning the monopoly of foreign trade (see present edition, Vol. 33, pp. 455-59). p. 479

⁵⁸⁶ In this letter Lenin expressed the hope that the plenum would adopt a decision confirming the unalterable principle of the foreign trade monopoly, since some of those who had voted against the monopoly at the October plenum had adopted a correct stand (see *Collected Works*, Vol. 54, Fifth Russian Edition, pp. 325-26). p. 480

⁵⁸⁷ See present edition, Vol. 33, pp. 460-61. p. 480

⁵⁸⁸ In his letter Lenin stressed the need for having the question of the foreign trade monopoly discussed at the plenum of the C.C. and having it raised at the next congress of the Party (see *Collected Works*, Vol. 54, Fifth Russian Edition, pp. 325-26). p. 480

⁵⁸⁹ On the night of December 16 Lenin's health took a sharp turn for the worse. Paralysis of the right arm and right leg set in. Then he began gradually to recover the use of his arm and leg.
Kozhevnikov, A. M.—Neuropathologist in attendance on Lenin. p. 480

⁵⁹⁰ In this letter Lenin expressed his views on the distribution of duties among the deputy chairmen of the C.P.C. and the C.L.D., and on the need for making brief notes during the reception of visitors; he also suggested that a meeting of deputies be held without him on the question of the Central Statistical Board (see *Collected Works*, Vol. 54, Fifth Russian Edition, p. 327). p. 481

⁵⁹¹ *Pakaln, P. P.*—chief of Lenin's bodyguard at Gorki. p. 481

⁵⁹² *Foerster O. R.*—German neuropathologist, Professor; consulted the physicians attending Lenin. p. 481

⁵⁹³ The plenum of the C.C., R.C.P.(B.) held on December 18, supported Lenin's proposals and confirmed the unalterable principle of foreign trade monopoly. The plenum adopted a special decision for him to be informed, by arrangement with his doctors, of the plenum's resolution and report. p. 481

⁵⁹⁴ On the night of December 23 paralysis of the right arm and right leg set in. p. 481

⁵⁹⁵ Lenin dictated his Letter to the Congress of the Party on December 23, 24, 25, 26, 29, 1922 and January 4, 1923 (see present edition, Vol. 36, pp. 593-97, 603-04). The letter dictated on December 23 was forwarded to Stalin by the secretariat the same day. p. 481

596   At this time the Tenth All-Russia Congress of Soviets was being held (from December 23 to 27, 1922).   p. 481

597   "All the articles and documents," Volodicheva wrote later, in 1929, "which Lenin dictated between December 1922 (the 20th) and the beginning of March 1923 were typed at his request in five copies, one of which he asked to leave for him, three copies to be given to Nadezhda Konstantinovna, and one to his secretariat (strictly secret). The copy to be sent to *Pravda* retyped fair with all his final corrections and changes was looked through by Lenin, after which it was passed on to Maria Ilyinichna. The three copies that Nadezhda Konstantinovna had received were also corrected. The rough copies were burnt by me. He asked that the sealed envelopes in which the copies of the documents were kept should be marked to the effect that they could only be opened by V. I. Lenin, and after his death by Nadezhda Konstantinovna. I did not write the words 'and after his death' on the envelopes. Lenin's copies were kept in a file and corded for more convenient use."   p. 482

598   B. V. Titlinov, *Novaya Tserkov* (The New Church), Petrograd, Moscow, 1923. After the corresponding entry in the "Books Issued Journal", librarian Manucharyants wrote the following note: "In January Nadezhda Konstantinovna asked for literature for Vladimir Ilyich on the co-operatives. Khinchuk sent the following: 1) Meshcheryakov. *Co-operation and Socialism.* 2) Chayanov, *Basic Ideas and Forms of Organisation of Peasant Co-operation.* 3) Tugan-Baranovsky, *The Social Foundations of Co-operation.* 4) Prokopovich, *The Co-operative Movement in Russia, Its Theory and Practice.*" and some other books.   p. 482

599   This refers to Lenin's article "Our Revolution (Apropos of N. Sukhanov's Notes)" (see present edition, Vol. 33, pp. 476-79).   p. 482

600   See present edition, Vol. 33, pp. 481-86. First variant—pp. 433-40 of this volume.   p. 483

601   *Khloplyankin M. I.*—Board member of the People's Commissariat for Labour.   p. 483

602   The next day (January 21) Volodicheva asked for the following magazines to be sent to Lenin: *Sotsialisticheski Vestnik* No. 1, *Sovremenniye Zapiski*, v. XIII and *Zarya* Nos. 9-10.   p. 483

603   The report of the Dzerzhinsky commission was discussed at a meeting of the Politbureau on January 25, 1923. The commission's proposals were endorsed.   p. 484

604   Lenin is referring to the books: P. M. Kerzhentsev. *Printsipi Organizatsii* (Principles of Organisation), Petrograd, 1922; O. A. Yermansky. *Nauchnaya Organizatsia Truda i Systema*

Taylora (The Scientific Organisation of Labour and the Taylor System), Moscow, 1922. These books are mentioned in Lenin's article "Better Fewer, But Better" (see Vol. 33 of this edition, pp. 487-502). On Yermansky's book see also Lenin's unfinished review "A Fly in the Ointment" (present edition, Vol. 33, pp. 368-69).   p. 485

605   *Reske, N. A.*—Board member of the People's Commissariat for Workers' and Peasants' Inspection.   p. 485

606   On February 1 the Politbureau allowed the materials of the Dzerzhinsky Commission on the Georgian question to be given out.   p. 485

607   Fotieva wrote down the following instructions of Lenin: "1) Why was the old C.C. of the C.P. of Georgia accused of deviationism. 2) What breach of Party discipline were they blamed for. 3) Why the Transcaucasian Committee is accused of suppressing the C.C. of the C.P. of Georgia. 4) The physical means of suppression ('biomechanics'). 5) The line of the C.C. (of the R.C.P.(B.)— *Ed.*) in Vladimir Ilyich's absence and in his presence. 6) Attitude of the Commission. Did it examine only the accusations against the C.C. of the C.P. of Georgia or also against the Transcaucasian Committee? Did it examine the 'biomechanics' incident? 7) The present situation (the election campaign, the Mensheviks, suppression, national discord)" (Central Party Archives, Institute of Marxism-Leninism of the C.C., C.P.S.U.).   p. 485

608   See present edition, Vol. 33, pp. 487-502.   p. 486

609   On February 2, through Krupskaya, Lenin asked for the following books to be obtained for him from M. P. Pavlovich: A. Y. Khodorov. *Mirovoi imperializm i Kitai (Opit Polit.-ekonom. issledovaniya)* (World Imperialism and China. An Essay at Politico-Economic Research). Shanghai, 1922, and M. P. Pavlovich. *Sovietskaya Rossia i imperialisticheskaya Yaponia* (Soviet Russia and Imperialist Japan). These books were delivered to Lenin in the evening together with A. M. Khinchuk's book *Tsentrosoyuz v usloviakh novoi ekonomicheskoi politiki* (Centrosoyuz Under the New Economic Policy), Moscow, 1922.   p. 486

610   This refers to the census of Soviet employees carried out in Moscow and Petrograd in October-November 1922.   p. 489

611   This refers to Lenin's "*The Proletarian Revolution and the Renegade Kautsky*".   p. 490

612   Apparently, on December 27 or 28 Lenin dictated his note on the subjects of his future work:
      "Memo:

"The letter about increasing the number of Central Committee members omits mention of the ratio of the members of the enlarged Central Committee to the Workers' and Peasants' Inspection.

"Subjects to be dealt with:

"1. Centrosoyuz and its significance in the light of the NEP.

"2. Correlation between Chief Board for Vocational Education and general educational work among the people.

"3. The national question and internationalism (in the light of the recent conflict in the Georgian party).

"4. The new book of public education statistics published in 1922." p. 491

613 Lenin asked, among others, for the following books (in Russian— *Ed.*): V. S. Rozhitsin. *Modern Science and Marxism.* Kharkov, 1922; S. Y. Semkovsky. *Marxism as a Teaching Subject. Report at the All-Ukraine Pedagogical Conference (July 1922).* Kharkov, 1922; M. Alsky. *Our Finances During the Civil War and NEP.* Moscow, 1923; S. N. Faulkner. *Turning-Point in the Crisis of World Industry.* Moscow, 1922; G. Tsiperovich. *By Ourselves! (Results of 5 Years of Economic Development).* Petrograd, 1922; L. Axelrod (Orthodox). *Against Idealism: A Criticism of Certain Idealistic Trends in Philosophical Thought. Collection of Articles.* Moscow-Petrograd, 1922; Arthur Drews, *Die Christusmythe.* Moscow, 1923; P. G. Kurlov. *The End of Russian Tsarism. Reminiscences of an ex-commander of the gendarmery.* Moscow-Petrograd, 1920; S. I. Kanatchikov. *Topics of the Day (Pages of Proletarian Ideology).* Petrograd, 1923; I. A. Modzalevsky. *Proletarian Mythmaking (On Ideological Deviations in Modern Proletarian Poetry).* Semipalatinsk, 1922. p. 492

614 Fotieva wrote down the following: "Vladimir Ilyich's instructions that a hint be given to Soltz (A. A. Soltz, member of the presidium of the Central Control Commission, R.C.P.(B.)—*Ed.*) that he (Lenin) was on the side of the injured party. Some one or other of the injured party was to be given to understand he was on their side.

"3 moments: 1. One should not fight. 2. Concessions should be made. 3. One cannot compare a large state with a small one.

"Did Stalin know? Why didn't he react?

"The name 'deviationist' for a deviation towards chauvinism and Menshevism proves the same deviation with the dominant-national chauvinists.

"Collect printed matter for Vladimir Ilyich."

Between February 15 and March 4 no entries were made in the Journal. p. 493

615 Lenin asked Trotsky to uphold the "Georgian case" at the plenum of the C.C. Trotsky, pleading illness, said he could not take upon himself such an obligation (see *Collected Works*, Vol. 54, Fifth Russian Edition, p. 329). p. 493

[616] This refers to Lenin's letter to Stalin, copies of which were sent
to Kamenev and Zinoviev (see *Collected Works*, Vol. 54, Fifth
Russian Edition, pp. 329-30).   p. 493

[617] Lenin stated in this letter that he was preparing a memorandum
and speech on the Georgian question (see *Collected Works*, Vol. 54,
Fifth Russian Edition, p. 330).   p. 493

[618] At this point the entries break off.
The text beginning with the words: "Nadezhda Konstantinovna asked..." is written in the Journal in shorthand; this was
deciphered by Volodicheva on July 14, 1956.   p. 494

NAME INDEX

A

Akhundov, R. A.—351
Alexinsky, G. A.—291
Algasov, V. A.—55
Alsky, A. O.—342
Andreyev, A. A.—301, 374
Antonov-Ovseyenko, V. A.—51
Aprelev, A. P.—66
Artyom (Sergeyev,* F. A.)—44
Arzhanov, M. M.—165
Avanesov, V. A.—137, 149, 160, 220, 222, 356
Avilov, N. P. (Glebov, N.)—184
Avksentyev, N. D.—49

B

Badayev, A. Y.—203
Balfour, Arthur James—37
Bauer, Otto—415
Bebel, August—127, 293
Belyakov, A. A.—128
Belenky, A. Y.—196-97
Bogayevsky, M. P.—69
Bogdanov, P. A.—343, 350, 351, 353, 357, 364
Bogdatyan, M. S.—278
Bogolepov, D. P.—86
Bonch-Bruyevich, V. D.—153
Brandler, Heinrich—322, 323
Briand, Aristide—392
Bubnov, A. S.—207

Brichkina, S. B.—206
Budyonny, S. M.—205, 206
Bullitt, William Christian—196
Bukharin, N. I.—40, 101, 119, 120, 121, 184, 201, 215, 221, 223, 224, 241, 242, 302, 320, 367, 393, 414, 427-28
Burdukov, A. A.—162
Burian, Edmund—328
Burov, Y. I.—161

C

Calvert, H.-S.—350, 352
Chernov, V. M.—273
Chervyakov, A. G.—267
Chicherin, G. V.—119-21, 144, 150, 206, 229, 232, 268, 340, 345, 390, 391, 392, 395, 401, 404, 410
Churchill, Winston Leonard Spencer—176, 178, 229
Chubar, V. Y.—305-06
Clausewitz, Karl von—327
Clemenceau, Georges Benjamin—176
Curzon, George Nathaniel—229, 250

D

Dabal, Tomasz—355
Danishevsky, K. Kh.—206
Daszynski, Ignazi—355

---

* Real names are given in parenthesis.

В. И. ЛЕНИН
СОЧИНЕНИЯ

Том 42

На английском языке

Printed in the Union of Soviet Socialist Republics

087480

practical   already accepted by
                   Russia
                   Finland
                   German Austria
                   Holland
                   Hungary

Please tackle this job *urgently*, and together with Bukharin draw up a *draft* on all these points. *Answer me at once, if only briefly.*

Greetings! *Lenin*

On no account must the Zimmerwaldists be taken as a gauge.

(αα) *Spartacusbund* (Germany)

The Communist Party of Finland
                "   "   German Austria
                "   "   Hungary

Social-Democrats αα of Poland and Lithuania
                "   "   Holland
                "   "   Russia
                "   "   Ukraine
                "   "   Estonia
                "   "   Latvia

ββ { The Tesnyaki of Bulgaria
     { Rumanian Party?

γγ ((the Lefts and the young in
    ((the Swiss Social-Democratic Party

ββ The Socialist Party of Scotland
αα the Left S.D. of Sweden
ββ the Norwegian S.D. Party
ββ the Danish S.D. group (Marie Nielsen) and the syndicalists, close to Bolshevism
γγ Loriot's group in France
ββ the "League" in the United States (or followers of Debs?)

We count on closer alignment and affiliation with { { the British Socialist Party... ββ
                       { the Italian Socialist Party...[122] ββ

Written December 27 or 28, 1918

First published in 1965 in the Fifth Russian Edition of the *Collected Works*, Vol. 50

Printed from the manuscript

INSTRUCTIONS FOR COMPILING
A READING BOOK
FOR WORKERS AND PEASANTS

Assignment: a reading book for workers and peasants to be compiled within a fortnight.

The book to consist of separate, complete, independent leaflets of two to four printed pages.

Wording must be very popular, designed for the ignorant peasant. Number of leaflets from 50 to 200; for the first issue—50.

Subjects: organisation of Soviet power, its home and foreign policies. For example: What is Soviet power? How to run the country. The law on land. The economic councils. Nationalisation of the factories. Labour discipline. Imperialism. The imperialist war. Secret treaties. How we offered peace. What we are fighting for now. What is communism? Separation of the church from the state. And so on.

Good old texts can and should be used, and old articles rewritten.

The reading book should provide material for public readings and home reading, for reprinting of separate texts and for translation (with slight additions) into other languages.

Written December 1918

First published June 1, 1936   Printed from the typewritten copy
    in *Pravda* No. 149

NOTES ON HELP TO KHARKOV[123]

1) Send maximum amount of money to Kharkov.

2) The S.E.C. to send textiles, etc., there in the most urgent manner....

3) Set up a Centre in Kharkov....

> Send people organisers, at least a few, familiar with food supply business.[124]

Written between January
    3 and 17, 1919

First published in 1933   Printed from the manuscript
in *Lenin Miscellany* XXIV

DRAFT DECISION FOR THE C.P.C.
ON THE CO-OPERATIVES[125]

I. Collect information on the actual implementation by the co-operatives of the basic line of Soviet policy, namely:

(1) not only co-operative organisation of the whole population, but the predominant role of the proletarian and semi-proletarian population in co-operative activities.

(2) such a system of supply and distribution as would really enable the poor (= proletarians + semi-proletarians) to derive benefit (goods, etc.) from the delivery of *all* surpluses of grain to the state.

ad 1 direct the Co-operative Department of the Supreme Economic Council and the Commissariat for Food, together with the Central Statistical Board to collect this information. Report in a fortnight.

II. Direct the Food Commissariat to draw up instructions concerning Soviet agents in the co-operatives and develop propaganda and organising work to this end.

III. Direct the workers' co-operatives to elect a majority of their own representatives to the Board of Centrosoyuz and make it possible to introduce *Communists* there experienced in practical work.

IV. Krestinsky—draft decree on consumers' communes.

Written January 28, 1919

First published in 1931
in *Lenin Miscellany XVIII*

Printed from the manuscript

THE STATE OF LIBRARY SERVICE

DRAFT DECISION FOR THE C.P.C.[126]

Direct the Library Department of the *People's Commissariat for Education* to publish monthly and forward to the C.P.C. brief factual information as to the implementation of the C.P.C.'s decisions of 7.VI.1918 and 14.I.1919 and the actual increase in the number of libraries and reading-rooms, and the growth of book distribution among the population.

Written January 30, 1919
First published February 1, 1919 in *Izvestia* No. 23

Printed from the manuscript

A CONCESSION
ON THE GREAT NORTHERN RAILWAY[127]

DRAFT DECISION FOR THE C.P.C.

1) The C.P.C. finds the direction of the railway and its general plan acceptable;

2) considers a concession to representatives of foreign capital generally, as a matter of principle, permissible in the interests of developing the country's productive forces;

3) considers the present concession to be desirable and its implementation a practical necessity;

4) to speed up a practical and final decision on this question, its sponsors to be asked to produce evidence of their declared contacts with solid capitalist firms capable of handling this job and shipping the materials;

5) an ad hoc commission to be directed to submit a final draft contract within a fortnight;

6) the Military Commissariat to be instructed within a fortnight to give its findings from the strategic and military point of view.

Written February 4, 1919
First published in 1933 in *Lenin Miscellany XXIV*

Printed from the manuscript

DRAFT DECISION FOR THE C.P.C.
ON THE QUESTION
OF ALLOTTING FARMS
TO INDUSTRIAL ENTERPRISES

The final decision on this question to be postponed until Tuesday.

The Commissariat for Agriculture to be asked to supply information on the following points by Saturday:

1) the number of state farms,

2) their organisation, and what has been done in this direction,

3) the number of agronomists,

4) actual sowing preparations,

5) the quantity of seeds actually available for sowing,

6) the number of agricultural machines.

The S.E.C. to be instructed to supply information 1) on the number of applications for land made by workers, 2) on the workers' experience in the organisation of agriculture.*

Written February 13, 1919

First published in 1959 in *Lenin Miscellany XXXVI*

Printed from the typewritten text supplemented by Lenin

RE DRAFT RESOLUTION
FOR THE C.C., R.C.P.(B.)
ON THE FOOD SURPLUS-APPROPRIATION SYSTEM
IN THE UKRAINE[128]

In issuing this directive, the C.C., R.C.P. proposes that the following established principle be adhered to: from the poor peasants—nothing, the middle peasants—moderately, the rich peasants—heavily.

* Points 5 and 6 of the original from which this document is published are in Lenin's handwriting. Points 1, 3 and 4, as well as Points 1 and 2 of the last paragraph were written by Lenin on the agenda of the C.P.C. meeting of February 13, 1919; they were incorporated without alteration into the text of the decision.—*Ed.*

We advise fixing the maximum surplus, *for example*, 500 million poods for the whole of the Ukraine, of which one-fifth or one-tenth share be assessed for requisitioning.

Written February 19, 1919

First published in 1933
in *Lenin Miscellany XXIV*

Printed from the manuscript

ON THE APPEAL
OF THE GERMAN INDEPENDENTS[129]

We seldom have a chance now of receiving foreign newspapers in Russia: the blockade with which the "democratic capitalists" of the Entente have surrounded us is apparently operating effectively. They are afraid to acquaint the educated workers of America, Britain and France with ignorant and uncivilised Bolshevism, they are afraid lest people in this land of uncivilised Bolshevism get to know of its successes in the West.

But despite the zealous efforts of the gendarmery of the new Holy Alliance to suppress it, the truth will out!

The other day I happened to see several numbers of the Berlin newspaper *Die Freiheit*, the organ of the so-called "independent" German Social-Democrats. The front page of No. 74 (for 11.II.1919) carried a lengthy appeal "To the Revolutionary Proletariat of Germany" signed by the Central Committee of the party and its parliamentary group. The ideas, or rather the lack of ideas, underlying this appeal are so characteristic of not only the German, but of the world's labour movement, that they deserve to be dwelt upon.

But first I should like to make a digression connected with personal reminiscences. Among the signatures of the parliamentary group of Independents I came across the names of Seger and Laukant, and they reminded me of what happened three years ago. I had occasion to meet Laukant at a meeting of the Zimmerwaldists in Berne.[130] This seemingly influential Berlin worker produced a dual impression: on the one hand, serious revolutionary work among the masses, on the other, an astonishing lack of theoretical* and appalling short-sightedness. Laukant did not like my sharp attacks on Kautsky (the ideological "leader" of the Independents, or rather leader of their non-ideology), but he did not refuse to help me when, doubtful of my unreliable German, I showed him the text of a short speech in German I had written,** in which I quoted the statement of the "American Bebel", Eugene Debs, to the effect that he would rather be shot than agree to vote for imperialist war loans, and that he would agree to fight only in a war of the workers against the capitalists. On the other hand, when, with furious indignation, I showed Laukant the passage from Kautsky's article in which that gentleman denounced the workers' street demonstrations as adventurism[131] (and that under Wilhelm II) Laukant shrugged his shoulders and answered with exasperating coolness: "Our workers don't read this as attentively as all that! I'm not obliged to agree with every line of Kautsky's, am I?"

Written in the second
half of February 1919

First published in 1933
in *Lenin Miscellany XXIV*

Printed from the manuscript

DRAFT DECISION
FOR THE COUNCIL OF DEFENCE
ON REGULATING RELATIONS BETWEEN
THE VECHEKA, THE RAILWAY CHEKA
AND THE COMMISSARIAT FOR RAILWAYS
AND A LETTER TO THE MEMBERS
OF THE COUNCIL OF DEFENCE

Decision of the Council of Defence

28.II.1919

In order to regulate relations between the Vecheka, the Railway Cheka and the Commissariat for Railways the following provisions are laid down:

---

* Apparently the word "interests" or "knowledg e" has been omit ted in the manuscript.—*Ed.*
** See Vol. 22 of this edition, pp. 125-26.—*Ed.*

Comrade Belyakov, from the Commissariat for Railways, to be delegated to the Transport Department of the Vecheka for permanent liaison and work.

The Commissariat for Railways to issue orders down the line that all complaints against the Cheka be addressed *exclusively* to C.R. Board member Belyakov.

The Cheka to be charged with supervising timely unloading of freights by the organisations and bodies concerned, and in the event of unloading work not being fulfilled in the time set by the Cheka, the guilty parties are to be called to account.

Local sections of the Railway Cheka to be given the right to use the railway telegraph (for payment) and made to bear strict responsibility for using it without need. Detailed instructions on the use of the telegraph and method of payment to be issued by the People's Commissar for Railways and the Chairman of the Vecheka by agreement.

The former premises of the railway police to be turned over to the Railway Cheka, and a special order to this effect to be issued by the C.R. Comrades Dzerzhinsky and Sklyansky to issue joint instructions concerning the eviction of military guards from these premises.

Food rations to be issued in the usual way to the Railway Cheka from the supplies of the railway food organisations.

So long as martial law introduced on the railways by the Council of Defence continues, the district transport departments of the Cheka are to be given the right to apply capital punishment to persons found guilty of bribery, theft of freights and railway material, and systematic abuse on the part of officials.

To Members of the Council of Defence

28.II.1919

The points I propose have been approved at a meeting I had with Comrades Nevsky and Dzerzhinsky on 28/II.

Please have them signed by all the members of the Council of Defence, so that this *extremely important* **agreement** may be put into effect immediately.

In the event of serious differences please send me *the text of amendments* at once by phoned telegram.

V. *Ulyanov* (*Lenin*)
Chairman, Council of Defence

First published in 1933
in *Lenin Miscellany XXIV*

Printed from the manuscript

SPEECH AT AGITATORS' COURSES OF THE MOTHER AND CHILD PROTECTION DEPARTMENT OF THE PEOPLE'S COMMISSARIAT FOR SOCIAL SECURITY

MARCH 8, 1919

Comrade Lenin began his speech by quoting the closing passage of the women students' letter and said that they should keep their word and create a strong army of the home front.[132] It was only with the help of the woman, her thoughtfulness and social awareness, that the new society could be consolidated. It was the lack of this social awareness among the mass of the women, he said, that had acted as a brake in previous revolutions.

Published in 1919
in the booklet (in Russian)
*People's Commissariat
for Social Security.
Report of the Mother and Child
Protection Department
May 1, 1918 to May 1, 1919*

Printed from the booklet text

ROUGH DRAFT FOR A C.P.C. DECISION ON THE PRINTING INDUSTRY DEPARTMENT OF S.E.C.

1) Commission for amalgamation and centralisation, and, in case of need, for drawing up a draft decree.

2) Statistical information, comparing printing-works
    (1) nationalised, in charge of the Printing Industry Department

(2) nationalised, in charge of various departments
(3) private enterprises
3) Assignment: increase threefold, term?
4) Report within a month?
5) Work discipline
6) Piece work
7) Factory Committees' attitude to managements.[133]

Written March 15, 1919

First published in 1933   Printed from the manuscript
in *Lenin Miscellany XXIV*

NOTES ON CO-OPERATION

Should not § 1 be thrown out?

Notes to § 2 and § 3 to be removed.

Not less than two-thirds of the membership of every co-operative should belong to the proletariat or semi-proletariat (i.e., to persons living solely or to the extent of not less than 50 per cent by the sale of their labour power).

Agencies of the workers' co-operatives send commissars to the co-operatives having over ten per cent of their members belonging to the propertied classes. The commissars have the right of supervision and control, as well as the right of veto, decisions thus vetoed being submitted for final settlement to the agencies of the S.E.C.

What form of expression may practical co-operation of the commercial and industrial employees' unions take?

What about introducing a number of substantial bonuses and benefits for co-operatives that have embraced the whole population?

Municipalities uniting the whole population around municipal shops.

Written in March, not later
than 16, 1919

First published in 1959   Printed from the manuscript
in *Lenin Miscellany XXXVI*

DRAFT RESOLUTION FOR THE C.C., R.C.P.(B.) ON SENDING GROUPS OF WORKERS OUT ON FOOD TRANSPORTATION JOBS

In view of the extreme danger threatening the Republic as a result of the aggravation of the food and transport crises, the C.C., R.C.P. resolves:

to charge Comrades Kamenev

Zinoviev

and Stalin

with organising groups of influential workers and forming trains by arrangement with the People's Commissariats for Food and Railways as well as with the Central Executive Committee, and sending them out on food transportation jobs.[134]

Lenin

Written in the second half
of March, not later than 28, 1919

First published in 1933
in *Lenin Miscellany XXIV*

Printed from the manuscript

DRAFT DECISION FOR THE COUNCIL OF DEFENCE ON SUPPLYING BREADSTUFFS TO THE RAILWAYMEN

The Commissariat for Railways makes known to the workers that receipt of 25 pounds, according to exact calculations, is fully guaranteed in the event of six million poods a month being transported. Much more than this can be transported. A strong effort must be made to increase the number of locomotives repaired. Over and above this *bonuses* will be issued for increased labour productivity in accordance with norms laid down by the All-Russia Trade Union Council.

Written March 31, 1919

First published in 1933
in *Lenin Miscellany XXIV*

Printed from the manuscript

ON THE QUESTION OF RELATIONS
WITH THE MIDDLE PEASANTS

Re *plan* of urgent measures in favour
of the middle peasant:

1) Special tax on *middle peasants* to be relaxed **at once.**
2) Party people to be sent out (3 from each gubernia committee) specially to work for *the middle peasants.*
3) Commissions to be set up in the centre (a number of them) and sent out to the local areas *to defend* the middle peasant.
4) Draw up and endorse plan for Kalinin's tours. Publish dates, places, reception of visitors, etc.
5) Participation in these tours (Points 4 and 5) by the People's Commissariats for *Justice, Internal Affairs, Agriculture,* and others.
6) Press campaign.
7) "Manifesto" in defence of the middle peasant.
8) Verification (and cancellation) of *coercive* measures for joining the communes.
9) Verification of *food* measures in the direction of relaxing requisitions, exactions, etc., from the *middle peasants.*
10) Amnesty.
11) "Identification of the kulak."
12) Surplus appropriation of grain and fodder.
13) Handicraftsmen and artisans recognised.

Written late March-early April, 1919

First published in 1933   Printed from the manuscript
in *Lenin Miscellany XXIV*

DRAFT RESOLUTION ON THE REPORT
ON THE DOMESTIC AND FOREIGN SITUATION
OF THE SOVIET REPUBLIC
AT THE EXTRAORDINARY PLENARY MEETING
OF THE MOSCOW SOVIET OF WORKERS'
AND RED ARMY DEPUTIES
APRIL 3, 1919[135]

This meeting of representatives of the working class and peasantry of the R.S.F.S.R. declares that the Soviet Republic has entered its most difficult month. The Allies are making their last desperate effort to crush us by force of arms. The food situation in the spring is the most difficult. The transport system is utterly disrupted.

Only the greatest effort can save us. Victory is possible. The revolution in Hungary has proved conclusively that the Soviet movement in Western Europe is growing and its victory is not far off. We have many allies all over the world, more than we imagine. We must hold on for another four or five difficult months in order to beat our enemies.

This meeting harshly condemns the Left Socialist-Revolutionaries,* the Mensheviks and the Right S.R.s who, while paying lip-service to Soviet power or protesting in word against the armed intervention of the Allies, are *in fact helping the whiteguards* when they agitate for strikes or for cessation of the civil war (although we offered peace to all![136]) or for concessions to freedom of trade, and so on.

This meeting declares that all those Mensheviks and Socialist-Revolutionaries who are prepared to help us in our difficult struggle shall be ensured full liberty as citizens of the Soviet Republic.

This meeting, however, declares relentless war upon those Mensheviks and Socialist-Revolutionaries who, like the literary and political groups *Vsegda Vperyod!*[137] and

---

* The first sheet of the manuscript is missing. The text up to the words "Left Socialist-Revolutionaries" is printed from the typewritten copy.—*Ed.*

Dyelo Naroda,[138] are *actually* impeding our struggle, actually *assisting* the whiteguards.

This meeting calls upon all workers, all workers' organisations and all working peasants to exert every effort to repel the enemies of Soviet power, to defend that power and improve the food supply and transport systems.

1. To enlist members of the middle section—i.e., people who are less experienced than the advanced workers and peasants—to replace the overworked advanced section.

2. To send more and more contingents of the advanced and rank-and-file workers out on food supply, transport and army work.

3. To enlist the largest possible number of politically conscious workers and peasants for work at the People's Commissariat for Railways and the State Control, in order to improve the functioning of these bodies and to eliminate bureaucracy and red tape.

4. To transfer as many people as possible from the starving cities to agricultural work, to vegetable gardening, to the rural districts, to the Ukraine, to the Don region, and so forth, in order to increase grain production.

All efforts to be exerted to assist the middle peasants, to put a stop to the abuses from which they so often suffer, and to render them comradely help. Those Soviet officials who refuse to carry out this policy—which is the only correct one—or who fail to understand it, must be immediately dismissed.

5. To combat all signs of weariness, faint-heartedness and vacillation, to enhearten in every way those who show such signs, strengthen their spirit, consciousness and comradely discipline. The working class and the peasantry of Russia have borne incredible burdens. The last few months have been incredibly difficult. But this meeting declares that the workers have not lost heart, that the working class remains at its post, that it will overcome all difficulties and maintain at all costs the victory of the Soviet Socialist Republic in Russia and throughout the world.

Written in April,
not later than 3rd, 1919

First published in 1963   Printed from the manuscript
in the Fifth Russian Edition   collated with the typewritten
of the *Collected Works*, Vol. 38   copy

MOTION TO ENDORSE THE DRAFT RESOLUTION OF THE C.C., R.C.P.(B.) CONTAINING DIRECTIVES FOR THE C.C. OF THE C.P.(B.) OF THE UKRAINE

I propose that the signatures of the C.C. Politbureau members be collected and these directives to the Ukrainian Communist Party and its C.C. for the Ukraine be endorsed. *Extremely urgent*.[139]

8/IV. *Lenin*

To the C.C. *O r g b u r e a u.* Forward urgently to the Ukrainian *C.C.**

Written April 8, 1919

First published in 1965
in the Fifth Russian Edition
of the *Collected Works*, Vol. 54

Printed from the manuscript

RE DECISION OF THE COUNCIL OF DEFENCE ON STEPPING UP WORK IN THE FIELD OF MILITARY DEFENCE[140]

Suspend for 3 months or substantially cut down those departments in the central and local commissariats that are not absolutely essential and that may provide useful workers for the army and the home front for the conduct of war, for food collection, agitation and so on.

Written in April,
not later than 21, 1919

First published in 1933
in *Lenin Miscellany XXIV*

Printed from the manuscript

POSTSCRIPT TO THE APPEAL TO HUNGARIAN INTERNATIONALISTS[141]

I fully subscribe to the text of the appeal and believe that the Hungarian proletarians at the fronts will bear in mind that another few months of struggle for the interests

* Marginal note added to the draft, apparently after it was endorsed.—*Ed.*

of the international proletariat will bring us victory—
a victory that will be decisive and real.

Lenin

Written April 23, 1919

First published in 1960
in the book
A. Kladt and V. Kondratyev,
Brothers-in-Arms
MOSCOW

Printed from the text
of leaflet
Russian translation from
the Hungarian

DRAFT DECISION
FOR THE C.P.C.'S ECONOMIC COMMISSION
ON ALLEVIATING THE POSITION
OF THE WORKERS[142]

1) More aid in kind to be rendered to workers' children.
2) Definite warehouses to be earmarked for *quick* registration and distribution of goods at a *moderate* price to the most needy workers *who do not receive* the minimum in money payment.
3) Ditto as regards rent.

Written May 2, 1919

First published in 1933
in *Lenin Miscellany XXIV*

Printed from the manuscript

SALARIES FOR SPECIALISTS
DRAFT DECISION

May 23, 1919

*Decisions Adopted by the C.P.C. Commission
at Its Meeting on 23.V.1919:*

1. Salaries over 3,000 rubles shall be appointed by the Board of each Commissariat, reported to the People's Commissariats for Labour and for State Control, and submitted to the Council of People's Commissars for endorsement.

2. Each People's Commissariat is obliged within a week to present a list of all employees who receive over 3,000 rubles a month.

3. Each Commissariat is obliged within a week to present a list of leading specialists and outstanding organisers who have to be paid over 3,000 rubles.

The Board of each Commissariat must declare in the case of each person 1) its assurance that he is an outstanding specialist in such-and-such a field; 2) exactly what outstanding organising job he is doing or is capable of doing.

4. On June 15 only those whose salaries have been endorsed by the Council of People's Commissars shall receive pay at the rate of 3,000 rubles and more.

5. The term within which salaries shall be endorsed by the Council of People's Commissars is to be fixed at not more than one week from the date of presentation.

6. Reports to be delivered by Lenin and Krasin.

7. Avanesov is directed not later than tomorrow, May 24, to submit theses or principles concerning salaries of over 3,000 rubles to non-outstanding specialists.

Please type *6—7* copies.

First published in 1945
in *Lenin Miscellany XXXV*

Printed from the manuscript

DRAFT DECISION
FOR THE COUNCIL OF DEFENCE
ON THE MOBILISATION OF SOVIET EMPLOYEES[143]

§ 1. All male employees of Soviet institutions between the ages of *18* and *45* [better more, as some will be exempted] to be mobilised for 4 months (from 15.VI to 15.X) and to be replaced by women or part of the work to be temporarily reduced.

Note to § 1. Only people who are ill or absolutely indispensable, but not more than 10 per cent, shall be exempted with the permission of a special commission.

§ 2. The mobilised men to be placed at the disposal of the military authorities. To present themselves (date).

§ 3. The mobilised men to answer for each other by collective liability and their families to be considered hostages in the event of their deserting to the enemy or failing to carry out assignments, etc.

§ 4. The mobilised men to form small groups, preferably of different professions, so that each group may take upon itself, in the rear and at the front, various tasks in connection with troop formation, ferrying, maintenance and so on.

§ 5. Each mobilised person is obliged to form for himself out of supplies received from C.E.C. and other stores a small collection of the most needful propaganda booklets and leaflets, with which he is duty bound to familiarise the soldiers and population and report every week on how he performs these duties.

§ 6. Each mobilised person, immediately on being mobilised, but not later than within ... days, is obliged to give detailed information as to his education, previous employment or occupation, places of former residence, knowledge of foreign languages, etc., in accordance with a programme to be specially drawn up.

Written not later
than May 31, 1919

First published in 1933   Printed from the manuscript
in *Lenin Miscellany XXIV*

DECREE OF THE COUNCIL
OF WORKERS' AND PEASANTS' DEFENCE
ON CALLING UP FOR MILITARY SERVICE
TRADE, INDUSTRIAL AND TRANSPORT WORKERS
AND OTHER EMPLOYEES

The call-up, by way of extra mobilisation, is announced for trade, industrial and transport workers and other employees. The order and date of the call-up as well as the number of persons to be drafted for military service are to be fixed by arrangement between the Revolutionary Military Council of the Republic, the Board of the Supreme Economic Council and the All-Russia Central Council of Trade Unions.*

Written May 31, 1919

Published June 15, 1919   Printed from the manuscript
in *Izvestia* No. 128

ORDER TO THE C.P.C. SECRETARIAT

19.VII.1919

The delay in endorsing the instructions concerning food parcels from the army[144] is an outrageous and intolerable piece of red tape.

It is necessary to ascertain who the culprits are and generally have this case investigated, first, in order to establish responsibility, second—and most important of all—in order to work out *practical* measures to make a repetition of this impossible.

I therefore order the institutions listed below, who were to have taken care of the speedy enforcement of the law on food parcels,

to immediately, rigorously and carefully investigate the cause of this red tape by collecting *all* relevant documents and questioning all persons concerned

and *submit to the C.P.C.* on Tuesday their reports together with their proposal of *practical* measures for eliminating red tape.

The institutions are:

Secretariat of the C.P.C. and Council of Defence
Central Committee of the Food Army
Food Commissariat
Military Commissariat
Commissariat for Post and Telegraph.

V. Ulyanov (Lenin)
Chairman, Council of People's Commissars

First published in 1942   Printed from the manuscript
in *Lenin Miscellany XXXIV*

---

* The top of the typed text of the decree signed by Lenin bears a note by him: "Off the record".—*Ed.*

DIRECTIVES TO THE COMMISSARIAT FOR AGRICULTURE RE MODIFICATION OF INSTRUCTIONS

The instructions of the People's Commissariat for Agriculture* are to be modified and effective control is to be exercised through all Soviet agencies in the spirit of the following propositions:

1) Landowners or estate managers to be positively prohibited from occupying posts in state farms of the same or neighbouring uyezds in which these persons resided during the rule of the landowners.

2) Lists to be kept of estate managers and employees at state farms and surveillance to be kept over them as strictly as over military experts in respect of their counter-revolutionary bent.

3) The number of representatives of uyezd and gubernia land departments in state farms to be increased and greater control exercised over them by these departments.

4) Greater attention to the workers' committees and their activities to be demanded of the trade union council.

5) Metayage and similar work in the state farms to be prohibited.

6) All state farm personnel to be prosecuted immediately in the event of their being unable to prove fulfilment by them of Article 59 of the Statute on Socialist Land Settlement, providing for *assistance* to be rendered to the local peasantry.

7) Forms of reporting and informing the local peasant population to be worked out for the state farms and workers' committees.

8) Monthly reports to the C.P.C. on fulfilment of the present rules to be demanded of the People's Commissariat for Agriculture and of the workers' committee in addition to those of 1 or 2 gubernia land departments of the most important gubernias.

---

* Here the following text was inserted in the manuscript by Lydia Fotieva, Secretary of the C.P.C.: "concerning the organisation and activities of the gubernia and district state farm administrations."—*Ed.*

9) The Central Statistical Board to extend its monographic description of the state farms by the inclusion of questions necessary for checking fulfilment of the above points.

10) Allocation of land to the state farms to be rechecked for possible excessive allotment of land or its seizure by non-proletarian organisations.

11) Nomination of candidates to the state farms by the gubernia and uyezd land departments to be made a general rule.

12) Instructions and measures to be submitted to the C.P.C. after preliminary consideration by a commission* Sereda, Sapronov, Vladimirsky, Tsyurupa, Milyutin and Golubev.**

Written in August,
not later than 5, 1919

First published in 1933
in *Lenin Miscellany XXIV*

Printed from the manuscript

DRAFT DECISIONS FOR THE C.C. POLITBUREAU ON MEASURES TO FIGHT MAMONTOV

1

Draft Resolution of the C.C. Politbureau

Attaching serious importance to Mamontov's[145] operations and considering the *speedy* destruction of his detachment an *urgent* matter, the Politbureau of the C.C. resolves:

1) once more to draw the attention of the People's Commissars for Post and Telegraph and for Railways to the necessity of exerting every effort to *improve post and telegraph connections in the area of Mamontov's* operations and *speed up the transportation of troops* in that area.

---

* Following this are the words "composed of" written in the manuscript by L. A. Fotieva.—*Ed.*

** Here the following text is inserted in the manuscript in Fotieva's handwriting: "The commission to be given a week. Its summoning and report to be entrusted to Sereda."—*Ed.*

2) Comrade Trotsky to be charged with
(a) drawing up a draft appeal by telegraph to the Party organisations of the given area with *a repeat appeal* for more energetic actions;
(b) taking part together with Comrade Lashevich (Lashevich retaining personal command) in all operations for routing Mamontov, to the extent of his complete liquidation, in order that the authority of the C.C. and the Revolutionary Military Council of the Republic may be displayed in all these operations with greater speed and determination[146];
(c) calling in volunteers against Mamontov from the gubernias of Tver, Kostroma, Yaroslavl and Ivanovo-Voznesensk.

2

Draft directives of the C.C. Politbureau to be drawn up at once.

It is considered politically essential
1) to speed up transportation of the Belebei Bashkir Division to Petrograd and effect this movement as energetically as possible;
2) Tula and the defence of the north generally against Mamontov being sufficiently covered, the 21st Division, in its known and greater part, is to be transferred to the Southern Front with the double objective of catching Mamontov from the south and taking part in the fighting on the Southern Front.

3

I propose the following addenda to the decision of the Politbureau (measures against Mamontov):
1) appointment of *chiefs of every section* (10 to 30 versts, etc.) in case of encirclement, of whom 1-2 to be Communists.
2) those refusing to leave the railway cars to be shot on the spot;
3) further draconian measures to tighten discipline.
The right of decision to *introduce* these measures to be given to *Lashevich + Trotsky*.

((Redirect before reaching Moscow.))

+3) *Speed up* dispatch of *each troop train* of the 21st Division to go into immediate action against Mamontov with the addition (*if necessary*) of Communists.

Written at the end
of August 1919

First published in 1942   Printed from the manuscript
in *Lenin Miscellany XXXIV*

INTRODUCTION
OF ONE-MAN MANAGEMENT IN LIEU
OF BOARD MANAGEMENT IN CENTROTEXTIL

DRAFT DECISION
FOR THE COUNCIL OF PEOPLE'S COMMISSARS[147]

1) The S.E.C. to be instructed to gradually reduce the number of Board members, and in particular to study the experience of one-man management either by Communists or by specialists with Communist commissars attached to them.

2) Side by side with Board discussion and decision, steps to be taken to gradually introduce personal responsibility for the performance of both definite kinds of work and separate operations.

3) The S.E.C. and other commissariats having industrial enterprises to report within 2 months on the *actual* fulfilment of these tasks (especially as regards the number of workers who are being taught practical management and their record of experience in this connection).

Written September 4, 1919

First published in 1945   Printed from the manuscript
in *Lenin Miscellany XXXV*

NOTE TO G. V. CHICHERIN
AND DECISION OF THE POLITBUREAU
OF THE C.C., R.C.P.(B.)
ON RELATIONS WITH THE ENTENTE COUNTRIES

Comrade Chicherin,

I am sending you the decision of the Politbureau.[148]

Yours,
Lenin

(1) **Certainly.**
(2) *Not* in the name of the Government.
(3) Hasten Litvinov's departure.
(4) Confine ourselves to Gorky's letter, *but not* allow him
to use the argument about the struggle being turned
into annihilation.

Members of the Politbureau: *Lenin**

Written in September,
not before 26, 1919

First published in 1965   Printed from the manuscript
in the Fifth Russian Edition
of the *Collected Works*, Vol. 54

DRAFT DECISION FOR THE C.P.C.
ON THE CONFLICT BETWEEN THE S.E.C.
AND THE COMMISSARIAT FOR STATE CONTROL[149]

The C.P.C. considers:

1) that the State Control should have recommended the
S.E.C. to close its legal departments, but should not have
applied a proscriptive order;

2) that the Board of the S.E.C. should immediately
take energetic measures to close its legal departments,

---

* The decision was signed also by Kamenev, Trotsky and Krestinsky (the latter with the stipulation "I agree reservedly").—*Ed.*

most of which are parasitical, and to prohibit members of these departments from being hidden away in other departments. Fulfilment to be reported to the Narrow C.P.C.[150] within a week;

3) the Commissariat for Justice to take legal action against members of the legal departments of the Food Commissariat and the S.E.C. for red tape. Fulfilment to be reported to the Narrow Council within a week.

Written September 30, 1919

First published in 1965
in the Fifth Russian Edition
of the *Collected Works*, Vol. 54

Printed from the manuscript

SUGGESTIONS ON THE QUESTION
OF CO-OPERATION[151]

Suggestions

1) that Soltz should devote himself entirely to non-commercial activities (literary, instructor's work, and so forth) in the co-operatives,

2) that if this cannot be published as a separate edition, it should be published, i.e., printed, in *Izvestia*, *Pravda* and **Bednota**,[152]

3) that *factual* information *be* **quickly** collected, from at least small districts, concerning the extent to which the decree[153] is being carried out in general (in all its parts) and particularly concerning the methods of purveyance and distribution (bodies, forms, conditions, exceptions to the rule and so on), and the transformation, or beginning of the transformation, of bourgeois co-operation into communist co-operation, etc.

Written October 9, 1919

First published in 1959
in *Lenin Miscellany XXXVI*

Printed from the manuscript

INTERVIEW WITH MOHAMMAD WALI-KHAN
AMBASSADOR EXTRAORDINARY OF AFGHANISTAN
OCTOBER 14, 1919[154]

NEWSPAPER REPORT

Comrade Lenin met the Ambassador in his private office with the words, "I am very glad to see in the red capital of the worker and peasant government the representative of the friendly Afghan people, who are suffering and fighting against imperialist oppression." To which the Ambassador replied: "I proffer you a friendly hand and hope that you will help the whole of the East to free itself from the yoke of European imperialism." During the talk that followed, Lenin said that Soviet power, the power of the working people and the oppressed, was striving towards the very goal the Afghan Ambassador Extraordinary had spoken about, but that it was necessary that the Moslem East should realise this and help Soviet Russia in her great war of liberation. To this the Ambassador replied that he could assert that the Moslem East realised this and the hour was not far off when the world would see that there was no room for European imperialism in the East.

Afterwards the Ambassador stood up and with the words: "I have the honour of presenting my Sovereign's letter to the Head of the free Russian proletarian Government and hope that the Soviet Government will give due consideration to what the Afghan Government is writing about," he handed Lenin the Amir's letter. Comrade Lenin answered that he accepted the letter with the greatest pleasure and promised shortly to give a reply to all the questions Afghanistan was interested in.[155]

Pravda No. 232 and   Printed from the *Pravda* text
Izvestia No. 232,
October 17, 1919

SPEECH TO IVANOVO-VOZNESENSK
COMMUNIST WORKERS
LEAVING FOR THE FRONT
OCTOBER 24, 1919[156]

REPORTER'S NOTES

In his speech Comrade Lenin described the general situation at our fronts and pointed out that it was the duty of every intelligent worker to render the greatest possible assistance to our fronts in the matter of proper supply of munitions, food, clothing, etc.

He expressed his conviction that the communist workers of Ivanovo-Voznesensk would be able to exercise a beneficial influence on the peasants in the front-line area and be a great help in conducting political work among the Cossacks.

Pravda No. 239,   Printed from the *Pravda* text
October 25, 1919

SPEECH TO ADULT-EDUCATION COURSE STUDENTS
LEAVING FOR THE FRONT
OCTOBER 28, 1919

The conference opened with a speech by Lenin. He greeted the students of the courses, who had resolved to go out to the front to help the Red Army, and gave a vivid description of the present situation on all the fronts and in the enemy's rear.

The bourgeoisie, both of Russia and the West, had begun to celebrate victory prematurely. The Red troops were driving Kolchak before them. Denikin was retreating from Orel. There was demoralisation among the White troops. In Denikin's rear there were uninterrupted uprisings. Today even the prosperous Cossacks were going against him.

Yudenich had scant forces, consisting mainly of Englishmen. Britain had given him a large fleet. Yudenich's offensive was intended to save Denikin, draw our forces off, but his plan failed—the workers of Petrograd had displayed examples of heroism. Europe was tensely watching the outcome of the struggle. The workers of France and Britain had already registered their protest against the attack upon Russia. Bolshevism in these countries was gaining ground. The elections in France were very significant in this respect.[157] Our chief attention was now directed to the Southern Front, where indescribably furious and sanguinary battles were raging, and where the fate of the revolution in the West as well as in Russia was being decided....

Denikin's officer corps was well armed. In view of the uprisings in their rear, they were putting up a desperate fight. But the worker and peasant masses were beginning to see things clearer and there was a strong upsurge among them. Our weakness was that we had too few knowledgeable organisers among the peasants and workers. That was why we had so many old officials, saboteurs, etc., in our institutions. It was necessary to advance the best workers from among the people, and give them knowledge....

It was important to have social-minded people capable of talking to the peasants, people who would raise the morale of the army, and therefore everyone going to the front should show an example of bravery and selfless dedication. Victory then will be ours. We shall put transport in order and bring in grain....

First published in 1960 in the journal *Kommunist* No. 6

Printed from the handwritten copy of the minutes

MOTION ON THE QUESTION
OF A SINGLE FORESTRY BODY[158]

(1) Mutual control of institutions*
(2) speed up assignment of lots
(3) employing the labour force of forestry specialists
(4) other measures to expedite and increase fuel supply
(5) should they be merged?**

Written November 11, 1919

First published in 1959 in *Lenin Miscellany XXXVI*

Printed from the manuscript

* Implying forestry institutions.—*Ed.*
** This refers to the setting up of a single forestry body.—*Ed.*

DRAFT DECISION FOR THE C.P.C.
ON POTATO PURCHASES[159]

The draft of the Food Commissariat and § 4 of the S.E.C. draft[160] shall be accepted as a basis.

A commission to be set up to work out the whole draft in detail in order to establish with absolute accuracy both the separate districts (in Food Commissariat's §§) and the concrete measures to reinforce the Food Army at definite centres, enlist the co-operation of the workers, determine the amount of necessary and possible deliveries of spirit and starch, and so on.

The commission shall precisely formulate the Food Commissariat's responsibility for fulfilment of all emergency measures and their enforcement in a revolutionary manner so that this responsibility can be taken into account in the C.P.C.'s future policy.

The commission to consist of Scheinman (+2 F.C.*)

Rykov
Schmidt
Kamenev
Avanesov (or a Vecheka man)
Markov

The commission to be given 2 days and the C.P.C. to meet on Friday.[161]

Written November 18, 1919
First published in 1933
in *Lenin Miscellany XXIV*

Printed from the manuscript

---

* Meaning two representatives from the Food Commissariat.—*Ed.*

NOTES AT A MEETING OF DELEGATES
TO THE SECOND ALL-RUSSIA CONGRESS
OF COMMUNIST ORGANISATIONS
OF THE PEOPLES OF THE EAST[162]

Meeting 21/XI.1919

A) Basic tasks: fundamental significance of the communist organisations and parties of the East.

B) Party-organisational questions.

Combine territorial C) State-administrative questions.
principle with exter-
ritorial

+Exterritoriality?

D) *Concrete questions of each nation*,
according to the extent of its
development, its special features, etc.

+ Closest alliance E) Methods and measures of contact
with the Russian *with the poor*, *with the working
working* masses. *people*, *with the exploited of
every* nation against its bureau-
crats, feudalists, bourgeoisie.

First published in 1933   Printed from the manuscript
in *Lenin Miscellany XXIV*

DRAFT RESOLUTION
FOR THE C.C., R.C.P.(B.) PLENUM

Decision of C.C. (29.XI.1919)

Most Urgent

Chicherin to draw up detailed theses for a brief report to
the Congress of Soviets on peace and the text of a declaration by the congress.[163] This text to contain a direct
proposal of peace and peace negotiations without mention-

ing terms (such a variant to be submitted as will confirm all previous peace proposals, but without committing us).

First published in 1959
in *Lenin Miscellany XXXVI*

Printed from the manuscript

RE DRAFT RESOLUTION
FOR THE C.C., R.C.P.(B.) PLENUM
ON THE COMPOSITION OF THE ALL-RUSSIA
CENTRAL EXECUTIVE COMMITTEE[164]

1) Do not include all the People's Commissars (as well as the Chairman of the C.P.C.) and deputy commissars.
2) Reduce the number of intellectuals and Soviet officials of the centre.
3) Considerably increase the number of workers and working peasants who are definitely in close touch with the non-Party mass of workers and peasants.
6) Keep strictly in line with the decision of the Party congress.[165]

Written November 29, 1919

First published in 1959
in *Lenin Miscellany XXXVI*

Printed from the manuscript

ON IMPROVING THE MANAGEMENT
OF RAILWAY TRANSPORT

DRAFT DECISION FOR THE COUNCIL OF PEOPLE'S COMMISSARS[166]

The C.P.C. directs the Commissariat for Railways to draw up within a week a detailed decree (or instructions) concerning the participation of workers and workers' organisations, especially the trade unions, in the management of the railways, in training workers for management, etc.

Written December 2, 1919

First published in 1933
in *Lenin Miscellany XXIV*

Printed from the manuscript

REMARKS ON DRAFT REGULATIONS CONCERNING THE BUREAU OF THE R.C.P.(B.) GROUP AT THE ALL-RUSSIA CENTRAL COUNCIL OF TRADE UNIONS[167]

1) Both Comrade Tomsky and the whole Bureau of the All-Russia C.C.T.U. group (this Bureau must be endorsed by the Central Committee of the R.C.P.) are to be invited without fail to the meetings of the Organising Bureau of the C.C., R.C.P. when any question concerning the trade union movement is under discussion.

2) The bureau of the A.C.C.T.U. group works out a detailed charter of its relationships with the Orgbureau of the C.C. This charter to be endorsed by the Orgbureau.

3) The "Regulations on the R.C.P. Group of the A.C.C.T.U." to be amended as follows
   in § 1 the word "guiding" to be thrown out[168]
   in §§ 3[169] and? the word "C.C." (of the unions) to be inserted.

Revise everything relating to the wording of the different paragraphs*

revise in the above order, accepting the draft as a basis, and making only editorial corrections.

Written December,
not before 4, 1919

First published in 1963   Printed from the manuscript
in the Fifth Russian Edition
of the *Collected Works*, Vol. 39

THE WORK OF THE FOOD SUPPLY AGENCIES

DRAFT RESOLUTION

A commission to be elected to consider the question.

The chief and most pressing task to be dealt with is, first, renewal and reorganisation of the staffs of the food

---

* The text from the word "amended" was crossed out in the manuscript by Lenin.—*Ed.*

supply agencies; second, injecting a spirit of initiative into the work of these organisations.

Practical steps for carrying out these tasks to be outlined as follows:

enlisting the participation of the workers' co-operatives on the broadest basis;

ditto the bourgeois co-operatives, though on a narrower basis;

developing the workers' food inspection more rapidly into an organisation of workers' co-operation in all fields of food supply work;

introducing a bonus system for different groups of office employees, workers and specially recommended persons from among all groups of the population, whose participation in the work should be permitted and encouraged.

The commission is not to be limited to these tasks, which are to be accepted by it as an approximate definition of its general line of work.

Non-food-supply staff workers
to be elected to the commission.
              I suggest for the commission
                     Kamenev
              V. D. Bonch-Bruyevich
                     Schmidt

Enlist without fail, not as a member of the commission	*Orlov*, author of the book *The Food Supply Work of the Soviet Government*

                     Yakovleva
                     Sosnovsky.

Written December 6, 1919

First published in 1933
in *Lenin Miscellany XXIV*   Printed from the manuscript

ROUGH DRAFT FOR THE C.P.C. DECISION ON MOSCOW'S FOOD SUPPLY[170]

("Statement of facts")

Labour rations?

exact information re grain-collecting places and state of transport

1) Agreement to be formally signed[171]

2) Daily reports to be reintroduced[172]

3) Workers to be mobilised on transport

{ task to be entrusted to Moscow Trade Union Council + Commissariat for Railways

4) Specially urgent: consider measures for transporting potatoes and controlling deliveries

5) Emergency issue (meat?) to be approved.

Written December 6, 1919

First published in 1933 in *Lenin Miscellany XXIV*

Printed from the manuscript

DRAFT C.P.C. DECISION ON GRAIN CONSIGNMENTS TO MOSCOW BY THROUGH TRAINS[173]

1) The Food Commissariat shall be found guilty of gross negligence in the performance of an extremely important assignment.

2) A complaint against the Commissariat for Post and Telegraph shall be formally lodged with the Chairman of the C.P.C. *within an hour* of complete failure to obtain a direct line and an answer by it.[174]

3) Inquiries shall be instituted into the conduct of the gubernia food commissars for non-fulfilment of or failure through bad organisation to fulfil the order of the People's Commissariat for Food.[175]

4) An official to be attached to the Food Commissariat to take proper charge of lines.

5) The C.P.C. to meet on Saturday* to check fulfilment and discuss a decision on delivery orders.

6) An explanation in writing to be demanded of the Post and Telegraph Commissariat in regard to the delay in delivering Food Commissariat telegrams, and an indication of measures or law amendments necessary to ensure the urgent transmission of the Food Commissariat's orders.

Written December 23, 1919

First published in 1933   Printed from the manuscript
in *Lenin Miscellany XXIV*

LETTER TO P. I. POPOV

(RE CONSUMPTION BY THE POPULATION OF THE R.S.F.S.R. BEFORE AND AFTER THE OCTOBER REVOLUTION) [176]

1

Comrade Popov,

Will you please—if it is not too much trouble to you—return the enclosed table to me with your remarks:

on the basis of statistical science and its modern data on Russia

(aa) could such a table be drawn up or not (on the strength, at least, of insufficient data)?

(bb) if it could, what would be the chief corrections?

(cc) would any of your specialists undertake to draw up such a table (even if with a wider amplitude of fluctuations)?

Yours,
Lenin

2

Assuming (in a round figure, for the sake of simplification and easy memorising) that the population of the R.S.F.S.R. = 50 million

* December 27, 1919.—*Ed.*

How do they eat? (today)	% of the popu- lation	How did they eat be- fore the war (before 1914-1917)? on the average, say, for 10 or 15 years before the war
a) 10 mill. workers = 50-60% of norm	20%	70-80% of norm
b) 20 mill. poor peasants = 70-80% of norm	40%	50-60% of norm
c) 15 mill. middle peas- ants = 90-100% of norm	30%	60-70% of norm
d) 4 mill. rich peasants = = 120-150% of norm	8%	or 90%? 100% of norm or 110-120%?
e) 1 mill. former land- owners, capitalists, high officials, etc. = 60-70% of norm	2%	150-200% of norm
	100%	

{ The norm to be considered the amount of bread, meat,
{ milk, eggs, and so on, a person needs according to science,
    i.e., the norm is not the amount of calories, but the
amount of food of a definite quality.

    By workers is to be understood industrial workers,
the non-worker urban population coming under the
corresponding groups c and d.

Social types:
  a) proletarian and semi-proletarian urban population
  b) ditto—rural
  c) middle peasantry and generally petty-bourgeois popu-
     lation nearest to it
  d) rich peasants and urban middle bourgeoisie
  e) higher classes.

Written late December 1919
  First published in 1933   Printed from the manuscript
in *Lenin Miscellany XXIV*

DRAFT DECISION
FOR THE C.P.C. ON THE QUESTION OF SUPPLYING THE WORKERS WITH CLOTHES AND FOOTWEAR[177]

The Narrow Council to be instructed immediately, but not later than Saturday,* to revise its decision, leaving its basic and general parts intact, but changing the figures of issue to the workers in accordance with the new military plans of army increase. Comrade Rykov to issue an exactly worded mandate to his representative and only he is to be admitted.[178]

Written December 30, 1919

First published in 1965
in the Fifth Russian Edition
of the *Collected Works*, Vol. 54

Printed from the manuscript

DRAFT DECISION FOR THE C.P.C.
ON INSTRUCTIONS CONCERNING PURVEYANCE OF RAW MATERIALS[179]

The Board of the S.E.C. to be directed, not later than Saturday,* to revise the instructions in such a manner as to ensure that the decision of the Seventh Congress of the Soviets will be fully carried out, in particular
1) on the question of the right of objection,[180]
2) the surplus-appropriation principle to be more fully and strictly applied;
3) rights and conditions for the display of local initiative and its stimulation to be worked out in detail;
4) methods for combating red tape to be worked out.
The full draft instructions mentioned in the decision of the Seventh Congress of the Soviets to be presented within a week.[181]

Written December 30, 1919

First published in 1933
in *Lenin Miscellany XXIV*

Printed from the manuscript

* January 3, 1920.—*Ed.*

RE TRANSPORT DEPARTMENT OF VECHEKA

DRAFT DECISION FOR THE COUNCIL OF DEFENCE [182]

16.I.1920

The Vecheka is to issue within three weeks detailed instructions not only governing the activities of the Transport Dept. of the Vecheka, but establishing strict responsibility of the Department's agents for oversight and failure to report cases of sabotage or profiteering.

In particular the agents of the T.D. of the Vecheka must be in contact with the communist and trade union cells of the truly proletarian section of the railwaymen who do not abuse their position for the purpose of systematic black-marketing.

First published in 1933 in *Lenin Miscellany XXIV*

Printed from the manuscript

DRAFT DECISION FOR THE POLITBUREAU OF THE C.C., R.C.P.(B.)

The People's Commissariat for Foreign Affairs is to adopt a policy of extreme restraint and mistrust towards the Azerbaijan Government in view of the latter's refusal to accept our offer of joint military operations against Denikin and the services it is rendering to the military forces of Britain operating against us in the Caspian Sea. While emphatically stressing our undeviating recognition of the right of the working masses of every nation to self-determination, the Commissariat for Foreign Affairs should vigorously protest against such conduct on the part of the Azerbaijan Government.[183]

Written in January, not before 17, 1920

First published in 1959 in *Lenin Miscellany XXXVI*

Printed from the manuscript

DECISION OF THE POLITBUREAU
OF THE C.C., R.C.P.(B.)
IN CONNECTION WITH THE ENTENTE'S ATTEMPT
TO START TRADE RELATIONS WITH RUSSIA
THROUGH THE RUSSIAN CO-OPERATIVES

In view of the Entente's intention to effect an exchange of commodities through the co-operatives with the patent design of using the co-operatives as an instrument for restoring capitalism, the C.C. instructs the Chairman of Centrosoyuz, the People's Commissariat for Food, the Chairman of the S.E.C. and the People's Commissariat for Trade to consider the question of the co-operatives very carefully from this angle and immediately work out measures ensuring full control on our part of the co-operative machinery primarily at all the points where such trade may be arranged (the Ukraine, the Soviet Far East).

Written January 17 or 18,
              1920

First published in 1963
in the Fifth Russian Edition,
of the *Collected Works*, Vol. 40

Printed from the typewritten
copy of the minutes·

DRAFT DECISION
FOR THE POLITBUREAU OF THE C.C., R.C.P.(B.)
ON THE COMMANDER-IN-CHIEF'S PROTEST
CONCERNING THE ORDER TO THE COMMANDER
OF THE TURKESTAN FRONT[184]

1) The order by Lenin and Trotsky given by telegram is found to be correct.
2) Exception taken to the form of this order is considered a case of undesirable military bureaucratism.
3) The Commander-in-Chief is to be notified that his verbal protest made through Comrade Smilga has been considered

and found incorrect. When an opinion is asked for, it should be given.

Written January 17 or 18,
1920
First published in 1965   Printed from the manuscript
in the Fifth Russian Edition
of the *Collected Works*, Vol. 54

POLITBUREAU OF THE C.C., R.C.P.(B.)
DIRECTIVES
ON A WORKERS' INSPECTION[185]

The Presidium of the All-Russia Central Executive Committee and the State Control Commissariat to be asked to be guided by the following directives of the C.C., R.C.P.:

1. No new bodies to be set up in any field of state administration, and the existing commissariats to be improved.

2. The Workers' and Peasants' Inspection to be developed, strengthened and extended in every way, all work being directed towards ensuring complete numerical predominance of workers and peasants in State Control.

3. No skilled workers, only unskilled workers, mainly women, to be enlisted in the Workers' Inspection.

4. A new draft of Workers' and Peasants' Inspection under the State Control Commissariat to be drawn up immediately with the co-operation of Avanesov and submitted to the Politbureau not later than 28.I.1920.

Written January 23, 1920
First published in 1928   Printed from the manuscript
in *Lenin Miscellany VIII*

DIRECTIONS CONCERNING THE WORK
OF THE PROPAGANDA-INSTRUCTOR
TRAINS AND STEAMERS[186]

1. Specifically:

1) Step up economic and practical aspects of the work of the trains and steamers by including agronomists and technicians in their political departments, by selecting technical literature, films on appropriate subjects, etc.

2) Production films (showing various branches of production), agricultural, industrial, anti-religious and scientific films to be made through the Film Committee, the film material to be ordered immediately from abroad through Comrade Litvinov. Telegraphic order to be given over Lenin's signature.

3) A large-scale volost map to be drawn up demonstrating all the work done and indicating the districts. This map to be exhibited to the public in open places.

4) Material received during trips to be worked up and diagrams, charts, etc., to be published.

5) Attention to be given to the need for a careful selection of films with due consideration of the effect of every film on the population during its demonstration.

6) The work of the trains and steamers to be extended beyond range of the tracks and riverbanks by making wider use of auxiliary forms of transport (motorcycles, motor-cars, bicycles) carried in the trains and steamers, as well by the use of local conveyances.

7) Agencies to be organised abroad for purchasing and shipping films, camera film and all kinds of photographic supplies.

8) Attention to be paid to the staffing of the trains and steamers.

9) Comrade Burov to be given the right in urgent cases where the activities of the All-Russia C.E.C.'s instructor trains and steamers are concerned to apply to Comrade Lenin directly and in less urgent cases to apply to Comrade Lenin through his secretary.

2. Generally:

1) A meeting of representatives of the All-Russia C.E.C., the C.C., the People's Commissariats and the political workers on the trains and steamers to be called immediately through the C.C. of the Party. This meeting is to consider the results of the work done by the trains and steamers and draw up regulations governing trips on behalf of the All-Russia C.E.C., the C.C. and the C.P.C.

2) These regulations to be put through the C.C. and the C.P.C. by Comrade Lenin.

3) A Special Standing Commission under the C.P.C. is to be summoned to take charge of trips in accordance with the drafted regulations.

Written January 25, 1920

Published in part in 1920
in the symposium
Agittrains and Steamers
of All-Russia C.E.C. *Their History,*
Apparatus, Methods and Forms,
Moscow

First published in full in 1932   Printed from the text of the book
in the book:
N. K. Krupskaya, *Collected Works,*
Vol. II,
"Political Educational Work"

DRAFT DECISION FOR THE C.P.C.
ON UNLOADING POTATOES
AND SNOW CLEARING OF MOSCOW'S STREETS
AND RAILWAY TRACKS[187]

1. The People's Commissariat for Food to be instructed within three days to draft a decision for resumption of the potato campaign and submit it to the C.P.C.[188]

2. Burdukov + Kamenev, Dzerzhinsky and Kursky to be instructed to present information concerning the number of adult and healthy men, their off-work hours and their possible employment for urgent jobs in the city, and a draft decision on their employment.

3. The Vecheka to be instructed to appoint a responsible and experienced investigator belonging to the Party to study the material relating to the unsatisfactory state of labour service organisation in Moscow both among the workers and office staffs.

Report to the C.P.C. to be made by Dzerzhinsky or his deputy within four days.

4. The People's Commissariat for Internal Affairs to be instructed to take more energetic steps to implement snow-clearing compulsory service and to report on this to the C.P.C. within three days.[189]

Written January 27, 1920
First published in 1933   Printed from the manuscript
in *Lenin Miscellany XXIV*

NOTES CONCERNING THE DRAFT REGULATIONS ON BONUSES FOR WORKERS AND OFFICE EMPLOYEES

1.II.1920

Regarding bonuses, I have strong doubts.

§ 4—absolutely arbitrary fixing of the standard (50%—exactly 50%—from "the best", i.e., given the best machines, etc. This is quite arbitrary. Can't we have it more exact? Publish standards for control? Or collect them for the scientific-technical department, etc., and publish in a bulletin?).

Account of results: top limit of bonuses. Accounts on this not provided for. Will this not virtually legalise gross abuses?

Consumers should be enlisted for standard control. Are there any examples of this? Among the co-operatives? and so on.

The draft is too sweeping, abstract, unbusiness-like; promises everything, verifies nothing.[190]

Lenin

First published in 1945   Printed from the manuscript
in *Lenin Miscellany XXXV*

SPEECH AT A CONFERENCE OF CHAIRMEN OF GUBERNIA AND UYEZD EXECUTIVE COMMITTEES FEBRUARY 1, 1920

At a meeting of executive committee chairmen preceding the opening of the session,[191] Lenin said, in dealing with the current situation:

In so far as the international situation stays as it is, and the whole course of events points to its stability, the tasks of economic activities should be advanced by us to the fore. As regards transport, we not only have to bring this to the fore, but simply drag this transport out by the ears, save it from imminent disaster. Trains carrying grain are stopping, we have more grain than we can transport. Military operations are often impeded through lack of transport. February is the most difficult month for transport, and we are simply heading for disaster.

We are threatened by a danger of transport dislocation more serious than in October, when Yudenich and Denikin were winning their biggest victories. More energy must be applied to save transport. We must carry out mobilisations here again and again. We shall have to rob a number of institutions of their workers and keep on robbing them to combat the chaos in transport.

The whole art of government and policy-making consists in being able to assess and know in good time where to concentrate your main forces and attention. We must now extricate transport in the course of two months. Unless we work the same miracle in two months with transport as we have done with Kolchak, disaster threatens us.

A number of vigorous and revolutionary measures are needed. This is a military and combat task and calls for combat action in military style.

Krasnaya Gazeta (Petrograd)   Printed from the newspaper text
No. 24, February 3, 1920

DRAFT DECISIONS FOR THE COUNCIL
OF DEFENCE ON THE STATE OF TRANSPORT

Meeting of 2/II.1920[192]

(1) $50 \to 100\%$ express goods trains.
(2) Kazan Railway.
(3) Samara-Zlatoust-Chelyabinsk
        ?
    {speed up food trains.
(4) Step up loading of food in Chelyabinsk district.
(5) Send top-level men out to the repair shops (of Petrograd and Moscow).

(6) Bonuses in the form of clothing outfits.

(7) Repair trains at the Western Front.

+ (8) Sending Arzhanov out.

+ (9) Military aides for railway superintendents.

— (10) 1 railway to be given to the army.

(11) Vecheka workers to be transferred to transport jobs.

(12) Repair works to be placed on same footing as transport works.

(13) Chuso* stocks handed over to the Food Commissariat are to be given to the transport workmen.

(14) Railway specialists from the C.P.W.** and other departments of S.E.C. and other bodies to be transferred to transport jobs.	mobi-lisa-tion

(15) Military forces to fight snowdrifts to be increased (40,000).

(16) ad 5 + members of the All-Russia C.E.C.

(17) Step up repair subbotniks.

(18) Martial law 30-50 versts.

(19) More personnel in volosts near the railway lines.

(20) Specially step up fuel work.

(21) Ask Orgbureau of C.C. to issue a Party circular and step up work in this direction.

(22) Revise rail freightage plan for increased food and fuel freights.

(23) Close some factories and switch them over for repairs.

(24) Prepare spades and mittens.

(25) Snowploughs and their distribution.

(26) Briefing of track maintenance agents.

POSTSCRIPT TO DECISIONS
OF THE COUNCIL OF DEFENCE
ON THE STATE OF TRANSPORT

I draw the particular attention of all leading Soviet workers to these decisions. The state of transport is

---

* Chuso (Chusosnabarm)—Extraordinary Representative of the Council of Defence for Army Supply.—*Ed.*

** C.P.W.—Committee of Public Works.—*Ed.*

desperate. Truly heroic and revolutionary measures are needed to save it.

2/II.1920 *Lenin*

First published in 1933   Printed from the manuscript
in *Lenin Miscellany XXIV*

PRIVILEGES FOR LOCOMOTIVE REPAIR WORKERS

DRAFT DECISION FOR THE C.P.C.[193]

1) Publish reports about goods trains as a reward for repairs.

2) Instruct the Commissariat for Railways to draw up such a plan of rewards as would provide only for essential repairs being made on goods trains, and not special repairs.

3) All data concerning goods train repairs to be collected and supplemented, and passed on to the Central Statistical Board to be worked up.

4) The A.C.C.T.U. and the Moscow, Petrograd, Ivanovo and Tver trade union councils to be charged with working up the question of using the best workshops for repairs all 24 hours of the day.[194]

Written February 5, 1920

First published in 1933   Printed from the manuscript
in *Lenin Miscellany XXIV*

SPEECH AT THE FOURTH CONFERENCE OF GUBERNIA EXTRAORDINARY COMMISSIONS[195] FEBRUARY 6, 1920

Comrades, you will now have to carry on your work under conditions when Soviet Russia is passing to a new phase of activities. You all know, of course, that these conditions of the transition period are due both to international and internal conditions, or rather to the changed situation both on the international and home fronts that has taken place recently.

The fundamental change is that the main forces of the whiteguard counter-revolution have been smashed after the defeat of Yudenich and Kolchak and after the victory over Denikin. We have to be cautious, though, since a hitch has recently occurred near Rostov and at Novocherkassk, and there is a danger that Denikin may recover. Nevertheless, the main victories create a new situation. Obviously, the bourgeoisie cannot seriously count on things taking a turn in their favour, all the more as the international situation, too, has changed greatly, changed to such an extent that the Entente has been obliged to lift the blockade. We have been able to conclude peace with Estonia. In this respect we have achieved a basic success which has greatly strengthened our position, and we shall probably secure peace with all the other border states, and then an invasion by the Entente will practically be ruled out.

Thus, the first acute moment of our struggle with the counter-revolution, with the whiteguard armed force, both overt and covert—this first acute period is apparently passing. It is more than likely, however, that attempts at one or another counter-revolutionary movement and revolt will be repeated, and, besides, the experience of the Russian revolutionary movement shows that attempts of a purely terrorist nature are often accompanied by a mass armed struggle, and therefore it is natural to expect that the counter-revolutionary armed officer force—an element probably most accustomed to handling and using arms—will not miss a chance to make use of these arms for their own ends.

So though the death sentence, after the capture of Rostov, has been abolished on Comrade Dzerzhinsky's initiative, a reservation was made at the very beginning that we do not by any means close our eyes to the possibility of restoring capital punishment. With us this is a matter of expediency. It goes without saying that the Soviet government will not keep the death penalty longer than is absolutely necessary, and by doing away with it, has taken a step that no democratic government of any bourgeois republic has ever taken.

You are aware that the great majority of the workers and peasants in all the outlying districts, who were under the yoke of the whiteguards, have come over to our side. The longer they were under that yoke the more strongly have they sided with us. And so we know that all the attempts of the bourgeoisie are doomed to failure. But that these attempts are possible, we know only too well from the two years' experience of Soviet power. We have seen tens of thousands of officers, landowner elements, stopping at no crimes, concluding agreements with the agents of imperialist foreign powers to blow up bridges. And we say that attempts like these will go on. With due consideration for the new general position of the state, we must nevertheless remain alert and remember that though the period of armed struggle on a big historical scale is coming to end, we must on no account exclude the possibility of our having to keep in a state of preparedness.

The problem set before the agencies of suppression of the counter-revolution, before the agencies of the Cheka, and still facing them today, is a complex and difficult one. On the one hand, they must realise and make allowance for the transition from war to peace, and, on the other, they must be on guard all the time, since we do not know how long it will take to secure a lasting peace; we must take into account what effect this new approach will have on the bourgeois sections of the population, we must bear in mind, test in practice what these changes will yield, and only after all this has been taken into consideration, introduce one or another modification on the basis of such practical experience.

In a word, we must continue to keep fighting fit to be able to repulse the enemy. There may possibly be attempts at invasion, Denikin may possibly fortify his position to continue the civil war, there may possibly be attempts at terror on the part of groups of counter-revolutionaries, and it is our duty to be always in fighting trim. While keeping in fighting trim, keeping the apparatus for suppressing the resistance of the exploiters alerted, we must take into account the new transition from war to peace and gradually change our tactics, change the nature of repressive measures.

This question, I believe, played no small part in your discussions, and you, of course, have much more to go on than I have in the matter of practical concrete decisions. I have no doubt that you will try to study this material in a concrete, practical way. You must work out in what direction the agencies for suppressing the counter-revolution are to modify their activities in the recently liberated parts of Russia, in Siberia and the Ukraine, how, in keeping with this, we are to change our activities. I shall not go into details or enlarge on this, because I have not had a chance to study the factual material, but I repeat—the important thing is to take into account the concrete facts that have come to light in the work of every Cheka. Moreover, the aim of such conferences is to enable you to discuss the factual material in greatest possible detail, so that local workers should not shut themselves up in their own narrow circle, but should be able, as a result of such an exchange of opinions, to devise more durable and lasting tactics.

I should like in particular to draw attention to a question that now confronts the agencies of suppression of the counter-revolution, the agencies combating espionage and profiteering, namely, to the bloodless front of labour, a question that is now becoming a key issue in the building up of Soviet power, in the strengthening of the workers' and peasants' rule and the revival of the ruined economy.

You know that the task of fighting Kolchak, Yudenich and Denikin, who have been supported by the Entente, the task of fighting the counter-revolutionary landowners and capitalists who were convinced up till now that their victory was secure, since the wealthiest Powers in the world were on their side—this task called for an exertion of all the country's strength, because the very existence of the Soviet Republic was at stake.

During these two years Soviet power can be said to have accomplished what is nothing short of a miracle, for in the struggle against international capital we have succeeded in winning such an incredible, such an amazing victory as the world has never known. This has happened because all our forces were closely united, because we had a real dictatorship of the proletariat in action in the sense that the vanguard, the best advance guard of the working class during these two years of Soviet government displayed unheard-of heroism and determination, while all the vacillating elements among the less developed section of the working class and the peasantry, who went through a long range of fluctuations, found themselves leaning more and more to our side. The more trials they went through, the sooner did they side with us.

To achieve such a concentration of forces we had to resort to measures of coercion in face of all the lamentations, regrets and complaints. Both before and after the October Revolution we held the view that the birth of a new order was impossible without revolutionary coercion, that all the regrets and complaints that we hear from non-Party petty-bourgeois intellectuals are simply reactionary. History, which is propelled by a fierce class struggle, has shown that when the landowners and capitalists felt that it was a question of the last decisive fight, they stopped at nothing.

History has shown that without revolutionary coercion victory cannot be achieved. Without revolutionary coercion directed against the avowed enemies of the workers and peasants, it is impossible to break down the resistance of these exploiters. On the other hand, revolutionary coercion is bound to be employed towards the wavering and unstable elements among the masses themselves.

Today we are witnessing the tremendous victory of the Red Army, but if we look back over the last two years of Soviet government and think of how we advanced towards these victories, we are bound to remember that the October Revolution started when the army was completely demoralised and there was a complete absence of any military organisation. We had no army, and were obliged to scrape one together, to weld, muster and build this army up anew by long hard work. And in building up this new disciplined Red Army we had to resort to revolutionary coercion. And this revolutionary coercion was quite rightly applied to self-seeking elements. At a time when the advanced section of the population were giving all their strength to the fight against the counter-revolution, at a time when thousands of them, with the greatest self-sacrifice, were laying down their lives on the fields of battle, the backward elements among the peasantry, who had received land, and the backward elements among the workers, were working only for themselves. At that time the advanced elements had to build up and strengthen the new discipline, which was maintained by revolutionary coercion and which could be so maintained only because the public-spirited section of the workers and peasants, of all the working masses, sympathised with this coercion, realised that without this iron discipline we could not have built up the Red Army, could not have held our own in the two years of struggle and generally could not have stood up against organised and united capital. In this respect, the tasks of cultivating discipline, maintaining discipline and rallying our forces to face the coming struggle—these tasks are now gradually being modified. At first we gave all our forces to the war, all the forces of the ruined country. This condemned the country to still greater ruin.

No one believed two years ago that Russia, a country ravaged by four years of imperialist war, could withstand another two years of civil war. In fact, if we were asked at the end of October 1917 whether we would survive two years of civil war against the world's bourgeoisie, I doubt whether many of us would have answered in the affirmative. Events, however, have shown that the energy which the worker and peasant masses developed proved to be greater than the people who had made the October Revolution believed. As a result, we have received—and the home fronts have shown us—a source of new strength considerably greater than anything we had counted on. At the same time this source has shown that the Red Army, which is capable of winning victories on the war fronts, is meeting with new obstacles on the home fronts—this is particularly the case in transport. Of course, things are bad with us as regards food, too, cold and hunger are worse than ever now, but with the liberation of the richest grain-producing gubernias the food situation is improving, and our chief crisis now is transport. It should be said that the same crisis exists in all the richest countries, who have never experienced such a long war. Even these countries are suffering from a shortage of railway cars. So you can imagine what is happening with us in Russia, who has been at war six years and had had her bridges and locomotives deliberately destroyed.

Our position, in this respect, is a very difficult one, of course, and the task of the Cheka's transport departments, of their whole organism, the efforts of all the revolutionary social-minded masses, are aimed at helping the country to extricate itself from this critical plight, which without exaggeration can be said to verge on catastrophe. Another thing to be borne in mind is that the state of the railways in February, what with the winter snowdrifts, is always worse, even during ordinary times, than at any other season. At present our transport crisis has reached a stage when the railways are threatened with a complete stoppage. Lately, Moscow has had only a three-day supply of bread, while dozens of trains have been held up through lack of fuel.

We are well aware of the methods for coping with this disastrous situation, which we have been using during two years of war. These methods are—raising the social consciousness of the masses and appealing directly to them. In every such crisis we deemed it our duty to appeal to the worker and peasant masses and describe to them the difficult situation that had arisen. We appealed to them and pointed out on whom the salvation of Soviet Russia depended and what effort was needed to concentrate on a single definite task. These tasks often changed while Soviet power was engaged in fighting its enemies, and a proper understanding of the state's position depends upon the ability to grasp what tasks have to be tackled in order to cope with the economic chaos and pass on to the normal work of economic organisation. Now, too, you know that most attention was given to explaining the critical position of the railways to the workers and peasants. A tremendous effort is needed here on the part of the proletariat and the peasantry. Such a thing as the delivery of fuel is a difficult problem, which cannot possibly be coped with unless the worker and peasant population give themselves to the task with enthusiasm, unless there is a spurt of collective mass effort such as we witnessed during the best period of the Red Army's victories. Today, for example, the delivery of fuel and the clearing of railway tracks meet with difficulties arising from the fact that the peasants were given a number of promises to compensate them for their food products. Naturally, deliveries require draft horses, and the peasants out there are unable to provide these, they are very unwilling and unfriendly, as they do not receive compensation in the way of a definite amount of goods; and we, owing to the almost complete stoppage of transport, are not in a position to give them any commodities worth speaking of. We say that the peasants should do this as a loan to their workers' and peasants' state in order to save the starving workers and put industry on its feet. The peasants should give this loan, because, for instance, in some places the peasantry are suffering terribly from a shortage of salt, while we have enormous stocks of this salt which we are unable to deliver since the railways do not cope with the task of transporting the absolutely essential amount of breadstuffs.

We have here a situation that calls for still greater discipline, for propaganda and agitation to educate and unite all the workers and peasants. The use of revolutionary coercion turns this discipline into something real and definite, showing that the class-conscious working class has set itself a definite practical task, which we shall see through to its conclusion. Just as in the period of our most difficult struggle against Yudenich, Kolchak and Denikin, when we advanced Communists, leading workers, to the front ranks, made great sacrifices, giving the lives of our best fighters and at the same time building up discipline and punishing self-seekers—we achieved the maximum exertion of the people's energy, and we won; so today, too, we must set ourselves the same aim and achieve it at all costs by the same methods if we are to save transport.

We have grain, salt, we have sufficient quantities of raw materials and fuel, we can put industry back on its feet, but this will take months of hard efforts, and in these efforts the agencies of the Cheka must become an instrument for carrying out the centralised will of the proletariat, an instrument of discipline such as we succeeded in creating in the Red Army.

And I am sure that after this meeting, in the practical work of your agencies, and here, too, you will come to an understanding of the role the uyezd transport departments of the Cheka are to play, of the way they should organise their work, how they should advance new people from their

midst in order to fight the profiteers and saboteurs, who
are more numerous among the railwaymen than anywhere
else. This is a task of your practical experience, a task you
will have to carry out by way of an exchange of opinions.
The railways are notable in that we have there a majority
of workers on a working-class level and a minority who
engage in profiteering, and here it is the task of the Transport
Cheka to secure a correct division of labour, responsibility
for economising labour power, and secure all this through
the efforts of the communist elements among the railwaymen.
Only by relying on these best masses shall we be able to
create a force that will cope with profiteers and gain the
upper hand over these elements, recruited during the worst
days of tsarism. To overcome this force inherited by us
from capitalism we have one means—that of tightening
discipline and developing revolutionary energy to the utmost.
The Cheka should rely on the communist groups, on the
trade unions—combine its work with propaganda and
agitation, evoke among the bulk of the railwaymen a conscious attitude towards this struggle.

And I am sure that by strict organisation and with our
previous experience to go on, we shall achieve in our work
results as good as those we achieved in the armed struggle.
(*Loud, continuous applause.*)

First published in 1957
in the magazine *Kommunist* No. 5

Printed from the shorthand
report

DRAFT RESOLUTION
ON THE UKRAINIAN BOROTBIST PARTY[196]

The Borotbists shall be qualified as a party, which,
by its propaganda aimed at splitting the military forces
and supporting banditism, is violating the basic principles
of communism, thereby playing directly into the hands
of the Whites and of international imperialism.

Also opposed to the interests of the proletariat is their
struggle against the slogan calling for a close alliance
with the R.S.F.S.R.

The whole policy must be systematically and steadily aimed at the dissolution of the Borotbists in the near future. To this end, not a single misdeed on the part of the Borotbists should be allowed to pass without being immediately and strictly punished. In particular, information should be collected concerning the non-proletarian and most disloyal nature of the majority of their party members.

The moment for their dissolution shall be determined within a short time by the Politbureau and communicated to the Ukrainian Revolutionary Committee.[197]

Written February 6, 1920

First published in 1945   Printed from the manuscript
in *Lenin Miscellany XXXV*

INTERVIEW WITH LINCOLN EYRE, CORRESPONDENT OF THE AMERICAN NEWSPAPER *THE WORLD*[198]

ALLIES PLAYING "CHESS GAME"

Of the Allies' reported decision to lift the blockade Lenin said:

"It is hard to see sincerity behind so vague a proposal, coupled as it seems to be with preparations to attack us afresh through Poland. At first glance the Supreme Council's proposition looks plausible enough—the resumption of commercial relations through the medium of the Russian co-operatives. But the co-operatives do not any longer exist, having been assimilated into our Soviet distribution organs. Therefore what is meant when the Allies talk of dealing with the co-operatives? Certainly it is not clear.

"Therefore I say that closer examination convinces us that this Paris decision is simply a move in the Allied chess game the motives of which are still obscure."

Lenin paused a moment, then added with a broad grin:

"Far obscurer, for instance, than Marshal Foch's intended visit to Warsaw."

I asked if he deemed the probability of a Polish offensive serious (it must be recalled that in Russia the talk was of a drive by the Poles against the Bolsheviki, not vice versa).

"Beyond doubt," Lenin replied, "Clemenceau and Foch are very, very serious gentlemen, and the one originated and the other is going to carry out this offensive scheme. It is a grave menace, of course, but we have faced graver ones. It does not cause us fear so much as disappointment that the Allies should still pursue the impossible. For a Polish offensive can no more settle the Russian problem for them than did Kolchak's and Denikin's. Poland has many troubles of her own, remember. And it is obvious that she can get no help from any of her neighbours, including Roumania."

"Yet peace seems nearer than before," I suggested.

"Yes, that's true. If peace is a corollary of trade with us, the Allies cannot avoid it much longer. I have heard that Millerand, Clemenceau's successor, expresses willingness to envisage commercial relations with the Russian people. Perhaps this heralds a change of front among the French capitalists. But Churchill is still strong in England, and Lloyd George, who probably wants to do business with us, dare not risk an open rupture with the political and financial interests supporting the Churchill policy."

UNITED STATES OPPRESSES SOCIALISTS

"And America?"

"It is hard to see clearly what is going on there. Your bankers seem to fear us more than ever. At any rate, your Government is instituting more violently repressive measures not only against the socialists but against the working class in general than any other government, even the reactionary French. Apparently it is persecuting foreigners. And yet, what would America be without her foreign workers? They are an absolute necessity to your economic development.

"Still, some American manufacturers appear to have begun to realise that making money in Russia is wiser than making war against Russia, which is a good sign. We shall need American manufactures—locomotives, automobiles, etc.—more than those of any other country."

"And your peace terms?"

"It is idle to talk further about them," Lenin returned emphatically. "All the world knows that we are prepared to make peace on terms the fairness of which even the most imperialistic capitalists could not dispute. We have reiterated and reiterated our desire for peace, our need for peace and our readiness to give foreign capital the most generous concessions and guarantees. But we do not propose to be strangled to death for the sake of peace.

"I know of no reason why a socialistic commonwealth like ours cannot do business indefinitely with capitalistic countries. We don't mind taking their capitalistic locomotives and farming machinery, so why should they mind taking our socialistic wheat, flax and platinum. Socialistic corn tastes the same as any other corn, does it not? Of course, they will have to have business relations with the dreadful Bolsheviks—that is, the Soviet Government. But it should not be harder for American steel manufacturers, for instance, to deal with the Soviets than it was for them to deal with Entente governments in their war-time munition deals."

EUROPE DEPENDENT ON RUSSIA

"That is why this talk of reopening trade with Russia through co-operatives seems to us insincere, or at least, obscure—a move in a game of chess rather than a frank, straightforward proposition that would be immediately grasped and acted upon. Moreover, if the Supreme Council really means to lift the blockade, why doesn't it tell us of its intentions? We are without official word from Paris. What little we know is derived from newspaper despatches picked up by our wireless.

"The statesmen of the Entente and the United States do not seem to understand that Russia's present economic distress is simply a part of the world's economic distress. Until the economic problem is faced from a world standpoint and not merely from the standpoint of certain nations or group of nations, a solution is impossible. Without Russia, Europe cannot get on her feet. And with Europe prostrate, America's position becomes critical. What good is America's wealth if she cannot buy with it that which she needs?

America cannot eat or wear the gold she has accumulated, can she? She can't trade profitably, that is, on a basis that will be of real value to her, with Europe until Europe is able to give her the things she wants in exchange for that which she has to give. And Europe cannot give her those things until she is on her feet economically."

WORLD NEEDS RUSSIAN GOODS

"In Russia we have wheat, flax, platinum, potash and many minerals of which the whole world stands in desperate need. The world must come to us for them in the end, Bolshevism or no Bolshevism. There are signs that a realisation of this truth is gradually awakening. But meanwhile not only Russia but all Europe is going to pieces, and the Supreme Council still indulges in tergiversation. Russia can be saved from utter ruin and Europe too, but it must be done soon and quickly. And the Supreme Council is so slow, so very slow. In fact, it has already been dissolved, I believe, in favour of a Council of Ambassadors, leaving nothing settled and with only a League of Nations which is nonexistent, still-born, to take its place. How can the League of Nations possibly come to life without the United States to give it backbone!"

I inquired as to whether the Soviet Government was satisfied with the military situation.

"Very much so," Lenin replied promptly. "The only symptoms of further military aggression against us are those I spoke of in Poland. If Poland embarks on such an adventure there will be more suffering on both sides, more lives needlessly sacrificed. But even Foch could not give the Poles a victory. They could not defeat our Red Army even if Churchill himself fought with them."

Here Lenin threw back his head and laughed grimly. Then he went on in a graver vein:

"We can be crushed, of course, by any one of the big Allied Powers if they can send their own armies against us. But that they dare not do. The extraordinary paradox is that weak as Russia is compared with the Allies' boundless resources she has not only been able to shatter every armed force, including British, American and French troops that they have managed to send against her, but to win diplomatic and moral victories as well over the cordon sanitaire countries. Finland refused to fight against us. We have peace with Estonia, and peace with Serbia* and Lithuania[199] is at hand. Despite material inducements offered to and sinister threats made against these small countries by the Entente, they preferred to establish pacific relations with us."

INTERNAL SITUATION HOPEFUL

"This assuredly demonstrates the tremendous moral force we hold. The Baltic states, our nearest neighbours, appreciate that we alone have no designs against their independence and well-being."

"And Russia's internal situation?"

"It is critical but hopeful. With spring the food shortage will be overcome to the extent at least of saving the cities from famine. There will be sufficient fuel then too. The reconstruction period is under way, thanks to the Red Army's stupendous performances. Now parts of that army are transformed into armies of labour, an extraordinary phenomenon only possible in a country struggling toward a high ideal. Certainly it could not be done in capitalist countries. We have sacrificed everything to victory over our armed antagonists in the past; and now we shall turn all our strength to economic rehabilitation. It will take years, but we shall win out in the end."

"When do you think Communism will be complete in Russia?" The question was a poser, I thought, but Lenin replied immediately:

"We mean to electrify our entire industrial system through power stations in the Urals and elsewhere. Our engineers tell us it will take ten years. When the electrification is accomplished it will be the first important stage on the road to the communistic administration of public

---

* This is a mistake on the part of the newspaper. Serbia was not at war with Soviet Russia. This obviously refers to Latvia.—*Ed.*

economic life. All our industries will receive their motive power from a common source, capable of supplying them all adequately. This will eliminate wasteful competition in the quest of fuel, and place manufacturing enterprise on a sound economic footing, without which we cannot hope to achieve a full measure of interchange of essential products in accordance with Communist principles.

"Incidentally, in three years we expect to have 50,000,000 incandescent lamps burning in Russia. There are 70,000,000 in the United States, I believe, but in a land where electricity is in its infancy more than two-thirds of that number is a very high figure to achieve. Electrification is to my mind the most momentous of the great tasks that confront us."

SCORES SOCIALIST LEADERS

At the close of our talk Lenin delivered himself, not for publication, however, of some cutting criticism of certain Socialist leaders in Europe and America which revealed his lack of faith in the ability or even desire of these gentry to promote world revolution effectively. He evidently feels that Bolshevism will come to pass in spite of, rather than because of, the "official" chieftains of Socialism.

Published in English
February 21, 1920
in the newspaper
The World No. 21368

First published in Russian
in 1957
in the journal *Kommunist* No. 15

Printed from the original
newspaper text

REMARKS
ON THE RESOLUTION OF THE EXECUTIVE
OF THE COMMUNIST INTERNATIONAL
ON THE BOROTBISTS

1) I strongly urge that the Borotbists be accused *not* of nationalism, *but* of counter-revolutionary and petty-bourgeois tendencies.

2) An accusation should be definitely added that they *do not* treat their Spilka schoolteachers (do not wage an

implacable struggle against them) the way we do *our* petty-bourgeois A.T.U.[200]

22.II.

Lenin

Written February 22, 1920

First published in 1933
in the book: N. N. Popov
*Outline of the History
of the Communist Party
(Bolsheviks)
of the Ukraine*, Kiev

Printed from the typewritten copy

DRAFT DECISION FOR THE C.P.C.
ON STOCKS OF COMMODITIES[201]

The People's Commissariat for Foreign Trade shall be instructed to make arrangements with the People's Commissariat for State Control and the Vecheka for combating hoarders of stocks and goods likely to serve, among other things, as exportable merchandise.

Written March 2, 1920

First published in 1933
in *Lenin Miscellany XXIV*

Printed from the manuscript

REMARKS
ON TROTSKY'S DRAFT THESES
"THE IMMEDIATE TASKS OF ECONOMIC
DEVELOPMENT"

Remarks on the Draft

Re § 1

a) Point 1 to be headed: *On Labour Enthusiasm*.[202] The words "raising the will to work" in the second line to be replaced by the words "*labour enthusiasm*".

b) Add

the principle establishing the strict responsibility of every staff worker (board member, manager, director, etc.) for the performance of a definite operation or job or task, a principle generally recognised and endorsed by many economic council and other meetings, should be persistently applied in practice without fail. Up till now this is not by any means being sufficiently practised.

c) The consumers—through the consumers' societies, etc.—should be systematically enlisted for control over production.

d) The Workers' and Peasants' Inspection should be encouraged to greater participation in control over production and distribution.

e) The fight against profiteering and red tape, as well as against bureaucratism, should be highlighted.

f) Every effort must be made to organise competition. Measures aimed at improving discipline and raising labour efficiency should include cuts in rations for offenders, etc.

g) The end of § 4 of Trotsky's text (nine last lines) should be removed or toned down, or worded in a more general form.

(These are my rough preliminary remarks.)

Lenin

3/III.

Written March 3, 1920

First published in 1934
in the book: *The Ninth
Congress of the R.C.P.(B.)
March-April 1920*

Printed from the manuscript

THE PROSECUTION OF MINORS[203]

NOTES AND AMENDMENTS TO THE DRAFT DECREE

1) The theory of delimitation is *no good.*

2) Courts and prisons are *corrupting.*

3) *Who* knows the psychology of children? The judges or expert opinion?

4) Special establishments?

5) Profiteers, etc.? *Recidive?*

———

1) Instruct the Commissariat for Justice by arrangement with the Commissariat for Public Health, the Commissariat

for Education and the Central Statistical Board to draw up forms of report for each case of juvenile delinquency.

2) Instruct the Commissariat for Education and the Commissariat for Public Health to step up activities in the organisation of medical and educational institutions for defective juveniles.

———

Instruct the Commissariat for Justice to exercise stricter supervision over the membership of the juvenile commissions and the way they fulfil their duties.

Written March 4, 1920

First published in 1933   Printed from the manuscript
in *Lenin Miscellany XXIV*

MEASURES FOR IMPROVING
THE ORGANISATION OF STATE FARMS[204]

DRAFT DECISION FOR THE C.P.C.

All work to improve the organisation and management of the state farms should be centred on strongly combating, first, the patently landowner-type abuses that have come to light in the application of money rent, métayage, and so on; secondly, the extremely low labour discipline and extremely low productivity of labour.

Exact information to be demanded of the gubernia land departments and state farms as to what measures they have taken in this direction and what practical results they have achieved. Responsible persons to be appointed answerable before a court of law for the carrying out of this decision and the elimination of abuses. If need be, the entire managing personnel of the worst farms should be replaced. Certain farms should be selected as specialised model farms of a producing or purely consuming type and data concerning the state of these farms to be recorded separately.

Written March 9, 1920

First published in 1933   Printed from the manuscript
in *Lenin Miscellany XXIV*

RESOLUTIONS OF THE POLITBUREAU
OF THE C.C., R.C.P.(B.)
CONCERNING BREACH OF PARTY DISCIPLINE
BY MEMBERS OF THE A.C.C.T.U. PARTY
GROUP[205]

The Politbureau, composed of Bukharin, Krestinsky and Lenin, discussed on 17.III.1920 the statement of the A.C.C.T.U. Party group signed by Tomsky and Lutovinov and found in their presence 1) that Comrade Krestinsky, in private conversations with Comrades Ishchenko, Glebov, Tomsky and Lutovinov, did not voice his misgivings about the awkwardness of the existing relations (namely, the sponsoring by members of the Party at non-Party congresses—and not at their communist groups—of resolutions that differ from the resolution of the C.C. of the Party) in respect of the decision passed by the C.C.

2) that Comrade Krestinsky had suggested that this question should not be dealt with by the Party group before its forthcoming discussion the next day at the Politbureau in the presence of members of the Party group's bureau;

3) that during these conversations Comrade Krestinsky had been rather hasty;

on the other hand,

that under the circumstances the discussion of this question at the Party group was highly out of place and bound to aggravate the conflict needlessly, or rather turn the difference of opinion between the C.C. and the Party group into a real conflict;

that the statement mentioned above is, in the eyes of every Party man, not only hastiness, but squabbling of a decidedly unsavoury nature;

therefore the Politbureau resolves that the members of the A.C.C.T.U. Party group bureau be asked

to have the Party group cancel its resolution and consider the incident closed.

———

The Politbureau, composed of comrades Bukharin, Lenin and Krestinsky, discussed on 17.III.1920 the abnormal situation arising from the fact that Party members sponsor resolutions at non-Party congresses which run counter to the decisions of the Party's C.C.

The Politbureau resolves that from the point of view of Party discipline this is decidedly wrong and impermissible.

Considering the quite exceptional circumstances, however (namely, the very early date of the forthcoming Party congress, the publication of Comrade Tomsky's theses, and the comparatively minor importance of the still moot question of collective management with or without one-man management in separate cases) it is recognised as a politically lesser evil that members of the A.C.C.T.U. Party group be permitted, pending the decision of the Party congress, to sponsor the resolution of that group at current congresses of the various trade unions.

Written March 17, 1920

First published in 1963
in the Fifth Russian Edition
of the *Collected Works*, Vol. 40

Printed from the manuscript

PREFACE TO THE ENGLISH EDITION
OF THE PAMPHLET
THE PROLETARIAN REVOLUTION
AND KAUTSKY THE RENEGADE[206]

Preface to the English Edition

The comrades who intend to publish my pamphlet against Kautsky in English, which has also been published in German,[207] have asked me to write a preface to the English edition.

I would prefer, in lieu of a short preface, to give a detailed analysis of one of the writings of J. Ramsay Macdonald, who, as far as I know, is one of the most influential and widely read of English writers of practically the same Kautskyan trend. Unfortunately, I was unable to obtain Macdonald's book *Parliament and Revolution*[208] which has short chapters on Soviet democracy and Soviet suffrage,

but the author's Kautskyan point of view is quite clear
from his article "Socialist Review Outlook" published in
The Socialist Review, October-December 1919, of which he
is the editor. Macdonald is not a Marxist, and the Marxist-
tinted opportunism characteristic of Kautsky is not typical
of England.

As I have no time just now to give a detailed analysis
of Macdonald's views, I shall confine myself to an attempt
at briefly describing his views as known to us from his
political activities, from the newspaper of his party (the
"Independent" Labour Party—independent in word and
fully dependent on bourgeois prejudices in deed), from his
magazine and in particular from the article just mentioned.

I shall first quote some of the most characteristic passages
from this article:

Describing the general political situation, Macdonald writes:
"...Never was honest service and labour held in lower esteem" (p. 306).
"...Our ships of war continuing the starvation of women and children.
We are in every mean and wicked conspiracy to subvert democracy
in Europe. Though the State is tottering on the verge of bankruptcy,
a Minister to gratify his personal vanity, and a small class of finan-
ciers to secure personal profit in the future, can add what will probably
amount to £ 100,000,000 further burden upon the British taxpayer,
for a Russian venture ..." (p. 307). "The storm in the teacup inside the
Parliamentary Labour Party, because Mr. Neil MacLean remained
seated during a theatrical display when the Prime Minister was being
welcomed for bringing in his pocket from Paris one of the worst instruments that ever terminated a war, shows this same proneness
?
in the Party to be stampeded by trivial fears." "The Labour Party has
to save itself from chastisement; it cannot allow handbills to be issued
against its candidates, headed: 'The Labour Party condones an
insult to our Gracious Sovereign.'" "Such a state of things," declares
brave Mr. Macdonald, "is not healthy; it contains no promise of great
reform...."*

Written not later than
      March 1920

First published in 1958   Printed from the manuscript
      in the journal
Voprosi Istorii KPSS No. 4

---

* Here the manuscript breaks off.—*Ed.*

ADDENDUM
TO THE DRAFT REGULATIONS ON SUBBOTNIKS[209]

I. AIMS AND PURPOSE OF SUBBOTNIKS

1) Subbotniks are a form of propaganda of the ideas of compulsory labour service and self-organisation of the working class.

2) Subbotniks should be a laboratory of forms of communist labour.

3) Subbotniks must be started primarily for important and urgent jobs.

4) Subbotniks should yield results not below established output rates, but participants should try to exceed these rates.

+a) Higher labour productivity
b)   "   work discipline
c) implementation of dictatorship of the proletariat
d) leadership of the peasantry
e) combating famine and economic chaos

Written not before the end of March 1920

First published in 1933 in *Lenin Miscellany XXIV*

Printed from the manuscript

TO MEMBERS OF THE POLITBUREAU OF THE C.C., R.C.P.(B.)

To Members of the Politbureau:

Please read this. *Interesting.*
I am *for seeking* a compromise with them.[210]

Lenin

Written between April 19 and May 6, 1920

First published in 1965 in the Fifth Russian Edition of the *Collected Works*, Vol. 54

Printed from the manuscript

NOTES CONCERNING THE DECREE
ON WORK RATIONS[211]

1

1) Title to be changed.

2) General public norm to be abolished.

3) The *work* ration, i.e., *for number of days worked*, to be made the basic ration.

4) The work ration to be divided into categories according to the lightness or heaviness of the work.

5) 1st category: mental and office work

6) 2nd   "   manual work

7) 3rd   "   heavy work, etc.

8) "Shock groups" (i.e., trades and enterprises of special importance for production) transferable, by decision of the C.P.C. (sometimes by special rules) and the Council of Defence, to categories 2, 3, and so on.

9) A special low norm to be fixed for non-working people, unemployed, traders, etc. *Exemptions*.

10) Special exemptions for children and the sick.

2

Title suggestions:

"Decree on Greater Uniformity of Food Rations and Work Rations As the Basis of the Whole Food System".

What was formerly called "general public norm" to be *changed* to

"norm for unemployed and small proprietors" or: self-employed citizens, people not working, etc. (or "small proprietors"), "people not working in Soviet enterprises or offices".

Advantage: (1) simplifies things tremendously in capital cities and all non-farming, industrial towns (as the *bulk* there work in Soviet enterprises or Soviet offices).

(2) In *non-industrial* towns we *clearly* set apart the population that is not working in Soviet enterprises or Soviet offices, *and this population should gradually be taken off rations* (either start a vegetable garden *of your own* or go to work in Soviet enterprises or Soviet offices).

> We *shall* *not* feed those who do not work in Soviet enterprises or Soviet offices.

Figure out under what system there will be *less food coupons* and the system itself more simple.

27/IV. 1920   *Lenin*

First published in 1945
in *Lenin Miscellany XXXV*   Printed from the manuscript

SPEECH AT THE STONE-LAYING CEREMONY FOR A MONUMENT TO KARL MARX MAY 1, 1920

NEWSPAPER REPORT

V. I. Lenin delivered a short but impressive speech on the significance of Karl Marx as a socialist leader.

"The working people were enslaved, despite political liberties. Now they are moving towards the workers' revolution, which will create a socialist society without landowners and capitalists. To Russia has fallen the great honour and joy of helping to establish this socialist society and a world Soviet Republic. Today, on this international festival of labour, when we wish to prove to everybody that we shall succeed in coping with the task of organising a socialist society of the working people, we honour the memory of Karl Marx. And I am confident that the laying of this monument to our great teacher will serve as a call impelling us to give all our attention to the need for working hard and long to create a society in which there will be no room for exploitation."

Izvestia No. 94 May 4, 1920   Printed from the newspaper text

SPEECH AT THE OPENING CEREMONY
OF THE ZAGORSKY WORKERS' PALACE
MAY 1, 1920

NEWSPAPER REPORT

Comrade Lenin devoted his short speech to reminiscences of Comrade Zagorsky, whom he had met abroad, where the deceased had lived as a political emigrant in 1907 and when Lenin visited the workers' circles of comrades living abroad and circles of Russian emigrants to read lectures and reports. Already in those days Comrade Zagorsky, who was secretary of the Geneva group of Bolsheviks, impressed one as being an energetic, clever man and a good organiser devoted heart and soul to the cause of the Party. When Zagorsky returned to Moscow in 1918 he threw himself into Party work and was shortly elected secretary of the Moscow organisation, at which honourable post he died during the explosion in Leontievsky Pereulok.[212]

Izvestia No. 94,
    May 4, 1920
and *Pravda* No. 95,
    May 5, 1920

Printed from the text
of the newspaper *Pravda*

SPEECH AT THE ELEVENTH ISSUE
OF RED COMMANDERS
OF THE FIRST MOSCOW MACHINE-GUNNERS
TRAINING COURSES
MAY 12, 1920

CHRONICLER'S RECORD

In a speech to the newly promoted Red commanders Lenin spoke about the things a Red commander should know when going out to the Western Front. A Red commander should remember that we were fighting, not the Polish workers and peasants, but the Polish bourgeoisie and landowners, as well as the capitalists of the Entente who stood behind them and controlled the Polish landed gentry. You know, Comrade Lenin said, that this war has been forced on us against our desire, but we are not going to let ourselves be crushed: better death than defeat.

K Novoi Armii
(To a New Army)
No. 6
June 1, 1920

Printed from the text
of the magazine *K Novoi Armii*

DRAFT DECISION
FOR THE COUNCIL OF PEOPLE'S COMMISSARS
ON THE PURVEYANCE OF RAW MATERIALS[213]

A commission to be set up, which shall, within a fortnight:

1) Devise measures for unifying all grain and raw material purveyance under a single department or by a sufficiently secure and expedient unification for this purpose of the respective departments. Use must be made of the co-operative machinery.

2) The commission, in particular, must examine the question of employing the Food Army and the internal security units for the purveyance of all kinds of raw materials; following this, the conditions and concrete dimensions for applying bonuses and exchange of commodities (as a rule, on a collective basis), in particular, returning to the peasants in the form of processed goods part of the raw materials delivered by them.

3) The application everywhere of the surplus-appropriation system in the purveyance of raw materials, as well as of fixed prices, is obligatory.

Written May 25, 1920

First published in 1945
in *Lenin Miscellany XXXV*

Printed from the manuscript

REMARKS ON THE DRAFT DECREE ON MEASURES FOR PROPER DISTRIBUTION OF HOUSING AMONG THE WORKING POPULATION[214]

In my opinion § 9 is unsuitable. People's Courts are weak.

The local sanitary departments (+labour commissariat) should be made:

    (a) to issue obligatory rules

    (b) *to punish*, without trial, by arrest up to 1 month and *compulsory labour* up to 2 months for uncleanliness, etc.

    (c) to organise *mass* control of cleanliness (through special *squads* of Soviet Deputies).

Lenin

Written May 25, 1920

First published in 1945   Printed from the manuscript
in *Lenin Miscellany XXXV*

ROUGH DRAFT DECISION FOR THE C.P.C. ON GRAIN RESOURCES[215]

26.V.1920

1) Express satisfaction at increased purveyance
2) monthly figures to be demanded
3) station deliveries to be kept separate from purveyances
4) help purveyors (§ 4)
5) step up deliveries (§ 5)
6) **vegetable garden?**

First published in 1945   Printed from the manuscript
in *Lenin Miscellany XXXV*

INTERVIEW WITH M. NAKAHIRA, CORRESPONDENT
OF THE JAPANESE NEWSPAPER *OSAKA ASAHI*[216]

He did not wait for our question, but started to speak of the relations between Japan and Russia—to the effect that it is regrettable that Japan does not seem willing to adopt an attitude of willingness to meet the Soviet Government's attitude of peace. The Soviet Government stands for peace, and therefore it recognises the neutral zone government.[217]

He then asked: "Is there a powerful landowning class in Japan? Does the Japanese farmer own land freely? Do the Japanese people live on food produced in their own country, or do they import much food from foreign countries?" He asked many other questions, showing his deep interest in living conditions in Japan.

Mr. Lenin next asked whether Japanese parents beat their children, and said he had read of this in a book. "Tell me whether it is true or not," said he, "it is a very interesting subject." I answered that there may be exceptions, but as a rule parents do not beat their children in Japan. On hearing my answer he expressed satisfaction and said that the policy of the Soviet Government is to abolish this condition. After that we asked about the revolution and subsequent developments.

In giving a résumé of Russian revolutionary history, he said: "Before the revolution, the working and peasant classes of Russia were extremely oppressed—in fact, their oppression was without parallel in past history. As a result of this most severe oppression, the revolutionary spirit of the poorer class gradually increased until it broke out in the revolution. But the organising capacity of the lower strata of Russia is comparatively weak and the degree of education lower than in any other countries. In spite of all this they could not be suppressed. But now, after two and a half years of experience, the Russian working and peasant masses have obtained a great deal of political and social discipline. The experience of this two and a half years can truly be compared with the development of several centuries."

At this point we asked why the Soviet Republic, in spite of its having repudiated the national debts of czarism, had promised to give Esthonia vast amounts of gold, when concluding peace. Smiling, Mr. Lenin said: "Esthonia has shown her good will toward the Soviet Government and therefore the Soviet Government has promised to pay her this gold. Moreover," he continued, "to deal with the propertied class is really a very difficult matter. The propertied class cares for nothing but its own material interests. For instance, look at America. America proposed a peace treaty with Soviet Russia. When we examined the treaty, we could not accept it because it was based on exploitation. So we rejected it. Of course we do not consider ourselves incapable. The Allied nations, rejecting recognition, attempt to interfere with Russia. There is reason to think that if the intervention of the Allies should continue, it will be profitable to the Bolsheviki.

"All in all, considering the prospects of Russia's industries, the situation is promising. If our electrical programme is attained entire industries can be electrified. The creative capacity of communism will be increased and will exert the greatest influence in solving these problems, and the development will be equal to that of several decades."

Transmitted by telegraph June 6, 1920

Published in Japanese June 13, 1920,
in *Osaka Asahi* No. 13814,
June 15, 1920,
in *Tokyo Asahi* No. 12211,
and in English in the magazine
Soviet Russia No. 6
August 7, 1920
First published in Russian
(translated from the English)
April 16, 1963 in *Izvestia* No. 91

Printed from the text in
Osaka Asahi
Translated from the Japanese

INTERVIEW WITH K. FUSSE,
CORRESPONDENT OF THE JAPANESE NEWSPAPERS
OSAKA MAINICHI AND *TOKYO NICHI-NICHI*

Lenin said on meeting Fusse that he was very glad to see him and that despite everything that had taken place in recent years between Russia and Japan and the fact that some people in Japan still took an uncompromising attitude towards Soviet Russia, he nevertheless took an optimistic view of future relations between the two countries. The Soviet Government had recognised the independence of the buffer state and "this, I hope," said Lenin, "would help restore peace in the Far East in the very near future."

Fusse started the interview by asking Lenin: "Last autumn you said the difficulties were over. Don't you foresee big difficulties ahead?"

I meant that our greatest difficulties were over; but, of course, there are still many difficulties confronting us.

Fusse: "You said it took capitalism many years to accomplish the transition from feudalism, therefore it would also take socialism many years to accomplish the transition from capitalism. Approximately how long do you think this will take?"

Generally, it is hard to fix dates; to overthrow the old order doesn't require much time, but you can't create the new order in a short time. We have launched our plan for the electrification of industry and agriculture; without electrification the communist order is impracticable, and our plan of electrification is designed for a period of ten years under the most favourable conditions. That's the shortest time we set for building up our new order.

Lenin then asked Fusse a number of questions concerning agrarian and class relations in Japan.

What kind of landowners does Japan have? What is the position of the landless peasant in Japan? Are there any peasant organisations? and so on. Lenin also showed an interest in the state of electrification and public education in Japan and how children were treated in Japan. When Fusse said that Japan took better care of her children than the West, Lenin remarked: "That's very important, in view of the fact that the practice of beating children in the schools has not yet been entirely eliminated in the so-called civilised countries of Europe, not even in a country like Switzerland."

After this Fusse again asked Lenin a number of political questions. *Fusse*: "How do you visualise good-neighbourly relations between socialist and capitalist states?"

Our terms of coexistence with capitalist countries were set forth at length in the draft treaty which the American representative, Mr. Bullitt, recently published in Washington. These terms were most unfavourable to us, and it was this that led the Allied governments to believe that our willingness to make concessions was a sign of weakness, and they started their intervention, as a result of which they suffered complete defeat. We routed Kolchak, Yudenich and Denikin.

Fusse: "Where does communism have more chance of success— in the West or in the East?"

So far, real communism can succeed only in the West, but it must be remembered that the West lives at the expense of the East; the imperialist powers of Europe grow rich chiefly at the expense of the eastern colonies, but at the same time they are arming their colonies and teaching them to fight, and by so doing the West is digging its own grave in the East.

Fusse: "What are the immediate tasks of the Soviet Government?"

First, to beat the Polish landowners, second, to secure a lasting peace, and then, third, to develop our economic life.

Transmitted by telegraph
June 4, 1920

Published in Japanese
June 10, 1920, in the newspaper
Tokyo Nichi-Nichi No. 15686

First published in Russian
in 1924 in a collection
of articles *Lenin i Vostok*
(Lenin and the East), Moscow

Printed from the text of the book
collated with the typewritten
copy of *K. Fusse*'s telegraphed
report

DECISION
IMPOSING A PENALTY ON E. Y. VEVER, MANAGER OF "GORKI" SANATORIUM

In a statement signed by Comrades Belenky, Ivanichev and Gabalin it has been established that by order of the Manager of the Sanatorium, Comrade Vever, a perfectly sound fir-tree was cut down in the sanatorium's park on June 14, 1920.

For causing damage to Soviet property I order Comrade Vever, Manager of the Sanatorium at the Soviet Gorki Estate, to be placed under arrest for 1 month.

Sentence to be executed by the Podolsk Uyezd Executive Committee on the understanding that

(1) should it be discovered that Comrade Vever had had no penalties previously imposed upon him, his sentence shall be suspended after a week's detention and he shall be warned that in the event of wrongful felling in the park, walks or woods or any other damage to Soviet property being allowed, he will be liable to further punishment over and above 3 weeks' arrest and to dismissal.

(2) The date on which sentence is to be carried out shall be determined by the Uyezd Executive Committee by arrangement with the Uyezd Land Department or the Management of the State Farms to ensure that farm work will not suffer in any way.

I instruct Comrade Belenky to bring this decision to the notice of Comrade Vever and his assistants, who are to sign that it has been announced to them and that any further similar offence will incur punishment for all workers and office staff, and not the manager alone.

I instruct the Uyezd Executive Committee to report to me what date they have fixed for the arrest and how the sentence has been carried out.

V. Ulyanov (Lenin)
Chairman, Council of Labour and Defence

14.VI.1920

First published in 1945
in *Lenin Miscellany XXXV*   Printed from the manuscript

SPEECH AT A MEETING
OF THE EXECUTIVE COMMITTEE
OF THE COMMUNIST INTERNATIONAL
JUNE 19, 1920
NEWSPAPER REPORT

Comrade Lenin put the question this way: what, in effect, does it mean to recognise the dictatorship of the proletariat. It means every day, in propaganda, agitation, speeches and articles, to prepare the proletariat for the conquest of power, for the suppression of the exploiters, the suppression of all the proletariat's opponents. Comrade Lenin, on the basis of various documents and newspapers, showed what a *gulf* existed between the Third International and the entire policy of the French Party.[218] He revealed all the rottenness of the Turatian wing of the Italian Party, which was preventing the party from adopting a correct line.

Pravda No. 133,
June 20, 1920
Izvestia No. 134
June 22, 1920

Printed from the *Pravda* text

DRAFT DECISION FOR THE POLITBUREAU OF THE C.C., R.C.P.(B.) ON THE TASKS OF THE R.C.P.(B.) IN TURKESTAN[219]

The theses and draft to be endorsed as a whole, but both to be amended in the direction of

(1) equalising land tenure of Russians and newcomers with that of local people;

(2) overcoming, ousting and subordinating Russian kulaks in the most energetic manner;

(3) not giving the Turkestan Commission[220] the right to alter decrees without obtaining the consent of the Turkestan Central Executive Committee and the Turkestan Council of People's Commissars and without consulting the centre;

(4) systematically considering, preparing and carrying out the transfer of power—gradually but steadily—to the local *Soviets of working people*, under the control of reliable Communists;

(5) the question of dividing the Republic into 3 parts not to be decided beforehand;

(6) the general task to be, not communism, but the overthrow of feudalism.

Written June 22, 1920
First published in 1959
in Lenin Miscellany XXXVI

Printed from the manuscript

MATERIAL FOR THE SECOND CONGRESS OF THE COMMUNIST INTERNATIONAL[221]

1

PLAN OF A RESOLUTION CONCERNING THE MEANING OF THE CONCEPT "DICTATORSHIP OF THE PROLETARIAT" AND THE FIGHT AGAINST THE "FASHIONABLE" DISTORTION OF THIS SLOGAN[222]

1. Precisely the revolutionary, and only the revolutionary part of the proletariat, to be organised into the party, and a similar part of the *party* promoted to its *leading* centres.

2. Systematic exposure to the masses of reformism and opportunism in the party and the labour movement.

3. Replacement of opportunist leaders in the party's sections, in the trade unions, in the co-operatives, in clubs, in cultural and educational and *all* other organisations of the proletariat by revolutionary leaders.

4. Formation of communist cells in all and every form of workers' and small-peasant organisations for systematic leadership of the entire labour movement (and part of the small-peasant movement) by the party.

=3?

5. Obligatory appointment of definitely revolutionary workers who are entirely free from traditions, habits and prejudices of peaceful work, parliamentarism and legalism, and who, even if extremely inexperienced, are (1) capable of fighting reformism and opportunism (2) and are in close touch with the rank and file of the proletariat and with its most revolutionary section—

— their appointment to top posts in the party in sufficient numbers, especially in the Party's C.C. and the *parliamentary group*, and in all the most important (for the Party) bodies.

6. Especially detailed subordination of the parliamentary group to the Party's Central Committee and the latter's strict supervision over it.

7. The people who are to be considered collaborationists, advocates of a bloc between the proletariat and the bourgeoisie

and proprietors, are not only those who put this idea into practice directly, who stand for a bloc in the government, etc., but also those who put it into practice *indirectly*, for instance, those who stand for equality between the working class and the class of petty proprietors, for equality in their points of view, etc.

8. Press organs of the reformists (or conciliation with reformism)...* *L'Humanite*,[223] should be closed down. The party should have 1 *central* organ of a definitely revolutionary trend—*not* like that of *Populaire*[224] or *Freiheit*.[225] The party's whole press is to be a single thought, a single trend, *preparation* for dictatorship.

9. Deeper into the masses. Not for the labour aristocracy, but for the untrained masses. Not only for the towns, but for the country. Agitation among the masses, not only propaganda (contra British Socialist Party).[226]

Free distribution of leaflets for the backward workers covered by contributions from the advanced.

Proletarians to go to the masses, to assist strikers and farm labourers.

10. Open analysis before the masses of mistakes and betrayals of the opportunist leaders (the strike of 20-21/VII. 1919, *etc.*).

Analysis in the press of *all* opportunist mistakes and weak speeches of parliamentarians, etc.

11. Systematic work on all occasions and in all respects in application to all spheres of life;

clarify *concrete* tasks of the dictatorship of the proletariat, viz.:

(a) suppression of the resistance of the exploiters (including the kulaks and saboteurs among the intellectuals);

(b) confiscation, since redemption payment now, after 1914-18, is impossible;

(c) special supervision over the exploiters and bourgeois intellectuals;

(d) immediate revolutionary improvement of life for the workers

---

* A word in the manuscript illegible.—*Ed.*

for all the exploited masses
for the small farmers
at the expense of the exploiters;
(e) neutralisation of the small proprietors

the middle peasants
artisans
small manufacturers
part of the bourgeois intelligentsia

i. e., with a view to preventing them going
over to the Whites;

(f) determination, capability, skill, special organisation
for suppressing resistance.

1. $\Sigma\Sigma = (\alpha)$ break down

(β) enthuse
(γ) neutralise.

12. Epuration...*

13. "Freedom of the press"? —"assembly"? —"the person"?
Party = the vanguard
$(\alpha\alpha)$ (1) revolutionary part
$(\beta\beta)$ (2) linked with the *masses*.

Immediate preparation $\Big($ 2. 3. 4. 5. 6 (+13). 7. $\alpha\alpha$
8. 9. 10. $\beta\beta$

Chief danger: Rights, i.e., undisplaced leaders.

3 parties (+ American Socialist Party[227]) (+Swiss
Socialist Party[228]). Immediate affiliation *impossible*.

Lefts. Their mistakes. Immediate affiliation *possible*.
Reformism in the Italian Party (maybe, + B.S.P.?)

NB

Committee on the French Party and press:

Lozovsky   Serrati
+ Bukharin   Deslinières
+ Guilbeaux   +
Sadoul

Written in July, not later
than 4, 1920
First published August 1, 1935
in the journal
The Communist International No. 22

Printed from the manuscript

* Purge.—*Ed.*

2

RE JACK TANNER'S SPEECH
AT THE SECOND CONGRESS OF THE COMINTERN[229]

Tanner's speech (Shop Stewards[230]) has made it quite clear
that:
1) a place should be made *within* the Third International
for *sympathisers*;
2) a *special* reservation should be made for Britain and
America to the effect that in spite of our contradictions
on parliamentarism we propose that
   (a) the mass movement in the form of the I.W.W. and
the Shop Stewards should remain *affiliated* to the
Third International; and
   (b) the question should be threshed out once more and
a practical *test* made to *improve* the socialist parties
which had agitated among the masses *insufficiently*
and *failed* to establish ties with them.

Lenin

Written July 23, 1920

First published in 1959   Printed from the manuscript
in *Lenin Miscellany XXXVI*

3

REMARKS ON THE REPORT OF A. SULTAN-ZADE
CONCERNING THE PROSPECTS OF A SOCIAL REVOLUTION
IN THE EAST[231]

1) Disintegration of the propertied exploiter classes
2) a large part of the population are *peasants* under
medieval exploitation
3) *small* artisans—in industry
4) deduction: *adjust* both Soviet institutions and the
Communist Party (its membership, special tasks) to the
level of the *peasant* countries of the colonial East.

This is the crux of the matter. This needs thinking about
and *seeking* **concrete** answers.

Written between July 24
and 29, 1920

First published in 1963   Printed from the manuscript
in the Fifth Russian Edition
of the *Collected Works*, Vol. 41

4

NOTES FOR THE COMMITTEE ON THE NATIONAL AND COLONIAL QUESTIONS

The use of *medieval particularism*? Too dangerous; not Marxist.

Modern national movements should be distinguished from "movements" (so-called *movements*) of a medieval nature.

Written in French in July,
not later than 28, 1920

Facsimile of the MS first
published in 1923 in the book:
H. Guilbeaux
Wladimir Iljitsch Lenin
Ein treues Bild seines Wesens,
Berlin

First published in Russian
in 1963
in the Fifth Russian Edition
of the *Collected Works*, Vol. 41

Printed from the facsimile
Translated from the French

DRAFT DECISION
FOR THE PLENUM OF THE C.C., R.C.P.(B.)
ON THE CONFLICT BETWEEN
THE PETROGRAD COMMUNE
AND THE PETROGRAD SOVIET[232]

1) Badayev for M.C.S.*

2) *Badayev to be rehabilitated (through the Orgbureau).*

3) A number of Petrograd food workers to be transferred to Moscow.

4) Petrograd to be placed under very strict supervision.**

5) Petrograd, Moscow and all other food points to be put on an equal footing in the distribution of bread and norms of issue.[233]

Written July 16, 1920
First published in 1965
in the Fifth Russian Edition
of the *Collected Works*, Vol. 54

Printed from the manuscript

---

* Moscow Consumers' Society.—*Ed.*

** Points 2 and 4 in the manuscript are crossed out. Point 4 was not included in the adopted decision.—*Ed.*

ANSWERS TO QUESTIONS
BY A. M. KRASNOSHCHOKOV,
FOREIGN MINISTER
OF THE FAR-EASTERN REPUBLIC[234]

1) Where to convene the congress?

Anywhere.

2) Principles of elections (is the "four-pointer" permissible)?[235]

It is.

3) Principles of constitution and economic policy?

Democracy permissible with slight privileges for Communists.[236]

4) Definition of official relations between Soviet Russia and the F.-E. Republic?

Friendship.

5) In view of non-compliance with C.C. directives by certain regions and the convocation in a few days' time of a preliminary conference, it is necessary to have a new exact formulation of the foundations of the Far-Eastern Republic and a definition of its authority.

Obey the C.C., otherwise we'll sack you.

Written in July, not before
17, 1920

First published in 1965
in the Fifth Russian Edition
of the *Collected Works*, Vol. 54

Printed from the manuscript

SPEECH AT A STONE-LAYING CEREMONY
FOR A MONUMENT TO KARL LIEBKNECHT
AND ROSA LUXEMBURG HELD IN PETROGRAD,
JULY 19, 1920[237]

NEWSPAPER REPORT

Comrades, in all countries communist leaders are suffering unimaginable sacrifices. They are dying by the thousand in Finland and Hungary and other countries. But no persecutions can arrest the growth of communism, and the heroism of fighters like Karl Liebknecht and Rosa Luxemburg gives us courage and faith in the complete victory of communism. (*Comrade Lenin's speech was drowned in thunderous cheers. The "Internationale" was sung.*)

Petrogradskaya Pravda No. 159   Printed from the newspaper text
          July 21, 1920

DRAFT DECISION FOR THE POLITBUREAU OF THE C.C., R.C.P.(B.) ON MAXIM GORKY'S ARTICLES IN THE JOURNAL *THE COMMUNIST INTERNATIONAL*[238]

I move the following resolution by a *collection of signatures* in the Politbureau:

The Politbureau of the C.C. considers the publication in No. 12 of *the Communist International* of Gorky's *articles* extremely inappropriate, especially the editorial, as there is not only *nothing* communist about these articles, but a good deal that is *anti*-communist in them. In future *such* articles must *on no account* be published in *the Communist International*.

*Lenin**

Written July 31, 1920

First published in 1965   Printed from the manuscript
in the Fifth Russian Edition
of the *Collected Works*, Vol. 54

PROPOSALS ON MILITARY QUESTIONS[239]

It having been certified that there remain (with Budyonny) not < 10,000,
1) I vote for taking the 6th Cavalry Division from Budyonny for the Wrangel front;

---

* The draft is signed also by L.D. Trotsky, N. N. Krestinsky and M.I. Kalinin.—*Ed.*

2) for reinforcing Budyonny's Mounted Army with those 3-4 thousand sabres which the Commander-in-Chief promises the South (*urgent*);

+ 4) more horses to be taken from the Byelorussian peasants to reinforce Budyonny's cavalry;

5) for replacing Gittis by Comrade Frunze *immediately* (see opinion of Commander-in-Chief and Tukhachevsky).

Lenin

Written in August,
not before 20, 1920

First published in 1959   Printed from the manuscript
in *Lenin Miscellany XXXVI*

DECISIONS OF THE POLITBUREAU OF THE C.C., R.C.P.(B.) ON THE ORDER OF THE REVOLUTIONARY MILITARY COUNCIL OF THE WESTERN FRONT[240]

The Politbureau rules that the action of Comrades Tukhachevsky and Smilga be severely censured. They had no right to issue their worse than tactless order, which undermines the policy of the Party and the Government.*

The Politbureau directs the R.M.C. of the Republic to immediately rescind the order of the R.M.C. of the Western Front and to reprimand the latter for their irregular action.** [241]

Written between August 20
and 24, 1920

First published in 1965   Printed from the manuscript
in the Fifth Russian Edition
of the *Collected Works*, Vol. 54

---

* By a note written at the top of the document Lenin instructed his secretary to have this decision telegraphed to the R.M.C. of the Western Front: "Brichkina, send this off by wire." Under the text of the decision he wrote: "Copies for Comrades Chicherin and Danishevsky."—*Ed.*

** This text was marked off by Lenin with a pencil and a note added: "Sklyansky has already been told."—*Ed.*

THE NINTH ALL-RUSSIA CONFERENCE OF THE R.C.P.(B.)

*SEPTEMBER 22-25, 1920*242

1

SPEECH ON THE IMMEDIATE TASKS OF PARTY DEVELOPMENT
SEPTEMBER 24

Comrades, I think that certain statements made during the debates and even certain speeches are worth mentioning if only because they obviously express not just overstrain, but overstrain bordering on hysteria and therefore giving a misplaced emphasis. I would not call it demagogy. It is physical overstrain to the point of hysteria. This applies mainly to the speeches by Lutovinov and Bubnov, in which there was less of demagogy than of overstrain. To some extent I think there were signs of overstrain in Medvedev's statement too. He said: "Now you have all started speaking about unhealthy symptoms, but before you used to deny it, you weren't telling the truth." I think this explanation is not quite correct, in fact it is quite incorrect. That the unhealthy symptoms we are talking about really exist—was hardly a secret. Without a doubt, the general situation was so grave that we couldn't find time till now for the Party, we had no chance to raise this question specially in the Party. Even now we raise it with difficulty, because the chance we are discussing here in our political talk—the chance of our being able to avoid a winter campaign—is extremely slender. The general situation of the Republic, as I mentioned, has improved to such an extent that we are now able to discuss things more calmly: there is no longer any question of suspending the conference the way we did several times when Kolchak and Denikin were advancing. There were Party congresses from which a number of leading workers went straight off to the front without waiting for them to end. Mind you, we seldom convene congresses, we seldom have a chance of discussing important issues at congresses—yet before we couldn't even see a congress through to the end, rarely though it was convened.

Today at any rate we can and ought to thresh things out without restricting ourselves. I should also like to say a word about Kalinin's attempts to present the case in a Marxist way. It seems to me that his arguments were a long step away from Marxism, and the correct Marxist view I think was given in the resolution of the Moscow Committee—which you have all, of course, read and which has been put out in a small pamphlet and printed in *Pravda*—and the letter of the Central Committee.

I should like to read out several lines, which I would offer to the committee (if it be decided to set one up), not in lieu of the Moscow resolution and the C.C.'s letter, but as supplementary material to them.* The resolution of the Moscow Committee I think—and all are agreed on this—deals with the question correctly. Allow me to quote those few words and dwell on them briefly. Here is the addendum: "The indescribably grave position of the Soviet Republic in the early years of its existence, extreme devastation and grave military danger, made it necessary to designate special "shock" (and therefore virtually privileged) departments and groups of workers. This was unavoidable, since the ruined country could not be saved unless resources and energies were concentrated on such departments and such groups of workers, without the strengthening of which the imperialists of the whole world would have certainly crushed us and prevented the Soviet Republic from even starting on economic construction...."

As regards the old specialists we have heard some very heated attacks here. The truth came out in Comrade Kutuzov's speech when he said that the proletariat saw no improvement of its position from Soviet Russia—if anything, it was often worse. That's true. But one must sort out the facts—for instance, that in Vienna, where there is no Soviet government, you have the same deterioration, to which you can add a moral humiliation a hundred times worse. But the rank and file cannot get this straight. Understandably, we are asked: What did we get in the course of these two years? And obviously, dissatisfaction with the old

---

* See pp. 212-13 of this volume.—*Ed.*

specialists is widespread. Naturally, the question whether we need specialists or not was a salient issue. We shouldn't forget, however, that without them we would not have had our army. We would have found ourselves in the same position as Hungary and the Finnish workers. That is how the matter stands. Without these specialists—I spoke about this in my political report—we would not have been able to take those elementary steps that helped us rise to a definite level. If we had failed to cope with this specialist business, we would not have had this, we would not have been able to make further progress. But now, when we have taken them in hand and harnessed them, when we know that they will not run away from us, but, on the contrary, are all running to join us, we shall now be sure that democratisation in the Party and the army will rise. I shall read further (reads the resolution)....

Point one (reads).* Here there is an addition. Comrade Tomsky said, referring to what we have often spoken about ourselves, that the rank and file should be brought to the fore, the leaders are tired, give the rank and file a chance. This could not be done at once, but it will be after another, maybe the twentieth, attempt. Failing this, Soviet Russia's cause would be hopeless. But we know that it is not hopeless, because we have new elements that are growing up. If the first attempts failed, we shall try and try again.

Point two (reads).* Here a rather sarcastic question was asked as to whether freedom of criticism would correspond to freedom to eat peaches.²⁴³ I have one measure as a possible guarantee, on the basis of the proposals made by the committee. At moments when the country is in danger, when Kolchak reached the Volga and Denikin Orel, there can be no freedoms. There are other things than this to be regretted. But the military situation is bad now, too, we see how fickle the fortunes of war are. We must put this question on the order of the day. But we cannot, we must not, promise that at moments of military danger we shall not act differently. We shall have to make a tremendous

* See p. 213 of this volume.—Ed.

effort again and no arguing about it, we shall have to stand firm, strain every nerve. We do not renounce this at all, and until we have an Italian victory we must not renounce it. And that's my reply to the peaches.

Point three (*reads*).* Here Comrade Preobrazhensky raised a question which Zinoviev raised too: Is regulation appropriate here and what is to be understood by it? I shall leave this question open, as it will be detailed in the committee. We shall see whether regulation is to be understood as detailed points or as the setting up of special bodies.

Point four (*reads*).* The speaker here said that this question had been raised by the committee but was rejected by its majority. I believe—I am putting this forward only in my own name—I believe that it should not be rejected, and if not accepted at once, at least it should first be considered. It has been pointed out here that 500 complaints have accumulated in the Orgbureau of the C.C. The Orgbureau has to distribute tens of thousands of people. Besides, there is not a single member of the Orgbureau who is not swamped with work, doing several jobs. Under these conditions one has to work with unknown quantities, and under such conditions you can only decide questions by intuition, a thing only experienced people can do, and even they often make mistakes. Taking into consideration these conditions, we want to find people with a length of Party membership of not less than fifteen years, who enjoy the Party's trust, who are unbiassed, and who would help in this business, while at the same time standing above the Orgbureau as regards independence, as they would be elected by the congress. I believe this step could be taken. To hamper the C.C.'s work or hold up the decision is impossible. There is no special provision for it, and we cannot offer it. There used to be a control commission in the German Workers' Party. How far that will be possible in our war situation—one cannot say. In any case we are in a position to take such a step, and the C.C. has taken that course.

The C.C.'s letter says: "Special Party commissions to handle relevant complaints should be organised at all

---

* See p. 213 of this volume.—*Ed.*

Gubernia Party Committees and made up of the most dispassionate comrades enjoying the general trust of the organisation." It speaks here of dispassionate comrades. For real militant activities—military, economic and organisational—passionate people are very often absolutely necessary, because without high passion they will not be able to work at high pressure, they will not solve the urgent problem facing the exhausted country. On the contrary, what we need here are people, who though they may not possess conspicuous administrative abilities, have a good knowledge of life. I doubt whether we shall be able to find enough of them for the whole of Russia, for all gubernias, and if the commissions which are now going to be set up and which you will set up under the Gubernia Party Committees prove to be unsuccessful, don't draw the conclusion that the whole enterprise is a failure. We may not find a sufficient number of comrades in the gubernias capable of holding out from congress to congress. If we don't find them in the gubernias, we shall find staunch comrades with a knowledge of life in the centre. I think we should not give up the idea of forming these bodies.

It may be said: Where is the guarantee that these bodies can exist? We are in a state of desperate civil war, where, generally speaking, there can be no question of any freedom of broad criticism and so forth. We have other things to think of, we must strain every effort to end the war. If the conditions of war were not what they are, the position would be different. Under the present conditions we cannot provide for a good many things; and we say straight out that in order to settle this question in a practical manner we cannot rely on the C.C., because it is swamped with work as it is. I doubt whether you will find a single C.C. member—I judge from my own experience—who doesn't feel over head and heels in debt as regards unfinished or skimped jobs. I can imagine no more effective guarantee of this plan being carried out than the creation of this commission, of a group of comrades capable of concentrating wholly on this job with the assurance that it will be entirely independent, handling affairs which no single member of the C.C., the Orgbureau, or the Politbureau is in a position to go into with any thoroughness. We may have a practical grasp of things, seeing that we are making some progress, that we have increased our grain collections from 60 to 260 million poods—but this proved insufficient to give us a Red Army that was not overexhausted, to give us workers who did not say, "What good has the Red Army done us, we are starving", and to give us a leadership that was not utterly worn out and does not stand in need of help from the rank and file. Nevertheless, we did make that progress, and that means that even in such a mass state of extreme fatigue the scale of this fatigue is beginning to diminish and we are entering a period when we can stop discussing the crust-of-bread question and pass on to weightier problems confronting us, which we all shall most certainly tackle.

First published in 1963
in the Fifth Russian Edition
of the *Collected Works*, Vol. 41

Printed from the shorthand record

2

DRAFT RESOLUTION ON THE IMMEDIATE TASKS OF PARTY DEVELOPMENT

Not in lieu of, but as supplementary *material* to the C.C.'s letter and the Moscow Committee's resolution:

The indescribably grave position of the Soviet Republic in the early years of its existence, extreme devastation and grave military danger, made it necessary to designate "shock" (and therefore virtually privileged) departments and groups of workers. This was unavoidable, since the ruined country could not be saved unless resources and energies were concentrated on such departments and groups of workers, without the strengthening of which the imperialists of the whole world would have certainly crushed us and prevented the Soviet Republic from even starting on economic construction.

This circumstance, coupled with the heritage of capitalist and proprietary habits and attitudes, which are so difficult to get rid of, explain the necessity for directing the Party's attention again and again to the struggle for implementing ...*

...the need for practical guarantees that the decisions of the Party, which is unanimous on the above-mentioned questions of principle, should not remain on paper. The conference therefore directs the Central Committee immediately to resolve, carry out and furthermore propose to the next congress of the Party that it endorse the following:

(1) the absolute obligatoriness of more frequent and wider meetings of Party members parallel with other measures for developing activity among the Party membership;

(2) literary organs to be set up, capable of carrying out a more systematic and wider criticism of the Party's mistakes and generally of criticism within the Party (discussion leaflets, etc.);

(3) precise practical rules to be drawn up on measures for eliminating the existing inequality (in the conditions of life, size of salaries, and so forth) between specialists and executives, on the one hand, and the rank and file, on the other—an inequality that violates democracy, is a source of demoralisation within the Party and lowers the prestige of Communists;

(4) it shall be found necessary to set up a Control Commission parallel with the Central Committee consisting of the most experienced, unbiassed comrades having the longest Party training and capable of carrying out strict Party control. The Control Commission elected by the congress of the Party should have the right to receive all kinds of complaints and examine them by arrangement with the Central Committee and if necessary by holding joint meetings with it or by submitting the question to the Party congress.

Lenin

24.IX.1920

First published in 1942
in *Lenin Miscellany XXXIV*   Printed from the manuscript

---

* One page of the manuscript is missing.—*Ed.*

3

PROPOSALS FOR THE RESOLUTION
ON THE IMMEDIATE TASKS OF PARTY DEVELOPMENT[244]

Re the composition of the Control Commission.
Adopt resolution of the C.C.:

that we nominate C.C. members to the Control Commission *only* at the desire of the Party conferences, considering it generally incorrect that these C.C. members are *not bound* by the decisions of the C.C. in their work within the Control Commission;

that C.C. members of the Control Commission do not vote in the latter when the matter specially concerns *their* departments or field of work.

As regards *transference*, add:
without detriment to those being transferred familiarising themselves with the matter in hand and without detriment to the work, i.e., only in such a manner as ensures that the management of affairs remains *always* in the hands of fully competent workers who guarantee success.

Lenin

Written September 29, 1920

First published in 1959   Printed from the manuscript
in *Lenin Miscellany XXXVI*

REPORT ON THE INTERNAL
AND EXTERNAL POSITION OF THE REPUBLIC
AT A MEETING OF ACTIVISTS
OF THE MOSCOW ORGANISATION OF THE R.C.P.(B.)
OCTOBER 9, 1920

There is no need to speak of our internal position at this meeting, since all the comrades are sufficiently informed about this from our press and from work in the local areas. Food collections are much bigger than they were last year, so are fuel collections, and these are the foundations of our work. We are worse off as regards supply, though. Some of the big factories can now be started, and the temper of the workers in them cannot be as hopeless as it was when the factories were at a standstill. Considering our economic situation, we can expect a change of heart.

I find it necessary to dwell on our external position, on the news of foreign policy. Poland is in the grip of a tremendous crisis: economically, Poland has suffered worse destruction than we have; politically, things have reached a point when even an opportunist party like the P.P.S.,[245] which has always conducted a vicious smear campaign against the Bolsheviks, protests against the brutal manner in which the government deals with the workers. In the territory which we are ceding to them under the peace treaty Poland will be able to rule only by violence. Among the worker and peasant masses of Poland there is a tremendous desire for peace. In offering Poland peace and making tremendous concessions we shall make the political parties realise that we were right, make them realise that we did not want war with Poland. By taking indemnities from us, Poland gains nothing. She will not receive the money—France will take it. Up till now this fact has been concealed in Poland, but the position is gradually being brought home to the workers, and we must see to it that it is brought home to them still more clearly. Therefore it is necessary that we now conclude peace. Besides, we shall win time and use it to strengthen our army.

On the Wrangel front the odds are in our favour, but at one time there was a grave danger to the Donets coal-field. Wrangel is frustrating our plan of a general offensive by dealing separate blows in various directions.

An, at first glance insignificant, incident is characteristic politically. Germany has allowed entry to Comrades Zinoviev and Bukharin to attend the forthcoming congress of the Independent Party in Germany. Maybe this is sheer provocation, but, on the other hand, there is no doubt that Zinoviev's arrival will speed up and deepen the split that had already started among the "Independents". Part of the breakaway "Independents" and up to a million members of the Communist Party of Germany will constitute an imposing revolutionary force. What is more, it will serve as immense propaganda material for all Europe.

The crux of the matter is that the imperialist policy of France now stands revealed—of France, who has always upset our peace talks and is now putting spokes in our wheel again. We must make use of every hour of the armistice to strengthen ourselves. We must step up our supply activities, achieve quick successes on the Wrangel front, and then we can hope to tear the web of diplomatic intrigues against us.

The situation in the Far East is such that Japan is bound to withdraw, since she cannot possibly face a winter campaign. This strengthens us. At the present time there is an American multi-millionaire in Moscow, who is negotiating a concession on Kamchatka. By granting this concession we shall aggravate relations between Japan and America.

In Turkestan and the Caucasus the situation is more complicated. Recently the Turks have started to move on Armenia with the aim of seizing Batum, and afterwards, perhaps, Baku. Obviously we must show the greatest caution in this matter. So far we have no information about military complications.

However great the disagreements between France and Britain, we cannot work on them now so long as we are having defeat instead of victory. Apparently, disagreements do exist. Britain wants to trade with us and we are trying to achieve this.

As to how our army is equipped with weapons I cannot say in any detail. There was a shortage of cartridges until recently, but the difficulties now have lessened. The work is on a strong foundation, it only has to be intensified still more. The Party organisations must help in this by working in the Party cells and through the trade unions.

As to what the chances are for victory, I cannot say just now, as the general feeling is hard to define at the moment. The disappointment is too great; six weeks have already passed since we started to retreat and we are still retreating. The thing is we are late with winter supplies; this has coincided with the defeat. Without doubt, we must make use of every moment of the armistice to strengthen ourselves.

We cannot set the tone for agitation until we know something definite. This meeting is already setting the tone.

According to Comrade Trotsky the question of Makhno has been very seriously discussed in military circles and it has been ascertained that we can expect nothing but a winning hand here. The reason is that the elements grouped around Makhno have already had experience of Wrangel's regime, and were not satisfied with what he could give them. Our agreement with Makhno is hedged around with guarantees that he will not go against us. We have the same picture here as with Denikin and Kolchak: as soon as they infringed upon the interests of the kulaks and the peasantry as a whole, the latter sided with us.

Unquestionably, the Poles, too, will use the armistice to strengthen themselves; maybe they will bring up munitions during that period, but that does not mean that we should not do the same.

So long as there is war, secret diplomacy must exist as a means of warfare. We cannot renounce it. An assessment of this diplomacy depends on a general assessment of the war.

First published in 1959 in *Lenin Miscellany XXXVI*   Printed from the shorthand record

ROUGH DRAFT OF A RESOLUTION ON PROLETARIAN CULTURE[246]

1. Not special ideas, but Marxism.

2. Not the *invention* of a new proletarian culture, but the *development* of the best models, traditions and results of the *existing* culture, *from the point of view* of the Marxist world outlook and the conditions of life and struggle of the proletariat in the period of its dictatorship.

3. Not apart from the People's Commissariat for Education, but as part of it, since the R.C.P. + Commissariat for Education = Σ Proletcult.

4. Proletcult's close link with and subordination to the Commissariat for Education.

5. No...*

Written October 9, 1920
First published in 1945   Printed from the manuscript
in *Lenin Miscellany XXXV*

---

* Here the manuscript breaks off.—*Ed.*

DRAFT DECISION
FOR THE POLITBUREAU OF THE C.C., R.C.P.(B.) ON THE TASKS OF THE R.C.P.(B.) IN LOCALITIES INHABITED BY EASTERN PEOPLES[247]

Having discussed the reports and communications made at a meeting of the Politbureau of the Central Committee with 27 delegates from the Baku Congress of the Peoples of the East,[248] on 13.X.1920, the Politbureau of the C.C. has decided:

1. To extend the work of the Council of Nationalities under the People's Commissariat for Nationalities; a report on this work to be made at the next meeting of the Council of People's Commissars.

2. To institute the strictest investigations into abuses and acts of violence committed by the local Russian population towards the Eastern peoples (especially the Kalmyks, Buryat-Mongols and so on) and to punish the offenders.

3. To issue in the name of the supreme Soviet authority a manifesto confirming the principles of the R.S.F.S.R.'s national policy and establishing more effective control over its full application.

4. To consider it necessary to carry out autonomy, in forms appropriate to the concrete conditions, for those Eastern nationalities which do not yet possess autonomous institutions, first and foremost for the Kalmyks and Buryat-Mongols. The Commissariat for Nationalities to be charged with this task.

5. On the agrarian question, to consider it necessary to restore to the mountaineers of the Northern Caucasus the lands they were deprived of by the Great Russians, at the expense of the kulak elements of the Cossack population, and to direct the C.P.C. immediately to prepare appropriate decrees.

6. To draw up instructions for all agents of the C.C. and the central Soviet authorities sent from Moscow to regions inhabited by Eastern peoples. The weight of emphasis

in these instructions to be made on clarifying the duty of the agents to act only through the local bodies consisting of representatives of the local working population, and to consider their chief task to be to fight against the bourgeois and pseudo-communist groups among the local population while at the same time giving support to the really communist groups and elements.

Written October 13 or 14, 1920

First published in 1958
in the journal
Voprosi Istorii KPSS No. 2

Printed from the manuscript

NOTES ON THE IMMEDIATE TASKS
OF THE PARTY

Principal questions after the termination of the war with Wrangel (and for the Party congress of 1921):

1) A drive against bureaucracy and red tape in Soviet institutions; checking real successes of this campaign;

2) Strengthening the socialist foundation: seven million trade union members. Equality in place of shock work.

Developing initiative on the part of seven million trade union members;

3) Links between the trade unions (A.C.C.T.U.) and the working, non-exploiting, non-profiteering peasantry. Forms and methods.

Strengthening connections between Soviet power and the peasantry.

Tractors and collective farms.

19.X.1920

First published in 1942
in *Lenin Miscellany XXXIV*

Printed from the manuscript

DRAFT DECISION
FOR THE COUNCIL OF LABOUR AND DEFENCE ON THE QUESTION OF RESTORATION OF THE BALTIC FLEET[249]

The Petrograd Soviet and specifically the Petrograd Council of Defence in the person of its chairman Comrade Zinoviev to be directed to give special attention to accelerating restoration work on the Baltic Fleet and co-ordinating the activities of all institutions capable of assisting in this matter, while at the same time eliminating all red tape and establishing effective control over the speedy progress of this work.

The report of the Presidium of the Petrograd Soviet and of Comrade Raskolnikov on the measures taken by them and the method of work adopted to be submitted within a fortnight by Raskolnikov and Sudakov (this may be done in writing).

Written October 23, 1920

First published in part
February 23, 1938
in *Pravda* No. 53

Published in full in 1963   Printed from the manuscript
in the Fifth Russian Edition
of the *Collected Works*, Vol. 41

DRAFT DECISION
FOR THE COUNCIL OF PEOPLE'S COMMISSARS ON THE WORK AND FOOD RATIONS FOR SOVIET EMPLOYEES[250]

Direct a commission of comrades
      Avanesov   +
      Nogin   Holtzmann
      Khalatov
      Gindin
      Fin

a) to collect information on the food supply of Soviet office employees of different departments compared with that of the workers (including unlawful supply);

b) to discuss measures for establishing greater uniformity and order in this field;

c) to submit a draft of personnel and regulations governing a commission for determining staffs of various institutions and studying work norms of Soviet office employees, their numbers, the results of their work, and so forth.

Written October 23, 1920

First published in 1959
in *Lenin Miscellany XXXVI*

Printed from the manuscript

DRAFT DECISION
FOR THE POLITBUREAU OF THE C.C., R.C.P.(B.)[251]

1. A very comprehensive and solemn printed statement concerning the Control Commission[252] to be issued within two days. Fulfilment by Bukharin and Dzerzhinsky.

2. Ask Dzerzhinsky and Preobrazhensky to work in the Control Commission not less than three hours a day in order to make it a really effective organ of Party and proletarian conscience.

3. "Discussion Leaflet" to be started immediately and given particular attention. Bukharin and Preobrazhensky to take special charge.

4. The Control Commission be recommended, as a special task, to adopt a careful and individualised attitude, often even in the form of a downright cure, towards representatives of the so-called opposition who have suffered a psychological crisis due to failures in their administrative or Party careers. We should try to calm them, explain things to them in a comradely manner, find them (without using the command method) suitable jobs congenial to their psychological nature, give them advice on this score, the directives of the C.C.'s Orgbureau, etc.

Written October 26, 1920

First published in 1959
in *Lenin Miscellany XXXVI*

Printed from the manuscript

November 1920-March 1923

ESTABLISHING CONTACTS BETWEEN
THE ECONOMIC COMMISSARIATS

1

DRAFT DECISION
FOR THE COUNCIL OF PEOPLE'S COMMISSARS[253]

A preliminary conference to be summoned to consider the question of linking the activities of all the economic commissariats.

All the economic commissariats, particularly the Commissariat for Food, the Supreme Economic Council, the Commissariat for Railways and the Commissariat for Agriculture, to be directed to submit to this conference by Monday, November 1, information concerning all existing inter-departmental economic commissions and a brief description of their work.

Written October 26, 1920

2

ROUGH DRAFT PROPOSALS

1) Direct the same trio (Avanesov + Larin + Popov)[254] to make a more accurate study of all the commissions as to their composition, nature of their work, etc., to classify them and formulate conclusions as to their necessary unification and simplification, and report to us on Saturday, November 6.

2) Direct (1) the Central Production Commission
        (2) the State Commission for Electrification
        (3) the Utilisation Commission
        (4) and the Commissariat for Agriculture

to prepare a report to our commission concerning the *nature* and *results* of their work *from the point of view of the general economic plan* of the whole R.S.F.S.R. and supply information at the *next sitting* (November 6) on the following points:

(a) by what date the report will be ready

(b) what are the main subjects (or the chief contents) of their report as far as the general economic plan of the R.S.F.S.R. is concerned (if possible, written theses of the report to be given).

Written November 1, 1920

First published in 1945 in *Lenin Miscellany XXXV*

Printed from the manuscripts

DRAFT DECISION FOR THE POLITBUREAU OF THE C.C., R.C.P.(B.) ON THE CHIEF COMMITTEE FOR POLITICAL EDUCATION[255]

The exact wording of the resolution of the Central Executive Committee speaks of "unification of *all work of political* education in the R.S.F.S.R".[256]

While definitely recognising the need for such unification, the Politbureau of the C.C.,R.C.P.(B.) establishes, first of all, that this unification can only be understood in the sense of preserving, strengthening and extending not only the independence of the Party organisation but its leading, guiding and preponderant position in regard to all fields of work without exception under the auspices of the People's Commissariat for Education.

The implementation of the C.E.C.'s resolution should be divided into two parts: a motion should be tabled immediately in the Council of People's Commissars for the unification of the institutions exactly enumerated in the resolution of the C.E.C.

This motion to be drafted not later than tomorrow, 29.X., by two members of the C.C.—Bukharin and Preobrazhensky.

The latter part of the task will cover: further unification of all parallel bodies of an educational nature in all the people's commissariats and elaboration of the organisational relations between the agitation and propaganda bodies of the R.C.P. and the educational bodies of the Commissariat for Education which are subordinate to them.

A report on this latter part, giving an accurate list of all parallel bodies in all the commissariats, is to be submitted to the Politbureau by Comrades Preobrazhensky and Bukharin.

Written October 28, 1920

First published in 1959   Printed from the manuscript
in *Lenin Miscellany XXXVI*

A LETTER TO MEMBERS OF THE C.C., R.C.P.(B.)

6/XI. 1920

To Members of the C.C., R.C.P.

Please consider and carry through at the plenum on 8.XI. a resolution that the report at the Congress of Soviets on 20/XII.20 on the second item of the agenda, namely, "The Basic Tasks of Economic Rehabilitation" be made by the Chairman of GOELRO (the State Commission for the Electrification of Russia), G. M. Krzhizhanovsky.[257]

We shall achieve effective implementation of the *general plan* of economic rehabilitation, which plan, without electrification, is nothing, and talk about "basic tasks" unrelated to this plan would not be serious.

For your preliminary information I enclose:

1) A copy of Krzhizhanovsky's memorandum "*Results of the Work of the State Commission for the Electrification of Russia*".

2) The booklet *Basis of Northern Region Electrification Project*, of which 3 copies for Trotsky, Rykov and Bukharin I can obtain tomorrow; the rest of the C.C. members should call up the switchboard, 2nd floor, if they wish to have copies.

3) Some electrification maps.

4) Proofs of the article: "Volga   1 copy to Comrade
   Area Electrification Plan"   Trotsky to be handed
                                 to Comrade Rykov and
                                 then to the remaining
                                 C.C. members

5) Stunkel's theses.

6) Krug's theses.

7) List of GOELRO material (over 200 works).

The sum of these documents shows clearly that we are fully able (by timely correction of the theses and plan of Krzhizhanovsky's report submitted on behalf of the C.C.) to get at the Congress of Soviets exactly what the Party and the country need, namely, a report on the "Basic Tasks of Economic Rehabilitation", which is both business-like and which sets forth the plan of work in a broad and attractive manner.

V. Lenin
Chairman, Council of People's Commissars

First published in 1959   Printed from the typewritten
in *Lenin Miscellany XXXVI*   copy

SPEECH AT AN ANNIVERSARY PLENARY MEETING OF THE SOKOLNIKI DISTRICT SOVIET HELD JOINTLY WITH REPRESENTATIVES OF THE FACTORY COMMITTEES AND INDUSTRIAL MANAGEMENTS OF MOSCOW NOVEMBER 7, 1920

Comrade Lenin said in his speech that the victory we had won was the most important of all. The international bourgeoisie had prevented us from engaging in productive labour, and all our energies in the course of three years had been engaged in war with them. Now we must win a victory on the home front. The bourgeoisie had diverted us from this work. Comrade Lenin spoke about the questions to be dealt with at the coming congress of Soviets—the questions of transport, agriculture, and so on. He said that all enthusiasm and discipline were to be switched over to the work of peaceful construction and the participation of the rank and file in this job was to be secured.

In addition, red tape and officialism had to be combated. Here, too, we had to win a victory, and there was only one way of doing that—by developing the consciousness and activity of the working masses themselves. In conclusion Comrade Lenin expressed the conviction that we would win a victory over cold and hunger.

Brief newspaper report
published November 9, 1920
in *Pravda* No. 251

First published in full in 1957
in the journal
Voprosi Istorii KPSS No. 1

Printed from the typed copy
of the minutes

DRAFT DECISION FOR THE PLENUM
OF THE C.C., R.C.P.(B.)
ON   PROLETCULT[258]

Confirming the resolution of the Politbureau, the C.C. approves in the main of the draft instructions drawn up in pursuance thereof by the Chief Committee for Political Education[259] and directs the Politbureau to edit it for a more exact expression of the main idea that the work of Proletcult in the field of scientific and political education merges with that of the People's Commissariat for Education and the Gubernia Education Departments, while in the artistic field (music, the theatre, fine arts and literature) it remains autonomous, and the leading role of the commissariat's organs, carefully screened by the R.C.P., is to be retained only for combating patently bourgeois deviations.

Written November 10, 1920

First published in 1958
in the journal
Voprosi Istorii KPSS No. 1

Printed from the manuscript

DRAFT DECISION
FOR THE PLENUM OF THE C.C., R.C.P.(B.)[260]

Zinoviev to be instructed to draw up detailed directives to Kopp and other comrades from the People's Commissariat for Foreign Trade and to the comrades working in Germany.

Mention to be made that we accept and highly appreciate the assistance of the rank-and-file workers in the execution of orders for Russia, including those workers who belong to the most reactionary of the trade unions.

At the same time we should expose the Legiens & Co., who want to make money out of this for themselves or their party, and give no money.

The text to be submitted to the Politbureau.

Written November 10, 1920

First published in 1959
in *Lenin Miscellany XXXVI*   Printed from the manuscript

DRAFT DECISION FOR THE C.P.C.
ON CONCESSIONS[261]

A commission composed of Comrades Lenin, Milyutin, Kursky, Lezhava and Sereda to be directed within a week* to revise and edit that part of the draft on concessions which is suitable for publication abroad, namely, first, the general decision, as a matter of principle, to grant concessions; second, a brief outline of the general economic and legal conditions for concessions; third, a list of concession objects with a sufficiently clear description of the economic significance of each object.[262]

Written November 16, 1920

First published in 1959
in *Lenin Miscellany XXXVI*   Printed from the manuscript

---

* The text from the word "composed" to the word "week" is in the handwriting of L. A. Fotieva.—*Ed.*

DRAFT DECISION OF THE POLITBUREAU
OF THE C.C., R.C.P.(B.)[263]

The Commissariat for Food to be directed, as a most important political and economic task, to regularly supply Baku with food to the extent of one hundred per cent of its requirements.

The food policy in Azerbaijan to be relaxed, namely, no grain at all to be taken from the peasants of Azerbaijan outside Mugan, and in Mugan itself with great care.

Frumkin to be directed immediately to report strict and punctilious execution of these directives twice a month to the Central Committee and the Council of Defence.[264]

A policy of utmost conciliation to be adopted towards Georgia, Armenia, Turkey and Persia, i.e., one directed most of all towards avoiding war.

We must not set ourselves the task of conducting any campaign against Georgia, or Armenia, or Persia.

The main task is to be that of guarding Azerbaijan and securing possession of the whole Caspian.

For this purpose the transference to Azerbaijan of no less than 7 divisions is to be speeded up in every possible way.

Propaganda, agitation, the development of the Committees of Poor Peasants,[265] and general Soviet activities in Azerbaijan to be stepped up in every way; for this purpose Comrade Stalin to be directed through the Orgbureau to dig up from everywhere he can the greatest possible number of Moslem Communists for work in Azerbaijan.

The Commissariat for Railways and the S.C.T.[266] to be directed to find means of transporting no less than 8 troop trains daily to Baku without affecting the supply of food to Russia.

Written November 27, 1920

First published in 1959   Printed from the manuscript
in *Lenin Miscellany XXXVI*

RE THESES OF A REPORT
AT THE EIGHTH ALL-RUSSIA CONGRESS
OF SOVIETS
ON IMPROVING THE ACTIVITIES
OF THE SOVIET AUTHORITIES
IN COMBATING BUREAUCRATISM[267]

Theses to be revised rather radically, on all points, in the direction of a very big reduction in the pledges, which are extremely vague, obscure and excessive

and the weight of emphasis to be placed on concrete, practical proposals realisable in a short time.

Supplementary to the theses, a draft resolution for the Eighth Congress of Soviets to be drawn up within a week.

Written November 27, 1920

First published in 1959
in *Lenin Miscellany XXXVI*

Printed from the manuscript

DRAFT DECISION FOR THE POLITBUREAU

(ON CHICHERIN'S MOTION THAT KRASIN BE TEMPORARILY RECALLED AND KRASIN'S INVITED OPINION)

In regard to the proposal of the People's Commissar for Foreign Affairs that Krasin's Mission be temporarily recalled from Britain[268] as a means of bringing pressure to bear on the British Government, the Politbureau makes no immediate decision on this matter and invites Krasin to give his opinion urgently. There is no question of a break with Britain, but merely that of pressure, for it is clear that Churchill, Curzon & Co. are dragging their feet and deceiving us, therefore, a temporary departure may prove very useful and intensify agitation by the Councils of Action.[269]

Written November 29, 1920

First published in 1965
in the Fifth Russian Edition
of the *Collected Works*, Vol 54

Printed from the manuscript

DRAFT DECISION FOR THE C.P.C.
ON DIRECT TAXES[270]

§ 1.   1) A commission to be instructed, within one week, to further examine the question of:

first, the possibility of repealing *local* monetary taxes and collecting accurate data both for the Petrograd and Moscow gubernias and, if possible, for other gubernias;

second, the necessity of preparing and carrying out simultaneously both the repeal of monetary taxes and the changeover from the surplus-appropriation system to the tax in kind.

§ 2.   2) The People's Commissariat for Internal Affairs to be directed to apply to the Presidium of the All-Russia Central Executive Committee requesting the latter to collect from all local executive committees information and material on all questions mentioned in § 1 for the Congress of Soviets.

§ 3.   3) The People's Commissariat for Finance to be instructed to submit to the Council of People's Commissars a draft decision on questions listed in § 1 depending on the decision of the commission.

Written November 30, 1920

First published in 1945   Printed from the manuscript
in *Lenin Miscellany XXXV*

DRAFT DECISION
FOR THE ECONOMIC COMMISSION
OF THE C.P.C.[271]

Considering it necessary, in view of the improvement in the internal and external position of the R.S.F.S.R., to focus the activities of the Council of Labour and Defence more than hitherto on the problems of economic development,

the C.P.C. asks the All-Russia Central Executive Committee to enact the following measures:

a) 1. To add a new member to the Council of Labour and Defence in the person of the People's Commissar for Agriculture.

sub-
sti-
tut-
ed

2. To direct the Council of Labour and Defence to discuss the idea of dividing its meetings into ordinary and special economic ones. *

c) 3. To extend the jurisdiction of the C.L.D. by including the following functions:

1) (a) co-ordination of all the work of the economic commissariats;

2) (b) endorsement and realisation of an integrated economic plan of the R.S.F.S.R.;

3) (c) directing the work of the economic commissariats in conformity with this plan, as well as establishing exemptions from this plan in case of need.

A subcommission to be directed to elaborate § 6 of its draft (in its final wording) and draw up an exact schedule of existing commissions which cover the work of the economic commissariats, showing their relations with and bearing on all the "special commissions" provided for in § 6.

Written December 1, 1920

First published in 1959
in *Lenin Miscellany XXXVI*   Printed from the manuscript

RE THE DRAFTING OF A DECREE
ON MEASURES FOR CONSOLIDATING
AND DEVELOPING PEASANT FARMING

NOTES TO THE COMMISSION MEMBERS

1) Number of representatives from the Peasant Assistance Committees to be increased....

2) The **Agriculture Commissariat's** wording of § 6 to be taken as a basis in determining the participation of the Peasant Assistance Committees.

3) The rights of the Sowing Committees to issue compulsory regulations are to be restricted and such issue is to be made subject to a preliminary discussion of intended measures by conferences of Peasant Assistance Committees both at uyezd, gubernia and regional levels.

---

* Point 2 in the manuscript is crossed out by Lenin.—*Ed.*

4) The paragraph concerning the requisitioning of seeds to be thrown out, the local bodies to be set the task of devising a form of protection of seed funds.

5) Section VII concerning penalties to be thrown out....

6) The major part of the draft to be transferred to instructions.

Written December 4, 1920

First published in 1945   Printed from the manuscript
in *Lenin Miscellany XXXV*

DRAFT DECISION
FOR THE POLITBUREAU OF THE C.C., R.C.P.(B.) ON THE TRADE AGREEMENT WITH BRITAIN[272]

The Politbureau approves the proposal of Comrade Chicherin on the question of the trade agreement with Britain and particularly emphasises:

that Krasin, without the special and explicit consent of the Central Committee, should on no account go beyond the text and letter of our Note of 29.VI on the questions of propaganda and debts[273];

all details to be dealt with at special talks on a peace treaty.

In motivation, reference to be made to their aid to Wrangel.[274]

Written December 4, 1920

First published in 1959   Printed from the manuscript
in *Lenin Miscellany XXXVI*

REPLY TO THE DEBATE ON CONCESSIONS
AT A MEETING OF ACTIVISTS OF THE MOSCOW ORGANISATION OF THE R.C.P.(B.) DECEMBER 6, 1920

Comrades, so many notes have been sent up that I cannot possibly answer them all. On the other hand, most of the arguments have already been refuted in the debate, so

I shall first comment on the booklet *On Concessions*.[275] I shall deal with this in greater detail. Comrade Lomov's one-and-a-half page preface deals with the subject all too briefly. Then there is the decree itself of November 23, which sets forth the idea of the interests of world economy. "The process of restoring the productive forces of Russia, and at the same time, of world economy as a whole, can be accelerated many times over by enlisting the co-operation of foreign state and municipal institutions, private enterprises, joint-stock companies, co-operative societies and workers' organisations of other countries in the extraction and processing of Russia's natural resources." Of course, this is merely of propaganda value, but it is economically indisputable. World economy has got to be restored. Capitalism acts in such and such a way, and we have our own proposals, but so far world economy remains capitalist.

We wanted to attract foreigners. Therefore the end of the decree lists these conditions:

Point One: "The concessionaire is to receive reward in the form of a share of the produce stipulated in the agreement with the right of exporting it abroad." Without this they won't go. The share is not specified. There will be a fight over this, we shall bargain and each of us will try to get the best of it. Comrades here said we shall have to keep our eyes skinned, and that's quite right.

Point Two: "In the event of special technical improvements being employed on a large scale the concessionaire will be granted trade priorities (such as the purchase of machinery, special agreements on large orders, etc.)." What do trade priorities mean? They mean we shall give this or that firm a priority agreement to the exclusion of another firm. And if the firm takes concessions, we can buy them out, we may pay them extra on the price. The main thing is that we shall be given machines. I think this consideration is clear enough, and here again we shall maintain elements of propaganda.

Point Three: "Depending on the nature and conditions of the concession prolonged concession terms will be granted to ensure full compensation for the concessionaire's risk and technical facilities invested in the concession." Here we have the duration of the concessions. It is quite an indefinite period, and we couldn't give Kamchatka on any other conditions, and Comrades Fedotov and Skvortsov are right about this being a special concession, which we are granting for important political reasons. In granting them under such conditions we are willingly giving away what we do not need ourselves, and we shall be no worse off for the loss of it neither economically nor politically.

Point Four: "The Government of the R.S.F.S.R. guarantees that the concessionaire's property invested in the enterprise shall not be subject to nationalisation, confiscation or requisition." Haven't you forgotten that we still have the law court? This is a well-considered phrase with which we were deeply concerned. We wanted to mention it at first, then thought better of it and decided to say nothing. Speech is silver but silence is gold. There won't be confiscation or requisition, but there remains the law court, and that court is ours, and if I am not mistaken it is composed of people elected by the Soviets. Personally, I hold anything but a gloomy view about our court being a poor one. So we shall make use of it.

Point Five: "The concessionaire shall have the right to hire workers and other employees for his enterprises in the R.S.F.S.R. with due observance of the code of labour laws or a special agreement guaranteeing workers definite conditions of work that protect their lives and health." There is nothing cautious here. If the workers go on strike and that strike is a reasonable one, we shall then be able secretly to support the strikers. What threat do the capitalists use? "We'll throw you out into the street and you will starve." But here they may find themselves getting a ration from somewhere or other, it all depends on us. We can and shall give it to them. And if the strike is a silly one, unreasonable, we'll have them up on the Soviet carpet and tell them off good and proper. It speaks here of a special agreement, but it is worded very carefully. By way of exception, however, it will have to be applied to Kamchatka, as we are not in a position to set up any Soviet bodies there. This is where Vanderlip was to demand a special agreement. We haven't even started yet to apply our own laws to Kamchatka.

Point Six: "The Government of the R.S.F.S.R. guarantees the concessionaire against any unilateral change in the terms of the concession agreement by any order or decree of the Government." We undertake not to change the terms of the agreement unilaterally, otherwise no one will sign it. This means there must be some go-betweens. Who? The neutral states are all capitalist states. Workers' organisations? We may have to invite Menshevik workers' organisations. In Western Europe they are in a majority. Maybe the Mensheviks will decide in turn—even number for the Bolsheviks, odd number for the capitalists. But if we don't come to terms, the agreement may be broken. That danger remains, but if it is a property agreement there is no harm in that. According to the basic principles of international law this is a private agreement, and you can break it, paying compensation, of course. If you broke it you've got to pay. There have been cases in the practice of international law when the ship of another country has been sunk by mistake during the war. It was taken for an enemy ship, but proved to be a neutral vessel. What is to be done? Pay up. The same here, as a last resort you buy yourself off. There still remains withdrawal from the war, though. War, of course, in the final analysis, is the ultimate argument. Of course, so long as there are capitalists in the world you must be prepared for war, once you have a socialist state. Further, we here are worrying now, but no one has taken a concession yet. When certain comrades say, "Ah well, this is the end, they'll all come crowding in now," I repeat, it's possible that no one will care to take it at all.

Section One: "Timber concessions in Western Siberia." The Northern Sea Passage is open for shipping, but we have no merchant fleet. A comrade says representatives have arrived, wishing to receive 6000 dessiatines in checkered order. The northern booklet says that if we take the extra electric stations of Petrograd we could use them for taking timber out of the northern districts and develop a production that would give us foreign currency to the value of five hundred thousand gold rubles a year. And total electrification, according to the estimate of the State Commission, will cost over a thousand million. It is a question whether we shall be able to do it. Concessions, however, will make this task easier. You don't go about offering concessions because you find life good, and when that life is a hungry

one, when you have to wangle things so as to give the people
a respite, you have to argue differently.

Section Three: "Mining concessions in Siberia." Siberia
is fabulously rich in copper. Copper has an extremely high
value in world economy and is one of the principal metals
used in electrification. We are offering a concession but
do not know who will take it. America or the Germans.
America will think that if she doesn't take it, Germany will.

When we carry through electrification we shall be a hundred
times stronger economically. We shall then speak a different
language. We shall speak about redemption. They know
that the socialist society is not only quick at creating
a Red Army, but can be quick in other things as well.

Further, separate concessions. Three million dessiatines
in the European part of Russia alone. Of these, over 800,000
dessiatines in the former Don Cossack Region. There are
no state farms or livestock. Whole stanitsas along the river
Ural are ruined, splendid virgin lands are lying idle.
Even if we give away three quarters of the wheat crop raised
there, we shall receive one quarter. We must strengthen our
transport and we can stipulate that tractors be delivered
cheaper.

If we cannot put three million dessiatines of magnificent
land to the plough, which will yield us 100 poods of wheat
per dessiatine—then what sort of farming is it? What sort
of policy is it?

The Italians are interested in this, and Italy is on the
eve of a revolution. In Italy the main argument against
a revolution is "We won't be able to feed ourselves, the
capitalist powers won't give us any food". But the socialist
power says, "I have three million dessiatines of land,
I have oil and benzine". You must realise that you can
agitate on various planes about capitalism being a dead
thing, and that it must be strangled. We have seen a good
deal. The European is living in the same conditions as
the Russian did when he went towards revolution from the
agonies of war. With them the war is over, they are living
by robbing other peoples. All the more weight does this
argument carry. They are unable to restore their economy,
and we offer them to start restoring it now. We have here
combined a political argument and socialist agitation, but

in a different form. You must learn to carry on agitation, otherwise your economic plans will come to nothing. And we are not only agitators, we are a Socialist Republic standing up to all the capitalist states in the world. You can't run your economy, but we can. There is a possibility of comparison here.

First published in 1963
in the journal
Voprosi Istorii KPSS No. 4

Printed from the shorthand
record

DRAFT DECISION
FOR THE PLENUM OF THE C.C., R.C.P.(B.)
ON THE REORGANISATION
OF THE PEOPLE'S COMMISSARIAT
FOR EDUCATION[276]

1. The post of Assistant People's Commissar to be instituted at the Commissariat for Education with all administrative functions concentrated in his hands.

3. General reorganisation of the Commissariat for Education is considered essential, but it should be more thoroughly prepared, particularly it should be discussed at a number of meetings in connection with the Congress of Soviets. Exact distribution of functions between the central and local bodies of the Commissariat for Education to be discussed and settled there.

4. It is considered necessary in principle to merge the secondary schools (or their higher forms) with technical vocational training under two indispensable conditions: 1) that general education subjects and communism in the technical vocational schools be extended; 2) that practical steps be taken immediately to pass over to polytechnical education, for which purpose use is to be made of every available electric station and suitable factory.

The implementation of this reform is to be deferred pending the general reorganisation.

5. Comrade Litkens to be appointed Assistant People's Commissar and made to devote no less than half his work

hours to the Chief Committee for Political Education until such time as this Committee is properly staffed.

6. The Orgbureau to be directed to speed up the staffing of the Chief Committee for Political Education and see to it that it is fully provided for in this respect.[277]

Written December 8, 1920

First published in 1959   Printed from the manuscript
in *Lenin Miscellany XXXVI*

DRAFT DECISION
FOR THE PLENUM OF THE C.C., R.C.P.(B.)
ON PRODUCTION PROPAGANDA

1) An All-Russia Bureau of Production Propaganda shall be set up under the All-Russia Central Council of Trade Unions,

on which the Commissariat for Education is to be more widely represented; the latter's apparatus is not to be transferred, but brought entirely to joint subordination with the All-Russia Bureau of Production Propaganda.[278]

Written December 8, 1920

First published in 1959   Printed from the manuscript
in *Lenin Miscellany XXXVI*

ADDENDA TO DRAFT DECISION
FOR THE C.C., R.C.P.(B.)
PLENUM CONCERNING
THE ORGANISATION
OF A SPECIAL PRODUCTION ORGAN[279]

1) Directives to be given to *Izvestia* and *Pravda* to become more of a *production* than a political organ and to teach *all* newspapers of the R.S.F.S.R. to do the same;

2) *Bednota* to be turned into a production newspaper featuring *concrete* material and aimed at bringing the peasants and workers, agriculture and industry, closer together.

Written December 20, 1920
First published in 1959
in *Lenin Miscellany XXXVI*

Printed from the manuscript

THE EIGHTH ALL-RUSSIA CONGRESS OF SOVIETS

DECEMBER 22-29, 1920[280]

1

REPLY TO THE DEBATE ON THE REPORT
ON CONCESSIONS DELIVERED TO THE R.C.P.(B.) GROUP
AT THE EIGHTH CONGRESS OF SOVIETS
DECEMBER 21

Comrades, I have received quite a few notes and shall briefly answer those to which no replies have yet been given. But first let me read to you a note of an informative nature, which I think is characteristic:

At the Arzamas uyezd congress, Nizhni-Novgorod Gubernia, a non-Party peasant declared the following concerning concessions, which we communicate to you as a characteristic sign: "Comrades, we are delegating you to the All-Russia Congress and declare that we, peasants, are prepared to endure hunger and cold and do our duty for another three years but don't sell Mother-Russia in the form of concessions!"

I think it would be very useful to quote this note in the official report to the Congress,* and it ought to be done because it shows a side of the question which the capitalists overlook, and in connection with which we have no need whatever to conceal the fact that there is a danger here, and we have to be on our guard against it. I have already mentioned that these reminders sharpen the attention of the workers and peasants. The fact that such reminders are coming from the midst of the illiterate peasantry is of special importance, as it stresses a task which is of excep-

---

* See Vol. 31 of this edition, p. 493.—*Ed.*

tional importance at the present time—I mean about your
having to examine the bills tabled in the Council of People's
Commissars for rendering assistance to peasant farming.
We must learn to convince the non-Party peasants, win
them over to our side and make them self-dependent. A note
like this shows that we have every chance of achieving
tremendous success here, and we shall achieve it.

Here is another note:

> Won't the capitalist concessionaires set the proletarian masses
> against the Soviet government, seeing that the economic crisis and
> chaos we are living through make it impossible for us to satisfy the
> needs of the workers the way the capitalists can?

I have said already that in the advanced countries, in
most of them, the workers are better provided for than ours,
yet the Russian workers in all the advanced countries are
all eagerness to come to Soviet Russia, although they are
well aware of the hardships the workers have to bear.

> Won't the Russian Ryabushinskys and the rest of the pack put
> in an appearance together with the English and American capitalists?

This has a bearing on the note which asks whether the
concessionaires will be exterritorial. Of course not, we shall
never grant them exterritoriality. This is granted only to
ambassadors, and even then on definite conditions. If
Ryabushinsky banks on hiding himself from the proper
authorities, I think he is mistaken.

Next, comrades, I want to tell you that Comrade Lezhava
reports: "Vanderlip has presented a mandate from about
a dozen big syndicates. This has been verified by our special
authorities here. It has already been corroborated by Krasin
in London, who has checked up on the seriousness of the
groups for whom Vanderlip is acting."

For the benefit of those comrades who ask why the agreement has not been published, I repeat that its publication
is not to our advantage, because the capitalists, who are
fighting among themselves, think there are far worse things
in that agreement. The hullabaloo about it in the press bears
this out. Let them go on believing it, we have no intention
whatever of disillusioning them. Those who wish to familiarise themselves with this agreement have every possibility of doing so. Besides, I mentioned that the agreement

will come into force after the new president of the United States of America has been sworn in. Our Party congress will be held in February.[281] Consequently, the Party will have every opportunity of controlling and deciding things.

Please explain, if you can, for how long Kamchatka has been let (or is proposed to be let) and is there an economic, apart from a political, advantage in this for the R.S.F.S.R. and in what form?

Kamchatka has not been let and cannot be let until March. The economic gain is that according to the draft agreement they are obliged to give us a share of the mineral wealth which they will extract.

In granting concessions do we not thereby admit the durability of the capitalist states and do we not consider our thesis concerning the earliness of a world revolution to be incorrect?

Bukharin has replied to this. It is not a question of our admitting their durability; the point is that gigantic forces are driving them to the brink. Our existence and speedy release from the critical situation and famine are a gigantic force and a factor of revolution more powerful than those farthings—a mere crumb from the point of view of world economy—which they will get from us. An extra hundred or thousand machines and locomotives are of tremendous importance to us, for it will mean that transport repairs, which Trotsky planned over a period of four and a half years and reduced to three and a half, will be reduced by another year. Reducing the economic chaos and famine by a year is of colossal importance to us.

What if Japan, to prevent us letting Kamchatka to America, goes and occupies it with her troops and declares it her own?

As a matter of fact she is in possession of Kamchatka right now, and if she could she would do it, but she can't because she is afraid of America.

Where will the capitalist get his labour force? Will he bring it with him? Hardly. If he is going to employ Russian workers, not only will these be under the thumb of the capitalist, but it will upset our labour market, and this, in turn, will upset our integrated economic plan.

I can't see how our economic plan will be upset by our workers going there to work. They won't be able to go there apart from the trade unions, apart from our economic organisations and our Party. The workers at the advanced capitalist enterprises will train our workers in the best methods of production. In submitting to capitalist conditions of work, our workers will subordinate them to our code of labour laws or to special restrictive agreements, and will not hesitate to quit if the conditions are bad. If the conditions are unfavourable, the workers will quit. Some comrades are afraid that the conditions will be good, others, that they will be bad. We shall look out, just like our workers and peasants, and take proper measures.

In granting concessions, when the concessionaires start working, will the activities of the R.C.P. in organising communist cells among those employed on the concession territory be open or only illegal?

Here is a wrong idea of concessions and concessionaires. The concessionaire is not an authority. He does not get any territory other than that to be used for economic exploitation. All government bodies and all courts of law remain only in the hands of the R.S.F.S.R.

Should unemployment in America force a revolution, won't our concessions be helping America to cope with this crisis, that is, hold up the revolution.

That argument has been disproved by Comrade Bukharin.

If the international bourgeoisie gets to know of the Soviet government's tactics in concessions, what will the position of the Soviet government be? Won't this be bad for us?

On the contrary, everyone in Europe has heard about the concessions, and the hullabaloo about it there only goes to show that the bourgeoisie is worried. They are anxious not to be late. All those capitalists who do not want to risk having dealings with Russia are now beginning to realise that they are lagging behind while the more enterprising people are getting in. And we are taking advantage of the contradictions among the capitalists.

Are there any plans or projects for concessions on large industrial enterprises in Moscow and in the centre generally? There is talk about three such concessions in Moscow, Yaroslavl and Lubertsi.

I know nothing about such concessions. There is an American factory in Lubertsi which has not been nationalised and never was, but there is no concession there. The only concession in the centre, which the S.E.C. comrades have spoken of as being possible, is a concession to the German chemists for developing dye works and letting one factory to them. In the Council of People's Commissars all were agreed it was possible, but this talk has had no practical consequences.

Germany is so far ahead of our country that during the imperialist war even the advanced countries found themselves in difficulties when the German chemical industry stopped supplying them. To get our chemical industry going we must be prepared to pay the German chemists well. The best way to learn is to grant the Germans a concession on one of our factories. No schools or lectures will help as much as practical work at a factory, where the workers can be trained in six months and then made to build another factory like it next door. To fear that the Germans of a single factory will do something to us, considering their international situation, is ridiculous. There were no differences of opinion in the C.P.C. In point of principle it is acceptable. Unfortunately, this question has not had practical results. I must stress the fact that we talk a great deal about concessions, but so far we have not succeeded in granting a single one. We shall consider it a great success if we manage to grant at least one, and you will see the concrete conditions of the concession.

Further.

What countries can be granted concessions? Can we give a concession to Poland?

We believe they can be granted to all countries, Poland included.

Couldn't the capitalists use the concessions to avert crises at home and thus stave off a social revolution?

If the capitalists could avert crises at home, then capitalism would be everlasting. They are decidedly blind pawns in the general mechanism—the imperialist war has shown that. Every month proves that the crisis of capitalism is deepening, disintegration throughout the world is spreading farther and farther, and Russia is the only country where an upswing towards a durable and serious improvement has started.

To sow dissension among the workers the concessionaires may place their workers in better conditions.

This won't increase dissension among our people, we have grown much stronger.

Will trade union groups be organised on the concessionaire's territory?

The concessionaires get economic exploitation, the authorities and laws remain Soviet ones.

Can you outline the conditions guaranteeing us against the danger of the Soviet state system being distorted and a capitalist set-up being introduced?

These conditions are the laws of the R.S.F.S.R. If a contracting party breaks them we have the right to cancel the agreement.

What is the gist of the tentative draft agreement with the American imperialists covering a concession on Kamchatka?

I said that the term of the concession is 50-60 years. We get a share of the produce, they the right to set up a military and naval base at the inlet near which there is an oil deposit.

You say that granting concessions to the capitalists of oppressed countries like Germany is more important than for other countries. But if the capitalists of oppressed countries use the concessions to improve their country's economic position, don't you think this will stave off the revolution in that country?

The international situation as regards revolution revolves around Soviet Russia's struggle against the rest of the world, the capitalist countries. To strengthen Soviet Russia and make her invincible—that is what matters most as far as the struggle of the oppressed and colonial countries is concerned.

What role in concessions does Turkestan cotton play?

So far there is no question of granting a concession on Turkestan cotton. This question was not discussed.

Will concessions be granted for the rehabilitation of industrial enterprises and for taking over railways?

Such exigencies are ruled out. The railways are a single integrated enterprise.

Has there been any question of concessions on slaughter-houses?

Not that I have heard of.

The protests against concessions in the local areas stand clearly revealed, not as healthy sentiments at all, but as patriotic feeling among a strong petty-bourgeois section of the countryside and among the urban middle classes.

The patriotism of a person who is prepared to go hungry for three years rather than surrender Russia to foreigners is genuine patriotism, without which we could not hold out for three years. Without this patriotism we would not have succeeded in defending the Soviet Republic, in doing away with private property and now getting as much as 300 million poods by means of the food surplus-appropriation system. This is the finest revolutionary patriotism. As for the kulaks being prepared to go hungry for three years to keep out the foreign capitalists, from whom they have something to gain—that is untrue. It is not the kulaks who are concerned, it is the non-Party middle peasant.

Isn't there a risk that in view of a possible war between America and Japan there is a likelihood of a serious attack on Soviet Russia by Japan? What shall we do then? Shall we fight off Japan in alliance with imperialist America, using her assistance as a real force?

Of course we shall—we have often said that an alliance with one imperialist state against another to consolidate the socialist republic is not objectionable in point of principle. An attack by Japan on Soviet Russia is much more difficult now than it was a year ago.

Please explain the Allies' policy towards Turkey and our relationships.

It is rather awkward, of course, to deal openly with this question in an official speech, as relations here are extremely confused. Everything here depends on the intricate play of relations in bourgeois Georgia, which is on the verge of catastrophe. The comrades who are interested in this will, I am sure, derive great benefit from the report by Comrade Meshcheryakov, Editor of *Pravda*, who has returned from Georgia, where he spent several weeks, if not months, and has collected highly interesting material on this Menshevik realm. Georgia is on the verge of disaster. The Turkish attack was planned against us. The Allies were making a pitfall for us, but fell into it themselves, because we have received Soviet Armenia.

The men at the top in Turkey are Cadets, Octobrists, Nationalists, who are prepared to sell us to the Allies. But that is an extremely difficult thing to do, because feeling among the Turkish people against the savage oppression by the Allies is running very high, and sympathy towards Soviet Russia is growing in proportion as we help the independent Azerbaijan Republic to carry out proper liberation of the Moslem peasants, who have driven out the landowners, but are afraid to take the land, and will shortly stop being afraid; when they do take the land the Turkish landowner won't last long.

We personally have been and will be peaceful in the extreme in the Caucasus, and for the information of our Caucasian comrades, we shall be very careful to avoid anything that may involve us in war. Our peaceful policy so far has been so felicitous, that the Allies are getting nervous, have started taking decisive steps against us, but are only getting them against themselves.

What is going to happen next to Georgia?

Even the Mohammedan Allah doesn't know that, but if we show self-restraint we have something to gain without running any risk.

We are asked whether there were any other concession objects besides Kamchatka. There have been no other concessions with Vanderlip.

Regarding press hand-outs. We can't do that, first because the printing-works are busy, and secondly so as not to make this material available to people abroad, where there is a desire to torpedo this undertaking of ours. So far we haven't got a single concession, a single agreement, and we must first get an agreement before speaking about dangers. We have nothing so far and are acting semi-legally.

How will things stand with concessions and with works and buildings erected by concessionaires in the event of a) their violating the laws of the R.S.F.S.R. b) war breaking out with a country of which the concessionaire is a subject, and c) with others?

In the event of an agreement being violated the concession-aire will be prosecuted under the laws of the R.S.F.S.R. In the event of war the concession agreement is broken and the property passes into the possession of the R.S.F.S.R. in accordance with military procedure.

The Russian bourgeoisie, who have escaped abroad, will be able to take part in the exploitation of concessions with their capital. Won't this lead to the old bosses coming back under the guise of foreign capital?

If an old boss takes a ride through the northern forests of European Russia under the guise of foreign capital we have nothing to fear. You will find many an old boss in the centre of Moscow. We have a thousand times less reason to fear a situation in which we shall have a list of all visiting foreigners, than those bosses who are operating at our enter-prises and who, unfortunately, have not been registered yet.

You have pointed out and underlined the political significance of concessions. That is understandable. But what the provinces are most worried about is this: with concessions there will be trade rela-tions. What threats and dangers to the Republic does this imply in the sense of disintegration and the blowing up of the Soviet system from within (perhaps increased profiteering, etc.) and what precautions can we take against it?

I have already spoken about that. We had a tremendous threat of profiteering in the shape of Sukharevka,[282] with which we waged a constant struggle. We understand, of course, that with the abolition of Sukharevka profiteering still remains, it remains wherever there is a small proprietor, and we have tens of millions of such proprietors. That is where the real danger lies, and not in big capital, which will be hedged around on all sides with special supervisions. It should not be forgotten that we shall have an agreement which we can always cancel at the risk—our greatest danger—of having to pay damages.

What is the position with regard to tsarist debts? Will the Allies agree to any transactions unless these debts are paid?

England already agrees not to demand the debts from us, since we have proposed the draft of a trade agreement to them. Under that draft trade deals are now starting and under it we are not obliged to repay debts. I say, England agrees, but France does not. And so we tell France that in

principle we do not refuse. The exact amounts of payments
will be discussed at a conference, at which we intend to
say: you, too, are responsible for the losses you have caused
us by your intervention. An ad hoc commission is working
on this question, and an initial estimate puts the figure
at ten thousand million in gold.

First published in 1963
in the journal *Kommunist* No. 6

Printed from the shorthand
record

2

SPEECH TO THE R.C.P.(B.) GROUP
AT THE EIGHTH CONGRESS OF SOVIETS
DURING THE DEBATE
ON THE REPORT
OF THE ALL-RUSSIA CENTRAL EXECUTIVE COMMITTEE
AND THE COUNCIL OF PEOPLE'S COMMISSARS
CONCERNING HOME AND FOREIGN POLICIES
DECEMBER 22

Comrades, allow me to begin by touching on certain
remarks made by speakers and answering notes, at least the
more important ones. From Comrade Korzinov's criticism
I have picked out the idea concerning engineers and agronomists. We must push forward with the training of engineers and agronomists from among the workers and peasants.
This is beyond all question, and the Soviet government is
taking steps in this direction, but we cannot count on very
quick results; it may not take as long as electrification, but
it will take at least several years; so it is wrong of Comrade
Korzinov to suggest that all other matters be set aside until
we have our own agronomists. Right now we have got to
find and get the best agronomists, call them to our meetings,
demand from them an account and thus single out the
industrious and educated men from the rest.

Comrade Korzinov has landed in the opposition for
opposition's sake when he says that the decree on concessions
should have been published earlier. But our work at the
Council of People's Commissars and the Council of Labour
and Defence is such that we have to react at once, and the

position with us is such that, given no differences of opinion in the C.C. and C.P.C., decisions are taken at once. If the decree on concessions is wrong,[283] then we should propose its repeal, because the chief concession with Vanderlip will not become a formal agreement until next March.

At the time we published this decree our main purpose was, and still remains, to conclude a trade agreement as quickly as possible and offer the bait of concessions to the capitalists. I dealt with this political aspect of the case in my report to the R.C.P. group and heard no objections at the time. I was therefore surprised when Comrade Ignatov, bent on being opposition-minded, said that we had slipped up on Vanderlip, that we hadn't found out who he was. I read the statement by the Deputy People's Commissar for Foreign Trade that all inquiries concerning the group Vanderlip represented had been made, had been confirmed abroad and remained unrefuted. Vanderlip himself had pointed out that no agreement could be concluded until after the presidential elections, when the Republican candidate would take office, since such an agreement would have to be sanctioned by the American Government.

This is an agreement under which the American Government is to receive a naval base. Consequently, even if this Washington Vanderlip, about whom Comrade Ryazanov went into such irrelevant details—as often happens with him—even if he did represent nobody and was just a swindler and the proposed agreement was to provide for the Government of the United States receiving a naval base aimed against Japan, there could be no question of our being swindled, as the President of the United States would really be a member of the Republican Party. After Vanderlip we shall be in a position to form a conclusive opinion about this trade agreement. Ignatov's entire criticism falls to the ground; he simply did not pay attention to what was said at our meeting.

Comrade Korzinov said that in the matter of Poland we should have given warning earlier. We have here an extremely difficult situation, and there was a moment when our troops were on the move and the Central Committee had reason to believe that despite the complicated situation we could achieve much by launching an offensive.

At such a time when, after Curzon's Note of July 11,[284] we had to give a reply within a few days, how could we be expected to call Party meetings to discuss the matter? Besides, every comrade knows that if we could have passed over to an offensive war at the right moment we would have done so without hesitation. And there would never have been any opposition to it anywhere. What we did see was an opposition in reverse, when we were accused of not pursuing a sufficiently active foreign policy. That there have been mistakes here, there is no doubt, but neither is there any doubt that arguing about them would be a sheer waste of time, as we have other things to think of besides our old activities. When time has receded, when all the documents and material will have been collected, we shall be able to fully appreciate our mistake. Therefore, I see nothing, absolutely nothing, in Comrade Korzinov's speech other than a desire to seek opposition. At another time, when we are in more favourable conditions, we shall make the same use of our successes. And so long as the Party does not forbid it, we shall always assume the offensive. I don't think that the Party or any of its members will propose a reverse policy at any meeting.

In regard to Comrade Gusev's remark, I must say that I made a mistake in introducing polemics in an official report, and therefore I have already suggested that this part of the report be deleted from the official text and greetings to Soviet Armenia added—through an unforgivable oversight on my part this was omitted in the report.

Comrade Gusev is wrong in saying that I boasted of my modesty—the point is that in passing over to a more serious practical integration of the economic commissariats and the implementation of a single economic plan, the thing we had to be afraid of was project-mongering.

Comrade Gusev says that I did not criticise his booklet[285] as a whole. But that is the central point: Comrade Trotsky and Comrade Rykov are invited to drop the departments and join the Council of Defence, which, not being a departmental body, will set up a new apparatus of its own. I cannot understand how, after three years of Soviet rule, one can raise and support such a question here. I am at a loss for words to express my perplexity. It is so ill-advised, it means knocking down the department in one place and setting it up in another. It means failure to understand what our apparatus is. I don't know whether Comrade Popov has managed to print the leaflet he gave me. It contains an extract from the 1920 census results. You know that this census has been satisfactorily carried out and has yielded a mass of valuable information concerning the number of Soviet office employees in Moscow. We took a similar census before this in 1919, but now we have a fuller one. It shows that we have no less than 230,000 office employees, of which 30,000, or even more, are in the most important commissariats, and 70,000 in the Moscow Soviet.[286] Try to imagine these figures, ponder over them, and then you will say to yourself—well, if you take an influential man, one who enjoys the greatest authority and has created a certain style of work in his department, take him out of that department and put him in charge of several united departments, you can expect nothing but chaos. Is that the way to fight bureaucratism? It is simply a frivolous attitude towards the work, absolutely unrealistic. I understand what a serious thing bureaucratism is, but no provision for its abolition is made in the Party Programme. It is not a problem for a congress, it is a problem for a whole epoch, and you have a special report devoted to this question.

Does anyone really believe that by a mere stroke of the pen, by taking comrades, who have created the best form of organisation in one or another of the most important departments, and transferring them to the Council of Labour and Defence, you will be getting a new department with indefinite powers that will not perform economically unifying functions. When the practical question arose in the Council of Labour and Defence as to what was economic and what was not, not only the Foreign Trade Commissariat, but the Finance Commissariat as well claimed that it was an economic commissariat. And can you conduct any economic work without the Commissariat for Public Health. Of course, when we shall have made big progress in economic reconstruction the relation of economic commissariats to non-economic ones may become different after we have achieved important successes in the work of changing our economic foundations. At present we have nothing of

the kind. Therefore, to treat the departmental question as
lightly as Gusev does—in other parts of the booklet, by
the way, he repeats some of the excellent ideas expressed
in his previous booklet[287]—is absolutely wrong.

I shall say nothing about Ryazanov's speech, which has
been sufficiently refuted by Kamenev. I shall merely mention
that both Ryazanov and Gusev, who has followed his bad
example, have been talking about having heard, perhaps
from me in the Council of People's Commissars, that
I wanted to, one said drown myself, the other said shoot
myself. If comrades are going to take a man at his angry
word, uttered when he is very tired, and make him speak
about it before an audience of a thousand, I don't think
these people can expect their speeches to be taken seriously.
(*Applause.*)

It's quite possible that we have a lot of vermicelli affairs
in the Council of People's Commissars—that's true. If
Maximovsky has made this an object on which to display
his oppositionist bent and made a special point of it, I must
say there is not and cannot be any government institution
which does not have to deal with vermicelli affairs. You
omitted to mention that the C.C. dealt with questions involving policy. So long as the ruling Party governs, so long
as this Party has to decide all questions concerned with
various appointments, you will not allow important state
appointments to be made by anyone but the ruling party.
When all is said and done, the question of who is to make
this or that policy is of secondary importance. Hasn't the
C.C. vermicelli affairs? Plenty of them. Aren't there agendas,
on completing which and running through a dozen items
of business, you would not only say you'd be glad to drown
yourself, but something worse still. I repeat, to catch me at
this sort of statement is not very difficult, but to come out
here and make it an object for an oppositionist stand and
speak against vermicellism is frivolous.

If, in a body which in general establishes only principles,
we attempted to set up a separate body to deal with petty,
practical, vermicelli affairs, we would only make things
worse. Because we would be tearing generalisation away
from the facts of life, and such a break would be sheer day-
dreaming and frivolity. Questions in the Central Committee

cannot be divided into questions of principle and trivial questions, because in every trifle a principle may be involved.

It is not a question of Ivan or Sidor. It is not a question of putting Sidor in Ivan's place or vice versa. What if they refuse? What if this Ivan and Sidor are both people's commissars—what's to be done then? The C.C. has a Secretariat, an Orgbureau, a Politbureau, finally, plenums of the Central Committee are held, and very often questions come before the Central Committee Plenum that are as trivial and tedious as anything, and some that you sit over for several hours until you feel like drowning yourself. But to draw a line between trivial questions and questions of principle is to undermine the very foundation of democratic centralism. At the same time it cannot be said that the Central Committee dumps its vermicelli onto other institutions. So far we have not been able to alter the Constitution and have been woiking autonomously. The fact that on some questions we have arrived at an agreement and on others there have been debates is only natural and inevitable, considering the apparatus we have. The fact that the C.C. is becoming an organ of control, and that in the general distribution of work it has fallen to Comrade Kalinin to supervise agitation and verification, and that he is required to give his personal impressions obtained during his trips and at work—this gives no grounds for shouting about the Council of People's Commissars referring all questions to the C.C and vice versa. It means introducing further confusion and turmoil while things remain essentially unchanged. The higher bodies are needed for the purpose of control and for turning down certain questions.

People here have spoken and complained about the Presidium of the All-Russia Central Executive Committee being swamped with business, and though it is our highest body, it is swamped with purely vermicelli affairs. But I would ask all those present here, how many of you have read a dozen reports of our proceedings? Who has read them from beginning to end? Probably no one, because they are dull, you can't wade through them. I must say that every member of our Party and every citizen of the Republic has a right to bring any question, any circumstance, however trivial, before the All-Russia Central Executive Committee. This question will go through the whole ladder, through the bureau, etc. till it gets to the C.E.C. Presidium, where it will be examined. And so it will be until the complete communist re-education of the working people, which will come within several decades after electrification has been finally completed. In this respect we are not afraid of changes.

I shall now deal with some of the notes. Comrade Minkin writes:

> Did Comrade Shlyapnikov inform the Council of People's Commissars of the disgraceful goings on at the Commissariat for Foreign Trade, or was this being kept for announcement at the Congress? If he did make such a statement, what has been done to eliminate them?

To answer this question I consulted Comrade Serebryakov who is better informed than I am. He was appointed by the Central Committee to the commission, the other members of which were Dzerzhinsky, Krestinsky and Lezhava, set up to take steps towards improving the relations between the Commissariat for Foreign Trade and the Commissariat for Internal Affairs, since our representatives abroad had information that these relations were anything but satisfactory. At my request Serebryakov gives the following answer to the note of delegate Minkin: "Comrade Minkin states ..." (reads).

After this commission a subcommission was set up. It is very easy to play at opposition, since there are disgraceful goings on with us in every commissariat, and the infelicitous mention of guarantees and 30,000 employees in the commissariat's technical publishing house is very characteristic in the sense that you can always find scandalously disgraceful things here. You will find the same thing in any division of the Red Army. Nevertheless our Red Army has been winning victories all the time.

The thing is to apply in good time to the institution that has to remedy matters, and not talk about it here, where we cannot collect accurate information about what Comrade Ryazanov has heard of this or that person and has not checked it or discovered the true facts. Is that democratic centralism? It is not at all democratic, and not at all centralism, but disorder and the introduction of chaos. Complaints should be lodged with Party bodies. If that body does not fulfil its duty it should be made to give a strict account of itself.

Among the notes that have been sent up there is the question of reducing the army. On this subject Comrade Trotsky will make a special statement, and you will decide whether this question should be dealt with today or at the next special meeting of the R.C.P. group. I can tell you that after an ad hoc commission on demobilisation headed by Trotsky and Dzerzhinsky was set up, the C.C. decided to start demobilisation, and this is now going on. It is being dealt with by the military department, and you will receive an exact report.

Is the Council of Labour and Defence regarded as an interim body called upon to unite the economic commissariats and then to be abolished, or is it the basis of a future integrated economic plan? Also, on what apparatus does the Council rely locally?

This question has not been settled, and we believe that to raise it now would be a waste of time. The order of the day now is a check-up of the organisation of the commissariats. The Council of People's Commissars has set up an organisational body which is to revise the apparatus of the People's Commissariats with a view to the tasks confronting them, and in this connection, to examine the question of staffs. To busy ourselves at the present time with setting up another apparatus in place of the Council of Labour and Defence is impossible until the question of electrification is settled. Various material on electrification will soon be handed out to you, and the Council of Labour and Defence will have to reckon with what the verification of this material and the reports will have to say. We now have an organ that we need, and, good or bad, we have in any case been working with it and coping with the tasks confronting us. We have no intention of embarking on reforms until we have practically tested how the integrated economic plan will be carried out. This is definitely a case of look before you leap.

Who is going to conclude concession contracts in the Far East, we or the buffer state, in either case—why?

This, comrades, is a delicate question. Buffer state[288]— it is such an embarrassing definition when we are asked:

You or the buffer? On the one hand we have the buffer, on
the other, the corresponding Party Bureau of the R.C.P.
The buffer's a buffer, it's to enable us to win time and
then beat the Japanese. I don't know whom Kamchatka
belongs to. Actually the Japanese are in possession, and
they do not relish the idea of our giving it away to the
Americans. We are consulted, our directives are complied
with, and nobody has protested against our negotiations
with Vanderlip, no single group of Party comrades has
considered the question important enough to demand its
being discussed at the plenum of the Central Executive
Committee and examined in the Control Commission.
This is the right of every Party member, and no one has
used this right. The person who has learned the facts which
led to the postponement of an agreement till March will
not try to make use of this right.

What is your view of the trade unions at the present moment in
connection with the concessions? Is it true that you stand for the
organisation of a trade union of peasants?

I must say that the Party's Programme mentions the
necessity of seeking new forms of trade unions that would
unite the poor sections of the peasantry.[289] This task has
been posed in the Party's Programme and I have often
pointed out that although we are not in a position at present
to solve this problem, we must not give it up. We must
not confine ourselves to the work of Vserabotzem,[290] which
is so weak, and which cannot give us outstanding workers.
So long as we have a levelling process taking place among
the peasantry, a levelling and unification of the working
peasants, the non-kulak section of the peasantry, this
problem cannot be removed from the order of the day of
socialist construction. To strengthen the work of the trade
unions we must extend them not only to the rural proletariat,
but to all the working peasantry. How this is to be done
we do not know yet. We have set this task in the Party's
Programme, we shall return to it many times and get it
settled in a practical manner from different aspects. That
is all I can say now on this question.

With the granting of concessions, the trade unions, naturally, will have important tasks imposed upon them—those

of checking, supervising, and maintaining contact with the workers who will be employed in these concessions. How this task will be handled in practice, I cannot say at the moment. To raise this question at the present time would be inadvisable, as the trade unions have more important tasks facing them.

In our fight against bureaucratism we certainly need the help of the trade unions. We must rely on them. This is basically provided for in the Party's Programme.[291] This shows what a long struggle is needed and what systematic work faces us. When we shall have data that in such-and-such a workmen's settlement the business of supervision is organised in such-and-such a way and definite results have been achieved, while in such-and-such a block, uyezd, etc. things are different—then we shall be able to weigh things, get them moving, and there will not only be talk about the "agitpotato" but we shall be in a position to check what steps have been taken in practice and on this ground apply practical measures that have already yielded results.

First published in 1963
in the Fifth Russian Edition
of the *Collected Works*, Vol. 42

Printed from the shorthand
record

3

SPEECH ON ADDENDA TO THE BILL OF THE C.P.C.
"ON MEASURES TO CONSOLIDATE AND DEVELOP
PEASANT FARMING"
DELIVERED TO THE R.C.P. GROUP
OF THE EIGHTH CONGRESS OF SOVIETS
DECEMBER 27

Comrades, the Central Committee today has examined the decision adopted by the group concerning the deletion of the words "individual householders" from the point of the resolution on agriculture which deals with improvement and premiums. The C.C. has passed the following resolution and authorised me to defend it.[292] (*Reads.*) There, comrades, you have the text of the C.C.'s decision. Allow me now to give the reasons why we simply could not agree with the group's decision. We had no doubts, and this was particularly stressed at the C.C. meeting, that the principal reasons the group was guided by in its decision to reject the idea of premiums for individual householders were the fear that we would give premiums to the kulak, and the desire to give priority to the village commune, the volost, the collective unit—to common labour, not the individual. With this we are in perfect agreement. We consider, however, that it would be wrong to let ourselves reject altogether the idea of premiums for individual farmers for reasons, which in themselves are quite correct, fundamentally indisputable to any Marxist and especially valuable from the point of view of the peasantry.

Allow me to give you some information from the history of the origin of this bill. I have been following its progress through the Council of People's Commissars fairly closely and must say that in the first draft, tabled by the Food Commissariat, the main accent, generally speaking, was on the hardworking farmer. The gist of Comrade Sereda's proposals was that it would be wrong to stake on the hardworking farmer, and that we should stake on the village commune, the collective body. The Council's attitude on this question—at least, mine—was that we had to weigh all the pros and cons and consult the local people. Indeed, it seemed wrong to me to reject premiums for individual farmers, but that the village commune had to be given priority—this might be all right if the local people with practical experience confirmed that it could and should be done. From this conflict of two points of view there emerged the formulation that was adopted for the bill of the Council of People's Commissars, namely, that both be retained and a ratio established between the two kinds of premiums. The details, as defined in the Council, were to be covered by instructions. In fact the decision of the Council says that the instructions are to be drawn up within a definite stated period by the Commissariat for Agriculture, co-ordinated with the Commissariat for Food and endorsed by the Council of People's Commissars. As an exception to the general procedure, when instructions are endorsed by a single order of the People's Commissar concerned, we arranged not only for verification—the participation of two People's Commissars—but specially added that the Council of People's Commissars demanded that the instructions be submitted to it for endorsement. Obviously, a great deal depended on the instructions.

After certain explanations given by comrades your decision not to give premiums to individual farms became clear to us. The Central Committee saw the point. The point is fear of unfair premiums, the giving of premiums to kulaks. Obviously, the best-run farms are those of the well-to-do peasants and the kulaks, and there are still plenty of these in the villages, on that score we haven't the slightest doubt. If we, in paying a premium for an efficient farm, did not take care to find out how that efficiency was achieved, then, naturally, the kulak would prove to have the best-run farm. And if we ignore the question as to how, at what price, economic improvement is achieved, we shall find the kulak receiving unfair privileges. If we reward him with the means of production, that is, with things that make for farm expansion, we shall find ourselves indirectly, and perhaps even not quite indirectly, boosting the kulaks, because, in rewarding an industrious farmer without considering whether or not he achieved his good results by kulak practices, and what is more, rewarding him with things like the means of production, that is to say, things he can use to strengthen his influence with, we shall, of course, be running counter to the basic provisions of not only the agrarian, but of all Soviet policy, and infringing the basic principle—that of supporting the interests of the working people against those of the kulaks. In doing so we shall really be seriously undermining the principles and foundations of all Soviet policy in general, and not only of agrarian policy.

But if we are to draw from this the conclusion that individual farmers should not be rewarded, then take the following example: we give bonuses to individual workers at factories and mills, where collective, socialised, labour has reached an incomparably higher level than in agriculture. What is to be done about the peasantry then? In a peasant country, where individual peasant labour predominates to the extent of nine-tenths, probably ninety-nine per cent, where we have twenty million peasant farms, we want to promote these farms and we must do so come what may. We know that their efficiency can be raised only after several long years of radical technical reform. We have learned something in our three years of practical work. We know how to build up the foundations of communism in agriculture—this can be done at the cost of a tremendous technical evolution. We clearly visualise that elaborated plan with located electric stations, we know the minimum-programme, the programme for the next ten years, but in this book on electrification we also have a maximum-programme, in which gigantic work is planned for years ahead. But now we have twenty million separate farms, which are run separately and cannot be run in any other way; and if we don't encourage them to raise productivity this would be grossly wrong, it would be clearly overdoing it, it means a refusal to see facts of reality that strike the eye, facts that we have to reckon with and be guided by. It would be desirable, of course, to have these farms rise through collectivism, by whole volosts, communes, etc. But how far that is possible at present is a thing we have to reckon with. If you, working in the local areas, support progress in this direction and raise a whole commune or a whole volost—all the better; in that case give them all that is best in premium payments. But are you sure that you will manage it, that it is not sheer fantasy, which in the practical work will lead to the greatest blunders?

That is why we propose to you the last part of the C.C's resolution reworded or amended as the practical workers may deem fit for inclusion in the resolution of the Congress of Soviets, so that this question should be decided by you and you should say here: premiums and rewards for individual farmers are acceptable under three known conditions. First, premiums for rural communes first and foremost, with householders coming second and receiving what remains—to this we agree. The second point says individual farmers who have achieved economic success by kulak practices should not be rewarded; it should not be a case of—you have made a go of it economically, you are to be rewarded. If anyone has achieved economic success, but employed a kulak method in doing so, whether in the form of a loan, the hiring of labourers, or profiteering—kulak practices sometimes dodge the law—if anyone has employed the slightest kulak method to achieve success, he is to forfeit reward of any kind. This is the second restriction which goes still further to meet your principled point of view as to combating the kulaks and supporting the working middle peasants and poor peasants. The third restriction— what is to be issued as premiums. They may be given in the form of means of production—things like implements and machines that serve to expand and improve the farm; articles of consumption may be issued, household articles of adornment, things that make the home brighter and life more beautiful. We say: "Give the individual farmers only consumer and household goods, and, of course, medals." You have already accepted the Order of the Red Banner.[293] As to the means of production, these may be given to individual farmers, but of such a type and on such conditions that they should not be usable for kulak purposes. No machines should be given, not even to the most hardworking farmer, not even if he has achieved success without the least resort to kulak practices. Machines should not be given, because by the very nature of their employment they require collective labour, and a farmer who receives a machine will not be able to use it by himself.

These are the considerations the C.C. was guided by and on the basis of which we have asked you to reconsider your decision, exchange opinions, and alter your decision if you deem it possible so as to allow individual farmers to be rewarded on the three conditions set forth above. If we do not accept this, we may not achieve needed results, since farm improvements cannot be carried out in a tired and ruined country without a special effort, and the hardworking farmers have to be rewarded. All hard work that contains no element of kulak practices should be rewarded. That is why we think that on considering these reasons you will agree to premiums subject to the three restrictive conditions mentioned above, which we think are really necessary in the interests of our economic development.

First published in 1959
in *Lenin Miscellany XXXVI*

Printed from the shorthand record

4

REPLY TO QUESTIONS AT THE MEETING
OF THE R.C.P. GROUP
OF THE EIGHTH CONGRESS OF SOVIETS
DECEMBER 27

Before answering the notes it must be stated definitely whether a formal difference of opinion exists between the congress group and the Central Committee. Dealing with what the first speakers have said here: we adopted a definite decision, intending to fight the kulaks, but at that time you did not have the methods of struggle outlined by us in the three addenda. What did the comrades who opposed these addenda say here? As a matter of fact they said nothing. The peasant Red Armyman who spoke here[294] said that the kulaks exist and they are growing, but we say definitely: if they are kulaks they will receive no reward. You are being asked to make that a law. Moreover, if the middle peasant achieves betterment individually, but may use it to become a kulak, he is not to receive a premium. What argument, then, has been advanced here against our reasons? None at all. It is reiterated that the kulak should not be rewarded. But we agree to that.

I shall deal now with the notes that have been sent up. The first one:

1) What will be the criterion for a "hardworking kulak" and a "hardworking middle peasant"?

2) If we do find that criterion here and work out a plan, how are we going to carry it out locally, all the more in places where the kulaks are still playing the leading role?

3) Where is the line to be drawn between rewarding a whole collective body and an individual farmer, or are both of them to be rewarded?

For one thing, the peasants know this better than we do. If the law bans any reward for people employing kulak practices, then this is broader than the notion of the kulak. The kulak is a man who generally uses kulak methods, and one or another kulak method is used by almost every middle peasant. That means we not only forbid premiums being given to kulaks but to any middle peasant as well, if he uses kulak methods, and these methods are endless in their variety. That crude method by which an extra horse was bought for five poods is not the only one.[295] Would a premium be given to a kulak like that? What makes you think that people in the country will close their eyes to this? As to the criterion for a hardworking kulak and a hardworking middle peasant, the local people know this perfectly well. We have no intention of writing a law about this, as it would mean writing a whole volume describing kulak practices, and people locally know this perfectly well.

Secondly, haven't we got uyezd committees of the Party, won't this thing be handled by the rural commune, by the volost land departments, by the Party cell? How can we speak about fighting the kulaks in the local areas if there are no fighting cells there? This argument is beyond me.

Thirdly, the law says that priority is given to the collective body with the individual farmer coming second. The differentiation will be made in greater detail by the Uyezd Party Committee and all the other bodies that exist locally.

The second note:

In introducing its amendment does the C.C. regard it as a political act, an incentive to the "hardworking peasants" to improve farming and industry in general so as to make it easier in the course of time to introduce collective cultivation? Will you please answer this?

In the first place, here is proof that there is nothing specially political in this question, something that should be kept from the non-Party peasants. Therefore I consider it quite right and think it should be made a custom to invite non-Party people to our group meetings on such questions. They will have no right of decision at the group meetings, but why not consult them? Our economic practice has shown that it is advisable to go over from individual to collective labour, but having experienced what this going means, we should not try to take it in our stride, but try to understand the need for doing it, the slower the going the better.

The third note:

I think the advocates of commune premiums ought to be asked whether they have enough ploughs and other implements to reward the commune with or not. If not, it's not worth talking about.

This argument is incorrect. Generally speaking, we have few articles usable as premiums, and so few ploughs that, as means of production, we shall not give them to individuals, but only to whole communes But why should we not, if we can, give a plough to a peasant who has worked hard to raise productivity? And who is to decide whether he is a kulak element or not? We must lend an ear to what people say lower down.

The next note:

Will you please, if possible, answer the following question right now on the back of this note. The Svyatiye Kresty Uyezd, Stavropol Gubernia, where I work, has had 10,000,000 poods of grain imposed on it for delivery by December 1,1920. We have delivered 3,200,000 poods. Owing to poor fulfilment we are widely practising confiscation of property from kulak elements, and so I ask you again, will you please tell us what we are to do? Should we carry out confiscation, or do it only as a last resort, so as not to ruin the farm?

This has no relation to the law we are discussing. Go on acting the way you have been doing. In strict conformity with the decree of the Soviet government and your own communist conscience go on freely acting the way you have been doing till now.

The next note:

How is the "hardworking kulak" to be distinguished from the concept of "hardworking peasant"?

Our bill covers all that, and your asking this is an abuse of question time.

Next we are asked:

Who can define a hardworking peasant and how, say in any village? If this is to be done by elected or authorised persons in the village, it will mean an abuse of elected and authorised persons.

I have already said that we must make use of our Party. We have the Committees of Poor Peasants, and in the Ukraine we have their counterpart.

1) Please consider this. Peasant farmers were given a premium for delivering hemp in 1920. They received 100 arshins of textiles each, but the village poor haven't received an arshin yet for 1920.

2) Is the fact taken into consideration that the system of premiums to individual farmers is an obstacle in the way of setting up collective farms and partly bolsters up the shaken foundations of capitalism in agriculture?

Comrades, you know that individual peasant farms with us are the foundations of capitalism, in a manner of speaking.

There is no doubt about that, and I pointed this out in my report, when I said straight out that the "Sukharevka" we had to fear was not the one that existed on Sukharevka Square or existed secretly on any other square, but the one that sits in the breast of every individual peasant farmer.* Can we get away from this in a year or two years? We cannot. But farming has to be improved right now. You are guided by excellent communist motives, but you want to jump from this floor to that top, and we say—it won't work, act more carefully and gradually

Further:

Why don't the Food Commissariat and other institutions give food products for bonuses to workers of Group 3?

I don't know why, but I should imagine it's because we have terribly little food products available for bonus payments.

Will you kindly answer this question: What does the C.C. of the R.C.P. think of the idea of rewarding the more well-to-do peasants, i.e., those who have large allotments which they work themselves? And at the same time, how do the land-poor peasants stand who have no chance of giving a good account of themselves because they have so little land?

Why does he have a large allotment? If it is unfair, why does the commune or the Land Department let him keep it? Because others are not able to cultivate it. So why punish him, if he works hard on it? If he uses kulak methods, don't let him do it, if he holds the allotment unfairly, take it away from him and give it to others, to those who will work it, but don't blame a man for having a lot of land. In Russia there is no private property, the land is distributed by you yourselves and by the commune. In Russia there are people who have large amounts of land. If the Party committee and the Soviet bodies see this and do nothing about it, they should be given the sack, but people should not be deprived of their premiums.

Two more notes. The first:

Will this point of the bill apply to the Ukraine?

* See p. 247 of this volume.—*Ed.*

I think it will, and I very much regret that not a single one of the comrades working in the Ukrainian Poor Peasants' Committees has spoken here. I think the premature closing of the debate a great mistake.

The second one:

If the R.C.P. congress group rejects the resolution of the C.C. shall we be worthy members of the R.C.P. or just showing our obstinacy?

My answer to this note is a document called "Rules of the Russian Communist Party". In Clause 62 of this document we read: "On matters relating to its inner life and current work the group is autonomous."[296] This means that all members of the group have the right and are bound to vote according to their conscience and not on the instructions of the C.C. If, in voting according to your conscience, you pass a second decision against the C.C's proposal, we are obliged, on the basis of Clause 62, to summon the Central Committee, and we shall do so at once, and you will send your representatives to attend its meeting. A serious question like this were best discussed two or three times to iron out serious differences of opinion between us. That is how matters stand, that is how we have to act. You have to vote now, not because the higher Party body has issued directives, but because you have either been persuaded or you have not.

Comrades here were wrong to say that things must have been in a poor way if Lenin has been sent to speak up for them. This is not true. The Party Rules define your rights exactly. That's one thing. Secondly, it isn't true because there was not a single difference of opinion on this question in the Central Committee, which said outright: We have been carried away by our struggle against the kulaks and have forgotten measure. Let us remind people about measure.

The C.C. appointed two comrades because these two members of the C.C. had occasion, during the discussion of the bill, to take a more active part in it than others and spoke in the debates. I handled all the drafts, and so did Preobrazhensky. That's why the two of us were appointed.

First published in 1963   Printed from the shorthand
in the Fifth Russian Edition   record
of the *Collected Works*, Vol. 42

5

ADDENDA TO THE RESOLUTION ON THE AGRARIAN QUESTION

Premiums to individual householders should,

first, come second compared with premiums to whole communes and collective bodies generally:

second, individual householders should be given premiums and generally rewarded only on the strict condition that the individual farmers have achieved their economic successes without the slightest use of kulak methods;

third, that individual householders receive premiums in the shape of medals, consumer goods, household goods, and so on; premiums in the shape of means of production are permissible for individual householders strictly on condition that only such means of production are issued as could under no circumstance be instrumental in turning the farmer into a kulak.[297]

Written December 27, 1920

First published in 1959
in *Lenin Miscellany XXXVI*

Printed from the manuscript

TO N. N. KRESTINSKY
FOR THE POLITBUREAU OF THE C.C., R.C.P.(B.)

Comrade Krestinsky

I propose:

1) that Kamenev and his commission (+ Stalin)[298] be given a *formal* assignment from the Politbureau, this *to be entered in the minutes.*

2) that Chervyakov be instructed to *urgently* draft a *detailed* letter of the C.C., R.C.P. on Byelorussia and a *decree* of the C.P.C. on the same subject (confidential).[299]

Written December 30 or 31, 1920

Lenin

First published in 1965
in the Fifth Russian Edition
of the *Collected Works*, Vol. 54

Printed from the manuscript

DRAFT RESOLUTION
FOR THE PLENUM OF THE C.C., R.C.P.(B.)
ON THE PEOPLE'S COMMISSARIAT
FOR AGRICULTURE[300]

Comrade Osinsky shall be authorised, together with the entire Board of the People's Commissariat for Agriculture, to draft and submit to the Council of People's Commissars and the next session of the All-Russia Central Executive Committee regulations governing both the commissariat in general and providing specially for broader and more systematic co-operation in the work by agricultural experts.[301]

Written January 4, 1921

First published in 1959
in *Lenin Miscellany XXXVI*   Printed from the manuscript

DRAFT RESOLUTION
FOR THE PLENUM OF THE C.C., R.C.P.(B.)
ON GEORGIA[302]

To Point 3

1) The People's Commissariat for Foreign Affairs to be directed to defer a break with Georgia, to systematically collect material concerning her violations of the agreement and to press our demands for transit of supplies to Armenia.

2) The Caucasian Front to be asked for information as to the state of preparedness of our available armed forces in the event of an immediate or imminent war with Georgia, this inquiry, mentioning Georgia's growing insolence, to be drafted by a committee consisting of Comrades Trotsky, Chicherin and Stalin.

3) Directives to be issued to the Revolutionary Military Council of the Republic and the Caucasian Front to be prepared for an emergency involving war with Georgia. The S.C.R.F.* to report as soon as possible to the Council

---

* The Supreme Council for Rail Freightage under the C.P.C.—*Ed.*

of Labour and Defence on the possibility of increasing troop transportation to and within the Caucasus.[303]

Written January 26, 1921

First published in 1965   Printed from the manuscript
in the Fifth Russian Edition
of the *Collected Works*, Vol. 54

DRAFT RESOLUTION
FOR THE POLITBUREAU OF THE C.C., R.C.P.(B.)
ON THE LETTER OF TSEKTRAN OFFICIALS[304]

The question being quite clear, I propose that we confine ourselves to questioning of members of the C.C. I move the following resolution:

"That at such short notice on the eve of the congress (both the congress of Tsektran and the congress of the R.C.P.) it is absolutely impossible and inadmissible to release anyone from work. The slightest instance of any "persecution", i.e., any polemics detrimental to the work of transport, which *develop* into attacks *destructive of discipline* will be severely punished by the C.C, which asks that all such instances be brought to its notice."

31.I.   *Lenin*

Written January 31, 1921

First published in 1959   Printed from the manuscript
in *Lenin Miscellany XXXVI*

ROUGH DRAFT RESOLUTION FOR THE C.P.C.
ON OIL CONCESSIONS

1) To be approved in principle (*both* in Grozny *and* Baku) and negotiations to be started....

2) A highly competent commission to be sent to Baku and Grozny and report back at the earliest moment.

1) Gubkin
2) Tikhvinsky[305]

Written February 1, 1921

First published in 1932   Printed from the manuscript
in *Lenin Miscellany XX*

DRAFT RESOLUTION FOR THE C.P.C.
ON CHECKING FULFILMENT
BY THE PEOPLE'S COMMISSARIATS
OF THE DECISIONS AND ASSIGNMENTS
OF THE C.L.D. AND THE C.P.C.

The Narrow Council to be directed to give greater attention to checking fulfilment by the People's Commissariats of the decisions and assignments of the C.L.D. and the C.P.C. in order that questions of special importance in point of practice and principle be referred to the Large Council.[306]

Written February 1, 1921

First published in 1965 in the Fifth Russian Edition of the *Collected Works*, Vol. 54

Printed from the manuscript

AMENDMENTS AND ADDENDA
TO THE DECISION OF THE C.L.D. ON COPING
WITH THE FUEL CRISIS[307]

(1) *interim* commission
(2) speed up and co-ordinate work
(3) relieve all members of this commission of all non-fuel work
(4) Form of brief accounts to be established in 2 days and submitted for endorsement to the Chairman of the C.L.D. on Monday,* the information in them to answer the following questions:

α) felling out-turn
β) haulage
γ) floatage
δ) loading
ϵ) receipts

Written February 11, 1921

First published in 1959 in *Lenin Miscellany XXXVI*

Printed from the manuscript

* Monday, February 14, 1921.—*Ed.*

DRAFT DECISION FOR THE C.P.C.
ON THE IMPORT PLAN[308]

1) The C.P.C. does not endorse the plan of imports submitted to it, as this plan is exaggerated at least fivefold.*
2) The C.P.C. directs the Council of Labour and Defence immediately to set up a General Planning Commission with the participation of experts and charge it (or its subcommission) with cutting down this plan and revising it with an eye to the practical use to which the purchases can be put under our present economic conditions. Final approval of the plan by the C.L.D.
3) Pending revision of this plan the People's Commissariat for Foreign Trade must restrict itself to one-fifth of this plan on each of the 71 main orders; to one-tenth in the case of the military department; with the indispensable condition that priority be given to the requirements of the fuel extracting and metallurgical industries. Exceptions with the permission of the C.L.D.

Written February 15, 1921

First published in 1959
in *Lenin Miscellany XXXVI*

Printed from the manuscript

DRAFT OF THE MAIN POINT
OF THE C.L.D. DECISION
ON THE GENERAL PLANNING COMMISSION[309]

*Personally to the Members of the C.L.D. from
Comrade Lenin*

As I am submitting to the C.L.D. tomorrow (18/II.) a draft decision concerning a General Planning Commission, I herewith present to you, for your information, a draft of the main point of this decision and a preliminary list of members

---

* Lenin crossed out Point 1 in the manuscript and wrote over it "Krasin's".—*Ed.*

(drawn up after consultation with Comrades Rykov and Krzhizhanovsky).* Please prepare your amendments or counter-proposals for the meeting of the C.L.D. on 18/II.

A General Planning Commission is being set up under the C.L.D. to work out an integrated state economic plan on the basis of the electrification plan approved by the Eighth All-Russia Congress of Soviets and to effect general supervision of this plan's realisation.

The primary economic tasks, especially those which have to be carried out in the near future, in the course of 1921, are to be elaborated by the General Planning Commission or its subcommission in the greatest possible detail, full account being taken of prevailing economic conditions.

Written February 17, 1921

First published in 1932   Printed from the typed copy
in *Lenin Miscellany XX*

SPEECH AT A MEETING
OF MOSCOW PARTY ACTIVISTS
FEBRUARY 24, 1921[310]

I am rather surprised at the nature of today's talk. I don't think this is the right political moment for it. We have to cope with the present situation, which has deteriorated both internally and internationally. Peace with Poland has not yet been concluded, and at home we have a growth of banditism and kulak revolts. As for food and fuel, things have gone from bad to worse. Last year we consumed 15 million poods of grain during the first half-year and 8 million in the second; this year we have used 25 million poods in the first half-year and are now obliged to cut the bread rations and are not even sure we shall be able to issue them regularly. Obviously our mistake was that we wrongly distributed the grain in the first half-year; we should not have increased its consumption to 25 million poods. There are no deliveries from Siberia now, because the kulak rebels have cut off the railway. Our Siberian comrades spoke of the possibility of

---

* See *Lenin Miscellany XX*, p. 24.—*Ed.*

a kulak uprising, but it is very difficult to determine the extent of it. It is not a war, in which one can weigh the forces engaged in it. The Siberian peasantry are not yet used to privations, although they are bearing less than the peasantry of European Russia, and there is now a break off in communications with Siberia and stoppage of deliveries. Between March 1 and 10, approximately, there will be no improvement in the food situation. We have left ourselves no stocks. The thing now is to hold out, to bear the present situation with the greatest possible firmness. There is a certain improvement in deliveries from the Caucasus, but there is a likelihood that things may get worse. Apparently the uprising in Armenia will quieten down,[311] but deliveries from the Caucasus can in no way compensate us for non-deliveries from Siberia, although pressure is being put on the South-Eastern Railway to make up the losses. This is sad news, but it can't be helped.

In the banditism one feels the influence of the Socialist-Revolutionaries. Their main forces are abroad; every spring they dream of overthrowing Soviet power. Chernov wrote about this recently in a Russian newspaper abroad. The S.R.s are connected with the local instigators. This connection is to be seen in the fact that the uprisings take place in the very districts from which we take grain. The surplus-appropriation system here met with tremendous difficulties. The same system is being applied in Siberia, but there they still have stocks left over from previous years.

The deterioration has spread to fuel as well. We have no exact figures, so no clear deductions can be made, nor can we determine the causes of the fuel crisis.

We have come to the conclusion that there exists discontent of a general nature. This discontent has to be caught from below, directly through the Party apparatus if it cannot be caught quickly through the administrative apparatus.

In addition to signs of bureaucratism, there are mistakes in the plan. The plan should be checked when it is drawn up by being discussed in the press and at meetings. We are obliged to stop enterprises and thereby upset the work of factories which do have fuel. What is the matter? Clearly, besides mistakes, the plan contains material for legal proceedings. Proletarian elements should be sent into the offices.

Undoubtedly, until the floating season is over, we shall not emerge from the fuel crisis. We must make the best possible use of sleighing and floating. The fuel crisis has affected the textile mills, too, and they are unable to fulfil even a minimum programme.

There are the difficulties arising from banditism and interrupted communication with Siberia. Smirnov's[312] report says they are coping with banditism out there but cannot promise an improvement in grain deliveries. Therefore, we should not disperse our attention in talk about the general situation, but concentrate our efforts on finding a way out of this situation.

A word or two about the situation in the Moscow organisation. Some comrades try to shift the blame for the squabbling on the majority of the Moscow Committee. If the minority are dissatisfied they can appeal against the conference decision to the Central Committee. I dont't know how the C.C. will decide the question, but my own opinion is that the minority is to blame. The resolution of the All-Russia Conference says that the opinion of the minority is to be reckoned with and that a discussion and debate is necessary within the Party.[313] At the gubernia conference in November elections to the Moscow Committee took place on this platform.[314] A two-room system was applied, and that is already a rift; such a state of affairs, though, can no longer be tolerated. We permitted criticism not for the sake of criticism, but to get a correct decision passed. Moscow has broken the record in discussions. In November there was talk about the Moscow Committee's wrong line, and 120 votes were given for it. During the discussion, when everyone put forward his own platform, the votes against the Moscow Committee were already less. What democracy is it, if a conference cannot elect the M.C.? After a three-month discussion the blame for the squabbling falls on those who are dissatisfied. Of course, there is the formal right to appeal against a decision, but it is the duty of revolutionaries to rally more closely at difficult moments and not abuse the formal right of appeal.

Sixty-seven Russian newspapers abroad tell us that the S.R.s and others count on setting us at odds in the spring at non-Party conferences. And at such a moment people talk about appealing against the decision of the conference. You have got to understand what you can appeal for, when and to what extent. We gave everyone a chance to have his say, we held a discussion—and the congress will decide, but now we are at our fighting posts. We have to rally and realise that one more step in the discussion and we are no longer a Party. While not for a moment denying the right to appeal, I say that we performed our duty even without the discussion and should do our duty now. We must send Communists to all the non-Party organisations and explain this difficult situation to them.

First published in 1963
in the Fifth Russian Edition
of the *Collected Works*, Vol. 42

Printed from the typewritten
copy of the minutes

NOTES ON THE QUESTION
OF MOBILISING RAW MATERIAL RESOURCES[315]

Meeting 26.II.1921

Raw Materials

	Previously		*1920*		*Yield was*	
Fibre						
cotton	725	thous. dessiatines	100	thous. dessiatines	12 m. poods	up to 22
flax	1.1	„	0.3	„	25.6	„
hemp	485	„	238	„	20	„
w o o l					6	„ (5)

	1920		Yield 1920	
fibre				
cotton	1.5	m. poods	0.9	m. poods
flax	2.9	„	2.0	„
hemp	4.5	„	1.3	„
w o o l	2.5	„	1.5	„

Hides	don't know... *there was?*	28.5 m. poods 1920-21 assessment 8.8 (30%) collected up to 1.II.1921

Furs 40 m. pelts—17.5 assessment
(70% from Siberia   (quota)
incl. 30% nomads)— 0.6 collected
              (=4%)
Turned over to the Food Commissariat in IX.1920, but it
is messing up the business, unable to organise an exchange
of goods with the nomads.

	Needed:
cotton	20-24 m. poods
wool	5 „ „
flax	12 „ „
hemp	15 „ „

$\Sigma = 56$ m. p. of all textile raw materials
$\Sigma = 56$ m. p.
our crops can cover 21% of requirements

Stocks 14.8 m. poods in warehouses (now II.1921)

Measures (remedies)*

1) freedom of local exchange of grain for flax, etc.;
2) principle of assessment stimulating the cultivator to
   increase his crops;
3) prohibit textile seeds from being processed for oil (now
   banned);
4) procure seeds from the population to increase cultivation
     {they are to be guaranteed a certain part of the yield;
5) premiums for improved processing;
6) ((organisational measure))
   secure widest possible co-operation of the population
   in improving raw material (artels, *associations*, etc.);
7) stimulation for small processing factories.
   wool:
8) premiums to Kirghizes, at least 1 arshin of textiles per
   pood of wool
   { 1.X.1920 it was handed over   }**
   { to Food Commissariat, which messed it up }

First published in 1932   Printed from the manuscript
in *Lenin Miscellany XX*

* The English word "remedies" is used by Lenin.—*Ed.*
** Lenin's pencilled note in the margin says: "Re raw material
show it to me at the C.P.C. when the question comes up."—*Ed.*

DECISION OF THE COUNCIL OF LABOUR AND DEFENCE
ON IMPROVING THE SUPPLY OF THE WORKERS[316]
28.II.1921

The Council of Labour and Defence resolves to take immediate and urgent steps to improve the supply of the needy workers in food and other necessaries, allocate funds for this purpose to the amount of up to *ten* million *gold* rubles and send a delegation abroad to purchase the necessary articles at once —the delegation to include representatives of the All-Russia Central Council of Trade Unions.

V. Ulyanov (Lenin)
Chairman, C.L.D.

First published in 1932
in *Lenin Miscellany XX*

Printed from the manuscript

PLAN OF A LETTER TO THE BAKU COMRADES[317]

Confidential

A Letter to the Baku Comrades

(On the question of concessions)

Preliminary plan:

1. Differences are beginning to arise on an extremely important question. (*Decision of the C.P.C.* 1921, its text.)
2. Concessions in Baku? example and crux of all differences, their "focus".
3-8. Counter-arguments (*A 1 — a 6*).
   + *8 bis.*
9. Examine and refute them.
10. Economic crux of the matter.
11. Gigantic political mistake.
12. Issue of principle.
13. Suggested agreement.
14. Conclusion.

NB

$$\left\{\left\{\begin{matrix}\text{a I} & \text{Chief phases of chief} \\ \text{II} & \text{``arguments'' (and chief} \\ \text{III} & \text{errors) of opponent}\end{matrix}\right\}\right\}$$

$$\left\{\left\{\begin{matrix}\text{IV} & \text{opponent's ``retreat''} \\ \text{V} & \text{``line of trenches behind} \\ \text{VI} & \text{which prejudice is trying to hide''}\end{matrix}\right\}\right\}$$

3. (a I) "Will not want to work for the capitalists, when others next door are working for themselves."

4. (a II) "Krasin is backed by Bogdatyan."

> Krasin: What, in point of principle, is the gist of the disputes concerning Krasin's personality? Simply "a bourgeois specialist"!

Specialists' deceit

$$\left(\begin{matrix}\text{question of the significance} \\ \text{of specialists and the attitude} \\ \text{towards them}\end{matrix}\right)$$

4 a. "Bourgeois specialist"? Out with him!
We must learn to use the "bourgeois specialist", learn to demand of him, to understand where his "strength" lies.

4 b. "Well-behaved communist musicians", who, may be a bit out of tune, but don't touch a drop.[318]

5.   (a III) "Private capitalism is a predator, only state power (nationalisation) is *capable* of running things rationally."

6.   (a IV) "It isn't proved that we shall not be able to obtain equipment ourselves."
(= we'll cope ourselves).

7.   (a V) Won't be able to control foreigners.

8.   (a VI) *Our* specialists say: "problematical" (what exactly is problematical and what must we *be able* to demand of the specialist).

8 bis (a VII) $\left\{\begin{matrix}\textit{Baku:} \text{ catastrophe.} \\ \textit{Grozny:} \text{ Variant.}\end{matrix}\right\}$

$1/_4$ of *oil wells*, gear, etc.—the **"rear"** of advanced capitalism.

10. Economic question: is advanced capitalism superior to us now in techniques and organisation?

10 a. Can we now set ourselves the task of coping on our own, or is this Left-wing childishness, or stupid doctrinairism?

10 *b.* Should the problem necessarily be put this way: in view of the gigantic danger of Soviet power's breakdown as a result of economic chaos and backwardness, the danger of *falling behind, not catching up,* the problem must be put only this way—*to catch up* by means of an alliance with foreign capital?

"If we give up $^1/_4$ and keep up with two-quarters — that is the *ideal,* which we shall not attain in a year, and if we do it in five years it will be a great victory."

This is a business-like, not infantile, way of putting the question.

11. Why does Σ mean a gigantic *political* error? Wrong evaluation of perspectives, *relations of classes* both in Russia (proletariat, peasantry, bourgeoisie) and **throughout the world.**

12. Economic significance $= (\alpha)$ bloc with *advanced state* capitalism against *petty-bourgeois* and *backward* element $= (\beta)$ bloc with one *imperialist* trust against another.

"Won't be able to control?" Who? Tsarist and bourgeois officials? We.

Give up $^1/_4$? Training ideal. Give up $^1/_4$, catch up with two-quarters (three-quarters unattainable ideal). Then in 30 years (average concession term) we shall have a peaceful victory, and in 15 probably buy it back.

Etwa:

13. § 1. Observation of up-to-date engineering rules.
§ 2. Import of breadstuff, clothes, and other consumer goods (for the workers of "their" enterprises).
§ 3. Import of machinery.
§ 4. All imports from abroad (§ 2 and § 3) give us one-quarter—one-third of the same product. (One "case" out of three falls to our lot.)
§ 5. We give a minimum (timber, for example) and for special payment.

§ 6. Our laws are compulsory.
§ 7. We give "him" 50-75% of oil.
§ 8. We feed up our workers and specialists in relays.
§ 9. We learn in earnest, and don't shout about "winning an easy victory".

14. ‖ Should we **try** to find such concessionaires on such conditions?
‖ This is the only right way of putting the question.

Written late February 1921

First published in 1959
in *Lenin Miscellany XXXVI*   Printed from the manuscript

NOTES ON ELECTRIFICATION

1

Significance of Electrification

1. Modern technics.
2. Restoration of productive forces. Increasing them.
3. Centralisation—maximum.
4. Communism = Soviet power + electrification.
5. General integrated plan: focussing the people's attention and energies.
6. Raising culture (of the working people).
6. Not simple literacy.

2

Towards Electrification

1) Decree endorsing the plan....
2) Mobilisation of technical forces.
⎧ Assembling both electrical engineering
⎪   and labour forces.
⎨ Utilisation of stations.
⎪ Agitation and propaganda.
⎪ Teaching of theoretical
⎩   and practical knowledge about electricity.
3) Decree on GOELRO.

4) Decree on Engineering Department....
5) Decree on All-Russia Electrical Engineering Congress.
6) Petrograd. Coal from abroad via Murmansk.

Written in February 1921

First published: 1—in 1942
in *Lenin Miscellany XXXIV*;
        2—in 1945
in *Lenin Miscellany XXXV*

Printed from the manuscript

ADDENDUM TO THE DRAFT DECISION
FOR THE C.P.C. ON AN OBLIGATORY
SCIENCE MINIMUM IN THE HIGHER SCHOOLS[319]

The following should be added, on the basis of the resolution of the Eighth All-Russia Congress of Soviets,
> *electrification plan*,
> its economic foundations,
> the economic geography of Russia,
> significance of and conditions for the plan's implementation.

Lenin

Written March 5, 1921

First published in 1945
in *Lenin Miscellany XXXV*

Printed from the manuscript

THE TENTH CONGRESS OF THE R.C.P.(B.)
MARCH 8-16, 1921[320]

1

OUTLINE OF A SPEECH AT A MEETING OF SUPPORTERS
OF THE "PLATFORM OF TEN"[321]

1) Top strata (bureaucratic) in the Workers' Opposition....
2) bottom strata, actually linked with the rank and file, really proletarian...

3) most resolute ideological struggle against the syndicalist and Makhayev deviation (at the top) of the
   Workers' Opposition

4) congress decision condemning in principle the syndicalist, anarchist, Makhayev deviation of the Workers'
   Opposition

5) congress decision (by roll-call vote) against leaving
   any faction or trace of factionalism

6) threat of expulsion from the Party and transference
   from the C.C. to alternate membership ((by decision
   of C.C. + Control Commission + all alternate members
   + two-thirds??))[322]

7) take really proletarian elements into the C.C.

8) **penetrate**, study, investigate, explore...

9) a number of speakers (at the congress) to put this
   line through should be elected **immediately**

10) *elect* a bureau of the "platform of Ten"...

11) resolution on the report of the C.C. (α) on greater unity
    and discipline generally, and in the C.C.; (β) on less
    bureaucratism in the Orgbureau

12) next meeting on the day of (or day after) arrival of
    the Petrograders (and Zinoviev)

+ 13) congress decision on press *reporting* of the Party
    congress: tone down factional disputes, demonstrate
    unity.

Written in March,
not later than 9, 1921

First published in 1959
in *Lenin Miscellany XXXVI*

Printed from the manuscript

2

REMARK ON THE AMENDMENT
OF RAFAIL (R. B. FARBMAN)
TO THE RESOLUTION ON PARTY UNITY
MARCH 16[323]

I don't think this amendment ought to be adopted. When
this discussion started we did not keep to the division in
Pravda —political articles got mixed up with discussion

articles. We say here in an emphasised but not ultimatum form that these should not be dragged into the press.

First published in 1921
in the book *The Tenth Congress
of the Russian Communist Party.
Verbatim Report*
(*March 8-16, 1921*), Moscow

Printed from the text of the book,
collated with the shorthand report

3

REMARK ON KISELYOV'S SPEECH
CONCERNING THE RESOLUTION ON PARTY UNITY
MARCH 16[324]

Comrades, I am very sorry that I used the word "machine-gun" and hereby give a solemn promise never to use such words again even figuratively, for they only scare people and afterwards you can't make out what they want. (*Applause.*) Nobody intends to shoot at anybody with a machine-gun and we are sure that neither Comrade Kiselyov nor anybody else will have cause to do so.

First published in 1933
in the book *The Tenth Congress
of the R.C.P.(B.)
March 1921*, Moscow

Printed from the text of the book,
collated with the shorthand report

4

REMARK ON MARCHENKO'S AMENDMENT
TO THE RESOLUTION
ON THE ANARCHIST AND SYNDICALIST DEVIATION
MARCH 16 [325]

To say this in the name of the congress is far too prohibitive. I move that this amendment should not be adopted, without, of course, depriving the C.C. of the right to recommend, and in case of need, to concentrate all this in C.C.

publications: but I think it would be too much to have a congress ban on the issue of such publications locally.

First published in 1921 in the book *The Tenth Congress of the Russian Communist Party. Verbatim Report* (*March 8-16, 1921*), Moscow

Printed from the text of the book, collated with the shorthand report

MOTION AT THE POLITBUREAU OF THE C.C., R.C.P.(B.) CONCERNING THE DRAFT DECISION FOR THE ALL-RUSSIA CENTRAL EXECUTIVE COMMITTEE ON THE ABOLITION OF MONETARY TAXES

I move that this be *withdrawn* (in view of the *introduction* of a tax in kind *and preparations* for a silver currency).[326]

16/III. *Lenin*

Written March 16, 1921

First published in 1959 in *Lenin Miscellany XXXVI*

Printed from the manuscript

DRAFT DECISION FOR THE POLITBUREAU OF THE C.C., R.C.P.(B.) ON PURVEYANCE IN TAMBOV GUBERNIA

19/III.

To be referred to members of the **Politbureau**

In reversal of the C.C.'s decision to suspend all purveyance in Tambov Gubernia, it is herewith resolved:

to allow purveyance in Tambov Gubernia only of bulky feed and only for the needs of the military forces operating there against the local bandits.[327]

Lenin

Written March 19, 1921

First published in 1959 in *Lenin Miscellany XXXVI*

Printed from the manuscript

MEETING OF THE COMMUNIST GROUP OF THE ALL-RUSSIA CENTRAL COUNCIL OF TRADE UNIONS

APRIL 11, 1921[328]

1

REJOINDER DURING THE DEBATE

We have just heard exceedingly diplomatic speeches on the part of Comrade Shlyapnikov and Comrade Ryazanov, who although they are now protesting very loudly, are nevertheless protesting so diplomatically that they would make highly satisfactory negotiators with concessionaires and with bourgeois states. We have come to a meeting at which I report on the disagreements that arose in the Central Committee and the Council of People's Commissars. The same disagreements will emerge here during the discussion.... These differences were resolved by the decision of the Tenth Congress, which says: "The decree of the C.P.C. shall be approved and a concession shall be granted in Baku and Grozny." We want to discuss this question here, that is why I asked that Shlyapnikov's and Ryazanov's proposal should be rejected, and they should have their inquisitiveness, not to say curiosity, gratified by the results of the ensuing debate.

First published in 1932
in *Lenin Miscellany XX*

Printed from the shorthand
record

2

REPLY TO THE DEBATE ON THE REPORT ON CONCESSIONS

Comrades, the question was raised here from the very outset whether our differences in regard to concessions were serious or not, and the desire was expressed, incidentally, by Comrade Shlyapnikov that more systematic information be given on each agreement. I'm afraid this is impracticable, if only for technical reasons. For instance, take the case

of peace treaties with different countries. After the general
directives, which at first were drafted in great detail, it so
fell out that a certain type of treaty with bourgeois countries
was adopted by tacit consent, the mass of details being left
to the representatives authorised to sign the treaty. And
most of these details are probably unknown to the majority
of the members of the Council of People's Commissars and
the Central Committee. The same here: we were dealing with
a question of principle and we thought there was a danger
of disagreements arising. Therefore the Party congress had
to step in, and therefore the present meeting, in which only
members of the Party are taking part, was a meeting called
for the purpose of mutual information. We have read out to
you what the Council of People's Commissars has adopted.[329]

The C.P.C.'s decision was adopted in spite of the motion
by two very prominent trade unionists. What other method
of information do the majority of the communist group
members have if not through such a meeting as this one? It
works out that there were less disagreements than we thought.
This is the most desirable thing for us. No minutes of this
meeting are being kept and we do not intend to have a press
discussion on it. Our purpose has been achieved.

In informing you of the decision of the Council of People's
Commissars, we are letting you know how we have accepted
the decision of the Party congress. The remaining differences
of opinion do not exceed those which arise from day to day
on various questions and are decided by a simple vote,
without becoming a hindrance to the work. Submission to
the majority in that case is not only a matter of form, but
an act that does not hinder further work. I think we have
achieved here a result in that no serious differences have come
to light, and partial differences will be ironed out in the
course of the work itself.

Comrade Ryazanov, characteristically, has tried to drag
in disagreements with the Workers' Opposition. He specially
chose a formulation that was intended to be a teaser, but
he failed in this, and none of the speakers fell for it.

One comrade sent in a note saying that we here are concluding a second Treaty of Brest. The first one had turned out
well, as to the second one, he has his doubts. This is partly
true, but the present agreement, in the field of economy

is something between the Brest Treaty and an agreement with any bourgeois state. We have already signed several such agreements, including a trade agreement with Britain. The one on concessions will be something between the Brest Treaty and such agreements with bourgeois states.

Comrade Ryazanov then passed a remark, quite correctly, which I should like to underline at the very outset. He said that if we want to grant a concession it was not meant to improve the position of the workers, but to raise the productive forces. Quite right! As to improving the position of the workers, we always stand by this. I have here a draft agreement with a Swedish corporation of ball-bearing plants written by the staff of the Supreme Economic Council[330] (*reads*).

This agreement does not stipulate any improvement in the condition of the workers. True, it is so worded that the Russian Government undertakes to supply the workers with everything they need, and if it fails to do this, the capitalists have the right to bring in workers from abroad. As to the ability of the Russian Government to fulfil everything the plan calls for as far as the workers are concerned, I think that neither we, nor the Supreme Economic Council, nor the Swedes can have any illusions on this score. At any rate, in this Comrade Ryazanov is quite right, for the main thing in concessions is not improvement of the workers' condition, but the raising of the productive forces and such a transaction under which we are making great sacrifices in order to increase output. But what are these sacrifices? I have been told that I gloss over these sacrifices, play them down. Comrade Ryazanov even tried to crack a joke on this score. I did not play down the sacrifices, I only said that we may have to give the capitalists not only hundreds, but thousands of per cent in profits. That's the whole gist of it!

If, as I assumed, on the basis of calculations by our specialists, we take 30-40 per cent of the oil, for instance, for ourselves, if the capitalist, out of every 100 million poods of oil which he produces, takes 50-60 million poods for himself, and possessing the transport, sells them at a profit of perhaps 1000 per cent, or maybe more, then the position is clear. And when I tried to find out from Krasin the terms of his agreement on the basis of his preliminary talks with the businessmen and tycoons, I asked: "Can one conceive of a type of agreement under which we stipulate a definite percentage of profit for the capitalist, say up to 80 per cent." He said: "It is not a question of the size of the profits, because these robbers now make as much as 1000 per cent, not 80."

To my mind, the sacrifices will be very heavy. We shall probably have to make great sacrifices if we are going to give concessions on ores or timber, if we are going to give away raw materials which they are so desperately in need of abroad, such as manganese ore, for example. Georgia has now become Soviet. The thing is to unite the Caucasian Republics into a single economic centre: the Georgian, Azerbaijan and Armenian Republics. Azerbaijan produces oil; it has to be transported via Batum through Georgian territory, so there will be a single economic centre.

According to one report, the Georgian Menshevik government had concluded a concession agreement, which, on the whole, is acceptable to us. Preliminarily, I could only get in touch with Georgian comrades and ascertain from a talk with Comrade Yenukidze, the Secretary of the All-Russia Central Executive Committee, who is himself a Georgian, that he had been there and concluded an agreement—true, not a concession agreement—with the Menshevik Georgian government granting us without resistance one-sixth of Georgia while retaining a guarantee of inviolability.[331]

After this agreement, to the signing of which Comrade Yenukidze was a party, they preferred nevertheless, despite the guarantee of inviolability, to quit Batum for Constantinople, so that we have gained by this in two ways, positively and negatively—in that we have acquired territory, not for Russia, but for Soviet Georgia—Batum and its environs—and in that we have lost a good many Mensheviks, who have left for Constantinople.

It appears that the Georgian Revolutionary Committee is inclined to confirm the concession on unworked coal-mines, which it considers a very important one. Two representatives of foreign powers were in Georgia and did not leave at the time of the Soviet coup—the Italian and the German—a most important circumstance, as it is desirable to develop relations with these countries, by means, among others, of concessions. Italy even had a concession agreement with

Georgia, while in Germany the situation is that some German capitalists own a tremendous per cent of the Chiatura manganese mines. The thing is to transfer the right of ownership to a lease or a concession, that is, to grant on lease to the German capitalists the very mines which they owned as property. Owing to the change in the political situation in the Caucasus, the circumstances are favourable for concession relations. The important thing for us is to force windows open one after another. The agreement with Britain[332] was that of a Socialist Republic with a bourgeois state, an agreement that imposed upon us a certain burden.

To the first state with whom we concluded an agreement we gave a much greater part of our gold fund than we have given to others. But the consequences have shown that thanks to this agreement we have forced open a window of sorts. It is from this point of view that we should judge every concession.

Germany and Italy, owing to their economic position, are obliged to seek an alliance with Russia. For Russia, an alliance with Germany opens up vast economic prospects, irrespective of whether or not the German revolution will soon win a victory there. We can come to terms even with a bourgeois government in Germany, because the Versailles Treaty has made Germany's position impossible, whereas an alliance with Russia opens up entirely different possibilities. Since Italy has no fuel resources of her own, they have taken a coal-mining concession in the Caucasus at coal-fields that have never been worked before. I should not be surprised to see the Germans hankering after oil concessions, as Germany has no fuel at all.

One of the comrades here said that the Kamchatka concession would not improve the condition of the workers. That is absolutely wrong. And Comrade Ryazanov was quite wrong when he tried to crack a joke about our dealings with Vanderlip turning out to be a Vander-slip. True, we made one mistake—our telegram to Harding. But since we have had no agreements or relations with America till now, there was no mistake on our part, and we only found out that Vanderlip had been boasting of his connections with the American Administration. Now it is quite possible that in sending our representatives to Canada, where we are to buy locomotives, that through this side door we may gain some access to the American market.

Negotiations for Kamchatka concessions are beginning to stir now, and it is quite wrong to say that these concessions will not improve the condition of the workers. If these concessions materialise, there will be an undoubted improvement in the condition of the workers, because we shall be receiving a certain deduction share, 2 per cent I believe, and when we have nothing at all, even 2 per cent is something. If we get 20,000 out of one million and use it for an exchange with the peasants, this will give us some of the products the workers need.

Further I wanted to point out that some of the remarks you have made here show that there are disagreements among the trade unionists, or rather perplexities, which are the only real danger and which we, among ourselves, perhaps by further discussions among the Party members, have to eliminate. For example, Comrade Marshev spoke about payment having to be made in cash, and not by coupons. As to the Amsterdamists[333] and whether they will attack us, we must come to an arrangement about this.

I recently re-read my pamphlet written in May 1918.* I quoted in it the Menshevik newspaper *Vperyod*[334] in which the Menshevik Isuv accused the Soviet government of agreeing to concessions, of having deals with bourgeois states. It is an old trick of the Mensheviks to blame us for granting concessions. Quite a few groups have already taken shape in this connection in Western Europe. The Communists understand that concessions are a treaty of Brest, which we are obliged to put up with because of the ruined state of a country with a predominantly peasant population. Everyone understands that regeneration of the country without a big industry is unthinkable.

The Communists of Germany understand why we have to give ground, but the Scheidemanns and the II$^{1}/_{2}$ International say that these concessions are proof of our complete failure, and I remember at a meeting last year I mentioned the American chauvinist Spargo,** who specialised in

---

* See Vol. 27 of this edition, pp. 323-54.—*Ed.*
** See Vol. 31 of this edition, pp. 414, 430.—*Ed.*

writing a heap of books about the Bolsheviks in the vein of our Alexinsky, and in connection with the concessions he all but performed a dance of triumph. I mentioned at the time that this was an utter distortion. Yesterday international capital was out to strangle us, and today we have a number of agreements with this international capital.

We are making sacrifices in giving away to foreign capital millions' worth of valuable materials from which they can make profits running into hundreds of per cent. These are sacrifices which we are making deliberately and consciously. But at the same time we should note that while allowing them to make any profit they like, we are receiving the advantages we need ourselves, i.e., increased output, and as far as possible an improvement in the condition of our workers, both those employed at the concession enterprises and those not so employed.

Comrade Shlyapnikov said here that it would be a good thing to grant a concession to Russian workers. The idea is absurd. We would then have to guarantee fuel, etc., a thing which we can't guarantee even to our most essential enterprises. We are bad off for fuel. The idea of a concession agreement with Russian workers, generally speaking, is permissible in principle, but such a solution of the problem for our big industry is not serious, since we cannot guarantee them anything, whereas foreign concessionaires can bring in supplies from abroad. That is what distinguishes the agreement with foreign capitalists. They have the world market, we have no secure economic base and would have to spend ten years creating it. This is what we must soberly take into account. All our people engaged in this problem have proved this situation.

We know that the electrification plan is the most economical one. We cannot lease our big factories to the Russian workers. We must stake here on small industry, develop it and not rail at our tax-in-kind measures the way Comrade Ryazanov does, or the author of that pamphlet which says that we are putting through anarcho-syndicalist laws.

As regards the development of small industry, we must take several steps, as we can get something out of it right now without state guarantees, and since we cannot guarantee even our most essential factories, we must do everything we can to develop small industry, which will give us a certain amount of produce which the peasants need.

On the question of cash or coupons I would say this: it would be something to fear if the capitalists had the power, but we have nothing to fear, since all the factories and enterprises are in our hands, and we haven't leased a tenth part of them to the capitalists. I repeat, we have nothing to fear from coupons, as the capitalists will be obliged to stock the goods we tell them to, not just salted fish, as was mentioned here, but such-and-such products. Since we are taking the norm of a foreign worker, we know that under this norm he gets even more and better products than the Russian worker does.

Comrade Shlyapnikov here said: "We have seen concessions." Both Comrade Shlyapnikov and many practical workers make this mistake. I have heard people say: "Your idea of concessions is schematic. The capitalist has always tricked the most experienced Russian lawyers." To be sure he did, when state power was in the capitalist's hands and he was all-powerful. What was that state power? A committee for the affairs of the propertied master class—that's what it was. A committee for the affairs of the landowners and capitalists—that was what the capitalist government was. But if we, having in our hands most of the factories, mills and railways, with our Party standing at the head—with communist cells below and Communists on top—if we do not hold our own in such conditions, then we might as well commit suicide. And that is panic!

We are not that bad though, I think, to allow ourselves to be tricked, and if we have already concluded several agreements in which the governments in France and Britain had the services of first-class bourgeois diplomats, and if even under these conditions we have not once been tricked, then why should we panic at the idea of being tricked by coupons? Let me remind you of the treaty of Brest. In what way was this treaty difficult? What were the difficulties of defence? When I was asked whether I had any hopes of our being able to fool the Germans, I was obliged, in my official capacity, to say that I did not. But now the treaty of Brest is past history.

I don't know whether the pamphlet Comrade Kamenev was preparing has come out (it deals there with Ludendorf), but I do know that Ludendorf has written a brilliant volume of memoirs in which ten pages are devoted to the Brest negotiations. When Kamenev and I read that chapter we said: "This is the best justification of the Brest Treaty." He tells how Trotsky and the others had driven them into a corner during the talks, how they were outwitted, and so on. We decided there and then that these pages had to be translated and published with a short preface by Comrade Kamenev, and the fact that this hasn't been done yet is a specimen of Soviet ineptitude. Or take a fact like this. We know that Comrade Joffe, our Ambassador to the German Government, was expelled from Germany on the eve of the revolution there. After this, don't try to guess who is going to trick whom. Don't let us lay down how many days will pass between the conclusion of the first concession agreement and the first big European revolution. That is why, on the question of agreements, I maintain that the comrades are absolutely wrong. There's nothing to worry about.

The agreements will say what goods they are to have and at what price. We can agree to any coupons or ration books. If they break the agreement we have the right to cancel it immediately. The agreement is a civil contract. I haven't gone into the question of what arbitration there is to be and who is to settle disputes, but I shall run through the initial draft of the agreement with the Swedish corporation. It says here: "Differences are settled...."

People here have brought academicians into play, and these will try to bring the lawyers into play. I remember Bebel saying that lawyers were the most reactionary and at the same time bourgeois, people. Of course, we can mend this somehow, but there is nothing at all to worry about. If the concessionaires were to lay down this condition we could accept it. Once the agreement stipulates precisely that there are to be such-and-such goods and payment on the ration book is to be made in such-and-such a way, we can agree to this, and the Socialist Republic has nothing to fear from coupons or ration books. It was further stated that Point 9 was bad because we would be drawing away from the international T.U.C.[335] Lozovsky threatened that the

Amsterdam people would slam us, but they will slam us all the same on all other points, and end up, as always, with slamming themselves.

You remember how the Mensheviks intended slamming us for having made the slightest concessions to the capitalists. When we wanted to overthrow capitalism, they said we would overthrow it only for a few days, but when we have overthrown it for a few years, they are trying to set another trap for us. They are trying to lure the enemy into a spot where he is sure to be beaten.

First they called us utopians, then invited us to jump from the fifth floor. We know that we have many small businesses. Petty proprietors are our opponents. The petty-bourgeois element is our most dangerous enemy. Brokers and leaseholders are the lesser enemy. Bureaucracy, too, and bureaucratic abuses are our enemy.

In regard to the point Comrade Lozovsky spoke about, I will say this—listen to it carefully. It says: "The trade unions shall not have the right to demand application of Russian pay rates or of Russian rules of employment to that category of workers." It speaks here of the Russian trade unions, and I am told about the international unions. Naturally, when the capitalists see the Russian terms, they say they are communist terms, ridiculous terms, and that the Russian trade unions have no right to demand Russian terms of employment, which are likely to be pretty stiff and far-fetched, but they do have a full right to apply international trade union agreements. This is good enough. Nothing is mentioned here about strikes, about their being banned. The thing is to be able not to mention everything before its time.

As to improving the condition of the Russian worker, Comrade Marshev and Tartakovsky have made an attack here, saying you won't be able to cope with the workers, you won't be able to make them work, because if you provide for one-fifth of them, the other four-fifths won't want to work under worse conditions. Do you mean to say we are dealing with workers who are so foolish, uncultivated and undisciplined? If so, then the only thing is to panic and commit suicide. If a hundred workers are underfed and we tell them that we can feed twenty, and no more, do you mean to say they will refuse it? So far we have not come up against anything like it. We have managed somehow to feed workers in certain branches of industry, but not all of them, yet the workers didn't all run away from these enterprises, whereas they all did from other enterprises. Can the Russian worker be so spoilt by the mistakes of Soviet power that he cannot figure out that it were better to feed at least 20 people than to make the whole hundred go hungry? There is a good deal here that ought not to be spoken about before its time. Why can't it be arranged for people to take turns in working for the capitalists? The workers would work six months, get working clothes, then give others a chance to feed up. Of course, we shall have to break down prejudices here.

When concessionaires come here, we must restrain our trade unions from making excessive demands. You know that the usual term of an agreement is a short one. In Europe there are no long-term agreements. The usual term is six months. In this way the workers will be able to feed up, get boots and clothes, then quit and make way for others.

Is it so impossible to arrange things so that a man works six months, feeds up, gets American boots and clothes, and makes room for the next man? It will be difficult, of course. It will demand a higher degree of organisation and discipline than we have, but it is not impossible. If we have contrived to keep a hold on the workers agai st an invasion of foreign capital during three years of terrible famine, do you mean to say we won't manage it this time? I realise only too well what difficulties confront us here. And therefore I say that concessions do not signify the advent of peace among the classes. Concessions are a continuation of the war among the classes.

If previously the war could be expressed in—I'll get you through starvation and you'll get nothing, now I say that I want to give the workers a pair of boots each, but I want them to work six months. And we'll fight for all the workers getting boots. We do not reject strikes, all this remains in our hands, if only we are reasonable and try to put the accent now on what we can do to attract the capitalists.

People here have talked about what a great danger this is, saying that the capitalist will come and trick us, but I assert that there is no danger, and that in the interests of raising

productivity it is desirable that he should come, because
he has a splendidly organised base and splendidly equipped
factories, where we can order the necessary parts without
having to buy them on the open market, where there is only
junk. The first-class factories have their orders booked up
for several years ahead. Even if we paid in gold we would
not receive anything, whereas a member of the syndicate
would get everything he wanted. We wouldn't mind paying
him extra if it meant improving the condition of at least
a small section of the workers and peasants, because each
extra product will go to the peasants in exchange for grain,
and that will create stable relations between the working
class and the peasantry.

Winding up, I would ask the trade unionists to waive
questions of principle and disputes. All these are idle disputes, sheer scholasticism. They should be dropped. Attention
should be wholly directed to those practical terms of concession agreements from which we, if we are sensible, may
derive benefit for ourselves. The trade unionists and Party
leaders should display here their inventiveness and practical
knowledge of conditions, of which we cannot and shall not
speak about in the press, because the Russian press is being
followed by the capitalists, just as during the Brest talks
we did not speak about the instructions that had been given
to Comrade Joffe. We shall give practical attention to the
practical methods by which we can derive benefit in the
way of improving the condition of the workers and peasants.
Every such improvement is of tremendous importance to us.
This is where the trade unionists should give their attention.
All trace of friction and prejudice should be eliminated.
It is a difficult business. So far no one has been willing to
conclude a concession agreement with us. They are all
expecting us to present impracticable demands.

We, therefore, on our part must use every effort to conclude several such agreements. Of course, we shall make
a number of mistakes. It is a new business. So far no socialist
republic has ever granted concessions to capitalists. But we
want the trade unionists to help us. There is vast scope here
for interpretations and pressure, including strikes, which
remain in our hands.

First published in 1932   Printed from the shorthand
in *Lenin Miscellany* XX   record

APPLICATIONS FOR FOREIGN TRADE ORDERS

DRAFT RESOLUTION FOR THE C.P.C.[336]

The State Planning Commission shall be directed to revise both the applications for orders to the amount of 38.9 million gold rubles and the remaining applications for foreign trade orders to allow only for such purchases in 1921-22 as are necessary for purveyance of essential minimum quantities of food and fuel based on the assumption of a worst possible harvest and worst possible conditions of fuel supply.

Written April 12, 1921

First published in 1932
in *Lenin Miscellany* XX   Printed from the manuscript

DRAFT DECISION FOR THE COUNCIL OF LABOUR AND DEFENCE ON "ALGEMBA"[337]

Set up a Commission of
    2 State Planning Commission   2 oilmen or fuel men
    2 Chief Oil Board   2 railway engineers
    ascertain within 2 weeks

1) what part of the Algemba railway work has been carried out;
2) ditto the pipeline;
3) in particular, present provision of rails and pipes, and the prospects of full provision;
4) the possibility of supplying fresh water to the Emba oilfields and other conditions for ensuring work on the Emba;
5) check comparative cost of delivering oil to the centre via Rakushi-Astrakhan by waterway and via Saratov by railway and pipeline;
6) possible and probable terminal date of Algemba railway and pipeline construction;
7) possibility, probability and cost of acquiring and delivering extra river and sea craft for the transportation of oil from the Emba via Rakushi-Astrakhan;
8) go into other aspects of the problem.

Written April 15, 1921

First published in 1959
in *Lenin Miscellany* XXXVI   Printed from the manuscript

ADDENDUM TO THE DRAFT DECISION
FOR THE C.P.C. "ON THE DISTRIBUTION
OF AGRICULTURAL MACHINES"[338]

No agricultural machines or implements are to be supplied unless there is effective control on the part of the Food Commissariat over receipt by the state of farm produce in exchange for such machines and implements.

The forms of control are to be laid down in special instructions by arrangement between the Agriculture and Food Commissariats.

The Agriculture and Food Commissariats shall be directed to consider and submit a plan for the most simple and economical way of delivering machines to the consumers.*

Written April 26, 1921

First published in 1932
in *Lenin Miscellany XX*

Printed from the manuscript

DRAFT OF A LETTER OF THE C.C., R.C.P.(B.)
ON THE ATTITUDE TO NON-PARTY WORKERS[339]

A circular to the gubernia committees to be drawn up and forwarded in cipher.

Contents:

the experience of non-Party conferences has fully proved that they have become an arena for agitation** by the Mensheviks and Socialist-Revolutionaries;

therefore, the greatest care must be taken in organising non-Party conferences, by no means allowing them to be held without thorough preparation at each respective factory. The Gubernia Party Committees should be answerable to the Party for the success of every non-Party conference.

Every Gubernia Party Committee is obliged to report to the Central Committee not only on the success of every non-

---

* The last paragraph is in the handwriting of L. A. Fotieva, apparently from Lenin's dictation.—*Ed.*

** The word "organisation" is written above the word "agitation" in the manuscript.—*Ed.*

Party conference, but prior to every non-Party conference, setting forth its conditions and preparedness.

At the same time it is absolutely essential to step up the work of preserving and developing the Communists' ties with the non-Party masses. For this purpose it is necessary:

not only to regularly hold general meetings for the rank-and-file workers and peasants, but arrange business reports to the rank-and-file workers and peasants by officials holding key posts. Such reports must be delivered at least once a month in order that the non-Party rank-and-file be given an opportunity to criticise the Soviet institutions and their work. Reports are to be made not only by Communists, but by all officials in top posts, first and foremost those of the food supply and economic council agencies.

Every gubernia committee is obliged to forward exact information monthly to the Central Committee about the number and progress of all these reports, as well as the demands made by the non-Party people at these meetings.

The C.C. will draw up more detailed instructions on the organisation of such reports, on the measures for checking ties with the masses, on the progress of the work for improving their condition, and on fighting the Mensheviks and Socialist-Revolutionaries, who are acting under the guise of non-Party people, etc.[340]

Written in April,
not later than 27, 1921

First published in 1932
in *Lenin Miscellany XX*   Printed from the manuscript

SPEECH AT A MEETING OF COMMUNISTS
AND CANDIDATE MEMBERS OF THE R.C.P.(B.)
OF THE KREMLIN AREA
MAY 9, 1921
(FROM THE MINUTES)

Comrade Lenin said in his report: You, as members of the Party, should read my pamphlet concerning the tax in kind,* which has now come off the press and is being dis-

---

* See Vol. 32 of this edition, pp. 329-65.—*Ed.*

tributed. He also pointed out that every member of the Party should not lose touch with the non-Party masses, as often happens with us. Each one of us, therefore, must keep closer to the non-Party masses and carry on more propaganda. In conclusion he said: All of you, who often read the newspapers and attend meetings and lectures, being more developed people, should do more work among the peasants, carry on agitation among them to explain the significance of the tax in kind. We shall then achieve better results.

First published in 1963
in the Fifth Russian Edition
of the *Collected Works*, Vol. 43

Printed from the typed copy
of the minutes

DRAFT DECISION FOR THE C.C., R.C.P.(B.)[341]

The C.C. of the R.C.P., having discussed Svanidze's telegram to Stalin No. 2031 dated 8/V, finds that the Georgian comrades are making a serious political mistake in not using an iron hand to put a stop to requisitions, confiscations, thefts and evictions of foreigners from their houses.

The C.C. resolves:

1) that the Georgian Revolutionary Committee be directed to issue immediately an order strictly prohibiting all such acts on pain of arrest and prosecution. A copy of this order to be sent to the C.C.

2) that the Georgian Revolutionary Committee immediately institute investigations, first, into the breaking open of the Germano-Caucasian Bank's store-room and the removal of documents. The guilty parties to be arrested. Documents to be returned. Secondly, ditto in regard to the goods of the Italo-Caucasian Bank. Thirdly, ditto in regard to the carload of textiles seized at Kutaisi.

3) that the Georgian Revolutionary Committee, by arrangement with the Command of the Caucasian Front, shall without delay appoint two of the most energetic, firm and resourceful Communists, one from the Caucasian Front, and one from the Georgian Revolutionary Committee, to supervise the cessation of requisitions, thefts, confiscations and evictions in regard to foreigners. The names of the

appointed men to be communicated to us by telegraph. The C.C. places responsibility for the enforcement of these measures upon Makharadze and Gittis. The two controllers to be invested with special powers and the right to make arrests for the slightest infringements. The two controllers to wire brief reports here weekly.

The C.C. draws the attention of the Georgian comrades to the extremely important significance of Georgia and her trade with Italy and Germany for the whole R.S.F.S.R., especially in view of America's and France's attempts to obstruct all our trade relations with foreign countries. Negligence in carrying out these directives will be regarded by the C.C. as a crime against Soviet power.

Written May 9, or 10, 1921

First published in 1959
in *Lenin Miscellany XXXVI*

Printed from the manuscript

DRAFT DECISION
FOR THE POLITBUREAU OF THE C.C., R.C.P.(B.)
ON MEASURES FOR ACHIEVING CONCENTRATION OF PRODUCTION[342]

1) The C.C. of the Metalworkers' Union and the All-Russia C.C.T.U. shall be directed to pay special attention to the swift implementation of the plan for closing down the greatest possible number of inefficient establishments with the aim of concentrating production in a small number of better organised enterprises.

The report on the exact plan, the closing down schedule and actual fulfilment to be made by Shlyapnikov and Medvedev or their deputies
by Kubyako
and by Holtzmann
by Andreyev
to the Council of Labour and Defence within a month

2) Shlyapnikov shall be directed to elaborate more concretely the most important and quickly realisable proposals of his draft.

Written May 11, 1921

First published in 1959
in *Lenin Miscellany XXXVI*

Printed from the manuscript

PLAN OF A SPEECH
AT A MEETING OF THE COMMUNIST GROUP
OF THE FOURTH
ALL-RUSSIA CONGRESS OF TRADE UNIONS[343]

PLAN OF A SPEECH 18/V

1. Rules of the R.C.P.: the Party and groups.
2. C.C. resolution—and its CONCEALMENT.
3. Ryazanov and his role. (Ryazanov's anti-Party resolution.)...
4. Tomsky and his *mistake or crime?*... ((*Composition of the Four.*))
5. The workers' extremely nervy, wrought up state, discontent:

Burden on the workers.
1920 surplus appropriation—on the peasants.
Alleviation for the peasants: still depends on the harvest.
For the workers: profound resentment at the spectacle of "lighters",[344] theft, and so on.

Written May 18, 1921

First published in 1959
in *Lenin Miscellany XXXVI*

Printed from the manuscript

PROPOSALS TO THE DRAFT DECISION
FOR THE C.C., R.C.P.(B.) PLENUM
ON CLAUSE 13 OF THE PARTY PROGRAMME[345]

Yaroslavsky and Bukharin to be instructed to revise the draft so as not to over-emphasise the question of combating religion (by throwing out § 7, for instance[346]) and to allow, under definite restrictive conditions, for religious, but honest and devoted Communists, to remain in the Party.

The fight against religion to be put on a more scientific footing.

(§ 10—out.[347])

Get it endorsed by the Politbureau.

Start the campaign after thorough preparation.

Written May 18, 1921

First published in 1965
in the Fifth Russian Edition
of the *Collected Works*, Vol. 54   Printed from the manuscript

DRAFT DECISION FOR THE C.L.D.
ON LOCAL ECONOMIC CONFERENCES,
ON REPORTING AND ON COMPLYING WITH
THE INSTRUCTIONS OF THE C.L.D.

1. Gubernia and uyezd economic conferences are to be organised everywhere, standing in the same relation to the gubernia and uyezd executive committees as the Council of Labour and Defence to the Council of People's Commissars. Managing offices or secretariats must be common ones. All the work is to be done through the apparatus of the corresponding departments without creating a special apparatus.

2. The village committees and village Soviets are to act as the local, lower bodies of the C.L.D., and in factory and urban communities these functions are to be assumed by the disctrict Soviets, the district economic conferences and the factory committees. The volost executive committees either completely fulfil the duties of volost economic conference or assign several of their members to form the volost economic conferences.

3. It is the obligatory duty of all the economic conferences to report on their activities to the C.L.D., such activities to be guided by the Instructions of the C.L.D. which are to be issued simultaneously with this decision.

The reports of the regional economic conferences, the gubernia and uyezd economic conferences must be printed in

no less than 100 copies (three of which are to be sent to the
C.L.D., one copy each to the leading public libraries, the
Rumyantsev Library in Moscow and the Public Library in
Petrograd, and one copy to the library of each gubernia
economic conference). Reports are to be submitted every two
months (three or four months?).

The reports of the lower bodies are to be in writing, one
copy for the gubernia economic conference and one for the
C.L.D.; to be submitted not less than twice a year.

The report to the C.L.D. must be accompanied by
systematically selected issues of the local newspapers or
cuttings from them devoted to questions of local economic
life, as well as all publications on these questions.

The co-operation of the local staff of the Central Statistical
Board and the Workers' and Peasants' Inspection should be
enlisted in compiling these reports.

Each local body is obliged immediately to appoint and
communicate to the C.L.D. the names of persons responsible
for the timely drawing up of the report in each of its sub-
sections and general collation, as well as the names of their
deputies.

4. The newspaper *Ekonomicheskaya Zhizn*[348] is to become
the organ of the C.L.D.

Following the same Instructions, it should regularly
publish summaries of local economic work alongside its
present coverage. The recording and study of practical
experience in all economic work in the R.S.F.S.R. and the
working out of general guidelines on the basis of such
experience must become the chief task of *Ekonomicheskaya
Zhizn*.

The editors must select and widen the circle of local
correspondents, both Party and non-Party, for the purpose
of information on the work done in the local areas.

It shall be the duty of the Central Distributing Agency
to accurately deliver two copies of *Ekonomicheskaya Zhizn*
to every gubernia, uyezd and volost library, and the duty
of these libraries to keep newspaper files of both copies
available for the whole population.

Written May 19-20, 1921

First published in 1959
in *Lenin Miscellany XXXVI*   Printed from the manuscript

DRAFT RESOLUTION FOR THE C.C., R.C.P.(B.)[349]

Decision of the C.C. (Politbureau) 22/V. 1921 on the Decisions of the R.C.P. Group of the Trade Union Congress

The Central Committee approves Comrade Chubar's theses (adopted by the group's bureau) and rejects Comrade Holtzmann's theses in view of the fact that the former far more correctly take into consideration the actual state of our resources, capabilities and means, which entail the necessity of planning slower realisation of our immediate aims.

The latter theses, those of Comrade Holtzmann, on the other hand, verge on the fantastic in many ways, they are out of touch with reality, which is also one of the failings of Comrade Larin, who zealously supports these theses.

The only important similarity between the two theses, practically speaking, is the idea expressed in the note to Point 3 of Chubar's theses* and in Point 6** of Holtzmann's theses, both comrades confirming here, and not disputing, the decision passed by the C.C. on 10.V.1921 in connection with the motion of Comrade Larin and the A.C.C.T.U.***

---

* Here is the text of this note:

"The whole above-mentioned system of distribution should be effected by way of experiment at several enterprises, where, in place of individual rationing issues, a system of collective supply should be introduced for the personnel of the enterprises on condition that they raise labour productivity."

** Here is the text of this 6th Point:

"Pending the formation of a wages food fund, the afore-mentioned system of distribution should be applied by way of experiment at several enterprises, where, in place of individual rationing issues a system of collective supply should be introduced for the workers of the enterprises, on condition that they raise labour productivity."

*** Here is the text of this decision. [350]

"The motion of Comrade Larin and the A.C.C.T.U. in the part relating to tariff policy shall be rejected and its authors asked to go into the matter more thoroughly with an eye, especially, to the possibility of ensuring a minimum of real food supply to a minimum of workers. Upon revision, the motion is to be submitted to the C.P.C. for the purpose of introducing at several enterprises, by way of experiment and in place of individual rationing issues, a system of collective supply on condition that labour productivity is raised."

The R.C.P. group of the Trade Union Congress, despite the recommendations of the Party's C.C., approved Holtzmann's theses by *567* votes, and rejected Chubar's theses, which collected *317* votes.

Not wishing to revoke the decision of the group on an issue that does not immediately affect the Government's policy—since this policy is predetermined by the decision of the C.C. of 10.V.1921, which, as pointed out above, is approved, and not disputed, by both Comrade Holtzmann and Comrade Chubar.—the Central Committee in this particular case waives its right of interference in the proceedings and decisions of the congress.

The C.C. confines itself to prescribing that this decision be announced at the group meeting and that the attention of the delegates be strongly drawn to the obligation they are taking upon themselves in adopting Holtzmann's resolution, namely, to display not only extraordinary heroism, but a degree of persistence, firmness and pertinacity in the fight against all habits, customs and conditions of life among the working-class masses far in excess of what is customary even in revolutionary times. It is now incumbent on the trade unions, on the strength of the decision they have made, to achieve an unusually rapid reduction in the number of enterprises and workers by concentrating the latter in a minimum of the best and biggest enterprises.

Written between May 17 and 22, 1921

Published in part in August 1921 in *Izvestia C.C., R.C.P.(B.)* No. 32

First published in full in 1959 in *Lenin Miscellany XXXVI*

Printed from the manuscript

REMARKS CONCERNING THE WORK PLAN OF THE C.C., R.C.P.(B.)[351]

It should be made the chief task of the All-Russia Conference[352] in May to prepare and collect material on the question of

1) closer contact between the Party organisations and the non-Party masses.

2) drawing non-Party employees into the work more widely and systematically.

3) reorganising the Workers' and Peasants' Inspection for combating bureaucratism and red tape, improving the condition of the workers and peasants and drawing non-Party people into Soviet work.

On all these points the conference should not only collect and study all the material of practical experience, but work out practical proposals for the C.C.

Reports at the plenary meeting

(α) 2-3 reports on the present (actual) **work** of the *C.C.* and the Party

(β) ditto on the plan of its reorganisation to meet the new tasks.

Written May 24, 1921

First published in 1932
in *Lenin Miscellany XX*   Printed from the manuscript

PLAN OF A SPEECH
AT THE TRADE UNION CONGRESS[353]

1. Passing examination from 3rd to 4th course.
2. From Narodnaya Volya[354] to Social-Democracy in Russia, from the Second to the Third International in the world.
3. 1st course: 1886-1903. ((17))
4. 2nd course: 1903-1917. ((14))
5. 3rd course: 1917-1921. ((4))
6. 4th course: 1921-? (1931)
7. "Not" our last and decisive fight. But ... near (years).
8. Victory on world scale difficult (bis. ter), but a dead certainty.
9. For capitalism, the capitalists—checkmate.
10. *Alias**: the cause of communism in Russia will be *secure*.
11. Discord arising from *private* property. Labour united against property.
12. India "does not count" Doch!
13. "Treaty of Versailles"?[355]

*   —Otherwise.—*Ed.*

13. *b i s.* International trade.
14. Difficulties *on economic front.*
15. Proletariat becoming declassed? Yes! Inferences? Ideology of small property owners.
16. Large-scale production and machines—proletariat's material and *psychological* base. Inde* *declassing.*
17. Politics plus, economics minus.
18. Self-discipline, partyism.
19. Economic front.
    Passing examinations: grain, fuel.   1917
       (tax in kind)   1918 ⎱
                                         1919 ⎰
                                         1920
                              versus 1921
20. We already have economic experience—go on building systematically, steadily, firmly.
21. Work discipline, higher labour productivity, work organisation, increased output, relentless fight against slipshod work and red tape.
22. By this sign shall ye conquer.

Written in May,
not later than 25th, 1921

First published in 1945   Printed from the manuscript
in *Lenin Miscellany XXXV*

TO THE MINER COMRADES OF THE PETROVSKOYE INDUSTRIAL GROUP[356]

Comrade Mezhlauk has told me of the great success in your work during April 1921: 294 poods per hewer compared with 291 poods in 1914. I congratulate our miner comrades on this outstanding success and send my best greetings. At this rate we shall overcome all difficulties and electrify the Donbas and Krivoi-Rog district, and that means everything.

With communist greetings,

V. Ulyanov (Lenin)

Written May 25, 1921

First published July 1921   Printed from the journal text
in the journal
Vestnik Rabochego Pravlenia
No. 9-10

* — Hence.—*Ed.*

TENTH ALL-RUSSIA CONFERENCE OF THE R.C.P.(B.) [357]

MAY 26-28, 1921

1

STATEMENT CONCERNING THE AGENDA
MAY 26

Comrades, as I have already told you, we intended to have a single item on the agenda in keeping with the nature of this conference, namely, the question of economic policy. The remaining reports were to be informational, so I did not prepare a political report, but I think this report will have to be dealt with on an economic plane. Therefore, in order to satisfy everybody, I suggest that supplementary questions be put to me after the report and I shall answer them in my summing-up speech. I repeat, I have made no preparations whatever on this question and cannot imagine what I would speak about if I had to apart from the question of the tax in kind.

First published in 1963
in the Fifth Russian Edition
of the *Collected Works*, Vol. 43

Printed from the shorthand
record

2

SPEECHES DURING THE DEBATE OF THE MOTION ON QUESTIONS OF THE NEW ECONOMIC POLICY
MAY 28

1

I believe this amendment[358] should not be adopted, because an explanation to the amendment would then be needed. Naturally, if there is a revolution in Europe we shall change our policy. Civil war, which such a revolution always involves, as you know, may in fact render our position even worse. Of course, this will be a short time, it is difficult, of course, to determine how long civil war in other republics

will last, but when it is over and won we shall change our
policy in the sense that we may say: we shall take nothing
in taxes, and only by commodity exchange. This has to be
made clear to the peasants, otherwise they will think:
what's this, back again to the surplus-appropriation system?
I believe, therefore, that it were best not to add anything
of this kind. Long years of revolution in Europe and civil
war will lead to commodity exchange without any tax at all.
This is stated in the resolution before the congress, which
says that the tax will gradually be reduced. This is the
point the forthcoming victorious revolution applies to, a
revolution which a long period of years turns into a short
one.

2359

Comrades, it was on this point that we had discussions
in the committee, where opinion was divided. At first
Milyutin objected to the words "anarchic commodity exchange to be combated" on the grounds that this would be construed as cavilling, and freedom to trade would, in practice,
be done away with. When this point was drawn up in its
present wording, which said: "anarchic commodity exchange
to be combated" since "it eludes all control and supervision" —
by this is meant the black-market "bagmen", and you know
that illicit trade is punishable in all countries where there
is freedom of trading, even in capitalist countries; on this
point we see eye to eye. In what way is it to be combated?
By having commodity exchange concentrated chiefly in the
hands of the co-operatives, to which is added: "without,
however, any restrictions on regular free market operations."
When this wording was adopted the committee unanimously
agreed that there was still a danger of free market operations
being restricted. This is a delicate matter, of course. We
don't want this ruling to restrict freedom to trade, but we
can't do without measures against illicit trade, specifically
against black-market bagmen and transport dislocation.
The committee thought of using a milder word than "combating", but then agreed that the target was only anarchic
commodity exchange that eluded all control on the part
of the state, all the more as this was qualified by the added

proviso, saying "without, however, any restrictions on regular free market operations". With this addition, the word "combat" is not too strong an expression. The amendment which the comrade here proposes is risky in the sense that we shall be defeating our own purpose. He throws out the words "without, however, any restrictions on regular market operations...."

3360

I think the state farms are not equal to this, they are still very weak. Let them improve a bit for another year, and the next year we shall see whether we can expand their initiative or not.

4

The last amendment is an unhappy one,[361] since the question of material resources is covered by Point 5: "Revision of (certain sections of) production programmes for large-scale industry with a view to increasing the manufacture of consumer goods and peasant household articles.

"Extension of the independence and initiative of each large establishment in the matter of disposing of financial and material resources. A precise decision to that effect to be submitted for approval to the Council of People's Commissars." Therefore, we shall not repeat this here. The question of material distribution, that of food, for example, is stated here quite definitely, without prejudice, of course, to the centre, because without it being gathered in the centre there can be no question of industry. As regards the first remark of the comrade who said that it was inappropriate just now to consider the question of the local economic conferences settled, as these might upset things—I have not heard anything about this. On the contrary, there have been demands to indroduce economic conferences everywhere, acting as commissions of the C.P.C. Every member of the C.P.C., every representative of the C.L.D. has the right of appeal to the C.P.C. Because we select the members of the C.L.D. from among the members of the C.P.C. itself, and locally, too, there are to be no special staffs, no special bodies, but the same offices and departments. The gubernia economic conference is a perfectly suitable form, which does not hamper, but facilitates the conference. As the Instructions say: "with leeway in modifying the main type, that is, the executive committees may assume all the functions and duties of the economic conferences ..." (*reads*), so that there is no ruling prescribing an absolutely hard-and-fast and single course of action. Besides, the resolution proposed by the commission says: "Adopt in principle." The commission[362] is meeting and functioning, its Chairman Osinsky tells us they have reviewed quite a number of points and already submitted them in writing. The work is of a difficult nature, and it will require another special commission. The fear that we shall be tying our hands by declaring that it is adopted in principle is therefore groundless.

5[363]

We have no objection; judging by the subject, however, it does not belong here, but to Point 6. [364] I propose that it be adopted in principle and placed under Point 6.

6[365]

These are mere details. The question should be raised at the session of the All-Russia Central Executive Committee and discussed with the people concerned. There can be no objection in principle, but generally speaking this is a detail.

7[366]

This fear is excessive here.

Point 7 of our resolution says "The need to maintain and enforce the apparatus for the full and expeditious collection of the tax in kind". Naturally, the tax in kind will be collected not by persuasion, it can be collected only by compulsion, and that is what the apparatus stands for. Today several important decisions and instructions have been signed, all aimed at preserving and strengthening the apparatus, from which we shall demand expeditious collection of the tax in kind. It is pointed out that we say here: "commodity exchange is brought to the fore" and the fear is expressed that the peasants will understand this as priority for commodity exchange. In that case we shall write: "holds a specially important place."

First published in 1963
in the Fifth Russian Edition
of the *Collected Works*, Vol. 43

Printed from the shorthand
record

TO ALL PEOPLE'S COMMISSARS
AND TO THE CHIEF
OF THE CENTRAL STATISTICAL BOARD

*Copies to the Chairman and Secretary
of the All-Russia Central Executive Committee*

28/V.1921

All People's Commissars should have printed copies of the circulated and distributed

Draft Instructions
of the Council of Labour and Defence

signed by Lenin and Chairman of the C.L.D Commission Comrade Obolensky (Osinsky).

This draft is being submitted to the session of the All-Russia Central Executive Committee opening at 1 p.m. on 30.V.1921.

All People's Commissars are obliged

1) by 2 p.m. on Monday, 30.V.1921, to prepare in writing their amendments and addenda to the Instructions on all points, items and subitems directly or indirectly applying to the commissariats concerned;

2) within the same time, to prepare an initial draft of items (for reporting) and subitems (i.e., a more detailed list of particular questions to be reported on). This applies to all commissariats without exception, to each People's Commissar on behalf of his respective commissariat.

This is obligatory, since the All-Russia C.E.C. will endorse the general Instructions consisting of two parts: a) the Instructions of the C.L.D. covering reports by the economic commissariats; b) Instructions of the C.P.C. covering reports of all commissariats without exception, economic and non-economic.

The latter reports will form the last, additional "Fifth Group of Questions". Each commissariat is to draw up a list of the most important questions for the report on the same pattern as the questions Nos. 1 to 27 contained in the draft Instructions of the C.L.D.

The reports will be printed in about 1000 copies by each Gubernia Executive Committee and each Uyezd Executive Committee (the technical possibilities of printing no less than 1 sheet a month by each uyezd have been ascertained by me and arranged with the Paper Industry Board. Printing and presentation of reports are planned for from 6 to 4 times a year, to be finally decided upon by the All-Russia C.E.C. simultaneously with the endorsement of these Instructions.

Each People's Commissar is obliged, by the above date (by 2 p.m. on 30.V.1921), to submit in writing, in 3-5 copies, a short list of the most important questions to be included in the report of the respective commissariat.

V. Ulyanov (Lenin)
Chairman, C.P.C.

To be communicated immediately, in writing or by telephone, with the commissar's signature of receipt, and in his absence, with that of his deputy, reporter or Board member.

First published in 1932   Printed from the manuscript
in *Lenin Miscellany XX*

BRIEF MONTHLY EXTRACTS FROM REPORTS

1. Current reports, which are to be practised in all departments, institutions, central boards, enterprises (including non-state enterprises), are to be submitted at least once a month.

2. These reports must be forwarded regularly and in good time to *Ekonomicheskaya Zhizn*, the *State Planning Commission* and the *Central Statistical Board* (apart from the higher administrative bodies, whose demands are to be met in any case).

3. Brief extracts from the reports (volume of output; number of workers; number of enterprises and similar essential information) are to be forwarded to *Ekonomicheskaya Zhizn*, the *Central Statistical Board* and the *State Planning Commission* (one copy to each).

4. *Ekonomicheskaya Zhizn* is to publish them immediately.

5. An analysis of these reports by essential industries is to be made by members of the editorial board of *Ekonomicheskaya Zhizn* (each member handling one industry), and by the S.P.C. and the C.S.B. (according to § 6 at present).

6. Periodical summarised reviews to be published by *Ekonomicheskaya Zhizn* at periods to be fixed by the editors, but not less than twice a year.

7. Simple diagrams to be made up monthly by the *C.S.B.*, the form to be worked out within a week. These diagrams according to the approved forms to be made up within a *week* of the forms' approval.

Written late May or
early June 1921

First published in 1945
in *Lenin Miscellany XXXV*

Printed from the manuscript

PROPOSALS ON A CHECK-UP AND PURGE OF THE R.C.P.(B.) MEMBERSHIP[367]

The chief group responsible for registration should be made up of old Party members (not less than 5-7 years in the Party), necessarily workers.

All members of the R.C.P. who are in any way dubious, unreliable, or who have failed to prove their stability, should be removed from the Party, with the right of re-admission upon further verification and test.

1) People who joined from other parties after X.1917;
2) members from among officials and functionaries who had

held office under the old governments; 3) people who had held posts involving any privileges; 4) state employees — these categories should all be subject to a thorough check-up, and workers, both Party and non-Party, who have had contact with the given member of the R.C.P. at his work, should be questioned.

Recommending members should be required to give an accurate written testimonial and should have among them several workers with a length of Party membership of 5-7 years.

Formalities should be reduced to a minimum in the case of real workers, actually working at their factory, and in the case of peasants engaged on their allotments; such people should not be troubled with reregistration.

Written in June,
not later than 21, 1921

First published in 1959
in *Lenin Miscellany XXXVI*

Printed from the manuscript

THE THIRD CONGRESS
OF THE COMMUNIST INTERNATIONAL

JUNE 22-JULY 12, 1921[368]

1

LETTER TO O. W. KUUSINEN
AND REMARKS ON THE DRAFT
"THESES ON THE ORGANISATIONAL ACTIVITIES
OF THE COMMUNIST PARTIES, ON THE METHODS
AND CONTENT OF THEIR WORK"

To Comrade *Kuusinen*

Urgent.

Address: from Finnish comrades
or at the Comintern.

10/VI.

Comrade Kuusinen,

I have read your article (3 chapters) and the theses with great pleasure.

I enclose my remarks in connection with the theses.

I advise you to immediately find a *German* comrade (a real German) to *improve* the German text (of the article and the theses). Perhaps this comrade, on your behalf, would read your article *as a report* at the Third Congress (it would be much more convenient for the German delegates to hear a *German*.[369]

My advice is—cross out the end (of the theses).

Re propaganda and agitation—much greater detail—especially on the press, but also on verbal propaganda.

I think you should definitely *take upon yourself* the report at *this* congress. I shall write to Zinoviev about this today.

Best regards,
Yours,
Lenin

Theses

(Thesis 6 or) § 6, 2nd par., last sentence
should read:

"... will inevitably inherit this tendency to a certain extent from ... environment...."

And the next sentence should read:

"... the Communist Party *should overcome* this tendency by systematic and persistent organisational work and *repeated* improvements and corrections...."

(Thesis 7 or) § 7:

It should be stated at greater length that this is exactly what is lacking in most of the legal parties of the West. There is no *everyday* work (*revolutionary* work) by *every* member of the Party.

This is the chief drawback.

To change this is the most difficult job of all.

But this is the most important.

§ 10.

This needs amplifying.

More details.

Examples.

The role of the newspaper.

"Our" newspaper compared with the *usual* capitalist newspaper.

Work for "our" newspaper.

Example: Russian newspapers of 1912-13.

The fight against the bourgeois papers. Exposure of their venality, their lies, etc.

Distribution of leaflets.

Home agitation.

Sunday outings, etc.

Far more details.

§ 11—far more details here too.

§ 13. Presenting reports and *discussion* of reports in the "cells".

Reports on hostile and *especially on petty-bourgeois* organisations (the Labour Party, the Socialist parties, etc.).

Greater detail about duties *among the mass* of the unorganised proletariat and of the proletariat organised in the yellow trade unions (including the II and II$^1/_2$ Internationals) *and the non-proletarian* sections of the *working people.*

§§ 26 and 27.

This is irrelevant.

This is not an "organisational question".

This subject had better be dealt with in a special article for the *Communist International*, say: "Organisational Questions in Revolutionary Periods" and so forth.

Or: "On the Question of Mounting Revolution and Our Corresponding Tasks" (on the basis of Russian and Finnish experience).

Written June 10, 1921

First published in 1958
in the journal
Problemi Mira i Sotsializma No. 3

Printed from the manuscript
Translated from the German

2

LETTER TO O. W. KUUSINEN AND W. KOENEN[370]

To Comrades Kuusinen and Koenen

9/VII.1921

Dear Comrades,

I read your draft theses on the organisational question with great pleasure. I think you have done a very good job. May I suggest just two addenda:

1) advice—control commissions consisting of the best, tried and experienced workers to be formed in all parties;

2) re spies—a special point in connection with the question of illegal work. Contents roughly as follows: the bourgeoisie is bound to infiltrate spies and provocateurs into the illegal organisations. A thoroughgoing and unremitting struggle should be waged against this, and a method of struggle to be specially recommended is a skilful combination of *legal* work with illegal, verification (of fitness for illegal work) *by means* of prolonged *legal* work.[371]

With communist greetings,

Yours,

Lenin

First published in 1958
in the journal
Problemi Mira i Sotsializma No. 3

Printed from the manuscript
Translated from the German

3

REMARKS ON THE DRAFT THESES ON TACTICS FOR THE THIRD CONGRESS OF THE COMMUNIST INTERNATIONAL

LETTER TO G. Y. ZINOVIEV[372]

The crux of the matter is that Levi in very many respects is *right politically*. Unfortunately, he is guilty of a number of breaches of discipline for which the Party has expelled him.

Thalheimer's and Béla Kun's theses are politically utterly fallacious. Mere phrases and playing at Leftism.

Radek is vacillating and has spoilt his original draft by a number of concessions to "Leftist" silliness. His first "concession" is highly characteristic: in § 1 of his theses *"Umgrenzung der Fragen"* he first had "winning the majority of the working class (*to the principles of communism*)" (mark this). Amended (verballhornt) to: "winning the *socially decisive sections* of the working class."

A gem! To weaken here, in such a context, the necessity of winning precisely the *majority* of the working class "to the principles of communism," is the height of absurdity.

To win power, you need, *under certain conditions* (even when the *majority* of the working class have already been won over *to the principles of communism*) *a blow* dealt at the decisive place by the majority of the socially decisive sections of the working class.

To modify, verballhornen, this truth in such a way that § 1 of the general tasks of the Communist International about winning the working class *to the principles of communism weakens* the idea about the necessity of winning the *majority* of the working class, is a classic example of Béla Kun's and Thalheimer's ineptitude (it looks all right, dammit, but it's all damn'd wrong) and of Radek's... *hasty complaisance.*

Radek's theses were much too long and boneless, and lacked a political central point. And Radek diluted them *still* more, spoilt them hopelessly.

What's to be done? I don't know. So much time and effort wasted.

If you don't want an open fight at the congress, then I propose:

1) that Thalheimer's and B. Kun's theses be rejected by exact voting this very day (since Bukharin assures me that the basic points have to be settled not later than today: they were better postponed) as being basically erroneous. Have this recorded. You will spoil everything if you don't do this and show indulgence.

2) that Radek's first draft, "unimproved" by any corrections, one specimen of which I have quoted, should be adopted as a basis.

3) that 1-3 persons be entrusted with cutting down the text and improving it so that it is no longer boneless (if that is possible!) and clearly, precisely and unequivocally puts into focus as the central ideas the following:

None of the Communist Parties anywhere have yet won the majority (of the working class), not only as regards organisational leadership, but to the principles of communism as well. This is the basis of everything. To "weaken" this foundation of the only reasonable tactic is *criminal irresponsibility.*

Hence: revolutionary explosions are possible nevertheless very soon considering the abundance of inflammable material in Europe; an easy victory of the working class—in exceptionable cases—is also possible. But it would be absurd now to base the tactics of the Communist International on this possibility; it is absurd and harmful to write and think that the propaganda period has ended and the period of action has started.

The tactics of the Communist International should be based on a steady and systematic drive to win the *majority of the working class*, first and foremost *within the* old *trade unions*. Then we shall win for certain, whatever the course of events. As for "winning" for a short time in an exceptionally happy turn of events—any fool can do that.

Hence: the tactic of the Open Letter[373] should definitely be applied everywhere. This should be said straight out, clearly and exactly, because waverings in regard to the "Open Letter" are extremely harmful, extremely shameful and **extremely widespread.** We may as well admit this. All those who have failed to grasp the necessity of the Open Letter tactic should be *expelled* from the Communist International within a month after its Third Congress. I clearly see my mistake in voting for the admission of KAPD.[374] It will have to be rectified as quickly and fully as possible.

Instead of spinning a long yarn like Radek, we had better have the whole text of the Open Letter translated (and in German quoted in full), its significance properly brought home and adopted as a model.

I would confine the *general* resolution on tactics to this.

Only then will the *tone* be set. The central idea will be clear. There will be no woolliness. No possibility of everyone reading his own meaning into it (like in Radek's).

Radek's original draft would then be cut down to a quarter, at least.

It is time we stopped writing and voting *brochures* instead of theses. Under this system partial mistakes are inevitable with any of us, even when the matter is indisputable. And when we have something boneless and disputable we are bound to make b i g mistakes and spoil the whole thing.

And then, if you have the itch for it, you can add a supplement: on the basis of such a tactic, specifically by way of example, precisely as an example and not as a principle, we add so-and-so and so-and-so.

Further.

To generalise Serrati and Levi into the same "opportunism" is stupid. Serrati is guilty; of what? It should be said clearly and precisely—on the *Italian* question, and not on the question of general tactics. Of having split with the Communists and not having expelled the reformists, Turati & Co. Until you have carried this out, Italian comrades, you are *outside* the Communist International. We are expelling you.[375]

And to the Italian Communists—serious advice and the *demand*: so long as you have not been able by persistence, patience and skill to **convince** and win over the majority of the Serratian *workers*, don't swagger, don't play at Leftism. "Fall Levi"* is not in general tactics, but in the appraisal of Märzaktion,** on the German question. Brandler says: there was a defensive. The government provoked it.

Assuming this is true, that it is a fact.

What deduction is to be drawn from this?

1) That all the shouting about an offensive—and there was any amount of it—was erroneous and absurd;

2) that it was a tactical *error* to call for a *general* strike once there was provocation on the part of the government, who *wanted* to draw the *small fortress* of communism into the struggle (the district in the centre where the Communists already had a majority).

3) Mistakes like this must be avoided in future, as the situation in *Germany* is a special one after the killing of 20,000 workers in the civil war through the skilful manoeuvres of the Right.

4) To call the defensive of hundreds of thousands of workers (Brandler says *a million*. Isn't he mistaken? Isn't he *exaggerating*? Why are there no figures by regions and cities???) a "putsch", and a "Bakuninist putsch" at that, is worse than a mistake, it is a breach of revolutionary discipline. Since Levi added to this a number of other breaches (list them very carefully and exactly) he deserves his punishment and has earned his expulsion.

The *term* of expulsion should be fixed, say, at six months at least. He should then be *permitted* to seek readmission

---

* The Levi case.—*Ed.*

** The March action.—*Ed.*

to the Party, and the Communist International advises that he be readmitted *provided* he has acted loyally during that time.

I have not yet read anything, apart from Brandler's pamphlet, and am writing this on the basis of Levi's and Brandler's pamphlets. Brandler has proved one thing—if he has proved anything—that the Märzaktion was not a "Bakuninist putsch" [for such *abusive language* Levi ought to be expelled] but a heroic defence by revolutionary workers, hundreds of thousands of them; but however heroic it was, *in future* such a challenge, provoked by the government, which, since I.1919, has already killed by provocations 20,000 workers *should not* be accepted until the Communists have the majority behind them all over the country, and not just in one small district.

((The July days of 1917 were not a Bakuninist putsch. For such an appraisal we would have expelled a person from the Party. The July days were an heroic *offensive*. And the deduction we drew was that we would not launch the next heroic offensive *prematurely*. Premature acceptance of a general battle—that is what the Märzaktion really was. Not a putsch, but a *mistake*, mitigated by the heroism of a defensive by hundreds of thousands.))

Concerning Šmeral. Can't we have at least 2 or 3 *documents*? There would be no harm in having at least 2 documents (2-4 pages each) on each country printed for the Comintern. What are the facts about Šmeral? about Strasser?

Do not forget one of the chief things—to delete from Radek's first theses everything relating to the "waiting party", to its censure. It must all come out.[376]

Regarding Bulgaria, Serbia (Yugoslavia?) and Czechoslovakia, the question of *these* countries must be put concretely, specially, clearly, and precisely.

If opinion is divided on this, I suggest convening the Politbureau.

10/VI.1921 *Lenin*

First published in 1965 in the Fifth Russian Edition of the *Collected Works*, Vol. 52

Printed from the manuscript

4

MOTION ON THE DRAFT THESES ON TACTICS

1) That Šmeral's designation and the whole end of the paragraph be crossed out;

2) That a Committee (or the Executive) be directed to draw up a detailed *letter* to the Czech Party containing a practical, lucid and *documented* criticism of what is *incorrect* in Šmeral's stand and what the editors of the Reichenberger *Vorwärts*[377] have to be more careful of.

Written in July,
not later than 9, 1921

First published in 1958
in the journal
Problemi Mira i Sotsializma No. 2

Printed from the manuscript

5

SPEECHES AT A MEETING
OF MEMBERS OF THE GERMAN, POLISH,
CZECHOSLOVAK, HUNGARIAN AND ITALIAN
DELEGATIONS
JULY 11

1

I read certain reports yesterday in *Pravda* which have persuaded me that the moment for an offensive is perhaps nearer than we thought at the congress, and for which the young comrades attacked us. I shall deal with these reports later, however. Just now I want to say that the nearer the general offensive is, the more "opportunistically" must we act. You will now all return home and tell the workers that we have become more reasonable than we were before the Third Congress. You should not be put out by this; you will say that we made mistakes and now wish to act more carefully; by doing so we shall win the masses over from the Social-Democratic and Independent Social-Democratic parties, masses, who, objectively, by the whole course of events, are being pushed towards us, but who are afraid of us. I want to cite our own example to show you that we must act more carefully.

At the beginning of the war we Bolsheviks adhered to a single slogan—that of civil war, and a ruthless one at that. We branded as a traitor everyone who did not support the idea of civil war. But when we came back to Russia in March 1917 we changed our position entirely. When we returned to Russia and spoke to the peasants and workers, we saw that they all stood for defence of the homeland, of course in quite a different sense from the Mensheviks, and we could not call these ordinary workers and peasants scoundrels and traitors. We described this as "honest defencism". I intend to write a big article about this and publish all the material. On April 7 I published my theses, in which I called for caution and patience.* Our original stand at the beginning of the war was correct: it was important then to form a definite and resolute core. Our subsequent stand was correct too. It proceeded from the assumption that the masses had to be won over. At that time we already rejected the idea of the immediate overthrow of the Provisional Government. I wrote: "It should be overthrown, for it is an oligarchic, and not a people's government, and is unable to provide peace or bread. But it cannot be overthrown just now, for it is being kept in power by the workers' Soviets and so far enjoys the confidence of the workers. We are not Blanquists, we do not want to rule with a minority of the working class against the majority."** The Cadets, who are shrewd politicians, immediately noticed the contradiction between our former position and the new one, and called us hypocrites. But as, in the same breath, they had called us spies, traitors, scoundrels and German agents, the former appellation made no impression. The first crisis occurred on April 20. Milyukov's Note on the Dardanelles showed the government up for what it was — an imperialist government. After this the armed masses of the soldiery moved against the building of the government and overthrew Milyukov. They were led by a non-Party man named Linde. This movement had not been organised

---

* See Vol. 24 of this edition, pp. 19-26.—*Ed.*
** Ibid., p. 40.—*Ed.*

by the Party. We characterised that movement at the time as follows: something more than an armed demonstration, and something less than an armed uprising. At our conference on April 22 the Left trend demanded the immediate over-throw of the Government. The Central Committee, on the contrary, declared against the slogan of civil war, and we instructed all agitators in the provinces to deny the out-rageous lie about the Bolsheviks wanting civil war. On April 22 I wrote that the slogan "Down with the Provisional Government" was incorrect, since if we did not have the majority of the people behind us this slogan would be either an empty phrase or adventurism.*

We did not hesitate in face of our enemies to call our Leftists "adventurists". The Mensheviks crowed over this and talked about our bankruptcy. But we said that any attempt to be slightly, if only a wee bit, left of the C.C. was folly, and those who stood left of the C.C. had lost ordinary common sense. We refuse to be intimidated by the fact that our enemies rejoice at our slips.

Our sole strategy now is to become stronger, hence cleverer, more sensible, more "opportunistic", and that is what we must tell the masses. But after we shall have won over the masses by our reasonableness, we shall use the tactic of offensive in the strictest sense of that word.

Now about the three reports:

1) The strike of Berlin's municipal workers. Municipal workers are mostly conservative people, who belong to the Social-Democrats of the majority and to the Independent Social-Democratic Party; they are well off, but are compelled to strike.[378]

2) The strike of the textile workers in Lille.[379]

3) The third fact is the most important. A meeting was held in Rome to organise the struggle against the fascists, in which 50,000 workers took part—representing all parties—Communists, socialists and also republicans. Five thousand ex-servicemen came to the meeting in their uniforms and not a single fascist dared to appear on the street.[380] This shows that there is more inflammable material in Europe than we thought. Lazzari praised our resolution on tactics. It is an

---

* See Vol. 24 of this edition, pp. 210-11.—*Ed.*

important achievement of our congress. If Lazzari admits it, then the thousands of workers who back him are bound to come to us, and their leaders will not be able to scare them away from us. "Il faut reculer, pour mieux sauter" (you have to step back to make a better jump). This jump is inevitable, since the situation, objectively, is becoming insufferable.

So we are beginning to apply our new tactic. We mustn't get nervy, we cannot be late, rather we may start too early, and when you ask whether Russia will be able to hold out so long, we answer that we are now fighting a war with the petty bourgeoisie, with the peasantry, an economic war, which is much more dangerous for us than the last war. But as Clausewitz said, the element of war is a danger and we have never been out of that danger for a moment. I am sure that if we act more cautiously, if we make concessions in time, we shall win this war too, even if it lasts over three years.

Summing up:

1) All of us, unanimously throughout Europe, shall say that we are applying the new tactic, and in this way we shall win the masses.

2) Co-ordination of the offensive in the most important countries: Germany, Czechoslovakia, Italy. We need here preparation, constant co-ordination. Europe is pregnant with revolution, but it is impossible to make up a calendar of revolution beforehand. We in Russia will hold out, not only five years, but more. The only correct strategy is the one we have adopted. I am confident that we shall win positions for the revolution which the Entente will have nothing to put up against, and that will be the beginning of victory on a world scale.

2

Šmeral seemed to be pleased with my speech, but he interprets it one-sidedly. I said in the committee that in order to find the correct line Šmeral had to make three steps to the left, and Kreibich one step to the right. Šmeral, unfortunately, said nothing about taking these steps. Nor did he say anything about his views on the situation. Concerning the difficulties, Šmeral merely repeated the old arguments and said nothing new. Šmeral said that I had dispelled his fears. In the spring he was afraid that the communist leadership would demand of him untimely action, but events dispelled these fears. But what worries us now is this: will things really come to the stage of preparation for the offensive in Czechoslovakia, or will they be confined merely to talk about difficulties. The Left mistake is simply a mistake, it isn't big and is easily rectified. But if the mistake pertains to the resolution to act, then this is by no means a small mistake, it is a betrayal. These mistakes do not bear comparison. The theory that we shall make a revolution, but only after others have acted first, is utterly fallacious.

3

The retreat made at this congress can, I think, be compared with our actions in 1917 in Russia, and therefore prove that this retreat must serve as preparation for the offensive. Our opponents will say that we are not saying today what we said before. It will do them little good, but the working-class masses will understand us if we tell them in what sense the March action is to be considered a success and why we criticise its mistakes and say that we should make better preparations in future. I agree with Terracini when he says that the interpretations of Šmeral and Burian are wrong. If co-ordination is to be understood as our having to wait until another country has started, a country that is richer and has a bigger population, then this is not a communist interpretation, but downright deception. Co-ordination should consist in comrades from other countries knowing exactly what moments are significant. The really important interpretation of co-ordination is this: the best and quickest imitation of a good example. That of the workers of *Rome* is a good example.

First published in 1958:
first speech in full,
second and third
in abridged form in the journal
Voprosi Istorii KPSS No. 5

Printed from the shorthand record
Translated from the German

ADDENDA TO THE DRAFT DECISION FOR THE C.P.C. ON COLLECTIVE PAY FOR EMPLOYEES OF STATE INSTITUTIONS[381]

POINT "A"

A five-man commission to be charged with collecting the fullest possible material for an estimation of both payments in kind and actual money payments, embracing all and every form of such payment without exception, including cab fares, etc., which are now being applied in Moscow's central institutions.

POINT "D"

Collective supply both for workers and office employees is to be introduced subject to the following rules:

1) each enterprise where collective supply is introduced concludes a special agreement with the Government;

2) under this agreement, the enterprise (in the person of its management and specially elected representatives) undertakes to steadily reduce the number of workers and office employees and raise their productivity, as well as work discipline to a normal level. An enterprise in industry corresponds to a department or subdepartment, etc., for state employees;

3) non-fulfilment of the agreement entails a penalty, including total loss of supply.

Written June 28, 1921
First published in 1932
in *Lenin Miscellany XX*   Printed from the manuscript

MOTION TO THE POLITBUREAU OF THE C.C., R.C.P.(B.) ON BONUSES FOR ENTERPRISES[382]

I propose to the Politbureau

Bonuses of up to 10,000 gold rubles be paid for the efficient organisation on commercial lines of a group of enterprises, departments and institutions.

8.VII.1921

Lenin

First published in 1932
in *Lenin Miscellany XX*   Printed from the manuscript

NOTES ON MEASURES FOR COMBATING FAMINE AND STEPPING UP ECONOMIC WORK[383]

If an area affected by crop failure and famine embraces a territory with a population of twenty-five million, should we not, by a number of revolutionary measures, take young men into the army from *this* particular area to the number of about 500,000 (or even perhaps up to 1 million?).

Purpose: to help out the famine-stricken population to some extent, as we shall feed some of them and perhaps help others by means of parcels which the men will send home. That is one thing. Secondly: locate these half a million in the Ukraine, where they can help to step up food supply work, in which they are deeply concerned, keenly aware as they are of the injustice of the gluttony practised by the rich peasants in the Ukraine.

The harvest in the Ukraine is estimated roughly (Rakovsky) at 550-650 million poods. Deducting *150* million poods for sowing and *300* (15 × 20 = 300) for feeding the family and the farm animals, we get a balance (550 − 450 = *1 0 0*; 650 − 450 = *2 0 0*) at an average of about *1 5 0 million poods*. If we post an army from the famine-stricken gubernias in the Ukraine this balance (tax + barter + special requisitions from the rich to help the starving) could be collected *in full*.

Measures should immediately be stepped up in the famine-stricken gubernias to collect raw materials (hides, hoofs, horns, bristles, etc., etc.) and it should be made a rule, incidentally, that not a pood of relief should be rendered either for seed or food unless payment is made in one or another form of raw materials or fallen wood fuel or similar stuff.*

To revive the work of the gubernia, uyezd and district economic conferences of Petrograd, Moscow, Ivanovo-Voznesensk and a few principal industrial centres not far from the two capital cities, could not 2-4 top-level workers of the

---

* In the manuscript this paragraph has been crossed out by Lenin.—*Ed.*

central departments be assigned to each of these economic conferences? These groups of, say, four people, could work together as a team, being selected from among the staff of one and the same central institution or being well acquainted with each other, and they could do regular work in these economic councils, say, an hour a day each, making 3-4 hours a day together?

The complete or partial transfer of workers of the non-economic commissariats to economic work could be arranged in this way: their work at the commissariat could be shifted to the extent of three-fourths or nine-tenths to third-rate assistants, whom they could supervise.

In Moscow (and afterwards in other places) *all* top-level Party workers should be mobilised for *economic* work in this way:

every top-level Party worker of a *non*-economic commissariat takes a *low-level economic* job, for which purpose he joins some factory committee (or house or block committee)—*no* organisation *higher* than that (in order to work at low-level)—and undertakes to devote no less than two hours a day to this work. Priority is to be given to the work of distributing foodstuffs, raising the level of the economic branch concerned, and fuel supply.

It is important that *each* worker's assignment should be precisely defined.

Should we not, simultaneously with the registration of top-level Party workers on 1.VII.1921, organise the registration of all members of the R.C.P. in Moscow (and perhaps in Petrograd as well?)? Enlist for this the services of the Gubernia Statistical Bureau. Obtain exact figures on the Party.*

Written in July,
not later than 9, 1921

First published in 1959
in *Lenin Miscellany XXXVI*   Printed from the manuscript

---

* This paragraph in the manuscript has been crossed out by Lenin.—*Ed.*

RE DRAFT DECISION FOR THE C.P.C.
ON THE ORGANISATION
OF COMMODITY EXCHANGE BY CENTROSOYUZ[384]

1) The next report to be made in a month's time.

2) The form of accountancy and its proper distribution to the local bodies, as well as fulfilment by the latter of their duties in making up these accounts, to be verified through the agent of the *Central Statistical Board.*

Term: 1 week.

3) Charge Centrosoyuz with submitting to the C.P.C. a number of decisions for more energetic action against anarchic commodity exchange.

Term: 1 week.

4) In the matter of equivalents, Centrosoyuz and its local agencies down to the rural commodity exchange stations should be allowed to conduct the business with greater freedom and introduce a system of high premiums for the amount and rate of turnover.

Term: 1 week for submitting to the Narrow C.P.C.

Written July 15, 1921

First published in 1932
in *Lenin Miscellany XX*   Printed from the manuscript

MOTION FOR THE C.C., R.C.P.(B.)[385]

I move:

1) that the matter be temporarily decided (today, 28/VII.) in favour of the Siberian Bureau;

2) that a resolution of censure be passed on the Siberian Bureau for patent breach of Party duty in not simultaneously forwarding the text of the motions tabled by the two other trends: the Siberian Bureau should have asked the two other trends officially and in good time for the texts of their proposals for submission to the C.C.;

3) that Omsk be asked to wire a brief formulation of the motions of the two trends by their spokesmen;

4) that the Party conference be postponed till 15/8;

5) that a C.C. member be found to sit in on the conference on 15/8.

28/7.

Written July 28, 1921

First published in 1959
in *Lenin Miscellany XXXVI*

Printed from the manuscript

PROPOSALS
TO F. E. DZERZHINSKY'S CONCLUSIONS ON THE STATE OF TRANSPORT[386]

§ 1. Greater attention to be paid to devising measures, etc.

2—4 The Orgbureau in co-operation with Comrade Rudzutak to deal with these questions urgently.

5— Elaborate and carry out administratively.

6— Measures for improving transport and ensuring closer contact between the Party apparatus and the railways.

Written August 8, 1921

First published in 1959
in *Lenin Miscellany XXXVI*

Printed from the manuscript

LETTER TO G. Y. ZINOVIEV
AND INSTRUCTIONS TO THE SECRETARY

Type 6 copies
and send to

1) Radek
2) me
3) Trotsky
4) Kamenev
5) Stalin
6) extra copy

To Comrade Zinoviev

13/VIII-1921

Obviously, we cannot properly organise in Russia a bureau for properly summarising and selecting information on the international labour movement. We haven't the people for it, nor the libraries, etc.

I suggest that such a bureau be set up in Germany. Employ one manager (a non-work-fit Communist, better still a *non*-Communist) plus 2 assistants (+ 2—3 typists).

A definite monthly sum should be earmarked for this purpose. We should try to arrange *legally*, under some trade name, something like *Zeitungskorrespondenz*, a supply of articles and copy to the newspapers.

Three Germans (knowing English, French, Italian and Czech—enough to start with) could of course be found. Radek, if I am not mistaken, even had someone in mind.

This bureau, if we could find efficient men to run it under contract (intellectuals in Germany are hard up, and we could select a good staff), would carry on systematic research work for us in *collecting* literary and special newspaper material and *working it up* on two cardinal and main points:

A) *international imperialism*;
B) *the international labour movement.*

We could (with Radek and with his help) probably find 2-3 dozen Communists doing journalistic work in all countries to act as contributors (and writer-consultants) to this bureau.

Such a bureau would work for a start in German (for the continent of Europe now undoubtedly the most international language); and at the first opportunity it would add to its publications translations into French and English. Russian translations could easily be arranged: we would simply give the job through official state channels to 2-3 bourgeois professors, so as not to divert communist forces on purely technical work.

On both these questions (*A* and *B*) the bureau should systematically keep abreast of the international literature, especially newspaper literature, and compile *lists of valuable books and newspaper articles* on these questions.

The most important thing here would be to detail and arrange these questions correctly—to compile a *rational* and classified *list* of these questions and supplement it in good time according to the needs of the moment.

And then—commentaries of not more than 3-10 lines on books and on very rare and specially important newspaper articles (1 out of 100, or maybe 1 out of 500), so that you can tell at once what to look for and what the respective book or article deals with.

The writer-consultants could write these commentaries (or rather a statement of the contents) easily, if the German centre organised this work and paid them for it.

Further, the bureau should run

a summary of important items of information from the newspapers and press-cuttings (at least 3-4 sets to begin with: one for the files, one for Moscow, and one extra set to meet any contingency).

With the help of *consultants* and Radek at their head, we could make up a list of subjects, for example:

— — shadings and controversial issues within communism;
— —   „   „   „   and on the *fringe* of communism ($II^1/_2$* and anarchists);
— —   „   „   „   also within the trade union movement;
— — elections and their statistics (or results) to judge the strength of the trends in the labour movement;
— — the history of outstanding strikes and "incidents" (demonstrations, actions, etc.) and so on.

I believe that, properly organised, this bureau would bring in a certain income, as its bulletins would be purchased by certain newspapers and libraries as important information material.

But this income, of course, would at best cover only a small part of the expenses. We can and should bear these expenses. All the material, as far as we are concerned, will serve the cause of public education and the work of propaganda and agitation.

Such a bureau can and should be organised. It can be very useful. Without it we have no eyes, ears or hands for participation in the international movement—and we do it casually, always *dependent* (for information) on someone who is closer, near at hand, who has happened to read about it, who has just dropped in, happened to mention it, and so on.

I propose that the Politbureau discuss this plan and set up a small commission for its *preliminary* drafting, say:

Radek
Trotsky
+ ?

* Meaning the Centrist $II^1/_2$ International.—*Ed.*

Perhaps only two would be better to start with. They *can enlist* the co-operation of Steklov and Béla Kun (and many others), *invite* to Moscow a candidate for the post of *bureau manager*, and then be able to make up *an estimate* and submit the whole *elaborated* plan to the Politbureau for consideration.[387]

16/VIII.   *Lenin*

First published in 1965   Printed from the manuscript
in the Fifth Russian Edition
of the *Collected Works*, Vol. 53

DRAFT DECISION FOR THE POLITBUREAU OF THE C.C., R.C.P.(B.) ON AN INSPECTION OF THE PEOPLE'S COMMISSARIAT FOR FOREIGN TRADE[388]

I move that the Politbureau resolve:

1) That the report be made.

2) That Unschlicht be appointed to make it.

3) That the report's *conclusions* serve as the Politbureau's decisions on its findings.

4) That the secret part be dealt with separately at a closed meeting.

23/VIII.   *Lenin*

Written August 23, 1921
First published in 1965   Printed from the manuscript
in the Fifth Russian Edition
of the *Collected Works*, Vol. 54

MOTION TO THE POLITBUREAU OF THE C.C., R.C.P.(B.) ON BRINGING UNGERN TO TRIAL[389]

I advise that greater attention be given to this case and the gravity of the charges be checked, and in the event of their being incontrovertibly proved, of which there seems to be no doubt, a public trial should be held with the greatest speed and the death penalty imposed.

Dictated over the telephone
      August 26, 1921
First published in 1945   Printed from the typed copy
in *Lenin Miscellany XXXV*

A NOTE TO E. VARGA
AND THESES ON THE ORGANISATION
OF AN INFORMATION INSTITUTE
ON QUESTIONS
OF THE INTERNATIONAL LABOUR MOVEMENT

Dear Comrade Varga,

I enclose my remarks. If you think it necessary, we can talk things over on the telephone.

Best regards,
Lenin
31/8

Tentative Amendments or Theses

To Comrade E. Varga's Project
for the Organisation of an Information Institute

1. Absolute and strict legality of the Institute for Berlin or Vienna conditions and for the whole of Western Europe, Britain and America.

2. Headquarters of the Institute—Berlin or Vienna or Copenhagen or Christiania.

3. No more than 20% of the Institute's working time and publications should be devoted to economic and social questions (both together 20%). 80% to political questions.

4. As far as political questions are concerned, the task of the Institute is only to collect objective data on questions that are legal and open to discussion.

5. The Institute must be completely independent of the respective Communist Parties.

6. The official name of the Institute should be, tentatively: Institute for the Study of Forms of Social Movement.

7. Instructions of a principle nature are to be given to the head (or to three heads, not more) of the Institute.

8. On the basis of verbal instructions of a principle nature the head is to work out detailed and absolutely legal instructions and submit them here in Moscow for endorsement by the Comintern Executive.

9. Reports to be submitted weekly or twice a week. Socio-economic appendixes monthly or tri-monthly.

10. The Institute must have no contacts whatever with the Russian embassies.

11. The Institute must begin in a small way. For the German-speaking countries, Scandinavia and the Slav countries—only the German language.

Activities may be extended to Anglo-Saxon and Romance countries only on the basis of a special agreement with a representative of each group of these countries. Agreement only here in Moscow.

12. The reports, or rather, publications, or correspondence of the Institute should be paid for by subscribers (newspapers libraries, etc.).

The basic principle should be—such an organisation of the Institute and such operation as would *compel all* labour newspapers of *all* trends to subscribe to the Institute's publications and pay for them. If this does not happen, it will be proof that the Institute is worthless.

13. Comrade Varga's project[390] should serve as initial draft instructions. In particular, two basic amendments to this project are needed: 1) § 3—*up*; 2) the political part should be considerably elaborated.

Some remarks to this Point 2:

(Appendix B.) §§ 3 and 4: Correspondence from factories? + money collected by the workers themselves?

+ questions of the *trade union movement* should be specially dealt with in detail from the political angle. Winning the trade unions is one of the most important political issues.

+ workers' co-operatives: *ditto* (to Section II, b)

+ all *transitional* political *formations* (like the workers' and farmers' party in the United States) are *especially* important.

+ Leaflets? Distribution? Circulation?

+ attitude to the 1914-18 war? *Extremely important.*

Section II, § a "revolutionary" (??) workers' parties like the Communist Workers' Party of Germany.

Name is wrong. They are *not* revolutionary. They should be called: semi-anarchist, anarchist or near-anarchist.

It is necessary to add: a split of anarchism all over the world in patriotic and internationalist questions; *for* the Soviet system; *against* the Soviet system.

(§ b). Parties of the II and $II^1/_2$ Internationals—**much more** *detailed*.

+ attitude to *own* colonies—and to *imperialism* in *practical* politics—*much, much more detailed.*

+ all pacifist and petty-bourgeois-democratic groups and trends—*much more detailed.*

And so on.

31/8.1921. Lenin

First published in 1965
in the Fifth Russian Edition
of the *Collected Works*, Vol. 54

Printed from the manuscript
Translated from the German

TO E. VARGA

Dear Comrade Varga,

I consider it incorrect to put the question that way (supplying information to the Comintern Executive *or* to the labour press *or* to both?).

We need *full* and *truthful* information. And the truth should not depend upon whom it has to serve.

We can accept only the division into *unofficial* information (for the *Comintern Executive* only) and *official* information (for everybody).

The former already exists and must exist *separately*; it must be improved.

The latter, to become good, requires good organisation in the *selection of facts* without a declaration that "we" are Communists.

If the *selection of facts* is full, exact and good, then the yellow labour press, too (especially the local and trade union newspapers) will certainly *buy* and pay for our material. If that does not happen it will be evidence of our *poor* legal work.

With communist greetings,
Lenin

1/IX.1921

First published in 1965
in the Fifth Russian Edition
of the *Collected Works*, Vol. 54

Printed from the manuscript
Translated from the German

DECISION OF THE POLITBUREAU
OF THE C.C., R.C.P.(B.) ON KEEPING
A RECORD OF WORKERS' DONATIONS IN EUROPE[391]

SEPTEMBER 2, 1921

a) The Russian members of the Executive shall be instructed to obtain a decision of the Comintern for organising accurate current statistics of workers' donations in Europe for sufferers of the famine in Russia and regularly publishing reports of such donations.

b) The Central Committee draws special attention to the need for stepping up agitation among the workers in Europe for contributing one-day's pay, as one of the most expedient forms of relief for the famine-stricken.

c) The Russian members of the Comintern shall be asked to submit a report on the progress of this propaganda to the Politbureau within a fortnight.

First published in 1964   Printed from the typed copy
in the Fifth Russian Edition   of the minutes
of the *Collected Works*, Vol. 44

A NOTE TO V. M. MOLOTOV
AND A DRAFT DECISION FOR THE POLITBUREAU
OF THE C.C., R.C.P.(B.) ON NOULENS' NOTE

Comrade Molotov,

Noulens is insolent to a degree. On the back of this sheet I propose a draft decision. If there is no agreement on this among us I demand that the whole Politbureau be convened tomorrow; I shall come down then. There can be no question of yielding here.

Lenin

4/IX.

I propose
this text of a Politbureau decision:

"Chicherin shall be instructed to draw up in reply to Noulens a sharply worded note of refusal in the form of a proclamation against the bourgeoisie and imperialism with special emphasis on the counter-revolutionary role of Noulens himself, with special mention of the cynically insolent nature of the proposal, before any agreement is reached, to send a commission of spies under the name of a commission of experts, specially ridiculing the idea of sending the commission question forms regarding winter crops by 4.IX., which we have already done ourselves on time, and specially ridiculing the 7 points and declaring that we shall either have dealings with governments à la Germany, or with persons—not those of the Noulens type, of course—on the basis of previous and clearly defined agreements. Special stress is to be laid on the fact that we cannot for a moment believe in the desire to help on the part of Messrs. Noulens *in view of such an approach to the matter as theirs.*[392]

Written September 4, 1921

First published in 1959
in *Lenin Miscellany XXXVI*   Printed from the manuscript

ADDENDUM TO THE DRAFT DECISION FOR THE POLITBUREAU OF THE C.C., R.C.P.(B.) ON DIRECTIVES TO THE PEOPLE'S COMMISSARIAT FOR FOOD[393]

Add:

(1) reduction of the number of recipient enterprises (receiving bread from the state);

(2) bread rationing not to be increased without special permission of the C.C.

Written September 5 or 6, 1921

First published in 1959
in *Lenin Miscellany XXXVI*   Printed from the manuscript

DRAFT DECISION
FOR THE POLITBUREAU OF THE C.C., R.C.P.(B.) ON SPENDINGS FROM THE GOLD FUND[394]

I move that the Politbureau resolve:

To ask the Presidium of the All-Russia Central Executive Committee:

1) To revoke the decision of the C.P.C. assigning $5^1/_4$ millions for orders to the firm of Armstrong.

2) To suspend the 10.9 million order for tank-cars, and instruct Kursky within a week to check this expenditure for conformity with all previous decisions of the Politbureau pertaining to the gold fund.

3) To instruct Kursky to carry out a similar check in regard to all allocations from the gold fund as from August 1921.

4) To instruct Alsky to devise a proper form of special accountancy covering spendings from the gold fund and special verification of each item of expenditure from the point of view of the decisions of the Politbureau (in co-operation with Molotov).

5) To instruct Kursky to personally ascertain from the documents whether allocations for Armstrong orders have been started, and if they have, what the legal position will be in connection with the annulment of the C.P.C.'s decision and the suspension of their fulfilment.

Lenin

Written September 7, 1921
First published in 1964
in the Fifth Russian Edition,
of the *Collected Works*, Vol. 44

Printed from the typed copy

DRAFT DECISION
FOR THE POLITBUREAU OF THE C.C., R.C.P.(B.) ON THE FREE SALE OF BOOKS FROM MOSCOW WAREHOUSE STOCKS[395]

1) Stock-taking of books in Moscow warehouses to be carried out jointly by the Moscow Soviet and the Chief Committee for Political Education;

2) The C.C.P.E. to be allowed to take such books from store as are needed for libraries, Moscow's interests being fully observed in the distribution of these books; to ensure that these interests are duly observed, the C.C.P.E. is obliged to satisfy the requirements of the Moscow Gubernia Committee for Political Education, which has the right to appeal against its decisions in the course of three days.

3) Pornography and books on religious subjects shall not be released for free sale, and shall be turned over to the *Paper Industry Board* as wastepaper.

4) The sale of foreign books shall be freely permitted.

Written September 13, 1921

First published in 1959
in *Lenin Miscellany XXXVI*

Printed from the manuscript

DRAFT DECISION
FOR THE POLITBUREAU OF THE C.C., R.C.P.(B.)[396]

Comrade Bogdanov shall be directed immediately to form a state trust of Ridder and Ekibastuz works and mines and all others economically linked with them, based on the utmost financial and economic autonomy and independence of local, Siberian, Kirghiz and other authorities, and direct subordination to the Supreme Economic Council.

Written September 14, 1921

First published in 1959
in *Lenin Miscellany XXXVI*

Printed from the manuscript

A NOTE TO V. M. MOLOTOV
WITH A MOTION FOR THE C.C., R.C.P.(B.)

Comrade Molotov,

From all sides I hear that recommendations (in connection with the Party purge[397]) are being given right and left as a favour.

I propose that a circular be published by the C.C. (by arrangement with and over the signatures of the Central Control Commission and the Verification Commission):

"Recommendations may be given only by those who have personally observed the work of the person recommended for at least one year, and have worked together with him in one or another Party organisation."[398]

15/IX.   *Lenin*

Written September 15, 1921

First published in 1939   Printed from the manuscript
in the journal
Proletarskaya Revolutsia No. 1

A LETTER TO V. V. KUIBYSHEV
AND A DRAFT ENGAGEMENT FOR WORKERS
GOING TO RUSSIA FROM AMERICA[399]

Comrade Kuibyshev,

I am sending you the draft of an undertaking which Rutgers and *all* his people down to each individual worker have to give (*in the event of* an agreement being signed).

If you are agreeable, put it to them.

Find a reliable *interpreter* (for all negotiations) who knows *both* languages *well*.

An agreement is essential, and it must be very precisely worded.

We must get *our own lawyer* (a Communist) to draw it up.

I suggest it be called an agreement for *handing over the management* of a number of factories, etc.

The technical examination results should be signed by *Stunkel* and several other experts *of repute*.

With communist greetings,
Lenin

Do the leaders and organisers of the enterprise agree to sign the following engagement and obtain the signatures of all the other people going to Russia from America:

1. We undertake to see to it and *collectively* answer for it that only such people shall *go* to Russia as are capable and willing to face a number of severe hardships involved in the rehabilitation of industry in a very backward and utterly ruined country.

2. Those going to Russia undertake to work their hardest and with the greatest efficiency and discipline exceeding those of capitalist standards, as otherwise Russia will not be able to outstrip capitalism or even catch up with it.

3. We undertake, in the event of any conflicts whatsoever to submit them for settlement to the supreme Soviet authority of Russia and faithfully abide by its decisions.

4. We undertake not to forget the extremely nervous state of the starving and exhausted Russian workers and peasants involved in our business and to render them every assistance with a view to establishing friendly relations and overcoming any distrust or envy.

Written September 22, 1921

First published January 20, 1929
in *Torgovo-Promyshlennaya Gazeta*
No. 17

Printed from the manuscript

DRAFT DECISION
FOR THE POLITBUREAU OF THE C.C., R.C.P.(B.)
ON THE QUESTION
OF THE FAR-EASTERN REPUBLIC

I move that we agree with Chicherin and authorise him to draw up *precise* and brief directives concerning the Far-Eastern Republic in the form of a *draft resolution*.[400]

Lenin

Written October 7 or 8, 1921

First published in 1959
in *Lenin Miscellany XXXVI*

Printed from the manuscript

RE DRAFT DECISION FOR THE C.C., R.C.P.(B.)
PLENUM

Work up the question of studying the composition of communist executives with a view to determining their suitability for work of various scope and scale, if only in the city of Moscow and one of the gubernias to begin with.[401]

Written October 8, 1921

First published in 1959   Printed from the manucript
in *Lenin Miscellany XXXVI*

DRAFT DIRECTIVES FOR THE POLITBUREAU
OF THE C.C., R.C.P.(B.)
ON THE ALLOTMENT OF LANDS
FOR SUGAR-BEET CULTIVATION
IN THE UKRAINE[402]

Directives

of the Politbureau on the allotment of lands in the Ukraine to the refineries for sugar-beet cultivation and on the compliance of the peasants on the lands adjoining the sugar refineries with compulsory crop rotation and fixed norms of culture.

1. This reform is to be carried out with the greatest care, no single step to be taken without practical verification that the business of beet cultivation is adequately provided for by a rational system of farming and by the peasant's own personal interest in the matter.

2. 400,000 dessiatines to be allotted to the refineries, this figure to be checked as to whether it is really necessary for ensuring properly organised large-scale factory farming.

The refineries to be made responsible for all the land allotted to them being rationally cultivated and utilised for the plants.

3. Compulsory crop rotation to be introduced on the peasant lands and obligatory norms of culture to be applied

to them only in those cases where beet crops have long been cultivated on these lands.

4. Strict care should be taken that the relations between the sugar refineries and the beet-cultivating peasants are based on a really voluntary agreement within the limits of an obligatory fixed beet-sowing area.

Written October 10, 1921

First published in 1959
in *Lenin Miscellany XXXVI*

Printed from the manuscript

DRAFT DECISION FOR THE POLITBUREAU OF THE C.C., R.C.P.(B.) ON SOCIAL INSURANCE[403]

The Presidium of the All-Russia Central Council of Trade Unions, jointly with the Supreme Economic Council, the People's Commissariats for Health and Social Security, shall be charged with working up the question of insurance for workers in connection with the new economic policy.

Written October 10, 1921

First published in 1959
in *Lenin Miscellany XXXVI*

Printed from the manuscript

NOTES ON YUGOSTAL[404]

Number of workers at these **3** works (both mining and metallurgical) minimum (in summer) 21,000 (roughly).

1. X. about *30,000* |||
Communists about *500* |||
Monthly pay-roll now:

$$216,000$$
$$+ \ 200,000 \ \text{coal}$$
$$+ \ 200,000 \ \text{overtime}$$

per month (12...*) $= \overline{616,000}$ rubles

* Undeciphered.—*Ed.*

Hewer = from 900,000 to $1^1/_2$ million
specialist (maximum) = $2^1/_2$ to 3 million
+ stealing or tips up to 10 million.

> 1 gold ruble = 40,000
> 75 gold rubles = 3 mill. Soviet rubles

Raise spec. pay by 1.I.1922:
maximum *40* million
= 1000 gold rubles a month.
"Commercial director" =
at *Head Office* of 3 works
(Yugostal)
= assistant manager...
(big businessman)
$\left(\left(\begin{matrix}\text{status of the highest,}\\\text{top-level specialist}\end{matrix}\right)\right)$
Marketing = his chief task.

Written in October,
after the 11th, 1921

First published in 1933
in *Lenin Miscellany XXIII*

Printed from the manuscript

A NOTE TO V. M. MOLOTOV
WITH A DRAFT DECISION
FOR THE POLITBUREAU OF THE C.C., R.C.P.(B.)
ON THE QUESTION OF AN AGREEMENT
WITH THE RUTGERS GROUP[405]

12.X.1921

Comrade Molotov,

I enclose material on the Rutgers business.

It is for the *Council of Labour and Defence* to decide.

I suggest that it *first* be decided in the C.C.—it is a political question. And the Politbureau *must* have its say, as it is a *gold* spending.

Please get the secretary to telephone *all* the members of the Politbureau who will each arrange for *one hour* in the course of which he will be able to familiarise himself with the material before Friday. Each one must look through it so that it can be settled on Friday.

Let the secretary make up a time-table and send the material round to each member of the Politbureau.

A difficult question:

for: *if* the Americans keep their word, it will be of tremendous benefit. In that case we shall not grudge *600,000* gold rubles.

against: will they keep their word? *Heywood* is half-anarchist. More sentimental than business-like. *Rutgers* may succumb to Leftism. *Calvert* is highly garrulous. We have no business guarantees whatever. Enthusiastic people, in an atmosphere of unemployment, may recruit a group of "adventurous spirits" who will end up in squabbles. We may then lose *part* of our 600,000 gold rubles (they will, of course, spoil and waste some of the property) and risk losing *up to 1 million gold rubles* **more**, because under § 8 (the end of it) we undertake

"to reimburse the equivalent of expenditures on machines and tools brought in by the said emigrant".

No small risk.

For: Smirnov I. N. and Maximov (of the Urals) are local people, and they are for it.

Against: Martens should know the Americans well, and he is against.

Lenin

Please arrange for all the members of the S.E.C. Presidium to be on phone call with the secretary of the C.C. on Friday from 12 to 4 p.m. in case they are called out to the C.C.

P.S. Please also send copies of this letter to all the members of the Politbureau.

First published in 1959
in *Lenin Miscellany XXXVI*

Printed from the manuscript

A LETTER TO POLITBUREAU MEMBERS
WITH A DRAFT DECISION
FOR THE C.C., R.C.P.(B.)
AND THE COUNCIL OF LABOUR AND DEFENCE
ON THE QUESTION OF RUTGERS' PROPOSALS

In my opinion, Rutgers' proposals cannot be accepted
now in their present form. But I should like to try a thing
like this: to make him *modify the group* (Rutgers + Heywood
+ Calvert). And modify the financial terms, too. We could
decide this way:

> while rejecting the proposals of Comrade Rutgers in
> their present form, i.e., the motion of Comrade Bogda-
> nov and the members of the S.E.C. Presidium who
> voted with him,
>
> the C.C. (and then the *C.L.D.* in administrative
> order) expresses an earnest wish that Comrade Rutgers'
> group should not regard this refusal as a final one and
> should revise their proposals on the following lines:
> α) modification of the group, the main group of sponsors,
> by adding to it 5-8 prominent representatives of the
> American labour union movement or other labour
> organisations; β) reducing our Government's expenses
> to the sum of $300,000 maximum; γ) cutting and
> specifying our expenses in the event of the agreement
> being cancelled.[406]

Lenin

Written between
October 12 and 15, 1921

First published in 1959   Printed from the manuscript
in *Lenin Miscellany XXXVI*

DRAFT DECISION FOR THE POLITBUREAU
OF THE C.C., R.C.P.(B.)
ON ASSIGNING A. G. SHLYAPNIKOV
TO FOOD SUPPLY WORK[407]

Confirm the decision of the Orgbureau; point out once
more the absolutely wrong behaviour of Comrade Shlyapnikov, who declared in the Orgbureau that he would not

comply; inquire of the Central Verification Commission and the Central Control Commission for how long they consider it possible to release Comrade Shlyapnikov for food supply work without detriment to the work of the Central Verification Commission.

Written October 14, 1921

First published in 1964
in the Fifth Russian Edition
of the *Collected Works*, Vol. 44

Printed from the manuscript

DRAFT DECISION
FOR THE POLITBUREAU OF THE C.C., R.C.P.(B.)[408]

1) Guseinov and Akhundov to be called out *immediately*.

2) It be strictly demanded that factional strife in Baku and Azerbaijan cease completely.

3) It be confirmed that those engaging in factional strife will be expelled from the Party.

4) The comrades sent to Azerbaijan from the R.S.F.S.R. shall be directed to check fulfilment.

5) Stalin shall be instructed to draw up by Monday draft directives on the implementation of the Communist Party's national policy in Azerbaijan.

6) In regard to Persia the strictest confirmation to be made at once.

Written October 15, 1921

First published in the journal
Voprosi Istorii KPSS No. 2

Printed from the manuscript

DRAFT DECISION
FOR THE POLITBUREAU OF THE C.C., R.C.P.(B.)
ON THE SETTING UP OF A SINGLE COMMISSION
ON CONCESSIONS

In view of offers from capitalists of neutral countries for concessions on some of the factories and branches of industry of the R.S.F.S.R., a committee of Comrades Trotsky, Bogdanov and Tsiperovich (with the right of the

Petrograd Gubernia Committee of the Party to replace him by another comrade) shall be directed to prepare a decision for the Politbureau abolishing all previous commissions on this matter and setting up a single directing commission to deal with these affairs in all their aspects.[409]

Written October 17, 1921

First published in 1959
in *Lenin Miscellany XXXVI*

Printed from the manuscript

A NOTE TO V. M. MIKHAILOV
WITH A DRAFT RESOLUTION
FOR THE C.C., R.C.P.(B.)
ON THE QUESTION OF AN AGREEMENT
WITH THE RUTGERS GROUP[410]

19.X.

Comrade Mikhailov,

I enclose the reply of the Rutgers group to the decision of the Council of Labour and Defence (i.e., the decision of the Central Committee).

I believe this is tantamount to an *acceptance* of our terms.

I am therefore enclosing a draft *decision for the C.C.* which please *circulate as quickly as possible* among the members of the Politbureau. *Very urgent.*

With communist greetings,
Lenin

In view of the fact that the group of sponsors (Comrades Rutgers, Heywood and Calvert) have accepted the terms proposed in the decision of *the C.L.D.* of 17.X., the Central Committee resolves and directs the C.L.D. to resolve:

The C.L.D. resolves:

1) that the agreement with the group be considered concluded;

2) that Comrade Bogdanov be directed to immediately draw up and submit to the chairman of the C.L.D. for signature telegrams giving the most urgent orders for laying in stocks of wood, timber, etc.;

3) that the Presidium of the S.E.C. be directed within two days to draw up the final text of a modified agreement for endorsement by the C.L.D. on Friday, 21.X.1921;
  4) that $5,000 be issued to Comrade Rutgers on Saturday, 22.X., according to the agreement, immediately after its endorsement by the C.L.D. on 21.X.

Further, without this being recorded as a decision of the C.L.D., the C.C. instructs Comrade Bogdanov, the Kuibyshev Commission, and the C.L.D. to modify the agreement in such a way that (1) *the C.L.D.* shall have the right to take part in the selection of extra candidates for the "Organising Committee" *before* and *for* the purpose of the final endorsement of this list; (2) the *total* sum of *all* the Soviet government's expenses *shall not exceed* $300,000; (3) in the event of the agreement being cancelled the Soviet authorities *shall not* incur any financial liabilities (or only such as shall be recognised as lawful by a court of the R.S.F.S.R. or *by the Central Executive Committee* of the R.S.F.S.R.).

Lenin

Written October 19, 1921

First published in 1959
in *Lenin Miscellany XXXVI*   Printed from the manuscript

PROPOSALS TO THE TEXT
OF THE DRAFT AGREEMENT
WITH THE A.R.A. ON THE ORGANISATION
OF FOOD PARCELS TO RUSSIA[411]

I agree. 19/X Lenin
(even if the aim is *trade*, we *should* make this experiment, as we are given a clear profit for the famine-stricken and the right of control; and the right of cancellation at 3 months' notice. Hence we should *not* charge for carriage and storage). A controller of ours (confirmed by the Politbureau) shall be appointed to the *A.R.A.* who combines reliability with an ability to control the w h o l e operation.

Written October 19, 1921
First published in 1959
in *Lenin Miscellany XXXVI*   Printed from the manuscript

A LETTER TO THE POLISH COMMUNISTS

19.X.1921

Dear Comrades,

Judging by the scrappy information concerning the growth of the communist movement in Poland that reaches our newspapers, and judging (still more) by the reports of some very prominent Polish comrades, the revolution in Poland is coming to a head.

A workers' revolution is brewing: the complete collapse of the P.P.S.* (in Russian—S.R.s and Mensheviks; in European—the II and II¹/₂ Internationals). The trade unions, one after another, are joining the Communists. The growth of demonstrations, and so on. Imminent and inevitable financial collapse. The gigantic failure of bourgeois democracy (and of the petty bourgeoisie) in Poland with the agrarian reform, a failure that is foredoomed, inevitable, and bound to push the majority of the rural population—the whole poor section of the peasantry—towards the Communists.

Financial collapse and shameless plunder of Poland by Entente capital (France and other countries) are bringing with them a practical exposure of national and Great Power illusions, an exposure that is strikingly clear and tangible to the *masses*, to the rank-and-file worker, to the rank-and-file peasant.

If this is so, then the revolution (Soviet revolution) in Poland is bound to win, and win soon. That being the case, the Government and the bourgeoisie must be prevented from strangling the revolution by bloody suppression of a *premature* uprising. You must not be provoked. You must wait for the tide to rise to its highest: it will sweep everything away and give victory to the Communists.

If the bourgeoisie kills 100-300 people, this will not ruin the cause. But if it is able to provoke a massacre, to kill 10-30 *thousand* workers, this *may* delay the revolution *even for several years.*

If it is important for the Government to hold elections to the Seim, then an effort should be made for the *Seim to*

---

* P.P.S.—the Polish Socialist Party.—*Ed.*

be won by the wave of the workers' revolution and the peasants' discontent.

Do not yield to provocation.

The revolution must be allowed to *grow to full* ripening of the fruit. The victory of Soviet power *from within* Poland will be a gigantic *international* victory. If Soviet power has, in my opinion, now won an international victory to the extent of 20-30 per cent, then with the victory of Soviet power *from within* Poland, we shall have a 40-50, perhaps even 51 per cent *international* victory of the communist revolution. For Poland is next door to Germany, Czechoslovakia and Hungary, and a Soviet Poland will undermine the *whole* regime built up on the peace of Versailles.

That is why the Polish Communists bear a responsibility before the whole world—that of keeping a firm grip on the helm of their ship and steering clear of provocations.

Is it worth while retaliating for the beating up of Dabal by Daszynski & Co.? Retaliation, if any, should be by beating up Daszynski, just like that, without any shooting or wounding. It may be worth while if it has the effect of teaching an insolent fellow a lesson at the hands of the workers, and stiffening the workers' spirit at the cost of a sacrifice of 5-10 of them (by imprisonment or execution). But maybe it is not worth while: would not the fact that *our* Dąbal had been brutally beaten up be *more useful* for the purpose of agitation among the *peasants*? Would it not be *more effective* in turning the sympathy of the *backward* peasants towards us than the thrashing of Daszynski? This should be weighed more carefully.

With communist greetings,
Lenin

First published April 22, 1962
in *Pravda* No. 112   Printed from the manuscript

DRAFT DECISION FOR THE POLITBUREAU OF THE C.C., R.C.P.(B.)[412]

Re § 4:

The People's Commissariat for Finance and the Finance Commission, as well as all comrades handling questions of home trade, shall be directed to select within the shortest possible time a group of people with long practical experience in capitalist trade for the purpose of consultation on currency questions. These comrades shall be asked, within two days, to report in writing whether they can fulfil this assignment and in what period of time.

Written October 20, 1921

First published in 1959
in *Lenin Miscellany XXXVI*　　　　　Printed from the manuscript

DRAFT DECISION FOR C.L.D.
ON FOWLER PLOUGHS[413]

1. Comrade Martens, Manager of the Metal Department of the S.E.C. shall be made personally responsible for fulfilment of the decisions of the *C.L.D.* on Fowler ploughs.

2. Comrade Martens shall be directed, within a week, to submit to the *C.L.D.* a written proposal containing a plan of work and concrete measures for its effective implementation.

3. The special three-man commission shall be liquidated, made to hand over all business to Comrade Martens within a week and submit a written report on its work.

4. The People's Commissariat for Justice shall be instructed to investigate, within a week, the red tape, mismanagement and wrong attitude to this business on the part of the Metal Department, also, especially, on the part of the three-man commission and other institutions.

Its report to be presented to the *C.L.D.*

Written October 21, 1921

First published in 1933
in *Lenin Miscellany XXIII*　　　　　Printed from the manuscript

DECISION OF THE C.L.D. ON THE QUESTION
OF REPORTS AND DIAGRAMS FOR THE C.L.D.[414]

OCTOBER 21, 1921

A commission consisting of comrades Gorbunov, Smolyaninov, Avanesov (with the right of replacement) and Krumin and with the co-operation of the Central Statistical

Board, the State Planning Commission and the appropriate departments, shall be directed

to submit to the C.L.D. within one week the draft of a decision calling for all departments to present statistical data and diagrams monthly to the C.L.D. pertaining especially to economic activities, their analysis, working up and formulation of practical conclusions.

Comrade Gorbunov or Smolyaninov to be charged with summoning the commission and reporting to the C.L.D.[415]

First published in 1933
in *Lenin Miscellany XXIII*

Printed from the typewritten
copy of the minutes

DRAFT DECISION FOR THE POLITBUREAU OF THE C.C., R.C.P.(B.) ON THE MANAGEMENT OF THE COTTON INDUSTRY[416]

Comrade Bogdanov jointly with Comrade Kamenev shall be charged with revising both drafts with a view to eliminating the red tape in both of them and establishing a system of efficient management on really commercial lines.

The two texts of the proposals to be juxtaposed and circulated among the members of the Politbureau.

Written October 27, 1921

First published in 1964
in the Fifth Russian Edition
of the *Collected Works*, Vol. 44

Printed from the manuscript

PLAN OF AN ARTICLE "COMMERCIAL ORGANISATION"[417]

Plan of an Article "Commercial Organisation"

Will this do for a slogan?

"Commerce"? = capitalism.

(α) "State capitalism". Its advantages.

(β) War conditions excluded "commerce".

(γ) The transition to "communism" was very often (both for war reasons and owing to almost absolute poverty and to mistakes, a number of mistakes) made without the intervening stages of socialism (communism *vs* socialism)

(δ) "Accounting and control"?

(ε) *Should pay for itself.*

$$c + v + s$$
$$s - \text{accumulation}$$
$$- \text{maintenance of the state}$$

Allgemein
Theoreti-
sches*

"War" = dictatorship of the proletariat.

variety of forms
- (α) Politics 25.X.1917—5.I.1918
- (β) Weltpolitik. Brester Frieden.**
- (γ) Civil war.
- (δ) Fighting "economic crisis", *i.e.*, the petty-bourgeois elements? post-war indiscipline? disintegration? inefficiency?

Condition for victory in war: supreme effort.

Commercial organisation =
= supreme effort
= reducing enterprises to a minimum, their concentration
= checking results
= "thrift".

Either—or:

aut 100,000 + 500,000
16...$^1/_4$ lb. for a peasant?***

aut supreme effort, reduction, "pressure" (?)
Had enough of indolence, slovenliness, petty profiteering, thieving, laxity.

Why not "thrift"?
- — freedom of trade
- — state capitalism
- — currency system.

Written in October
or November, 1921
First published in 1959
in *Lenin Miscellany XXXVI*

Printed from the manuscript

* General theoretical propositions.—*Ed.*
** World politics. The peace of Brest.—*Ed.*
*** These figures have not been deciphered.—*Ed.*

DRAFT DECISIONS FOR THE C.P.C.
ON THE FINANCIAL PLAN
AND PLAN OF EMISSION FOR 1922

1

1) The Finance Commission shall be directed to submit by Tuesday, 15.XI., an estimate in gold rubles covering all and every form of revenue, including the tax in kind, fuel, etc., etc.,

— to submit a calculation in gold rubles showing distribution of expenditure by commissariats (absolute figures)—in comparison with similar figures before the war (average for 5 or 10 years) and with approximate figures for 1919 and 1920.

2) To submit 2 variants: 240 and 300 million gold ruble volume of emission.

3) To compare quota distribution of the general budget (both material and monetary) with the distribution of rations under the food plan of the *C.L.D.*

4) Drawing up of the budget on the basis of the given plan (with an emission variant of 240 million gold rubles) to be started at once.

5) Assignment for the State Planning Commission? The Central Statistical Board? or an enlarged commission?

6) Time limit—20.XII.

7) Could we not publish some of the Finance Commission's *findings*?

especially calculation (in goods) of the pre-war ruble, and so on.[418]

Written November 5, 1921

First published in 1959
in *Lenin Miscellany XXXVI*   Printed from the manuscript

2

1) The Finance Commission and the State Planning Commission shall be directed to complete the estimate of revenue and expenditure on the broad terms at present accepted by the Finance Commission, as well as the comparison ordered by the C.P.C. in its decision of November 5.

2) These calculations to be presented in the form of summarised statements viewed as preliminary data for shaping the state budget for the year 1922.[419]

Written November 18, 1921

First published in 1945
in *Lenin Miscellany XXXV*   Printed from the manuscript

TALK WITH A DELEGATION
OF THE MONGOLIAN PEOPLE'S REPUBLIC[420]
NOVEMBER 5, 1921

1st question of the Mongolian delegation: "Comrade Lenin, what do you think about the establishment of a People's Revolutionary Party in our country and what is most important for us?"

Comrade Lenin outlined to our delegation our country's international situation and pointed out that owing to the M.P.R.'s geographical position the imperialist powers, in case of war, would try to seize our country and use it as a jumping-off ground for military operations against another country. Therefore, Lenin said, the only right way for every working person in your country was to fight for state and economic independence in alliance with the workers and peasants of Soviet Russia. This fight could not be carried on isolatedly, therefore the establishment of a party of Mongolian arats was a pledge of success in their struggle.

The Mongolian delegation's second question: "Will the national liberation struggle be victorious?"

Comrade Lenin's answer:

"I have been in the revolutionary movement myself for thirty years and I know by experience how difficult it is for any people to liberate themselves from their external and internal enslavers. Although Mongolia is a cattle-breeding country and the bulk of her population are nomad herdsmen, she has achieved great progress in her revolution, and most important of all, has made good these successes by creating a People's Revolutionary Party of her own, whose aim is to become a mass party uncluttered by alien elements."

The Mongolian delegation's third question: "Ought not the People's Revolutionary Party be transformed into a Communist Party?"

Comrade Lenin's reply:

"I should not recommend it, because one party cannot be 'transformed' into another." Comrade Lenin explained the essence of a Communist Party as a party of the proletariat, and said: "The revolutionaries will have to put in a good deal of work in developing state, economic and cultural activities before the herdsman elements become a proletarian mass, which may eventually help to 'transform' the People's Revolutionary Party into a Communist Party. A mere change of signboards is harmful and dangerous."

Comrade Lenin elaborated on the idea that it was possible and necessary for the M.P.R. to follow a non-capitalist path of development, the main condition for which was hard work on the part of the People's Revolutionary Party and the Government, so that this work and the increased influence of the Party and the authorities would result in a growth of the number of co-operatives, in the introduction of new forms of economic activity and national culture, and would rally the arats behind the Party and the Government in the interests of the country's economic and cultural development. It was only from the islets of the new economic way of life created by the efforts of the Party and the Government that the new non-capitalist economic system of arat Mongolia would take shape.

First published in 1934
in the book *The Ninth Congress
of the Mongolian People's
Revolutionary Party*
(September 28-October 5, 1934)
Ulan-Bator, *Modern Mongolia*
Publishing House

Printed from the text
of the book

DRAFT DECISION FOR THE POLITBUREAU OF THE C.C., R.C.P.(B.)

It shall be recognised that the resolution of the First All-Russia Conference on the cultural and educational work of the trade unions is at variance with the resolution of the Tenth Congress of the R.C.P. on the Chief Committee for Political Education and its relations with the All-Russia Central Council of Trade Unions (§ 2).[421]

The resolution of the Congress of Gubernia Political Education Departments[422] shall be confirmed as a whole and the Chief Committee for Political Education shall be directed, within a month and in agreement with the A.C.C.T.U. to draw up detailed practical instructions giving concrete definitions of the forms of "joint" work by both institutions and the forms in which the trade unions and their bodies are to "use" the "apparatus and staff" of the Chief Committee for Political Education.[423]

Written November 8, 1921

First published in 1964
in the Fifth Russian Edition
of the *Collected Works*, Vol. 44

Printed from the manuscript

A NOTE TO V. M. MIKHAILOV WITH A DRAFT DECISION FOR THE POLITBUREAU OF THE C.C., R.C.P.(B.)[424]

Comrade *Mikhailov*,
Please have this sent round to the members of the Politbureau.
My personal opinion is that the whole of V. Milyutin's plan should be *rejected* as being worthless and absolutely unconsidered.
I propose it be *rejected*.

Lenin

9/XI.

Written November 9, 1921

First published in 1959
in *Lenin Miscellany XXXVI*

Printed from the manuscript

A NOTE TO V. M. MIKHAILOV WITH A DRAFT DECISION FOR THE POLITBUREAU OF THE C.C., R.C.P.(B.) ON FOOD SUPPLY WORK IN THE UKRAINE[425]

9/XI.

Comrade Mikhailov,
Please send this round to the members of the Politbureau and return to me.

I propose this decision for the Politbureau.

The Politbureau impresses upon the Central Committee of the Communist Party of the Ukraine that full, 100%, food collections in the Ukraine are of absolutely paramount importance to the R.S.F.S.R. Similarly the delivery to us of 57 million poods. Immediate and energetic measures are to be worked out for achieving this aim and all decisions are to be reported.

Brief fortnightly reports by telephone are to be made on the progress of food collection and delivery to the R.S.F.S.R.

Lenin

Written November 9, 1921

First published in 1959
in *Lenin Miscellany XXXVI*

Printed from the manuscript

RE DRAFT DECREE
"ON PENALTIES FOR FALSE DENUNCIATIONS"[426]

I propose an addendum raising the penalty
  α) to not less than so many years
  β) for deliberately false evidence or a reply *in writing* (or evasion of a question under certain conditions) after the pattern of Meineid* in Germany, but without the Eid.**

Lenin

Written between November
14 and 24, 1921

First published in 1945
in *Lenin Miscellany XXXV*

Printed from the manuscript

REMARKS ON THE DRAFT DECREE
"ON THE INTRODUCTION OF PAYMENT
FOR NEWSPAPERS"

Addendum necessary either in the form of a number of §§ on control (*strictest*) of circulation free of charge,

---

* —perjury.—*Ed.*
** —oath.—*Ed.*

or make this obligatory by special instructions (one §
on this).[427]

15/XI.   *Lenin*

Written November 15, 1921
First published in 1959   Printed from the manuscript
in *Lenin Miscellany XXXVI*

A NOTE TO V. M. MOLOTOV
WITH A MOTION FOR THE POLITBUREAU
OF THE C.C., R.C.P.(B.)

Viva voce voting

26.XI.1921

Comrade Molotov,

Could you try to settle two questions in the Politbureau
by telephone:

1) That Sokolnikov be appointed member of the Board
of the People's Commissariat for Finance and member of the
Finance Commission *on condition* that he remains *Chairman
of the Turkestan Bureau* and is obliged to *travel* to Turkestan
when necessary until things there have been fully put in
order. (If this does not get a majority, I shall have to put
the matter for consideration to the whole Politbureau).

2) Today we rejected my motion offhand[428] and I agreed
to withdraw it. But I now see that I was too hasty and
I renew it:

That 1) Pyatakov; 2) Rukhimovich; 3) Bogdanov (or
his deputy Smilga) be directed to submit to the Politbureau
within two weeks a plan (or regulations or theses) of relations between the gubernia economic conferences and
the large enterprises located in the given gubernia and
subordinated directly to the centre in Moscow.[429]

[We ourselves cannot draft it. It is a *universal* question.
All the commissariats will have to be questioned. It must
be worked up quickly. Start with the Donets Gubernia
Economic Conference.]

                                                                Lenin

First published in 1959   Printed from the manuscript
in *Lenin Miscellany XXXVI*

A LETTER TO A. D. TSYURUPA WITH A DRAFT RESOLUTION FOR THE ALL-RUSSIA CENTRAL EXECUTIVE COMMITTEE AND A NOTE TO THE MEMBERS OF THE POLITBUREAU OF THE C.C., R.C.P.(B.)

28/XI.

Comrade Tsyurupa,

My plan has matured:

In addition to the post of Deputy Chairman of the Council of Labour and Defence held by Rykov (with the right of casting vote in the Council of People's Commissars) the post of second deputy chairman of the C.L.D. is instituted on equal terms. Tsyurupa is appointed to this post and released from the Food Commissariat.

The rights of these deputies: a casting vote in the C.P.C. and the *C.L.D.*; the chairing of the meetings in the absence of the chairman. *All* the rights of C.P.C. chairman as far as participation in all boards and institutions is concerned, and (inter alia) the right to give instructions in regard to the practical work (subject to immediate execution) to People's Commissars and to members of their boards, etc. (with the knowledge and consent of the commissars of the government departments concerned) *on questions pertaining to the integration and direction* of the economic commissariats' activities.

That is how I conceive the official decision of the *All-Russia Central Executive Committee*.[430]

The task is to integrate and improve the *economic work* AS A WHOLE, especially *in connection with and through the State Bank* (trade) and the *State Planning Commission*.

To make a *first-hand* study of the specific features and work of all the economic commissariats and an acquaintance with *all the members* of their boards and a number (10-100) of local and regional top workers in this field.

To *personally* attend *important* board meetings of the respective commissariats, the State Planning Commission, the State Bank, Centrosoyuz, *etc.* and check *personally*, at the choice of the Deputy Chairmen of the C.L.D., those functions which are considered *most vital* or of special topicality.

For how long these posts will be, "we shall see": perhaps 3-4 years, perhaps 30 years.

One of the objects is to develop a highly trained type of instructor-inspector to check and *organise* all economic work at all economic institutions centrally and locally.

The deputy chairmen conduct their work *through the apparatus* of the existing commissariats, having only the *Managing Department of the C.L.D.* as *their own* body (4-5 C.L.D. business managers with 1-2 assistants and 1-2 secretaries to each assistant).

The business manager of the C.L.D., his assistants and secretaries form the *sole* single staff of the *C.L.D.* as a whole and of both its deputy chairmen.

Let me have your reply not later than **WEDNESDAY.** *Return this.*

With communist greetings,
Lenin

To members of the Politbureau: I have received A.D. Tsyurupa's consent to this *tentative* plan and ask all the members of the Politbureau to read it. I want to put it before the Politbureau tomorrow, 1.XII.

30.XI.   *Lenin*

Written November 28 and 30, 1921

First published in part in 1933
in *Lenin Miscellany XXIII*
   Published in full in 1964   Printed from the manuscript
in the Fifth Russian Edition
of the *Collected Works*, Vol. 44

ROUGH DRAFT OF A DECISION
FOR THE POLITBUREAU OF THE C.C., R.C.P.(B.)
ON THE VECHEKA

1st: jurisdiction to be narrowed
2nd: right to arrest still narrower
3rd: term < 1 month

4th: more weight to courts or only through the courts
5th: name
6th: pass > radical relaxations[431] through the *All-Russia Central Executive Committee.*

Written December 1, 1921

First published in 1959
in *Lenin Miscellany XXXVI*

Printed from the manuscript

DRAFT DECISION
OF THE POLITBUREAU OF THE C.C., R.C.P.(B.)
ON THE TACTICS OF THE UNITED FRONT

a) That the line of joint action with the workers of the Second International proposed by a number of Communist Parties of the Communist International and introduced by Zinoviev, Radek and Bukharin be approved. The latter to be directed within two days to set forth this line clearly in a draft resolution to be circulated among the members of the Politbureau.

b) That Comrade Bukharin be directed to write and show the Politbureau an article summing up the experience of the R.C.P. in the Bolsheviks' struggle against the Mensheviks and the blocs between them.[432]

Written December 1, 1921

First published in 1964
in the Fifth Russian Edition
of the *Collected Works*, Vol. 44

Printed from the manuscript

DRAFT DECISION OF THE C.L.D.
ON THE COMMISSION FOR THE UTILISATION
OF MATERIAL RESOURCES[433]

a) The draft of the State Planning Commission shall be adopted as a basis and the latter directed within a week to submit a revised draft with amendments to §§ 2 and 3, as well as results of the work called for in § 5.

Written December 2, 1921

First published in 1959
in *Lenin Miscellany XXXVI*

Printed from the manuscript

DRAFT DECISION FOR THE POLITBUREAU
OF THE C.C., R.C.P.(B.)[434]

The Food Commissariat shall be directed to preserve the main group of specialists (as indicated by the S.E.C.) in the flour mill administration and carry out the maintenance programme for large flour mills under the control of the S.E.C.

Written December 5, 1921
First published in 1959
in *Lenin Miscellany XXXVI*

Printed from the manuscript

REMARKS TO THE THESES
ON A UNITED FRONT

Comrade Zinoviev,

I have read the rough draft of the theses and have no objections.

The paragraph on the history of Bolshevism should be amplified and partly modified. It is incorrect to say there was a split only in 1910. It should be stated that the formal splits with the Mensheviks in the spring of 1905 and in January 1912 alternated with the semi-unity and unity of 1906 and 1907 followed by that of 1910 not only because of the vicissitudes of the struggle but also under pressure from the rank and file, who demanded check tests through their own experience.

I think this should be stated more explicitly and concretely on one page.[435]

6/XII.

Lenin

Written December 6, 1921
First published in 1945
in *Lenin Miscellany XXXV*

Printed from the typewritten
copy

LETTER TO THE PROPAGANDA
AND ACTION COUNCIL
OF THE PEOPLES OF THE EAST[436]

Dear Comrades,

I heartily welcome your forthcoming publication. I am very sorry that ill-health prevents me from contributing an article. I hope that the business of attracting the best representatives of the working people of the East will make faster and wider progress thanks to your newspaper. The destiny of all Western civilisation now largely depends on drawing the working masses of the East into political activities.

With best wishes and greetings,

Lenin

Chairman, Council of People's Commissars
of the R.S.F.S.R.

Dictated by telephone
not before
December 17, 1921

First published April 22, 1957
in *Pravda* No. 112

Printed from the secretary's
notes

COMMENTS ON THE DRAFT RESOLUTION
FOR THE ELEVENTH CONFERENCE
OF THE R.C.P.(B.)
ON THE PARTY PURGE

With regard to Zalutsky's draft resolution on the Party purge I would like to make two remarks.

1) In section 3 §a Zalutsky proposes that enrolment into the Party be suspended for 6 months. I think this is wrong. I would propose, on my part, not to suspend enrolment, but to lay down stricter conditions, namely: a long term of probation. If an eighteen-month term for real workers is considered too long, it can be reduced, say, to nine, or even six months, as Trotsky proposes. In the case of such short terms, however, I think we should require a qualified

majority in the bodies making enrolment decisions, for
instance, that it should require a majority of not less than
four-fifths to have the term of enrolment reduced, this four-
fifths majority to be demanded not only from one Party
body (the local cell making the admission), but from several
bodies for the sake of mutual control (for example, from
the Gubernia Party Committee in addition to the local
cell, and so on). I would have nothing whatever against
admission into the Party being made easier for genuine
workers, but unless very strict conditions are laid down
for determining who is to be considered a worker of large
industry, we shall immediately find a mass of riff-raff
crawling through the hole again. As regards Red Armymen,
I think we should have stricter conditions, since, for one
thing, most of them are not workers, but peasants, and
secondly, these people are too young and need testing.

2) In Section 4 §a Zalutsky proposes a revision of the
plans of work among the Young Communist League. I believe
stricter conditions should be laid down on this point to make
sure that the members of the Y.C.L. admitted to membership of the Party have, first, really studied seriously and
learnt something, and secondly, that they have a long record
of serious practical work (economic, cultural, etc.).[437]

Lenin

Dictated over the telephone
December 22, 1921

First published in 1959
in *Lenin Miscellany XXXVI*

Printed from the secretary's
notes (typed copy)

SPEECHES AT A MEETING
OF NON-PARTY DELEGATES TO THE NINTH
ALL-RUSSIA CONGRESS OF SOVIETS
DECEMBER 26, 1921[438]

1

Comrades, having decided to continue our talk—I think
we have no doubts on this score—I just want to say that
it is now about half past eight and we can sit on till half
past nine or even later. We must pick a question which we

are most interested in. If, as one comrade said here, it is the agrarian question, then I say—let us distribute our time on those questions which are most important for you. My business here, as I understand it, is mainly to listen and make notes. What I wanted to tell you I have already told you at the congress. I am trying to take down notes as to what gubernia, what uyezd the complaints come from and what most of them are about. I think the time should be distributed in such a way that after the question of compulsory carting tax has been dealt with, we should figure out what questions seem most important so that delegates from different gubernias can have time to have their say on them. My business here is to make as detailed notes as possible in order to know what the non-Party delegates have spoken about. In any case, it will be very difficult for me to answer some of the questions that will be put here, as I have no information at hand and cannot give an immediate reply. That is why I suggest choosing questions which are considered the most important and on which delegates will speak from the floor, the way the carting tax question has been raised, and I shall write down every statement made by local people.

2

Comrades, it is very difficult for me to say even a few words on this question, because all the questions that have been put here I am writing down with a note of what gubernia they come from, but without exact information from the institution concerned I am unable straight off to answer the questions that have been put here. The comrade from the Commissariat for Labour who has just spoken, found it much easier because he has before his eyes a published law and an explanation of what mitigations the enforcement of that law will yield. Without information from the commissariats concerned I can give no definite answers to some of the questions that have been put here.

A number of notes have been sent up. One of them is from a Ukrainian comrade from Kiev, who asks why I have never visited the Ukraine. It is a long journey to the Ukraine, and a difficult one to undertake.

One comrade asks, who is going to pay for the horses killed in the carting service. I have made a note of that question. The comrade has already answered in a general way.

Two notes have been handed up on the question of the tax in kind and about it being impossible for the needy peasant to buy textile goods. Naturally, the peasants in all gubernias these days have many difficulties like these to bear. Without information from the institution concerned I am unable to answer this sort of question just now.

Can we help and to what extent can we help? I repeat, that at the moment I can give no reply. It seems to me that the most important thing that has been said here on the question of carting service is—as far as I can gather from a glance at my notes (and I have written down briefly what each of the comrades has said here)—the most important thing, to my mind, are the instances of abuse and irregularities on the part of the Zheleskoms.[439] Most of the complaints have been about the stints assigned by the Zheleskoms being heavy, about the hard time peasants are having, about there being far too many irregularities in the distribution and assignment of jobs, especially at a time when they are simply harmful to the peasants' farm work. I have made notes of all these remarks, and a note that when the last three-week campaign was held, all comrades from the centre were sent out to the local areas. I asked for exact information on all irregularities connected with fuel work, and on all abuses, as well as a number of reports to be collected. I have already begun to receive letters about this, but recently, owing to ill-health, which made me confine myself only to a general report at the congress, I have not been able to deal with these letters myself. This will be entrusted to another comrade, who is temporarily taking my place, but we shall definitely collect all the information that has come in during the last three-week campaign. The complaints about the irregularities and abuses of the Zheleskoms I consider, on the whole, undoubtedly correct. One of the principal reasons why it was decided to introduce the carting tax which the comrade from the Labour Commissariat has spoken about here is that, unless the amount of work to be done is properly determined (this attempt is being

made by the fixing of a six-day period of work in the law),
unless this is properly determined in the law, abuses by the
gubernia logging committees and the Zheleskoms are bound
to take place and will be very difficult to combat. But when
the law definitely declares, as it now does, how many work
days are required and there will be a known set task fixing
how much work is to be done in the given number of days,
the abuses will be much easier to combat. Naturally, the
fight against abuses by these bodies in the gubernias and
uyezds is no easy job, especially when, as a comrade here
pointed out, many of the old employees, the former landowners and former timber contractors have wormed their
way into these bodies. A stricter eye must be kept on this
in the local areas and we must have more comrades from
among the non-Party peasants in the Central Executive
Committee, who could be applied to in the event of a complaint failing to reach its destination, and who would raise
the question at a sitting of the C.E.C. and demand an
investigation into the abuses. These measures will be put
through at this congress in any case. The number of C.E.C.
members from among the non-Party peasants, as comrades
taking part in the congress have told me, will definitely
be increased. By this means it will be possible to keep
an eye on abuses by the Zheleskoms and easier to combat
them when there will be more non-Party peasant members
in the C.E.C. I repeat, I am making a note of all the remarks
that are made here and shall write to the appropriate commissariat or economic council about each of them in order
to have proper measures taken. I cannot of course give
a reply offhand to each particular question without getting
the information from the commissariat concerned.

3

I have asked Comrade Kalinin for two minutes to clear
up any misunderstanding that his words may have caused.[440]
I am sure he did not intend to impute to me the idea that
I ever suggested burning prayer-books. Needless to say,
I never suggested such a thing and never could. You know
that according to our Constitution, the fundamental law

of our Republic, freedom of conscience in respect of religion is fully guaranteed to every person.

Another word to the comrade who spoke about the very difficult situation in some of the uyezds of Vyatka Gubernia. These uyezds are in the famine-stricken area. Our main hope now will be in the agreement which the American Government has offered us. We shall conclude it within the next few days. Under this agreement the American Government offers twenty million dollars. We shall give ten million, making thirty million dollars altogether—that is, sixty million gold rubles. This is a sizable sum. Most of the spring crop area, if not all of it, will be sown. In addition we are sending men to Canada. I think we shall be able to spend an extra sum from the gold fund to buy a little more seed. The main problem now, of course, is the famine, the dearth of fodder. The sowing of spring crops must be done as fully as possible. Every effort in this direction will be made. (*Applause.*)

First published in 1933
in *Lenin Miscellany XXIII*

Printed from the shorthand
record

DRAFT THESES
ON THE ROLE AND FUNCTIONS
OF THE TRADE UNIONS
UNDER THE NEW ECONOMIC POLICY[441]

The Plenum of the C.C., R.C.P. on 28.XII.1921 considered the question of the role and functions of the trade unions under the New Economic Policy. The plenum heard the reports of Comrades Rudzutak, Andreyev and Shlyapnikov (the planned report by Comrade Lutovinov was not made owing to failure to call the reporter out in time). After an exchange of opinions it was decided to submit the original draft theses of Comrades Rudzutak and Andreyev to a committee of these two comrades with the addition of Lenin and to charge this committee with drafting theses for endorsement by the Politbureau.

(Several lines will be added to this *after* approval of the draft by the committee and then the Politbureau.)

DRAFT

1. THE NEW ECONOMIC POLICY
AND THE TRADE UNIONS

The New Economic Policy introduces a number of important changes in the position of the proletariat and, consequently, in that of the trade unions. These changes are due to the fact that in their entire policy of transition from capitalism to socialism the Communist Party and the Soviet government are now adopting special methods to implement this transition and in many respects are operating differently from the way they operated before: they are capturing a number of positions by a "new flanking movement", so to speak; they are drawing back in order to make better preparations for a new offensive against capitalism. In particular, a free market and capitalism, both subject to state control, are now being permitted and are developing; on the other hand, the state enterprises are being put on what is called a profit basis, i.e., they are in effect being largely reorganised on commercial and capitalist lines.

2. STATE CAPITALISM IN THE PROLETARIAN STATE
AND THE TRADE UNIONS

The proletarian state may, without changing its own nature, permit freedom of trade and the development of capitalism only within certain bounds, and only on the condition that the state regulates (supervises, controls, determines the forms and methods of, etc.) private trade and private capitalism. The success of such regulation will depend not only on the state authorities, but also, and to a larger extent, on the degree of maturity of the proletariat and of the masses of the working people generally, on their cultural level, etc. But even if this regulation is completely successful, the antagonism of class interests between labour and capital will certainly remain. Consequently, one of the main tasks that will henceforth confront the trade unions is to protect in every way the class interests of the proletariat in its struggle against capital. This task should be openly put in the forefront, and the machinery of the trade unions must be reorganised, modified or supplemented accordingly; strike funds, and so on should be formed, or rather, built up.

3. THE STATE ENTERPRISES THAT ARE BEING PUT ON A PROFIT BASIS AND THE TRADE UNIONS

The conversion of state enterprises to what is called the profit basis is inevitably and inseparably connected with the New Economic Policy; in the near future this is bound to become the predominant, if not the sole, form of state enterprise. Actually, this means that with the free market now permitted and developing, the state enterprises, will to a large extent be put on a commercial, capitalist basis. This circumstance, in view of the urgent need to increase the productivity of labour and make every state enterprise pay its way and show a profit, and in view of the inevitable rise of narrow departmental interests and excessive departmental zeal, is bound to create a certain conflict of interests between the masses of workers and the directors and managers of the state enterprises, or the government departments in charge of them. Therefore, it is undoubtedly the duty of the trade unions, in regard to the state enterprises as well, to protect the class interests of the proletariat and the working masses against their employers.

4. THE ESSENTIAL DIFFERENCE BETWEEN THE CLASS STRUGGLE OF THE PROLETARIAT IN A STATE WHICH RECOGNISES PRIVATE OWNERSHIP OF THE LAND, FACTORIES, ETC., AND WHERE POLITICAL POWER IS IN THE HANDS OF THE CAPITALIST CLASS, AND THE CLASS STRUGGLE OF THE PROLETARIAT IN A STATE WHICH DOES NOT RECOGNISE PRIVATE OWNERSHIP OF THE LAND AND THE MAJORITY OF THE LARGE ENTERPRISES AND WHERE POLITICAL POWER IS IN THE HANDS OF THE PROLETARIAT

As long as classes exist, the class struggle is inevitable. In the period of transition from capitalism to socialism the existence of classes is inevitable; and the Programme of the

Russian Communist Party definitely states that we are taking only the first steps in the transition from capitalism to socialism. Hence, the Communist Party, the Soviet government and the trade unions must frankly admit the existence of a class struggle and its inevitability until the electrification of industry and agriculture is completed— at least in the main—and until small production and the supremacy of the market are thereby cut off at the roots. It follows from this that at the present moment we can under no circumstances abandon the idea of the strike struggle, we cannot, as a matter of principle, conceive the possibility of a law that makes compulsory state mediation take the place of strikes.

On the other hand, it is obvious that under capitalism the ultimate object of the strike struggle is to break up the state machine and to overthrow the given class state power. Under the transitional type of proletarian state such as ours, however, the ultimate object of the strike struggle can only be to fortify the proletarian state and the state power of the proletarian class by combating the bureaucratic distortions, mistakes and flaws in this state, and by curbing the class appetites of the capitalists who try to evade its control, etc. Hence, the Communist Party, the Soviet government and the trade unions must never forget and must never conceal from the workers and the mass of the working people that the strike struggle in a state where the proletariat holds political power can be explained and justified only by the bureaucratic distortions of the proletarian state and by all sorts of survivals of the old capitalist system in the government offices on the one hand, and by the political immaturity and cultural backwardness of the mass of the working people on the other. When the law courts and all other organs of the state are built on a class basis, by the working people themselves, with the bourgeoisie excluded from the electorate, the normal method of settling conflicts between labour and capital, between employed and employers, will more and more often find expression in the working people turning directly to the state authorities.

5. REVERSION TO VOLUNTARY TRADE UNION MEMBERSHIP

The compulsory wholesale signing up of all workers for membership in the trade unions is no longer consistent with the present degree of socialisation achieved in industry or with the level of development of the masses. Compulsory membership has moreover introduced a certain degree of bureaucratic distortion into the trade unions themselves. It is absolutely essential to revert for a fairly considerable length of time to the practice of voluntary membership in the trade unions. Under no circumstances must trade union members be required to subscribe to any specific political views; in this respect, as well as in respect of religion, the trade unions must be non-partisan. All that must be required of trade union members in the proletarian state is that they should understand comradely discipline and the necessity of uniting the workers' forces for the purpose of protecting the interests of the working people, and that they should keep faith with the working people's government, i.e., the Soviet government. The proletarian state must encourage the workers to organise in trade unions both for legal and material reasons; but the trade unions can have no rights without duties.

6. THE TRADE UNIONS AND THE MANAGEMENT OF INDUSTRY

Following its seizure of political power, the principal and fundamental interest of the proletariat lies in securing an increase in output, an enormous increase in the productive forces of society. This task, which is clearly formulated in the Programme of the Russian Communist Party, is particularly urgent in our country today owing to post-war ruin, famine and economic dislocation. Hence, the speediest and most enduring success in restoring large-scale industry is a condition without which no success can be achieved in the general cause of emancipating labour from the yoke of capital and securing the victory of socialism. To achieve this success in Russia, in the conditions at present obtaining in that country, it is absolutely essential that all authority in the factories be concentrated in the hands of the management. The factory management, usually built up on the principle of one-man responsibility, must have authority independently to fix and pay out wages, and also distribute rations, working clothes, and all other supplies; it must enjoy the utmost freedom to manoeuvre, exercise strict control of the actual successes achieved in increasing production, in making the factory pay its way and show a profit, and carefully select the most talented and capable administrative personnel, etc.

Under these circumstances, any direct interference by the trade unions in the management of the factories must be regarded as positively harmful and impermissible.

It would be absolutely wrong, however, to interpret this indisputable axiom to mean that the trade unions must play no part in the socialist organisation of industry and in the management of state industry. Their participation in this is necessary in the following strictly defined forms.

7. THE ROLE AND FUNCTIONS OF THE TRADE UNIONS IN THE BUSINESS AND ADMINISTRATIVE ORGANISATIONS OF THE PROLETARIAN STATE

The proletariat is the class foundation of the state making the transition from capitalism to socialism. In a country where the small peasantry is overwhelmingly predominant the proletariat can successfully fulfil this function if it very skilfully, cautiously and gradually establishes an alliance with the vast majority of the peasantry. The trade unions must collaborate closely and constantly with the government, all the political and economic activities of which are guided by the class-conscious vanguard of the working class—the Communist Party. Being a school of communism in general, the trade unions must, in particular, be a school for training the whole mass of workers, and eventually all working people, in the art of managing socialist industry (and gradually also agriculture).

Proceeding from these principles, the trade unions' part in the activities connected with the business and administrative organisations of the proletarian state should take the following main forms:

(1) The trade unions should help staff all the business and administrative bodies connected with economics by nominating their candidates for them and casting a consultative vote; the trade unions take part in these bodies too, not directly, but through the members of the higher state bodies, the members of business boards, members of the factory managements (where collegiate management is practised), managers, their assistants, etc., nominated by them and endorsed by the Communist Party and the Soviet government.

(2) One of the most important functions of the trade unions is to promote and train factory managers from among the workers and the masses of the working people generally. At the present time we have scores of such factory managers who are quite satisfactory, and hundreds who are more or less satisfactory, but very soon, however, we must have hundreds of the former and thousands of the latter. The trade unions must much more carefully and persistently than hitherto keep a systematic register of all workers and peasants capable of holding posts of this kind, and thoroughly, efficiently and from every aspect verify the progress they make in learning the art of management.

(3) No less important is the participation of the trade unions in all the planning bodies of the proletarian state. In addition to participating in all cultural and educational activities and in production propaganda, the trade unions must also, on an increasing scale, enlist the working class and the masses of the working people generally for all branches of the work of building up the state economy; they must make them familiar with all aspects of economic life and with all details of industrial operations—from the procurement of raw materials to the marketing of the product; give them a more and more concrete understanding of the single state plan of socialist economy and the worker's and peasant's practical interest in its implementation.

(4) The drawing up of wage rates and scales of supplies, etc., is one of the essential functions of the trade unions in the building of socialism and in their participation in the management of industry. In particular, disciplinary courts should steadily improve labour discipline and proper ways of promoting it and achieving increased productivity; but they must not interfere with the functions of the People's Courts in general or with the functions of factory managements.

This list of the major functions of the trade unions in the work of building up socialist economy, should, of course, be drawn up in greater detail by the competent trade union and government bodies. The most important thing is that the trade unions should consciously and resolutely avoid direct, inexpert, incompetent and irresponsible interference in administrative matters, which has caused no little harm, and should start persistent, practical activities calculated to extend over a long period of years and designed to give the workers and all the working people generally *practical training* in the art of *managing* the economy of the whole country.

8. CONTACT WITH THE MASSES—
THE FUNDAMENTAL CONDITION FOR ALL TRADE UNION ACTIVITY

Contact with the masses, i.e., with the overwhelming majority of the workers (and eventually of all the working people), is the most important and most fundamental condition for the success of all trade union activity. In all the trade union organisations and their machinery, from bottom up, there should be instituted, and tested in practice over a period of many years, a system of responsible comrades—who must not all be Communists—who should live right among the workers, study their lives in every detail, and be able unerringly, on any question, and at any time, to judge the mood, the real needs, aspirations, and thoughts of the masses. They must be able without a shadow of false idealisation to define the degree of their class-consciousness and the extent to which they are influenced by various prejudices and survivals of the past; and they must be able to win the boundless confidence of the masses by a comradely attitude and concern for their needs. One of the greatest and most serious dangers that confront the numerically small Communist Party, which, as the vanguard of the working class, is guiding a vast country in the process of transition to socialism (for the time being without the direct support of the more advanced countries), is isolation from the masses, the danger that the vanguard may run too far ahead and fail to "straighten out the line", fail to maintain firm contact with the whole army of labour, i.e., with the overwhelming majority of workers and peasants. Just as the very best factory, with the very best motors and first-class machines, will be forced to remain idle if the transmission belts from the motors to the machines are damaged, so our work of socialist construction must meet with inevitable disaster if the trade unions—the transmission belts from the Communist Party to the masses— are badly fitted or function badly. It is not sufficient to explain, to reiterate and corroborate this truth; it must be backed up organisationally by the whole structure of the trade unions and by their everyday activities.

9. THE CONTRADICTIONS IN THE STATUS OF THE TRADE UNIONS UNDER THE DICTATORSHIP OF THE PROLETARIAT

From all the foregoing it is evident that there are a number of contradictions in the various functions of the trade unions. On the one hand, their principal method of operation is that of persuasion and education; on the other hand, as participants in the exercise of state power they cannot refuse to share in coercion. On the one hand, their main function is to protect the interests of the masses of the working people in the most direct and immediate sense of the term; on the other hand, as participants in the exercise of state power and builders of the economy as a whole they cannot refuse to resort to pressure. On the one hand, they must operate in military fashion, for the dictatorship of the proletariat is the fiercest, most dogged and most desperate class war; on the other hand, specifically military methods of operation are least of all applicable to the trade unions. On the one hand, they must be able to adapt themselves to the masses, to their level; on the other hand, they must never pander to the prejudices and backwardness of the masses, but steadily raise them to a higher and higher level, etc., etc.

These contradictions are no accident, and they will persist for several decades. For one thing, these contradictions are inherent in every school. And the trade unions are a school of communism. We cannot count, until the lapse of several decades, on the majority of the workers achieving the highest level of development and discarding all traces and memories of the "school" for adults. Secondly, as long as survivals of capitalism and small production remain, contradictions between them and the young shoots of socialism are inevitable throughout the social system.

Two practical conclusions must be drawn from this. First, for the successful conduct of trade union activities it is not enough to understand their functions correctly, it is not enough to organise them properly. In addition, special tact is required, ability to approach the masses in a special way in each individual case for the purpose of raising these masses to a higher cultural, economic and political stage with the minimum of friction.

Second, the aforementioned contradictions will inevitably give rise to disputes, disagreements, friction, etc. A higher body is required with sufficient authority to settle these at once. This higher body is the Communist Party and the international federation of the Communist Parties of all countries—the Communist International.

10. THE TRADE UNIONS AND THE SPECIALISTS

The main principles on this question are set forth in the Programme of the Russian Communist Party; but these will remain paper principles unless constant attention is paid to the facts which indicate the degree to which they are put into practice. Recent facts of this kind are: first, cases of the murder of engineers by workers in socialised mines not only in the Urals, but also in the Donets Basin;

second, the suicide of V. V. Oldenborger, chief engineer
of the Moscow Waterworks.*

The Communist Party and the Soviet government as
a whole bear a far greater share of the blame for cases of
this kind than the trade unions. It is not a question now
of establishing the degree of political guilt, but of drawing
certain political conclusions. Unless our leading bodies, i.e.,
the Communist Party, the Soviet government and the trade
unions, guard as the apple of their eye every specialist who
does his work conscientiously and knows and loves it—even
though the ideas of communism are totally alien to him—
it will be useless to expect any serious progress in socialist
construction. We may not be able to achieve it soon, but
we must at all costs achieve a situation in which specialists—as a separate social stratum, which will persist until
we have reached the highest stage of development of communist society—can enjoy better conditions of life under
socialism than they enjoyed under capitalism insofar as
concerns their material and legal status, comradely col-
laboration with the workers and peasants, and in the intel-
lectual plane, i.e., finding satisfaction in their work, realising
that it is socially useful and independent of the sordid
interests of the capitalist class. Nobody will regard a government department as being tolerably well organised if it
does not take systematic measures to provide for all the
needs of the specialists, to reward the best of them, to
safeguard and protect their interests, etc., and does not
secure practical results in this. The trade unions must
conduct all the activities of the type indicated (or systematically collaborate in the activities of all the government
departments concerned) not from the point of view of the
interests of the given department, but from the point of
view of the interests of labour and of the economy as a whole.
With regard to the specialists, on the trade unions devolves
the very arduous duty of daily exercising influence on the
broad masses of the working people in order to create proper
relations between them and the specialists. Only such
activities can produce really important practical results.

---

* Here is the report about this in *Pravda* for 3.I. 1922: ((quote
the full text on p. 4)).[442]

11. THE TRADE UNIONS AND PETTY-BOURGEOIS INFLUENCES ON THE WORKING CLASS

Trade unions are really effective only when they unite very broad strata of the non-Party workers. This must give rise—particularly in a country in which the peasantry largely predominates—to relative stability, specifically among the trade unions, of those political influences that serve as the superstructure over the remnants of capitalism and over small production. These influences are petty-bourgeois, i.e., Socialist-Revolutionary and Menshevik (the Russian variety of the parties of the II and $II^1/_2$ Internationals) on the one hand, and anarchist on the other. Only among these trends has any considerable number of people remained who defend capitalism ideologically and not from selfish class motives, and continue to believe in the non-class nature of the "democracy", "equality" and "liberty" in general that they preach.

It is to this socio-economic cause and not to the role of individual groups, still less of individual persons, that we must attribute the survivals (sometimes even the revival) in our country of such petty-bourgeois ideas among the trade unions. The Communist Party, the Soviet bodies that conduct cultural and educational activities and all Communist members of trade unions must therefore devote far more attention to the ideological struggle against petty-bourgeois influences, trends and deviations among the trade unions, especially because the New Economic Policy is bound to lead to a certain strengthening of capitalism. It is urgently necessary to counteract this by intensifying the struggle against petty-bourgeois influences upon the working class.

The End

Discuss together with the theses.

Give this to Comrade Molotov **without rewriting**.

This is the end of the publishable theses, i.e., the draft of them that is being submitted to the commission and then the Politbureau.

I suggest that the resolution contained in Comrade Rudzutak's draft be adopted by a special decision of the Politbureau in the following wording:

The Politbureau directs the Orgbureau to set up under the Orgbureau of the Central Committee a special commission to check and replace some of the leading officials (and if possible all communist functionaries) in the trade union movement for the purpose of intensifying the struggle against petty-bourgeois, S.R., Menshevik and anarchist influences and deviations. This commission to complete its work (or most of it) by the next, Eleventh, congress of the R.C.P. and submit its report to the Party congress.[443]	Not for publication

4.1.1922 *Lenin*

Written December 30, 1921—
January 4, 1922

Published with amendments   Printed from the manuscript
January 17, 1922
in *Pravda* No. 12

MEMO TO V. M. MOLOTOV
FOR THE POLITBUREAU OF THE C.C., R.C.P.(B.)
WITH DRAFT DECISIONS

To *Comrade Molotov* for the **Politbureau**

In view of the utter inadequacy (or reticence?) of the report in *Pravda* on 3.I.1922 concerning the suicide of *Oldenborger* and the investigations into this case

I propose the following decision for the Politbureau:

1) that the Moscow Soviet be asked to apply to the Presidium of the All-Russia Central Executive Committee in order to have all those persons mentioned in the commission's findings brought to *trial*;

2) that the Presidium of the A.C.E.C. be asked to grant this request immediately and

3) — to give this wide publicity in the *whole* Soviet press;

4) that the People's Commissariat for Justice be directed (under the personal responsibility of Comrade Kursky and an appointed public prosecutor) to handle this case skilfully, impressively and with special care;

5) that the Orgbureau be directed to set up a special Party Court to try the whole *communist group* of the Waterworks. (Some to be expelled from the Party for good or for a time, some to be severely reprimanded, depending on the measure of their guilt.) The trial to be held in an impressive public manner.

+ 6) that *Izvestia* and *Pravda* be instructed to highlight this outrageous affair in a number of strong articles.

4.I.1922   *Lenin*

Another draft resolution:

All cases of the murder of engineers (and specialists) at Soviet enterprises shall be reported to the Politbureau together with the results of the investigations ((the Supreme Economic Council, the A.C.C.T.U., etc., through the *C.L.D.*)).[444]

P.S. This is scandalous: we should ring the tocsin.

First published in 1959   Printed from the manuscript
in *Lenin Miscellany XXXVI*

MOTION FOR THE POLITBUREAU
OF THE C.C., R.C.P.(B.)
ON ALLOCATION OF FUNDS
TO THE NIZHNI-NOVGOROD RADIO LABORATORY

(Re the request of Dovgalevsky for 50,000 gold rubles to be allocated to the Nizhni-Novgorod Radio Laboratory)

I support the request and ask Comrade Molotov to put this to the vote of the Politbureau. I ask the Politbureau members to bear in mind the exceptional importance of the Nizhni-Novgorod Radio Laboratory, the tremendous services it has already rendered and the great use it can be to us in the near future both in military matters and in propaganda work.[445]

Lenin

Dictated over the telephone
January 12, 1922

First published in 1959   Printed from the secretary's notes
in *Lenin Miscellany XXXVI*   (typewritten copy)

DIRECTIVES ON THE FILM BUSINESS

The People's Commissariat for Education should organise the supervision of all film showings and systematise this business. All films shown in the R.S.F.S.R. should be registered and numbered at the Commissariat for Education. A definite proportion should be fixed for every film-showing programme:

a) entertainment films, specially for advertisement or income (of course, without obscenity and counter-revolution) and

b) under the heading "From the life of peoples of all countries"—pictures with a special propaganda message, such as: Britain's colonial policy in India, the work of the League of Nations, the starving Berliners, etc., etc. Besides films, photographs of propaganda interest should be shown with appropriate subtitles. The privately owned cinemas should be made to yield a sufficient return to the state in the form of rent, the owners to be allowed to increase the number of films and present new ones subject to censorship by the Commissariat for Education and provided the proper proportion is maintained between entertainment films and propaganda films coming under the heading of films "From the life of peoples of all countries", in order that film-makers should have an incentive for producing new pictures. They should be allowed wide initiative within these limits. Pictures of a propaganda and educative nature should be checked by old Marxists and writers, to avoid a repetition of the many sad instances when propaganda with us defeated its own purpose. Special attention should be given to organising film showings in the villages and in the East, where they are novelties and where our propaganda, therefore, will be all the more effective.[446]

Dictated January 17, 1922

First published in 1925 in the magazine *Kinonedelya* No. 4

Printed from the notes of N. P. Gorbunov (typewritten copy)

MOTION FOR THE POLITBUREAU OF THE C.C., R.C.P.(B.) ON M. I. KALININ'S TRIP TO THE UKRAINE[447]

To Comrade Molotov for all the members of the Politbureau

Please put to the vote of the Politbureau the following motion: that Comrade Kalinin be directed immediately to make a round of the richer grain gubernias of the Ukraine to collect aid for the victims of the famine. The expedition to be fitted out with great thoroughness to enable it to carry out effective agitation for relief collections by means of photographs, films, demonstration of witnesses and sufferers from the famine-stricken areas, etc. Personal responsibility for the practical organisation of the expedition to be imposed upon

1. Kalinin for the political side of the business

2. a specially appointed practical worker endorsed by the Politbureau who would really be capable of putting through and organising the business properly.

Kalinin together with the whole expedition shall leave within 3 days.

Lenin

Dictated over the telephone January 27, 1922

First published in 1945 in *Lenin Miscellany XXXV*

Printed from the secretary's notes

MOTION FOR THE POLITBUREAU
OF THE C.C., R.C.P.(B.)

To Comrade Molotov for All Members
of the Politbureau

I think that "Bespartiiny" in today's *Pravda* is proposing a perfectly correct and timely plan.[448]

I move that a commission be set up to elaborate it immediately and put it into effect as quickly as possible, this commission to consist of Molotov (replaceable by somebody appointed by the Secretariat of the Central Committee or the Orgbureau), Yakovenko, Teodorovich and the "Bespartiiny" in question.

Lenin

Dictated over the telephone
January 27, 1922

First published in 1959   Printed from the secretary's
in *Lenin Miscellany XXXVI*   notes

DRAFT DIRECTIVES
TO THE DEPUTY CHAIRMAN
AND ALL MEMBERS OF THE GENOA DELEGATION[449]

1.II.1922

To Comrade Molotov for members of the Politbureau

I propose that the following directives to the deputy chairman and all members of the Genoa delegation be endorsed:

1. All members of the delegation should be posted in a general way on all political and financial questions that are likely to be brought up at the conference. Moreover, every member of the delegation should make a special and thorough study of one of the most important diplomatic and one of the most important financial questions.

Chicherin and Litvinov are to be charged with drawing up an assignment of these questions among all the members of the delegation (with the exception of sick members like Rudzutak, etc.).

2. Every member of the delegation must prepare for the meeting on 22.II (with the Politbureau of the C.C.) the briefest (maximum 2-3 pages telegraphic style) of summaries of his programme of views and policies on all cardinal questions, both diplomatic and financial.

3. Chicherin and Litvinov are to see to it that the appropriate literature in different languages is collected and handed out to the members of the delegation together with a systematic collection of documents in the Russian language.

4. In view of the special importance and special difficulty of financial questions, Chicherin and Litvinov, by arrangement with the People's Commissariat for Finance, the State Planning Commission and A. D. Tsyurupa, are to draw up a list of financial experts and a plan of work distribution among them; this to be done within 1 week.

5. All members of the delegation must be *perfectly familiar* with Keynes's book (*The Economic Consequences of the Peace*) and with similar bourgeois and bourgeois-pacifist books and *parts of books* (Lansing on the "imperialist" nature of the war and the peace of 1918, and so on). Preparations should be on these lines: speeches and statements should give the *communist* point of view in a nutshell, set forth in such a way as to intimate that although we are Communists and hold such-and-such communist views we wish to cite non-Communists to this audience and to pose the question of annulling all debts and so forth from the bourgeois standpoint (see 6 and 7).

6. All speeches and statements by our delegates at the conference should be calculated in advance in such a way that whatever the course or the outcome of the conference (even in the event of its speedy failure, which we, of course, should try to prevent), there would be, as a result, a brief but clear statement of the sum total of communist views (on questions of international relations and economics) and a detailed statement of bourgeois and bourgeois-pacifist views on the irreconcilable contradictions of the imperialist world (and the imperialist peace).

7. It is highly probable, almost certain, that all the bourgeois delegates at the conference will immediately form a silent but strong bloc for attacking us on account of Georgia and with all the usual accusations of petty-bourgeois and big bourgeois diplomacy and democracy. We should be prepared for this in advance and make sure that we are the first to attack (apart from our main object of dividing the different countries and setting them by the ears). The initiative in taking the offensive should be done mostly in a veiled form, for example by "hinting" (or by bourgeois quotations from relevant works) at the most painful and shameful points of imperialist relations (Korea; Amritsar; public flogging of revolutionaries in India; Lloyd George's speech against Briand at Cannes concerning "assassinations" and so on and so forth).

8. In view of the repeatedly proven desire on the part of our specialists in general and the Menshevik-minded ones in particular to fool us (very often successfully) by turning their foreign trips into a holiday and a means of strengthening whiteguard ties, the Central Committee proposes to limit ourselves in this case to an absolute minimum of fully reliable experts, each of whom is to present a guarantee in writing from the People's Commissar concerned and from several Communists. Forty-five is the top limit. The list of experts and of all members to be submitted for approval to the C.C. within $1^1/_2$ weeks. This § to be taken charge of by Comrades Litvinov, Joffe and Chicherin. They are also to choose a business manager who will not permit night work and such-like scandalous practices.

I move the following addendum to the draft theses of *directives* for the Genoa delegation:

9. Our delegates should cite § 1 of the Cannes terms in their speeches and statements as often as possible, this citing to be done, first, exclusively in the wording of *Petit Parisien*, i.e., using the words "system of property" and not just "system"; secondly, these words and this § to be given an extended meaning as if implying recognition of the inevitability of the capitalist system of property being replaced by the communist system of property, as if the only point at issue "between us" now remains the question of when this replacement will be effected and in

what manner, i.e., by the Russian method of 1917-20 or by the Lloyd George method of "truncated revolution" of the 1921 Irish type or the 1922 Egyptian type.[450]

Lenin

First published in 1964
in the Fifth Russian Edition
of the *Collected Works*, Vol. 44

Printed from the manuscript

LETTER TO N. I. BUKHARIN AND G. Y. ZINOVIEV

To Comrades Bukharin and Zinoviev

We must consider beforehand what people, preferably those with a ready tongue, are going to represent the Comintern at the conference with the II and II$^1/_2$ Internationals.[451] We must also consider beforehand the basic questions of tactics and strategy to be employed at this meeting.

The list of questions to be dealt with at the meeting should be considered beforehand and drawn up in agreement with each of the parties attending the meeting. On our part we should include in this list only questions that have a direct bearing on practical joint action by the working masses and touching on matters that are recognised as indisputable in the official press statement of each of the three participants. We must explain at length the reasons why we confine ourselves to such questions in the interests of a united front. In the event of the yellow fraternity raising mooted questions of policy, such as our attitude to the Mensheviks, the question of Georgia, etc., we should adopt these tactics: 1) declare that the list of questions can be drawn up only by a unanimous decision of all three participants; 2) declare that in drawing up our list of questions we were guided exclusively by the desire for unity of action by the working masses, which unity could be achieved immediately even under existing deep-seated political differences; 3) declare that we fully agree to questions such as our attitude to the Mensheviks, the question of Georgia and any other questions being raised by the II and II$^1/_2$ Internationals, provided that they agree to the following questions being raised: 1) the renegade attitude of the II and II$^1/_2$ Internationals to the Basle Manifesto; 2) complicity of these same parties in the murder of Luxemburg, Liebknecht and other Communists of Germany through the bourgeois governments which those parties support; 3) a similar attitude of these parties to the murder of revolutionaries in the colonies by the bourgeois parties which the II and II$^1/_2$ Internationals support, etc., etc. We should prepare a list of these and similar questions beforehand and also prepare beforehand theses and speakers on various important questions of this nature.

We must find occasion to declare officially that we regard the II and II$^1/_2$ Internationals only as inconsistent and vacillating participants of a bloc with the counter-revolutionary world bourgeoisie, and that we agree to attend a meeting on the united front for the sake of achieving possible practical unity of direct action on the part of the masses and in order to expose the political error of the II and II$^1/_2$ Internationals' entire position, just as the latter (the II and II$^1/_2$ Internationals) have agreed to attend a meeting with us for the sake of achieving practical unity of direct action by the masses and in order to expose the political error of our position.

Lenin

Dictated over the telephone
February 1, 1922

First published in 1959   Printed from the secretary's
in *Lenin Miscellany XXXVI*   notes (typewritten copy)

DRAFT DECISION
FOR THE POLITBUREAU OF THE C.C., R.C.P.(B.)
IN CONNECTION WITH THE GENOA CONFERENCE

To Comrade Molotov (for the members of the Politbureau)

I draw attention to the article "The Genoa Conference" by Y. Klyuchnikov in No. 13 of *Smena Vekh*,[452] and propose:

1. That the question of enlisting Klyuchnikov's services as an expert be discussed jointly with the members of the delegation.

2. That it be made incumbent upon the whole delegation to see to it that several articles on the same subject as that dealt with in Klyuchnikov's article are published in our press, only at greater length and in fuller detail so as to cover the ground thoroughly.

3. That every person who wishes to go as an expert from Russia or who has been nominated for this post be made within 10 days to prepare an article dealing in detail with Russia's relations with foreign countries in his selected field. Those articles (or such parts of them) which contain no confidential matter should immediately be published in our press.

4. That Chicherin and Litvinov be made responsible for reporting the distribution of subjects for the articles and the names of the writers under Points 1 and 2 to the Politbureau within one week.

Lenin

Dictated over the telephone
February 4, 1922

First published in 1959
in *Lenin Miscellany XXXVI*

Printed from the secretary's
notes (typewritten copy)

ON THE PUBLICATION OF A TELEGRAM
REPORTING THE PAMPHLET BY PARVUS[453]

1

To Comrade Molotov
(for members of the Politbureau)

I propose that an inquiry be made as to who was responsible for publishing in our newspapers the other day a telegram giving a summary of Parvus's writings.

When the guilty party has been ascertained, I propose that the ROSTA* manager of that department be severely reprimanded and the journalist directly responsible should be dismissed, for only a perfect fool or a whiteguard could use our newspapers for advertising such a scoundrel as Parvus.

Lenin

Dictated over the telephone
February 4, 1922

First published in 1945
in *Lenin Miscellany XXXV*

Printed from the secretary's
note (typewritten copy)

* ROSTA—Russian Telegraph Agency.— *Ed.*

2

DECISION OF THE POLITBUREAU
OF THE C.C., R.C.P.(B.)
MARCH 11, 1922

The Politbureau recognises that the publication of such a telegram was improper, as it gave the impression of advertising Parvus, and the editors of Party and Soviet newspapers are directed to refrain from publishing such telegrams in future.

First published in 1964   Printed from the typewritten
in the Fifth Russian Edition   copy of the minutes
of the *Collected Works*, Vol. 44

DRAFT DIRECTIVES OF THE C.C., R.C.P.(B.)
FOR THE SOVIET DELEGATION
TO THE GENOA CONFERENCE[454]

I propose the following draft of C.C. directives:

Without endorsing the list of experts, the C.C. directs the candidates nominated in it to submit within a week a précis of *programme* and *tactics* (on questions that come within the terms of reference of the given expert) for *the whole* Genoa Conference. All People's Commissars are obliged within 2 days to give *written* testimonials and guarantees for their candidates nominated as experts. Should the experts disgrace themselves in Europe they and the People's Commissars will be held responsible.

In furtherance of the directives concerning the Genoa Conference *I propose the following*:

1. Without pre-determining in what form and at what time the speeches of our delegation should be made, the C.C. considers that the delegation is definitely obliged to develop a full, independent and integral programme on all cardinal issues.

2. This programme should be a bourgeois-pacifist programme with the reservation, timely and clearly expressed

by our delegation, that we do not put forward here a communist programme—the only one that is in keeping with our views—(set it forth briefly) because we wish to put before the other delegations, who hold fundamentally different views, a number of palliatives and measures of a reformist type which have already been proposed in parts in Britain and other capitalist countries by people who share bourgeois views. Under certain conditions this programme of palliatives could serve to mitigate the present difficult situation (the only real way out of which is possible given a final break with all the principles of capitalist property).

3. A tentative list of the main points of this programme:

(1) annulment of all debts;

(2) application of the "Irish" solution to all colonies and dependent countries and nations;

(3) radical revision of the Versailles Treaty;

(4) the granting of loans on favourable terms to the countries most ruined by the war and too weak to recover their own feet, while being most important for world economy as eventual suppliers of vast quantities of food and raw materials;

(5) establishment of a unified international gold unit for the currency systems of a number of countries and measures to introduce this unit;

(6) an agreement among a number of countries on measures to combat inflation and depreciation of money (enumerate some of these measures);

(7) agreement among a number of countries on measures for coping with the fuel crisis and on measures for the most rational and economical use of power resources on the basis of unified planned electrification;

(8) the same in regard to the most urgent measures for reorganising and improving international transport to handle deliveries of raw materials and food.

And so on.

4. Such a programme should be elaborated in speeches, and if this is impossible, printed in 3-4 European languages and handed out to the delegates and the press (if only in the form of a précis). (In any case it should be printed.)

5. Only such people should be admitted as experts who are capable of developing, and making out a case for such

a programme (in one or another part of it) and who have *proved this capability*. The experts will have to have their programmes and plans printed *for Europe over their own signatures*. ((Such a programme will evoke comment in the press of the Third International, whose articles will say: this attempt "to convince" will do no harm, but practically it is useless, because what is *needed* is a *revolution*; and in the press of the II and II^1/$_2$ Internationals—we shall see what they have to say.))

Written February 6, 1922

First published in part
April 24, 1962
in *Pravda* No. 114

First published in full in 1964   Printed from the manuscript
in the Fifth Russian Edition
of the *Collected Works*, Vol. 44

MEMO TO V. M. MOLOTOV WITH A MOTION FOR THE POLITBUREAU OF THE C.C., R.C.P.(B.)

Comrade Molotov,

Please put two proposals for the Politbureau to the vote by telephone:

1) Not to publish the decision of the Politbureau on the figure of a single grain tax pending a new decision after the State Planning Commission has completed and submitted its calculations.

(Krzhizhanovsky yesterday complained to me bitterly that they had been doing a big job on these calculations, but it was broken off without him having even been given a hearing. Please give him another 3-4 days and do not publish until then.)

2) The newspaper *Kooperativnoye Dyelo* to be closed down. Arrangements to be made with *Ekonomicheskaya Zhizn* for using the material.[455]

Lenin

Written February 11, 1922

First published in 1945   Printed from the manuscript
in *Lenin Miscellany XXXV*

MARKS ON N. L. MESHCHERYAKOV'S LETTER AND A DRAFT DECISION FOR THE POLITBUREAU OF THE C.C., R.C.P.(B.)

...Now as regards the newspaper *Kooperativnoye Dyelo*.

?? 1) The Board of Centrosoyuz, which consists only of Communists, says that the newspaper is necessary if the co-operatives are to fulfil their difficult and new organising work and carry out the trade tasks imposed upon them.

2) The paper's editorial board consists only of Communists: I, Sarabyanov, Shvetsov, Kutuzov-Ilimsky, etc.

?? 3) A delegation of Western co-operators is coming to Russia. The closing of the newspaper will be taken advantage of by the old co-operators and will make co-operative work difficult.

4) The closing of the newspaper will be exploited at the Genoa Conference.

ha—ha!! 5) So far there has been nothing hostile to Soviet power or communism in the paper...

February 11, 1922   *N. Meshcheryakov*

To Comrade Molotov for the *Politbureau*:

in view of the obvious flimsiness of Comrade Meshcheryakov's arguments, I propose:

1) that the Board of Centrosoyuz be directed to replace the daily newspaper *Kooperativnoye Dyelo* with a *weekly*;

2) the personnel and funds thus released should be used wholly for improving the activities of headquarters in supervising and helping to develop proper trade by the co-operatives locally;

3) reports on the fulfilment of § 2 to be made monthly to the Politbureau;

4) more contributions to be made to *Ekonomicheskaya Zhizn*

14/II   *Lenin*

Written February 14, 1922

First published in 1959
in *Lenin Miscellany XXXVI*

Printed from the manuscript

LETTER TO MEMBERS OF THE POLITBUREAU OF THE C.C., R.C.P.(B.) WITH REMARKS TO THE DRAFT RESOLUTION FOR THE FIRST EXTENDED PLENARY MEETING OF THE COMINTERN EXECUTIVE ON PARTICIPATION IN A CONFERENCE OF THE THREE INTERNATIONALS[456]

To Comrade Molotov
(for members of the Politbureau)

I move the following amendments to the draft resolution sent in by Zinoviev concerning the Comintern's participation in the planned conference of all the workers' parties of the world. After the words: "unity of action among the working class masses which could be achieved immediately, despite fundamental political differences," the phrases following this should be deleted up to the words: "that the working-class masses demand unity of action". The phrase beginning with these last words should be recast as follows: "the class-conscious workers, who are perfectly well aware of these political differences, nevertheless, together with the vast majority of the workers, desire and demand unity of action on practical issues most urgent and close to the interests of the workers. There can be no doubt about this now in the mind of any conscientious person" and so on.

My second amendment is that the phrase beginning with the words: "all controversial issues to be avoided and questions that are not open to argument to be brought into focus" should be amended as follows: "and while postponing for a time the more controversial questions and bringing into focus the less controversial, both sides, or rather all three international organisations taking part in the conference, will naturally count on the ultimate victory of their points of view."

My chief amendment is aimed at deleting the passage which calls the leaders of the II and II 1/2 Internationals accomplices of the world bourgeoisie. You might as well call a man a "jackass". It is absolutely unreasonable to risk wrecking an affair of tremendous practical importance for the sake of giving oneself the extra pleasure of scolding scoundrels, whom we shall be scolding a thousand times at another place and time. If there are still people at the enlarged meeting of the Executive who have not grasped the fact that the tactic of the united front will help us to overthrow the leaders of the II and II$^{1}/_{2}$ Internationals, these people should have an extra number of popular lectures and talks read to them. It may be necessary to have a specially popular pamphlet written for them and published in French, say, if the Frenchmen have not yet grasped Marxist tactics. Finally, it were better to adopt this resolution, not unanimously, but by a majority (those who voted against we would afterwards put through a special, thorough and popular course of enlightenment) than run the risk of spoiling a practical affair for the sake of a few political youngsters who tomorrow will be cured of their infantile disorder.

Lenin

Dictated over the telephone
February 23, 1922

First published in 1964
in the Fifth Russian Edition
of the *Collected Works*, Vol. 44

Printed from the secretary's
notes (typewritten copy)

DRAFT DECISION FOR THE C.C., R.C.P.(B.)
ON THE TASKS
OF THE SOVIET DELEGATION AT GENOA

Only for circulation among members of the Politbureau

Draft decision for the C.C.

1. The C.C. recognises as correct the appraisal of the situation and the tasks (of our delegation at Genoa) as given in the theses of Comrade Litvinov.

2. The C.C. fully empowers Vice Chairman Chicherin to act as chairman of the delegation.

3. In the event of Comrade Chicherin's illness or departure his powers shall be vested in turn in one of the two trios:

a) Litvinov, Krasin, Rakovsky; b) Litvinov, Joffe, Vorovsky.

4. Our delegation should try to evade the question of acceptance of the Cannes terms. Failing this, and in the event of our being presented with a direct ultimatum, we should try to work Krasin's formula: "All countries recognise their state debts and undertake to compensate damage and losses caused by the acts of their governments."

If this does not work either, we should make for a break, declaring definitely that we are prepared to recognise private debts, but that, not wishing to play hide-and-seek, we point out that we consider them covered, together with the whole sum of our obligations, by our counter-claims. We accept no chief umpire between us and all the bourgeois countries, since the dispute is between two systems of property.

If we have to break, we should make it perfectly clear that the main and sole reason for the break is the greed of a handful of private capitalists, Urquhart, etc., whom the governments serve.

As a maximum concession these capitalists can be offered: a preferential right to concessions (i.e., if we grant X a concession on their former property wholly or in part on such-and-such terms, we undertake to give it to its former owner on the same terms).

5. In view of the possibility of the bourgeois trying to prevent us from developing our programme, we should make every effort in the very first speech to set forth, if not develop, this programme, or at least outline it (and immediately publish it in greater detail).

6. In our programme we should, without concealing our communist views, confine ourselves to a brief and passing mention of them (for instance, in a subordinate clause), and to a forthright statement to the effect that we do not consider this the right place to preach our views, since we have come for trade agreements and for an attempt to reach an agreement with the pacifist section of the other (bourgeois) camp.

By the pacifist section of that camp (or some other well-chosen polite expression) we should make it clear that we mean the petty-bourgeois, pacifist and semi-pacifist democrats of the II and II$^1/_2$ International type, and the Keynes type, etc.

One of our main, if not principal, political tasks at Genoa is to single out this wing of the bourgeois camp from the rest of the camp, try to flatter that wing, make it known that we consider possible and desirable not only a trade, but a political agreement with them (as one of the few chances of capitalism's peaceful evolution towards the new order, which we, Communists, do not greatly believe in, but which we agree and consider our duty to help try out, as representatives of one power in face of a hostile majority of other powers).

Everything possible and even impossible should be done to strengthen the pacifist wing of the bourgeoisie and increase if only slightly its chances of success at the elections. This first and foremost. Secondly, to disunite the bourgeois countries that will be united against us at Genoa—such is our dual political task at Genoa, and not at all the development of communist views.

7. Every attempt should be made to develop at length and publicise as widely as possible (in print, if not in speeches) the plan for the rehabilitation of the national economy in Russia and in Europe—in the spirit of the State Planning Commission's researches and on the basis of these researches.

8. If the bourgeois camp in Genoa presents an ultimatum to us not to touch on questions of pacifism, but to speak only on narrow trade subjects, we should express our regret, but comply with this ultimatum, saying that we had two aims at this conference—a pacifist aim and a trade aim. This will leave only one.

9. The C.C. leaves it to the delegation to elaborate the pacifist programme, confining itself to the general directive that they should try to develop it as broadly as possible in order to split the pacifist camp of the international bourgeoisie away from the gross-bourgeois, aggressive-bourgeois, reactionary-bourgeois camp.

10. On the question of trade and concessions (including the question of loans), the forests of the North, etc., should be put forward as the principal guarantee. We agree to no derogation of the rights of our state. No agreements

are to be signed without the special consent, by telegraph, of the Central Committee.[457]

Lenin

Written February 24, 1922

First published in 1964
in the Fifth Russian Edition
of the *Collected Works*, Vol. 44

Printed from the manuscript

MEMO TO V. M. MOLOTOV
FOR MEMBERS OF THE POLITBUREAU
OF THE C.C., R.C.P.(B.)
WITH A DRAFT DECISION
ON THE NOTE TO ITALY

Comrade Molotov for Members of the Politbureau

I think the question of Genoa is clear after the memos of Chicherin, Joffe, Krasin and Litvinov.

I propose a draft decision.

Plan: all members of the Politbureau attempt to come to an agreement *in writing*. Failing this, all meet and sit for 1 hour *alone* (and without a secretary).

Then 1 or 2 hours with the delegation and finis.

24.II. *Lenin*

I move: That the Politbureau direct Comrade Chicherin to send a Note to Italy, a longish, meticulously courteous Note, but with plenty of digs in it hinting that it is not we who are violating one of the first "conditions", the 8.III convocation, that we propose 1) confirming 8.III; but if (2) the majority are against, we protest and propose 15.III.[458]

Lenin

Written February 24, 1922

First published in 1964
in the Fifth Russian Edition
of the *Collected Works*, Vol. 44

Printed from the manuscript

AMENDMENTS AND REMARKS
TO THE DRAFT REGULATIONS
ON THE NARROW C.P.C.[459]

this is un-Russian	.... 10. All decisive resolutions of the Narrow Council of People's Commissars, viz., those deciding a question in substance,
This is the wrong word, *clerical* or *pertaining to clerical*—would be *better*	other than those mentioned in Article 5, are referred to the C.P.C. All particular decisions of an incidental nature, such as: sundry investigations, collection of necessary material, forwarding papers to the departments concerned all kinds of answers to inquiries from government departments addressed to the Narrow Council, as well as management and business affairs of the C.P.C. are passed finally by the Narrow Council in its own name and are not referred to the Large Council.

+ I advise the addition of: a representative of the Moscow Soviet must always be called in on all questions that concern him.

+ *all* the People's Commissariats concerned must always be called in.

Written in February 1922

First published in 1945
in *Lenin Miscellany XXXV*

Printed from the manuscript

DRAFT DECISION FOR THE POLITBUREAU
OF THE C.C., R.C.P.(B.)
ON THE SWEDISH LOAN[460]

I move: that in principle it be approved and that the Foreign Trade Commissariat be directed to continue negotiations *on the understanding, however,* that (1) no final decision is made without the Politbureau (which should retain

the right of *refusal*); (2) an attempt is made to contract
a *similar loan* on better terms with another (Italian) *offerer*.

13/III. *Lenin**

Written March 13, 1922

First published in 1965
in the Fifth Russian Edition
of the *Collected Works*, Vol. 54
Printed from the manuscript

LETTER TO MEMBERS OF THE POLITBUREAU OF THE C.C., R.C.P.(B.) WITH PROPOSALS ON THE DRAFT DIRECTIVES OF THE COMINTERN EXECUTIVE FOR THE COMINTERN DELEGATION TO THE CONFERENCE OF THE THREE INTERNATIONALS[461]

Zinoviev
Stalin
Kamenev and other members of the Politbureau:

I propose
p. 11 (2nd part) (re changing attitude towards the
Mensheviks) should be thrown out.
We cannot speak of this even provisionally just now.
In my opinion the directives should be amended this way:
AA) If you wish to raise the most controversial questions,
i.e., those that evoke the greatest hostility of the
III International towards the II and II$\frac{1}{2}$ Internationals, then we agree on condition
(a) that the list of questions be arranged with us
(b) ... and the most detailed rules of procedure
in discussing the rights of the III International;
these rights to be safeguarded in greatest detail,
etc., etc.

---

* The draft was signed also by Kamenev and Stalin; Trotsky abstained.—*Ed.*

BB) We, on our part, propose raising *only* the least controversial questions with the aim of attempting partial, but joint **action** by the rank and file of the working class.

If they accept *AA*, we shall insert: a **general** appraisal by us of the II and II¹/₂ Internationals, the *sum* of our accusations against them, etc., etc.

Further: on 25.III, i.e., at the preliminary meeting, our delegates should be extremely discreet, *so long as* there is still hope of achieving our purpose, **i.e.,** enticing all 3 Internationals ((the II and the II¹/₂)) into a general conference.

We should not make a break at once because of its *composition*, and in any case we should not break without getting in touch with Moscow, unless it is something **glaringly** mean, *absolutely* intolerable.

Lenin

Written March 14 or 15, 1922

First published in part in 1958
in the book
*O Deyatelnosty V. I. Lenina
v 1917—1922 g.*
(*Lenin's Activities in 1917-1922*),
Moscow

Published in full in 1959
in *Lenin Miscellany XXXVI*

Printed from the manuscript

LETTER TO THE POLITBUREAU
OF THE C.C., R.C.P.(B.)
WITH A DRAFT OF DIRECTIVES
TO COMRADES TRAVELLING ABROAD

Comrade Molotov for members of the Politbureau

In view of Comrade Radek's trip abroad, and *Comrade Sosnovsky's, too, I hear,*

—in view of the fact that a *flair for diplomacy is not one of the strong points* of these most valuable and important workers, I propose that the following directive be issued by the Politbureau:

"The Politbureau impresses upon all comrades travelling abroad that the present moment calls, on the one hand, for the greatest restraint in utterances and talks about the Mensheviks and the Socialist-Revolutionaries, and, on the other hand, for a relentless struggle against and the greatest distrust towards them (as the most dangerous *de facto* accomplices of the whiteguards)".

17/III.   *Lenin*

P.S. Please get this *voted by telephone.*[462]

Lenin

Written March 17, 1922

First published in 1964
in the Fifth Russian Edition
of the *Collected Works*, Vol. 45

Printed from the manuscript

LETTER TO THE POLITBUREAU OF THE C.C., R.C.P.(B.)[463]

Comrade Molotov for members of the Politbureau

This is not the first time that the Moscow Committee (and Comrade Zelensky too) is showing *indulgence* towards communist criminals, who deserve to be hanged.

This is done "by mistake". The danger of this "mistake", however, is enormous. *I move*:

1. That Comrade Divilkovsky's proposal *be adopted*.

2. That the Moscow Committee be severely reprimanded for being *indulgent* to Communists (the form of indulgence —a special commission).

3. That it be confirmed to all Gubernia Party Committees that for the slightest attempt to "influence" the courts in the sense of "mitigating" the responsibility of Communists, the C.C. will *expel* such persons *from the Party*.

4. That a circular be issued notifying the People's Commissariat for Justice (copies to the Gubernia Party Committees) to the effect that the courts are obliged to punish Communists *more severely* than non-Communists.

People's judges and members of the Board of the Commissariat for Justice who fail to observe this are to be *dismissed from office*.

5. That the Presidium of the All-Russia Central Executive Committee be asked to *inflict* a reprimand on the Presidium of the Moscow Soviet in the press.

Lenin

18.III.

P. S. It is a crying shame, disgraceful—the ruling Party defends "its own" scoundrels!!

Written March 18, 1922

First published November 20, 1962   Printed from the manuscript
     in *Pravda* No. 324

NOTE TO N. P. GORBUNOV
AND PROPOSALS ON THE QUESTION
OF THE CO-OPERATIVES[464]

Comrade Gorbunov,

Read this, make a note of it for yourself and forward it *immediately* to Comrade Molotov for the members of the *Politbureau*, then for *Tsyurupa* and *Rykov*.

In my opinion, the co-operatives are not the trade unions.

The co-operatives should remain obligatory as regards membership.

Contributions should be voluntary. If our co-operatives will carry on trade (and not play at publishing dailies in which idle chatter-mongers engage in political twaddle, which everyone is fed up with), then trading should yield an income. Those who make contributions will receive an income.

Everybody should be a member of the co-operatives. We need this for the future. I don't see how this interferes with anything.

Shares are voluntary. Those who have paid their contributions should receive a share of the profit.

Conclusion: I think the matter should be postponed; it should not be raised at this session.

Lenin

18/III.

Written March 18, 1922

First published in 1959   Printed from the manuscript
in *Lenin Miscellany XXXVI*

AMENDMENTS AND REMARKS TO THE DRAFT DECLARATION OF THE SOVIET DELEGATION AT THE GENOA CONFERENCE[465]

Comrade Molotov

With reference to Comrade Chicherin's motion entitled "Elements of a first speech at the Conference" I propose the following amendments:

1) Lines 7 and 8 down on the first page—I propose that we speak about "systems of property" and not just politico-economic systems.[466]

2) On the same page, lines 8 and 9 up—all mention of "inevitable forcible revolution and the use of sanguinary struggle" must definitely be thrown out; instead we should speak only of the fact that we Communists do not share the views of the pacifists—a fact which is sufficiently well known from communist literature—but having come here as merchants, we positively consider it our duty to give our fullest support to any attempts at a peaceful settlement of outstanding problems.

3) On the same page, 2nd and 3rd lines up—the words stating that our "historic conception includes the use of forcible measures" should definitely be deleted.

4) Page 2, 2nd and 3rd lines down—the words about our historic conception being definitely based on the inevitability of new world wars should be definitely deleted.

Under no circumstance should such frightful words be used, as this would mean playing into the hands of our opponents. We should confine ourselves only to mentioning that the views of the Communists do not coincide with the views of such pacifists as the states we are beginning negotiations with, such statesmen as Henderson, Keynes, etc., but that we consider it our duty, in order to achieve the economic agreement we are desirous of concluding, to do everything in our power for the broadest possible fulfilment of at least a certain part of this pacifist programme.

Lenin

Dictated over the telephone
March 23, 1922
First published in 1964
in the Fifth Russian Edition
of the *Collected Works*, Vol. 45

Printed from the secretary's
notes (typewritten copy)

ELEVENTH CONGRESS OF THE R.C.P.(B.)
MARCH 27-APRIL 2, 1922 [467]

1

PROPOSAL TO THE DRAFT RESOLUTION
ON THE REPORT
OF THE R.C.P.(B.) DELEGATION IN THE COMINTERN

The purpose and sense of the tactics of the united front consist in drawing more and more masses of the workers into the struggle against capital, even if it means making repeated offers to the leaders of the II and $II^1/_2$ Internationals to wage this struggle together. When the majority of the workers have already established their class, i.e., their Soviet, and not "general national" (i.e., in common with the bourgeoisie) representation, and have overthrown the political domination of the bourgeoisie, then the tactics of the united front, of course, cannot require co-operation with parties such as that of the Mensheviks (the "R.S.D.L.P.") and the S.R.s (the "Party of Socialist-Revolutionaries") for these have turned out to be opponents of Soviet power. Influence upon the working-class masses under Soviet rule has to be extended *not* by seeking co-operation with the *Mensheviks and S.R.*s, but in the manner mentioned above.[468]

Written between March 29
and April 2, 1922

First published in 1959
in the journal
Voprosi Istorii KPSS No. 2

Printed from the manuscript

2

SPEECH ON THE QUESTION
OF PRINTING ADVERTISEMENTS IN *PRAVDA*
APRIL 2[469]

Comrades, an almost fatal mistake has occurred here. I have risen to a point of order (as the chairman made clear) and not to make a closing speech. I have taken the floor to ask the congress to waive standing orders and procedure. There is a rule that after a decision has been passed there can be no interference on that question. I ask the congress to give me 4 or 5 minutes in order to oppose the decision that has been wrongly passed here.

When I heard that the congress had passed this decision and when I heard that Comrade Ryazanov had defended it ... (*Ryazanov*: "That is not so.") All the better—at least one absurd decision has by-passed Ryazanov. If we were dealing here with an innocent young lady of some twelve summers, who had learned only yesterday that there was such a thing in the world as communism, and she would have put on a frilly white frock with red ribbons and said that Communists were just pure tradesmen—that would be funny, and we could enjoy a hearty laugh over it, but seriously, what are we doing? Where will *Pravda* get the money to make up for the advertisements we have deprived it of? I ask—how much money does *Pravda* need to keep up with *Izvestia*? You don't know? Nor do I!

First published in 1931   Printed from the shorthand
in the Second and Third editions   record
of the *Collected Works*, Vol. XXVII

3

NOTES AT THE CONGRESS MEETING
APRIL 2

Sedoi:
α) ... Contradictions, abnormality, inconsistency....
β) "*greatest trust*" and!!?

1) Groundlessness of the accusation that the C.C. is persecuting the former *Workers' Opposition*
2) refusal to do positive work
3) concentration on playing at opposition
4) behaviour at metalworkers' congress
5) ditto after the congress
6) is there such a division within the former *Workers' Opposition*, which makes the Party draw a line between the majority who are working loyally in the Party, despite

difference in views, and the minority (perhaps even an insignificant one) who are behaving in a definitely unloyal manner.

Written April 2, 1922

First published in 1959   Printed from the manuscript
in *Lenin Miscellany XXXVI*

DRAFT DECISION
FOR THE PLENUM OF THE C.C., R.C.P.(B.)
ON ORGANISING THE WORK OF THE SECRETARIAT

The C.C. directs the Secretariat to strictly fix and adhere to the schedule of official reception hours and to publish it; the secretaries are to make it a rule not to personally undertake any work other than major tasks of a principled nature, and to turn such work over to their assistants and technical secretaries.

Comrade Stalin is directed to immediately find himself deputies and assistants relieving him of work (other than general management and guidance of a principled nature) in government offices.

The C.C. directs the Orgbureau and the Politbureau to submit within a fortnight a list of candidates for members of the Board and deputy commissars of the Workers' and Peasants' Inspection.[470]

Written April 3, 1922

First published in 1959   Printed from the manuscript
in *Lenin Miscellany XXXVI*

NOTES
TO THE POLITBUREAU OF THE C.C., R.C.P.(B.)
WITH DRAFT DECISIONS

1

Comrade Molotov, please put this article and my following proposals to the vote of the Politbureau by sending them round to the members.

1. That there is no objection to having this article of Lenin's published in *Izvestia* and *Pravda* on Tuesday.

2. That directives be given to the Soviet and Party press to appraise the Berlin agreement from this angle, and to dwell at special length on the factual existing links between the S.R.s and Mensheviks, the Right wing of both these parties, and the international bourgeoisie.

3. That the publication for the said purpose in all European languages of Savinkov's pamphlet *Fighting the Bolsheviks* and of S. Ivanovich's pamphlet *The Twilight of Russian Social-Democracy* should be speeded up and a detailed account given of how these pamphlets prove the real ties that exist between the Right-wing Mensheviks and S.R.s and international reaction.

4. That Comrade Trotsky be directed to see to it that these and similar materials are published in all languages with appropriate comments as quickly as possible.

5. That Comrade Radek be asked by wire to return to Moscow as soon as possible with the full minutes of the Berlin Conference.

6. That Comrade Bukharin shall be forbidden to return to Russia until he has completed his cure.

Lenin

Dictated over the telephone
April 9, 1922

First published in 1964   Printed from the secretary's
in the Fifth Russian Edition   notes (typewritten copy)
of the *Collected Works*, Vol. 45

2

Comrade Stalin
for the Politbureau

In view of Comrade Zinoviev's proposal, I now vote for not having Radek called back, but asking instead for all the detailed minutes of the Berlin Conference to be forwarded through the diplomatic mail.

I object most emphatically to Bukharin's coming here, as this will needlessly interfere with his medical treatment.[471]

Lenin

Dictated over the telephone
April 10, 1922

First published in 1964   Printed from the secretary's
in the Fifth Russian Edition   notes (typewritten copy)
of the *Collected Works*, Vol. 45

REMARKS AND PROPOSALS
TO THE DRAFT DECISION
FOR THE COMINTERN EXECUTIVE FOLLOWING
THE CONFERENCE
OF THE THREE INTERNATIONALS[472]

LETTERS TO G. Y. ZINOVIEV

1

On Point 1 I propose the addendum: dwell at greater length 1) on the real links between our Mensheviks and S.R.s and the common front of the landowners and bourgeoisie against the Soviet government, special attention being given for this purpose to Savinkov's pamphlet *Fighting the Bolsheviks* (Warsaw, 1920) and S. Ivanovich's pamphlet *The Twilight of Russian Social-Democracy*, as these booklets very clearly reveal what is known, of course, from a number of other documents—namely, that Right-wing Mensheviks and S.R.s take refuge behind the name of a common party, as a matter of form, while in fact they act quite independently; 2) pay special attention to showing up the identity of our Mensheviks and S.R.s with the leaders of the II and II$^1/_2$ Internationals, the highly pernicious nature of Otto Bauer's recent pamphlet, which virtually proposes and preaches panic retreat in the face of capitalism. Such preaching we regard as tantamount to preaching panic flight at the front during war.

Point 2, I accept.

Re Point 3:

I have my doubts about this, as I believe that a precisely worded ruling calling for unanimity should save us from making mistakes, while general appeals on subjects clarifying the points endorsed at the Berlin Conference (defence of Soviet Russia, etc.) will be extremely useful to us, as we shall repeatedly make use of them in future to expose the muddle our opponents have got themselves into.

Re Point 4—I definitely support this.

Re Point 5—I have no objection.

Re Point 6:

The purport of this point is not clear to me. I believe that the Berlin agreement should be ratified immediately upon receipt of the official text of the adopted decisions, or, better still perhaps, it should be ratified at once with the reservation that the text being ratified was the one that was published in *Pravda* on 9/IV.

I would particularly ask you to arrange for the full text of the minutes of the Berlin Conference to be dispatched as quickly as possible by special courier and to check whether these minutes have been signed by the official representatives of each of the three Internationals.

Lenin

Dictated over the telephone
April 11, 1922

First published in 1959   Printed from the secretary's
in *Lenin Miscellany XXXVI*   notes (typewritten copy)

2

Comrade Zinoviev,

The following should be added to those points of the Comintern Executive's decision on which we exchanged notes this morning:

Criticism of the policy of the II and $II^1/_2$ Internationals should now be given a somewhat different character, namely, this criticism (especially at meetings attended by workers who support the II and $II^1/_2$ Internationals, and in special leaflets and articles written for them) should tend to be of a clarifying nature, made with particular patience and thoroughness, so as not to scare away these workers with harsh words, and bring home to them the irreconcilable contradictions between the slogans their representatives have adopted in Berlin (for example, the fight against capital, the eight-hour day, defence of Soviet Russia, aid to the famine-stricken) and the entire reformist policy.

Perhaps, before publishing this, we ought to verify whether the Berlin decisions have been ratified by the II and $II^1/_2$ Internationals.

Lenin

Dictated over the telephone
April 11, 1922

First published in 1959   Printed from the secretary's
in *Lenin Miscellany XXXVI*   notes (typewritten copy)

INTERVIEW WITH THE CORRESPONDENT
OF *THE NEW YORK HERALD*[473]

In his talk with the correspondent of the American newspaper *The New York Herald* on the subject of the Genoa Conference, Lenin stated:

This Conference should be guided only by one economic principle. Russia is well aware of what she can expect from the bourgeois states. The present state of affairs cannot continue any longer. It is disastrous both for Russia and for the whole world.

Russia stands in need of trade with the bourgeois states. On the other hand, the bourgeois governments are well aware that the economic life of Europe cannot be adjusted without Russia.

However, those who intend to offer humiliating terms to the Russian delegation at Genoa are deeply mistaken. Russia will not allow herself to be treated as a vanquished country. If the bourgeois governments try to adopt such a tone towards Russia they will be committing the greatest folly.

Krasnaya Gazeta (Petrograd)
No. 84, April 14, 1922

Printed from the newspaper
text

DECISION OF THE POLITBUREAU
OF THE C.C., R.C.P.(B.)
ON THE PUBLICATION OF THE WORKS
OF G. V. PLEKHANOV

APRIL 27, 1922[474]

Comrade Kamenev shall be directed to talk over with Comrade Ter and make arrangements for the publication of Plekhanov's revolutionary works in one volume.

First published in 1964
in the Fifth Russian Edition
of the *Collected Works*, Vol. 45

Printed from the typewritten
copy of the minutes

DRAFT DECISION
FOR THE POLITBUREAU OF THE C.C., R.C.P.(B.) ON PRESENTATION TO THE C.C. OF SUMMARISED INFORMATION CONCERNING THE TAX IN KIND

1) The Commissariat for Food
2) The Commissariat for Agriculture
3) The Central Statistical Board
4) The State Planning Commission
   agricultural section

shall be directed to present to the C.C. within four days a summary of information on the tax in kind, length not more than *1 page*, containing a clear and precise summary of the amount of the tax in kind collected in 1921-1922 and that expected in 1922-1923 as mentioned in the press.[475]

Written May 11, 1922

First published in 1964
in the Fifth Russian Edition
of the *Collected Works*, Vol. 45

Printed from the manuscript

NOTE TO J. V. STALIN
WITH A DRAFT DECISION FOR THE POLITBUREAU OF THE C.C., R.C.P.(B.) ON THE QUESTION OF THE FOREIGN TRADE MONOPOLY[476]

Comrade Stalin,

In view of this, please get a directive passed through the Politbureau by *collecting the votes* of members that "The C.C. reaffirms the monopoly of foreign trade and resolves that a stop be put everywhere to the working up of the question of merging the Supreme Economic Council with the Commissariat for Foreign Trade. All People's Commissars to sign confidentially" and return the original to Stalin. No copies to be made.

15/V.   *Lenin*

Written May 15, 1922

First published in 1959
in *Lenin Miscellany XXXVI*

Printed from the manuscript

ADDENDUM TO THE DRAFT PREAMBLE
TO THE CRIMINAL CODE OF THE R.S.F.S.R.
AND A LETTER TO D. I. KURSKY[477]

Draft

PREAMBLE TO THE CRIMINAL CODE OF THE R.S.F.S.R.

... 5. Pending the establishment of conditions guaranteeing Soviet power against counter-revolutionary encroachments upon it, the revolutionary tribunals shall be given the right to apply × capital punishment for crimes under Articles 58, 59, 60, 61, 62, 63+64...... of the Criminal Code).

×) Add also Articles *64* and *65* and *66* and *67* and *68* and *69*.

××) Add the right, by decision of the Presidium of the All-Russia Central Executive Committee, to commute the death sentence to deportation (for a term or for life).

×××) Add: death penalty for illicit return from abroad.

Comrade Kursky,

I think the application of the death sentence should be extended (commutable to deportation). See *1st line down*—to all forms of activity by the Mensheviks, *S.R.s and so on*;

to be formulated so as to identify these acts with those of the *international bourgeoisie* and their struggle against us (bribing the press and agents, working for war and so on).

Please return urgently with your comments.

15/V.   *Lenin*

Written May 15, 1922

First published in part   Printed from the manuscript
in 1937 in the journal
Bolshevik No. 2

Published in full in 1964
in the Fifth Russian Edition
of the *Collected Works*, Vol. 45

LETTER TO THE SECRETARIAT
OF THE C.C., R.C.P.(B.) ON THE QUESTION
OF REDUCING THE RED ARMY[478]

I think it should be put on the agenda and a reduction by one-fourth announced, the reason given being that a real, if only small and not very reliable, step towards a truce has been made at Genoa.

Lenin

Dictated over the telephone
May 20, 1922

First published in 1959   Printed from the secretary's notes
in *Lenin Miscellany XXXVI*   (typewritten copy)

LETTER TO J. V. STALIN
FOR THE POLITBUREAU OF THE C.C., R.C.P.(B.)
WITH A DRAFT DECISION ON THE COMPOSITION
OF THE ALL-RUSSIA C.E.C.

Comrade Stalin for the *Politbureau*:

The session of the All-Russia Central Executive Committee has shown how wrongly the A.C.E.C. is constituted. The great majority of its members are officials.

I propose that the Politbureau pass a decision:

"To recognise as essential that no less than 60 per cent of the members of the A.C.E.C. should be workers and peasants not occupying any official posts in government bodies; that no less than 67 per cent of the A.C.E.C.'s members should be Communists; a three-man commission consisting of Comrades Kalinin, Yenukidze and Kamenev, be directed to work up this question for the next plenum of the C.C. To be passed first through the Politbureau, then to the Plenum of the C.C. for enactment by the next All-Russia Congress of Soviets.[479]

23/V.1922   *Lenin*

First published in 1959   Printed from the manuscript
in *Lenin Miscellany XXXVI*

TO THE FIRST CONGRESS
OF WORKING WOMEN OF TRANSCAUCASIA[480]

I greet the First Congress of working women of Trans-caucasia. Thank you for electing me. I cannot attend owing to illness.

Lenin

Written in May, not
later than 26th, 1922

Published on May 29, 1922
in the newspaper
Bakinsky Rabochy (Baku Worker)
No. 117

Printed from the newspaper
text

ON THE ESTABLISHMENT OF THE U.S.S.R.

LETTER TO L. B. KAMENEV
FOR MEMBERS OF THE POLITBUREAU[481]

26.IX.

Comrade Kamenev, Stalin has probably already sent you the resolution of his commission on the entry of the independent republics into the R.S.F.S.R.

If he has not, please take it from the secretary at once, and read it. I spoke about it with Sokolnikov yesterday, and with Stalin today. Tomorrow I shall see Mdivani (the Georgian Communist suspected of "independent" senti-ments).

In my opinion the matter is of utmost importance. Stalin tends to be somewhat hasty. Give the matter good thought (you once intended to deal with it, and even had a bit to do with it); Zinoviev too.

Stalin has already consented to make one concession: in Clause 1, instead of "entry" into the R.S.F.S.R., to put:
   "Formal unification with the R.S.F.S.R. in a Union
   of Soviet Republics of Europe and Asia."

I hope the purport of this concession is clear: we consider ourselves, the Ukrainian S.S.R. and others, equal, and enter with them, on an equal basis, into a new union, a new federation, the Union of the Soviet Republics of Europe and Asia.

Clause 2 needs to be amended as well. What is needed besides the sessions of the All-Russia Central Executive Committee of the R.S.F.S.R. is a

"Federal All-Union Central Executive Committee of the Union of the Soviet Republics of Europe and Asia."

If the former should hold sessions once a week, and the latter once a week (or once a fortnight even), this may be easily arranged.

The important thing is not to provide material for the "pro-independence" people, not to destroy their *independence*, but to create another *new storey*, a federation of *equal* republics.

The second part of Clause 2 could stand: the dissatisfied will appeal (against decisions of the *Council of Labour and Defence*, and the *Council of People's Commissars*) to the Federal All-Union Central Executive Committee, *without thereby suspending* implementation (just as in the R.S.F.S.R.).

Clause 3 could stand, but its wording should be: "amalgamate in *federal* People's Commissariats whose seat shall be in Moscow, with the proviso that the respective People's Commissariats of the R.S.F.S.R. have their authorised representatives with a small staff in all the Republics *that have joined the Union of Republics of Europe and Asia.*"

Part 2 of Clause 3 remains; perhaps it could be said to emphasise equality: "by agreement of the *Central Executive Committees* of the member republics of the Union of the Soviet Republics of Europe and Asia."

Let's think about Part 3: perhaps we had better substitute "*mandatory*" for "desirable"? Or perhaps insert *conditionally* mandatory at least in the form of a *request for instructions* and the authority to decide without such instructions solely in cases of "specially urgent importance"?

Clause 4 could perhaps also be "amalgamate by agreement of the Central Executive Committees"?

Perhaps add to Clause 5: "with the establishment of joint (or general) conferences and congresses of a *purely consultative* nature (or perhaps of a *solely* consultative nature)?

Appropriate alterations in the 1st and 2nd comments.

Stalin has agreed to delay submission of the resolution to the Political Bureau of the Central Committee until my return. I shall arrive on Monday, October 2. I should like to see you and Rykov for about two hours in the morning, say 12 noon to 2 p.m., and, if necessary, in the evening, say 5-7 or 6-8.

That is my tentative draft. I shall add or amend on the strength of talks with Mdivani and other comrades. I beg you to do the same, and to reply to me.

Yours,
Lenin

P. S. Send copies to *all* members of the Political Bureau.

Written September 26, 1922

First published in 1959
in *Lenin Miscellany XXXVI*   Printed from the manuscript

TO THE CONGRESS OF TEXTILE WORKERS[482]

10.X.1922

Dear Comrades,

I apologise for having had to let you down. I had the toothache, which not only kept me from my work just when I had started it, but kept me fretting for a whole week. All meetings (at congresses) have to be cancelled again for a week.

I am very sorry that I cannot meet you at your congress. I hope that Comrade Kutuzov will tell you everything in detail and convey to you my best greetings and wishes.

Yours,
Lenin

Published in 1922 in the book   Printed from the facsimile
Report of the Fifth All-Russia   in the Special Edition
Congress of the Textile   of the newspaper *Golos Tekstilei*
Workers' Trade Union.   (Voice of the Textile Workers)
October 6-11, 1922, Moscow   January 25, 1924

ADDENDA TO THE TERMS OF THE AGREEMENT
WITH L. URQUHART[483]

1) Further: the territory of the concession should be reduced, definitely ensuring to the R.S.F.S.R. a part of Ekibastuz that will be sufficient for the Urals (not less than one-fourth or one-sixth);

2) most important: the sums payable to Urquhart should be cut so that our receipts should not be deferred until 1934 (?).

Lenin

3) What are these amendments for? For *approximate* directives to our agents?

For.
Lenin

Written not before
October 25, 1922

First published in 1959   Printed from the manuscript
in *Lenin Miscellany XXXVI*

THESES ON THE CO-OPERATIVE BANK[484]

1) Premiums for size of transactions and uyezd coverage;

2) ditto—deposits;

3) participation in the bank of leading agricultural communist co-operators for purposes of control and drive;

4) stimulation of the Co-operative Bank by the State Bank by way of reduced %;

5) allocation of a certain sum by the State Bank.

Written November 2, 1922

First published in 1964   Printed from the manuscript
in the Fifth Russian Edition
of the *Collected Works*, Vol 45

TO THE TEXTILE WORKERS OF PETROGRAD[485]

3.XI.1922

Dear Comrades,

I thank you sincerely for the woollen blanket you have sent me. I find it excellent. I am very sorry I was unable to see Shorov.

My best greetings,
Yours,

V. Ulyanov (Lenin)

First published in 1945
in *Lenin Miscellany XXXV*

Printed from the manuscript

MOTION FOR
THE POLITBUREAU OF THE C.C.,R.C.P.(B.)
ON THE REDUCTION OF THE ARMY

Comrade Stalin

Please obtain today a viva voca vote of the Politbureau members on this motion of mine:

that Comrade Trotsky's plan for submitting to the Government a proposal for reducing the army by 200,000 men in the course of January be endorsed;

that Comrade Trotsky be asked to state what period he considers possible for such a question to be introduced to the C.P.C. in the form of a completed draft.[486]

13/XI.1922

Lenin

First published in 1964
in the Fifth Russian Edition
of the *Collected Works*, Vol 45

Printed from the typewritten
copy

TO THE RUSSIAN COLONY IN NORTH AMERICA[487]

Comrade Reichel, a representative of the American Society for Technical Aid for Soviet Russia, told me about the incorrect view on the New Economic Policy prevalent among some members of the Russian colony in North America.

This incorrect view could, I believe, be the result of deliberate misinterpretation of this policy by the capitalist press and the ridiculous tales spread by the embittered whiteguards, who have been driven out of Soviet Russia, as well as by the Mensheviks and Socialist-Revolutionaries.

In Europe these tales about us and especially about our New Economic Policy are falling into disuse. The New Economic Policy has changed nothing radically in the social system of Soviet Russia, nor can it change anything so long as the power is in the hands of the workers—and that Soviet power has come to stay, no one now, I think, can have any doubt. The malignity of the capitalist press and the influx of Russian whiteguards in America merely prove our strength.

The state capitalism, which is one of the principal aspects of the New Economic Policy, is, under Soviet power, a form of capitalism that is deliberately permitted and restricted by the working class. Our state capitalism differs essentially from the state capitalism in countries that have bourgeois governments in that the state with us is represented not by the bourgeoisie, but by the proletariat, who has succeeded in winning the full confidence of the peasantry.

Unfortunately, the introduction of state capitalism with us is not proceeding as quickly as we would like it. For example, so far we have not had a single important concession, and without foreign capital to help develop our economy, the latter's quick rehabilitation is inconceivable.

Those to whom the question of our New Economic Policy—the only correct policy—is not quite clear, I would refer to the speeches of Comrade Trotsky and my own speech at the Fourth Congress of the Communist International* devoted to this question.

Comrade Reichel has told me about the preparatory work which the Society for Technical Aid is doing to organise American agricultural and other producers' communes who wish to come out to work in Russia and intend to bring with them new instruments of production, tractors, seeds of improved cultures, and so on.

---

* See Vol. 33 of this edition, pp. 418-32.—*Ed.*

I have already expressed my gratitude to the American comrades in my letters to the Society for Technical Aid and the Society of Friends of Soviet Russia in connection with the very successful work of their agricultural communes and units in Russia in the summer of 1922.*

I take this opportunity to thank you once more on behalf of the Soviet Government and to stress the fact that of all the forms of aid *the aid* to our agriculture and improvement of its technical methods is the most important and valuable for us.

V. Ulyanov (Lenin)
Chairman, Council of People's Commissars

Written November 14, 1922
Published January 10, 1923
in the newspaper *Russky Golos* No. 2046,
New York

Printed from the typewritten copy collated with the newspaper text

DRAFT RESOLUTION
FOR THE FOURTH CONGRESS
OF THE COMINTERN ON THE QUESTION
OF THE PROGRAMME
OF THE COMMUNIST INTERNATIONAL[488]

Proposals adopted at a meeting of the C.C. Five
(Lenin, Trotsky, Zinoviev, Radek, Bukharin)
November 20, 1922

1. All the programmes are handed to the Executive of the Comintern or to a committee appointed by it for detailed working up and study.

The Executive of the Comintern is obliged within the shortest possible time to publish all the draft programmes forwarded to it.

2. The congress confirms that all the national parties which do not yet have their own national programmes must immediately start drafting them so that they may be submitted to the Executive not later than within three months of the next congress, which shall endorse them.

* Ibid., pp. 380, 381.—*Ed.*

3. The necessity of fighting for transition demands subject to appropriate reservations making these demands dependent on concrete conditions of place and time should be stated explicitly and categorically in the national programmes.

4. The theoretical basis for all such transition or limited demands should be definitely stated in the general programme, the Fourth Congress declaring that the Comintern emphatically condemns both the attempts to represent the inclusion of limited demands in the programme as opportunism, and all and any attempts to use limited demands to obscure and side-track the basic revolutionary task.

5. The general programme should clearly state the basic historical types of transition demands of the national parties depending on cardinal differences of economic structure, as for example, Britain and India, and such-like.[489]

First published in 1965
in the Fifth Russian Edition
of the *Collected Works*, Vol 54

Printed from the typewritten
copy

PROPOSALS FOR THE DISTRIBUTION
OF FUNCTIONS BETWEEN THE DEPUTY CHAIRMEN
OF THE C.P.C. AND THE C.L.D.[490]

Distribution of functions between the Deputy Chairmen:

1. One deputy takes the *C.L.D.*, the other two the *C.P.C.* monthly.

2. They divide the People's Commissariats between them according (or similar) to the spring list of 1922.

3. Work already started (for example, the trusts—the Trust Commission; account of expenditure on heavy industry) is to be continued by Comrade Kamenev.

4. Each deputy chairman undertakes a check of staffs;— a certain part weekly or fortnightly (to be calculated and scheduled in such a way that each check is devoted in turn to one or another People's Commissariat;—now top,

now bottom;—that each check is documented by a detailed statement in writing; those parts of the unchecked commissariats which do not carry out similar reductions and improvements ordered for other commissariats shall incur a penalty, including arrest and dismissal).

4/XII.1922 *Lenin*

First published in 1959
in *Lenin Miscellany XXXVI*   Printed from the manuscript

RE DRAFT PROPOSAL FOR THE POLITBUREAU OF THE C.C.,R.C.P.(B.) ON THE REPORT OF THE STATE SUPPLIES COMMISSION

All schools, including teachers and pupils, to have their requirements in bread fully provided for over and above the given calculations, and Comrades Kamenev, Tsyurupa and Yakovleva to figure out exactly what amount of bread should be earmarked for this purpose, with the addition of a minimum, specially verified, quantity for office employees.

Another 1 million gold rubles to be added for school expenses.[491]

Lenin

Written December 6 or 7, 1922
First published in 1959
in *Lenin Miscellany XXXVI*   Printed from the typed copy
signed by Lenin

PROPOSAL FOR THE PLENUM REGARDING THE POLITBUREAU STANDING ORDER

1. The Politbureau meets on Thursdays from 11 to 2 (not later).

2. If any questions remain outstanding, they are to be dealt with either on Friday or on Monday during the same hours.

3. The agenda of the Politbureau should be forwarded to members not later than 12 o'clock on Wednesday. Material (in written form) pertaining to the agenda should be sent in within the same period.

4. Additional questions may be introduced on the day of the meeting only on the following conditions:
   a) in cases of absolute urgency (especially diplomatic questions),
   b) only in writing,
   c) only in cases where no objection is raised by any single member of the Politbureau.

The latter condition regarding non-objection to new questions being introduced in the agenda may be waived only in the case of diplomatic questions which brook no delay.

Lenin

Dictated over the telephone
December 8, 1922

First published in 1945   Printed from the secretary's
in *Lenin Miscellany XXXV*   notes (typewritten copy)

PROPOSALS CONCERNING THE WORK ROUTINE OF THE DEPUTY CHAIRMEN AND THE CHAIRMAN OF THE C.P.C.

Work Routine of the Deputy Chairmen and the Chairman of the C.P.C.

1. Working hours: 11-2, 6-9; together with the C.P.C. chairman on *Monday and Tuesday*, *Thursday and Friday*.

2. Special meetings of all the deputies and the chairman of the C.L.D. (minus the Politbureau, C.P.C. and C.L.D.) on these days and at these hours whenever there is need, but *generally not less than* twice a week for one hour. This hour to be fixed on the eve not later than 9 p.m.

3. All the work of the deputies is divided into:
   (a) close supervision over the work of the Narrow C.P.C.;
   (b) similar supervision over the work of the business meetings of the *C.L.D.*

(it is necessary to resume the business meetings of the *C.L.D.* in order to disengage the deputies for other more important work. The business meetings are *not* chaired by the deputies but *their* signatures *alone* endorse the decisions of these meetings);

(c) chairmanship at those parts of the *C.P.C.* and *C.L.D.* meetings where the chairman of the *C.P.C.* does not preside;

(d) participation in the Financial Committee (plus Sokolnikov and his deputy and the chairman of the Narrow C.P.C.; the latter need not attend all meetings of the Financial Committee).

(Perhaps arrange a meeting of the Financial Committee once a week for one hour chaired by the *C.P.C.* chairman? Think this over.);

(e) determining the agenda of all bodies, including the Narrow C.P.C., and the order of priority, the most important questions being chosen by all four under the chairmanship of the C.P.C. chairman;

(f) close supervision of the various People's Commissariats and their apparatus both by means of instructions to the People's Commissars and their deputies personally and by means of studying their apparatus top and bottom;

(g) the commissariats, for this purpose (Point *f*), are allocated among the deputies, such allocation to be endorsed by the chairman of the *C.P.C.*

4. All the above-mentioned work is distributed among the deputies in such a way that each of the three (and if need be their assistants from among the business managers) handles a definite job *for two months* and afterwards *changes it* for another.

(This is necessary in order that all the deputies may acquaint themselves with the *entire* apparatus and in order to achieve real unity of management.)

5. The draft of such a distribution among the three deputies is to be drawn up by them immediately and approved by all four.

6. Since the work of improving and correcting the whole apparatus is far more important than the work of chairmanship and the chatting with Deputy People's Commissars and

People's Commissars, which has up till now fully occupied all the deputies' time, it is necessary to arrange and strictly carry out a practice under which each deputy, *for not less than two hours* a week, "goes down to the bottom", makes a personal study of all the various parts of the apparatus, top and bottom, and the most unexpected ones at that. The official record of such a study, made, confirmed and communicated (in certain cases) to *all* government departments, should lead to a *reduction* in staff and tighten up discipline throughout our state machinery.

Lenin

Written December 9, 1922

First published in 1945
in *Lenin Miscellany XXXV*

Printed from the manuscript

LETTER TO L. B. KAMENEV, A. I. RYKOV AND A. D. TSYURUPA
ON THE DISTRIBUTION OF WORK BETWEEN THE DEPUTY CHAIRMEN OF THE C.P.C. AND THE C.L.D.

Comrades Kamenev, Rykov and Tsyurupa

Owing to a recurrence of my illness I must wind up all political work and take a holiday again.[492] Therefore our disagreements with you lose their practical significance. I must say, however, that I utterly disagree with Rykov's practical addendum, and I move the exact opposite against it—namely, that reception should be quite free, unlimited and even extended.[493] I am leaving the details until a personal meeting.

To a considerable extent I disagree also with the distribution of the commissariats. I think this distribution should be more closely adjusted to the ability for purely administrative work on the part of the various deputies; in my opinion, the chief fault of your yesterday's distribution consists in the lack of such adjustment.[494] The functions of chairmanship and supervision of the proper legal wording of both legislative acts and decisions of the Financial Committee and so forth should be far more strictly separated from the functions of checking and improving the administrative apparatus. Comrade Kamenev is more suitable for the former functions (i.e., chairmanship, supervision of proper wording, etc.) whereas the purely administrative functions are more in Tsyurupa's and Rykov's line.

For the general reason mentioned above I must defer this question until my return from leave. But please bear in mind that I give my consent to your proposed distribution, not for three months (as you suggest), but pending my return to work, should this take place earlier than within three months.

I see that your distribution has overlooked such an important organ as *Ekonomicheskaya Zhizn*, which needs someone to keep a special eye on it. I think this could best be done by Rykov

Lenin

13.XII.1922

Dictated over
the telephone

First published in 1959
in *Lenin Miscellany XXXVI*

Printed from the secretary's
notes (typewritten copy)

MATERIALS TO THE ARTICLE
"HOW WE SHOULD REORGANISE THE WORKERS' AND PEASANTS' INSPECTION"*

1

PLAN OF AN ARTICLE
"WHAT SHOULD WE DO WITH THE W.P.I.?"

1. — Our state apparatus as a whole is most closely tied, most imbued with the old spirit.

In this way we may better renovate it.

---

* See Vol. 33 of this edition, pp 481-86.—*Ed.*

2. — Such a type of apparatus as that directly connected with the Central Committee makes for the greatest mobility.

3. — It enjoys greatest authority.

4. — Won't that make for too many C.C. members?

5. — The conference nature of the C.C. plenums has already grown out of our previous Party building.

6. — A ruling is possible limiting attendance of C.C. members at meetings of higher government bodies (the C.P.C., C.L.D., All-Russia Central Executive Committee, etc.).

7. — It is possible to arrange their taking turns in attending these meetings.

8. — It is possible to arrange their taking turns at the meetings of the Board of the Workers' and Peasants' Inspection.

9. — Possible objections to this plan: too many inspectors, too much supervision, too many chiefs having the right to demand an immediate reply and tearing the staff away from their direct duties, etc.

10. — Answer: we propose an unusual type of personnel for the W.P.I.

11. — How account for the fact that the Commissariat for Foreign Affairs has a better type of staff? And what are the conditions for making a similar renovated apparatus out of the W.P.I.?

12. — The W.P.I. should start right away organising the work on new lines, guided by five years experience.

13. — New organisation of work on the part of the C.C. Secretariat (training new members of the C.C. in all the details of administration).

14. — Better organisation of Politbureau meetings will come about in the course of the work itself.

15. — Important gain from increasing the number of C.C. members—lessening of the personal and casual element in its decisions, etc.

Dictated not later than
January 9, 1923

First published in 1959
in *Lenin Miscellany* XXXVI

Printed from the secretary's
notes (typewritten copy)

2

WHAT SHOULD WE DO WITH THE W.P.I.?

Without a doubt, the W.P.I. is an enormous difficulty for us. So far nothing has come of it, and the question of its organisation and even its expediency remains a question.

I think that those who doubt whether there is any need for it are wrong. At the same time, however, I do not deny that the problem presented by our state machinery and the task of improving it is very difficult and far from being solved.

With the exception of the People's Commissariat for Foreign Affairs, our state apparatus is largely a survival of the past, and least of all affected by any drastic change. It has only been slightly touched up on the surface. In all other respects, in order to get it to work properly, it has always been necessary for the workers' and peasants' state—a state built entirely on new lines—to concentrate members of the Party in it throughout the hierarchical framework.

It is worth remembering how we acted in the critical moments of the civil war, how we concentrated our best Party forces in the Red Army, how we resorted to the mobilisation of the advanced workers from among the Party ranks—in order to confirm what has been said.

And so, I believe, as a result of all our attempts to reorganise the Workers' and Peasants' Inspection there emerges the conclusion that we have not made one more attempt. Namely, we have not tried to put this matter into the hands of our workers and peasants, by placing them at the head of our Party as members of the Central Committee.

I visualise this reform of the W.P.I. in the following manner: some 50 to 75 workers and peasants, fully tried and trusted as to conscientiousness and devotion, are elected to the C.C. of the Party in addition to the other C.C. members. At the same time, the staff of the W.P.I. should be reduced at last (at long last!) to several hundred, consisting, on the one hand, of persons with most experience in W.P.I. work in general, i.e., persons who are most familiar with the general supervision of our apparatus of highly skilled specialists and who have a knowledge of both our apparatus and of the principles and problems of office work organisation, methods of verification and investigation—and, on the other hand, of persons of the purely secretarial, auxiliary staff.

The task of the new members of the C.C., who have fully equal rights with the other members of the C.C., is, by long hard work, to make a study of and improve our state machinery. All the other members of the W.P.I. staff are to help them in this, some as persons most familiar with this machinery and with the work of the W.P.I., others as employees of the secretarial type.

At the same time the People's Commissariat of Workers' and Peasants' Inspection could remain the same commissariat it has been up till now. The new members of the C.C. could be considered temporarily attached to it. The People's Commissar of the W.P.I. could retain his present rank, position and rights along with the members of his Board.

What do we stand to gain from such an organisation? First of all, we would drop once and for all the practice of new reorganisations undertaken on the basis of an inadequate study of our apparatus. Secondly, we would enhance the authority of this commissariat both by means of enlisting members of the C.C. to it and by reducing its staff to a few hundred members. From the present position, under which the members of the People's Commissariat of the W.P.I. as a general rule live on sops from the inspected institutions, we would pass immediately to a position under which the maximum independence of the W.P.I. employees would be guaranteed either by a very high salary (this could be achieved by reducing the number of the staff to a few hundred very highly skilled and tested top-level workers), or by those assistants of a purely secretarial type, who would be under the constant control and supervision of both the above-mentioned members of the C.C. and of the few specialists left by us after careful screening of the commissariat's staff

The new members of the Central Committee would be assigned the task of making a closer and more careful study of our machinery of state in all its ramifications, including, incidentally, the state trusts.

This job cannot be done quickly. No definite time limit, therefore, would be set for them. On the other hand, they could reckon on several years work by alternating members of the C.C. working on the same assignment, i.e., by a decision of a Party congress we would guarantee to members of the C.C. the possibility of working at this job for several years and then returning to their former jobs.

Lenin

January 9, 1923

Taken down by M. V.

WHAT SHOULD WE DO WITH THE W.P.I.?
(continuation)

I foresee that this plan will evoke no end of objections, most of which will be prompted by the vicious howl of the worst of the old elements in our state apparatus, who have remained really old, that is, pre-revolutionary. They will say that this will lead to nothing but complete chaos in the work, that the C.C. members, not knowing what to do, will loiter about the commissariats and government offices, interfering everywhere with the work, demanding explanations, etc., etc.

I think that the nature of these objections clearly betrays the source they come from, and are hardly worth answering. Obviously, if we had in mind an ordinary type of staff, some of these objections might be warranted. But the thing is, we do not have in mind the usual type of staff for this commissariat, but single out for it the best workers, who, on verification by the Party congress, deserve to be elected to the C.C. In this way, I believe, we guarantee that the staff of the People's Commissariat of the W.P.I. will be as good as the best of our commissariats, namely, the People's Commissariat for Foreign Affairs. How do we account for the Commissariat for Foreign Affairs having the best staff of employees? In the first place, because diplomats of the old stamp could not remain there to any noticeable degree; secondly, because we selected people there anew, selected them by entirely new standards, by their fitness for the new tasks; thirdly, because there, in the Foreign Commissariat, we do not have, as in other commissariats, that plethora of haphazardly selected employees who, practically speaking, have inherited all the old qualities of officialdom; and fourthly, because the Foreign Commissariat is working under the direct guidance of our Central Committee. This, as a matter of fact, is the only one of our commissariats that has been fully renovated and that is really working for the workers' and peasants' government and in the spirit of that government, and not merely giving the impression of working for it, while actually, in the main, working against it or in the wrong spirit.

Now what conditions are we faced with in our attempt to make a truly renovated apparatus out of the W.P.I.? The first condition—conscientiousness, will be fully ensured by selection; the second condition is the high qualities of the staff members as regards their devotion to the cause and their abilities; the third condition is their closeness to the highest Party body and their equal rights with those who lead our Party, and, through it, the whole of our state apparatus.

It may be said that no amount of conscientiousness or Party authoritativeness can make up for what, in this case, is the most important thing, namely, knowledge of one's business, knowledge of our state apparatus, and knowledge of the way it should be remodelled.

My reply to this is that one of the essential conditions of my proposal is that we are not to expect quick results in the work of the new commissariat and anticipate that this work will go on for many years. The question then boils down to organising the work of the new commissariat.

And here I feel justified in presuming that both our Party workers and the people now in charge of the W.P.I. have accumulated sufficient experience, sufficient knowledge, sufficient ability and other qualities to properly organise the training of the new C.C. members, and a practical training at that, i.e., by combining their familiarisation with all the details of our state apparatus with a study of what modern science has achieved in the bourgeois states as regards efficient organisation of every kind of staff work.

Lenin

January 13, 1923
Taken down by L. F.

WHAT SHOULD WE DO WITH THE W.P.I.?

(continuation 2)

I assume that it goes without saying that the W.P.I. will start at once, on the basis of five years experience, organising the work on new lines; that it will divide the new workers into a number of groups and assign the work among these groups systematically; that it will divide these groups into: periodically employed people making a practical study of foreign experience; into people engaged in theoretical work and studying the results of modern science in the field of organisation of labour generally and managerial work in particular. It will arrange for all the W.P.I. workers to go through the jobs assigned to them, systematically working from the bottom upwards, performing varied functions in varied fields of administration, in varied localities, in varied conditions of work as regards nationalities, and so on.

In short, I assume that the comrades in the W.P.I. have learned something during these five years and will be able to apply the knowledge they have gained to the new organisation of the commissariat. Moreover, it should not be forgotten that we have, I believe, three scientific institutions carrying out research into problems of work organisation (the Central Institute of Labour, a special group under the W.P.I. and a group under the Military Commissariat). A meeting of these three groups was held recently,[495] and it is to be hoped that their work will now proceed in a more efficient manner and in a better team spirit than heretofore.

What is the new work organisation that I propose on the part of the Secretariat of our C.C.? Naturally, the increased number of C.C. members will require a new organisation of the work. I must point out, however, that actually we have already passed to a form of organisation of our C.C. plenums after the type of highest conferences. The thing now is to organise the training of these new C.C. members in all Central Committee work and familiarise them with the work of the leading state institutions. If we are late with this, we shall not be fulfilling one of our main duties, namely, that of taking advantage of our being in power in order to teach the best elements of the working people all the details of administration. Such measures as making better arrangements for the meetings of our Politbureau, holding them twice a week and reducing the length of sittings, better preparation of all the documents for these meetings and arranging for these documents to be at the disposal of all the members of the C.C. in good time. These measures now follow from the entire course of the work and are essential, so much so that any kind of objection to this is hardly conceivable. Naturally, this will call for an increase in expenditure on secretarial type personnel, but to grudge the money for these expenses would be most unwise.

Besides, frankly speaking, an important advantage in increasing the number of C.C. members I consider to be the diminished chances of a personal, incidental element being introduced in its decisions; these decisions will be better prepared, the endorsements made at such meetings will be more thoroughly verified, and as a result there will be greater stability in our C.C., both as regards the continuity of its work and its power to resist splits that might arise from insufficient contact of this body with the masses.

Lenin

January 13, 1923

Taken down by L. F.

Dictated January 9 and 13, 1923

First published in 1959
in *Lenin Miscellany XXXVI*

Printed from the secretary's
notes (typewritten copy)

APPENDIX

QUESTIONNAIRE FOR DELEGATES
OF THE NINTH CONGRESS OF THE R.C.P.(B.)

1. Name in full: Vladimir Ilyich Ulyanov
                         (Lenin)

2. No. of delegate's card $\frac{\text{voting}}{\text{debating}*}$:   381

3. What organisation do you belong to (Uyezd, Gubernia):
       Moscow

4. Membership of your organisation: 35,000

5. How were you elected (at gubernia conference, uyezd conference, general meeting, etc.) and when:
       Moscow city conference

6. Number of Party members represented at the gubernia conference, uyezd conference, or general meeting, at which you were elected to the congress: 35,000

7. Age: 50

8. Education: university

9. Former profession (state definitely), or what professions do you know:
                former: barrister's assistant
                publicist

10. Nationality: Russian

11. Family status: married

       Party work.

12. When did you become a member of the R.C.P. (year, month):
       in 1893

---

* The word "debating" is crossed out by Lenin.—*Ed.*

13. What All-Russia Party congresses did you attend:
Practically all, I believe

14. What Party work have you done, when and where:
member of the C.C. and editor of the Central Organ

15. How long have you been doing illegal Party work:
1893-1917

16. What Party work are you doing now:
member of the C.C.
Chairman of the C.P.C. and the Council of Defence

17. Did you belong to any other party before joining the R.C.P., when and how long: no

Soviet administrative work.

18. What Soviet administrative work have you done, when, where:
Chairman of the C.P.C. and the Council of Defence

19. What Soviet administrative work are you doing now: the same

20. What trade unions did you belong to, and when, and what t.u. do you belong to now: none

21. Were you persecuted for doing Party work, when and on what occasions:
was arrested in 1887, 1894 and 1900

22. Where were you at the beginning of the February revolution (in exile, penal servitude, prison, abroad, in military service, factory employment, etc.):
in emigration (in Zurich)

23 How long were you in prison: 14 months plus several days

   „   „   „   „   in exile: 3 years
   „   „   „   „   penal servitude: I was not
   „   „   „   „   in emigration: 1900-1905 and 1908-1917

Signed: *V. Ulyanov (Lenin)*
29th of March, 1920

First published in 1934 in the book
The Ninth Congress of the R.C.P.(B.)
Moscow (facsimile)

Printed from the form filled in
by Lenin

REREGISTRATION FORM FOR MEMBERS
OF THE MOSCOW ORGANISATION
OF THE R.C.P.(B.)

1) Name in full: Vladimir Ilyich Ulyanov

2) Age: 50   years

3) Place of birth (gubernia, town, uyezd, volost, village):
town of Simbirsk

4) Parents' profession and their address: dead

5) Members of your family (by age) and number of dependents:

wife   51

brother   45

sister   44

6) Do you own immovable property (land allotment, house) or means of production and where: no

7) Nationality: } Russian
8) Mother-tongue: }

9) In what languages, besides Russian, do you speak, read, write (underline):

French, German, English; all 3 poorly

10) Basic profession: litterateur

11) What education did you receive and where:

a) General   ⌠ High School
b) Special   ⎱ Passed university extern examinations
               ⎰ in 1891 at law faculty

12) Have you been abroad, when and where:

1895; 1900-1905; 1907-1917 in emigration (Switzerland, France, England, Germany, Galicia)

13) What localities of Russia do you know well:

I lived only on the Volga and in the capital cities

14) Were you in military service in the old army (rank, unit and how long):　no

15) Did you take part in fighting and were you wounded (where and when):

no

16) In what enterprise or office are you working at the present time (its address and telephone No.), in what post:

C.P.C.

17) What salary do you get and are you doing any by-work:

$13^1/_2$ thousand (13,500)[496]

by-work—literary

18) How long have you been a member of the R.C.P.:

since its foundation and earlier (1893)

19) Did you join during Party Week:　—no—

20) What organisation originally admitted you to membership of the R.C.P.:

see § 18

21) Did you attend lectures on socio-political questions, where, when, and did you take a course in the rudiments of political knowledge and what grade:

— —

22) What Party cell do you belong to:

Kremlin subdistrict

23) Were you on party trial, when and what for:

by the Mensheviks in the R.S.D.L.P. during splits

24) Did you belong to any other party, what party and when and in what capacity:　no

25) What documents or certificates do you have testifying that you were in our illegal Party organisation:

history of the Party—document

26) Chief places of previous work:

1. Before the February revolution:

        a) civil work:

        b) Party work:

2. Before the October Revolution:

        a) civil work:

        b) Party work:

abroad and Petrograd

27) What was your part in the February revolution:

    apart from general Party work, none

        (in emigration)

28) Ditto in October Revolution: member of the C.C.

29) Were you subject to repressive measures for political crimes, where and when, and what sentence did you serve:

    arrest   1887 (several days)

       ,,   1895-1897 (14 months and 3 years

       ,,   exile in Eastern Siberia)

              1900 (several days)

30) What trade union did you belong to, where and when:

        none

31) What trade union do you belong to at present (give No. of membership card): none

32) Did you hold elective office after the February revolution and where:

    a) Administrative: Chairman of the C.P.C.

    b) Trade Union: no

    c) Party: member of the C.C.

    d) Factory:

    e) Army units: } no

    f) Others:

33) Did you undergo military training (army rank) and are you registered in the Special Detachment, if so in what company and what number: no

34) Were you mobilised in the Red Army, when, by what organisation and under what arrangement (general mobilisation or Party mobilisation), how long were you at the front and where (indicate exactly), what duties did you perform, did you take part in the fighting, were you wounded, when and where: no

35) Were you mobilised for transport work, when and by what organisation: no

36) What Party and administrative work can you do (organiser, administrator, lecturer, propagandist, culture worker, etc.):

— —

37) Did you ever address big meetings and preside at them:

yes

38) What Party work are you doing at the present time:

member of the C.C.

39) What further information do you wish to give:

— —

40) Your address and telephone No :

Kremlin. Upper switchboard

41) What works of Marx, Engels, Lenin, Kautsky and Plekhanov have you read:

practically all works (of underlined authors)

42) On what subjects did you have occasion to address the workers and peasants or read lectures:

mostly political

43) Do you write articles for the newspapers, where and on what subjects:

seldom, on political subjects

44) Can you write leaflets and appeals, and what have you written in this field:

Yes. Rather too numerous to list

45) In what field of knowledge do you feel strongest and on what subjects can you read lectures or conduct lessons:

mostly on political questions

(Signed:)   *V. Ulyanov (Lenin)*

17/IX.1920

First published in 1926
in the book: *"Personal File"*
R.C.P. B. Member V. I. Ulyanov (Lenin)
Moskovsky Rabochy Publishing House,
Moscow-Leningrad

Printed from the form filled in
by Lenin

QUESTIONNAIRE FOR DELEGATES
OF THE NINTH ALL-RUSSIA CONFERENCE
OF THE R.C.P. (BOLSHEVIKS)

1. Name in full: Vladimir Ilyich Ulyanov

2. No. of delegate's card $\frac{\text{debating}}{\text{voting}}$ not yet received

3. By what organisation delegated: Central Committee

4. Age: 50 years

5. Education: university

6. Former profession (state definitely) or what professions do you know:
litterateur

7. Nationality: Russian

8. When did you join the R.C.P. (year, month):
1893, formally 1898

9. What Party work are you doing at the present time:
Member of the C.C.

10. What administrative work are you doing at the present time:
Chairman of the C.P.C. and Chairman
of the Council of Defence

11. What trade unions do you belong to:
none

12. Did you belong to any other party before joining the R.C.P. when and for how long: no

Signed: V. Ulyanov (Lenin)

20.IX. 1920

First published in 1959
in *Lenin Miscellany XXXVI*

Printed from the form filled in
by Lenin

QUESTIONNAIRE FOR DELEGATES
OF THE TENTH ALL-RUSSIA CONGRESS
OF THE R.C.P.

1. Surname:	Ulyanov (Lenin)
2. First name and patronymic:	Vladimir Ilyich
3. What Party organisation do you belong to (gubernia, town, uyezd army, division):	C.C., R.C.P. Moscow
4. No. of delegate's card $\frac{voting}{debating}$	No. 21. debating [497]
5. How were you elected (at gubernia conference, uyezd conference, army conference, division conference, general meeting, etc.) and when:	from the C.C. debating delegate
6. Number of Party members represented—at gubernia, uyezd, army, division conferences at which you were elected to the congress:	C.C. of 19 people
7. What All-Russia Party congresses did you attend:	all except that of July 1917 (or August?)
8. Date of birth:	1870

9. State of health or disablement:	in good health
10. Family status (number of members of the family and dependents):	wife and sister live together with me
11. Nationality:	Russian
12. Mother-tongue:	Russian
13. What other languages do you know and how well	English, German, French poorly; Italian very poorly
14. What localities of Russia do you know well and how long did you live there:	best of all the Volga district where I was born and lived till 17
15. Were you abroad (when, where and how long):	in a number of countries of Western Europe 1895; 1900-1905; 1908-1917
16. Military training:	none
17. Education (at what educational establishments did you study; did you graduate, if not how many classes or courses did you complete):	graduated Petrograd University (passed extern examinations), law faculty in 1891

18. Basic occupation up to 1917:	litterateur
19. What trades do you know:	none
20. What occupations were you engaged in after 1917 apart from Party, administrative, trade union and other similar work:	apart from those listed, only literary work
21. What trade union do you belong to at the present time:	Journalists' Union

22. What work have you been doing since 1917—administrative, military, trade union, business (apart from Party) work:

When (date from/to, indicate month/year)	Where (gub., uyezd, town, army, div.)	In what agency	In what post
from X. 1917 to III. 1921	Moscow	C.P.C. and C.L.D.	chairman

23. What work—administrative, military, business, trade union are you doing at the time of filling in this form (apart from Party work):

When (date from/to, indicate month/year)	Where (gub., uyezd, town, army, div.)	In what agency	In what post
since X. 1917	Moscow	C.P.C. and C.L.D.	chairman

24. How long have you been a member of the R.C.P.(Bolsheviks):	since 1894
25. Did you belong to any other parties, if so, to which, when and for how long:	no

26. Did you take part in the revolutionary movement before 1917:

When (date from/to)	Where (gub., uyezd, town)	In what organisation	What work
1892-1893	Samara		
1894-1895	St. Petersburg		
1895-1897	prison	illegal S.D. circles, and after the founding of the R.S.D.L.P. its member	
1898-1900	Siberia (Yenisei Gubernia)		
1900-1905	abroad		
1905-1907	St. Petersburg		
1908-1917	abroad		

27. Were you subject to repressive measures for revolutionary activities (when, on what occasions):	1887 arrest; 1895-1897 arrest; 1898-1900 Siberia; 1900 arrest

28. How long were you in:

prison	several days
penal servitude	+ 14 months
exile	I was not
emigration	three years
	9-10 years

29. What Party work have you been doing since 1917:

When (date from/to, indicate month/year)	Where (gub., uyezd, town, army, div., etc.)	In what agency	In what post
from X. 1917 to III. 1921	Moscow	C.C.	member C.C.

30. What Party work are you doing at the time of filling in this form:

When (from what date)	Where (town, gub., uyezd, army, div.)	In what agency	In what post
from X. 1917 to III. 1921	Moscow	C.C.	member C.C.

31. Were you on trial before a Court of Law of the RSFSR or a Party court (when, where, on what charge):	no

7th of March 1921

Delegate's signature:

V. Ulyanov (Lenin)

First published in part
January 21, 1926
in the newspaper *Na Smenu*
(Sverdlovsk) No. 5

Published in full in 1932
in *Lenin Miscellany XX*

Printed from the form filled in
by Lenin

QUESTIONNAIRE FOR DELEGATES
OF THE ELEVENTH ALL-RUSSIA CONFERENCE
OF THE R.C.P.(BOLSHEVIKS)

1. Name in full: Ulyanov (Lenin) Vladimir Ilyich

2. With what voice (voting or <u>debating</u>) are you attending?

3. Delegate's card: No. 1

4. What organisation delegated you: C.C., R.C.P.

5. What All-Russia Party conferences and congresses did you attend as a voting delegate:

congresses: all, except those of 1898   conferences:
and the summer of 1917   practically all

6. Year of birth: 1870

7. Nationality: Russian

8. Education (elementary, secondary, <u>higher</u>)

9. a) Basic profession and speciality up to 1917:
        litterateur

   b) How many years have you worked at this profession:
        from 1894 to 1917, i.e., 23 years

10. a) Principal means of livelihood before 1914:

   literary earnings and salary from the Party

   b) during 1914-1917:   ditto
   c) during 1917-1921:   ditto up to 25.X. 1917. After
                           25/X salary from the Soviet
                           Government

11. What administrative work are you doing at present:

   Chairman of the C.P.C. and C.L.D.

12. What part are you taking at present:
   a) in co-operative work ⎫ I am not taking any actual part
   b) in trade union work ⎬

13. What Party work are you doing at the present time:

   member of the C.C., R.C.P.

14. When did you join the R.C.P.:   in 1895

15. Did you previously belong to any other parties, if so when and
   to which: no

16. Were you subject to repressive measures for revolutionary
   activity (when):

      arrest and exile in 1887; arrest and exile
      to Eastern Siberia 1895 (XII) — 1900

   How long were you:

   1) in prison: for several days in 1887 and 1900; 14 months
                              1895-1897

   2) in penal servitude: not at all

   3) in exile: three years (Yenisei Gubernia, Minusinsk
                              Uyezd)

   4) in emigration: 1900-1905 and 1908-1917

                        Signed: *V. Ulyanov* (*Lenin*)

   14th of December 1921

First published in 1959   Printed from the form filled in
in *Lenin Miscellany XXXVI*   by Lenin

ALL-RUSSIA CENSUS FORM FOR MEMBERS OF THE R.C.P.(B.)

February 13, 1922

| C.C.,R.C.P.
STATISTICAL DEPT.
Form "A"
No. 38 | ALL-RUSSIA CENSUS
OF MEMBERS
OF THE RUSSIAN
COMMUNIST PARTY
(BOLSHEVIKS)
1922 | Workers
of the World,
Unite! |

1. Location of Party cell: $\frac{town}{vil.}$ Moscow $\frac{uyezd}{volost}$ Zam-district

   $\frac{gub.}{region}$ Kremlin area No. 1

2. Name of enterprise (office, army unit) at which the cell is organised: C.P.C., Party card 224,332

3. Name of Party organisation which issued the card: Zam-district committee

4. Surname: Ulyanov (Lenin)

5. First name and patronymic: Vladimir Ilyich

6. Sex: M. 7. Date of birth: born in 1870; age: 52 years

8. Spoken language: Russian 9. What other languages can you freely speak: I can freely speak in none

10. a) Do you hold any religious beliefs (convictions)? (yes, no) specify which: No

    b) If you are an atheist, state since what age: 16

11. Number of members of the family (excluding the signer):
    dependents: two
    working: two

12. Education: a) can you read and write (yes, no): Yes
    b) if you studied or are studying, state: —

Table I. Educational Qualification

Type of school (2-class rural zemstvo, 4-class town school; technical vocational school; evening motor classes; aviation classes, high school); university; Party school). Out-of-school education to be indicated by the words "self-taught", "home-taught"	How many years did you study	Did you finish school (yes, no, finished such-and-such a class, still studying)
13	14	15
a. Finished classic school in 1887 b. and passed university finals c. at extern law faculty in 1891	8 years (in classic school)	Finished classic school. Passed extern university finals

16. If you have a desire to study, what would you take up (reading and writing, the sciences, arts, trades — specify which):—

Table II. Social and National Origin

Relation to the signer	Basic profession or occupation, post, rank	Trade status (employer; self-employed, wage-worker, professional man, houseowner, housewife)	Nationality
17	18	19	20
1. Grandfather (on father's side)	I don't know		
2. Father............	Director of elementary schools		
3. Mother............	—		

21. At what age did you start earning your own living: at 27 (approximately); as employee or self-employed: litterateur
22. a) Basic profession and speciality before 1917: litterateur
    b) How many years have you worked at this profession:

    about 20 (1897-1917)

23. Principal source of income before 1914:
    literary work and salary from the Party.
    in 1914-1917: Ditto

Table III. Record of Employment from 1917 to Date

Work period	Place of work				Length of employment			
	Name of enterprise (office, army unit) where you have worked no less than 3 months and where you are working at present	Town or gubernia	Kind of occupation	Employed, elected, appointed	Period, from/to		Total employment	
					Month year	Month year	Years	Months
24	25	26	27	28	29	30	31	32
A. From 1917 to time of entering present employment	a	....	.....	....	....	.....	---	---
	b	....	.....	....	....	.....	---	---
	c	....	.....	....	....	.....	---	---
	d	....	.....	....	....	.....	---	---
	e	....	.....	....	....	.....	---	---
B. At time of filling in this form:	a. from X. 1917 Chairman C.P.C.	Moscow		By appointment	from 25. X. 1917		4	3
	b.		.....	....	....		---	---

33. Last monthly pay: (monetary): wage category 17, basic rate .... rubles, total pay 4,700,000 rubles

Table IV. Length of Party Membership

Name of Party and Group	Status in the organisation ("professional", committee member, Committee Secretary, organiser, agitator, propagandist; combat-squad member, technical worker, rank-and-file member)	Place of work (town, gubernia)	Period of Party membership		
			Joined (year, month)	Quitted (year, month)	Total length of Party membership (in years and months)
34	35	36	37	38	39
R.C.P.(B.)	professional, C.C. member	Moscow	1895 (actually)	—	about 27 years

Table V. Revolutionary Record

Participation	Number of occasions
40	41
1. In economic strikes	—
2. In political „	—
Total	
3. In street political demonstrations	—
4. In students' movements	(1887)
5. In illegal circles	many
6. In illegal mass rallies and meetings	many
7. In May Day rallies	
8. In armed uprisings and partisan actions	—
9. In Party conferences	} In practi-
10. In Party congresses	} cally all

42. Prison record: a) length of imprisonment: years 1 months 2; in administrative exile: years 3 months —; deportation years — months—; political emigration: years about 10 months ....; number of escapes: —

43. a) What newspapers and magazines did you read in 1921 (name them): various

    b) Regularly, occasionally, never: irregularly

    c) If you never read, state why (no newspapers, no time, no interest) —

    d) If you do read state where (at home, at work, at a library, reading-room, on paper stands: at home

44. a) How long have you been a member of a trade union: from 19............

    b) Do you take part at the present time in trade union work (yes, no): no

    c) If you do, specify what:

Table VI. Military Record as Serviceman and Political Commissar

In what army	Arm of service and specialty (infantry, cavalry, artillery, sappers, engineers)	Military rank (private, company commander)	Length of service				Number or occasions of				
			Date, from/to		Total service		Participation		Wounds		Military awards
			Month, year	Month, year	Years	Months	In skirmishes	In hand-to-hand fighting	Firearm	Cold steel	
45	46	47	48	49	50	51	52	53	54	55	56
1. In tsarist army	✗ 0										
2. In White army											
3. In Green army											
4. In Red army											

57. If you were not in military service, did you undergo General Military Training (yes, no): No

58. When were you demobilised month——— of, year 19 ———

59. a) If you are a town dweller or a worker do you maintain any contacts with the village (yes, no) ———
    b) If so, specify (I have a farm, a market garden, a bee-garden, etc., of my own or in partnership with other persons) ———
    c) What is your part in this business (personal labour, financial support) ———

Notes:

Town of *Moscow* -- February 13, 1922

V. Ulyanov (Lenin)

First published in part
(facsimile of the first page)
in 1924 in the magazine
Ogonyok No. 7

First published in full
(facsimile) in 1926 in the book:
I. G. Lazyan
"Personal File" of R.C.P.(B.)
Member V. I. Ulyanov (Lenin),
Moskovsky Rabochy Publishing
House, Moscow-Leningrad

Printed from the form filled in
by Lenin

QUESTIONNAIRE FOR DELEGATES
OF THE ELEVENTH CONGRESS
OF THE R.C.P.(BOLSHEVIKS)

1. Name in full:......Vladimir Ilyich Ulyanov*

2. Are you attending as debating or voting delegate:

3. Delegate's card No.:

4. What organisation have you been delegated by:......Moscow

5. Age:.....52 years

6. Nationality:......Russian

7. Education:......university

8. What social group do you belong to (worker, peasant, office employee):

9. How long have you worked at your profession: 28 years as litterateur

10. What Party work are you doing at the present time:
member of the C.C.,R.C.P.

11. What administrative work are you doing at the present time:
Chairman of the C.P.C. and C.L.D.

12. What part are you taking at the present time:
    a) in the co-operative movement ⎫ no part
    b) in the trade union movement ⎭

13. When did you join the R.C.P.:......at its foundation (1895)

14. Did you previously belong to any other parties, when, which:
No

Signed: *V. Ulyanov (Lenin)*

27th of March 1922

First published in 1930
in *Lenin Miscellany XIII*   Printed from the form filled
                                                  in part by Lenin

----

* The answers printed in small type are in the handwriting of Lenin's sister Maria.—*Ed.*

JOURNAL
OF LENIN'S
DUTY SECRETARIES[498]

November 21, 1922-March 6, 1923

November 21, morning (entry by N. S. Alliluyeva).

In the morning Vladimir Ilyich received Gorbunov.[499] After 11.30 Kamenev; meeting at 6 o'clock.[500] There have been no orders. Lydia Alexandrovna [Fotieva] has a paper[501] for voting* which Vladimir Ilyich asked to be reminded of from 5-6 p.m. in order to have a talk with Stalin. But Lydia Alexandrovna kept it and said that the explanations he wished to receive from Stalin she would give him herself, so there was no need to remind him, but Lydia Alexandrovna would remind him. Kamenev 10.15-10.45.

November 21, evening.

Haskell—11.30 ⎫
Stalin—12.30 ⎬ appointment for November 22**
Re Haskell and Lers (interpreter), orders given to the commandant's office.

November 22, morning (entry by N. S. Alliluyeva).

I. Morning no orders. Appointments kept.

[For] the evening—Kivdilo and Brodovsky at 6 o'clock (workers of the porcelain works),*** will be received in the following order: at 6 they will arrive at Gorbunov's office and he will interview them and inform us, and then Vladimir Ilyich will drop in for a minute.

An order has to be given concerning the pass (through the Troitsky Gate).

Notes in the "Execution" column:

* Voted. Passed on to the Politbureau. Chicherin and Stalin informed. Volodicheva.

** Haskell [502]—through Kamenev. Lers—interpreter. Stalin—carried out. Both received.

*** Kivdilo and Brodovsky have been notified through Zax,[503] all information about them can be got from Zax.

II. Vladimir Ilyich has given a letter, strictly confidential, concerning Haskell's proposal, to be sent round to all the members of the Politbureau and Chicherin. Eight copies have been sent to Nazaretyan[504] to be circulated for voting.* Check with Burakova[505]—received.

III. Gorbunov's papers addressed to the presiding committee of the Fifth All-Russia Congress of the Soviet Employees Trade Union[506] to be given to Vladimir Ilyich to sign (to be returned to Gorbunov after signing).

November 23, morning (entry by N. S. Alliluyeva).

At 11 in the morning Vladimir Ilyich has a meeting of the Politbureau up to 2.30.[507] So far no orders have been given.

If Vladimir Ilyich asks about the letter to Hoover he is to be told that Chicherin is seeing to that himself. Haskell is leaving today at 7.20. The letter will be handed to him through Lander (as Vladimir Ilyich asked). No reception for the evening so far.

November 23, evening (entry by S. M. Manucharyants).

At 5.40 Vladimir Ilyich was in his office. Asked for the packet from Sklyansky[508] and when the Politbureau minutes would be ready and how this was being handled technically. I got in touch with Sklyansky, who promised to deliver the packet in the morning of November 24.

6.45 packet to Sokolnikov.[509]

8.05 Vladimir Ilyich wanted to talk with Stalin, who proved to be engaged at a meeting of the Central Committee Secretariat. Vladimir Ilyich said: "either in the evening or the morning, there's no need to bother him now." At 8.30 he left.

Vladimir Ilyich looked through all the new books. I gave Vladimir Ilyich the packet from Zinoviev[510] and the material from Zax. Vladimir Ilyich asked for the agenda of the meeting of the Large Council of People's Commissars and gave a letter to be translated from Russian into English. At 10.05 Vladimir Ilyich left.

Note in the "Execution" column:

* Forwarded 15/20 min. No. 8565.

November 24, *morning* (entry by N. S. Alliluyeva).

Vladimir Ilyich wanted to receive Meisner (of the Fishing Industry Board), he may possibly receive him today—so far it is unknown.

Possibly this evening or tomorrow in the daytime Vladimir Ilyich will receive Sklyansky and Pantsendjansky on the question of the ship-repair programme.* [511]

Vladimir Ilyich asked that Earsman and Garden[512]—delegates of the Australian Party, should be kept on phone call this evening from 5 to 9, they will be waiting in the "Luxe" 294, can be called through the commandant's office.

Burakova phoned, asked that Chicherin's proposal concerning Vorovsky's wire about the Straits be given to Vladimir Ilyich for voting.** [513]

November 24, *evening* (entry by S. M. Manucharyants).

Before the meeting Vladimir Ilyich received Kamenev. From 6 to 7.30 Vladimir Ilyich was at the meeting of the Council of Labour and Defence.[514] The question of the composition of the commission in connection with the statement by the C.C. of Georgia was handed to Vladimir Ilyich from the Politbureau for voting.[515] Vladimir Ilyich did not vote.

Passed on the voting on the Straits to be forwarded to the Politbureau. 7.30-8.30 Sklyansky, and then Krzhizhanovsky—at the flat.

November 25, *morning* (entry by N. S. Alliluyeva).

Vladimir Ilyich is unwell,[516] he stayed only five minutes in his office, dictated three letters over the phone,[517] to which he wanted inquiries made later for answers.

Maria Ilyinichna [Ulyanova] said that he should not be bothered in any way—if he asked about the answers himself, then inquiries should be made in the proper quarters. No reception, no orders so far. There are two packets from Stalin and Zinoviev[518]—but this to be kept under the hat until special instructions and permission are given.

Notes in the "Execution" column:
* Sklyansky was received.
** Forwarded to Politbureau in the evening.

November 25, evening.

Came at 6 o'clock. Spoke on the telephone for several minutes. A. D. Tsyurupa was with him from 6.30 to 7.30. Afterwards, left immediately, asking that all Kamenev's papers on his desk in two folders should be sent to Tsyurupa,[519] and the articles on the Urquhart concession to Chicherin.[520] This has been done. (But part of the materials is with Nikolai Petrovich [Gorbunov] or in the files.)

Chicherin asked Vladimir Ilyich to be told that he would like to receive personal instructions concerning the Urquhart concession. He (Chicherin) is leaving tomorrow evening. This has to be reported first thing in the morning on Sunday. (Not yet reported.)

8.30 to 8.45 telephone conversation. Gorbunov asked for all the materials concerning the trusts, questions of financing and information from Kamenev's secretariat to be passed on to him, as Vladimir Ilyich had asked him to show them to Tsyurupa. I have already sent Tsyurupa the opinions on the trusts and the information from Kamenev—Tsyurupa has received them and asked they should be left with him for a time to study. Apparently, Nikolai Petrovich has given him some other materials.

I have not shown the packets. But they are all apparently very important. Lydia Alexandrovna ought to be consulted about this.

November 26, Sunday, morning (entry by S. M. Manucharyants).

Vladimir Ilyich arrived at 12, spoke on the telephone, sorted out the books, took several with him. Left at 1.30, taking V. Milyutin's report[521] and other papers.

November 26, Sunday, evening (entry by S. M. Manucharyants).

Vladimir Ilyich came at 6.50, spoke on the telephone. At 7.30 Tsyurupa arrived. At 8.30 Tsyurupa left, and so did Vladimir Ilyich.

November 27, morning (entry by N. S. Alliluyeva).

Vladimir Ilyich was in his office round about 12, asked for no one and shortly went away. Through Nadezhda

Konstantinovna asked for all the materials on foreign trade. All sent to his flat. No orders so far, no reception. No packets either.

November 27, evening (entry by M. A. Volodicheva).

Gorbunov asked, if possible, that the paper from Zinoviev in connection with Münzenberg[522] be given to Vladimir Ilyich to sign (if received) and the materials on foreign trade to be passed on to him (Gorbunov), since Vladimir Ilyich had asked him to show them to Tsyurupa. But today Vladimir Ilyich has not given them. They are at his flat. No orders from Vladimir Ilyich. A little after 6 I gave orders to the commandant's office to admit Kramer[523] to the flat. Quite a few packets. Among them the mail from Berlin.

November 28, morning (entry by N. S. Alliluyeva).

Vladimir Ilyich did not come to his office, spoke twice on the phone with Lydia Alexandrovna.* Asked for Sorokin's article in *Ekonomicheskaya Zhizn* for November 26[225] concerning 159 directives**—then gave orders to Lydia Alexandrovna; no orders for the evening so far. I am not leaving the packets either.

November 28, evening (entry by S. M. Manucharyants).

At 7.45 Vladimir Ilyich asked to get hold of Avanesov[526] and ask him whether he could phone him. Phoned a second time and gave his number. I told Vladimir Ilyich that Avanesov was at a board conference of the Workers' and Peasants' Inspection. "Then don't trouble, I'll ring you in the morning." There was a paper for Vladimir Ilyich to sign from Gorbunov to the Presidium of the All-Russia Central Executive Committee, copies to Bogdanov[527] and Fomin[528] on the question of the All-Russia C.E.C. revising the decision to transfer the creosoting works from the Supreme Economic Council to the People's Commissariat for Railways.[529] Vladimir Ilyich signed it (at his flat and passed it on to the Secretariat).

Notes in the "Execution" column:

* See supplementary card.[524]

** Article cut out, pasted and sent to his flat.

November 29, morning (entry by N. S. Alliluyeva).

Vladimir Ilyich was in his office at 12.20, sent for Stalin, who sat till 13.40. No orders for the evening. No packets either so far.

November 29, evening (entry by M. A. Volodicheva).

Notice from the Politbureau (8812) that the question of the Union Republics will be discussed at the Politbureau tomorrow (sent not for information, but for consideration).[530]

Vladimir Ilyich phoned from 5.30 till 6. Asked whether the paper on the ship-repair programme had been received from Stalin. Talked for several minutes on the phone with Kamenev. Dictated over the phone his views on the ship-repair programme which he asked to be sent to Stalin and Kamenev (this has been done).[531]

Asked whether a telegram had been sent to Haskell in London. The duty secretary in Chicherin's office answered in the affirmative.* He will send confirmation in writing tomorrow morning. Vladimir Ilyich has been informed.

Avanesov was from 7.50 to 8.55. They talked in Vladimir Ilyich's office. Left at 9. During the talk with Avanesov inquired what date the plenum of the Central Committee was fixed for. Tomorrow this question is on the order of the day of the Politbureau (together with the agenda), and at the last plenum of the C.C. it was decided to time the plenum to the Congress of Soviets. This has been reported to Vladimir Ilyich.[532]

November 30, morning (entry by N. S. Alliluyeva).

Vladimir Ilyich came to his office at 1.10, phoned and asked for No. 763 of *Posledniye Novosti* [Latest News] for October 13. He was interested in Peshekhonov's article there.[533] I found it and took it to his flat. Vladimir Ilyich was in his office exactly five minutes and went home at once. No orders. No packets either. Lydia Alexandrovna asked to make a note—just for information—that Haskell's and Chicherin's packets addressed to Vladimir Ilyich had been handed to Kamenev.

Note in the "Execution" column:

* Copy of the telegram mailed to Haskell over Litvinov's signature. Received November 30.

November 30, evening (entry by S. M. Manucharyants).

Vladimir Ilyich came to his office at 6.45, asked what news there was and when the Politbureau meeting ended. I told Vladimir Ilyich that there were some new books. He asked to bring them to him. Returned the newspaper *Posledniye Novosti* for October 13.

At 7.55 Adoratsky[534] came to see Vladimir Ilyich, sat till 8.40. Vladimir Ilyich spoke on the telephone. Asked for the minutes of the Politbureau. I gave them to him. Vladimir Ilyich asked that the Politbureau minutes be put away. He asked that special care be taken of Engels's book "Political Testament".[535] Handed over the new books he had looked through. Vladimir Ilyich left at 9.

December 1, morning (entry by N. S. Alliluyeva).

Vladimir Ilyich phoned Lydia Alexandrovna at 11.20, asked to see Molotov at 12.*

Molotov and Syrtsov[536] called, were together from 12 till 1.30. No orders for the evening so far. No packets either.

December 1, evening (entry by S. M. Manucharyants).

Vladimir Ilyich arrived at 5.30, and at 5.45 Tsyurupa came.

Earsman, Garden and interpreter Voitinsky came at 7 o'clock and left at 8.40. Vladimir Ilyich left at 8.45.

December 2, morning (entry by N. S. Alliluyeva).

Vladimir Ilyich arrived at 12.30, stayed only 10 minutes, sent for Lydia Alexandrovna. Asked her to collect the materials on the Fishing Board for his interview with Knipovich,[537] which he asked to arrange for 7 p.m. The materials are with Gorbunov, see to it that they should all be here by 6 o'clock. Orders have to be given at all posts for Knipovich to be let through, as he has no pass.

The doctor was with Vladimir Ilyich in the morning and told him that once or even twice in two months Vladimir Ilyich had to go away for several days for a rest. On Tuesday he did not permit him to preside, but would permit him

---

Note in the "Execution" column:

* Molotov's appointment made for 12 He kept it.

on Thursday, but not for long—and after Thursday he was to go away positively for several days.

Gorbunov phoned and asked that Vladimir Ilyich be told at the first opportunity that Rykov had left Tiflis on December 1 by express train. Vladimir Ilyich has to be told this as he is very interested in it.

Vladimir Ilyich asked for Kamenev to see him at 8 p.m. (he phoned at 14.05).

Lydia Alexandrovna has to be reminded to find out from Vladimir Ilyich exactly what article of Kin's[538] he spoke to Tsyurupa about, as the latter can't find it.

December 2, evening.

From 6.30 in his office; from 7 to 8—Knipovich; from 8 to 9.15—Kamenev.

Gave English letter and asked to find out when Earsman was leaving. Inquiries made of "Luxe" commandant Kaizer, who said that Earsman would probably not be leaving today and that tomorrow he would report the exact day of his departure.* This, should then be reported to Vladimir Ilyich and the letter given to him.

Signed the letter to Münzenberg**[539] with the reservation that he does not agree to the beginning of the letter which is incorrectly worded in German. Asked for a copy to be left with him (No. 8579) in the Secretariat.

He has a letter to Svidersky to be signed, we have a copy. If he signs it, it is to be forwarded to destination.[540]

Gorbunov has handed in press cuttings***; one folder with fresh material, the other older. These are materials for Vladimir Ilyich's speech at the Congress of Soviets, which he asked to be collected. I think Lydia Alexandrovna should be asked whether it can be handed to him on Sunday.

Vladimir Ilyich asked that inquiries should be made of Belenky[541] as to when (exactly) Rykov and Dzerzhinsky

---

Notes in the "Execution" column:

* Kaizer reported: Earsman does not know himself when he is going away, but will spend a long time here, possibly even a few months.

** The letter has been delivered to Münzenberg through Gorbunov. M. Volodicheva.

*** Put on Vladimir Ilyich's desk.

are arriving.* He is very interested in this. I have not made inquiries of Belenky.

Vladimir Ilyich has been told that Frumkin is preparing the material and will send it in on Monday morning or Sunday evening.[542]

Vladimir Ilyich asked Gorbunov several times for Mikhailovsky's memo on the financial question. Nadya [Alliluyeva] must have it. He asked that both memos, Mikhailovsky's and Krasnoshchokov's[543], should be returned to him when finished with. Left at 9.30.

December 3, morning (entry by S. A. Flakserman).

Vladimir Ilyich came to his office at 2 p.m. Asked for the stenographer. Volodicheva was not at home, and Vladimir Ilyich said we shouldn't trouble to look for her as he did not have much writing to do and would do it by hand. Reported to Vladimir Ilyich: Belenky's information about the arrival of Rykov and Dzerzhinsky, also Kaizer's report on when Earsman is leaving. Vladimir Ilyich asked to find out through Voitinsky of the Comintern, who knows English, when Earsman wants the memo.

Vladimir Ilyich stayed in his office 20 m. and left.

December 3, Sunday evening (entry by S. A. Flakserman).

Vladimir Ilyich came to his office at 6 p.m.

Belenky reported that according to the information received from the People's Commissariat for Railways Rykov left Baku on December 3 and was expected at Rostov on December 5. A wire has been sent to Dzerzhinsky for checking. I did not tell Vladimir Ilyich.

6.45. Vladimir Ilyich asked to tell Avanesov that he received his letter, read it and would like to talk with him first over the phone.[544] Pass message on tomorrow morning.

At 7 p.m. Vladimir Ilyich left his office.

Note in the "Execution" column:

* Belenky reported that Dzerzhinsky was leaving Tiflis round about December 8, would stop on the way for inspections and be in Moscow round about December 13. Rykov left Tiflis on December 2 and will be here on December 4 in the morning. (As regards Rykov, he will check again and phone). Belenky phoned again and said that Rykov would be here at 6 p.m. today, said he would check it again and phone up. He has made inquiries down the line.

December 4, morning (entry by N. S. Alliluyeva).

Vladimir Ilyich came to his office at 11.05. Asked to get exact information on Rykov's arrival.* At 10.40 Vladimir Ilyich phoned to ask that Avanesov be invited at 11 a.m. Avanesov arrived at 11.15, left at 12.10. Talk was on the question of foreign trade. At 12.30 Vladimir Ilyich went to Gorbunov's office,[545] then came back and began to dictate to Volodicheva over the telephone, went home at 2. At 6 p.m. Vladimir Ilyich will be seeing Kolegayev[546] (telephone 174—14 or through Trotsky's switchboard).

When Rykov arrives (if Vladimir Ilyich is in the country by that time, he is leaving on Thursday) he is to be put through to Vladimir Ilyich.** At 5.50 Zhukov[547] is to be with Lenin for 10 minutes. From 7 to 8 Frumkin, from 8.15 to 9 Tsyurupa (tentatively, if this time is inconvenient to Vladimir Ilyich, then tomorrow at 11 or 12.30 a.m.).

December 4, evening (entry by S. M. Manucharyants).

At 5.30 Vladimir Ilyich dictated to Volodicheva a letter to Litvinov and greetings to the Third Congress of the Young Communist International.[548] Dialled and asked me what I have for the day, told him the schedule of reception. At 5.50 Kolegayev went in, on the closing of the theatres, up to 6.10. Soon after Zhukov went in with Holtzmann[549] and Lavrentyev, up to 6.50, talked about electrical industry. After them Frumkin went in at 6.50 till 7.25 on the question of foreign trade. At 7.30 Vladimir Ilyich left his office, at 8 o'clock he came into his office. Vladimir Ilyich asked about Litvinov's answer. Asked for Haskell's wire. Handed over the book by the Spaniard Cesar Reyes, asked that the inscription and contents of the book be translated.[550] The commission made up of Zinoviev, Trotsky and Bukharin met on December 4 (today) in the evening, to whom was sent a copy of Vladimir Ilyich's notes (addressed to

---

Note in the "Execution" column:

* I phoned Belenky, asked him again to find out exactly. Promised to answer this evening.
** Watch this.

Bukharin) on the question of the tasks of our delegation at the Hague:[551]

At 9 o'clock Vladimir Ilyich left his office.

December 5, morning (entry by N. S. Alliluyeva).

Litvinov reported that there was confirmation of receipt of the telegram by Haskell through our mission. Tell Vladimir Ilyich.

Vladimir Ilyich came to his office at 10.45, asked whether the Bukharin-Zinoviev-Trotsky commission had met. I told him it had that night; he left at 1.40.

At 6 o'clock Vladimir Ilyich is to receive the Czechoslovak workers (see list).[552] Orders have to be given to all posts to let them through; they have passes to the Kremlin (for 15 m.). They have been notified.

Popov[553] is coming at 7 for half an hour (notified). There should be a written report from Litvinov concerning receipt of the telegram by Haskell.

December 5, evening (entry by M. A. Volodicheva).

From 6 to 6.45 the Czechoslovaks: Josef Hans, Hamosta, Fránek, Richtér, Chapěra, with Antselovich.[554]

From 7 to 8 Popov (on the census). Several minutes break (went home). At 8.20 Tsyurupa in his office. Left at 9.25.

December 6, morning (entry by N. S. Alliluyeva).

Vladimir Ilyich came to his office a little after 11. He asked Lydia Alexandrovna to write several letters on his behalf (to Yakovleva, Kamenev, Tsyurupa[555]). Asked to be put through to Stalin, made arrangements to see him. At 12.40 Stalin came, sat with him till 2.20. Asked to invite Eiduk at 7.30, Dovgalevsky[556] at 6, Bogdanov at 7. After Stalin he wanted to talk with Meshcheryakov.*[557]

At 2.25 Vladimir Ilyich went home, Kamenev phoned, said he was sending a packet addressed to Comrade Lenin, has to be handed to him directly.**

Notes in the "Execution" column:

* He did not, as he was kept late.

** Received at a quarter to five and put on the desk. Volodicheva.

December 6, evening (entry by M. A. Volodicheva).

Kamenev's letter read by Vladimir Ilyich at 6 o'clock. From 6.05 to 6.30 Bogdanov; from 6.55 to 7.20 Eiduk; from 7.25 to—Dovgalevsky.

For 15-20 minutes dictated his reminiscences of N. Y. Fedoseyev.[558] Left a little after 9. Reminiscences at his request forwarded to Anna Ilyinicha [Yelizarova] (see copy of forwarding note).

December 7, morning (entry by N. S. Alliluyeva).

Vladimir Ilyich came to his office at 10.55; at 11 the Politbureau meeting started with Kamenev in the chair. Vladimir Ilyich attended.[559] Vladimir Ilyich left the meeting to go home at 2.20.

December 7, evening (entry by S. M. Manucharyants).

Vladimir Ilyich came to the office at 5.30, talked with Stalin and others over the phone, gave various orders for the Politbureau[560] and Yakovleva.[561] Left for Gorki at 6.15, taking with him current papers.[562]

December 8, morning (entry by N. S. Alliluyeva).

At 12.10 Vladimir Ilyich phoned Lydia Alexandrovna, talked with her about yesterday's decisions of the Politbureau.

At 12.15 the following were sent to Vladimir Ilyich with Belenky: 1) minutes of the Politbureau No. 39[563] and 2) list of key-post executives of all-Russia and district level (from Syrtsov). Vladimir Ilyich wanted to phone a little later and dictate something.

December 8, evening (entry by S. M. Manucharyants).

Vladimir Ilyich phoned at 5.35, dictated to Volodicheva[564]; at 5.50 Lydia Alexandrovna spoke with Vladimir Ilyich, who voted on three Politbureau questions: the wire from Vorovsky, Mdivani, Chicherin dated December 7, 1922,[565] the composition of the commission to examine the resolutions for the Tenth Congress of Soviets, and greetings to the All-Ukraine Congress.[566] Dictated standing order for the Politbureau.[567] Agrees to putting off the plenum.[568] Finished speaking at 6.20. Medicine from Berlin sent.

December 9, morning (entry by N. S. Alliluyeva).

No orders left in the evening. Maria Ilyinichna phoned, saying that Vladimir Ilyich was going to dictate something at 5.45, and at 6 he was to talk with Rykov—the latter has arrived and is sitting at home. No orders. Some packets have come in.

December 9, evening (entry by M. A. Volodicheva).

Vladimir Ilyich phoned at 6.05, gave instructions. His letters concerning the work of the deputies[569] sent off to Rykov, Stalin, Tsyurupa and Kamenev.

Belenky is to bring a packet for Vladimir Ilyich from Kamenev.

Vladimir Ilyich's letter in French will be returned by Souvarine this evening.[570]

Vladimir Ilyich is being sent: 1) his letter on the work of the deputies (original, copy and copy of the old decree[571]), letter from Zetkin and medicine.

December 10, morning.

Nothing from Vladimir Ilyich.

December 10, evening.

Phoned a little after 6, asked to be put through to Stalin. Voted on the telegram from Kirov, Vasilyev and Poluyan concerning the S.R.s.[572]

Send by hand, at first opportunity, Vladimir Ilyich's letter to Lazzari in French, corrected by Souvarine; it has been left at the gate; at 8.45 Vladimir Ilyich asked to send Frumkin his letter asking for his comments on Avanesov's theses. Sent. Find out tomorrow morning from Frumkin when he is sending his comments.[573]

Also make inquiries of Gorbunov first thing in the morning (see copies Nos. 8605 and 8606).[574]

The letter to Lazzari should not be sent specially. To be sent only by hand. Vladimir Ilyich said so.

December 11, morning (entry by N. S. Alliluyeva).

No orders given. Vladimir Ilyich did not phone once. Check the temperature in his office, to be no less than 14 degreees. (R.)

December 11, evening (entry by S. M. Manucharyants).

There have been no orders. Vladimir Ilyich did not phone once.

December 12, morning (entry by N. S. Alliluyeva).

Vladimir Ilyich arrived in Moscow at 11, came to his office at 11.15, stayed there a short time and went home before 12. At 12 he was to see Rykov, Kamenev and Tsyurupa.*

Vladimir Ilyich left his office at 2 o'clock. Rykov, Kamenev and Tsyurupa sat with him till 2.

For the evening so far nothing.

December 12, evening (entry by M. A. Volodicheva).

Vladimir Ilyich in his office at 5.30. Spoke on the phone for several minutes. Gave a letter to the Italian Lazzari to be sent off and asked to see to it that the person taking it was a trustworthy comrade. Dzerzhinsky from 6 to 6.45.[575]

Stomonyakov[576]—(question of the foreign trade monopoly)—7.45.

Left at 8.15.

Vladimir Ilyich's letter to Lazzari forwarded to Souvarine ("Luxe", 23). He will make arrangements with reliable comrades and let us know about it tomorrow morning, or better still will phone him**.

December 13, morning (entry by L. A. Fotieva).

Doctors came at 11. Ordered complete rest, he was to leave town.[577]

Round about 12 sent for Fotieva for winding up affairs. Dictated letters: to the Central Committee concerning Rozhkov,[578] to Frumkin, Stomonyakov and Trotsky concerning foreign trade,[579] and to his deputies concerning distribution of functions.[580] At 12.30 Stalin came, left at 2.35.

Note in the "Execution" column:

* Saw them.

** Check carefully at Vladimir Ilyich's request. Souvarine signed for the letter, his personal signature received.

December 13, evening (entry by L. A. Fotieva).

At 5.55 sent for Fotieva. Told of Frumkin's and Trotsky's answers. Arranged to see Krzhizhanovsky at 12 on December 14. Dictated, from 7.30 to 8.25, a letter to the plenum of the Central Committee on the question of foreign trade.[581] Wanted to see Frumkin, but cancelled the engagement. Fairly good humour, joked. Only worried about the winding up of affairs.

December 14, morning (entry by L. A. Fotieva).

Phoned at 11, spoke with Fotieva about yesterday's letter on foreign trade, asked not to give it to anybody, as he had an addition to make. Inquired whether Krzhizhanovsky was coming. Phoned again at 11.10.

At 1.10 asked to be put through to Yaroslavsky.[582] As Yaroslavsky could not be found, put off his talk or interview with him for the evening. At 2.25 sent for Fotieva, gave her a note for Avanesov to be sent to him together with the letter on foreign trade.[583] Gave orders for the letter, when returned, to be sent to Frumkin, whom he would probably receive in the evening. Was very pleased to hear of the Politbureau's decision concerning Rozhkov, laughed and said that this was very good news.[584] Outwardly in good humour, jokes and laughs.

December 14, evening (entry by M. A. Volodicheva).

Vladimir Ilyich phoned at a quarter to six. Asked about the Politbureau minutes. Said he intended to dictate. Asked to be put through to Yaroslavsky. (Yaroslavsky was with him). At 7 o'clock, the doctor. Frumkin came, but did not see Vladimir Ilyich. At a little past eight Vladimir Ilyich inquired whether he was there. Asked Lydia Alexandrovna to remind him about Frumkin tomorrow at 12, when Frumkin would be seeing Tsyurupa. Asked to find out whether all the materials concerning the foreign trade monopoly had been sent to Trotsky and handed over those he had been keeping. They have to be shown to Lydia Alexandrovna. Vladimir Ilyich's letter concerning Bukharin's letter has been sent to Stalin and Trotsky at Vladimir Ilyich's request. *[585] The addition, as he said, he would write separately.

Note in the "Execution" column:

* Does it have to be sent to Frumkin?

Before 8 told Lydia Alexandrovna that he would dictate: 1) a letter to Zinoviev concerning Rozhkov in Pskov; 2) to Kamenev concerning the Union of Socialist Republics; 3) an addition to the letter on foreign trade.

Repeated round about 9 o'clock that he reserved the right to phone up to 10 o'clock. Round about 10 Maria Ilyinichna phoned and said that Vladimir Ilyich would not dictate today.

December 15, morning (entry by L. A. Fotieva).

Phoned at 11.50. Asked for copies of yesterday's letters. Sent for Fotieva and gave a letter he had written to Trotsky, telling Fotieva to type it herself and send it off, keeping a copy in a sealed envelope in the secret files.[586] He found it very difficult to write, asked that the original be destroyed but it is preserved in the secret file together with the copy.

Gave instructions about his books. Technical, medical and other books to be separated and sent back, books on agriculture to be turned over to Maria Ilyinichna, those on production propaganda, labour organisation and pedagogics to Nadezhda Konstantinovna, fiction to be kept until claimed, and publicist, political books, memoirs, etc., to be kept for him.

He also gave orders that all the minutes of the Finance Committee be turned over to him with a memo of the secretary, not too long, but neither too short, from which he could get a clear idea of the work of the Finance Committee. Not very cheerful, said he was feeling worse, had not slept that night.

December 15, evening (entry by L. A. Fotieva).

Phoned at 8.30. Dictated (first over the telephone, then invited me over to his flat) letters to Stalin and Trotsky. To Stalin concerning his possible speech at the Congress of Soviets.[587] To Trotsky on a categorical protest against the question of foreign trade being removed from the agenda of the plenum, should that be contemplated.[588] He finished round about 9.

December 16, morning (entry by L. A. Fotieva).

At 11-11.45 doctors called (Kramer and Kozhevnikov[589]). Nadezhda Konstantinovna sent down the letter to the deputies which she had taken down, apparently, yesterday evening or today before the doctors came.[590] Pakaln[591] says that Vladimir Ilyich has no wish to go to Gorki, saying that the journey by aero-sleigh was tiring and you could not go down by car. Pakaln tells that every day at 9.30 a dog (Aidu) is brought to him with whom he plays and is very fond of. A telegram has arrived from Foerster[592] confirming that before addressing the congress he should have no less than 7 days complete rest. Vladimir Ilyich did not phone once and has given no orders.

December 16, evening (entry by L. A. Fotieva).

Nadezhda Konstantinovna phoned asking that Stalin be told in Vladimir Ilyich's name that he would not address the Congress of Soviets. On being asked how Vladimir Ilyich was feeling, she said middling, he looked all right, but then it was difficult to say. She also asked, on his instructions, to phone Yarovslavsky secretly and ask him to make notes of the speeches of Bukharin and Pyatakov, and if possible others at the plenum, on the question of foreign trade.

December 18, morning (entry by N. S. Alliluyeva).

A meeting of the Central Committee plenum is on. Vladimir Ilyich is not attending, he is ill—no orders or instructions.

December 18, evening.

The plenum is in session. Vladimir Ilyich is not attending. With the evening session the plenum is closed.[593]

December 23 (entry by M. A. Volodicheva).

A little after 8 Vladimir Ilyich called me to his flat. In the course of 4 minutes he dictated. Felt bad. Doctors called.[594] Before starting to dictate, he said: "I want to dictate to you a letter to the congress. Take it down".[595] Dictated quickly, but his sick condition was obvious. Towards the end he asked what the date was. Why was I so pale, why wasn't I at the congress,[596] was sorry that he was taking up the time that I could have spent there. I received no more orders.

December 24 (entry by M. A. Volodicheva).

Next day (December 24) between 6 and 8 Vladimir Ilyich called me in again. Warned me that what he had dictated yesterday (December 23) and today (December 24) was strictly confidential. He emphasised this again and again. Demanded that everything he was dictating should be kept in a special place under special responsibility and to be considered categorically secret. He then added another order.[597]

Sukhanov's "Notes on the Revolution", Volumes III and IV, were taken for Vladimir Ilyich.

December 29.

Through Nadezhda Konstantinovna Vladimir Ilyich asked that lists of the new books be made up. The doctors have allowed him to read. Vladimir Ilyich is reading Sukhanov's "Notes on the Revolution" (Volumes III and IV). Vladimir Ilyich is not interested in fiction. He asked that the lists be made up by sections.

January 5, 1923.

Vladimir Ilyich asked for lists of new books as from January 3 and Titlinov's book "The New Church".[598]

January 17 (entry by M. A. Volodicheva).

Vladimir Ilyich called me in for half an hour between 6 and 7. He read and made corrections to his notes on Sukhanov's book on the revolution. In the course of 10-15 minutes dictated a continuation on the same subject.[599]

Was pleased with the new stand that made it easier for him to read books and his own manuscripts.

When dictating the sentence "Our Sukhanovs..." he paused at the words "... never even dream ..." and while pondering the continuation, jokingly remarked: "What a memory! I have completely forgotten what I was going to say! Dash it! Extraordinary forgetfulness!" He asked me to type the notes at once and give them to him.

Watching him during dictation for several days running I noticed that he did not like to be interrupted in the middle of a sentence, as he lost the thread of his thoughts.

January 18 (entry by M. A. Volodicheva).

Vladimir Ilyich did not send for me.

January 19 (entry by M. A. Volodicheva).

Vladimir Ilyich sent for me round about 7 and a little after 8. Dictated his second variant about the Workers' and Peasants' Inspection ("How We Should Reorganise the W.P.I."[600]) for about 30 minutes. Said he wished to get it finished as quickly as possible.

January 20.

Vladimir Ilyich called me in today between 12 and 1 o'clock. Read his article "How We Should Reorganise the W.P.I." Made amendments and additions to it.

Said that Nadezhda Konstantinovna would give him information relating to one part of his article, and asked Lydia Alexandrovna to find out the same thing: what and how many bodies there were dealing with the scientific organisation of labour, how many congresses had been held on the subject and what groups had been represented at them. Was there any material in Petrograd? (Khloplyankin[601] had sent the same material as Nadezhda Konstantinovna had, a little more detailed.)

Asked for a full list of books.[602] I was with him for about 30 minutes.

January 21 (entry by M. A. Volodicheva).

Vladimir Ilyich did not send for me.

January 22 (entry by M. A. Volodicheva).

Vladimir Ilyich called me in for 25 minutes (from 12 to 12.25). Made corrections in the 2nd variant of the W.P.I. article. Finally chose this variant. As his time was limited he was in a great hurry. Asked me to put the article in order, retype it and give it to him by the evening. Nadezhda Konstantinovna, when letting me in, said he had stolen several minutes to look through the article. Nadezhda Konstantinovna told me that the nurse (on duty) had not wanted to let me in to him. After I had left, Nadezhda Konstantinovna came into the secretariat to tell me Vladimir Ilyich's request "to leave a space in the places, if any, which I had not managed to take down". She said that Vladimir Ilyich, being in a hurry, imagined that I had difficulty in following him. I asked him to be told that I had taken it all down, and if I had any doubts I would do as he had asked.

January 23 (entry by M. A. Volodicheva).

Vladimir Ilyich sent for me between 12 and 1 o'clock. Once more glanced through the article mentioned above and made slight changes. Asked me to insert them in his copy and ours and give one to Maria Ilyinichna for *Pravda*. Article corrected and handed to Maria Ilyinichna before 3 o'clock. He asked whether Lydia Alexandrovna had come back and whether our holidays were over?

January 30 (entry by L. A. Fotieva).

On January 24 Vladimir Ilyich sent for Fotieva and gave instructions to ask Dzerzhinsky or Stalin for the materials of the commission on the Georgian question and to make a detailed study of them. This assignment was given to Fotieva, Glyasser and Gorbunov. Object—report to Vladimir Ilyich, who wanted this for the Party congress. Apparently, he did not know the question was up at the Politbureau.[603] He said: "Just before I got ill Dzerzhinsky told me about the work of the commission and about the 'incident', and this had a very painful effect upon me."

On Thursday, January 25, he asked whether the materials had been received. I answered that Dzerzhinsky would not be arriving until Saturday. Therefore I had not yet been able to ask him.

On Saturday I asked Dzerzhinsky, he said Stalin had the materials. I sent Stalin a letter, but he was out of town. Yesterday, January 29, Stalin phoned saying he could not give the materials without the Politbureau. Asked whether I had not been telling Vladimir Ilyich things he was not to be told—how was it he was posted about current affairs? For instance, his article about the W.P.I. showed that certain circumstances were known to him. I answered that I had not been telling anything and had no reason to believe he was posted about affairs. Today Vladimir Ilyich sent for me to learn the answer and said that he would fight to get the materials.

On January 26 Vladimir Ilyich gave instructions for Tsyurupa, Svidersky and Avanesov to be told that if they agree with his article, they should arrange a number of conferences and discuss by way of preparation for the congress whether or not a plan should be drawn up, a synopsis of textbooks (apparently on the normalisation of labour). Do they know the books by Kerzhentsev and Yermansky?[604] There is a plan of scientific organisation of labour, there is a normalisation department at the Workers' and Peasants' Inspection.

Today he asked what answer Tsyurupa had given, whether he, Svidersky, Avanesov, and Reske[605] agreed with the article. And other members of the Board? I said I did not know this. He asked, wasn't Tsyurupa dilly-dallying, procrastinating, was he frank with me. I said I had not had a chance to speak to him yet, I had only given him the instructions, which he said would be duly carried out.

On January 24 Vladimir Ilyich said: "First of all, about this 'secret' job of ours—I know that you are deceiving me." To my assurances to the contrary, he answered: "I have my own opinion about that."

Today, January 30, Vladimir Ilyich said that yesterday, on asking whether he could address the congress on March 30, the doctor had answered in the negative, but had promised that he would be up by that time and within a month would be allowed newspapers. Reverting to the question of the Georgian commission, he said, laughingly: "That is not newspapers, so I can read it now." Apparently not in a bad humour. No compress on his head.

February 1 (entry by L. A. Fotieva).

Today Vladimir Ilyich sent for me (at 6.30 p.m.). I told him the Politbureau had permitted the materials to be given out.[606] He gave instructions what to pay attention to and generally how to use them.[607] Vladimir Ilyich said: "If I were at large (at first he made a slip, then repeated, laughing: if I were at large) I would easily do all this myself." It had been estimated that their study would take 4 weeks.

He asked what the attitude of Tsyurupa and the others was towards his article. I answered, according to the directions of Tsyurupa and Svidersky, that Svidersky was fully in agreement. Tsyurupa approved it in the part referring to the enlistment of Central Committee members, and doubted whether it was possible for the Workers' and Peasants' Inspection to discharge all its present functions with a staff reduced to 300-400 people. I do not know Avanesov's point of view. Tomorrow there is to be a meeting of the whole Board.

He asked whether the question of the article had been up before the Central Committee. I answered that I did not know this. Vladimir Ilyich was satisfied with these reports.

February 2 (entry by M. A. Volodicheva).

Vladimir Ilyich sent for me at 11.45. Dictated article "Better Fewer, But Better".[608] Finished at 12.30.

Asked Lydia Alexandrovna to come every other day. When asked, "At what time", he said that he was now a free man. Casually mentioned that the only time that was ruled out was from 2 to 5; said 6 might do, or to arrange it with his sister.

I had not seen him since January 23. Outwardly, a considerable change for the better: fresh, cheerful looking. Dictates, as always, excellently: without halts, seldom at a loss for words, speaks, gesticulating, rather than dictates.[609] No compress on his head.

February 3 (entry by L. A. Fotieva).

Vladimir Ilyich sent for me at 7 o'clock for a few minutes. Asked whether we had looked through the materials. I answered that only externally and that they were less than we had expected. Asked whether this question had been up before the Politbureau. I answered that I had no right to talk about it. Asked: "Have you been forbidden to speak precisely and particularly about this?" "No, I have no right generally to talk about current business." "So this is current business?" I realised that I had made a slip. I repeated that I had no right to talk. He said: "I heard about this business from Dzerzhinsky before I got ill. Has the commission reported to the Politbureau?" "Yes, it has. The Politbureau has endorsed its decision as far as I remember." He said:

"Well, I think you will make your report in about three weeks, and then I'll send them a letter." I answered: "We may not manage it in three weeks." The doctors came (Foerster, who had just arrived, Kozhevnikov and Kramer) and I went away. Looked cheerful and buoyant, perhaps somewhat excited at Foerster's visit—Foerster had not seen him for some time.

February 4 (entry by M. A. Volodicheva).

Vladimir Ilyich sent for me today round about 6 o'clock. Asked whether I did not mind him calling me on holidays. ("You must take a rest, too, sometimes, mustn't you?")

Dictated continuation of his article "Better Fewer, But Better" for over half an hour. Looked fresh, voice cheerful. No compress. Ended with the words: "Well, that'll do for the time being. I'm a bit tired." Asked me to type it out and phone him when I had finished, as he would probably continue the article that day; said it was an old habit of his to write with the manuscript in front of him, otherwise he found it difficult to write.

Nadezhda Konstantinovna told me that the German doctor (Foerster) had seen him, had told him a lot of pleasant things, allowed him to do gymnastic exercises and allowed him extra time for dictating articles, and that Vladimir Ilyich was very pleased.

At 8 o'clock he sent for me again. He did not dictate, however, but looked through what he had written and made amendments. When he had finished he said that before sending the article to the press he wanted to show it to Tsyurupa and perhaps some other members of his board and intended to make certain additions to these thoughts of his. Dictated more slowly than usual. Compress on his head. Face went pale. Obviously tired.

February 5 (entry by M. A. Volodicheva).

Today Vladimir Ilyich called me in at 12 o'clock. I was with him three-quarters of an hour. Dictated slowly. In one place, finding difficulty to express himself, he said: "It doesn't go smoothly with me today somehow, not briskly" (he stressed the word). Asked for his article "How We Should

Reorganise the W.P.I." Read it for 3 or 4 minutes in silence.
Then he continued a little longer and decided to stop, saying
he would call me in today at 4 or 5, maybe 6 o'clock.

February 5, evening (entry by M. I. Glyasser).

Vladimir Ilyich sent for Lydia Alexandrovna at 7 o'clock
(ten to 7), but as she was indisposed he sent for me.

Asked whether we had started sorting out the materials
of the Georgian commission and by what date we planned
to finish this work. I answered that we had distributed the
materials and begun to read them, and as for the date, we
expected to keep the deadline he had given us, that is, three
weeks. He asked how we intended to read the materials.
I said we had come to the conclusion that it was necessary
for each of us to read everything. "Is that your unanimous
decision?" "Yes." Vladimir Ilyich began to figure out how
much time was left until the congress. When I said a month
and 25 days, he said that this term was probably sufficient,
but if extra information was required, it might prove too
little, all the more considering that it would take still
longer to go to the Caucasus. He asked how much each of us
was working, and said that in case of need we could use
Volodicheva and Shushanika Manucharyants. Then he asked
whether the decision for all to read everything had been
formally adopted. I answered that we had no record of this
decision in writing and asked whether he had anything
against it maybe. He said that he would like us all to read
everything, of course, but the tasks of our commission were
very indefinite. On the one hand, he would not like to give
us too much trouble, but on the other, we have to reckon
with the need for widening these tasks as the work progresses.
It may be necessary to obtain additional material. He asked
where the materials were being kept, how we use them,
whether we would make a brief summary of all the materials
and whether we would have it typed ("wouldn't it be too
much trouble?"). Finally, Vladimir Ilyich decided that
in the course of the next week we would decide how much
time we needed and in what form we would handle these
materials, and in handling them we would be guided by the
necessity of drawing up a general survey of all the data on
the points which the commission had mapped out as well

as on those questions which he would put to us in the course of the work.

Then Vladimir Ilyich ordered inquiries to be made of Popov as to how things stood with the working up of the census materials of the Central Statistical Board in Petrograd, Moscow and Kharkov (if a census in the last-named city was carried out), and by what date he intends to have them worked up and whether they would be published.[610] Vladimir Ilyich would like to see them in print before the Party congress; he considers that in view of the special importance of this census the materials ought to be published even though those of previous censuses had not been published and Popov had only sent Vladimir Ilyich the tables. Popov, therefore, had to be got moving. An official inquiry should be sent to him about this, following a preliminary talk.

I was with Vladimir Ilyich altogether 20 minutes. I was seeing him for the first time since his illness. I thought he looked well and cheerful, only slightly paler than before. Speaks slowly, gesticulating with his left hand and stirring the fingers of his right. No compress on his head.

February 6, evening (entry by M. A. Volodicheva).

Vladimir Ilyich called me in between 7 and 9. I was there for about an hour and a half. First he began to read his article "Better Fewer, But Better". The corrections, made in red ink, put Vladimir Ilyich in a good humour (not the corrections themselves, but the way they were inserted!). The article at his request had not been retyped, and the first deciphered copy had had the corrections added to it which Vladimir Ilyich had made during his reading. The corrections having been made not in proof-reader style, but in the ordinary secretarial way, Vladimir Ilyich, on second reading, found this inconvenient. He asked that the next time the whole thing should be retyped anew. Running through the article, Vladimir Ilyich made passing remarks, spoke about his old habit of writing and not dictating; that he understood now why stenographers do not satisfy him ("did not satisfy him," he said); that he was accustomed to seeing his manuscript in front of him, stopping, pausing to think over difficult passages, passages in which he had "got stuck", walking up and down the room, even running away to take a walk somewhere; that even now he often felt like seizing a pencil and writing or introducing corrections himself.

He recollected how he tried to dictate an article of his to Trotsky's stenographer back in 1918, and how, when he felt himself getting "stuck", he "plunged" on in confusion with "incredible" speed, and how this led to his having had to burn the whole manuscript, after which he sat down to write himself and wrote "The Renegade Kautsky",[611] with which he was pleased.

Vladimir Ilyich talked about all this very gaily, laughing his infectious laugh. I had never seen him in such a mood. He went on dictating part of this article. Dictation lasted 15-20 minutes. He stopped the dictation himself.

February 7 (entry by L. A. Fotieva).

Vladimir Ilyich sent for me. Spoke on 3 questions.

1) On the results of the census (asked to be shown the proofs of the census book. I said there would have to be Stalin's permission for this).

2) On the Georgian commission. Asked how the work was getting on, when we would finish reading, when we would get together, and so on.

3) On the Workers' and Peasants' Inspection. Did the Board now intend to make any decision, "to take a step of state importance" or was it putting things off until the congress. Said he was writing an article, but was not getting on with it at all, nevertheless he was thinking of revising it and giving it to Tsyurupa to read before sending it to the press. Gave instructions to ask Tsyurupa whether he was to hurry up with this article or not.

Today Kozhevnikov said that there was a tremendous improvement in Vladimir Ilyich's health. He was now moving his arm and had begun to believe himself that he would regain the use of it.

February 7, morning (entry by M. A. Volodicheva).

I was with Vladimir Ilyich at about 12.30. Said that he would dictate on any subjects and arrange the material at some future time. Dictated on the subject of 1) how Party and administrative bodies could be merged, and 2) whether it was convenient to combine educational activities with official activities.

At the words "And the more abrupt the revolution ..." he stopped, repeated them several times, obviously struggling with them; asked me to help him, re-read the preceding passages, laughed and said "Here I've got completely stuck, I'm afraid, make a note of that—stuck on this very spot!"

To my remark that I was his unavoidable evil for a short space of time, as he would soon be able to write himself, he said: "Oh, that won't be so soon!" His voice sounded weary, with a hint of pain in it.

February 7, evening (entry by M. A. Volodicheva).

Vladimir Ilyich called me between 7 and 9. Was with him for about an hour and a half. Completed the sentence at which he had stopped yesterday. Said: "I shall now try to develop the next subject." There and then asked about the subjects he had already noted previously[612]; when these were read out, he remarked that one of them he had forgotten (on the correlation between the Central Board for Vocational Education and the general educational work among the people). Dictated the general part of his article "Better Fewer, But Better". Dictated fast and freely, without difficulty, gesticulating.

On finishing, said he would try later to fit this part in with his article as a whole. Tired. In the evening I learned from Nadezhda Konstantinovna that Vladimir Ilyich would not dictate tomorrow; he intended to read.

February 9 (entry by L. A. Fotieva).

In the morning Vladimir Ilyich sent for me. Confirmed that he would move the question of the Workers' and Peasant's Inspection at the congress. As for the census, he was worried whether the tables would be printed the way they should be. Agreed to my suggestion that instructions for having this checked should be put through Kamenev or Tsyurupa. The assignment to be given to Krzhizhanovsky or Svidersky. Mood and appearance excellent. Said that Foerster was inclined to allow him to receive visitors rather than newspapers. On my remarking that this really would seem to be the best from the medical point of view, he said very gravely after a thoughtful pause that in his opinion it would be worse precisely from the medical point of view, because printed matter could be read and done with, whereas visits evoke an exchange.

February 9, morning (entry by M. A. Volodicheva).

Vladimir Ilyich called me in a little after 12. Said the retyped stuff pleased him better. Read the part of the article he had dictated yesterday, made practically no corrections. On finishing, said: "I think I've made a good job of it." I had the impression that he was very pleased with that part of his article. Asked me to take down the end: "That is how I link up ...", etc. I stayed for about an hour.

February 9, evening.

Vladimir Ilyich sent for Lydia Alexandrovna. Nadezhda Konstantinovna asked her to be given the general part of the article, as Vladimir Ilyich wanted her to read it.

February 10 (entry by L. A. Fotieva).

Called me in a little past 6. Asked that the article "Better Fewer, But Better" be given to Tsyurupa to read, if possible within 2 days.

Asked for listed books.[613] Looks tired, speaks with great difficulty, losing the thread of his thoughts and confusing words. Compress on his head.

February 12 (entry by L. A. Fotieva).

Vladimir Ilyich is worse. Bad headache. Called me in for several minutes. According to Maria Ilyinichna, the doctors had upset him so much that his lips quivered. Foerster the day before had said that he was emphatically prohibited newspapers, visitors and political information. Asked what he meant by the latter, Foerster replied: "Well, this, for example. You are interested in the census of Soviet employees." The fact that the doctors knew about this upset Vladimir Ilyich. Apparently, furthermore, Vladimir Ilyich had the impression that it was not the doctors who gave instructions to the Central Committee, but the Central Committee that gave instructions to the doctors.

Talked with me about the same 3 subjects, pleaded a headache. I said jokingly that I would treat him by suggestion and in two days he would have no more headaches.

February 14 (entry by L. A. Fotieva).

Vladimir Ilyich sent for me a little after 12. No headache. Said that he was quite well. That his was a nervous illness, that sometimes he felt quite well, i.e., his head quite clear, but sometimes he felt worse. Therefore we had to hurry with his requests, as he wanted to put some things through without fail in time for the congress and hoped that he would manage it. But if we dragged it out and thus ruined the business, he would be very very annoyed. The doctors came and we had to break off.

February 14, evening.

Called me in again. Impediment in speech, obviously tired. Spoke again on the three points of his instructions. In special detail on the subject that agitated him most of all, namely, the Georgian question. Asked to hurry things up. Gave certain instructions.[614]

March 5 (entry by M. A. Volodicheva).

Vladimir Ilyich did not send for me until round about 12. Asked me to take down two letters: one to Trotsky,[615] the other to Stalin[616]; the first letter to be telephoned personally to Trotsky and the answer given to him as soon as possible. As to the second letter, he asked it to be put off, saying that he was not very good at it that day. He wasn't feeling too good.

March 6 (entry by M. A. Volodicheva).

Asked about a reply to the first letter (reply over the telephone was taken down in shorthand). Read the second letter (to Stalin) and asked it to be handed to him personally and receive the answer from his own hands. Dictated a letter to the Mdivani group.[617] Felt bad. Nadezhda Konstantinovna asked that this letter to Stalin should not be sent, and it was held up throughout the 6th. On the 7th I said I had to carry out Vladimir Ilyich's instructions. She spoke to Kamenev, and the letter was handed to Stalin and Kamenev, and afterwards to Zinoviev when he got back from Petrograd. Stalin's answer was received immediately on receipt of Vladimir Ilyich's letter (the letter was handed to Stalin personally by me and his answer to Vladimir Ilyich dictated to me). The letter has not yet been handed to Vladimir Ilyich, as he has fallen ill.[618]

First published in 1963
in the magazine
Voprosi Istorii KPSS No. 2

Printed from the secretaries'
notes

NOTES

1 *Vikzhel*—the All-Russia Executive Committee of the Railwaymen's Trade Union, which was set up at the First All-Russia Inaugural Congress of the Railwaymen held in Moscow in July-August 1917. The Executive was controlled by the Mensheviks and Socialist-Revolutionaries. After the victory of the armed uprising in Petrograd this Executive Committee became a bulwark of the counter-revolution. Taking refuge behind statements declaring its neutrality and calling for cessation of the civil war, Vikzhel hindered the dispatch of revolutionary troops from Petrograd to Moscow, where fighting was still going on for the establishment of Soviet power, and threatened to stop railway traffic. On October 29 (November 11), 1917, Vikzhel adopted a resolution calling for the establishment of a new, "homogeneous socialist government" to include representatives of all the parties "from the Bolsheviks to the Popular Socialists". Vikzhel's counter-revolutionary policy and actions were strongly disapproved by the rank and file. At the All-Russia Emergency Congress of the Railwaymen held in January 1918 Vikzhel was dismissed, and a new governing body of the Railwaymen's Union, Vikzhedor, was elected in which the Bolsheviks formed the preponderant majority.   p. 35

2 The Draft Decree on the Requisition of Articles of Warm Clothing for the Soldiers at the Front was discussed and approved at a meeting of the Petrograd Soviet of Workers' and Soldiers' Deputies on November 8 (21), 1917. Lenin's addenda in regard to the requisitioning of articles of warm clothing were taken into consideration in the final wording of the decree (see *Pravda* No. 184, November 22 [9], 1917). On the question of "the requisition of flats of the rich to relieve the needs of the poor". Lenin's amendment formed the basis of a Draft Decree on Installing the Families of Red Armymen and Unemployed Workers in the Flats of the Bourgeoisie and on the Normalisation of Housing which was approved at a meeting of the Petrograd Soviet on March 1, 1918 (see *Izvestia* No. 38, March 2, 1918).   p. 36

3 This refers to the elections to the Constituent Assembly in the Petrograd Electoral Area held between November 12 (25) and 14 (27), 1917. These elections, the preliminary results of which became known on November 15 (28) and the final results the next

day, gave the Bolshevik Party 424,000 votes and 6 seats in the
Constituent Assembly (out of the twelve assigned to Petrograd);
the Cadets received 247,000 votes (4 seats); the Socialist-
Revolutionaries 152,000 votes (2 seats, one of them won by the
Left S.R.s).

The terms "President of the Council of National Commissioners"
and "Social Revolutionists" used by the correspondent are better
known as "Chairman of the Council of People's Commissars" and
"Socialist-Revolutionaries". p. 36

[4] At the elections to the district councils of Petrograd held at the
end of May and beginning of June 1917 the Bolshevik tickets
received 20 per cent of the votes. At the elections to the City Council
of Petrograd on August 20 (September 2) the Bolsheviks received
33 per cent of all the votes. In speaking of the September elections
Lenin was probably referring to the elections to the district councils
of Moscow (held on September 24 [October 7], 1917) at which
the Bolsheviks received 51 per cent of all the votes. This voting,
Lenin pointed out, "is in general one of the most striking symptoms
of the profound change which has taken place in the mood of the
whole nation" (see present edition, Vol. 26, p. 80). p. 37

[5] *Cadets*—members of the Constitutional-Democratic Party, the
chief party of the big bourgeoisie in Russia. Founded in October
1905. p. 37

[6] *Socialist-Revolutionaries* (S.R.s)—a petty-bourgeois party formed
in Russia at the end of 1901 and beginning of 1902. After the
victory of the bourgeois-democratic revolution of February 1917
the S.R.s, together with the Mensheviks and Cadets, were the
mainstay of the bourgeois Provisional Government.

At the end of November 1917 the Left wing of the party founded
a separate Left Socialist-Revolutionary Party. The Left S.R.s
formally recognised the Soviet Government and entered into an
agreement with the Bolsheviks, but very soon turned against
Soviet power. p. 37

[7] This draft was written at a meeting of the Council of People's
Commissars during the discussion of the question of salaries for
People's Commissars and was adopted with slight amendments.
It was published as a decree of the C.P.C. "Remuneration for
People's Commissars and High-Ranking Office Employees and
Officials" on November 23 (December 6), 1917, in *Gazeta Vremennogo
Rabochego i Krestyanskogo Pravitelstva* (Newspaper of the Provi-
sional Workers' and Peasants' Government) No. 16.

The question of remuneration for specialists was subsequently
revised by the Party and the Soviet Government. The decree
of the C.P.C. of January 2 (15), 1918, on "Rates of Pay for High-
Ranking Officials" (see p. 52 of this volume) specified that the
restriction in salaries for People's Commissars did not imply a ban
on higher rates of pay for specialists. The need for making this

change in the general system of remuneration was recognised in a decision of the All-Russia Central Executive Committee dated April 29, 1918.   p. 37

8 This draft was adopted at a meeting of the C.P.C. on November 19 (December 2), 1917.   p. 38

9 After the arrest of General Manikovsky, the general management of the War Department was taken over by N. I. Podvoisky, People's Commissar for Military Affairs, and members of the Commissariat's Board B. V. Legran, K. A. Mekhonoshin and E. M. Sklyansky.

On November 30 (December 13) the C.P.C. passed a decision to release Manikovsky and Marushevsky on parole.   p. 38

10 On November 25 (December 8), 1917 the 6th Tukum Regiment of Lettish riflemen posted in Valka was ordered to Petrograd, and on November 28 (December 11) it was doing garrison duty in the vicinity of the Smolny and the Taurida Palace.   p. 39

11. These theses were written by Lenin in connection with the drafting of a decree for the nationalisation of urban real estate. The draft was endorsed at a meeting of the C.P.C. on November 23 (December 6), 1917, and published on November 25 (December 8) in *Gazeta Vremennogo Rabochego i Krestyanskogo Pravitelstva* No. 18 under the heading "Draft Decree Abolishing Private Ownership of Urban Real Estate (Adopted by the Council of People's Commissars)". The decree was endorsed on August 20, 1918 at a meeting of the All-Russia Central Executive Committee and published in *Izvestia* No. 182 on August 24.   p. 39

12 This draft was written by Lenin in connection with the discussion at a meeting of the Council of People's Commissars on November 27 (December 10), 1917 of his proposal for organising "a special commission to carry out a socialist policy in the financial and economic fields". The draft was adopted with slightly altered wording.   p. 40

13 The Special Defence Council was formed on August 17 (30), 1915 "to discuss and co-ordinate measures to defend the state and ensure a supply of munitions and other materials for the Army and Navy" (Osobiye soveshchaniya i komitety voennogo vremeni [Special Councils and War-time Committees], Petrograd, 1917, p. 7).

By a decree of the Council of People's Commissars dated December 11 (24), 1917 the Special Defence Council was charged with "the annulment of defence orders or their reduction to a normal peace-time level, and, in connection therewith, the demobilisation of the factories and their switchover to peace-time production" (*Dekrety Sovietskoi Vlasti* [*Decrees of the Soviet Government*], Vol. 1, Moscow, 1957, p. 214).   p. 40

[14] Lenin's notes "Demonstration Slogans" are an amendment to the appeal of the Petrograd Soviet "To the Workers and Soldiers of Petrograd" which was published on November 28 (December 11), 1917, in *Pravda* and *Izvestia*. The Cadets had arranged a demonstration for that day with the intention of forcing the opening of the Constituent Assembly and carrying out a counter-revolutionary coup.

The attempt of the counter-revolutionary bourgeoisie, under the leadership of the Cadets, to seize power was frustrated by the measures taken by the Council of People's Commissars and the Petrograd Soviet.   p. 41

[15] *Chernov, V. M.* (1876-1952)—one of the leaders of the S.R. Party. In 1917 he was Minister of Agriculture in the bourgeois Provisional Government. After the October Revolution he was one of the organisers of anti-Soviet revolts.   p. 41

[16] This draft was written by Lenin following an anonymous accusation to the effect that Y. S. Hanecki had been in the employ of a German commercial firm. For Lenin's letter on this question to the C.C. of the R.S.D.L.P.(B.) see *Collected Works*, Fifth Russian Edition, Vol. 50, pp. 14-16.   p. 41

[17] The question of Alexandro-Grushevsky Mining District was discussed at a meeting of the C.P.C. on December 9 (22), 1917.
p. 44

[18] *Monotop*—Russian abbreviation for Donets Fuel Monopoly Trade Council, which was set up by the Provisional Government in 1917. After the October Revolution Monotop pursued a policy of sabotage in the matter of supplying fuel to the railways and industrial enterprises in the central part of Soviet Russia.
p. 44

[19] This draft was written by Lenin in connection with the discussion at a meeting of the C.P.C. held on December 13 (26), 1917, of a report on the work of the Conciliation Board set up by the C.P.C. on December 11 (24) to examine the question of rates of pay for employees of government offices; the draft was endorsed with a slightly modified wording. On the strength of this decree the C.P.C. circulated an order to all the People's Commissariats establishing as from November 1 (14), 1917, new increased rates of pay for these employees; the People's Commissars were directed to introduce immediately the necessary changes in the salary estimates for 1918.   p. 45

[20] This draft was submitted by Lenin and adopted at a meeting of the C.P.C. on December 15 (28), 1917 during the discussion of the question of work stoppage at the Putilov Works; it was published as a decree of the C.P.C. in the *Gazeta Vremennogo Rabochego i Krestyanskogo Pravitelstva* No. 35, under the heading "The Organisation of a Commission of Practitioners".
p. 45

[21] Lenin's motion was discussed at a meeting of the C.P.C. on December 18 (31), 1917, and a ruling adopted: "To endorse Lenin's instructions and Gorbunov's proposal to close the agenda half an hour before the appointed meeting and to oblige the People's Commissars to fulfil this under a written engagement" (Central Party Archives of the Institute of Marxism-Leninism of the C.C. of the C.P.S.U.).   p. 46

[22] This draft was written by Lenin in connection with the discussion of a statement by F. E. Dzerzhinsky, Chairman of the All-Russia Extraordinary Commission (Vecheka), at a meeting of the C.P.C. on December 19, 1917 (January 1, 1918). Dzerzhinsky protested against the action of I. Z. Steinberg, People's Commissar for Justice, and V. A. Karelin, member of the Board of the People's Commissariat for Justice, both of them Left S.R.s.

The evening before, at a meeting of the C.P.C., Lenin received a report that the Vecheka had arrested a group of members of the counter-revolutionary Constituent Assembly Defence Union on the premises of the Free Economic Society, during an illegal attempt on their part, made in defiance of the decree of the C.P.C., to open a "session" of the Constituent Assembly. The C.P.C. had decided to detain the arrested men in custody until their identity was established. Steinberg and Karelin visited the scene, but instead of carrying out the decision of the C.P.C. they released all the arrested persons without even notifying the Vecheka. Their action ran counter to the agreement between the Central Committees of the Bolsheviks and the Left S.R.s for conducting a common line in the C.P.C. and was a violation of the obligation to pursue a Soviet policy which the Left S.R.s had taken upon themselves when joining the C.P.C.

The C.P.C. endorsed the draft resolution written by Lenin.   p. 46

[23] The Dzerzhinsky Commission (Vecheka)—the All-Russia Extraordinary Commission for Combating Counter-Revolution and Sabotage; the other commissions referred to were: the Committee of Inquiry of the Petrograd Soviet, the Naval Committee of Inquiry and the Committee for Combating Drunken Riots.   p. 46

[24] *Kerensky, A. F.* (born 1881)—a Socialist-Revolutionary; after the February bourgeois-democratic revolution of 1917 was minister, then head of the bourgeois Provisional Government and Supreme Commander-in-Chief. After the October Socialist Revolution he fought against the Soviets; escaped abroad in 1918.   p. 48

[25] *Kornilov, L. G.* (1870-1918)—a general of the tsarist army. In July-August 1917 Supreme Commander-in-Chief. In August 1917 headed a counter-revolutionary revolt aimed at restoring the monarchy. He was one of the organisers, and subsequently commander of the whiteguard Volunteer Army on the Don.   p. 48

[26] *Avksentyev, N. D.* (1878-1943)—one of the leaders of the Socialist-Revolutionary Party. After the February revolution of

1917 he was Minister of the Interior in Kerensky's government, and later chairman of the counter-revolutionary Provisional Council of the Russian Republic (Pre-parliament). p. 49

27 *Lieberdans*—an ironical nickname attached to the Menshevik leaders Lieber and Dan and their followers after Demyan Bedny, the satirical poet, had written a satire on them in 1917 entitled "Lieberdan". p. 49

28 *Savinkov, B. V.* (1879-1925)—an S.R.; after the February Revolution Deputy Minister of War; then Military Governor-General of Petrograd. After the October revolution he organised a number of counter-revolutionary uprisings. p. 49

29 *Novaya Zhizn* (New Life)—a daily newspaper, published in Petrograd from April 18 (May 1), 1917 to July 1918; sponsored by Menshevik internationalists and writers grouped around the magazine *Letopis* (Chronicle). The paper adopted a hostile attitude to the October Socialist Revolution and the establishment of Soviet power. From June 1, 1918, appeared in two editions—in Petrograd and Moscow. Both were closed down in July 1918. p. 49

30 This refers to the statement by S. A. Lozovsky, then Secretary of the All-Russia Central Council of Trade Unions, addressed to the Bolshevik group in the Central Executive Committee. It was published in the newspaper *Novaya Zhizn* No. 172 for November 4 (17), 1917. In December 1917 S. A. Lozovsky was expelled from the Bolshevik Party. He was reinstated in December 1919. p. 50

31 Lenin is referring to S. A. Lozovsky's articles "The All-Russia Congress of Trade Unions" and "The Trade Unions and Soviet Power" published in *Professionalny Vestnik*, Nos. 7 and 8, 1917.

Professionalny Vestnik (Trade Union Herald)—a journal, organ of the All-Russia Central Council of Trade Unions; appeared from September 1917 to March 1919 in Petrograd. p. 50

32 *Kaledin, A. M.* (1861-1918)—a general of the tsarist army, Don Cossack chieftain. Active participant in the Kornilov revolt in August 1917. After the October Revolution he was one of the leaders of the Cossack counter-revolution on the Don. p. 51

33 *Antonov-Ovseyenko, V. A.* (1884-1939)—commanded the Soviet troops against Kaledin and the Central Ukrainian Rada at the end of 1917 and beginning of 1918. p. 51

34 This motion of Lenin's was adopted at a meeting of the C.P.C. on January 2 (15), 1918, during the discussion of an inquiry by A. G. Shlyapnikov, People's Commissar for Labour, concerning the rates of pay for high officials of the factory managements. p. 52

³⁵ Lenin is referring to the decree of the C.P.C. of November 18 (December 1), 1917, on "Remuneration for People's Commissars and High-Ranking Office Employees and Officials". The draft of the decree was written by Lenin (see p. 37 of this volume, and Note No. 7).   p. 52

³⁶ This motion was adopted at a meeting of the C.P.C. on January 14 (27), 1918. The decree was an attempt to enlist the co-operation of the All-Russia Food Council, which set itself against the People's Commissariat for Food and sabotaged the measures of the Soviet authorities. The first Soviet Food Congress, which opened in Petrograd on January 14 (27) and was attended by delegates to the Third All-Russia Congress of Soviets, abolished the Food Council and other organisations handling the food business, and concentrated this business in the hands of the Soviet authorities.
                                                       p. 52

³⁷ On January 11 (24), 1918, the C.P.C., on the motion of I. Z. Steinberg, People's Commissar for Justice, instituted an investigation into the activities of the Committee of Inquiry under the Petrograd Soviet, and suspended this Committee pending the results of the investigation. On January 14 (27) the C.P.C. examined the statement of the chairmen of the Committee of Inquiry M. Y. Kozlovsky and P. A. Krasikov asking the C.P.C. to reconsider its decision, and ordered the Inspection Commission set up by it to submit the results of its investigation within forty-eight hours. It also passed a decision to send an inquiry to the C.C. of the Left Socialist-Revolutionary Party concerning the resolution of the Petrograd Committee of the Left S.R.s to the effect that it would not be represented on the Committee of Inquiry. It was in connection with this resolution that Lenin wrote his inquiry.
   The findings of the commission investigating the activities of the Committee of Inquiry were discussed at meetings of the C.P.C. On January 21 (February 3) the C.P.C. adopted the draft decree written by Lenin (see pp. 55-56 of this volume); on February 26 the C.P.C. found that "all accusations of bribery and other crimes or improper conduct against the leading members of the Committee of Inquiry are without foundation" and considered the investigation into the activities of the Committee of Inquiry to be closed, and its leading members Krasikov, Kozlovsky, Lindeman, Mitzgendler and Rozin to be reinstated in their posts (*Decrees of the Soviet Government*, Vol. I, Moscow, 1957, p. 499; see also p. 62 of this volume).   p. 53

³⁸ This draft, written by Lenin, was endorsed at a meeting of the C.P.C. on January 15 (28), 1918.   p. 54

³⁹ This refers to § 51 of the "Regulations for the Democratisation of the Navy" endorsed by an order of the Supreme Naval Board on January 8 (21), 1918. It stated that "all orders of the central bodies, both those of the naval department and the state authorities, as well as the orders of any committees whatso-

ever... shall be fulfilled in the fleet or sea flotillas only if confirmed by the Central Committee of the Navy..." (Central Party Archives of the Institute of Marxism-Leninism of the C.C. of the C.P.S.U.).   p. 54

40 The question of salaries for post and telegraph employees was examined at a meeting of the C.P.C. on January 16 (29), 1918. Lenin's draft decree on this subject was adopted by the C.P.C.
                                                                               p. 54

41 These draft decisions were written by Lenin during the discussion at the meeting of the C.P.C. of the report of the presidium of the first Soviet All-Russia Food Congress, which opened in Petrograd on January 14 (27), dealing with the organisation of a single centre for handling the food problem. The resolution of the congress testified to the important progress achieved in rallying the food supply workers behind the Soviet government. At the same time the C.P.C. was informed of disagreements between the People's Commissar for Food A. G. Schlichter, on the one hand, and the presidium of the food congress, the All-Russia Food Council (elected in November 1917 at the food congress in Moscow) and the Food Department of the Supreme Economic Council, on the other. It was in this connection that Lenin wrote his second draft.
   The first was adopted by the C.P.C., but the second was not included in the minutes of the meeting (see pp. 52-53 of this volume).   p. 55

42 This document bears Lenin's note: "Adopted unanimously". The decision of the C.P.C. in a slightly different wording was published in *Izvestia* No. 17 on January 23 (February 5), 1918.   p. 56

43 The original draft was drawn up by the Board of the People's Commissariat for Agriculture and then submitted for editing to a committee of the Third All-Russia Congress of Soviets. Lenin, who was a member of this committee, put in a good deal of work in editing this draft. His addendum, in a slightly modified wording, was incorporated in the law as Article 26, constituting Section V headed: "Establishment of Norms of Land Tenure in Allotting Land Plots for Building, for Agricultural Industries, for Cultural-Educational Purposes, etc." (see *Decrees of the Soviet Government*, Vol. I, Moscow, 1957, p. 414).   p. 56

44 This addendum was written by Lenin during the discussion at the meeting of the C.P.C. on January 30 (February 12), 1918, of the draft decree concerning the setting up of an inter-departmental extraordinary commission for guarding the railways—"in order to ensure a regular supply of food and articles of prime necessity to the population". Lenin's addendum was incorporated in the adopted decree as § 5 (see *Decrees of the Soviet Government*, Vol. I, Moscow, 1957, pp. 453-54).
   On the report of the above commission the C.P.C. also passed a decision based on Lenin's proposals published below (see pp. 57-58 of this volume).   p. 57

[45] This decision was passed by the C.P.C. at its meeting on January 31 (February 13), 1918, on the report of Y. M. Sverdlov concerning the elimination of sabotage by former government officials.

p. 58

[46] This telephone message, printed from Lenin's manuscript, found its way into the Central Party Archives of the Institute of Marxism-Leninism of the C.C. of the C.P.S.U. in 1948. p. 59

[47] The decision of the C.P.C. was communicated to the German Government in Berlin at 7 a.m. on February 24. Nevertheless, in reply to the radio-telegram of N. V. Krylenko, Supreme Commander-in-chief of the Soviet troops, proposing that the armistice, previously concluded, should be considered in force, the German command stated that it was no longer valid. The German troops continued to advance right up to March 3, when the peace treaty was signed. p. 60

[48] On January 14 (27), 1918, a revolution started in Finland and power passed into the hands of the proletariat. In February, on the initiative of the workers' government of Finland—the Council of People's Representatives—negotiations were commenced for signing a peace treaty between the Russian and Finnish socialist Republics. The draft treaty drawn up by the Russo-Finnish Conciliation Board was discussed at meetings of the Council of People's Commissars held on February 25, 27 and 28. The treaty was signed by representatives of the contracting parties on March 1.

Lenin took an active part in drawing up the treaty. He talked with the delegates of the Finnish workers' government, who had been authorised to sign the treaty, and he edited the draft (see *Lenin Miscellany XXI*, pp. 241-43).

This was the first treaty in history between two socialist republics, an example of a new type of international relationships—fraternal, friendly relationships between equal sovereign states where the working class had come to power. p. 61

[49] Lenin's draft was endorsed at the meeting of the C.P.C. held on February 25, 1918. p. 61

[50] Lenin's motion was adopted at the meeting of the C.P.C. on February 27, 1918.

§ 13 of the "Treaty Between the Russian and Finnish Socialist Republics" stated that "The Russian Federative Soviet Republic grants all the political rights of Russian citizens to Finnish citizens residing in Russia who belong to the working class or to the peasants who do not employ other people's labour, if they live on the territory of Russia for the purpose of engaging in labour occupations.

The Finnish Socialist Workers' Republic, for its part, undertakes to give citizens of the Russian Federative Soviet Republic in Finland every facility to enjoy political rights, special consideration being given to the interests of the working population who have no permanent domicile" (*Decrees of the Soviet Government*, Vol. I, Moscow, 1957, p. 508). p. 62

[51] This draft was written by Lenin and adopted by the C.P.C. at its meeting on February 26, 1918, as an amendment to the decision of the C.P.C. concerning investigations into the activities of the Committee of Inquiry under the Petrograd Soviet. p. 62

[52] The shorthand record of the C.P.C. meeting from which these speeches are printed is kept in the Central Party Archives of the Institute of Marxism-Leninism of the C.C. of the C.P.S.U. It was read back in 1962 for the Fifth Russian Edition of Lenin's *Collected Works*. p. 63

[53] This refers to the proposal made by representatives of the C.C. of the Water Transport Workers Trade Union that the management of water transport be concentrated in the hands of the Trade Union.

At the meeting of the C.P.C. on March 4, 1918, the question of setting up a water transport management board was discussed. According to the decision of the C.P.C. the management of water transport was entrusted to the Supreme Economic Council, under which a Waterways Department was being set up; the Board of this Department was to consist of representatives of the S.E.C., the C.P.C., the Water Transport Workers Trade Union and the regional economic councils.

The C.P.C. rejected the anarcho-syndicalist demands of the water transport workers. On Lenin's motion the C.P.C. decided to immediately set up a Board on the basis of § 3 of the C.P.C.'s decision of February 27, to temporarily increase the number of trade union representatives on the Board, and take steps to immediately dispatch currency notes to pay the wages of the workers on the Volga and the Mariinsk system. The chief points of this decision of the C.P.C. were drafted by Lenin (see p. 66 of this volume). p. 63

[54] Lenin is referring to the Decree of the C.P.C. on the Nationalisation of the Merchant Fleet adopted on January 23 (February 5), 1918. The decree was published on January 26 (February 8) in *Gazeta Vremennogo Rabochego i Krestyanskogo Pravitelstva* No. 18. p. 63

[55] This draft was written by Lenin and endorsed at the meeting of the C.P.C. on March 4, 1918, following a discussion of the question of organising a Water Transport Management Board. (For Lenin's speeches at this meeting see pp. 63-66 of this volume.) p. 66

[56] The reference is to § 3 of the Decree Concerning the Administration of the Merchant Marine and Inland Water Transport adopted at a meeting of the C.P.C. on February 27, 1918 (see *Decrees of the Soviet Government*, Vol. I, Moscow, 1957, pp. 501-02). p. 66

[57] This refers to the allocation of funds for repair work on the Volga and Mariinsk system. p. 66

58 A photo copy of the typewritten text of this interview with a post-script in Lenin's own handwriting (as well as an English translation of it) was published in 1932 in the book: R. H. Bruce Lockhart, *Memoirs of a British Agent*. The copy of the typewritten text of the interview bears the following note by Lenin: "23/III given to Ransome" (Central Party Archives of the Institute of Marxism-Leninism of the C.C. of the C.P.S.U.).

Daily News—a bourgeois newspaper published in London from 1846 to 1928.   p. 67

59 Lenin is referring to the speech of A. Balfour, the British Foreign Minister, in the House of Commons on March 14, 1918, in which the latter tried to cover up the true aims of the Japanese intervention by hypocritically alleging that in occupying Siberia with the consent of the Allies, and seizing the Siberian railway, Japan would be preventing a German invasion of northern Asia.
p. 67

60 The draft decree instituting state control over all forms of insurance was discussed at the meeting of the C.P.C. on March 23, 1918. The decree was adopted with amendments. Lenin's proposals formed the basis of § V of the decree. In addition Lenin clarified the heading of the decree as follows: Decree on the Establishment of State Control Over All Forms of Insurance *Other Than Social* (*viz., Compulsory State*) *Insurance* (the italicised words were added by Lenin). The decree was published on April 2, 1918, in *Izvestia* (see *Decrees of the Soviet Government*, Vol. II, Moscow, 1959, pp. 5-11).   p. 68

61 This was dictated to a stenographer by Lenin on March 23-28, 1918. His work on the article was apparently connected with the forthcoming discussion in the Central Committee of the R.C.P.(B.) of the plan for developing socialist construction. In his opening speech at the plenary meeting of the C.C. held on April 7 Lenin stressed that the revolution was living through a "new period". The Central Committee instructed Lenin "to draw up theses concerning the present situation and submit them to the C.C." In connection with this decision Lenin wrote his "Theses on the Tasks of the Soviet Government in the Present Situation" (this was the heading given in the manuscript of Lenin's work *The Immediate Tasks of the Soviet Government*; see present edition, Vol. 27, pp. 236-77).

For chapters X (end), XI, XII and XIII see Vol. 27 of this edition, pp. 203-18. Part of Chapter IV and chapters V, VI, VII, VIII, IX and the beginning of Ch. X of the original version of the article "The Immediate Tasks of the Soviet Government" were first published in Vol. 36 of Lenin's *Collected Works*, Fifth Russian Edition. Chapters I, II, III and the beginning of Ch. IV have not yet been found.   p. 68

62 This draft was proposed by Lenin at a meeting of the Council of People's Commissars on March 26, 1918, at which A. G. Shlyapnikov reported on the All-Russia Congress of Inland Water Transport Workers held in Moscow on February 14-26, and at which the Draft Decree on the Management of Water Transport on the Volga presented by Y. Larin was discussed. Lenin's motion was adopted by the C.P.C.

The Nizhni-Novgorod Congress of Water Transport Employees mentioned in the decision was held in March 25-April 10, 1918.

p. 85

[63] *Kavomar*— the Board of Management of the Caspian-Volga-Mariinsk System—was organised under the Decree on the Management of Water Transport on the Volga for administering the nationalised fleet and all freight and passenger traffic. By a decision of the C.P.C. dated May 18, 1918, providing for the reorganisation of the water transport management bodies, Kavomar was abolished and its functions transferred to Glavvod—Chief Water Board.

p. 85

[64] This draft, proposed by Lenin during the discussion of the question of "The Organisation of Control Over Expenditure by all Departments of the Supreme Economic Council", was adopted at the C.P.C. meeting on March 26, 1918. p. 85

[65] The Draft Decree on the Procedure To Be Followed by the Various Commissariats in Sending Their Commissars and Agents Out to the Provinces submitted by the People's Commissariat for Internal Affairs was discussed at the meeting of the C.P.C. on April 1, 1918. The C.P.C. asked all the commissariats to consider the draft and give their comments. On April 5 the decree was endorsed with Lenin's addenda and on April 11, 1918, it was published in *Izvestia* (see *Decrees of the Soviet Government*, Vol. II, Moscow, 1959, pp. 58-59). p. 87

[66] The joint meeting was held to discuss the project for setting up a trust ("The National Company") proposed by a group of capitalists headed by A. P. Meshchersky, Managing-Director of the "Sormovo-Kolomna" Industrial Association. The Board of the Supreme Economic Council passed a decision on April 14, 1918, to break off negotiations with Meshchersky; on April 18, the Council of People's Commissars turned down Meshchersky's project and decided to carry out the nationalisation of the works. A resolution in favour of nationalisation was passed also by the conference of delegates of the machine-building works held May 12-18, 1918 (see present edition, Vol. 27, pp. 388-89). p. 88

[67] *The First Congress of Soviets of the Don Republic*, which proclaimed itself the supreme Soviet authority on the Don, was held on April 9-12, 1918. It was attended by 750 delegates. Lenin was elected honorary chairman. The resolution referred to by Lenin was adopted on April 12 by an overwhelming majority, the Mensheviks' motion receiving only 2 votes. The congress approved the Soviet Government's peaceful policy and stressed in the resolution that it regarded the Don Republic as part of the R.S.F.S.R.

and considered it its chief task to work for the rehabilitation of the national economy and the creation of a Red Army. The congress declared the working Cossacks' readiness to defend Soviet power.   p.   88

68 This document was incorporated in the Decree on the Registration of Shares, Bonds and Other Interest-Bearing Securities, the draft of which was edited, supplemented and supplied with a heading by Lenin and endorsed after discussion by the C.P.C. on April 18; it was published on April 20 in *Izvestia* No. 78 (see *Decrees of the Soviet Government*, Vol. II, Moscow, 1959, pp. 130-38). p.   89

69 The question of providing funds for financing the sugar-beet sowing campaign was raised by the Chief Sugar Committee; this request was supported by the Congress of Sugar Industry Workers, which was held jointly with representatives of the land committees. The C.P.C. on April 17, 1918, discussed the application tabled by the Supreme Economic Council for twenty million rubles to be allocated to the Chief Sugar Committee and endorsed Lenin's draft decision in this connection.   p.   89

70 This text, with slight amendments, was incorporated in the Decree on the Institution of an All-Russia Evacuation Commission adopted by the Council of People's Commissars on April 19, 1918. The decree was published in the newspapers *Znamya Truda* and *Izvestia* on April 23 and 24, 1918 (see *Decrees of the Soviet Government*, Vol. II, Moscow, 1959, pp. 140-42).   p.   90

71 The draft decree was on the agenda of the C.P.C. sitting of April 22, 1918, but its consideration was postponed until the next meeting. The addendum to it was introduced by Lenin after he had examined the draft. On April 23 the C.P.C. adopted the decree *in toto* with Lenin's addendum and the next day finally endorsed it with certain amendments (a new clause was inserted). Therefore Lenin's addendum in the text published in *Izvestia* No. 84 for April 27, 1918, applies to § 7 of the Decree on Supplying Agriculture With Implements and Metals (see *Decrees of the Soviet Government*, Vol. II, Moscow, 1959, pp. 169-72).   p.   91

72 The draft decree was considered at a meeting of the C.P.C. Commission on April 25, 1918. The commission approved the decree on May 2, 1918, and on the same day it was endorsed by the C.P.C. with this addendum of Lenin's and published on May 10 in *Izvestia* No. 91 (see *Decrees of the Soviet Government*, Vol. II, Moscow, 1959, pp. 212-16).   p.   91

73 This document was written by Lenin in connection with the question, raised by the leaders of the Left S.R.s M. A. Spiridonova and V. A. Karelin, that control of the People's Commissariat for Agriculture be handed over completely to the Left Socialist-Revolutionaries, with the Bolsheviks retaining merely political

representation. See also Lenin's memorandum on this subject to the C.C. of the R.C.P.(B.) (*Collected Works*, Vol. 50, Fifth Russian Edition, Document 133).

On May 3, 1918, the C.C. of the Russian Communist Party rejected the claims of the Left S.R.s. p. 92

74 This draft decision was adopted by the C.P.C. on May 9, 1918, during the discussion of a decree granting extraordinary powers to the People's Commissariat for Food. p. 93

75 The fuel question was discussed at a meeting of the C.P.C. on May 24, 1918, the reporters being N. I. Solovyov on behalf of the Fuel Department of the Supreme Economic Council and S. S. Dikansky on behalf of Moskvotop. p. 93

76 This draft of Lenin's was adopted at a meeting of the C.P.C. on May 25, 1918, which discussed the question of transferring motor transport to the Motor Section of the Transport Department of the S.E.C. p. 93

77 This document was adopted by the C.P.C. without amendment and incorporated in its decision on the private purveyance of food supplies which was published on June 1 in *Izvestia* No. 110 (see *Decrees of the Soviet Government*, Vol. II, Moscow, 1959, pp. 344-48).

Prodput—Central Food Bureau of the People's Commissariat for Railways.

Prodvod—Central Food Bureau of the Chief Water Board (of the People's Commissariat for Railways). p. 94

78 The draft "Regulations for the Management of the Nationalised Enterprises" drawn up by the Supreme Economic Council were discussed on May 28 and 30, 1918, at a meeting of the Organisation of Production Section of the First All-Russia Congress of Economic Councils. After a lengthy discussion, the section, under pressure from the "Left" Communists, adopted the Regulations, which ran counter to the policy of the Party and the Government. On learning of the speeches of the "Left" Communists on the question of management of the nationalised enterprises (see *Collected Works*, Vol. 50, Fifth Russian edition, p. 84) and reading the Regulations drafted by the section, Lenin proposed that they be examined at the Conciliation Board specially set up on June 2 and at which the C.P.C. was represented by V. I. Lenin and the S.E.C. by A. I. Rykov and G. D. Veinberg. The Conciliation Board revised the Regulations on the basis of Lenin's comments published here. Despite the "Left" Communists, the congress, by a majority, adopted the draft of the Conciliation Board. p. 96

79 This draft decision was adopted the same day it was written.

Lenin's letters, speeches, articles and notes, as well as his draft decisions for the C.P.C. and other documents relating to library organisation, have been collected in N. K. Krupskaya's book, *Chto pisal i govoril Lenin o bibliotekakh* (What Lenin Wrote and Said About Libraries), Moscow, 1956. p. 96

80 These proposals of Lenin's were written apparently at a meeting of the Council of People's Commissars on June 8, 1918, when the draft was under consideration. The draft decree was adopted with substantial amendments. The All-Russia Central Executive Committee endorsed the decree on June 11 and *Izvestia* published it on June 16, 1918 (see *Decrees of the Soviet Government*, Vol. II, Moscow, 1959, pp. 412-19). The Committees of Poor Peasants were instituted by this decree. An appraisal of them was given by Lenin in his speech at the First All-Russia Congress of Land Departments, Poor Peasants' Committees and Communes on December 11, 1918 (see present edition, Vol. 28, p. 338). p. 97

81 This formulation applies to § 2 of the draft decree. In conformity with Lenin's proposal, it was worded as follows: "The right to elect and be elected to the volost and village Committees of Poor Peasants shall be enjoyed by all without restriction, both by local villagers and newcomers, with the exception of avowed kulaks and rich farmers having surpluses of grain or other food products, having trade or industrial establishments, and employing farm-hands or hired labour, etc.
"*Note*: Those employing hired labour for farm work not exceeding the subsistence norm may elect and be elected to the Committees of Poor Peasants" (*Decrees of the Soviet Government*, Vol. II, Moscow, 1959, pp. 416-17.) p. 97

82 On June 10, 1918, the Council of People's Commissars heard the reports of M. P. Pavlovich and A. I. Rykov concerning endorsement by the presidium of the Supreme Economic Council of the composition of the Committee of Public Works (instituted by Decree of the C.P.C. of May 9, 1918). The present text constituted § 2 of the C.P.C. decision on this question. p. 98

83 This draft was adopted the same day by the C.P.C. following the report of Deputy People's Commissar for Railways V. I. Nevsky. On June 18 the C.P.C. endorsed a 9-man Board consisting of 4 Bolsheviks, 2 internationalist Mensheviks and 3 Left Socialist-Revolutionaries. p. 98

84 Lenin here refers to the Statute on the Management of Railway Communications in the Russian Socialist Federative Soviet Republic approved by the All-Russia Central Executive Committee on June 8, 1918, and published in *Izvestia* No. 122 on June 16 (see *Decrees of the Soviet Government*, Vol. II, Moscow, 1959, pp. 365-67). p. 98

85 This draft was adopted at a meeting of the C.P.C. on June 15, 1918, on the question of advancing money to the Central

Committee of the Textile Industry under the Supreme Economic Council (Centrotextil) for the purchase of flax (see also pp. 118-19 of the volume). p. 99

86 Lenin's draft on the question of issuing funds to the Supreme Economic Council for the purchase of raw materials by the Chief Committee for the Tanning Industry was adopted by the C.P.C. on June 15, 1918. p. 99

87 The interview with Lenin was reported to the newspaper the same day by a special telegram, but for technical reasons it was received late and was not published until July 4, 1918. Following this, a summary of the interview was published on July 6 in *Leipziger Volkszeitung* No. 155.

Folkets Dagblad Politiken—newspaper of the Swedish Left Social-Democrats, was published in Stockholm from April 1916 (up to November 1917 it was called *Politiken*). In 1921 it became the organ of the Communist Party of Sweden; after the split in the party in October 1929 the newspaper passed into the hands of the party's Right wing. Publication ceased in May 1945. p. 101

88 This refers to the disarming of the anarchists by the security forces in Moscow on the night of April 12, 1918. This measure was necessitated by the fact that the various groups of anarchists served as a screen for counter-revolutionary and criminal elements who terrorised the population by their raids and robberies and took refuge in the villas which the anarchists had seized. The anarchists in Petrograd, who failed to comply with the demand for the surrender of firearms, were disarmed on April 23, 1918.

Anarkhia (Anarchy)—an anarchist literary and socio-economic newspaper published in Moscow from September 1917 to July 1918; by order of the Vecheka it was closed down on April 13; publication was resumed on April 21, 1918. p. 102

89 On July 2, 1918, the C.P.C. heard an out-of-order statement by Lenin concerning "the need for meeting the peasants' requirements in agricultural machines" and adopted this draft decision in this connection (Central Party Archives of the Institute of Marxism-Leninism of the C.C. of the C.P.S.U.). p. 103

90 This refers to the Fifth All-Russia Congress of Soviets (held in Moscow July 4-10, 1918). p. 103

91 This draft decision was adopted by the C.P.C. on July 8, 1918, in connection (as recorded in the minutes) with the inquiry of "The Chairman of the Council of People's Commissars to Comrade Lunacharsky and Comrade Malinovsky concerning the reasons for non-fulfilment by them of the decision of the Council of People's Commissars expressed in the 'Decree on the Removal of Monuments Erected to the Tsars and Their Servants and the Projecting of Monuments of the Russian Socialist Revolution'"

(Central Party Archives of the Institute of Marxism-Leninism of the C.C. of the C.P.S.U.).

On this question see also present edition, Vol. 35, p. 360, and Vol. 50, Documents 131, 140, 189, of Lenin's *Collected Works*, Fifth Russian Edition.   p. 103

92 This document was embodied in Article 20, Section 2 of the Constitution of the R.S.F.S.R. adopted on July 10, 1918, at the Fifth All-Russia Congress of Soviets.   p. 104

93 Lenin addressed a meeting in the large hall of the Racing Society at Khodynka on the evening of July 26, 1918. The hall was crowded to overflowing with workers and Red Armymen. A soldier made a speech on behalf of the First Reserve Artillery Brigade in which he said that in the person of Lenin they greeted the Council of People's Commissars and were ready to defend the workers' and peasants' government at the Council's first call. The resolution proposed after Lenin's speech was adopted unanimously with one abstention. In conclusion Znamensky briefly acquainted the audience with Lenin's biography. p. 104

94 This draft decision was adopted with slight amendments at the meeting of the C P.C. on August 22, 1918.   p. 106

95 Point 1 of this decision of the C.P.C. was published in *Izvestia* on August 23, 1918.   p. 107

96 It has not been possible to establish what document this proposal refers to.   p. 107

97 The question of introducing a tax in kind was raised by Lenin in his "Theses on the Food Question" written on August 2, 1918 (see present edition, Vol. 28, pp. 45-47). The draft decree for imposing a tax in kind on the farmers was first introduced at a meeting of the C.P.C. on September 4. It was discussed again at a meeting of the C.P.C. on September 21. It was probably during these meetings of the Council that Lenin jotted down his "Main Provisions of the Decree" and his remarks on the draft. (For Lenin's documents connected with the drafting of the decree at this and other meetings of the Council of People's Commissars— notes, calculations, plan of a speech at the Council meeting— see also *Lenin Miscellany XVIII*, pp. 148-50.) The decree in its final form was adopted by the C.P.C. on October 26, endorsed by the All-Russia Central Executive Committee on October 30 and published in *Izvestia* on November 14, 1918. The extension of foreign military intervention and the civil war prevented this measure from being implemented.

Lenin's principles for an income tax in kind drafted in 1918 were elaborated and embodied in the food tax in the spring of 1921, which marked the post-war transition to peaceful economic construction on the basis of the New Economic Policy. The

·decree on the tax in kind adopted in October 1918 was mentioned by Lenin in his report on the political work of the C.C. at the Tenth Congress of the R.C.P.(B.), when dealing with the question of replacing the surplus-appropriation system by a food tax (see present edition, Vol. 32, p. 187).   p. 107

[98] Article 12 of the "Basic Law on the Socialisation of the Land" endorsed by the Third All-Russia Congress of Soviets on January 18 (31), 1918, and adopted at the session of the All-Russia Central Executive Committee on January 27 (February 9) runs as follows: "The distribution of land among the working people shall be carried out on an equalised labour basis in such a manner that the subsistence and labour norm adapted in the given area to the historically established system of land tenure should not exceed the available manpower on each individual farm and at the same time should allow the farmer's family to make a fairly comfortable living." Article 17 of the Law says: "The surplus income derived from naturally fertile superior plots as well as from their more advantageous location for marketing, shall be placed at the disposal of the Soviet authorities to be used for public needs" (*Decrees of the Soviet Government*, Vol. I, Moscow, 1957, pp. 408-09).   p. 108

[99] At a meeting of the C.P.C. on October 15, 1918, the People's Commissariat for Food tabled a proposal that 40 million rubles be allocated for the upkeep of the Poor Peasants' Committees, apparently for a period of six months at the rate of 6.5 million rubles per month. In view of the impending amalgamation of these committees with the local Soviets, Lenin proposed a 2-month allocation of funds ("$2 \times 6^1/_2 = 13$"). The C.P.C. adopted Lenin's proposal for the allocation of 13 million rubles; the other proposals of Lenin's were also included in the decision of the C.P.C. (see *Decrees of the Soviet Government*, Vol. III, Moscow, 1964, pp. 593-95).   p. 109

[100] This was written by Lenin in connection with the discussion by the C.P.C. of the report of the Board of Three on logging under the Supreme Economic Council. All Lenin's proposals were incorporated in the decision adopted by the C.P.C. on this question. The latter allocated 100 million rubles for logging operations, demanded an account of their expenditure within a week and ordered the Board of Three, within the same period, to submit more concrete information on the questions formulated by Lenin.   p. 109

[101] On November 8, 1918, the Extraordinary Sixth All-Russia Congress of Soviets, on the report of People's Commissar for Justice D. I. Kursky, passed a decision on revolutionary legality based on Lenin's theses, which were approved by the Party's Central Committee. The decision was published in *Pravda* on November 10.   p. 111

102 On June 5, 1918, *Izvestia* published a decree of the C.P.C. placing the educational institutions and establishments of all departments under the jurisdiction of the People's Commissariat for Education. On November 19, 1918, the People's Commissariat for Social Security submitted to the C.P.C. (the question was reported by A. I. Ulyanova-Yelizarova) a draft decree leaving the children's homes under the jurisdiction of this commissariat. It was in connection with this discussion that Lenin wrote his draft decision, which was adopted with slight changes.
p. 111

103 § 3 of the C.P.C.'s Decree of June 5, 1918, ordered the People's Commissariat for Education to form special commissions of representatives of the departments concerned and of the Commissariat for Education to make arrangements for the turnover of the educational institutions and establishments, including the institutions of pre-school education.   p. 111

104 The draft decree on the organisation of supply for the population was discussed at a meeting of the C.P.C. on November 12, 1918, and finally endorsed by the C.P.C. on November 21. Lenin's addenda were included in the adopted text of the decree, which was published in *Izvestia* on November 24.

The question of the co-operatives' participation in the organisation of supply for the population as dealt with in the draft decree with Lenin's addenda to it, was misunderstood by some of the leading food supply workers. Lenin clarified this question in a speech delivered at a meeting of delegates from the Moscow Central Workers' Co-operative on November 26, 1918, in a report on the attitude of the proletariat to petty-bourgeois democrats made at a Moscow Party workers' meeting on November 27, and in his reply to the discussion (see present edition, Vol. 28, pp. 196-200, 213-16, 221-24).

See also present edition, Vol. 35, p. 376, and Vol. 50, Fifth Russian Edition, Document 378.   p. 112

105 *The Council of Defence* (Council of Workers' and Peasants' Defence) was set up by the All-Russia Central Executive Committee on November 30, 1918, as a special organ of the Soviet state vested with full powers in the matter of mobilising the country's forces and resources in the interests of defence. Lenin was appointed Chairman of the Council of Defence.

The documents published here were written by Lenin at the first meeting of the Council of Defence on December 1, 1918. First Lenin outlined the immediate tasks of the Council and the agenda for its first sitting (Document 1). Then he jotted down a number of proposals for elaborating these questions, formulating more detailed proposals on the food question (Documents 2 and 3). Lenin's proposals were reflected in the decisions of the Council of Defence adopted at its sitting (see *Lenin Miscellany XVIII*, pp. 243-45).   p. 112

[106] On Point 4 of the agenda ("On the Mobilisation of Intellectuals") L. B. Krasin was instructed to draw up a draft decision for the mobilisation of technical personnel; L. B. Krasin, V. I. Nevsky and N. P. Gorbunov were instructed to draw up draft regulations on questionnaires to be submitted to the C.P.C. p. 113

[107] The Council of Defence passed a decision for the fuel question to be considered by a special five-man commission, which was to be summoned by Lenin. The commission met on December 2, 1918 (see the next document). p. 113

[108] This draft was written by Lenin apparently at a meeting of the Fuel Commission set up by the Council of Defence (see previous Note). It took into account the opinions expressed by the commission members. Lenin's draft was adopted by the commission and included in its minutes. In the Minutes of the Fuel Commission points 1, 2, 3, 4 are given under a special heading "Decisions of the Commission Having the Force of Defence Council Decisions". Lenin's draft, endorsed as a decision, was signed also by Defence Council members J. V. Stalin and V. I. Nevsky.

p. 114

[109] The State Bank held up the issue of currency notes from the special fund reserved to the Chief Timber Board. p. 114

[110] In the course of a discussion of the work of the railways at a meeting of the Council of Defence on December 1, 1918, a commission was set up to deal with questions relating to the activities of the transport department of the Vecheka. The commission, chaired by Lenin, held its first meeting on December 3. This rough draft was probably made by Lenin during the meeting. All points of these proposals with the exception of the two last paragraphs were later crossed out by Lenin. The commission's decisions were formulated on the basis of Lenin's proposals.

p. 115

[111] This refers to the leadership of the boards of the gubernia and railway Chekas. p. 115

[112] On the basis of Lenin's proposals the commission decided to instruct the People's Commissariat for Railways together with a representative of the Vecheka to revise the regulations governing the Transport Department of the Vecheka in respect of non-interference by the Vecheka in the commissariat's technical and management functions. On the question of the relationships between the Vecheka, the Railway Cheka (Transport Department of the Vecheka) and the Commissariat for Railways see the draft decision of the Council of Defence (pp. 127-29 of this volume). p. 115

[113] By decision of the commission the right to participate in judicial investigations through their delegates was granted to the People's Commissariats and the Party Committees of the R.C.P.(B.). p. 115

[114] This rough draft was made by Lenin in connection with the discussion by the Council of Defence of N. P. Bryukhanov's report concerning the speeding up and increase of food purveyance. Lenin's proposals were incorporated in the Council's decision on this question (see *Lenin Miscellany XVIII*, pp. 246-47).

p. 115

[115] The draft Regulations introduced by N. P. Bryukhanov were discussed at the meeting of the C.P.C. on December 5, 1918. Lenin's draft decision and remarks in this connection were apparently jotted down during the discussion, but were then crossed out by him. However, the amendments adopted at the meeting and incorporated in the draft Regulations coincide with his drafts.

p. 116

[116] On December 4, 1918, during the discussion of the question of introducing a third shift at the Tula cartridge and small arms factories, the Council of Defence set up a special commission to deal with this matter. The commission on cartridges met on December 5 and was attended by V. I. Lenin, L. B. Krasin (Chairman of the Extraordinary Commission on Red Army Supply), E. M. Sklyansky (Vice-Chairman of the Revolutionary Military Council of the Republic), Commander-in-Chief I. I. Vatsetis, and representatives of the Chief Artillery Board, the Tula Cartridge Factory and others—altogether 17 people. The commission passed decisions having the force of Defence Council decisions; they were based on the measures outlined by Lenin in his notes (see *Lenin Miscellany XXXIV*, pp. 55-57).

p. 117

[117] This refers to the setting up of committees on a parity basis for convening a congress of bank employees, which was to form a single union of bank employees in place of the two existing trade unions—the All-Russia Credit Business Workers Trade Union (Banktrud) and the R.S.F.S.R. People's Bank Workers Union (Bankosotrud). On December 2, 1918, the question of the relationships between the two unions was discussed at a special conference presided over by Lenin. The Congress of Bank Employees was held in the beginning of January 1919. p. 118

[118] This document was written by Lenin in connection with the discussion of V. P. Milyutin's report concerning the financing of Centrotextil (Central Committee of the Textile Industry under the S.E.C.) at a meeting of the C.P.C. on December 14, 1918. Lenin's proposals were reflected in the decision which the C.P.C. adopted in this connection.

p. 118

[119] Points 1 and 3 were crossed out by Lenin. A comparison with the text of the decision as recorded in the minutes gives grounds for presuming that Lenin did not cross out the points which were accepted by the C.P.C.

p. 119

120 Lenin's letter to Chicherin was written in connection with the
     preparations for the first congress of the Comintern.
         Already at the beginning of the first world war, when the collapse
     of the Second International occurred as a result of most of the
     leaders of the socialist parties in the West adopting a social-
     chauvinist stand, Lenin put forward the idea of founding a new,
     truly revolutionary International and pressed forward with
     a campaign to unite the Left socialist forces in the international
     labour movement. The victory of the October Socialist Revolu-
     tion and its growing impact upon the international revolutionary
     movement, and the emergence of Communist Parties or groups
     in a number of capitalist countries made this task more urgent
     than ever and created favourable conditions for its solution.
         The urgent need for uniting the Communists was further dictated
     by the fact that the opportunist, social-chauvinist leaders had
     made an attempt to revive the Second International. The leader-
     ship of the British Labour Party had addressed a proposal to the
     socialists of all countries to convene in Lausanne on January 6,
     1919, an international socialist conference to rehabilitate the
     Second International. In reply to this proposal the Central Com-
     mittee of the Russian Communist Party (Bolsheviks) circulated
     on December 24, 1918, a radio-telegram calling on all revolu-
     tionary internationalist elements to refuse to take part "in
     conferences of enemies of the working class wearing the mask of
     socialism" (*Pravda* No. 281, December 25, 1918). At the same time
     Lenin, as his letter to Chicherin shows, raised the question of
     convening without delay an international conference of Commu-
     nists and Left Social-Democrats with the aim of founding the
     Third International.   p. 119

121 This refers to E. Fuchs, a member of the Central Council of the
     Spartakusbund. He arrived in Moscow from Berlin at the end
     of December 1918 to inform Lenin of the situation in Germany.
                                                              p. 119

122 A report was drawn up for Lenin on December 31 characterising
     the parties and organisations mentioned in his list. In addition
     to those given by Lenin the report gave the names of eight more
     organisations. It also suggested inviting representatives of the
     Chinese, Korean and Persian revolutionary workers to the con-
     ference in the capacity of guests.
         The same day Lenin received the draft of an appeal "To the
     First Congress of the Communist International" written at his
     request and in keeping with his proposals. Lenin made a number
     of important amendments to the draft.
         In January 1919 the draft appeal "To the First Congress of
     the Communist International" was submitted by Lenin at a meeting
     of representatives of a number of communist and socialist parties
     and organisations. After a discussion, the meeting adopted the
     draft. The appeal was published in the press on January 24,
     1918.

The First Congress of the Communist International was held on March 2-6, 1919 (see present edition, Vol. 28, pp. 453-77).
p. 121

[123] These notes were written at a time when the Soviets were being restored in Kharkov. The city, which had been occupied by Petlyura, was liberated by the Soviet troops on January 3, 1919.
p. 122

[124] The question of sending people to Kharkov was discussed at a meeting of the Council of Defence on January 17 and 27, 1919.
p. 122

[125] This draft was introduced by Lenin and adopted with slight amendments at a meeting of the C.P.C. on January 28, 1919.

The draft decree on consumers' communes mentioned in Point 4 was adopted by the C.P.C. on March 16 and published in *Izvestia* No. 60 on March 20.

Lenin's addendum to Point 1 was written in the margin probably after the writing of the draft decision as a whole. The beginning of Point 1 of the C.P.C.'s decision of January 28 was worded as follows: "Direct the Co-operative Department of the S.E.C. and the People's Commissariat for Food together with the Central Statistical Board to collect within the shortest possible time information concerning the actual implementation by the co-operatives of the basic line of Soviet policy".
p. 123

[126] This draft was adopted at a meeting of the C.P.C. on January 30, 1919, and published on February 1 in *Izvestia* No. 23.
p. 123

[127] The question of granting a concession to build the Great Northern Railway was discussed at a meeting of the C.P.C. on February 4, 1919. The Council adopted Lenin's motion with certain amendments.

According to the project of the concession's sponsors the new line was to link the Ob with Petrograd and Murmansk via Kotlas. No contract for this railway was concluded.
p. 124

[128] This document was incorporated almost *in toto* in the resolution of the C.C. of the Russian Communist Party adopted on February 19, 1919.

On March 11, 1919, the C.C. adopted a new detailed resolution on the food policy in the Ukraine. On one of the pages of the typewritten text of this resolution, which is kept in the Central Party Archives of the Institute of Marxism-Leninism, Lenin had written: "Endorsed 11.III. at the Bureau of the C.C. of the R.C.P. as a directive for the Ukrainian R.C.P. and the Ukrainian Soviet Government. 11. III. 1919. Lenin".
p. 125

[129] Lenin's unfinished article "On the Appeal of the German Independents" was written in the latter part of February 1919. The appeal is criticised in § 21 of Lenin's theses on bourgeois democracy and the dictatorship of the proletariat (see present edition, Vol. 28, p. 467).
p. 126

130 Lenin is referring to the meeting of the enlarged International Socialist Commission (*Internationale Sozialistische Kommission*) held in Berne on February 5-9, 1916. It was attended by 22 delegates from the internationalists of a number of countries: Germany, Russia, Italy, Norway, Austria, Poland, Switzerland, Bulgaria and Rumania. Lenin took an active part in the proceedings. The meeting adopted an appeal "To All Affiliated Parties and Groups" denouncing the participation of socialists in bourgeois governments, the slogan of "Defence of the fatherland" in the imperialist war, and voting for war loans; it pointed to the necessity of supporting the labour movement and preparing mass revolutionary action against the imperialist war. The appeal, however, suffered from inconsistency in that it failed to demand a break with social-chauvinism and opportunism. In voting for the text of the appeal, the members of the Zimmerwald Left declared at the meeting that although they did not consider all its points satisfactory, they were voting for it because they regarded it as a step forward in comparison with the decisions of the First International Socialist Conference at Zimmerwald. The meeting fixed the date for convening a second international socialist conference.   p. 126

131 The reference is to Kautsky's article "*Fraktion und Partei*" published in *Die Neue Zeit* No. 9 for November 26, 1915.   p. 127

132 The women attending the courses wrote a letter to Lenin asking him to address their meeting. They concluded their letter with a pledge to take the places of their husbands, brothers and sons who had joined the Red Army.   p. 129

133 This draft was written by Lenin in connection with the discussion of the question of the Printing Industry Department of the S.E.C. at a meeting of the C.P.C. on March 15, 1919. The Council's decision was formulated on the basis of Lenin's proposals. For the text of this decision see *Lenin Miscellany XXIV*, p. 24.   p. 130

134 The need for sending the best workers out on food and transportation jobs had been dealt with by Lenin in his speech at a joint session of the All-Russia Central Executive Committee, the Moscow Soviet and the All-Russia Trade Union Congress on January 17, 1919 (see present edition, Vol. 28, pp. 403-04).
    Lenin's draft was adopted by the C.C. of the R.C.P.(B.); it was signed also by C.C. members L. B. Kamenev, G. Y. Zinoviev, J. V. Stalin, Y. D. Stasova, N. N Krestinsky, M. F. Vladimirsky, N. I. Bukharin, V. V. Schmidt and F. E. Dzerzhinsky. p. 131

135 *The Extraordinary Plenary Meeting of the Moscow Soviet of April 3, 1919*, was held jointly with representatives of the district Soviets, factory committees and trade union executives in connection with the aggravation of the food situation in Moscow and the

consequent agitation carried on among the railwaymen by the
Mensheviks and Socialist-Revolutionaries. The latter called upon
the railwaymen to strike and sabotage work in the railway repair
shops. This counter-revolutionary agitation led to a strike in
the shops of the Alexandrovsky Railway, as a result of which the
central workshops were closed on March 31 by order of the People's
Commissariat for Railways and work in them was not resumed
until April 3, after the kulak elements had been dismissed.

Lenin made a report at the meeting on the domestic and foreign
situation of the Soviet Republic. A report on the state of railway
transport was made by L. B. Krasin, and on the food policy
by A. I. Svidersky. Speakers in the debate denounced the
counter-revolutionary agitation of the Mensheviks and Socialist-Revolutionaries. In winding up the debate, A. V. Lunacharsky
moved the resolution on the domestic and foreign situation of
the Soviet Republic drafted by Lenin. This volume contains
the original version of this draft resolution. The meeting of the
Moscow Soviet also adopted a special resolution branding the
counter-revolutionary agitation and approving the measures
taken by the Commissariat for Railways in regard to the
Alexandrovsky railway shops.

For Lenin's report and resolution see present edition, Vol. 29
pp. 255-74.   p. 133

136   In January 1919 the Soviet Government made two offers of peace
(on the 12th and 17th). On February 4 it notified the Governments
of Great Britain, France, Italy, Japan and the U.S.A. by radio
that it was ready to attend the proposed peace conference on
Princes Islands.   p. 133

137   *Vsegda Vperyod!* (Ever Forward!)—a Menshevik newspaper published in Moscow; in 1918 one issue appeared, and in 1919 it was
published from January 22 to February 25.   p. 133

138   *Dyelo Naroda* (People's Cause)—organ of the S.R. Party, published
in Petrograd, then at intervals in Samara and Moscow under
different names from March 1917 to March 1919. After the October
Socialist Revolution the paper adopted an anti-Soviet attitude.
It was closed down for counter-revolutionary activities.

                                                                                 p. 134

139   Lenin's proposal was written on the draft resolution of the C.C.
of the R.C.P.(B.). The draft, with Lenin's corrections, is signed
by V. I. Lenin, N. N. Krestinsky, and J. V. Stalin. The resolution
states: "An essential condition for success in the conduct of the
war is unconditional unity of action on all fronts, which, in turn,
demands unity of Red Army command on all fronts, unity of Red
Army supply on all fronts and unity of transport management
of all railways, since transport is of primary importance in the
conduct of war." The resolution stresses the need for the strictest
directives being given to the Commissariats for the Army and
the Navy as well as to the supply agencies of the Soviet Republics—

"in order that these independent commissariats work exclusively in strict conformity with the directives given by the appropriate Commissariats of the R.S.F.S.R., since only in this way can the necessary unity, dispatch and accuracy be achieved in the fulfilment of all orders and operations."

The resolution goes on to say that "the most urgent task in the Ukraine is to make maximum use of fuel, metals, existing factories and workshops, and also stocks of food". Pointing out that the whole industry of the Ukraine was concentrated in the eastern part of the republic and that the transfer of the Economic Council from Kharkov to Kiev had adversely affected the rehabilitation of transport and of the mining and manufacturing industries of the Ukraine, the C.C. of the R.C.P.(B.) recognised the need for the Economic Council as well as the Special Commission for Army Supplies of the Ukraine being located in Kharkov or having competent agencies in Kharkov authorised to deal directly with Moscow and to receive money appropriations directly from Moscow. The C.C. of the Party emphasised that "the Ukrainian railways are an inseparable part of the Russian railway network and are managed by the People's Commissariat for Railways from Moscow." The resolution also states that "the People's Commissariat for State Control of the R.S.F.S.R. should cover all institutions in the Ukrainian Soviet Republic" (Central Party Archives of the Institute of Marxism-Leninism of the C.C. of the C.P.S.U.).

This resolution of the Party's Central Committee was an important step towards strengthening unity in military affairs among the Soviet Republics. On April 24, 1919, in connection with Commander-in-Chief I. I. Vatsetis's memorandum on the military situation in the R.S.F.S.R., urging the need for uniting the armed forces of the Soviet Republics and subordinating them to a single command, Lenin wrote to E. M. Sklyansky asking him to urgently "draft the *text* of the C.C. directive to all "nationals" concerning military *unity* (unification)" (*Collected Works*, Vol. 50, Fifth Russian Edition, Document 528). For "Draft C.C. Directive on Army Unity" see present edition, Vol. 29, pp. 404-05. The military union of the Soviet Republics was officially implemented on June 1, 1919, by a decree of the All-Russia Central Executive Committee "On the Unification of the Soviet Republics of Russia, the Ukraine, Latvia, Lithuania and Byelorussia for Fighting World Imperialism". p. 135

[140] On April 21, 1919, Lenin made a report "On Stepping Up Work in the Field of Military Defence" at a meeting of the Council of Defence. The document printed here is apparently a rough draft of the concluding part of the resolution on this question. p. 135

[141] This postscript was written to Béla Kun's appeal on behalf of the Soviet Government of Hungary to the Hungarian soldiers serving in the Red Army. "You, Hungarian internationalists,"

the appeal stated, "who are fighting on Russian soil against the bands of Kolchak and counter-revolution, are also fighting for the Hungarian Soviet Republic just as your comrades are doing in Hungary, for Hungary and Russia today form a single whole." This appeal was issued in April 1919 in Hungarian and promulgated on the civil war fronts.

The Central Party Archives of the Institute of Marxism-Leninism of the C.C. of the C.P.S.U. have the text of the postscript in Russian in the handwriting of L. M. Karakhan. It runs: "I whole-heartedly support the appeal of our Magyar comrades. I hope the interests of the international cause will come first with our Magyar comrades. We must hold out another few months and victory will be assured. Lenin".   p. 135

142 This draft was written at the second meeting of the Economic Commission of the C.P.C. on May 2, 1919, in connection with the discussion of measures to alleviate the position of the workers.
                                                                    p. 136

143 On May 31, 1919, the Council of Defence considered questions relating to mobilisation. The Council endorsed the decree drafted by Lenin (see pp. 138-39 of this volume) and decisions directing the People's Commissariat for Food to provide the mobilised men with food and ordering the conscription status of employees in all departments and institutions to be checked with the object of placing at the disposal of the military command all such persons who were liable for service in the armed forces and who could be replaced without great detriment to the work by persons who were not liable or by women.   p. 137

144 The Council of Defence on May 24, 1919, passed a decision allowing Red Armymen of frontline units operating in the rich grain-producing districts to send food parcels to their families in the famine-stricken areas. The Council ordered the Central Committee of the Food Army to submit not later than June 1 a draft of detailed instructions for the implementation of this decision. The draft was endorsed by the Council of Defence on July 23, 1919.   p. 139

145 Mamontov's mounted corps was launched by Denikin for attacks behind the lines of the Soviet troops on the Southern Front. On August 10, 1919, Mamontov's cavalry broke through the front in the vicinity of Novokhopersk and raided several towns and villages. This cavalry raid created a threat to the Soviet troops, made offensive operations difficult and interfered with army control and supply in a number of places. The Party and the Government took emergency measures to fight Mamontov's cavalry. On August 23 the Council of Defence declared martial law in Ryazan, Tula, Orel, Voronezh, Tambov and Penza gubernias, on the territory of which all power was vested in the Revolutionary Committees. These were responsible for organising defence against whiteguard attacks and suppressing counter-revolutionary

actions. Lenin attached great importance to the organisation of Mamontov's defeat. The latter's corps was routed in October-November 1919.   p. 141

[146] Lenin had repeatedly demanded that the Revolutionary Military Council of the Republic, headed by Trotsky, take drastic measures to fight Mamontov's troops. On September 16, 1919, Lenin wrote: "Inaction against Mamontov. Evidently, there has been one delay after another. The troops marching on Voronezh from the North were late. We were late in transferring the 21st Division to the South. We were late with the armoured cars. Late with communications.... Apparently our R.M.C.R. 'gives orders', without being interested in or able to follow up *fulfilment*. This may be our common vice but in military affairs it simply means destruction" (see present edition, Vol. 35, pp. 420-21). p. 142

[147] The draft decision was adopted by the C.P.C. at its meeting on September 4, 1919.   p. 143

[148] The decision of the Politbureau accompanying Lenin's note was adopted in connection with Chicherin's letter to Lenin dated September 26, 1919, in which Chicherin asked for instructions on the following points: 1) could an appeal be made without the decision of the C.C. of the R.C.P.(B.) to the workers of the Entente countries to bring pressure to bear on their Governments not to interfere in the Soviet state's negotiations with the Baltic states for concluding peace treaties? 2) Should we make new peace proposals to the Entente countries in the name of the Soviet Government? "This," wrote Chicherin, "would be construed as a sign of weakness.... On the other hand, it would give an opening to the opponents of intervention, especially to the trade unions"; 3) Could we take advantage of Litvinov's proposed trip to a neutral country to negotiate an exchange of prisoners of war with the English representatives in order to "throw out a feeler on the question of peace"? 4) In the event of Litvinov's mission being a failure would it be worth while asking A. M. Gorky, who intended to make an appeal for peace, to mention in his letter "our invariable desire for peace and to point out to the Governments of the Entente the risk of the struggle being turned into annihila-

tion"? (underlined by Lenin). "However," wrote Chicherin, "we

should much prefer an official peace proposal ..." (Central Party Archives, Institute of Marxism-Leninism of the C.C. of the C.P.S.U.). On this question see also V. I. Lenin, *Collected Works*, Vol. 51, Fifth Russian Edition, Document 85.   p. 144

[149] The conflict arose through an order of the People's Commissariat for State Control to do away with nine legal departments of the S.E.C. The latter lodged a complaint against the State Control with the Narrow Council of People's Commissars. The C.P.C. endorsed the decision of the Narrow Council in this connec-

tion on September 30, 1919, and adopted Lenin's motion with slight amendments, namely: Point 3 was added, reading: "The same to be demanded of all committees within a fortnight", while Point 3 of Lenin's draft was endorsed as Point 4 of the decision worded as follows: "The Commissariat for Justice to institute investigations with the object of taking legal action against members of the S.E.C.'s legal departments for red tape. Fulfilment to be reported to the Narrow Council within a week (Central Party Archives, Institute of Marxism-Leninism of the C.C. of the C.P.S.U.).   p. 144

150 The Narrow C.P.C. was set up in December 1917 to relieve the agenda of the C.P.C. of minor questions; it had the status of a C.P.C. commission. All the decisions unanimously adopted by the Narrow Council were signed by Lenin and acquired the force of C.P.C. decisions; in cases of disagreement the business was referred to the C.P.C.   p. 145

151 The *suggestions* were written in connection with a meeting of the communist groups of Centrosoyuz and the Food Commissariat arranged by the C.P.C. and chaired by Lenin on October 9, 1919.   p. 145

152 *Bednota* (The Poor)—a peasant daily, published in Moscow from March 27, 1918 to January 31, 1931. The newspaper was founded by decision of the C.C. of the R.C.P.(B.) in lieu of the newspapers *Derevenskaya Bednota* (The Rural Poor), *Derevenskaya Pravda* (Rural Truth) and *Soldatskaya Pravda* (Soldiers' Truth). The newspaper carried on an active campaign to strengthen the alliance between the working class and the peasantry, to organise and rally the mass of the poor and middle peasants behind the Communist Party and the Soviet Government. *Bednota* played an important role in promoting the political education and raising the cultural level of the labouring peasantry, in advancing public-spirited activists from among the rural poor and the middle peasantry, and training a numerous army of rural correspondents. On February 1, 1931, *Bednota* merged with the newspaper *Sotsialisticheskoye Zemledeliye* (Socialist Agriculture).   p. 145

153 The reference is to the Decree "On Consumers' Communes" passed by the Council of People's Commissars on March 16, 1919.   p. 145

154 The Afghan Embassy Extraordinary headed by the Ambassador Extraordinary Mohammad Wali-Khan arrived in Moscow on October 10, 1919. On October 12 the Ambassador, accompanied by Chief Judge of the Afghan Army Saifurrahman-Khan and the Secretary of the Embassy visited the People's Commissar for Foreign Affairs. He was received by the Board of the Commissariat in full attendance. On October 14 Lenin received the embassy in the presence of representatives of the People's Commissariat for Foreign Affairs. The talk between the Ambassador and Lenin lasted over half an hour.   p. 146

[155] Replies to the questions raised in the letter of Amir Amanullah Khan were given in the Soviet Government's letter dated November 27, 1919, signed by Chairman of the Council of People's Commissars V. I. Lenin.
p. 146

[156] The speech was made at Trade Union House in Moscow to communist workers of Ivanovo-Voznesensk who were on their way to the front. On October 3 a town Party meeting had been held in Ivanovo-Voznesensk at which every Party member was called upon to spare no effort to defeat Denikin's army, and the Party organisations were called upon to start mobilising Communists for the front. On October 9 the Bureau of the Ivanovo-Voznesensk Gubernia Committee passed a decision to announce a general Party mobilisation. In a short period about 350 men were mobilised. The first group was seen off on October 22 and arrived in Moscow on October 24. In a letter to the Revolutionary Military Council of the Southern Front Lenin wrote: "I heartily recommend the bearer, Comrade Stepan Nazarov, a Bolshevik whom I have known personally for a long time.

"Together with other Ivanovo-Voznesensk comrades they formed a *well-planned organised* group (of from 300 to 500 men) for giving all-round service to and raising the morale of a whole army.

"I heartily recommend the comrades and request you earnestly to take all steps not to lose sight of them, but make proper and careful use of them" (*Collected Works*, Vol. 51, Fifth Russian Edition, Document 121).
p. 147

[157] Referring to the Chamber of Deputies election campaign, which started in October 1919.
p. 148

[158] At its meeting on November 11, 1919, the C.P.C. discussed a draft decree for the establishment of a single forestry body. The Council rejected the draft and set up a commission consisting of representatives of Glavleskom (Chief Timber Committee), the People's Commissariat for Agriculture and the People's Commissariat for Internal Affairs, with instructions to put into effect Lenin's proposals as here set forth. The decree was endorsed by the C.P.C. on November 21, 1919, and published in *Izvestia* on November 29, 1919.
p. 148

[159] This draft decision was adopted by the C.P.C. on November 18, 1919.
p. 149

[160] Simultaneously with the draft of the Food Commissariat the C.P.C. discussed the draft of the Supreme Economic Council on the same question. Point 4 of the S.E.C. draft read: "The starch and treacle factories shall be allowed to make contracts with the peasants for the delivery of potatoes, and to issue 1 pound of produce for every processed pood" (*Lenin Miscellany XXIV*, p. 140).
p. 149

161 The decree on potato purchases drafted by the commission was endorsed by the C.P.C. on Saturday, November 22, 1919, with amendments proposed at its meeting.   p. 149

162 This congress, convened by the Central Bureau of Communist Organisations of the Peoples of the East under the C.C., R.C.P.(B.), was held in Moscow from November 22 to December 3, 1919. On the eve of the congress, November 21, a preliminary meeting of Central Committee members with a group of delegates was held with Lenin presiding. The congress was attended by 71 voting delegates and 11 delegates with a consultative voice. On the opening day of the congress Lenin delivered a report on the current situation (see present edition, Vol. 30, pp. 151-62). The resolution adopted on his report was submitted to the presidium "for concretisation and drafting of the chief theses that should serve as a basis for work in the East". The congress heard the report on the work of the Central Bureau of Communist Organisations of the Peoples of the East, reports from the local areas, the report of the Central Moslem Military Collegium and others. The congress outlined the tasks in the field of Party and Soviet work in the East and elected a new Central Bureau.   p. 150

163 G. V. Chicherin's report on the international situation was delivered to the Eighth All-Russia Conference of the R.C.P.(B.). The conference adopted the resolution on the international situation drafted by Lenin. In his report on the activities of the All-Russia Central Executive Committee and the Council of People's Commissars to the Seventh All-Russia Congress of Soviets Lenin proposed this resolution as a draft resolution of the congress (see present edition, Vol. 30, p. 231). It was unanimously adopted by the congress as a peace proposal to the countries of the Entente.   p. 150

164 This document formed the basis of the resolution adopted by the Plenum of the C.C., R.C.P.(B.) on November 29, 1919, on the composition of the All-Russia Central Executive Committee, which was to be elected at the Seventh All-Russia Congress of Soviets.   p. 151

165 Lenin is referring to the decision of the Eighth Congress of the R.C.P.(B.) on the question of organisation. The section dealing with Soviet construction stated that the composition of the All-Russia C.E.C. should be changed and its membership should consist largely of people from the local areas who conduct regular work among the peasants and workers (see *The Eighth Congress of the R.C.P.(B.). March 1919. Minutes*, Moscow, 1959, p. 427).   p. 151

166 The draft decree on improving railway transport in connection with military freightages was discussed at a meeting of the C.P.C. on December 2, 1919. During this discussion Lenin introduced his motion, which was incorporated in § 10 of the decree. With this addendum and other amendments the decree was adopted by the C.P.C. and published in part in *Izvestia* No. 281 for December 14, 1919.   p. 151

167 Lenin's remarks were used as a basis for the decision of the Polit-bureau of the C.C., R.C.P.(B.) which discussed the Draft Regulations at its meeting on December 27, 1919.   p. 152

168 § 1 of the Draft Regulations stated that the R.C.P. group at the A.C.C.T.U. was the guiding Party organisation of the entire Russian trade union movement.   p. 152

169 § 3 of the Draft Regulations read as follows: "With a view to co-ordinating the actions of all the all-Russia industrial unions and carrying out the line of the Communist Party in the trade union movement in a more effective and organised manner, all existing and newly created Party groups in the all-Russia industrial unions shall be directly subordinated to the Party Group at the A.C.C.T.U."   p. 152

170 The question of Moscow's food supply was discussed at a meeting of the C.P.C. on December 6, 1919. The Council's decision on this question was formulated on the basis of Lenin's rough draft.   p. 154

171 This refers to the agreement between the Commissariat for Railways and the Food Commissariat on the question of the transportation of grain from the producing to the consuming areas. "The agreement," stated the Council's decision, "should ensure regular deliveries to Moscow of such a quantity of breadstuffs as was necessary for its class ration distribution" (Central Party Archives, Institute of Marxism-Leninism of the C.C. of the C.P.S.U.).   p. 154

172 This refers to the daily reports to the C.P.C. concerning the supply of breadstuffs to Moscow and the movement of potato freights for Moscow.   p. 154

173 Lenin wrote this draft in connection with the discussion, at a meeting of the C.P.C. on December 23, 1919, of the question of the Kazan, Simbirsk and Samara gubernia food commissars' failure to carry out the order of the Food Commissariat concerning grain consignments to Moscow by through trains. The draft was adopted by the Council with certain amendments. p. 154

174 From the reports of speakers it transpired that one of the principal reasons for non-fulfilment of the order was the delay on the part of the Commissariat for Post and Telegraph in giving the Food Commissariat a direct line for communicating with the local areas. This point was adopted by the Council in the following wording: "In all cases of non-receipt of a direct line the guilty party shall be that commissariat, which, not having received

the line in the course of an hour for carrying out an important
assignment, shall have failed to complain about it to the Chairman of the C.P.C." (*Lenin Miscellany XXIV*, p. 147).   p. 154

175 This point was adopted by the C.P.C. in the following wording:
"The Commissariat for Justice is instructed to institute
investigations to determine the culpability of the gubernia food
commissars and other officials guilty of non-fulfilment of the
Food Commissariat's order for through trains with grain to
be consigned to Moscow or of failure to fulfil same through bad
organisation" (*Lenin Miscellany XXIV*, p. 147).   p. 155

176 The data given by the Central Statistical Board were used by
Lenin in the Central Committee's report to the Ninth Congress
of the R.C.P.(B.) (see present edition, Vol. 30, p. 460). p. 155

177 On December 23, 1919, the Narrow Council of People's Commissars
examined the question of supplying the workers with clothes and
footwear. It decided to use for this purpose part of the stocks
reserved for the Red Army, but in a manner that would not be
detrimental to the army. At the end of December the Central
Army Supply Administration was to have issued to the Food
Commissariat from army stores 30,000 pairs of leather boots, while
the S.E.C. undertook to deliver to the Food Commissariat every
fortnight 20 per cent of all the boots manufactured in the country.
     Apparently this decision of the Narrow Council met with
objection on the part of the Presidium of the S.E.C., as a
result of which the C.P.C. passed a decision based on this draft
of Lenin's.   p. 157

178 This motion was adopted by the C.P.C. in the following wording:
"Comrade Rykov shall give an exact mandate to his representative for all meetings on the question of working clothes and
delegate only him."
     The question was examined a second time by the Narrow
Council on January 3, 1920, this time in the presence of Chairman
of the S.E.C. A. I. Rykov, who was ordered to supply monthly
to the Food Commissariat's agencies, as from January 1, 1920,
not less than 40,000 pairs of men's working boots, not counting
clogs, bast sandals and felt boots.   p. 157

179 The draft instructions were discussed and adopted by the C.P.C.
the same day they were written.   p. 157

180 This alludes to the decision of the Seventh All-Russia Congress
of Soviets on state organising activities, with special reference
to the commissariats' right of objection to managers of Soviet
Executive Committee sections.   p. 157

181 Under a resolution of the Seventh All-Russia Congress of Soviets
the S.E.C. was to frame instructions defining the rights and

duties of the central and local bodies of the S.E.C. in respect
of state factories of special importance, trustified enterprises,
etc.   p. 157

182   This motion was adopted by the Council of Workers' and
      Peasants' Defence at its meeting on January 16, 1920, after dis-
      cussion of a report "On the Reorganisation of the Special
      Committee for Imposing Martial Law on the Railways and the
      Transport Department of the Vecheka".   p. 158

183   On January 2, 1920, the Soviet Government proposed to the
      Mussavatist Government of Azerbaijan an agreement for joint
      action against Denikin. This offer was turned down.
         Following a report by the People's Commissar for Foreign
      Affairs G. V. Chicherin on the possibility of peace negotiations
      with Azerbaijan made at a meeting of the Politbureau
      on January 17 and 18, 1920, the latter adopted Lenin's motion
      on this question.   p. 158

184   This draft decision was adopted by the Politbureau of the C.C.,
      R.C.P.(B.) on January 17-18, 1920, in connection with the pro-
      test of the Commander-in-Chief concerning the telegram with
      Lenin's postscript which the Chairman of the Revolutionary
      Military Council of the Republic L. D. Trotsky sent to
      M. V. Frunze, Commander of the Turkestan Front and G. K.
      Voskanov, Commander of the 4th Army, on January 17, 1920. The
      telegram asked for energetic steps to be taken to build the Emba
      Railway and rebuild the Krasny Kut-Alexandrov Gai railway
      to a wide gauge (see *Collected Works*, Vol. 51, Fifth Russian
      Edition, Document 207).   p. 159

185   The question of reorganising the State Control Commissariat into
      a Workers' and Peasants' Inspection was raised at the end of
      1919 and discussed at the Seventh All-Russia Congress of Soviets.
      A commission consisting of representatives of the State Control,
      the All-Russia Central Council of Trade Unions and the All-
      Russia C.E.C. was set up to draft regulations governing the
      Workers' and Peasants' Inspection. Opinion in the commission
      being divided, the question was referred to the Politbureau,
      which passed its decision on January 23, 1920, on the basis of
      the directives moved by Lenin.   p. 160

186   These directions were written by Lenin on Y. I. Burov's report
      summarising the work of the propaganda-instructor trains and
      steamers of the All-Russia Central Executive Committee. The
      latter's Propaganda-Instructor Trains and Steamers Department
      reported on February 3, 1920, that in accordance with the
      directions the Department had established contact with the
      Film Committee and set up a preliminary commission to draft
      the regulations governing propaganda trips on the trains and
      steamers of the All-Russia C.E.C.   p. 160

187 This draft was written at a meeting of the C.P.C. during the discussion of the report by A. A. Burdukov, Chief of Moscow Military District and the Moscow City Garrison, concerning the unloading of potatoes at the Moscow Railway Junction and snow clearing on Moscow's streets and railway tracks. Lenin's draft was endorsed by the C.P.C. p. 162

188 The following decision was adopted at the meeting of the C.P.C. on January 31, 1920: "Resumption of the potato campaign shall be postponed until the spring when, simultaneously with the seed campaign, the People's Commissariat for Food shall undertake in the course of April and May 1920 to satisfy the requirements of Moscow in food potatoes to the amount of 560,000 poods" (Central Party Archives, Institute of Marxism-Leninism of the C.C., C.P.S.U.). p. 162

189 The report on measures taken by the Commissariat for Internal Affairs to implement compulsory service in connection with snow clearing was made to the C.P.C. on January 31, 1920. The Council passed a decision to set up a commission under the chairmanship of F. E. Dzerzhinsky which was to be made responsible for the conduct of this business. p. 162

190 Point 4 of the draft regulations on bonuses for workers and office employees, about which Lenin had his doubts, was worded as follows: "§ 4. Standard output shall be established on the basis of technically possible output under the best technical conditions of production, provided the means and implements of production are in a normal condition. In view, however, of the general conditions prevailing in industry, a deduction should be made from this technically possible standard, but in no case more than 50 per cent, after which the actual standard of productivity, varying with the different trades, enterprises and groups, shall be fixed."

At its meeting on February 1, 1920, the Narrow C.P.C. resolved that "the draft decision on bonuses shall be returned to the People's Commissariat for Labour for revision in accordance with Comrade Lenin's directions".

A decision "On the Procedure for Endorsing Bonus Projects" was adopted by the Council of People's Commissars on June 8 and published in *Izvestia* on June 10, 1920. p. 163

191 This refers to the *first session of the All-Russia Central Executive Committee, seventh convocation*, held in Moscow on February 2-7, 1920. On February 2 Lenin delivered his report at the session on the work of the A.C.E.C. and the Council of People's Commissars (see present edition, Vol. 30, pp. 315-36). p. 163

192 This draft was incorporated *in toto* in the decisions of the Council of Defence dated February 2, 1920, which, over Lenin's signature, were circulated to all government departments with Lenin's

postscript (see pp. 165-66 of this volume). The C.D. decisions
were published in *Lenin Miscellany XXIV*, pp. 64-67.   p. 164

193 This draft was moved by Lenin at a meeting of the Council of
     People's Commissars on February 5, 1920, in connection with
     L. B. Krasin's report on the question of granting privileges to
     workers engaged on locomotive repairs and the production of
     spare parts for transport.
         The following resolution was adopted on the report: "The
     S.E.C., the Commissariat for Food and the Commissariat for
     Railways are instructed to examine in detail the question of
     all privileges applying to workers engaged in locomotive repairs
     and the production of spare parts for transport, and to present
     a list of factories to the C.P.C."   p. 166

194 The question of *"using the best workshops for repairs all 24 hours
     of the day"* was discussed at a meeting of the C.P.C. on March 16,
     1920. The question of intensive and uninterrupted work on the
     repair of locomotives was raised by Lenin in connection with the
     catastrophic state of railway transport, and this led to a number
     of other questions being discussed at the same Council meeting,
     namely: the possibility of placing an order abroad for locomo-
     tives and spare parts for repairing railway transport, and an
     inspection of factories and works engaged in the repair of goods
     train cars and engines.   p. 166

195 *The Speech at the Fourth Conference of Gubernia Extraordinary
     Commissions* was delivered by Lenin at the morning plenary
     session on February 6, 1920. The conference was called at a time
     when the Soviet Republic, having defeated Kolchak, Denikin
     and Yudenich, had gained a temporary respite and was in a
     position to tackle its economic problems.
         The conference was attended by 69 voting delegates and
     7 delegates with a consultative voice. All the delegates were
     Communists, the majority of the 69 voting delegates having
     joined the Party long before the revolution. Most of the delegates
     were workers.   p. 166

196 *Borotbists*—members of a petty-bourgeois nationalist party,
     Borotba, formed in May 1918 after a split in the Ukrainian Social-
     ist-Revolutionary Party. So called from the name of the Party's
     central organ *Borotba* (Struggle). In March 1919 assumed the
     name of Ukrainian Socialist-Revolutionary Party of Communist
     Borotbists, and in August that of the Ukrainian Communist
     Party of Borotbists. Its leaders, among others, were V. Blakitny,
     G. Grinko and A. Shumsky. There were a good many counter-
     revolutionary followers of Petlyura in the ranks of the party,
     who, under cover of revolutionary phrases and declarations to the
     effect that they stood on the communist platform, came out
     against the dictatorship of the proletariat and pursued a policy
     aimed at splitting the united revolutionary front of the working

peoples of the Ukraine and Russia. For Lenin's appraisal of the Borotba Party see pp. 180-181 of this volume.

The Borotbists twice applied to the Executive of the Communist International asking to be admitted to membership of the Comintern and to be recognised as the main communist party in the Ukraine. The Comintern passed a special decision on this question on February 26, 1920, proposing to the Borotbists that they dissolve their party and merge with the Communist Party (Bolsheviks) of the Ukraine. The resolution said that the Executive of the Communist International could only regard the desire to found a second parallel party as an attempt to split the ranks of the working people.

The growing influence of the Bolsheviks among the peasantry and the successes of the Soviet government in the Ukraine forced the Borotbists to decide on voluntary dissolution.

The Fourth Conference of the Communist Party (Bolsheviks) of the Ukraine, held March 17-23, 1920, agreed to admit the Borotbists into its ranks, all the newly enrolled members being reregistered. Eventually, however, many Borotbists resumed their anti-Soviet activities and headed the struggle of the counter-revolutionary bourgeois-nationalist elements in the Ukraine.

p. 174

[197] The manuscript further contains a note by Lenin reading: "Trotsky and Rakovsky are instructed, not later than tomorrow, to word this resolution more accurately and transmit it tomorrow by coded telegraph to the Ukrainian Revolutionary Committee."

p. 175

[198] This interview was given by Lenin in the middle of February 1920, at a time when Soviet Russia, having gained a peaceful respite, was planning the country's economic rehabilitation and reconstruction, and when the Soviet Government embarked on a broad programme for establishing diplomatic and commercial relations with the capitalist countries. Lincoln Eyre of *The World* was sent to Russia to obtain an interview from Lenin, and was received by him in the company of cameraman Victor Kubes. The interview was conducted in English, first in Lenin's private office, then at his rooms in the Kremlin. It lasted an hour and touched on questions of topical interest. Lenin's interview was published in *The World* and reprinted by many newspapers in Western Europe and America.
p. 175

[199] The *Peace Treaty between the R.S.F.S.R.* and Lithuania was signed in Moscow on July 12, 1920. The Peace Treaty between the R.S.F.S.R. and Latvia was signed at Riga on August 11, 1920.
p. 179

[200] In referring to the Ukrainian Spilka teachers Lenin has in mind the Schoolteachers' Union of the Ukraine, which was controlled by Petlyura elements.

Spilka—Ukrainian Social-Democratic Union.

ATU—All-Russia Schoolteachers' Union.
p. 181

201 This draft was adopted at the meeting of the C.P.C. on March 2, 1920, during the discussion of Krasin's report on the question of foreign trade. It is connected with Point 17 of the theses on foreign trade, reading: "A commission consisting of representatives from the Commissariat for Foreign Trade, State Control and the Vecheka shall be set up to ascertain and reserve the Republic's stocks of commodities suitable for foreign trade" (Central Party Archives, Institute of Marxism-Leninism of the C.C., C.P.S.U.).
p. 181

202 Point 1 of Trotsky's draft theses was headed "The Will to Work" (see *The Ninth Congress of the R.C.P.(B.). March-April 1920. Minutes.* Moscow, 1960, p. 533). p. 181

203 The draft decree on the prosecution of minors introduced by the Commissariat for Education was discussed and endorsed with Lenin's Amendments at the meeting of the Council of People's Commissars on March 4, 1920. The decree was published in *Izvestia* No. 51 for March 6 under the heading: "Cases of Juveniles Accused of Socially Dangerous Acts". p. 182

204 Lenin proposed this draft at a meeting of the C.P.C. during a discussion of the question of the state farms. The Council instructed S. P. Sereda, People's Commissar for Agriculture, "to submit the exact text of all decisions on this question and the draft decision drawn up in this connection". The Draft Decision on Measures for State Farm Organisation drawn up by the People's Commissariat for Agriculture was endorsed by the C.P.C. on April 15, 1920. p. 183

205 At a joint meeting of the Party groups of the All-Russia Central Council of Trade Unions and the Moscow C.T.U. on March 15, 1920, N. N. Krestinsky, Secretary of the C.C., R.C.P.(B.), declared that since the stand taken by the A.C.C.T.U.'s Party Group and its responsible leaders on the question of collective and one-man management differed sharply from that of the Party's Central Committee, he proposed in the name of the Party's C.C. that none of the group's members should deliver reports at trade union congresses in favour of collective management.

Members of the group's bureau, at a closed meeting, emphatically protested against such interpretations and methods of enforcing Party discipline and applied to the C.C. of the R.C.P.(B.) asking to be allowed to move resolutions at trade union congresses on behalf of the A.C.C.T.U.'s Party Group. Their statement was discussed at a meeting of the C.C.'s Politbureau, which adopted Lenin's draft resolutions. p. 184

206 Lenin did not finish his preface. The pamphlet *The Proletarian Revolution and Kautsky the Renegade* came out in English at the end of March 1920 without a preface. p. 185

207 The German pamphlet N. Lenin. *Die Diktatur des Proletariats und der Renegat Karl Kautsky* came out at the end of December 1919.   p. 185

208 Lenin received Macdonald's book later. It stands in his private library with his marginal notes. Lenin specially marked those passages in the book in which Macdonald tried to play down the class contradictions of capitalist society. These marginal notes were published in *Lenin Miscellany XXIV*, pp. 253-85.
                                                                                p. 185

209 The "Regulations on Subbotniks" were drafted by A. N. Sokolov, a member of the staff of the Central Committee of the R.C.P.(B.). They were prepared, apparently, for the first anniversary of the launching of the subbotniks (anniversary date May 10, 1920).
                                                                                p. 187

210 Lenin's note was written in connection with the decisions of the Twelfth Conference of the Bund held April 12-19, 1920. The resolutions of this conference with Lenin's marks are to be found in the Central Party Archives of the Institute of Marxism-Leninism of the C.C., C.P.S.U. In the resolution "On the Present Situation and the Tasks of Our Party" Lenin marked off the following passage: "14. Summing up the experience of the last year, the Twelfth Conference of the Bund finds: 1) that the Bund, in principle, had adopted the communist platform since the Eleventh Conference, 2) that the Programme of the Communist Party, which is also the programme of the Soviet government, corresponds with the fundamental platform of the Bund, 3) that a 'united socialist front' with principled opponents of Soviet power, who draw a line between the proletariat and its government, is impossible, 4) that the moment has come when the Bund can relinquish its official oppositional stand and take upon itself responsibility for the Soviet government's policy."

At the same time, the resolution on organisational questions stated that "the logical consequence of the political stand adopted by the Bund is the latter's entry into the R.C.P. on the same basis as the Bund's membership of the R.S.D.L.P." (underlined by Lenin). The conference authorised the C.C. of the Bund to see to it, as an essential condition, that the Bund preserve within the R.C.P. the status of "an autonomous organisation of the Jewish proletariat" (marked off by Lenin).

On May 6, 1920, the Politbureau of the C.C., R.C.P.(B.) discussed the question of "The Conditions for the Bund's Admission to Membership of the R.C.P." and resolved: "that Kamenev, Stalin and Preobrazhensky be authorised to receive the representatives of the Bund and hear their proposals" (Central Party Archives, Institute of Marxism-Leninism of the C.C., C.P.S.U.).

At its Thirteenth Conference in 1921 the Bund decided to dissolve itself, and part of its membership joined the R.C.P.(B.) on the basis of the rules of admission.   p. 187

211   The *Decree on the Introduction of Work Rations* was adopted by
the Council of People's Commissars on April 30, 1920 and published on May 4 in *Izvestia* No. 94.   p. 188

212   This refers to a bomb explosion in the building of the Moscow
Committee of the Party in Leontievsky Pereulok. The bomb
was thrown by Left Socialist-Revolutionaries on September 25,
1919.   p. 190

213   This draft was adopted at the meeting of the C.P.C. on May 25,
1920.   p. 191

214   The text of the decree, amended in accordance with Lenin's
remarks, was adopted at the meeting of the C.P.C. on May 25,
1920 and published in *Izvestia* on June 4, 1920.   p. 192

215   Lenin's proposals outlined in this rough draft were incorporated
in the Decision of the Council of People's Commissars of May 27,
1920.   p. 192

216   This interview took place in Lenin's private office in the Kremlin on June 3, 1920. Writing from Moscow, Nakahira reported:
"I interviewed Mr. Lenin at his office in the Kremlin. Contrary
to my expectation, the decoration of the room is very simple.
Mr. Lenin's manner is very simple and kind—as if he were greeting an old friend. In spite of the fact that he holds the highest
position, there is not the slightest trace of condescension in his
manner." (*Osaka Asahi* No. 13814 for June 13, 1920.) The next
day, as Nakahira mentions in his later reminiscences, he brought
the text of his interview to Lenin, who read it carefully and
made several corrections.
   Lenin's interview given to another Japanese correspondent,
K. Fusse, and printed lower down, took place on June 3 or 4.
Possibly both correspondents were received by Lenin together.
Fusse says the interview lasted about twenty minutes. A. N. Voz-
nesensky, Chief of the Eastern Department of the People's Commissariat for Foreign Affairs, was present at the interview.
   Fusse's interview with Lenin was reported on June 26, 1920,
in the Socialist-Revolutionary newspaper *Volya* published in
Vladivostok. The text of the interview given in this volume was
first published in Russian in 1924 in the collection of articles
Lenin i Vostok (Lenin and the East) and afterwards in the First
Edition of Lenin's *Collected Works* (Vol. XX, Part II). It was
not included in the 2nd, 3rd and 4th (Russian) editions of the
Collected Works.   p. 193

217   This refers to the *Far-Eastern Republic* set up in April 1920 on
the territory of the Trans-Baikal, Amur, Maritime and Kamchatka regions and Northern Sakhalin. In form a bourgeois-
democratic state, in essence it pursued a Soviet policy in keeping
with the interests of Soviet Russia, which needed a prolonged
respite on her Eastern Front and wanted to stave off war with

Japan. At the same time, the creation of a buffer state in the Far East was made necessary by force of circumstances. As Lenin pointed out, "circumstances made necessary the creation of a buffer state, the Far-"Eastern Republic. We are well aware of the unbelievable sufferings that the Siberian peasants are enduring at the hands of the Japanese imperialists and the atrocities the Japanese have committed in Siberia" (present edition, Vol. 31, p. 465).

After the interventionists and whiteguards were driven out of the Soviet Far East (except Northern Sakhalin), the People's Assembly of the Far-Eastern Republic voted for entry into the R.S.F.S.R. on November 14, 1922.   p. 193

[218] The reference is to the *French Socialist Party.*

At the outbreak of the imperialist world war the Party's reformist leadership adopted a social-chauvinist stand of open support of the imperialist war and participation in the bourgeois government. There was a Centrist trend in the Party headed by Jean Longuet, which took a social-pacifist stand and pursued a policy of conciliation with the social-chauvinists. There was also a Left, revolutionary wing in the Party which took an internationalist stand and was represented chiefly by its rank and file.

After the October Socialist Revolution a sharp struggle developed within the Party between the open reformists and Centrists on the one hand, and the Left, revolutionary wing, on the other—the latter strengthened by rank-and-file workers who joined the Party en masse. At the Party's congress in Tours in December 1920 the revolutionary wing received a majority. The congress adopted a decision for the Party to join the Communist International and founded the Communist Party of France. The majority of reformists and Centrists broke away from the Party and formed a separate party, retaining the old name of French Socialist Party.   p. 198

[219] Lenin's draft was adopted with slight amendments at a meeting of the Politbureau of the C.C. on June 22, 1920, at which the theses and draft resolution on the Turkestan Republic drawn up by a special commission were discussed. For this commission's draft with Lenin's remarks see Lenin's *Collected Works*, Vol. 41, Fifth Russian Edition, pp. 433-36.   p. 198

[220] The Turkestan Commission of the All-Russia Central Executive Committee and the Council of People's Commissars of the R.S.F.S.R. was set up on October 8, 1919. Its members were G. I. Boky, F. I. Goloshchokin, V. V. Kuibyshev, Y. E. Rudzutak, M. V. Frunze and S. Z. Eliava. The commission was vested with the powers of a Government and Party body and was sent to Turkestan to give all possible aid to the local Communists and the working people of Turkestan in overcoming that country's political, economic and cultural backwardness, con-

solidating Soviet power and strengthening the union between the peoples of Turkestan and Soviet Russia. One of the commission's tasks was to correct mistakes made during the implementation of the national policy in Turkestan.

The Turkestan Commission carried out a number of measures for strengthening the local Party organisations and combating dominant-nation chauvinism and local nationalism. Important issues were those concerning the principles of Turkestan autonomy, relations with the federal bodies, and the forms and methods of Party organisation.   p. 198

221 *The Second Congress of the Communist International*, which laid the foundations of the Comintern's programme, tactics and organisation was held from July 19 to August 7, 1920, in Soviet Russia. The opening session was held in Petrograd and the subsequent sessions, beginning with July 23, in Moscow. The congress was attended by 169 voting delegates and 49 delegates with a consultative voice representing 67 workers' organisations of 37 countries. Apart from delegates representing the Communist Parties and organisations of 31 countries, there were delegates from the Independent Social-Democratic Party of Germany, the socialist parties of Italy and France, Industrial Workers of the World (Australia, Britain and Ireland), the National Confederation of Labour of Spain and other organisations. The R.C.P.(B.) was represented at the congress by 64 delegates.

All the preparatory work for convening the congress was directed by Lenin, who attached great importance to this international congress of communist and workers' organisations. An important role in defining the tasks and working out the political line of the Comintern was played by Lenin's book *"Left-Wing" Communism—an Infantile Disorder*, written for the opening of the Second Congress. Lenin wrote the "Preliminary Draft Theses on the National and Colonial Questions (For the Second Congress of the Communist International)", "Preliminary Draft Theses on the Agrarian Question (For the Second Congress of the Communist International)", "Theses on the Fundamental Tasks of the Second Congress of the Communist International" and "The Terms of Admission into the Communist International" (see present edition, Vol. 31, pp. 144-51, 152-64, 184-201, 206-11).

The congress adopted the following agenda: 1) The International Situation and the Fundamental Tasks of the Communist International; 2) The Role and Composition of the Communist Parties Before and After the Conquest of Power by the Proletariat; 3) The Trade Unions and the Factory Committees; 4) the Question of Parliamentarism; 5) The National and Colonial Questions; 6) The Agrarian Question; 7) The Attitude to the New "Centrist" Trends and Terms of Admission Into the Communist International; 8) The Charter of the Communist International; 9) Organisational questions (legal and illegal organisations, women's organisations, etc.); 10) The Communist youth movement; 11) Elections; 12) Miscellaneous.

At the opening session of the congress Lenin delivered a report on the international situation and the fundamental tasks of the Communist International (see present edition, Vol. 31, pp. 215-34).

Lenin took an active part in the work of most of the committees—those on the national and colonial questions, on the agrarian question, on terms of admission into the Communist International, and on the international situation and the tasks of the Comintern.

Lenin also made a speech at the congress on the role of the Communist Party, delivered a report of the Committee on the National and Colonial Questions, speeches on the terms of admission into the Communist International, on parliamentarianism and on affiliation to the British Labour Party (ibid., pp. 235-63).

The congress adopted Lenin's theses as a resolution, passed a resolution "On the Role of the Communist Party in the Proletarian Revolution", in the formulation of which Lenin took an active part, and adopted other resolutions, the "Terms of Admission Into the Communist International" and the Charter of the Comintern. The congress also adopted the Manifesto of the Second Congress of the Communist International. In addition it published a number of appeals: "The Third International to the Trade Unions of All Countries", "To the Workers of Petrograd", "To the Red Army and Red Navy of the R.S.F.S.R.", "Against the Executioners of Hungary", "To the Proletarian Men and Women of All Countries", and others.

The Second Congress of the Comintern played a tremendous role in the development of the international communist movement. After the congress Lenin pointed out that "communism has become the central to the working-class movement as a whole" (see present edition, Vol. 32, p. 180).   p. 199

222   This is one of Lenin's rough drafts for his "Theses on the Fundamental Tasks of the Second Congress of the Communist International".   p. 199

223   *L'Humanité*—a daily newspaper, founded in 1904 by Jean Jaurès as the organ of the French Socialist Party. During the First World War it was controlled by the extreme Right wing of the party.

From December 1920, after the split in the French Socialist Party, the paper became the central organ of the French Communist Party.   p. 200

224   *Le Populaire*—a newspaper founded by the French Centrists; published from 1916 in Limoges and from July 1917 in Paris. In 1921 it became the organ of the French Socialist Party. It is now controlled by the Right socialists.   p. 200

225   *Die Freiheit*—a daily, organ of the Independent Social-Democratic Party of Germany, published in Berlin from November 15, 1918 to September 30, 1922.   p. 200

[226] *The British Socialist Party* was founded in 1911, in Manchester, as a result of the amalgamation of the Social-Democratic Party with other socialist groups. Its small membership and its poor links with the masses gave the B.S.P. a somewhat sectarian character. During the First World War a sharp struggle developed within the Party between the internationalists (William Gallacher, Albert Inkpin, John Maclean, Theodore Rothstein and others) and the social-chauvinists headed by Hyndman. Within the internationalist trend there were inconsistent elements who took a Centrist stand on a number of issues. In February 1916 a group of B.S.P. leaders founded the newspaper *The Call*, which played an important part in uniting the internationalists. The annual conference of the B.S.P., held in Salford in April 1916, condemned the social-chauvinist stand of Hyndman and his supporters, who then left the Party.

The British Socialist Party welcomed the Great October Socialist Revolution. Its members played an important part in the «Hands off Russia» movement. In 1919 the overwhelming majority of its organisations (98 against 4) declared for affiliation to the Communist International. The British Socialist Party, together with the Communist Unity Group, formed the core of the Communist Party of Great Britain. At the First (Unity) Congress, held in 1920, the great majority of the B.S.P. local organisations entered the Communist Party.   p. 200

[227] *The American Socialist Party* was formed in July 1901 at a congress held in Indianapolis as a result of the amalgamation of groups that had broken away from the Socialist Workers' Party and the Social-Democratic Party of the U.S.A.; one of the organisers of the latter was Eugene Debs, a popular figure in the U.S. labour movement. He was also one of the founders of the new party. The party had a socially mixed membership made up of native-born and immigrant workers, as well as small farmers and people of petty-bourgeois origin. The party's Centrist and Right-wing opportunist leaders (Victor Berger, Morris Hillquit and others) denied the necessity of the proletarian dictatorship, renounced revolutionary methods of struggle, and reduced all party activities mainly to participation in election campaigns. During the First World War (1914-18) three trends appeared in the Socialist Party: the social-chauvinists, who supported the imperialist policy of the Administration; the Centrists, who opposed the imperialist war only in word; and the revolutionary minority, who took an internationalist stand and carried on a struggle against the war.

The Party's Left wing, headed by Charles Ruthenberg, William Foster, William Heywood and others, relying on the proletarian elements, waged a struggle against the party's opportunist leadership, for independent proletarian political action and the formation of industrial trade unions based on the principles of the class struggle. In 1919 a split took place in the Socialist Party. The breakaway Left wing founded the Communist Party of